NEW YORK

AN ILLUSTRATED HISTORY

NEW YORK

AN ILLUSTRATED HISTORY

EXPANDED EDITION

NARRATIVE BY
RIC BURNS
AND
JAMES SANDERS

PICTURE EDITOR
LISA ADES

ALFRED A. KNOPF
NEW YORK 2003

BASED ON "NEW YORK:
A DOCUMENTARY FILM"
DIRECTED BY RIC BURNS
PRODUCED BY LISA ADES
AND RIC BURNS
WRITTEN BY RIC BURNS
AND JAMES SANDERS

WITH
CONTRIBUTIONS BY
CAROL BERKIN
MARSHALL BERMAN
ROBERT A. CARO
DANIEL CZITROM
KENNETH T. JACKSON
DAVID LEVERING
LEWIS
PHILLIP LOPATE
ROBERT A. M. STERN
MIKE WALLACE

This Is a Borzoi Book
Published by Alfred A. Knopf

Copyright © 1999, 2003 by
Steeplechase Films, Inc.

Library of Congress Cataloging-in-
Publication Data
New York : an illustrated history /
[compiled] by Ric Burns and James
Sanders with Lisa Ades.
p.   cm.
Includes bibliographical references.
ISBN 1-4000-4146-5 (hc.) /
0-375-71032-9 (pb.) (alk. paper)
1. New York (N.Y.)—History.
2. New York (N.Y.)—History—
Pictorial works.   I. Burns, Ric.
II. Sanders, James.   III. Ades, Lisa.
F128.3.N585   1999
974.7'1—dc21   99-23569
                                CIP

Manufactured in Singapore

Published November 5, 1999

First Paperback Edition,
September 30, 2001

Expanded Edition, September 2003

The text of this book was set
in Bembo.

Composition and color separations
by North Market Street Graphics,
Lancaster, Pennsylvania

Printed and bound by
Imago, Singapore

Designed by Wendy Byrne

Endpapers: Skyline of midtown
Manhattan from Welfare (later
Roosevelt) Island, 1950.

Page i: Photographer atop a new
skyscraper on lower Fifth Avenue,
about 1910.

Pages ii–iii: Workers on the cables of
the Brooklyn Bridge, 1914.

Pages iv–v: Workmen constructing
the Woolworth Building, 1912.
The Municipal Building, also under
construction, rises on the left.

Pages vi–vii: The Lower East Side,
looking north along Mulberry
Street from Baxter Street, 1900.

This page: World War I Victory Arch
and the Flatiron Building, 1919.

Opposite: Pine and Henry streets,
looking toward the Manhattan
Bridge, March 6, 1936 (Berenice
Abbott).

Pages x–xi: Looking south on Fifth
Avenue from 57th Street, atop a
double-decker bus, about 1930.

Page xiv: Dancers atop the Chanin
Building, with the Chrysler
Building beyond, 1930.

CONTENTS

Evening is coming fast, and the great city is blazing there in your vision in its terrific frontal sweep and curtain of star-flung towers, now sown with the diamond pollen of a million lights, and the sun has set behind them, and the red light of fading day is painted upon the river—and you see the boats, the tugs, the barges passing, and the winglike swoop of bridges with exultant joy—and night has come, and there are ships there—there are ships—and a wild intolerable longing in you that you cannot utter.

Thomas Wolfe, 1933

INTRODUCTION: CITY OF DESIRE

There's a place in New York City—not so much little known as little visited—at the southern end of Ward's Island, one of the in-between places in the city, an island in the stream between Manhattan, Queens, and the Bronx where the waters of the Harlem River and the waters of Long Island Sound meet the tidal surge of the East River to form a treacherous nebula of current that the boatmen call Hell Gate.

At the very bottom of the island—which for the past sixty years or so has served mainly as a footing for the mighty Triborough Bridge, an epic human construct, Pharaonic in scale, that stitches together the North American continent and the wayward rocky forms of Manhattan and Long Island—lies an out-of-the-way park that happens to command one of the most stunning views in a city of infinitely breathtaking prospects.

Sitting in a car in the fading light of day one evening in late November 1996 after a long day of driving around the city and talking about New York—the massive tower of the Queens suspension bridge soaring into the twilight overhead—tired and exhilarated by the day and the cold, hypnotized by the afterglow behind the astonishing city, we stared at the circling, silvering tides below Hell Gate and at the darkening skyline of Manhattan beyond—brightening as dusk fell into the most sublime of human constructs—spellbound by the power and beauty and heartbreaking mystery of the modern world, and by the unfathomably huge city that is still its capital.

This book, like the twelve-hour film series to which it is a companion, has its origins in that spectacle—in the tremendous surge of longing, exhilaration, and wonder it evokes, and in the attempt to make sense of the human forces that in the course of nearly four hundred years have brought it into being.

Gazing upon New York is, of course, one of the ritual acts of our culture and, like gazing upon Mount Rushmore or Niagara Falls or the Grand Canyon, is almost an aspect of American citizenship. And understandable enough, for there is nothing in the world quite like it. For generations now, the dark beauty and inimitable power of the city have stirred men and women to the bottom of their souls, seeming the very embodiment of all ambition, all aspiration, all romance, all desire. New York has dazzled—and sometimes dazed—onlookers since the dawn of the modern age: inciting, defeating, and reigniting the imaginative energy of citizens and visitors alike as they have struggled to embrace and comprehend and somehow come to terms with it.

"The firmament that is New York," the writer Luc Sante once said, "is greater than the sum of its constituent parts. It is a city and it is also a creature, a mentality, a disease, a threat, an electromagnet, a cheap stage set, an accident corridor. It is an implausible character, a monstrous vortex of contradictions, an attraction-repulsion mechanism so extreme no one could have made it up."

"The city is like poetry," E. B. White remarked, in much the same spirit, half a century ago now. "The island of Manhattan is without any doubt the greatest human concentrate on earth, the poem whose magic is comprehensible to millions of permanent residents but whose full meaning will always remain elusive."

Like millions of others before us, then, we have gazed upon New York rapturously and in wonder, and its immense and extravagant presence has confronted us, as it has so many others, with the most basic questions. Where did such a thing come from? How did it get to be that way? What forces converged to make it possible? What does it tell us about ourselves as a people? Is there any way of explaining something so dense, complex, incomprehensibly vast, multiple, and overpowering?

This book was created amid the production of a twelve-hour documentary film series on the history of New York, a circumstance that has profoundly conditioned every aspect of its form and content. Film—no matter how conventional or experimental—is first and foremost a profoundly narrative medium; indeed, it is perhaps the most insistently and inevitably narrative of all art forms and for all its apparent modernity curiously old-fashioned in its commitments to the arrow of time. We know this from the physical form of film itself—a river of light and shadow that runs through the camera and projector at twenty-four frames per second, implacably, unstoppably, from the beginning to the end. The obligation of every film, whether twelve minutes or twelve hours long, is that it have one strong central narrative at its core.

Our first challenge in the series itself, then, and in this book, was to find and craft a narrative that could somehow encompass the nearly four hundred years and four hundred square miles and millions upon millions of people that collectively constitute the sprawling, impossibly complex history that is New York. Indeed, in the course of the nearly seven years my partners, James Sanders and Lisa Ades, and I spent working on the project, nothing proved more continually invigorating than the effort expended in seeking to grasp and forge that narrative, both on paper and on film— an intensely collaborative effort and, in the end, a deeply gratifying one.

Every great city is, of course, in some sense also a great story. The city of New York, unparalleled in its size, grandeur, and complexity, has engendered, over the course of its turbulent and spectacular history, a story that is nothing less than an urban epic—as richly peopled, as dramatically plotted, and as movingly profound as any great fiction.

It is a story rich in superlatives. New York has contained, over time, the world's largest population, the tallest buildings, the longest bridges, the busiest subways and port. Its mixtures of people and cultures are the most diverse in the world. It has more newspapers, magazines, publishers, theaters, art galleries, and restaurants than anywhere else. More gold bullion lies beneath a single street in Lower Manhattan, Maiden Lane, than in all of Fort Knox. More than a third of the entire world's monetary transactions pass electronically through New York every day of the year.

It is a story rich in contradictions. The wealthiest of American cities, New York has also been since the middle of the nineteenth century home to the greatest number of urban poor. The most relentlessly commercial of cities, embodying what Joseph Schumpeter once called the "creative destruction of capitalism," it has also—and partly for that reason—been more aggressive than any other city in America in looking for ways to mitigate the excesses of the capitalist system. The grandest of all public arenas, it is also a patchwork of small communities, at once the most cosmopolitan of places and yet the most parochial. To many foreigners it represents America; to many Americans, it represents all that is foreign. A city that relentlessly tears itself down and rebuilds itself, embodying all that is new, it nevertheless has the richest historic heritage of any city in the country. A crucible for all cities, offering a stunning vision of the future, it also offers a remarkable window onto the past. It is the ultimate city of money and the ultimate city of the imagination, and in its story from the very start money and imagination have been inseparable and intertwined.

Like all great stories, it begins at the beginning, at the time of the city's founding by the Dutch in the early seventeenth century. Unlike Puritan Boston and Quaker Philadelphia, New York was founded not as a religious establishment but as a business colony. The first colonists—all employees of the Dutch West India Company—came to New Amsterdam not to find God but to collect beaver skins and so devoted were they to making money that it took eight years to get around to building the first church on the island. As a result of that unswerving and fundamental commercial dedication, there were from the very beginning no rules—religious, ideological, or otherwise—governing who was to be included and who was to be excluded from the old Dutch colony.

And so in they came. Within two decades of its founding, the enterprising colony had begun to give rise to one of the most diverse civic cultures ever. By 1644, eighteen languages could be heard on the streets of New Amsterdam. Peter Stuyvesant himself, an almost truculently bigoted Calvinist, would have vastly preferred to keep out Lutherans and Catholics and did try to refuse entry to twenty-

two Jews in 1654. But he was overruled by the board of directors of the Dutch West India Company, who reminded him that he was running a business colony, that the labor shortages were bad enough, and that if word got out that people were being excluded from the colony, the scarce supply of labor would grow scarcer still.

From the very start, in other words, a profound relationship was established in New York between commerce and diversity—between what were called by the nineteenth century capitalism and democracy—and, from that day to this, those forces have been alive in the history and culture of New York as they have in no other city.

Melding cultures, classes, races, ideologies, and lifestyles from around the world, New York emerged by the turn of the twentieth century as the most complex and intensely interactive environment in history—a unique public arena that has condensed the widest variety of human endeavor and the fullest range of human experience within perhaps the greatest of human constructs.

No other city has more vividly embodied the problems and possibilities of a relentlessly commercial, increasingly pluralistic society. No other city has so continuously extended and challenged the American democratic experiment by gathering together in one place every conceivable class, constituency, race, religion, and ethnic group—all drawn into the vortex of New York's transforming economic engine, and charged, whether they wished to be or not, with the responsibility of building a workable common culture. In the end, for all its flaws and foibles, the city remains today what it has been for nearly four centuries: the supreme human laboratory, where the most challenging experiment of modern times continues to be carried out—the exhilarating, often harrowing experiment to see if all the world's people can live together in a single place.

To say that a city has a story, that it can be grasped by a single master narrative, is to suggest that one can see the city as a whole and understand what has made it grow. What forces or tides—human, geographical, spiritual, cultural, and economic—have shaped the history of New York? How can one grasp the whole of the history of this, or indeed of any, city? Given the enormous welter of events, how can one make sense of a city as a whole?

In its existence, many stories—many histories—many master narratives—have been put forward to make sense of New York.

There are geological narratives that take geography as destiny and chart the city's implacable rise from the harbor—when all is said and done, one of the three greatest natural deep-water ports in the world.

There are economic narratives that chronicle the arc of New York's trajectory from the periphery of one global economic system dominated by Europe to the very center of another, dominated by America. Or that chart the ceaseless ebb and flow of the boom and bust cycles of capitalism itself, the rise of eras of wild prosperity and speculation, followed by catastrophic downturns, hardship, depression—and recovery again.

There are socioeconomic narratives that chart the conflict and tension between two rival social logics in New York—one associated with the relentlessness of capitalism, the other with the myriad democratic movements that have sought to provide an alternative to that logic. "New York," the historian Mike Wallace has said, "is on the one hand a place where free market capitalism has been given its widest latitude, and yet it's also the place where the consequences of that system have been called most sharply into question and efforts made to rein it in."

There are high modernist narratives, like that of the brilliant Dutch architect Rem Koolhaas, who has described the rise of Manhattan "as the product of an unformulated theory, Manhattanism, whose program [is] to exist in a world totally fabricated by man, to live inside fantasy." Or like that of the equally brilliant American urbanist Marshall Berman, for whom New York became in the course of the nineteenth and twentieth centuries the epicenter of what Karl Marx meant when he wrote that "All that is solid melts into air"—a place where, perhaps more than anywhere else, the awesome, dissolving forces of modernity have made continuous change and transformation the only constant in the modern world.

We have tried in our film and book to avail ourselves of all these stories—to follow their trajectory from time to time or at least to catch a glimpse of them in flight. But in the end, for better or for worse, the film itself has led us back toward a simpler, and certainly a more romantic story—a narrative of wonder and simple rapture, a poetic narrative of New York—one that is mesmerized by the power and tragicomic glory of the tremendous creativity and collective achievement the city has embodied over time.

In the end, for all the complexity of the city's history, that narrative can be easily summarized.

Founded at the dawn of the modern age, when Europeans first coursed out across the globe, New York was fated to become the ultimate city of dreaming and desire, a place of passage and transformation, of possibility and exchange, of mingled cultures and identities—the place where above all others people from around the world would come to shed tradition, realize ambition, make themselves new.

Consecrated to the power of commerce and money, supercharged by the most astonishing influx of peoples the world has ever seen, it would give rise to a unique culture of transformation.

No place would project itself more relentlessly into the future. No place would embody more powerfully the cre-

ative and the destructive forces of modern life. No place would embrace more completely the American experiment in capitalism and democracy—until in the end, the story of New York would be nothing less than the story of America itself rising.

And yet for a place so ruthlessly modern, it was fated to become the most haunted city on earth, haunted not only by the past but by the future: by the shadow of all that once was, and all that had never come to be, and all that is struggling still to be born.

The story of New York in this sense presents a collective, and even mythic, human epic—the metropolis as Prometheus, who stole the fire of the gods in order to remake the world. This poetic grasp of the city has its roots in the old sense of the word *poesis*—"to make" or "to fabricate." In this sense, New York might perhaps best be seen as a history of modern men and women making and remaking their own world after their own lights.

Ezra Pound, of all people, saw this aspect of the city's character burning in the night sky over New York in the autumn of 1913 and expressed it as well as anyone ever has.

Is "New York," he wondered, "the most beautiful city in the world? It is not far from it. No urban nights are like the nights there. I have looked down across the city from high windows. It is then that the great buildings lose reality and take on magical powers. Squares and squares of flame, set and cut into the ether. Here is our poetry, for we have pulled down the stars to our will."

We hope in this book, as in the film it accompanies, to have caught glimpses of the poetry Pound saw and to have conveyed some sense of his wonder in the modern world.

Ric Burns, New York City, July 1999

Two years after this book was first published, New York City and with it much of the contemporary world were changed utterly, in the space of less than two hours, on the morning of September 11, 2001. In the epilogue to this revised edition—a companion to the eighth episode of our series, *New York: A Documentary Film*—we have sought to chronicle the epic story of the rise and fall of the World Trade Center, within the context of New York's long and fateful relationship with the rest of the world.

Ric Burns
James Sanders
June 2003

The Landing of Henry Hudson, Robert W. Weir, 1838. Painted more than two centuries after Hudson's ship, the *Half Moon*, arrived in New York Harbor, this romantic tableau depicts the fateful moment in September 1609 when Native Americans of the lower Hudson Valley rowed out to meet the European visitors they called *swanekken*— "people of the salt water."

THE COUNTRY

1609–1825

AND THE CITY

Most of the big shore places were closed now and there were hardly any lights except the shadowy, moving glow of a ferryboat across the Sound. And as the moon rose higher the inessential houses began to melt away until gradually I became aware of the old island here that flowered once for Dutch sailors' eyes—a fresh, green breast of the new world. Its vanished trees . . . had once pandered in whispers to the last and greatest of all human dreams; for a transitory enchanted moment man must have held his breath in the presence of this continent . . . face to face for the last time in history with something commensurate to his capacity for wonder.

F. Scott Fitzgerald, *The Great Gatsby*

Fifty thousand years ago, roaming glaciers a thousand feet thick chiseled out the riverbeds, waterways, and rocky land formations that comprise the harbor of New York—with Hong Kong and San Francisco, one of the three greatest natural ports in the world. The Lower Bay alone affords superb refuge from the open sea.

Through the narrows, however, lies a *second* harbor, the Upper Bay—an enormous, tranquil body of water, entirely sheltered from the rough wind and waves of the Atlantic, that forms the heart of an intricate network of rivers, bays, inlets, and estuaries—and nearly 800 miles of interior shoreline.

SAFE HAVEN

On April 17, 1524, Giovanni da Verrazano—an Italian explorer hired by the French to find a faster route to the riches of the Orient—steered his hundred-ton ship, the *Dauphine,* into the outer bay of New York Harbor, anchoring just off the sandy shore of present-day Staten Island. The first European explorer ever to set eyes upon the great harbor, the veteran Florentine sailor was not impressed. "A pleasant place," he recorded in his diary, "not without some riches." But it was not the fabled Northwest Passage he had been commissioned to find, and when a sudden storm blew up, Verrazano quickly weighed anchor and left, without actually setting foot upon dry land himself.

Eighty-five years later, on September 12, 1609, Henry Hudson, an English explorer hired by the Dutch to find a faster route to the Orient, steered his eighty-ton ship, a three-masted, flat-bottomed galliot called the *Halve Maen* (the *Half Moon*) through the narrows that Verrazano had never bothered to enter, and into an astonishing inner bay: a vast sheltered expanse of water just a few miles from the rough winds and surging currents of the North Atlantic.

The local inhabitants, who called themselves the Lenape, rowed out to meet them, trying to keep pace with the strange-looking vessel as it made its way across the bay—"eight and twentie Canoes, full of men women and children," one of Hudson's officers, Robert Juet, reported, "seeming very glad of our comming. . . . Then wee Anchored, and saw that it was a very good Harbour for all windes, and rode all night. The people of the Countrey came aboord of us, making shew of love, and gave us Tabacco and Indian Wheat, and departed for that night; but we durst not trust them."

Mesmerized by the sublime beauty of the place, Hudson moved on—sailing to the mouth of the mile-wide river that flowed into the habor from the north, then pushing his tiny vessel ninety miles upstream, hoping it led to China. It didn't. But though he had failed to find the Northwest Passage, Hudson had stumbled upon something even better: one of the best and biggest natural harbors in the world, and the main entrance to the most abundant continent on earth.

Hudson soon set sail for home, a perilous four-thousand-mile, three-month crossing made materially more uncomfortable by his unruly Dutch and English crew. By winter, however, the seasoned explorer had managed to send back to Amsterdam tantalizing tales of the rich bounty in fur, timber, and crops waiting to be harvested in the New World. "The land is the finest for cultivation that I ever in my life set foot upon," he wrote in an official report to his clients, the directors of the Dutch East India Company. "Were our own industrious farmers to settle here, they would soon transform this wilderness into a Paradise where no man need ever go hungry. . . . Never have I beheld such a rich and pleasant land."

Of all the early explorers, Hudson was first to grasp the immense potential of the remote and lonely place that would one day give rise to the greatest city on earth—though he himself would never again see the great bay, or the majestic waterway that would bear his name. Two years later, in 1611, he set sail again to find the Northwest Passage, up by present-day Hudson's Bay, in northern Canada. There, his crew mutinied again, in earnest this time, and he was last seen bobbing alone in a small skiff, on which he had been cast adrift in the open sea.

In the dramatic history about to unfold, geography would prove to be destiny—more, perhaps, than in the history of any other city on earth. Following Hudson's lead, other navigators would explore the contours of a harbor unlike any other. With eight hundred miles of pristine shoreline, comprising seven bays, four river mouths, and four estuaries, it was a vast and intricate meeting of land and water—a "safe and convenient haven," the Dutch chronicler Adriaen van der Donck reported in 1650, "wherein a thousand ships may ride in safety." Washed by three powerful currents at once, from the river, the ocean, and the Long Island Sound, it was a self-sustaining wonder—arguably the greatest natural port in the world—that never needed dredging and that was seldom bound by fog or blocked by ice. Over the next two hundred years, as Europeans took hold of the spectacular natural resource the last ice age had left behind, that port would arise—moving inexorably from the periphery of one European empire toward the center of another, only

The determined and resourceful English navigator Henry Hudson—one of the premier explorers of his day—dedicated his whole career to finding the fabled Northwest Passage to India. He had already made two unsuccessful voyages, sailing for an English firm called the Muscovy Company, when in the spring of 1609 the Dutch East India Company hired him to make another attempt. For his third trip, Hudson personally outfitted his new ship, the *Half Moon,* which while modest in size— just 63 feet long and 17 feet wide at the beam— offered the era's most advanced hull and sail design.

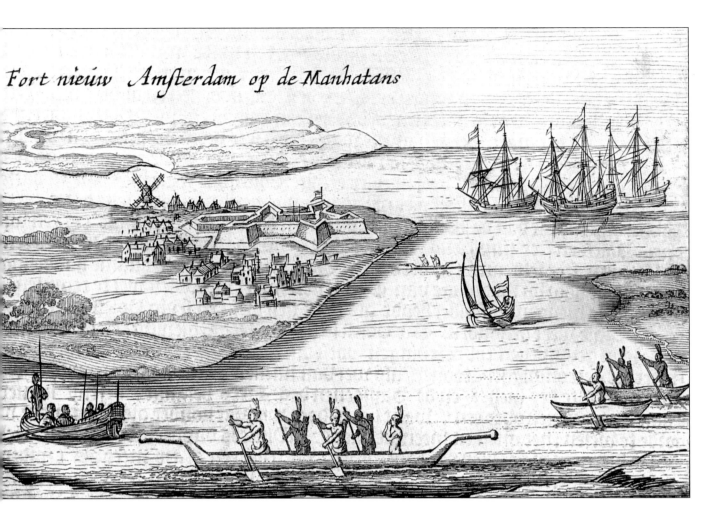

Fort nieuw Amsterdam op de Manhatans

The earliest known view of the city (inadvertently printed backward when an engraving of it was made in 1651) was probably drawn in 1626 by Kryn Frederycks, a civil engineer hired to lay out the original Dutch settlement at the foot of Manhattan. Frederycks depicted the colony's 30-odd houses and windmill accurately enough, but the imposing five-bastioned fortification—laid out by Frederycks himself in 1625—was never completed. A less ambitious four-sided earthwork was finished in 1628, at the foot of present-day Broadway, across from the Bowling Green.

to become the undisputed commercial capital of a new American empire emerging in the New World.

But no one, not even Henry Hudson, could have imagined what would have to transpire for that destiny to be fulfilled: native peoples displaced and all but destroyed—rival empires displacing each other—until the Old World had at last been cast off and replaced by a new kind of culture, capable of transforming geography itself.

NEW AMSTERDAM

The Dutch sprang into action—spurred on by Henry Hudson's glowing reports of a fur-trading paradise, and eager to beat out their archrivals, the English, to the spoils of the North American continent.

In 1621, a consortium of merchants from five Dutch cities laid claim to an enormous tract of land along the middle Atlantic seaboard, stretching all the way from the Delaware River in the

south to the Connecticut River in the north, including the entire Hudson River valley. They called the sprawling territory Nieuw Neder-landt—New Netherland. From one end to the other, the new colony was to be owned and operated by a giant corporation called the Dutch West India Company—the Atlantic wing of a vast trading empire that stretched around the globe.

Sailing the fastest ships on the ocean and opening up markets from Singapore to South America, Holland had by the third decade of the seventeenth century eclipsed France, Spain, and Portugal, and threatened to overtake England itself as the most sophisticated maritime power in the world. The English writer and novelist Daniel Defoe thought he understood their secret. "The Dutch," he wrote, "must be understood as they really are—the Middle Persons in Trade, the Factors and Brokers of Europe. They buy to sell again, take in to send out, and the greatest Part of their vast Commerce con-

Few civic legends have enjoyed wider currency or longer appeal than the celebrated $24 deal that stands at the threshold of New York City's history. Conjured from a bewildering tangle of fact, fantasy, wishful thinking, and legend, it remains to this day a potent—if almost comically dog-eared—foundation myth for a city devoted as no other to the business of buying and selling. That some kind of transaction actually took place is virtually certain—though no deed of sale has survived. On November 5, 1626, a merchant with the Dutch West India Company named Pieter Jansen Schagen wrote that the colonists had "bought the

island Manhattes from the wildmen for the value of sixty guilders." From the simple language of Schagen's report a profusion of half-truths would spring in the centuries to come. In 1846, one early historian came up with the now-famous $24 figure—using anachronistic exchange rates that were subsequently never revised. (A Dutch bank recently re-calculated the rate using current dollars, and came up with the somewhat less memorable figure of $669.42). In 1877, another layer of myth was added when yet another historian confidently declared that the Dutch had paid the Indians in "beads, buttons, and other trinkets"—an

undocumented assertion that has been a staple of accounts ever since. Infinitely pliable, the story has been used to deride Native Americans for making the worst real-estate deal in history—and to mock the Dutch, for purchasing something the local Indians considered impossible to own. Handed down from generation to generation, the story of the deal has become part of American folklore—and often the only anecdote from early New York familiar to those outside the city. If lacking the grandeur of older myths of origin—such as that of Romulus and Remus who, suckled by wolves, went on to found Rome—the

worldly tale perfectly captures the spirit of the great commercial city—locating its beginnings not in military conquest or divine intervention but in a business deal (and one involving, moreover, the quintessential New York business—real estate). In the end, however, the essence of the story's enduring appeal may lie in the simple touch of wonder it evokes, at the sheer scale and completeness of the transformation that turned a few square miles of primeval forest into the most valuable and densely built-up parcel of land in the world.

sists in being supply'd from All Parts of the World, that they may supply All the World again." No matter how far it came or how large it grew, the colony the Dutch were about to found would forever after be animated by the original Dutch genius for transaction and exchange.

In the spring of 1624, the first boatload of Dutch colonists arrived to establish a permanent presence in the harbor. One hundred and ten men, women and children in all, in thirty different families, the newcomers were mostly not Dutch at all but French-speaking Protestants, called Walloons. They chose as the headquarters of their operations the slender rugged island at the head of the bay—"the key and principal stronghold of the country," one man said—and called it Manna-hata, after an old Indian word, thought by some to mean "island of hills," and by others, "place of general inebriation."

The encampment thrown up at its southern tip they named New Amsterdam, after Holland's largest city, where the company's board of directors resided. By the spring of 1625, the newcomers had managed to put up a few bark cabins on the east side of the island, sheltered from the wind, along with a stone counting-house, a brewery, a mill, an earthwork fortification, called Fort Amsterdam, and a small fur-trading post.

Hundreds of Lenape already made their home on the island. To facilitate fur trading with them, the Dutch colonists soon widened an ancient hunting trail that ran north from the fort, calling it Heere Straat, and later Breede Wegh. It would become Broadway.

A business proposition from the very start, New Amsterdam was the original company town—its citizens all company employees, and its director general a company appointee, commanded by the terms of his charter "to do all that . . . the increase of trade shall require." So intent were the new colonists upon making money, they would not get around to building a church for almost a decade. For eight years, the weekly services of the Dutch Reformed Church had to be conducted in a loft space above the company mill.

In 1626, two fateful events took place. On May 26, the colony's director general, Peter Minuit, called together the leaders of all the local tribes and had bundles of goods distributed to them—axes, probably, along with farm implements, sewing trinkets, and cloth. We "have bought the island Manhattes from the wildmen," the Dutch merchant Pieter Jansen Schagen later reported in a letter to Amsterdam, "for the value of sixty guilders." In fact, the Dutch had paid far more than the twenty-four dollars of legend, but still little more than five hundred dollars for all fourteen thousand acres of Manhattan real estate.

The Lenape, whose ancestors had lived on the island since the end of the last ice age, thought the arrangement temporary.

One month later, in June 1626, a ship carrying the first eleven African slaves arrived from Angola. They were quickly put to work building the fort and clearing land for Dutch farmers.

"The colony is now established on Manhattan," a visiting physician and journalist named Nicolaes van Wassenaer announced at the end of 1626. "A fort has been staked out by Master Kryn Frederycks, an engineer. It is planned to be of large dimensions. . . . Every one is busy about his own affairs. Men work there as in Holland; one trades, upwards, southwards and northwards; another builds houses, the third farms."

That year, by van Wassenaer's count, 7,246 beaver skins, 675 otter skins, 48 mink, and 36 wildcat were bought in trade from Native American trappers along the Hudson Valley and shipped back to Holland from New Amsterdam.

"There is great traffic in the skins of beavers, otters, foxes and minks, wild cats and the like," a company official named Johannes de Laet confirmed in a report to his colleagues back in Amsterdam. "The land is excellent and agreeable, full of noble forest trees and grapevines, and nothing is wanted but the labor and industry of man to render it one of the finest and most fruitful lands in that part of the world."

As the fur trade expanded, other settlements began to spring up around the harbor. In 1635, Dutch colonists began laying out the village of Breuckelen, named for a town back in Holland and linked by rowboat to Manhattan. Four years later, a Danish sea captain named Jonas Bronck

*New England has captured American
history. It has made 1620 the great date, the
Mayflower the great argosy. Yet . . . Dutch-
men were comfortably settled in Manhattan
when the first boatload scrambled ashore on
Plymouth Rock. And where the Puritans
who had dared greatly for freedom of
worship persecuted the slightest forms of dissent . . . the Dutch colony welcomed their
exiles. . . . In consequence colonists of every
faith, Huguenots, Swedish and German
Lutherans, Scotch Presbyterians, English
Independents, Moravians, Anabaptists,
and Jews gathered there. . . . Indeed, the
"polyglot boarding-house," derided in our
time as a latter-day plague, is of ancient lineage, while the most inherently American
doctrines of religious toleration, of personal
freedom are our Netherlandish, our New
Amsterdam, our Manhattan heritage.*

Ernest Gruening, *The Nation*,
November 29, 1922

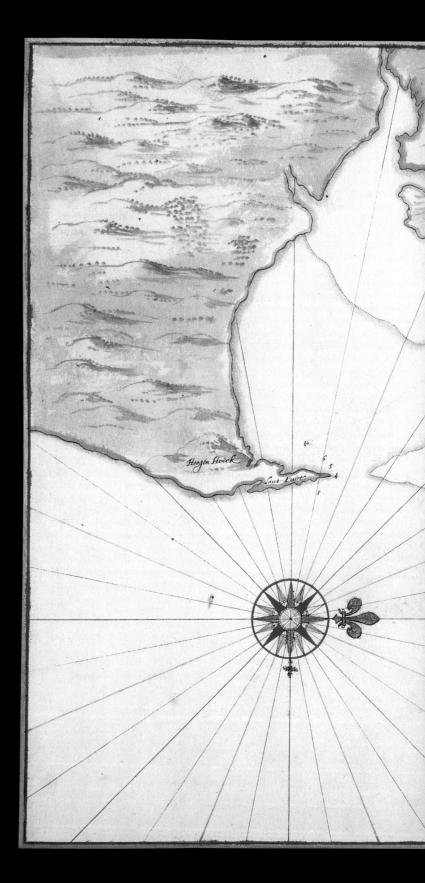

Encompassing much of
what would eventually
become the five boroughs
of New York City, the
"Manatus Map"—drawn
in 1639 by a cartographer
named Johannes Ving-
boom—was probably cre-
ated to boost Dutch set-
tlement in the remote
colony—in part, by adver-
tising the availability of
attractive sites for farm-
steads and estates. Ori-
ented east-west rather
than north-south, with

the shoreline of present-day New Jersey at the top, the map is filled with hauntingly familiar names, beginning with the "Eyland Manatus" itself. "Staten Eylant," named for the Dutch States General, the governing body of the Netherlands, guards the entrance to the inner harbor. Across the Narrows, "Conyn Eylent," named for the wild rabbits that once abounded there, protrudes like the nub of an eraser from the foot of present-day Brooklyn. Running along the west side of Manhattan is the "Noort Rivier," or North River, the original name for the lower Hudson and one used by seamen well into the twentieth century. The key provided at the lower right reveals, among other things, that number 43 on the map—across the Harlem River from Manhattan, in what is now the Bronx—marks the site of Jonas Bronck's "bouwerie" or estate. The wealthy Danish farmer's name would eventually be extended to the entire borough.

settled his family on a sprawling plantation north of Manhattan. It would eventually be known simply as "the Broncks."

But despite the company's high hopes for quick profits, the remote and lonely colony struggled to take hold. Four thousand miles from the mother country, New Amsterdam was on the far edge of the known world, and though the officials of the Dutch West India Company did what they could to attract new colonists—including offers of free passage and free tracts of land—few Dutch citizens were willing to come. In desperation, company officials sent over indentured servants, orphans from Dutch poorhouses, and more slaves, but it did little to ease the chronic labor shortage in the colony. More than a decade after being founded, New Amsterdam was home to just four hundred people, a startling percentage of whom seemed to be smugglers, pirates, prostitutes, and drunks.

Director generals came and went. When yet another, Willem Kieft, arrived in 1638, he was dismayed to find windmills standing idle, and company farms and storehouses in disrepair. Pigs could be seen rooting in the foundations of the crumbling fort, and one in four dwellings, Kieft estimated, was being used as a tavern.

And there was worse trouble to come. As the fur trade began to fall off, the Dutch colonists cleared more land to make way for farms—

sparking anger and resentment among the Lenape. In 1643, Director General Kieft—whose harsh style of rule had earned him the nickname "Willem the Testy"—tried to tax the Lenape, and when they resisted, launched a brutal year-long war against them, resolving, he said, to "wipe the Indians' chops" once and for all.

On February 26, 1643, a platoon of Dutch soldiers acting on Kieft's orders fell on two unsuspecting Lenape villages, butchered eighty men, women, and children in their sleep, then marched back to Fort Amsterdam with the severed heads of their victims. Before the year was out, hundreds of Indians and dozens of Dutch settlers had died in what was called the Year of the Blood.

"Our fields lie fallow," one colonist grimly recorded in 1644, "our dwellings are burnt; the crops which the Lord permitted to come forth during the past summer remain in the field standing and rotting. . . . We have no means to provide necessaries for wife and children; and we sit here amidst thousands of Indians and barbarians, from whom we find neither peace nor mercy."

The board of directors of the Dutch West India Company had had enough. In 1645, Willem Kieft was recalled to Amsterdam to answer for his actions, but died before he could

Newcomers approaching New Amsterdam from the south in 1653 could already see the fruits of Stuyvesant's new regime. The most prominent silhouettes on the spartan skyline of Manhattan included the company windmill; the twin gables of the Dutch Reformed Church the director general had erected inside the perimeter of the renovated fort; and—down by the newly constructed wharf—the cantilevered armature of the colony's weighing beam, which sometimes did double duty now as a whipping post and gallows.

NIEUW AMSTERD.
op t Eylant Manhattans.

Peter Stuyvesant at 50 (below), in a 1660 portait by Henrick Couturier. Among the least-loved and most effective leaders the city would ever see, the puritanical, one-legged ex-soldier was legendary for his fiery temper and unbending style of rule. He often "burst into a violent rage," one Dutch merchant complained, "if we in our advice didn't fall in with his humor." But whether his colonists liked it or not, Stuyvesant brought order to the unruly backwater, and during his 17 years as director general ruthlessly bullied the town's fiercely independent citizenry into making New Amsterdam a going concern.

get there when his ship was caught in a storm off Wales, and sank with everyone on board. On the other side of the Atlantic, the colony he had so incompetently governed was falling apart—its population stagnant, drunkenness and petty crime increasing, and morale at an all-time low. The experiment was failing.

DIRECTOR GENERAL

On the island of Manhate, and in its environs, there may well be four or five hundred men of different sects and nations: the Director General told me that there were men of eighteen different languages; they are scattered here and there on the river, above and below, as the beauty and convenience of the spot has invited each to settle: some mechanics however, who ply their trade, are ranged under the fort; all others are exposed to the incursions of the natives, who in the year 1643, while I was there, actually killed some two score Hollanders, and burnt many houses and barns full of wheat.

Father Isaac Jogues, 1646

In the spring of 1647, New Amsterdam got a new director general. A tall, thirty-seven-year-old ex-soldier and minister's son, who had lost his right leg to a cannonball during a naval battle in the West

Indies, he had been hastily transferred up from the Dutch colony at Curaçao by the company's worried board of directors.

Iron-willed, short-tempered, and rigidly puritanical, Peter Stuyvesant had strict orders to clean up the colony. "I shall govern you as a father his children," he told the stubborn and unruly colonists upon arrival, and it was soon apparent he meant every word he said.

He quickly made peace with the Lenape, then, to improve public safety, formed the city's first regular police force—a detail of nine men, authorized to patrol New Amsterdam's unlit streets after dark with orders to "pursue, attack and capture . . . robbers or others who would wish to inflict injury and damage." To improve public morals, he banned drinking on Sundays, outlawed knife fighting in public, and imposed stiff fines for missing church, for driving wagons too fast on Broadway, and for fornicating with the Indians.

It was the beginning of a long and stormy relationship between the director general and his colonists. Though they bitterly resented his harsh style of rule, under Stuyvesant's guidance the colony began to take hold.

Recognizing that New Amsterdam could never thrive on fur and farming alone, he sought to give it a new economic base—slaving. In the years to come, the colony would become a crucial depot for plantations in the Caribbean and the mainland American South, its merchants running slaves, along with molasses and rum, in and out of Africa, the West Indies, and North America.

In less than a decade, Stuyvesant managed to transform the disorderly backwater into a self-respecting town, with its own canals and windmills, three hundred forty row houses, and a population of fifteen hundred. Under his auspices, the city's first school was founded, along with the first post office, hospital, jail, almshouse, orphanage, and coroner's office. Making use of the company's growing supply of African slaves, he had the rocky shoreline trimmed with a neat bulkhead so that ships could anchor closer to shore, then ordered construction of the colony's first pier.

In 1653, the rigid director unbent far enough to let the fiercely independent citizens of New Amsterdam set up a rudimentary deliberative body of their own, separate from company rule. In February, the first municipal government in North America was convened, on the island of Manhattan. The fledgling board of five schepens, or aldermen, met in a tavern that had been hastily converted for use as a city hall.

Their first act was to authorize the construction of an imposing 2,340-foot wall, stretching all the way across the island, from the East River to the Hudson—to keep out hostile Indians and the English. Separating the bustle of the city from the infinitely spreading wilderness beyond, the wall rehearsed the essential idea of Manhattan: the concentration of resources within an enclosed space, to maximize human and commercial potential.

> *The sweet ruler that influences the wisdom, power, and appearance of man, of animals, and of plants, is the air. Many name it the temperament, or the climate. The air in the New Netherlands is so dry, sweet, and healthy that we need not wish that it were otherwise. In purity, agreeableness, and fineness, it would be folly to seek for an example of it in any other country.*
>
> Adriaen van der Donck, 1653

> *They all drink here, from the moment they are able to lick a spoon. . . . The women of the neighborhood entertain each other with a pipe and brazier; young and old, they all smoke.*
>
> Nicasius de Sille, 1653

Despite Stuyvesant's heroic efforts, New Amsterdam could never grow fast enough to compete with the chain of English colonies rapidly expanding to the north and south of the New Netherlands. Desperate to ease the chronic labor shortage in the colony, Stuyvesant reluctantly agreed to let in almost anyone willing to work, though it offended his sense of order.

By 1654, company officials reported hearing eighteen languages on the streets of New Amsterdam, including English, French, Irish, German, Spanish, Polish, and Portuguese, and as the colony became a kind of global village, Stuyvesant feared it would become too diverse to govern. "The English and French colonies are populated by their own countrymen," he lamented in 1661, "and consequently bound together more firmly and united; while [we in] New Netherland are peopled by the scrapings of all sorts of nationalities, who have [not] the least interest in the welfare and maintenance of the commonwealth."

Stuyvesant's chief advisor, an austere Calvinist minister named Johannes Megapolensis, agreed that the worrisome influx of foreigners had to stop somewhere. The colony was already on the verge of becoming "a Babel of confusion," he wrote. "For as we have here Papists, Mennonites, and Lutherans among the Dutch; also many Puritans or Independents, and many Atheists . . . who conceal themselves under the name of Christians; it would create a still greater

New Amsterdam had acquired a reputation for loose morals and bawdy behavior before it was two decades old. One newcomer in 1638 was appalled to discover that almost one in four structures in the tiny colony served as "grog shops or houses where nothing is to be got but tobacco and beer." Peter Stuyvesant labored tirelessly to put an end to debauchery and drunkenness in Manhattan—with little success. The city would never live down its reputation for boisterous high spirits and rowdy behavior— satirized in the nineteenth-century painting *Peter Stuyvesant's Army*.

Peter Stuyvesant did everything he could to stop the proliferation of Lutherans, "Papists," and Mennonites in New Amsterdam. In 1656, he publicly rebuked a Mennonite shoemaker named William Wickendam for baptizing converts in the East River, then expelled him from the colony. The incident became the subject of John Whetten Ehninger's 1850 painting, *Peter Stuyvesant and the Cobbler.*

confusion if the obstinate and immovable Jews came to settle here."

But they soon did. In September 1654, twenty-three Sephardic Jews arrived in New Amsterdam, seeking refuge from the Spanish Inquisition in Brazil. It was the last straw. Stuyvesant immediately petitioned the board of directors of the Dutch West India Company in Amsterdam to have them turned away—insisting, he wrote, that "none of the Jewish nation . . . be permitted to infest New Netherland."

The refugees filed a counterpetition, requesting, they wrote, "that your Honors be pleased not to exclude but to grant the Jewish nation passage to and residence in that country; otherwise this would result in a great prejudice to their reputation. Also that . . . the Jewish nation be permitted . . . to travel, live and traffic there, and . . . enjoy liberty on condition of contributing like others."

To Stuyvesant's dismay, his own petition was overturned. Reminding him that he was running a business colony, not a religious establishment, and that the investors of the Dutch West India Company included several wealthy

Jews, the company directors chastised Stuyvesant for his intolerance, and insisted that no one be turned away.

"The consciences of men," they wrote in a later statement of policy, "ought to be free and unshackled, so long as they continue moderate, peaceable, inoffensive and not hostile to government. Such have been the maxims of . . . toleration by which . . . this city has been governed; and the result has been, that the oppressed and persecuted from every country have found among us an asylum from distress. Follow in the same steps and you shall be blessed."

Stuyvesant grudgingly gave in. The Jews were allowed to stay, though prohibited from worshipping in public. On September 12, 1654, the first Rosh Hashanah service in North America was held in a private house on the corner of what became Broad Street and Mill Lane, in New Amsterdam. It was the beginning of Congregation Shearith Israel, the oldest existing Jewish congregation in the New World.

Without intending to, the tiny Dutch outpost on the edge of the world had begun to pioneer a new kind of society, unlike any other in North America. The English Puritans who

REDRAFT
of
THE CASTELLO PLAN
NEW AMSTERDAM
in
1660

JOHN WOLCOTT ADAMS
I. N. PHELPS STOKES
1916

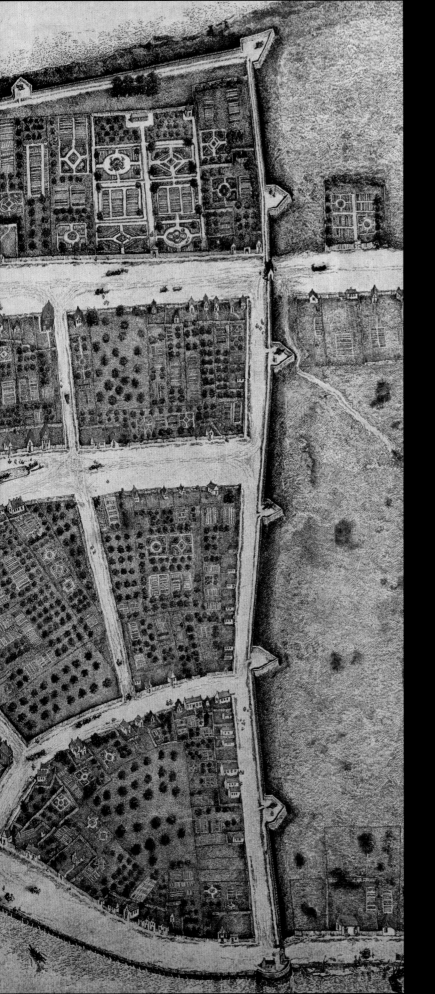

Prepared in the summer of 1660 by New Amsterdam's surveyor general, Jacques Cortelyou, the celebrated Castello Plan—named for the Florentine villa where it was rediscovered in 1900—offers a breathtaking aerial view of the colony in the last years of Dutch rule. To a startling degree, the footprint of the modern financial district is plainly legible in the lineaments of the baroque colonial plan. Then as now, Breede Wegh—later Broadway—ran south to the Bowling Green. The gently curving canal that once cut into the heart of the closely built-up town runs along the path of present-day Broad Street, nearly all the way up to the 2,340-foot wall—built where Wall Street now stands.

With its limits sharply defined on all sides by the man-made wall and two great rivers, the city was a kind of miniature Amsterdam, whose density and compactness made it convenient for business and easy to defend. In the lovingly detailed view, 342 houses and buildings can be seen, along with the stout ramparts of Fort Amsterdam, the company pier and windmill, and the tidily laid out gardens, orchards, and backyards. "This place, the Manhattans," a Dutch sea captain named Jacob Jansen Hays wrote on September 30, 1660, one month after the Castello Plan was made, "is quite rich of people, and there are at present full over 350 houses, so that it begins to be a brave place."

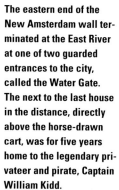

The eastern end of the New Amsterdam wall terminated at the East River at one of two guarded entrances to the city, called the Water Gate. The next to the last house in the distance, directly above the horse-drawn cart, was for five years home to the legendary privateer and pirate, Captain William Kidd.

Looking southeast toward the East River waterfront, along the Heere Gracht—the tiny creek Peter Stuyvesant had deepened and widened into a canal. Allowing goods and supplies to be brought directly into town, the picturesque canal was one of the touches that most reminded the colony's Dutch citizens of their homeland. Perhaps for that very reason—or because in low tide, the canal tended to become a pestilential ditch—English officials ordered it filled in and paved over in 1676, 12 years after taking over the colony.

founded Boston five years after New Amsterdam began, demanded religious obedience from all their citizens and banished those who would not conform. The business-minded Dutch, by contrast, were willing to accept people of any faith—including those of no faith at all—as long as they were willing to work. In the centuries to come, the city's greatest challenges—and greatest strengths—would always come from its extraordinary diversity.

ENGLISH DOGS

In the end, Dutch rule would prove remarkably brief—lasting just forty years, from 1624 until 1664. And yet in that time they would give the city much of its enduring character: its unswerving commitment to business and commerce, its willingness to take in almost anybody—and its openness to change.

But the colony never became quite as profitable as the directors of the Dutch West India

Company had wished, and, with each passing year, grew increasingly vulnerable to the encroachments of Holland's archenemy, the English.

For years, tension between the two great powers had been on the rise. In 1658, one hundred outraged English sea captains, galled by Holland's prowess on the high seas, bitterly denounced the greed and incivility of their rivals, in a petition to Oliver Cromwell. "The Dutch eat us out of our trade at home and abroad," the injured mariners wrote. "They refuse to sell us a hogshead of water to refresh us at sea, and call us 'English Dogs,' which doth much grieve our English spirits. They will not sail with us, but shoot at us, and by indirect courses bring their goods into our ports."

In 1664, friction between the two superpowers came to a head—in North America. With English colonists expanding aggressively northward from Virginia and southward from Massachusetts through Connecticut, Britain moved to perfect its thousand-mile hold on the Atlantic seaboard, and rid the American continent once and for all of its rival.

On the morning of August 27, 1664, four heavily armed English warships sailed into the harbor, ready to take the Dutch colony by force, if necessary.

Peter Stuyvesant climbed painfully to the top of Fort Amsterdam and made ready for battle. "I would rather be carried to my grave" than surrender, he said. But before a shot could be fired, Stuyvesant was handed a petition that had been signed by ninety-three leading merchants of the town—including his own son. It urged him to consider the "absolute ruin and destruction" that the British guns could rain down on their closely built-up, wood-and-brick town, and implored him to surrender without a struggle.

There was nothing he could do. Facing hopeless odds and an indifferent citizenry, Stuyvesant gave up without a fight. In a solemn ceremony a week later, the blue, white, and orange colors of the Netherlands were struck for the last time and—with drums beating and flags flying—Stuyvesant led his troops out of the fort forever.

In the years to come, the man who first brought order to the city and thus secured its future would retire to a sprawling estate north

By the time New Amsterdam was renamed in his honor, James Stuart, Duke of York (right), was already playing an aggressive role in British colonial policy. In early 1664, eager to oust the Dutch from North America, he convinced his brother, King Charles II, to proclaim him proprietor of the territory occupied by the New Netherlands—then quickly ordered a British fleet across the ocean to lay claim to his new "possession."

of town, and tend a fruit farm on land that would one day be Greenwich Village.

The English governor who replaced him, Richard Nicolls, shrewdly did everything he could to ease the transition between the two empires. Dutch legal customs, he assured the brand-new English subjects, would remain intact; Dutch officials if they chose could stay in office; and Dutch itself could still be used for the purpose of transacting business. The royal governor even graciously offered free passage back to Holland for any Dutch citizen unwilling to accept English rule.

No one took him up on it. Virtually overnight, the town had traded allegiance from one empire to another, and for decades would remain poised between two identities, neither entirely English nor entirely Dutch.

Two days after the English takeover, on August 29, 1664, New Amsterdam was officially renamed New York, in honor of the Duke of York, the brother of King Charles II, to whom the colony had been promised as a birthday present.

The day after that, everyone went back to work, as if nothing much had happened after all.

THE HAND OF GOD

To say something of the Indians, there is now but few upon the Island, and those few no ways hurtful but rather serviceable to the English, and it is to be admired, how strangely they have decreast by the Hand of God, since the English first setling of those parts; for since my time, where there were six towns, they are reduced to two small Villages, and it hath been generally observed, that where the English come to settle, a Divine Hand makes way for them, by removing or cutting off the Indians either by Wars one with the other, or by some raging mortal Disease.

Daniel Denton, 1670

Though the British signed treaties of friendship with the Lenape after taking control of the colony in 1664, the displacement of the original inhabitants continued. Within a handful of years, they had been forced to relinquish all lands within the boundaries of present-day New York City. By the end of the eighteenth century, almost all of the Lenape were gone, having succumbed to disease, or moved up the Hudson Valley in search of open land.

Increasingly, the few that remained intermarried with whites, and they rarely taught their children the old language and ways. One by one, the last surviving speakers of Algonquian would die off, ending all living connection to the native culture that had once thrived throughout the region.

Looking back, later historians of New York would be awestruck by how swiftly the aboriginals had been swept aside—an ultimately annihilating confrontation that would haunt

What race first peopled the island of Manhatta? They were, but are not. The wild children of nature, unmolested by the white man, roamed through its forests, and impelled their light canoes along its tranquil waters. But the time was near at hand when these domains were to be invaded by strangers who would lay the humble foundations of a mighty state, and scatter everywhere in their path exterminating principles which would never cease to act until the whole aboriginal race should be extirpated.

E. Porter Belden, 1849

Native Americans along the Atlantic seaboard—depicted in an early English illustration by John White called *The Manner of Their Fishing* (above)—had settled over much of what would become the five boroughs of New York City, with settlements in present-day Queens at Rockaway (whose name meant "sandy place"), Maspeth ("bad water place"), and Jamaica ("beaver place"), as well as in Brooklyn, at Canarsie ("grassy place").

the city's history down to the present day. In the end, it would be the fate of New York's original inhabitants to be remembered—when they were remembered at all—as place-names, in what had become the most completely man-made environment on earth.

NEW YORK

For 119 years, England would rule New York, as the colony moved steadily from the periphery of one European empire toward the center of another. What for the Dutch had been a second-rate outpost of empire was for the English the strategic missing link in a chain of colonies stretching the length of the Atlantic seaboard.

Slowly but surely the new English governors brought the colony into the imperial system: reorganizing the lands around the harbor and naming them after members of the royal family.

The flatlands surrounding Brooklyn were named Kings County, in honor of King Charles, and the region to the north, Queens, in honor of his wife, Catherine. Staten Island was named Richmond after the Duke of Richmond—the king's bastard son.

New York has first a chaplain . . . of the Church of England; secondly, a Dutch Calvinist; thirdly, a French Calvinist; fourthly a Dutch Lutheran. Here be . . . few Roman Catholics, abundance of Quaker preachers . . . Singing Quakers, Ranting Quakers, Sabbatarians, Anti-Sabbatarians, some Anabaptists, some Independents, some Jews; in short of all sorts of opinions there are some, and the most part, of none at all.

Governor Thomas Dongan, 1687

The number of Inhabitants in this Province are about 3000 families, whereof almost one halfe are naturally Dutch a great part English and the rest French. . . . As to their Religion they are very much divided. [A] few of them intelligent & sincere but the most part ignorant & conceited, fickle & regardless. As to their wealth & disposition thereto [the] Dutch are rich & sparing, the English neither very rich nor too great husbands, the French are poor and therefore forced to be penurious: As to their way of trade & dealing they are all general cun-

ning and crafty but many of them not so just to their words as they should be.

John Miller, 1695

Though they did everything they could to ease the transition, the English found it no easier than the Dutch to keep order in the fractious, mongrel colony.

In 1685, Charles II died, and his brother, James, the Duke of York, succeeded him as king. One of his first acts was to attempt the administrative merger of New York with its neighboring colonies New Jersey, Pennsylvania, and New England—provoking a storm of protest from Dutch New Yorkers, who feared that their heritage would be drowned in a sea of Englishness. In 1689, a forty-nine-year-old merchant named Jacob Leisler led a populist takeover of the colony with the support of its Dutch citizens. The English reconsidered the merger, but not before Leisler's Rebellion was brutally put down. In May 1691, Leisler and his chief confederate were tried, convicted, and sentenced to be publicly executed at a gallows on Park Row—where, the royal governor, Henry Sloughter, stipulated, they were to be "hanged by the Neck and being Alive their bodys be Cutt Downe to the Earth; that Their Bowells be taken out and they being Alive, burnt before their faces; that their heads shall be struck off and their Bodys Cutt in four parts."

> *The city of New York is a pleasant, well-compacted place, situated on a*
> *commodious river which is a fine harbor for shipping. The buildings brick generally,*
> *very stately and high. . . . The insides of them are neat to admiration. The English*
> *go very fashionable in their dress. But the Dutch, especially the middling sort, differ*
> *from our women. . . . Their fingers are hooped with rings, some with large stones*
> *in them of many colors as were their pendants in their ears.*
>
> Sarah Kemble Knight, 1704

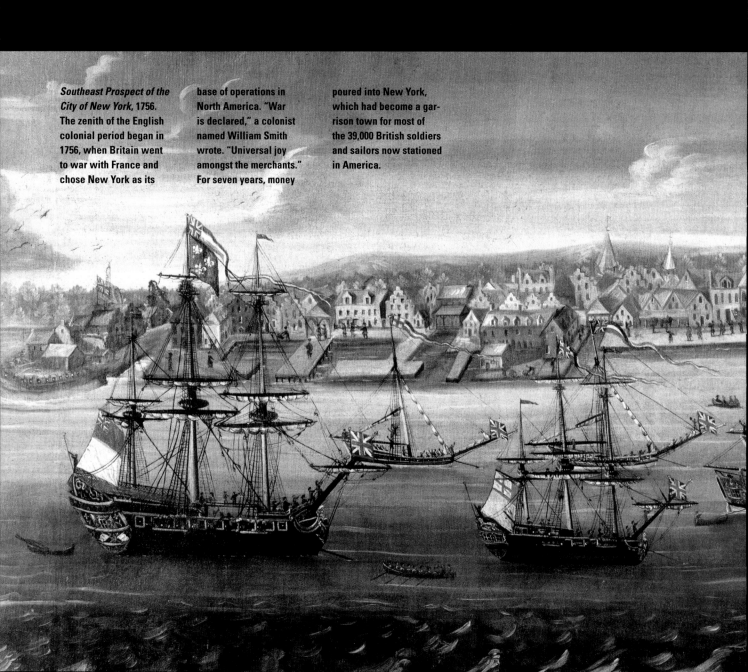

Southeast Prospect of the City of New York, 1756. The zenith of the English colonial period began in 1756, when Britain went to war with France and chose New York as its base of operations in North America. "War is declared," a colonist named William Smith wrote. "Universal joy amongst the merchants." For seven years, money poured into New York, which had become a garrison town for most of the 39,000 British soldiers and sailors now stationed in America.

South East View of the City of New York, 1768, based on a drawing by Thomas Howdell. In contrast to the busy waterfront along the East River, the city's western districts (right) were almost pastoral. "The eye of a European," the French visitor St. Jean de Crevecoeur wrote in 1772, "is agreeably surprised to see . . . these rocky shores planed down, turned into delightful gardens, ornamented with elegant houses, pretty retreats, planted with fruit trees, and become meadows and cultivated fields." The prominent building at the center of this 1768 view is King's College—later Columbia.

A few years later, trouble erupted again, when a new monarch, Queen Anne, placed her own cousin, an imperious viscount named Edward Hyde, Lord Cornbury, in charge of the volatile colony. Petitioning the queen for his dismissal, Cornbury's enemies did everything they could to ruin his reputation—accusing him of embezzling public funds, persecuting Presbyterians—and, it was later said, of having a special liking for women's clothing. "It was not uncommon," one of his detractors supposedly charged, "for him to dress himself in a woman's habit, and then to patrole the fort in which he resided. Such freaks of low humour exposed him to the universal contempt of the people." "I represent a woman," Cornbury was said to have retorted, "and ought in all respects to resemble her as faithfully as I can." No one would ever be sure whether the viscount had been the target of an elaborate political smear campaign, or whether his predilection for dresses was genuine. One way or the other, after four years he was removed from office and returned to London.

Despite all the problems, including a string of startlingly incompetent governors, membership in the British Empire brought with it enormous benefits to the port city, as England soon surpassed Holland as the greatest maritime empire on earth, and pulled New York into the mainstream of its rapidly expanding network of global trade.

By 1699, the royal governor was able to boast that New York was "the growingest town in America." That year, the old Dutch wall was pulled down to make way for new houses, and a new lane paved over it, called Wall Street. In the surrounding countryside new settlements arose, and old ones expanded: Greenwich Village, two miles to the north, named for a town outside London, and five miles beyond that, Harlem, a farming community named for a suburb of Amsterdam.

The immense potential of the harbor, protected by the world's most powerful navy, and connected to Britain's global trade routes, began to shift and stir. Year by year, the number of ships sailing from New York surged upward, from thirty-five a year at the end of Dutch rule to more than *seven hundred* a century later. Year by year, New York's merchants grew richer, shipping timber and grain to Britain—carrying manufactured goods from England to Africa—and importing ivory, gold, slaves, molasses, and rum back from Africa and the West Indies.

By 1740, New York had become the third largest port in the British Empire, second only to Philadelphia and London itself.

The heart of the port city was the East River waterfront, where an entire world centered on shipping and commerce had blossomed alongside the dock. There were shipwrights, coopers, sailmakers and rope makers, linen weavers, sugar refiners, tanners and printers, Irish clock-

In 1717, the village of Brooklyn was little more than a cluster of houses near the ferry slip to Manhattan, seen here in a detail from William Burgis's six-foot-long panoramic engraving of the harbor, published that year. James Hardwick's "publick house of entertainment" can be seen on the right, one of more than 100 taverns and drinking establishments located around the harbor.

makers, British coach makers, German metal-workers, and wigmakers, barbers, and hairdressers from Italy. Women often worked side by side with men, or ran shops of their own, as milliners, dyers, menders, and scourers. Blanche White, an upholsterer whose shop combined furniture making with undertaking, proudly advertised "funerals furnished with all Things necessary, and proper Attendance as in England."

With a population of nearly eleven thousand, New York was home now to people from everywhere—an uneasy assortment of old Dutch families and English merchants, colonial administrators and sailors, smugglers and privateers, Protestants and Catholics, free blacks and slaves. Packed into a bustling and surprisingly picturesque enclave still confined to the foot of the island, they formed a physically compact if far from harmonious society, with a high degree of mingling of the classes.

There were taverns everywhere, at least in part because of Manhattan's inadequate supply of groundwater. One count put the number of licensed taverns in 1740 at more than 150. Wealthier merchants gathered at places like the King's Arms, the Merchants' Coffee House, and the White Lion up near Broadway. Sailors, free blacks, and slaves congregated at rougher inns and tippling houses down by the docks. One indignant townsman complained of a particularly unsavory establishment called the "Sign of the Dog's Head in the Porridge Pot," where, he said, "the scum of society" gathered each evening in a "slovenly" setting.

The taverns served as the unofficial nerve center of the city. There, customers received mail, found employment, auctioned goods, conducted business, and pored over the latest British newspapers (and after 1725, the *New York Gazette* and the *Weekly Journal,* the first papers ever published in Manhattan)—exchanging news and gossip, and complaining about everything from the undrinkable water, to the inadequacies of the latest royal governor, to the most recent trade restrictions imposed by Parliament.

By the winter of 1741, however, there was only one topic on anybody's mind in the taverns of New York—the series of mysterious fires that had begun breaking out all over the city. In the weeks and months to come, as panicked

officials searched frantically for the guilty parties, the colony would explode—over an issue that had troubled it from the beginning.

REBELLION

Ordered, that this Board request his Honor the Lieutenant Governor to issue a proclamation, offering a reward to any white person that should discover any person or persons lately concerned in setting fire to any dwelling-house or storehouse in this city . . .
Daniel Horsmanden, 1741

The slave presence in the city was as old as the colony itself. More than any other settlement north of Maryland, New York had depended since the days of the Dutch upon slave labor, and the profits of the slave trade.

Peter Stuyvesant, understanding how crucial slaves were to the functioning of New Amsterdam, had repeatedly petitioned the directors of the Dutch West India Company to send more. "They ought to be stout and strong fellows," he instructed in 1660, "fit for immediate employment on this fortress and other works; also, if required, in war against the wild barbarians, either to pursue them when retreating, or else to carry some of the soldiers' baggage."

Whether serving as farmhands, as domestic servants, or as the backbone of the colony's public workforce, most Dutch slaves had been owned by the company—which had extended some liberties to them, including the right to sue in court, to start their own families, to own their own land, if only on the outskirts of town, and, in some cases, to win partial freedom as they reached old age.

Under the much harsher conditions of English rule, however, even those slender perquisites disappeared. Henceforth, all slaves were considered chattel—forever—and the few that were freed, permanently barred from owning land or houses.

And, crucial as African workers had been under the Dutch, they would become even more vital to the English economy, both as unpaid members of the workforce and as commodities to be bought, sold, and rented. By 1711, the trade in Africans had grown so brisk in New York that a special slave exchange had to be established down by the East River to handle the volume of business.

Some New Yorkers considered the practice barbaric. "Slave-holding depraves the mind," one Quaker minister said, "with as great certainty as cold congeals water." But year by year, as slavery was bound ever more intimately into the routine of daily life in the city, the demand for African laborers grew. By the end of the second decade of the eighteenth century, one in five New Yorkers was owned by other New Yorkers—two thousand men, women, and children in all.

Each morning, African slaves could seen making their way to the market at the foot of Wall Street, where while waiting to be rented out as day laborers and domestic servants they exchanged news with free blacks, and looked for every chance they could to break free.

Tension in the city began to rise. "On Sundays, while we are at our Devotions," an Anglican minister named Elias Neau worried, "the streets are full of Negroes, who dance and divert themselves." Each May, crowds of black New Yorkers, both freemen and slaves, filled the streets during Pinkster—a Dutch holiday adapted to suit African customs—and "Election Day," in which a black king was temporarily elected, and paraded through the shanty district at the northern edge of town. As the slave population grew, white slave owners feared the consequence of free blacks mingling with their property. The frequent meeting of "Negroe Slaves at the houses of free negroes," one colonial magistrate complained, "hath been the occasion of great disorder."

Incidents of violence began to break out. In 1712, twenty-five blacks set fire to a building on the east side of the island, then ambushed the whites who came to extinguish it. The uprising was quickly suppressed, and the conspirators hunted down and executed—"some . . . burnt," the royal governor reported, "others hanged, one broke on the wheele, and one hung live in chains in the town, so that there has been the most exemplary punishment inflicted that could be possibly thought of." New regulations were passed, further restricting the movement of slaves in the city, but it only served to bolster the desire for freedom.

In the winter of 1741, decades of rising tension between slave owners and slaves came to

Brought in by the West India Company in 1626 to build roads and fortifications and clear land for white farmers, Africans were the second oldest group in the city, after the Dutch. Still numbering fewer than 100 when this drawing of *Nieu Amsterdam* was made in 1643 (left), the slave population grew rapidly after the arrival of Peter Stuyvesant, who sought to make the slave trade a mainstay of the colony's economy and kept 40 slaves himself.

The deck of the *Brookes,* an English slave ship of the late eighteenth century (upper right), was often jammed with 300 unwilling passengers to the New World.

In 1711, an open shed along the East River at the foot of Wall Street (lower right) was pressed into service as a municipal slave market. Each morning, white householders gathered there to rent laborers and domestic servants, or to buy or sell slaves outright.

U AMSTERDA

Cum Privilegio Ordinum Hollandiæ et West-Frisiæ

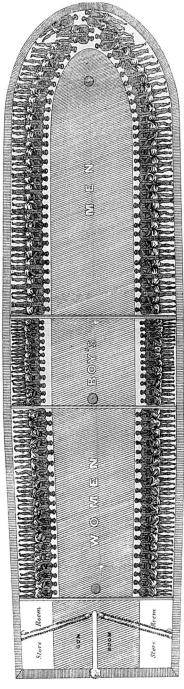

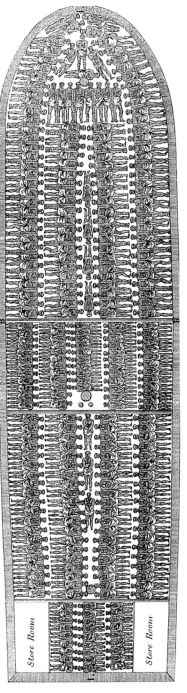

a head. Reports of uprisings in other colonies had already brought white fears to the breaking point, when in February, a tobacconist's shop was burgled, followed by a series of unexplained fires that struck the King's Chapel, the barracks of the royal army, and the homes and businesses of prominent New Yorkers.

Suspicion immediately fell on New York's black population. "The recorder taking notice of the several fires which had lately happened in this city," Daniel Horsmanden, the presiding judge, wrote, "must necessarily conclude, that they were occasioned . . . by some villainous confederacy of latent enemies amongst us." In March, as city magistrates searched for someone—anyone—to blame, a seventeen-year-old Irish servant girl named Mary Burton came forward to testify against her employer—an Irish Catholic tavernkeeper named John Hughson, whose establishment was a favorite meeting place for slaves and free blacks. Prompted by the offer of a hundred-pound reward, Burton told wild tales of a "Negroe plot" to burn the city and overthrow the government, leveling one charge after another—against Hughson, his wife, and a growing list of alleged black conspirators, describing lurid rituals with knives and Catholic Bibles.

A wave of hysteria swept through the city. Some blacks had almost certainly been involved in fomenting trouble, but with almost no evidence to go on, colonial judges ordered a massive roundup of black New Yorkers and put them on trial for their lives. In the weeks to come, the reign of terror visited on the city's black population, and anyone suspected of conspiring with them, would be worse than the Salem Witch Trials half a century before.

"We have 70 Negro's in Custody," Daniel Horsmanden wrote, "and 'tis feared that most of the Negro's here (who are very numerous) knew of the Late Conspiracy to murder the Christians; six of them have been their own Executioners by shooting and cutting their own Throats; Three have been Executed according to Law; one burnt, a second broke upon the wheel and a third hung up alive. . . . [W]e shall not be quite safe, till that wicked race are under more restraint or their number greatly reduced within this."

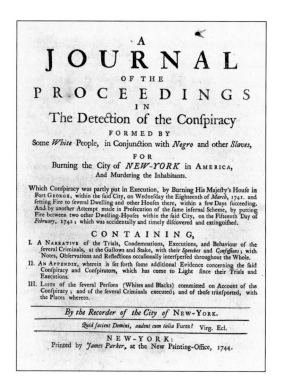

A
JOURNAL
OF THE
PROCEEDINGS
IN
The Detection of the Conſpiracy
FORMED BY
Some *White* People, in Conjunction with *Negro* and other *Slaves*,
FOR
Burning the City of *NEW-YORK* in AMERICA,
And Murdering the Inhabitants.

Which Conſpiracy was partly put in Execution, by Burning His Majeſty's Houſe in Fort GEORGE, within the ſaid City, on Wedneſday the Eighteenth of *March*, 1741. and ſetting Fire to ſeveral Dwelling and other Houſes there, within a few Days ſucceeding. And by another Attempt made in Proſecution of the ſame infernal Scheme, by putting Fire between two other Dwelling-Houſes within the ſaid City, on the Fifteenth Day of *February*, 1742 ; which was accidentally and timely diſcovered and extinguiſhed.

CONTAINING,
I. A NARRATIVE of the Trials, Condemnations, Executions, and Behaviour of the ſeveral Criminals, at the Gallows and Stake, with their *Speeches* and *Confeſſions* ; with Notes, Obſervations and Reflections occaſionally interſperſed throughout the Whole.
II. AN APPENDIX, wherein is ſet forth ſome additional Evidence concerning the ſaid Conſpiracy and Conſpirators, which has come to Light ſince their Trials and Executions.
III. LISTS of the ſeveral Perſons (Whites and Blacks) committed on Account of the Conſpiracy ; and of the ſeveral Criminals executed ; and of thoſe tranſported, with the Places whereto.

By the Recorder of the City of NEW-YORK.

Quid facient Domini, audent cum talia Fures? Virg. Ecl.

NEW-YORK:
Printed by *James Parker*, at the New Printing-Office, 1744.

. . . require a labour perfectly Herculean. The Dogs I intend are that real canine Species, which, with their dismal Howlings, disturb the repose of the Healthy, break the interrupted slumbers of the sick, add fresh Horrors to the night and render it perillous to traverse our streets after the sun is sunk beneath our Horizon.

Letter of Complaint, *New York
Independent Reflector*, 1753

*The nobleness of the town surprised me. . . .
I had no idea of finding a place in America,
consisting of near 2,000 houses, elegantly built
of brick, raised on an eminence and the streets
paved and spacious, furnished with commodious quays and warehouses, and employing some
hundreds of vessels in its foreign trade and fisheries—but such is this city that very few in
England can rival it in its show.*

An English Naval Officer, 1756

The frontispiece of Daniel Horsmanden's *Journal of the Proceedings of the Detection of the Conspiracy* (left), published in 1744. In February 1741, decades of simmering racial tension in New York exploded when a series of suspicious fires convinced white authorities that a general uprising of the slave population was imminent. Horsmanden, the city recorder and a Supreme Court justice, directed the brutal wave of official violence that followed. Three years later, stung by charges that the circumstances surrounding the so-called "slave uprising" had been grossly exaggerated, he wrote a lengthy defense of his judgment and actions.

In all, 160 blacks and 21 whites were arrested. Over two dozen slaves were tortured, hanged, or burned at the stake. Medieval punishments banned decades before in the legal treatment of whites were resurrected to wring "confessions" from black suspects and to terrify innocent slaves into naming other alleged conspirators.

By June, the reign of official violence had subsided. No one would ever know how deep the conspiracy had gone—or whether there had even been a conspiracy at all. Following the murderous reprisals, slave unrest in New York City went underground. It would take nearly a century more for all black New Yorkers to win their freedom.

But it would not be long before English rule was challenged again—not by African Americans this time, but by a restless alliance of merchants, artisans, and sailors. When that happened, the proud "royal colony" would begin a long journey—out of empire, out of the past, and into the future.

THE ROYAL COLONY

To the editor: It appears, Sir, from the most accurate calculation, that we have in this City, at least a thousand dogs: I do not mean of the human Kind, for the extirpation of those would

By 1763, New York had been riding on a tide of prosperity for almost two decades. For seven years, as Great Britain waged war against the French and Indians in Canada, the strategically located port had been the staging ground for the English armed forces, which month after month, year in and year out, streamed up and down the Hudson.

The war had proved to be a windfall for the colony's merchants. "I can plainly see," Benjamin Franklin wrote, passing through Manhattan in 1756, "that New York is growing immensely rich, by Money brought into it from all Quarters, for the pay and subsistence of the troops." By the time of Franklin's visit, the thriving port had outstripped Boston in size and, though still smaller than his hometown, Philadelphia, presented what one man called "a more urban appearance" than either of its rivals.

With its compact skyline dominated by the Anglican spires of Trinity Church and newly founded King's College, the "royal colony" was acknowledged up and down the Atlantic seaboard to be the most English of all Britain's American settlements. "There are under three thousand [houses] at this time," a visiting British army officer observed in 1764, "about 300 stores, 12 churches and places of Worship, and perhaps 20,000 inhabitants,—here are more Negroes than in any Northern province, and by being the Seat of Government, Civil and Military, and the place to which all the money for the Exigencies of America is sent from Britain—[New York] is rich."

Never again would membership in the British Empire bring the city such rewards. Within months, as the French and Indian War came to an end, the British troops would disappear, along with the lucrative war contracts. "The tipling soldiers," a merchant named John Watts lamented, "are gone to drink in a warmer region." Two years later, the English government—nearly bankrupt after a decade of waging war in North America—would attempt to force its thriving colonies to share in the cost of their own defense. The modest proposals shortly put forward in the House of Commons would unleash a storm of protest—and carry New York and its sister colonies out of the British Empire forever.

STAMP ACT

The merchants of this City are come to a Resolution to which 400 of us have set our hands that unless the Stamp Act is repealed that we shall not sell any European goods that are shipped after 1 January 1766.

Evert Bancker, 1765

It began in the spring of 1765, when Parliament passed the Stamp Act, a special levy on virtually every document printed in the American colonies. Taxing without colonial consent no fewer than forty-three different kinds of business transaction—including legal contracts, handbills, shipping orders, college diplomas, newspapers, liquor licenses, marriage licenses, and playing cards—it struck at the very heart of New York's vibrant merchant culture. Though always the most royal of British colonies, the city erupted almost immediately into angry, injured protest.

"If . . . the Interest of the Mother Country and her Colonies cannot be made to coincide," a New York newspaper boldly declared, "then the connection between them ought to cease." The night before the act was to take effect on November 1, 1765, two hundred merchants gathered at the City Arms Tavern on Broadway and vowed to resist the hated law. The next day, offices throughout the city were closed,

flags flown at half-mast, and black crepe hung from the gaming tables in the coffeehouses. In the evening, an angry mob of two thousand sailors, artisans, apprentices, and free blacks gathered on the New York Commons, marched to the royal governor's home on the Bowling Green, hanged and burnt him in effigy, then set his carriage on fire.

Parliament backed down. Within months, the House of Commons had voted to repeal the Stamp Act. Four years later, in 1770, grateful New York merchants erected a huge bronze statue of King George III in the middle of the Bowling Green to affirm their loyalty to the British Crown.

But in the coming years more "intolerable acts" were passed, along with more taxes—on sugar, molasses, and tea—and anger at Great Britain flared again. Without anyone fully realizing it, the first steps had been taken toward complete separation from the mother country.

REVOLUTION

With all the opulence and splendor of this city, there is very little good breeding to be found. . . . We have been treated with an assiduous respect; but I have not seen one real gentleman, one well-bred man, since I came to town. At their entertainments there is not conversation that is agreeable; there is not modesty, no attention to one another. They talk very loud, very fast and altogether. If they ask you a question, before you can utter three words of your answer, they will break out upon you again, and talk away.

John Adams, 1774

In June 1773, an illegitimate sixteen-year-old boy from the West Indian island of Nevis landed in New York, burning to make a name for himself. "Like a seed blown by happy chance onto perfect ground," a biographer later said, the young Alexander Hamilton arrived in the city on the eve of an extraordinary transformation. In many ways the quintessential New Yorker—an immigrant eager to escape the past and reinvent himself—he would in the years to come do everything in his power to hurry New York on toward its ultimate destiny.

He was, John Adams later wrote with more venom than accuracy, "The bastard brat of a Scots pedlar." Abandoned at seven by his way-

Alexander Hamilton (below), the brilliant bastard son of a bankrupt Scottish nobleman, born in the West Indies, was in many ways the quintessential New Yorker: an immigrant eager to escape his past and reinvent himself in the restless port city.

ward father, a bankrupt Scottish nobleman—then all but orphaned at eleven by the death of his mother—by twelve Hamilton was working in the St. Croix office of a New York–based shipping company, run by a prosperous merchant named Nicholas Cruger. The slightly built, strikingly brilliant boy was soon running the entire operation, confidently selecting trade routes, dispatching vessels, and handling thousands of pounds' worth of inventory and payroll. Recognizing his gifts, Cruger and a local Presbyterian clergyman sent him north to be educated in the American colonies.

By the time Hamilton had enrolled at King's College in the autumn of 1773, New York had become one of the most divided places in America: at once a bastion of loyalty to the English Crown and a breeding ground of patriotic fervor—though even many vocal supporters of the patriot cause shrank from the prospect of complete separation. "I see, and I see it with fear and trembling," a New York lawyer named Gouverneur Morris wrote, "that if the disputes with Great Britain continue, we shall be under the worst of all possible dominations; we shall be under the domination of a riotous mob."

But Hamilton had no doubts. Convinced the future lay not with kings but with the power of commerce and free men, he threw himself almost immediately into the whirlwind of debate sweeping through the colony—joining a patriot group called the Sons of Liberty and publishing an incendiary pamphlet, calling on New Yorkers to defy the English Parliament and lay claim to their natural rights as free men.

"Our contest with Britain," he declared in December 1774, "is founded entirely upon . . . this interesting question: whether the inhabitants of Great Britain have a right to dispose of the lives and properties of the inhabitants of America—or not?" The seventeen-year-old college sophomore and pamphleteer was soon mesmerizing crowds on the Commons with his passionate, closely reasoned political oratory. Loyalist New Yorkers were horrified by Hamilton's rhetoric, but to groups like the Sons of Liberty he quickly became, one man said, "our oracle."

March, 1775. The people here are very much divided, and Party spirit is very high. Politics,

Politics, Politics! Men, women, children, all ranks and professions are mad with Politics.
Dr. Robert Honyman

Loyalists and patriots alike were stunned, however, when in the spring of 1775, Hamilton's call to arms was heeded—sooner than even he could have imagined. On Sunday, April 23, a frantic messenger came galloping into town down the Post Road from Boston. Blood had been shed at Lexington and Concord; the American Revolution had begun. Exultant New York patriots immediately seized city hall, the customhouse, and the guns of the city arsenal, and celebrated that night with a fireworks display and a noisy parade down Broadway.

Despite the high spirits, a feeling of unease stole over Manhattan, as the prospect of war drew near. Even the most ardent of patriots could see that the island city would be all but defenseless before the guns of the British navy. "The past week has been one of commotion and confusion," a local pastor and English loyalist named Ewald G. Schaukirk wrote in late April. "Fear and panic seized many of the people, who prepared to move into the country." In the weeks and months to come, thousands of New Yorkers would abandon the city, loyalists boarding ships bound for England, patriots sending their wives and children into the surrounding countryside.

By August, entire sections of town had been boarded up. Wall Street's coffeehouses, once bustling with customers, no longer bothered to light their candles. "Some of the streets look plague-stricken, so many houses are closed," Pastor Schaukirk reported toward the end of the month. Before the year was out, New York City's population had dropped by more than 80 percent, from twenty-five thousand to barely five thousand people.

Alexander Hamilton was among those who chose to stay. On hearing the news of Lexington and Concord, he abandoned his studies and was soon turning out for military maneuvers with his King's College classmates in a Manhattan churchyard. In the months to come, he threw himself into the revolution—stealing cannon from the British battery at Fort George and forming a company of gunners called the First New York Artillery. By the spring of 1776, his energy and brilliance had brought him to

Still a compact settlement at the southern tip of Manhattan, New York had expanded well beyond the old boundaries of New Amsterdam by 1767, the year this superbly detailed map by a British army officer named Bernard Ratzer was surveyed. At the far northern edge of town, the Commons, or Fields—the site of present-day City Hall Park—marked the start of the Post Road from Boston. Down that lane, in April 1775, horsemen brought extraordinary news from Lexington and Concord, that the American Revolution had started.

the attention of General George Washington—who would soon promote the young immigrant to the rank of colonel and count him among his closest aides.

By 1776, Washington himself was in Manhattan, along with most of the ill-equipped Continental army, which he had hastily brought down from Boston—certain that when the British army came to crush the rebellion they would strike New York first. The island city, John Adams of Massachusetts declared, was "a kind of key to the whole continent"—with its vast harbor and mile-wide river reaching deep into the hinterland, the strategic hinge of North America.

"Should they get that Town and the Command of the [Hudson] River," Washington grimly wrote, "they can stop the intercourse between the northern and southern Colonies, upon which depends the Safety of America."

All spring, American soldiers under Washington's field commander, General Charles Lee, labored to reinforce the island's defenses. The few civilians left in town watched apprehensively as cannon were hauled through the streets, and the streets themselves torn up to make earthworks, redoubts, and trenches. "General Lee is taking every necessary step to fortify and defend this city," a merchant named Frederick Rhinelander wrote. "To see the vast number of houses shut up, one would think the city almost evacuated. Women and children are scarcely to be seen in the streets. Troops are daily coming

A View of the Attack against Fort Washington and Rebel Redoubts near New York on the 16th of November 1776 (left). On November 16, 1776, a battalion of British solders crossed the Harlem River from the Bronx and attacked Fort Washington, the last patriot stronghold at the northern tip of Manhattan (visible on the ridge at the center of this view, drawn by Captain Thomas Davies of the Royal Regiment of Artillery). From across the Hudson in New Jersey, Washington looked on as 2,000 of his men fought valiantly to hold off the superior British forces—without success.

On July 9, 1776, a defiant throng of patriotic citizens and soldiers marched down to the Bowling Green and pulled the huge bronze statue of King George III from its pedestal (right). The French printmaker who published this engraving a few months later blithely made up most of the features of the city he had never seen. The statue of King George was in fact an equestrian piece, not a standing figure; the oddly turbaned, half-naked "Indian" rioters resembled no known American patriots; and the surrounding buildings were those of a grand European capital rather than the modest brick dwellings of colonial New York.

in; they break open and quarter themselves in the houses they find shut up. Necessity knows no law."

As the days and weeks ticked by, New Yorkers waited anxiously for the British ships to come. "I feel for you . . . my . . . New York friends," one newspaper editor wrote, "for I expect that your city will be laid in ashes."

On the morning of June 29, 1776, the citizens of New York and Brooklyn awoke to an astonishing sight. "I was upstairs," wrote Daniel McCurtin, an American private stationed in Brooklyn, "and spied as I peeped out the Bay something resembling a wood of pine trees trimmed. I could not believe my eyes. I thought all London was afloat."

During the night, a hundred British warships had sailed into the harbor. In the weeks to come, nearly 500 vessels—including 330 transport and supply ships carrying ten thousand British sailors and an army of thirty-two thousand men—would drop anchor in the bay. It was the greatest land-sea expeditionary force mounted by Great Britain until the invasion of Normandy in World War II. It would take six weeks for the

giant force to disembark and take up positions on Staten Island.

Across the bay, New Yorkers braced for war. On July 9, 1776, as British warships assembled in the harbor, the Declaration of Independence was read aloud for the first time in Manhattan, to a large crowd of troops and civilians gathered on the Commons. Afterward, a cheering throng marched down Broadway to the Bowling Green, knocked the royal crowns from the iron fence posts, then pulled down the gilded statue of King George III, put up just six years before. The two tons of British lead were melted down to make 42,088 American musket balls.

Attempting to hold the island city against the most powerful navy in the world, George Washington faced an all but impossible strategic and tactical challenge. He knew he had to defend Manhattan, at all costs. To do that, however, he would also have to defend the heights of Brooklyn on the far side of the East River—from whose high bluffs the British guns could rain down a devastating fire on the town. To defend Brooklyn Heights, however, he would have to split his forces and move most of his

men off Manhattan onto Long Island—and risk being cut off by General William Howe's vastly superior British forces.

It was an immense gamble—but Washington had no choice. On August 22, the British commander began ferrying twenty thousand troops, including five thousand Hessian mercenaries, from Staten Island to Gravesend Bay, five miles south of Brooklyn. On August 25, with British forces moving north, Washington rushed seven thousand of his soldiers over to the Brooklyn side and ordered them to dig in along the highlands south of the little village.

The next day, on August 26, 1776, the battle for New York began. For the Americans, it was a disaster. Washington's raw recruits were no match for the battle-tested British regulars, who thrust north from Flatbush, while a second unit swung east through Jamaica Pass, completely outflanking the American position near present-day Prospect Park. The American troops wavered, fought bravely where they could, then retreated under a withering fire, until their backs were pressed against the East River.

In just two days, Washington lost nearly two thousand men—more than a quarter of his army.

On the rain-soaked night of August 29, 1776—with his beleaguered forces in disarray and the British army poised for the kill—the American commander gambled everything on an extraordinary military maneuver. With the fate of the new nation hanging in the balance, Washington commandeered every skiff and fishing boat he could lay his hands on, and ferried his exhausted men across the East River to Manhattan—in total darkness, without a sound, in less than seven hours.

The British forces, just a few dozen yards away, never even heard them. Escaping through the fog to the temporary safety of Manhattan, the battered American army survived to fight another day.

Certain he could no longer defend the city, the commander-in-chief now reluctantly changed his strategy. For six weeks he led a bloody retreat up the length of Manhattan, fighting rearguard actions along a country lane that would one day be upper Broadway, and on the Harlem Heights, where Columbia University now stands. From the porch of his field headquarters at the Morris mansion in upper Manhattan, nine miles to the north, he could just make out the Union Jack flying over the city he could not save. In November, with the British army in hot pursuit, Washington's forces abandoned Manhattan completely.

For seven long years, the Revolutionary War raged. New York was no longer a city but a British garrison—the largest military base on earth, home to a handful of uneasy American patriots and more than ten thousand British troops and officers.

Despite Washington's fears, the fall of New York did not spell disaster for the American cause.

Though the British held the harbor, they never got complete control of the Hudson and spent much of the war bottled up near Manhattan.

The streets of New York never saw fighting again. But the destruction New Yorkers had for so long feared came anyway. Early on the morning of September 21, 1776, just four days after the British occupation began, a fire broke out near Whitehall Slip. Patriot arsonists were suspected, but whatever the cause, the fire's progress was abetted by the wartime conditions. The church bells that might have sounded the alarm had long since been melted down to make patriot bullets, and most of New York's fire brigade had gone off to fight with General Washington. Unchecked, the fire moved north, carving a path of destruction nearly a mile long, soon engulfing the tallest structure in town, Trinity Church, whose 140-foot-high wooden steeple, one witness said, "resembled a vast pyramid of fire."

"Several Women and Children perished in the Fire," the New-York Mercury reported, "their Shrieks, joined to the roaring of the Flames, the crash of falling Houses, and the wide spread Ruin which everywhere appeared, formed a scene of Horror grand beyond all Description, and which was still heightened by the Darkness of the Night."

By morning, the entire city west of Broadway had been reduced to a blackened ash heap. "The destruction was very great," one Loyalist New Yorker lamented—"between a third and a fourth of the City is burnt. All that is west of the New Exchange, along Broad Street to the North River, as high as the City Hall, and from

As George Washington's forces prepared to retreat from New York, members of his staff debated whether or not to burn the city behind them. No order to do so was ever given, but the timing of the terrible fire that began on September 21, 1776—seen in a period engraving, raging at its height—prompted both sides to suspect arson. "Providence," Washington said, "or some good honest fellow, has done more for us than we were disposed to do for ourselves."

Ruin of Trinity Church, 1780, from a drawing by Thomas Barrow, 1776. First erected in 1698 and enlarged 40 years later, Trinity Church was completely destroyed in the great fire and remained in ruins throughout the British occupation. Soon after the city was reoccupied by the Continental army in November 1783, plans for reconstruction were begun.

thence along the Broad Way to King's College, is in Ruins. Our Distresses were great before, but this Calamity has encreased them tenfold. Thousands are hereby reduced to beggary."

In all, 493 buildings had been destroyed— along with a hundred more two years later, when a second great fire ripped through the city. "What a Pity it is to see such a fine City as this almost half Burned to ashes," an Irish visitor observed in 1782, "and to see now nothing remaining but the bare walls of fine Churches & other Public Buildings."

As the war ground on, the years of misuse
and neglect began to take a toll on the once-
proud city. Even districts untouched by the fires
were soon all but unrecognizable. Along the
East River, the formerly bustling wharves, now
idle and unused, began to rot and crumble into
the river. Public buildings and once-grand mansions were converted for use as army barracks,
military hospitals, and headquarters for the
British general staff.

An atmosphere of unreality fell over the
occupied town. During the winter months,
while fighting was suspended, the English officers and their wives diverted themselves with
formal teas and fancy dress balls. Nearby, meanwhile, thousands of New Yorkers, rendered
homeless by the fires, huddled miserably in tents
and huts, in a makeshift community called Canvas Town.

"Wood often could not be purchased for
money," Fredericka Riedesel, the wife of the
senior Hessian commander, wrote, "if by chance
a little was for sale, it cost ten pounds by the
cord. . . . The poor were obliged to burn fat,
in order to warm themselves and cook their
meals."

But little by little, the tide of battle turned,
as Britain slowly wearied of chasing Washing-
ton's tiny, elusive Continental army. In 1778,
France entered the war on the American side.
Dutch bankers helped, too, loaning millions of
dollars to help the patriot war effort. By 1780,
Loyalists by the thousands were flooding into
New York, seeking refuge from the advancing
American forces. Thousands of slaves poured
in, too—spurred on by British offers to eman-
cipate any slave willing to declare loyalty to the
Crown. To free themselves in the war for Amer-

ican freedom, blacks had been obliged to join the other side.

By 1782, almost every British soldier in the colonies had been withdrawn to New York City—the last British stronghold on the American continent.

Finally, in the fall of 1783, the English capitulated completely. "The soldiers in the barracks just opposite our house marched off," Pastor Schaukirk recorded. "Last night a strong watch was kept for fear of accidents or mischief. Today all the British left New York and General Washington with his troops marched in and took possession of the city."

On November 25 that year—exactly seven years after he had been forced to abandon the city—George Washington led his army triumphantly back into New York. The British commander surrendered to him inside the old fort at the foot of Manhattan—where Peter Stuyvesant had surrendered the Dutch colony to the British 119 years before. The Union Jack was lowered. The Stars and Stripes were raised, crowds cheered, and cannon boomed.

New York was an American city, at last—though no one yet knew precisely what that would mean.

RUINS

Rich when they left this city they have returned poor, having little other property than the paper evidences of their patriotism. While in exile, they pleased themselves with the hope of one day returning to those peaceful mansions. . . . The day arrived, and they returned—to what?—to heaps of rubbish, and half-ruined houses—to poverty, and to the dread of future wretchedness.

An Anonymous Citizen, 1786

When New York's war-weary citizens returned after seven years, they were shocked by what they found.

During seven years of British occupation, the colonial city had been all but destroyed. Thousands of Loyalist families were gone forever, and the hulks of half-ruined mansions were visible everywhere. The handsome beech trees and orchards that had lined the colonial city's streets were gone, and the very streets themselves rendered impassable by earthworks and

trenches. At the head of Wall Street, the blackened skeleton of Trinity Church was all that remained of the tallest structure in town.

No other American city had experienced anything like it. Philadelphia had emerged from the Revolution largely intact; so had Boston. New York, by contrast, lay in ruins: its economy shattered, its leadership depleted, its population scattered and demoralized. And yet somehow, in the next half century or less, the devastated colonial trading post would arise from the ashes of the American Revolution to become the most important metropolis in the Western Hemisphere—on its way to becoming the wealthiest and most powerful city on earth.

THE CAPITAL

With remarkable speed, New York sprang back to life, as people by the thousands flocked into the city. Just two years after the end of the Revolution, the population had rebounded completely, doubling from twelve thousand to twenty-four thousand in twenty-four months, and rapidly surpassing its prewar peak. As the population rose, citizens new and old threw themselves into the task of rebuilding the city from one end to the other. At the southern tip of the island, the old British guns were dismantled and Fort George itself demolished, its stones used as landfill to create an elegant promenade, called the Battery.

One by one the symbols of royal rule were discarded. Crown Street was quickly renamed Liberty Street. King Street became Pine Street, and Queen Street, Pearl. Less than a year after the British surrender, Alexander Hamilton's old alma mater, King's College—from which he had never graduated—reopened under a new charter and with a proud new American name, Columbia.

Jacques-Pierre Brissot de Warville, a French businessman who visited New York in the years after the war, was amazed by the energy the revolution had unleashed in the city. "Let those men," he wrote, "who doubt the prodigious effects that liberty produces on man, and on his industry, transport themselves to America. What miracles will they here behold! Whilst everywhere in Europe the villages and towns are falling to ruin . . . new edifices are here arising

First in War, First in Peace, and First in the Heart of His Countrymen; George Washington's Inauguration, engraved by Montbaron and Gautschi. At noon on April 30, 1789, George Washington took the oath of office as the first president of the United States, from the second-floor balcony of Federal Hall overlooking Wall Street. The ceremony was delayed at the last minute while frantic officials, who had forgotten to bring a Bible for the swearing in, ransacked nearby shops and houses to find one. A large crowd filled the intersection of Wall and Broad streets to witness the historic event, cheering wildly when Chancellor Robert R. Livingston, filled with emotion after administering the oath of office, cried out, "Long Live George Washington, president of the United States!"

on all sides. . . . I walked out by the side of the [Hudson] River; what a rapid change in the space of six weeks! . . . On all sides, houses are rising, and streets extending: I see nothing but busy workmen building and repairing."

To a remarkable degree, the key to New York City's rise—and with it the rise of America itself to urban greatness—would lie in the hands of one man: the brilliant, combative immigrant from the West Indies, Alexander Hamilton—whose meteoric ascent as Washington's aide had stunned everyone except Hamilton himself.

Less than a week after the British surrender, Hamilton had joined the flood of New Yorkers coming back into the city, bringing along his wife, Elizabeth, and their infant son. They settled in a house at 57 Wall Street, where he opened his own law firm, having passed the bar exam in just three months, then organized the city's first bank, the Bank of New York, which soon opened for business a few doors away.

In January 1785, new neighbors arrived. The brand-new Continental Congress, unable to decide on a permanent home, set up temporary headquarters in New York City—at 40 Wall Street, right next door to the Hamiltons. Thrilled to be at the center of the action, Hamilton hoped it would stay there.

Though forty-nine locations would eventually be considered, many Americans thought New York the most logical choice for the nation's capital. Everything a capital city would need was already there, from hotels and restaurants and boardinghouses to scriveners and printers and lawyers. At a time when travel by ship was far faster and more reliable than horse-drawn coaches on badly rutted dirt roads, the island city—roughly equidistant between New England and the South, and already connected by ship to every point along the eastern seaboard—was the most convenient, central, and readily accessible place in America.

But Hamilton had higher reasons for favoring New York—the city, after all, where he himself had been allowed to rise. In cities like New York, he argued, the human possibilities were greater—the flow of commerce more abundant—the exchange of ideas more open and creative—than anywhere else in the country. It was in cities that men of talent and ability rather

John Trumbull's portrait of Alexander Hamilton, painted in 1806—two years after Hamilton had died—is the basis of the likeness that appears on the ten-dollar bill. Other than Benjamin Franklin, Hamilton is the only non-presidential figure to appear on any American paper currency in common circulation—a testament to his crucial role in establishing the nation's financial system.

than family or ancestry would be able to flourish and rise, and upon that, he was sure, the future vitality of the republic depended.

In the spring of 1789, Hamilton's hopes came one step closer to being realized, when the newly formed federal government began assembling in lower Manhattan.

At noon on April 30, George Washington was sworn in as the first president of the United States—in New York City, from the balcony of the old city hall, which New Yorkers had lavishly renovated, and optimistically renamed Federal Hall.

Washington quickly brought in Thomas Jefferson to be Secretary of State—though the Virginian loathed New York, which he later called "a cloacina of all the depravities of human nature."

Hamilton—just thirty-two—was named Secretary of the Treasury. Though the appointment came through on a weekend, he went right to work—hurrying to his new office in the Treasury Department on Broadway—a few steps from the new Trinity Church, now nearing completion.

"More than any other man," one opponent later admitted, Hamilton "did the thinking of the time." In the months to come, with an impatience and single-minded tenacity that could be "highly disagreeable," another colleague said,

Thomas Jefferson (seen here in a portrait by Charles Willson Peale) arrived in Manhattan in early 1790 to take up his post as the nation's first Secretary of State. Deeply mistrustful of cities, and especially New York, he violently opposed Alexander Hamilton's vision of America as a gloriously commercial, and ultimately urban, nation.

Hamilton began mapping out the practical blueprint for a new kind of nation. At a time when 90 percent of America's economy was still agricultural, Hamilton imagined a nation whose wealth would come not from farms, plantations, and slave labor but from cities like New York—from banking, commerce, manufactured goods, and immigrant toil.

The brilliant, radical program he submitted to Congress that winter aroused a storm of protest—from southern planters like Jefferson and James Madison, but also from Hamilton's own Wall Street neighbor and archenemy, Aaron Burr, whose career Hamilton considered it his "religious duty to oppose."

It was the beginning of a fateful split in American society, one that would pit country against city, farm against factory—and eventually, South against North.

Fearing the disorder and diversity of large cities, and dreading the very concentration of money and power Hamilton hoped to encourage, Jefferson was sure the New Yorker's plans would create an urban colossus in the north, that would crush the South while corrupting the nation's moral fiber. "[L]et our workshops remain in Europe," he declared. "It is better to carry provisions and materials to workmen there, than bring them to the provisions and materials, and with them their manners and

principles. The mobs of great cities add just so much to the support of pure government, as sores do to the strength of the human body."

Certain the future of the nation lay not in the city but in the countryside—where a nation of like-minded yeoman farmers could spread peacefully across the continent—Jefferson proposed moving the capital out of New York to a new rural setting on the Potomac, across the river from his native Virginia.

Torn between two incompatible visions of the future, unable to determine even where its own home should be, Congress was soon hopelessly deadlocked. It was an open question, one member warned, "whether this government is to exist for the ages, or be dispersed among contending winds."

In the spring of 1790, the struggle came to a dramatic climax—over a volatile issue crucial to Hamilton's entire program for the new nation. Sure that the future of the republic depended upon sound public credit, Hamilton desperately wanted the federal government to assume responsibility for the enormous debts incurred by the individual colonies during the Revolutionary War. Most southern states, including Virginia, had already paid theirs off, but many northern ones, including New York, had not—badly compromising the new nation's credit at home and around the world. Federal assumption of the debts, Hamilton knew, would bolster the flow of capital into the country, encourage public confidence in the new national government, and jump-start his ambitious economic programs.

All spring, Hamilton lobbied tirelessly for federal assumption of the state debts. All spring, southerners—uneasy with any expansion of federal power and disinclined to pay a second time debts they had already discharged—fought him at every turn.

On the evening of June 20, 1790, with the U.S. government hovering on the brink of bankruptcy, Hamilton went to Jefferson's house on Maiden Lane in lower Manhattan, hoping to find some way out of the crisis. Over a glass of madeira after dinner, as the intense young New Yorker insisted yet again that the federal government pay off the state debts, Jefferson made a fateful offer. Jefferson would use his influence to persuade the other southerners not to block federal assumption of the debt—if Hamilton would agree to move the capital of the new nation away from New York to the rural site Jefferson had proposed along the Potomac, after a ten-year layover in Philadelphia.

Hamilton agreed. "The project of Philadelphia & Potomac is bad," he later explained to a disappointed colleague, Congressman Rufus King of New York. "But it will insure the funding system and the assumption; agreeing to remain in New York will defeat it." Though he regretted seeing the capital move from what he considered its natural home in Manhattan, he knew that what the government did was more important than where the government did it. "Power without revenue is a bauble," he said.

Known after as "the deal," the simple swap of power for money had profound consequences for the future of New York. Never again in its history would the city be asked to represent the entire spectrum of the nation's political interests. Nor would it be weighted down with the symbolic obligations and ceremonial trappings a national capital entailed. Henceforth, New York would go it alone, and dedicate itself unswervingly to what since the days of the Dutch had come most naturally: making money.

Some New Yorkers were devastated by the loss of the capital. But Hamilton was philo-sophical. To fund the huge new debt he had gotten the federal government to assume, he immediately had the Treasury Department issue $80 million in government bonds, and soon money was pouring into New York City, as the trade in stocks and bonds soared.

No one had ever seen anything like it. "Abundant streams of revenue gushed forth," Daniel Webster later observed; Hamilton had "touched the dead corpse of public credit and it sprang upon its feet." To handle the new volume of business, a group of merchant brokers began meeting regularly under a buttonwood tree on Wall Street—exchanging quotations and trading stocks on the open sidewalk.

On May 17, 1792, two dozen brokers and speculators gathered under the same tree to formalize their association—agreeing to a system of standard minimum fees for the buying and selling of securities. Known thereafter as "The Buttonwood Agreement," it would be the closest New York's acquisitive citizenry would ever come to their own Constitution or Declaration of Independence:

We, the Subscribers, Brokers for the Purchase and Sale of Public Stock, do hereby solemnly promise and pledge ourselves to each other, that we will not buy or sell from this day for any person whatsoever, any kind of Public Stock, at a less rate than one quarter per cent Com-

View of Broad Street, George Holland, 1797. When the national capital left New York in 1790, Federal Hall (the large building at the end of Broad Street) resumed its humbler function as city hall. In the years to come, the surrounding streets, still lined mostly with houses, including one of the last remaining Dutch-style gabled structures in the area—on the right, dated 1698—would become home to the city's rapidly growing financial community.

Among the prominent figures in post-Revolutionary New York was the lawyer, politician, and businessman Aaron Burr, seen crossing Wall Street with his daughter in a latter-day painting by Jeannie Broomscombe.

mission on the [face] value and that we will give a preference to each other in our Negotiations. In Testimony whereof we have set our hands this 17th day of May at New York, 1792.

It was the beginning of the New York Stock Exchange. Almost single-handedly, Alexander Hamilton had kicked into life the most powerful economic engine on earth.

Three years later, in 1795, Hamilton left public office and threw himself back into the commercial life of the city—nurturing his law practice and, in 1801, founding the *New-York Evening Post*. Following the election of his old nemesis, Thomas Jefferson, in 1800, he left government entirely, retiring to his handsome estate in upper Manhattan to watch his city grow.

By 1804, its population had more than doubled in less than a decade, climbing to eighty thousand. That year, for the first time in its history, New York surpassed Philadelphia. It was now indisputably the most populous city in the United States—though Hamilton himself would not be around to savor the triumph.

Late that spring, he was challenged to a duel by his bitter enemy, Aaron Burr, an ambitious and powerful New York politician whose career Hamilton had spent a lifetime trying to destroy, with considerable success. Forbidden from dueling in New York, thanks to a law Hamilton him-

self had helped pass after his own son had been killed in a duel, the two men retired on the morning of July 11, 1804, to Weehauken, New Jersey, across the Hudson River from the rolling hills and woodlands of Manhattan. When the crucial moment came, Hamilton's shot went wide. Burr's struck Hamilton in the right side, inflicting a mortal wound. The next afternoon, after more than thirty hours of excruciating pain, Alexander Hamilton died in the parlor of a friend's house on Jane Street, in Greenwich Village.

All New York turned out to mourn him. On July 13, 1804, after one of the largest funeral processions in the city's history, Hamilton was buried with full military honors in the graveyard of Trinity Church—just across Broadway from Wall Street, in the heart of the city whose future he had done so much to secure.

He was just forty-seven years old. New York was on its way. In the century to come, the world that would rise up around Hamilton's final resting place would be a stunning monument to the magnitude of his achievement.

AMERICA'S CITY

Everything in the city is in motion; everywhere the shops resound with the noise of workers. . . . One sees vessels arriving from every

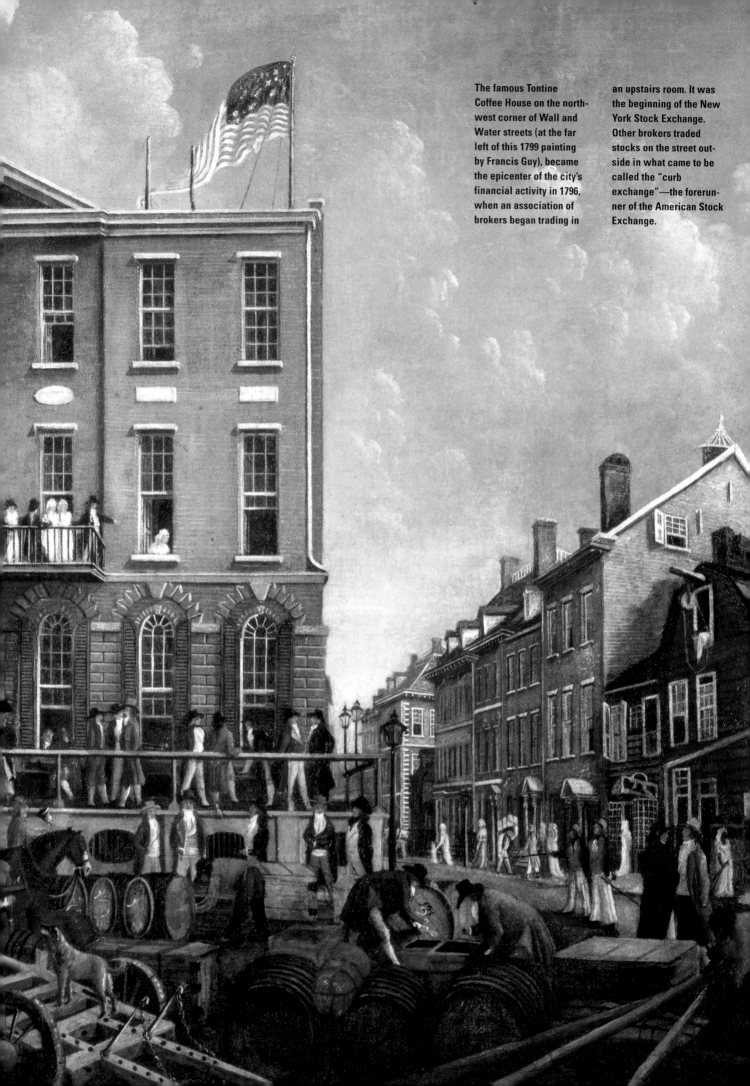

The famous Tontine Coffee House on the northwest corner of Wall and Water streets (at the far left of this 1799 painting by Francis Guy), became the epicenter of the city's financial activity in 1796, when an association of brokers began trading in an upstairs room. It was the beginning of the New York Stock Exchange. Other brokers traded stocks on the street outside in what came to be called the "curb exchange"—the forerunner of the American Stock Exchange.

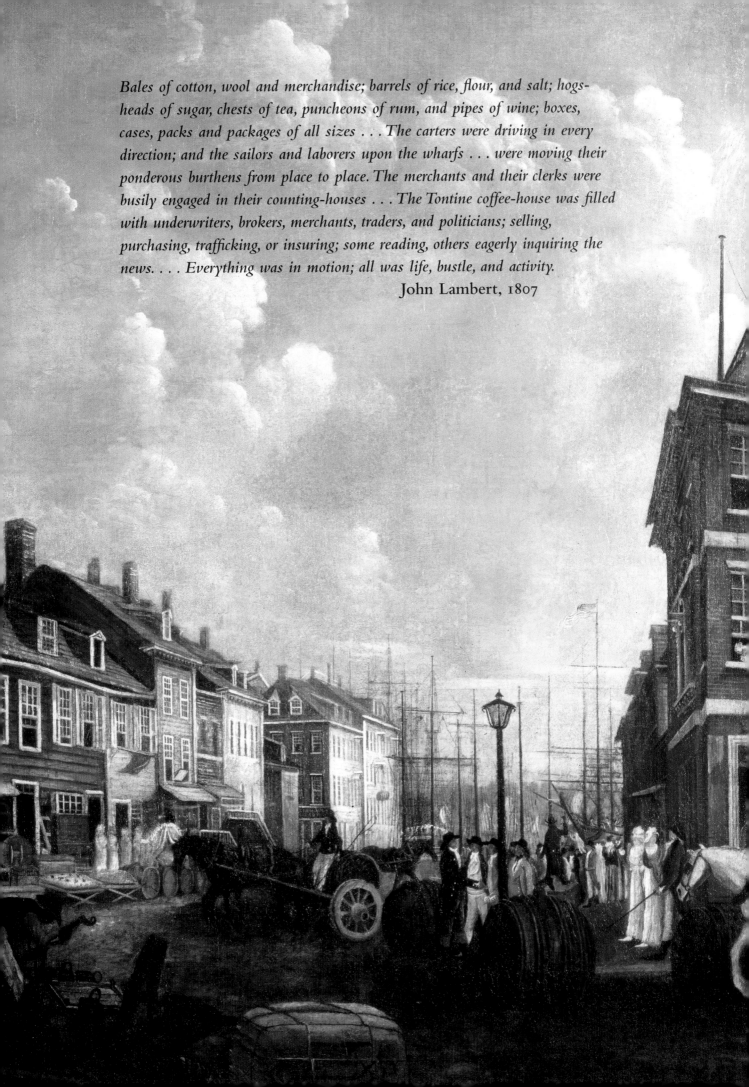

Bales of cotton, wool and merchandise; barrels of rice, flour, and salt; hogs-heads of sugar, chests of tea, puncheons of rum, and pipes of wine; boxes, cases, packs and packages of all sizes . . . The carters were driving in every direction; and the sailors and laborers upon the wharfs . . . were moving their ponderous burthens from place to place. The merchants and their clerks were busily engaged in their counting-houses . . . The Tontine coffee-house was filled with underwriters, brokers, merchants, traders, and politicians; selling, purchasing, trafficking, or insuring; some reading, others eagerly inquiring the news. . . . Everything was in motion; all was life, bustle, and activity.

John Lambert, 1807

part of the world, or ready to depart. This still new city . . . is the queen of commerce and the sovereign of the seas.

François Marie Perrin du Lac, 1801

The daily lives of its merchants astounded outsiders. They breakfasted at eight or half past, and by nine were in their counting-houses, laying out the business of the day; at ten they were on their wharves, with aprons round their waists, rolling hogsheads of rum and molasses; at twelve, at market, flying about as dirty and diligent as porters; at two, back again to the rolling, heaving . . . and scribbling. At four they went home to dress for dinner; at seven, to the play; at eleven, to supper, with a crew of lusty Bacchanals who would smoke cigars, gulp down brandy, and sing, roar, and shout in the thickening clouds . . . till three in the morning. At eight, up again, to scribble, run, and roll hogsheads. What a day's work this would have been for a Carolinian!

John Bernard, 1797

Almost two hundred years had elapsed since European sailors had first set eyes on the vast and tranquil harbor—in which, they dreamed, a thousand ships might one day ride in safety.

Now, at last, the vision of the old Dutch explorers was about to become a reality. In the next twenty years, New York would rise to become one of the greatest centers of shipping and commerce the world has ever seen. Along the way, New Yorkers would show the world how to transform nature, obliterate geography, and alter time and space itself.

In 1807, a transplanted Pennsylvanian named Robert Fulton launched the world's first practical steamboat off the west side of Manhattan. It looked like a "backwoods sawmill," one man said, "mounted on a scow and set on fire." But it freed ships forever from the tyranny of the wind.

In 1810, a sixteen-year-old boy from Staten Island named Cornelius Vanderbilt purchased a secondhand sailboat with a hundred dollars he had borrowed from his mother and started his own ferry service to Manhattan. Mockingly called "the Commodore" by his rivals, Vanderbilt had begun what would eventually become the greatest shipping empire in the world.

In 1817, a shipping company called the Black Ball Line came up with a startlingly simple idea that would revolutionize commerce around the world. On October 27, the owners announced a special new packet service connecting New York and Liverpool: ships that would "sail from each place on a certain day in every month throughout the year"—a "regular succession of Vessels," the company promised, that would "positively sail, *full or not full.*" The novelty was not the route but the regularity. Up until then, ships had typically lingered at dockside until the weather was acceptable, or the hold was full, or the crew was mustered, or the captain was ready. But on the bitterly cold morning of January 5, 1818, at 10:00 a.m. precisely, Captain James Wilkinson of the Black Ball Line gave orders for the *James Monroe* to cast off from Pier 23 on South Street—into a driving snowstorm, with only a few barrels of apples and flour on board, along with eight passengers and a mailbag. The first scheduled maritime departure in history, it was the beginning of the world's first shipping *line*—a regular service running back and forth, month in and month out. For the first time, businessmen could make firm commitments, certain that their goods would arrive "on time"—a phrase that now made its way into the language. New York's merchants had invented the idea of a schedule.

The Black Ball Line's packet service blossomed rapidly. As the innovation drew more and more business to the city, other lines were founded, and soon New York's ships were leaving for Liverpool once a week. Within six years, the city completely dominated the nation's trade—shipping more goods overseas than Boston, Philadelphia, Baltimore, Norfolk, and Savannah combined. Not content with that, its merchants widened their lead still further by linking the city's transatlantic services to its fleets of fast-moving coastal steamers that plied the Atlantic seaboard.

No other port could match it. It was soon cheaper for southern merchants to "trans-ship" cotton through New York than directly to England. The great northern port had become the clearinghouse for southern cotton. Soon, a third of all the merchant tonnage in the world was sailing from South Street, whose two-mile stretch of piers, countinghouses, supply houses, and shipyards had become, one man said, a "for-

At one o'clock, on Sunday, August 17, 1807, Robert Fulton's first steamboat cast off from a Hudson River dock in Greenwich Village. As a curious crowd of onlookers watched from shore, the strange-looking vessel built up speed despite a countervailing breeze, and soon "overtook many sloops and schooners beating to windward," one witness wrote, "as if they had been at anchor." Within two weeks, the steamboat—christened the *Clermont* in 1810— was in commercial service, carrying paying customers to Albany and back.

Arrival of the Great Western Steam Ship, off New York, on Monday, 23 April 1838. The arrival of two English steamships on the same day in April 1838— the *Sirius* at noon, followed by the *Great Western* four hours later—marked the start of regular steamship service between New York and England. Cheering crowds lined the Battery to welcome the brave new ships, which cut the time it took to cross the Atlantic from the three weeks to ten days. A 19-year-old law student and fledgling diarist named George Templeton Strong strolled down to the Battery to catch a glimpse of the new vessels—which, he said, "created quite a sensation, and the Bay is all alive. Hurrah for the Advance of Mind!"

On a cold February morning in 1784—just ten weeks after the British departed at the end of the Revolutionary War—a 360-ton ship called *Empress of China* cast off from Pier 14 in the East River, bound on a 14,000-mile voyage to the Far East. On her return, 15 months later, she brought not only a bounty of tea, porcelain, and silks but evidence that England's century-long hold on the China trade had been broken. Untethered from the privileges and constraints of Britain's unwieldy global empire—free at last to develop markets of their own—New York merchants swiftly reached out to the ends of the earth and, with remarkable speed, created a new kind of commercial empire.

The heart of that empire was a two-mile stretch of East River waterfront, known around the world as the Street of Ships. By the 1820s, every available space along the west side of South Street had been taken over by a bewildering parade of counting-houses, warehouses, marine insurers, importers, commission merchants, jobbers, chandleries, coopers, sailmakers, and taverns—the bright commercial facades confronting a bristling forest of docked ships, the line of bowsprits angled above the bustling street like lances or pikes.

Out on the long wooden piers, merchants conducted fast-paced auctions next to mountains of crated goods, while textile manu-facturers from New England and Great Britain huddled around bursting bales of southern cotton, inspecting the merchandise and haggling over price. At the far northern end of South Street, the piers and countinghouses gave way to giant sheds, launchways, and a new innovation called a "marine railway"—the nation's first dry dock. With fourteen major shipyards, New York City had become the largest shipbuilding center in America, soon to be home to innovative designers like William H. Webb and Brown & Bell, renowned for their trim, sturdy vessels—packets, schooners, steamers, and sleek clippers.

For visitors, nothing was more startling about South Street than its casual cosmopolitanism. At a time when most Americans knew little of what happened more than a few miles from their own front doors, South Street connected New Yorkers to the most far-flung reaches of the globe. Each week, exotic goods from China—perfume, silks, tea, china—were unloaded on the piers, alongside linen from Ireland, cutlery from England, bonnets and gowns from France, casks of port and sherry from Portugal and Spain, ivory from the Guinea coast, coffee from Brazil. Destination placards in front of each ship advertised distant ports of call, the flags and ensigns of two dozen countries flew from the halyards, and a babble of foreign languages could be heard. South Street crews included scores of black sailors from the West Indies, Africa, and New York itself, as well as a host of young Chinese men—who by the 1830s had begun to build their own homes in New York, just a few blocks from the piers—the earliest Chinese community in America.

Brooklyn remained largely rural in the early years of the nineteenth century—even as business in the restless port city across the harbor was booming as never before. By 1802 the year William Burch created this bucolic view, the East River waterfront across from Brooklyn had become a forest of masts, and ships sailing from New York were carrying nearly ten times the value in goods they had handled a dozen years before.

est of masts." "All streets," New Yorkers said, "lead to South Street."

> Business along our streets and docks is now unusually brisk, and the warehouses and stores begin to be crowded with European and Indian goods. The importations this season are like to be larger than for many years past, and are arriving on time. No less than five ships arrived here yesterday from the single port of Liverpool.
>
> The Repertory, September 25, 1810

Whoever visits New York feels as he does in a watchmaker's shop; everybody goes there for the true time, and feels on leaving it as if he had been wound up or regulated anew. . . . He hears a clicking, as it were, on all sides of him, and finds everything he looks at in movement, and not a nook or corner but what is brim-ful of business. Apparently there is no inactivity; that is, no person is quiescent both in body and mind at once. The reason of this is, that the lazy are excited by the perpetual motion of the

This tranquil view of the foot of Cortlandt Street shows one of the dozens of merchant houses that by 1819 lined the South Street waterfront along the East River. "Every thought, word, look and action of the multitude seemed to be absorbed in commerce," an English traveler named John Lambert wrote a few years earlier.

John Jacob Astor, a blunt and acquisitive German-born fur trader, amassed the first great fortune in the history of the United States, speculating in real estate in upper Manhattan. At the peak of his buying spree, he owned more than 300 separate parcels of land, including the real estate under Times Square and much of the Lower East Side.

Washington Irving was just 26 years old when he wrote the city's first best-seller—a whimsical blend of fact and fiction called *A History of New York, from the Beginning of the World to the End of the Dutch Dynasty*. He would go on to give New York its most enduring nickname—"Gotham," for a mythical town in northern England, whose citizens were legendary both for their foolishness and their guile.

busy, or at least compelled to bestir themselves to avoid being run over.

Theodore Dwight, 1833

Propelled by the immense power of the port, Manhattan began to move north. "The progress of this city is, as usual, beyond all calculations," wrote Senator Jonathan Mason of Massachusetts, passing through in 1804. "Seven hundred buildings erected in the last twelve months; and Broadway, beyond all dispute, is the best street . . . in America."

One by one the sprawling Dutch farms and English estates north of town began to be divided into smaller and smaller lots, sold to builders and speculators, and filled with houses as fast as streets could be laid down. In the process, Manhattan real estate—now among the most expensive in the world—became for the first time not just something to build upon but a major industry in itself, and a source of enormous profit. An English traveler sojourning in the city in the first decade of the century was startled by the money to be made in the Manhattan real estate market. "New York," he wrote, "has rapidly improved in the last twenty years; and land which then sold for fifty dollars is now worth 1,500."

In 1800, John Jacob Astor, a thirty-seven-year-old German-born fur trader, began buying up every piece of undeveloped land he could lay his hands on. The first to grasp the most obvious fact of Manhattan's future development, Astor saw more clearly than anyone else that the city had only one way to grow—northward. In one year alone, he expended nearly $200,000 on empty tracts of land north of the city limits. Less a builder than a speculator, Astor did little to improve the properties he purchased, patiently waiting instead for the city to move north before selling his holdings at a breathtaking profit—then buying still more land, even farther to the north.

Single-minded, relentlessly acquisitive, and notoriously crude, Astor stunned the city's polite society with his appalling manners—mixing peas and ice cream, then eating them with a knife, then wiping his hands on the tablecloth.

But, at least to his face, no one said a word, as, gambling on the future of New York, Astor transformed his already enormous fortune into

an empire of extraordinary proportions. At the peak of his buying spree, the methodical, insatiable millionaire owned more than three hundred parcels of land on Manhattan, including most of the Lower East Side and all of the land under what became Times Square. More than any man of his era, he had learned how to turn the future itself into a commodity, and it made him the richest man in the nation—by far. At the time of his death in 1848, the second-richest man in America was worth $10 million. By then, John Jacob Astor was worth $25 million. "His very name," Herman Melville wrote, "rings like unto bullion."

Even on his deathbed, the old man's appetite for real estate remained unquenched. "Could I begin life again, knowing what I know now," he said, seeing what the city had become, "I would buy every foot of land on the island of Manhattan."

Virtue has been regarded as the guiding principle or principal strength of a republic. That of the American Republic appears to be a frantic love of money. It is a result of the political equality which reigns there, and which, leaving people no other distinction besides wealth, invites them to acquire it by every possible means.

Louis-Felix de Beaujour, 1806

KNICKERBOCKERS

Everything in New York seemed to be changing now, with sometimes disorienting swiftness. Most of the old Dutch city had long since been destroyed by the two great fires during the Revolution, but each week brought news that another piece of the city's heritage had disappeared.

As New Yorkers wrenched themselves free of the past to make way for the future, a yearning for history grew.

In 1804, the New-York Historical Society was founded. Five years later, in 1809, a curious volume called *A History of New York, from the Beginning of the World to the End of the Dutch Dynasty* went on sale in the city's bookstores. Presented as the work of an elderly Dutch gentleman named Diedrich Knickerbocker, its author was in fact a twenty-six-year-old native New Yorker named Washington Irving—who had been born in the year of the English surrender and who once wrote a promotional pamphlet for John Jacob Astor himself.

"I was surprised," Irving said, "to find how few of my fellow-citizens were aware that New York had ever been called New Amsterdam, or had heard of the names of its early Dutch governors, or cared a straw about their ancient Dutch progenitors."

To rectify the situation, he set out to reinvent the past for a city busy inventing the future. Mingling in his writings historical figures, like Peter Stuyvesant, with fictional ones, like Rip Van Winkle, Irving created a mythical origin for the bustling, forward-looking city—reimagining the unruly Dutch colony as an enchanted fairyland of canals and windmills that the Dutch themselves would scarcely have recognized.

Irving's fictional *History* rapidly became the city's first best-seller, and Irving himself the first man in America to earn his living solely by his pen. "Father Knickerbocker" was adopted as the unofficial symbol of the city, and soon even the oldest colonial families were calling themselves Knickerbockers—proudly tracing their lineage back to a man who never existed.

MAGNUS APOLLO

If it had done nothing more, New York City would have remained forever after the greatest port on the Atlantic seaboard. But a larger destiny lay in store—and to achieve it, two immense obstacles would have to be overcome.

One was the geography of Manhattan itself—whose rugged natural landscape hindered orderly growth, with its swamp-covered lowlands and rocky granite outcroppings. The other was the geography of the American continent—to whose vast fertile plains and endless natural abundance the city's merchants still had no easy access.

The man who would attempt to solve both problems—and in so doing stake a claim to being the greatest New Yorker of all time—was a six-foot-three-inch patrician politician, so brilliant and commanding that friends and enemies alike called him Magnus Apollo. In ten terms as mayor and three as governor, De Witt Clinton would do more to shape the future of the city than anyone else in its history. To do that, he would first have to bring order out of chaos—then reach westward and transform geography itself.

"He seemed to be a hundred persons in one," one admirer said. The son of a long line of New York lawyers and politicians, and the first man to graduate from King's College under its new name, Columbia, he went on to be schooled in the intricacies of city and state politics—as secretary to his uncle, George Clinton, the first

No one grasped the commercial and cultural potential of New York City more than De Witt Clinton, (opposite) the brilliant and commanding scion of a long line of distinguished lawyers and politicians, seen here at age 51 in an 1820 painting by John Wesley Jarvis.

In 1811, at a time when New York still huddled below Canal Street at the foot of Manhattan, a three-man commission—appointed in part by De Witt Clinton—came up with one of the most audacious and far-sighted urban visions ever conceived. On a map more than eight feet long, the Commissioners' Plan

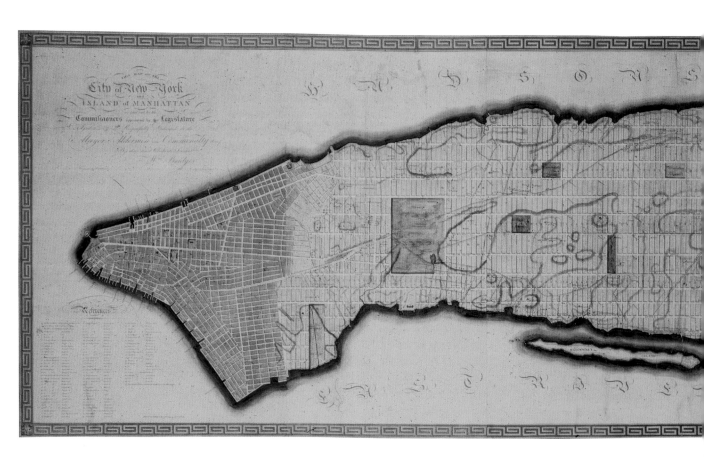

governor of the state, and as an assistant to Alexander Hamilton. An ardent admirer of Hamilton's—and heir to his tremendous vision of the city—Clinton had survived his own duel in New Jersey, two years before Hamilton's, with a protégé of Aaron Burr's.

A pragmatic idealist who knew how to get things done, in a quarter century of public life Clinton would extend Hamilton's extraordinary vision of New York as the metropolitan center of an emerging American empire—capable of rivaling the greatest cities of Europe.

Appointed mayor in 1803, the thirty-four-year-old Clinton set right to work, overseeing construction of a new city hall, then helping found the New-York Historical Society, the New York Academy of Sciences, the Free School Society, the Orphans Asylum, and a dozen other institutions.

But Clinton had a larger plan for the island city, which was already lurching northward—"breaking," he observed, "with irresistible force into all parts of the country." In 1807, to bring order to the chaotic spasms of uncoordinated growth, he oversaw the creation of a special commission to come up with "a final and conclusive" plan for the development of the island.

Four years later, in 1811, the commissioners unveiled their plan. On a single giant map, more than eight feet long, they had projected

a breathtaking urban vision that would shape the future of Manhattan for centuries to come. "A blueprint for the island's manifest destiny," the architect Rem Koolhaas later wrote, the Commissioners' Plan would prove to be the "most courageous act of prediction in Western civilization: the land it divides, unoccupied; the

projected an astonishing vision of the city's future: a single giant grid, 155 streets long and 12 avenues wide, covering almost all of Manhattan Island with more than 2,000 blocks. In the decades to come, as the Commissioners' Plan was filled in with startling speed, only one rogue avenue—Broadway—would be allowed to deviate from the strict rectilinearity of the grid. The only other significant difference from the city the commissioners imagined would be the inclusion, half a century later, of a giant "central park."

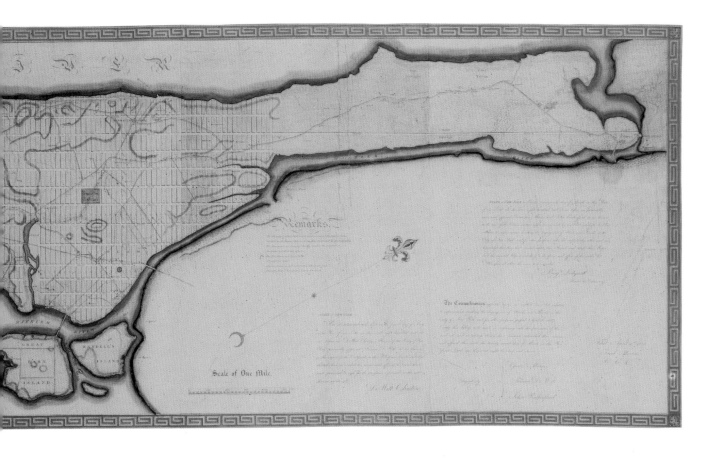

population it describes, conjectural; the buildings it locates, phantoms; the activities it frames, non-existent."

At a time when the city was still huddled at the southern tip of Manhattan, the commissioners proposed leveling the island's entire natural topography and replacing it with a single massive grid, 12 avenues wide and a 155 streets long, covering 11,000 acres with more than 2,000 blocks.

There had been grids before, but never on this scale. At a time when the city's population was still less than a 100,000 people, Clinton's plan envisioned a giant metropolis of more than a million. If realized, it would transform Manhattan into the most populous city on earth. "It may be a subject of merriment," the commissioners acknowledged, that they had "provided space for a greater population than is collected at any spot this side of China."

With its thousands of blocks, each more or less identical to every other, the grid anticipated a profoundly democratic city—and, with its hundreds of streets leading down to the rivers, a relentlessly commercial one.

"One of the first objects which claimed their attention," the commissioners noted, "was whether they should confine themselves to . . . rectangular streets, or . . . adopt some of those supposed improvements . . . circles, ovals, and stars, which certainly embellish a plan, whatever may be their effects as to convenience and utility. . . . They could not but bear in mind that a city is to be composed principally of the habitations of men, and that strait-sided and right-angled houses are the most cheap to build, and the most convenient to live in. The effect of these plain and simple reflections was decisive."

In the end, only one maverick avenue—Broadway, running the entire length of the island—would be permitted to deviate from the strict rectilinearity of the grid, whose right-angled lots, the commissioners explained, would make them easy to buy, sell, and build upon.

"It may be a matter of surprise," the commissioners acknowledged, "that so few vacant spaces have been left, and those so small, for the benefit of fresh air and consequent preservation of health. . . . But those large arms of the sea which embrace Manhattan Island render its situation, in regard to health and pleasure, as well as to the convenience of commerce, peculiarly felicitous." The endless miles of waterfront, the commissioners argued, and thousands of private backyards would satisfy all the city's recreational needs. The absence of park space would haunt the city for decades to come.

View of Broadway, New York City, **Axel Leonhard Klincköwstom, 1819. The center of civic and cultural life in New York in 1819 was the elegant stretch of Broadway sweeping north past city hall, itself completed only seven years before. Philip Hone, a wealthy auctioneer considered New York's leading citizen, lived in a stately brick row house directly across from city hall. The second house north of St. Paul's Chapel (whose fluted columns can be seen at far left) was the home of John Jacob Astor. In 1834, Astor ripped his own house down—along with the rest of the block—to make way for the enormous new Astor House hotel.**

In its optimism and unbounded faith in the future, the Commissioners' Plan was without parallel in the history of urban planning. Yet even that audacity was nothing compared to that of another proposal De Witt Clinton put forward that same year—not an eight-foot map, but a 363-mile-long ditch that, if completed, would transform forever New York's relation to the entire American continent.

CANAL

As yet we only crawl along the outer shell of our country. The interior excels the part we inhabit in soil, in climate, in every thing. The proudest empire in Europe is but a bauble compared to what America will be, must be, in the course of two centuries—perhaps of one.

Gouverneur Morris, 1800

For years, New York's merchants had been dreaming of the immense wealth locked in the continent's interior. But though they now dominated every point on the compass but one, to the west the Appalachian and Allegheny mountains rose like a great wall, dividing the Atlantic coast from the heartland of the country.

With no waterway through them, the only way across was overland, on horse-drawn carts over steep, rutted trails, that often required weeks of travel. As late as 1811, it cost more to ship a ton of goods thirty miles inland than all the way to England.

That very year, De Witt Clinton put forward a daring solution. If nature had provided no river to the west, New Yorkers would simply build one. Taking advantage of the fact that the only natural gap in the Appalachian Mountains ran through Upstate New York, Clinton proposed building a barge canal that would connect the Hudson River to Lake Erie. Linking New York Harbor to the western shores of the Great Lakes a thousand miles inland, it would bring the bounty of an entire continent to the city's doorstep.

The scope of the project was mindboggling—an artificial waterway unlike anything undertaken since the days of the ancient Egyptians. At a time when most canals in America were under 2 miles long, and the longest 27, Clinton's canal would have to run well over 350 miles, across the rugged wilderness of Upstate New York. At $6 million, the cost alone was nothing less than staggering—fully three-quarters of the entire federal budget.

Thomas Jefferson himself had blocked federal funding for the scheme, pointing out that Congress had refused to fund a pet project of General Washington—a thirty-mile canal along the gentle banks of the Potomac—"because the small sum of $200,000 necessary to complete it cannot be obtained from the General Government, the State Government, or from individuals. And you talk of making a canal *three hundred and fifty miles through the wilderness*! It is

With the building of the Erie Canal—a special project of De Witt Clinton's and the crowning glory of his career—New Yorkers perfected the extraordinary geographical advantages the ice age had given them. A shallow, unprepossessing ditch—seldom more than 40 feet wide and 12 feet deep, but running 363 miles across the rugged wilderness of upstate New York—the canal connected the Hudson River at Albany to the Great Lakes at Buffalo—giving the port of New York a direct water link to the heartland of the North American continent.

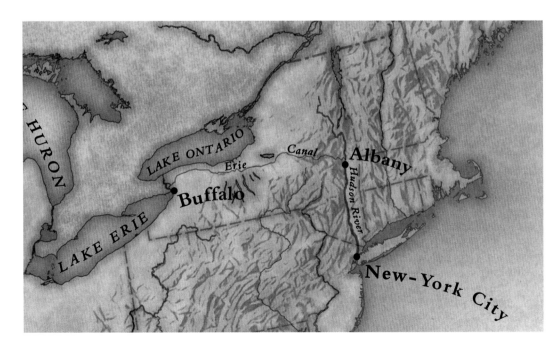

a splendid project, and may be executed a century hence. It is little short of madness to think of it at this day."

To Clinton's dismay, the New York State legislature agreed, and so did President James Madison, who warned that the canal's enormous cost would bankrupt the federal government. But Clinton would not be deterred. The Erie Canal, he insisted, would make New York "one of the most splendid commercial cities on the face of the earth."

Appealing directly to the public, he lobbied ceaselessly for what his detractors called "Clinton's Big Ditch"—holding mass rallies in New York City, and circulating a petition eventually signed by more than a hundred thousand New Yorkers. The canal, he declared to a crowd of potential investors in 1815, would pass "through the most fertile country in the universe [and] convey more riches on its waters than any other canal in the world.... It remains for a free state

to . . . erect a work more stupendous, more magnificent, and more beneficial than has hereto been achieved by the human race."

To pay for it all, he himself devised an ingenious scheme for using public funds to raise private financing: making millions of dollars' worth of government bonds attractive to New York bankers and brokers, by simply backing them with a modest state tax on salt. It showed once and for all that great public works could be built in a democracy.

In the spring of 1817, after years of maneuvering, Clinton finished securing the final funds for his gigantic undertaking. On July 4, work on the Erie Canal began.

Nine thousand men in all worked on the vast project—most paid less than a dollar a day, wielding picks and shovels to carve a sinuous channel forty feet wide, twelve feet deep, and hundreds of miles long. To oversee the work, Clinton had appointed three judges and a school-

Called "the Grand Canal," "the Great Western Canal," and "Clinton's Big Ditch" during its seven years of construction, the Erie Canal—seen here (opposite) in an 1832 watercolor by John William Hill—was America's first school of engineering. Teaching themselves as they went along how to build an "artificial river," scores of engineers and workmen gained the skills they would need to open up an entire continent. As the massive effort neared completion in 1822, Thomas Jefferson—who as president had refused to provide federal funds for the project—wrote to De Witt Clinton. "Many, I dare say," he said, "still think with me that New-York has anticipated, by a full century, the ordinary course of improvement."

Four views along the Erie Canal. "The novelty of seeing large boats drawn by horses upon waters artificially conducted," one man wrote in 1820, as the first completed sections of the canal were opened to traffic, "through cultivated fields, forests and swamps, over ravines, creeks and morasses, and from one elevation to another, by means of ample, beautiful, and substantial locks, has been eminently exhilarating."

teacher, none of whom had ever seen a canal before. Undaunted, they went right to work—building, one man said, "by guess and by God," teaching themselves as they went along the science of building rivers, inventing devices to fell trees, extract stumps, and cut through thick roots.

By the spring of 1825, the canal was nearly done. At a ceremony honoring the completion of the locks at Lockport, New York, the Reverend F. H. Cuming was filled with wonder at the magnitude of Clinton's accomplishment. "The mountains have been levelled," he declared, "the vallies have been filled; rivers and gulfs have been formed over them, by the exertions of art, a channel in which the waters of the distant Hudson, the waters of the still more distant Atlantic, will unite with the waters of the remote west, and constitute a river."

On October 26, 1825—on budget, and at least three years ahead of schedule—the entire undertaking was complete. "The longest canal in the world," one journalist declared, had been "built in the least time, with the least experience, for the least money, and to the greatest public benefit."

"The great Erie Canal," another man said, "has defied nature and used it like a toy." With its eighty-three locks and eighteen aqueducts—including an eight-hundred-foot waterbridge over the Genesee River—it was the greatest construction feat of its day.

It had also worked nothing less than an economic miracle. Where it had once taken three weeks to move a ton of wheat from Buffalo to New York, it now took less than eight days—and the cost had been cut from a hundred dollars to less than six.

At the opening celebrations, De Witt Clinton—governor now, and the undisputed hero of the day—poured a keg of water drawn from Lake Erie into New York Harbor. The symbolism was lost on no one. All America now met in New York.

"It may be confidently asserted," Clinton declared in his speech that day, "that this canal, as to the extent of its route, as to the countries which it connects, and as to the consequences it will produce, is without a parallel in the history of mankind." He went on to utter a fateful prediction:

Junction of the Erie Canal and Northern Canal, by John William Hill, circa 1830. "Everything on the Canal is life and motion," a Boston traveler wrote in 1845, two decades after the waterway was completed. "Every moment the boats passed loaded with western produce." "For twenty years," the editor of the *Albany Argus* observed that same year, "the wealth of the teeming West has poured down that avenue, and already has placed New York on an eminence as the Commercial Emporium of America. So long as New York remains at the head of the western trade, it must irresistibly advance in wealth, influence and population, until she be known not only as the great city of America, but as the *great city of the world*."

Every word Clinton spoke would come true. Almost overnight, the Erie Canal transformed New York, and with it the nation. Before Clinton's great achievement, most of the bounty of the American hinterland had flowed south down the Mississippi River, and observers could be forgiven for assuming that New Orleans was destined to become the chief metropolis of the nation.

The canal changed that forever, capturing the goods and produce of the Great Plains and Middle West and sending them streaming east toward New York City, along what soon became the nation's central commercial corridor. To collect and process the immense flood of commerce, mighty cities would soon arise along the shores of the Great Lakes—Chicago, Detroit, Cleveland, and Buffalo—great cities in themselves, to be sure, but subsidiaries still to the great hub of New York, through which much of the wealth of the entire nation would soon be passing.

In the years to come, the Erie Canal would pull the nation together as never before, becoming the spine of an emerging industrial North, with New York as its focus. Along the way, the great city—no longer merely a thriving seaport but the funnel of the Western world—would become a fulcrum between the Old World and

The growing prosperity of the early-nineteenth-century city was reflected in the increasingly comfortable life—in both town and country—of its merchant elite. In Manhattan, wealthy New Yorkers founded clubs, learned societies, private libraries, and elegant places of amusement—such as the fashionable Park Theater, shown (left) in an 1822 painting by the artist John Searle. Commissioned by a wealthy New York merchant named William Bayard, the painting offers a composite view—the theater's stalls cozily filled with Bayard's circle of friends, all members of New York's tightly knit ruling class. (Bayard himself stands in the first row of boxes, just to the left of the woman whose shawl spills over the rail. Three seats to her right, wearing a white bonnet and facing forward, sits Mrs. De Witt Clinton.) Outside the city, meanwhile, in the rolling landscapes of Brooklyn and Staten Island, New York merchants built sprawling estates overlooking the Upper Bay and the Narrows—such as the country house and grounds on the eastern edge of Staten Island, shown (below) in a view by the German artist August Köllner.

the New, the principal point of connection between Europe on one side and the American continent on the other.

Irrevocably linked now to the great heartland as well as to the South, New England, and the world across the ocean, New York City quickly became the first real center in America. With astonishing foresight and determination, De Witt Clinton had first imagined the great metropolis New York might become, then reshaped the geography of an entire continent to make it inevitable.

> *We do not think that we can be charged with exaggeration when we state that there is not a city in the world which, in all respects, has advanced with greater rapidity, than the city of New York, in the last ten years. Whichever way we turn, new buildings present themselves to our notice. In the upper wards particularly, entire streets of elegant brick buildings have been formed on sites which only a few years ago were either covered with marshes, or occupied by a few straggling frame huts of little or no value. . . . [Last year,] the number of vessels arriving at this port aggregated 1,217, of which 1,097 were American, 91 British, and the remainder Dutch, French, Swedish, Spanish, Portuguese and other nationalities, having on board 4,999 passengers and laden with the products of our sister states, of the European nations, the West Indies and the new republics of South America. On the 1st of January 1824, there were 326 vessels in our harbor.*
>
> New-York Evening Post,
> January 8, 1824

> *I never saw more industry, or more general application to business of every description, than in this city. Turn which way you will, mechanics, carvers, carpenters, bricklayers, ship-carpenters, cartmen, all is one continual bustle, from morning till ten o'clock at night. No wonder New-York outstrips all her rivals!*
>
> Mrs. Anne Royall, Alabama, 1824

Following the completion of the Erie Canal, New York would surge into the future—its citizens confident they had left the chaos of nature behind. In many ways they had. But in the turbulent decades to come, as tens of thousands, then hundreds of thousands of newcomers streamed into the growing port, New Yorkers would confront a different kind of chaos—the chaos of man—and that would prove even more difficult to tame.

Between 1825 and 1860, New York City would grow as no city had ever grown before. Even New Yorkers habituated to change would soon feel uncannily like Washington Irving's Rip Van Winkle, who awoke after a night's sleep to discover that twenty years had passed, and that everything around him had utterly changed. Irving himself would awake one morning to find the city he had once known gone forever.

> *August 29th, 1847. My dear Sister: New York, as you knew it, was a mere corner of the present huge city and that corner is all changed, pulled to pieces, burnt down and rebuilt—all but our little native nest in William Street, which still retains some of its old features; though those are daily altering. I can hardly realize that within my term of life, this great crowded metropolis, so full of life, bustle, noise, shew and splendor, was a quiet little City of some fifty or sixty thousand inhabitants. It is really now one of the most rucketing cities in the world.*

ALEXANDER HAMILTON, THE NEW YORKER WITH A NATIONAL VISION

CAROL BERKIN

While the sons of Virginia planters and Massachusetts ministers daydreamed over their Latin books or copied etiquette rules into their journals, fifteen-year-old Alexander Hamilton was busy increasing the profits of a thriving West Indian trading company. The young Hamilton's formal education was undoubtedly spotty, but his knowledge of shipping costs, payrolls, international markets, and local credit conditions was finely tuned. Born without the benefit of wealth, or a good family name, isolated on the small islands of Nevis and St. Croix, Hamilton learned early in his life to take advantage of the assets he had: brilliance, quick comprehension, rigorous self-discipline, boundless ambition and energy, great power of persuasion, and bold vision. And, like many young people of limited resources and limitless talent in later centuries, in 1773 Alexander Hamilton made his way to New York City.

Armed with little but letters of introduction to his employer's New York business contacts, Hamilton immediately began pursuit of his first goal: a respectable formal education. His mentors predicted a long and arduous college preparatory course, but Hamilton, like most New Yorkers, felt he had little time to waste. He buried his head in history books, classic philosophy tracts, and introductory texts on geography and mathematics. Book in hand, he could be seen pacing the floor day and night, reciting material aloud, committing it to memory, and often arguing with himself the merits and flaws of the text. If his learning style was idiosyncratic, it was clearly effective. Within a year he had been admitted to Manhattan's King's College, an urban, upstart rival to the more hallowed halls of Princeton, Yale, and Harvard. Like most institutions in New York, the college reflected the factional—not to say fractious—politics of the city. With a conservative Anglican as president and liberal Protestant dissenters on the board of trustees, King's wisely produced a secular curriculum. Educators at other institutions condemned King's as shockingly liberal—but it suited Hamilton perfectly.

In college, Hamilton devoured the influential and sophisticated works of Grotius, Locke, Hobbes, and David Hume, only occasionally distracted by the raucous sounds from the taverns and brothels on nearby Greenwich and Church streets. He was a model student, yet he was never a scholar, for he valued the practical application of any theory far more than its aesthetics. And, because his basic inclination was activist, not academic, he soon abandoned reading about revolution and started agitating for it.

Hamilton had been a thousand miles away when Parliament began its attack on New Yorkers' "rights as Englishmen," yet his commitment to the revolutionary camp came easily. He could not fail to see that his own future and the future of an independence movement were intertwined, for a dramatic break with the past, the elimination of an old political order, and the creation of a new one, might well put a premium on those very qualities he had to offer: talent, commitment, and an unerring ability to transform the theoretical into the practical.

Hamilton quickly demonstrated his rhetorical and literary skills, popularizing the central radical argument that government was a contract between rulers and the ruled, designed to protect rather than endanger a citizen's innate and inalienable human rights, including the right to resist tyranny. New Yorkers were amazed to learn that the firebrand who wrote "The sacred rights of mankind are not to be rummaged for, among old parchments, or musty records. . . . They are written, as with a sunbeam, in the whole volume of human nature, by the hand of the divinity itself; and can never be erased or obscured by mortal power" was a twenty-year-old immigrant. The Declaration of Independence was not yet drafted, but Alexander Hamilton had already emerged as New York's champion of independence.

Hamilton gladly shouldered the mantle of political radicalism, but he remained a social conservative. Throughout his life, he maintained an unshakable conviction that men of breeding, education, and wealth deserved to dominate their society—so long as they welcomed into their ranks those men who earned, rather than inherited, their position. Being more clever, more talented, more driven than most, Hamilton believed in a "natural" social hierarchy, an ascending order that separated the "unthinking populace" from gentlemen, born or made. This was no simple arriviste view of the world; it was the cultural credo of a new class of English and American men who opposed legal and tradition-bound restraints on social mobility but rejected social equality. Thus, Hamilton abhorred the legal restraints imposed by black slavery, but he abhorred the chaos inherent in democracy as well.

In the spring of 1776, Hamilton put down his pen and took up a sword. He was a total novice, but a novice with confidence: he quickly lobbied for a military commission, read a few books on artillery, borrowed funds from friends and acquaintances, and joined the ill-fated defense of the city as captain of an artillery company. Only a few years earlier, on the island of St. Croix, Hamilton had confessed to a friend his dreams of winning notice as a military hero. War, he observed, was a certain path to glory. The American Revolution proved him right.

Hamilton's bravery and skill had indeed won him notice. Yet General Washington's invitation for the young New Yorker to serve as his aide-de-camp was based as much on Hamilton's rumored organizational skills as on his military record. Realizing that there was little glory in a desk job, Washington sweetened his offer with the promise of a promotion to the rank of lieutenant colonel. Wisely, if somewhat reluctantly, Hamilton accepted, for he understood the social advantages of the position. As a member of Washington's most intimate military "family," Hamilton was immediately courted by New York political figures eager for reliable news of the war. And, as a high-ranking officer, his credentials as a gentleman were secured, despite his obscure background or his modest finances. Typically, Hamilton acted to profit from these new advantages. In 1780, he married Elizabeth "Betsey" Schuyler, oldest daughter of General Philip Schuyler, one of New York's wealthiest land owners and a powerful force in New York politics. The Hamilton-Schuyler match was universally appreciated by the savvy New York elite; Betsey's family had added the most exciting new face on the public scene to their intimate circle while the immigrant from the West Indies had parlayed talent, charm, and genius into permanent social status.

The years with Washington did more, however, than secure Hamilton's social standing. They shaped his political perspective and fashioned his political identity. Working daily to coordinate the war effort and to forge and maintain a viable army, Hamilton learned to "think continentally." His exposure to committed nationalists such as the brilliant financier Robert Morris led Hamilton to envision a role for himself beyond the local political world of New York. Like Morris, Hamilton saw clearly the connections between practical fiscal matters and national destiny: without sound public credit, a stable monetary system, a uniform trade policy, effective taxation and revenue-raising programs, the new nation could not hope to fulfill its economic promise, take its place among the nations of the world, or prevent what he viewed as social anarchy within its domestic borders. In Hamilton's judgment, the nation's first government, the Articles of Confederation, was woefully inadequate to the task of ensuring American greatness.

In 1781, Hamilton resigned his military post and by 1782, he had moved temporarily to Albany to begin the study of law. Typically, he was impatient with the profession's expectation of extended training and preparation, and just as typically, he found a way to accelerate the process. He buried himself in James Duane's ample private legal library and immediately devised a strategy to master the fundamentals

of English-based American law. Working at a furious pace, he wrote his own practice manual, summarizing procedures and creating logical categories for essential aspects of legal theory and practice. The resulting 177 pages was a perfect distillation of the craft. As summer began, he paced and recited until he had memorized the entire manual. By July, he had passed the bar exam and before the year was out, opened a practice in New York City.

Although his legal career flourished, Hamilton's intellectual energies were focused on the national political scene. As early as 1781, he had begun to set down on paper a vision—and a practical agenda—for America's future. In shaping his national political agenda, Hamilton relied upon his own keen observation of the world around him as much as he did upon political theorists. His basic political axiom—that all men were knaves driven by private interests, and therefore a successful government must harness this self-interest—may have been distilled from philosophical treatises of writers like David Hume. But for Hume, the value of harnessing individual selfishness to ensure the public good was a theory; for a New Yorker like Hamilton it was a political reality. In the early years after independence, he had watched the city's political enemy, Governor George Clinton, win the loyalty of many wealthy urbanites by allowing holders of the rapidly devaluing Continental securities to trade them for state bonds. In the process, Clinton made New York a creditor of the Confederation, and thus a state that could ignore the national government's repeated requisition of funds. Although Hamilton believed the city's interest would be better served by a champion of commerce rather than a spokesman for upstate landed interests, he appreciated Clinton's strategy. Clinton's secure hold on the reins of state power, more than any philosopher's argument, convinced Hamilton that citizens' self-interest could serve political ends.

New York state politics taught Hamilton another critical, practical lesson: landed interests and commercial interests rarely coincided. Like most of the city leaders, he blamed many urban problems on a dominant upstate gentry who believed land was the only legitimate source of wealth and who held the merchants, entrepreneurs, and financiers of the city in contempt. The landed gentry's control over the governorship and the legislature led to laws and policies that Hamilton considered shortsighted, including the harassment of former loyalists, many of them his clients, who chose to take their capital and their talents away from the state. The effective national government taking shape in Hamilton's mind would actively pursue policies supporting the commercial interest despite agriculture's reluctance.

Hamilton admired, and carefully studied, the Bank of England, which he believed facilitated England's rapid progress in commerce and manufacturing. He came to the

conclusion that it could be duplicated to serve American interests. Soon after the British evacuated the city, he led a small, determined group of merchants and lawyers in a successful fight to charter a Bank of New York. Throughout the early years of the Confederation, while Jefferson was waxing lyrical and Adams legalistic, Hamilton was assessing which institutions and policies would help America take advantage of its most plentiful resources: land, entrepreneurial skills, and a social fluidity that encouraged people with talent and ambition to rise to the top. Despite his pragmatism, he was perhaps more visionary than either man. Certainly he was more farsighted than most of the men who would come to be known as the founding fathers. In a country that was overwhelmingly agrarian, he saw that the future lay in manufacturing and industry. In a society still suspicious of cities, still fearful of urban mores and morals, Hamilton voiced the cosmopolitan conviction that "city air breathes free," that in an urban setting like New York ideas circulated more freely, energy was better harnessed, merit was rewarded. Surrounded by political leaders who obsessed over the concentration of power, he saw the benefits of collective and cooperative efforts by government, the wealthy, and the nation's entrepreneurs. In the midst of political dialogue that seemed fixated on the inevitability of tyranny, he was confident that national leaders would not oppress the citizenry.

Between the ratification of the articles and the calling of the Constitutional Convention in 1787, Hamilton worked tirelessly for governmental reform. Like a political impresario, he arranged for like-minded political leaders of several states to meet to discuss aspects of the nation's "crisis." In 1786, a rebellion by western Massachusetts farmers against the state's taxation and property foreclosure policies turned the political tide in Hamilton's favor. Shays's Rebellion, as this rural protest was called, raised the specter among the planter elite of slave uprisings and led northern leaders to fear a breakdown in the social order. By the summer of 1787, the Constitutional Convention had convened in Philadelphia.

Hamilton was among the New York delegates to the Constitutional Convention. But his attendence was irregular. The long, heated debates over the internal structure of the government interested him little; he cared less about how its branches were organized and far more about getting it organized quickly so that policies could be put in place. He leaped into action, however, when it came time to see the Constitution ratified. As a New Yorker, he knew one of the toughest battles would take place in his own state.

Federal Hall, Archibald Robertson, 1798. In 1789, the imposing structure had been remodeled by Major Pierre-Charles L'Enfant, in anticipation of the arrival of the federal government.

Northeast Corner of Wall and William Streets, New York City, Archibald Robertson, 1798. As Alexander Hamilton's economic policies took hold, the northeast corner of Wall and William streets became known as Bank Row. The Bank of the United States, Hamilton's brainchild, was located in the modest brick row house at number 52—two doors down from the Bank of New York at number 56, which Hamilton had founded 15 years before.

There was little reason, after all, for a prospering New York to cede political decision-making powers, revenue-raising policy, and trade regulation to a national government.

New York voters sent a clear message as they elected the delegates to the state ratifying convention. Voting sixteen thousand to seven thousand against ratification, they elected forty-six anti-Federalists and only nineteen Federalists (largely from New York City and surrounding areas) to the convention. Although Hamilton joined James Madison and John Jay in a prodigious written defense of the Constitution, later known as *The Federalist Papers,* Hamilton had little faith that reasoned debate would change many delegate votes. The battle was tactical, not rhetorical, and in New York the anti-Federalists were well organized and well disciplined. Governor Clinton himself orchestrated the anti-Federalist opposition from outside the convention. Hamilton helped write and push through a resolution calling for a clause-by-clause discussion of the Constitution, a strategy designed to stall the vote until news from outside the convention halls broke down the anti-Federalists' resolve. The plan worked, as the nine states needed for the Constitution

to go into effect were won and the powerful state of Virginia voted yes. Hamilton then dealt the anti-Federalists the final blow, joining with Jay in a tactic that has been resorted to many times since 1787: he threatened that New York City would secede from the state if its demands were not met. On July 26, 1788, New York ratified the Constitution by a vote of 30 to 27.

The city celebrated extravagantly—honoring not only the Constitutional victory but also the heroic efforts of Alexander Hamilton. The centerpiece of the city's long and elaborate parade was a float representing the ship of state and bearing the name the *Hamilton*. But this popular acclaim paled beside what soon followed: President George Washington invited Hamilton to shape the new nation's economic policies as Secretary of the Treasury. Here was the opportunity that Hamilton's entire life seemed to be preparing him for, and he felt more than ready. An upstart from the Caribbean, with no pedigree, he was prepared to lead an upstart nation into greatness.

Hamilton immediately gave up his legal practice and eliminated all private sources of income. He wanted no taint of self-interest as he established policies and institutions based on the self-interest of others. He served from 1789 to 1795, laying out a coherent program that came to be known as the Hamiltonian system. Under his direction, the new government moved to establish its credit at home and abroad by assuming all remaining state debts from the Revolutionary War, pledging to pay the now-enlarged national debt at face value, and taking steps to do so by funding it. In this brilliant financial and political move, Hamilton provided the federal government with a justification for revenue raising or taxation, diminished the powers of the states, and tied the well-being of wealthy government creditors to the success of the new Constitutional government. Victory in these matters did not come easily. But, having honed his skills in the fractious political world of New York, he knew how to bargain for what he wanted: he traded the location of the nation's capital for the direction of its economy.

Hamilton's relentless pursuit of his goals—and his success in achieving them—turned former political allies into enemies. James Madison, his comrade-in-arms in the struggle over ratification, renounced Hamilton's *Report on Public Credit* and his fiscal policies as immoral; Thomas Jefferson condemned the creation of the Bank of the United States as unconstitutional. Anticommercial interests in the Congress blocked Hamilton's most aggressive program, set forth in his *Report on Manufactures,* which would have committed the federal government to actively assist in the growth of American industry. By 1795, conceding that his effectiveness was ended, Hamilton resigned from office and returned to New York City. The leading architect of the American capitalist system was only thirty-seven years old.

While Virginia gentlemen such as George Washington spoke fondly, and often, of retiring to the peaceful solitude of country life, Hamilton had a New Yorker's restless energy. Retirement was unthinkable; activity was essential. His political views might not be popular, especially his outspoken support of Britain rather than revolutionary France, but he continued to express them and to maneuver behind the scenes within the Federalist party. He threw himself into his legal practice, taking on an ever increasing number of cases each year. Friends, however, believed that frustration and disappointment were changing Hamilton: he seemed to be a driven man, overextended in his law practice, impolitic in chosing his causes, prospering yet depressed and sullen.

Between 1797 and 1804, he suffered a series of personal blows that may have accounted for his changed character far more than any shift in political fortunes. In 1797, a Republican newspaper editor exposed an adulterous affair Hamilton had carried on with Maria Reynolds in 1787. Hamilton was forced to issue a response, admitting that his private life was blemished but insisting that his integrity in office was unassailable. The Reynolds exposé placed a strain on Hamilton's marriage and his relationship with his extended New York family. Soon afterward, the Hamiltons retreated to a new home, the Grange, eight miles north of the rancor and political intrigues of New York City. He became a commuter, traveling into the city to his law offices each day. Although he kept his hand in city affairs, founding the *New-York Evening Post* as an outlet for Federalist views, he could not fail to feel he lived on the margins rather than at the center of American public life.

On November 20, 1801, Hamilton's fragile peace of mind was shattered by the death of his nineteen-year-old son, Philip, killed in a duel with a Republican lawyer. The loss of "the brightest, as well as the ablest, hope of my family," drove Hamilton into despair. He spoke of Philip's death as "an event, beyond comparison, the most afflicting of my life," and then saw the tragedy widen as his oldest daughter, Angelica, became permanently deranged over her sibling's death. Hamilton wrote stoically to his wife that they "lived in a world full of evil," but to his friend Gouverneur Morris, he confided his bitterness at not only his personal but his political fate. "Mine is an odd destiny," he wrote this old ally in local and national politics: "Perhaps no man in the United States has sacrificed or done more for the present constitution than myself—and . . . I am still laboring to prop the frail and worthless fabric. Yet I have the murmurs of its friends no less than the curses of its foes for my reward. What can I do better than withdraw from the Scene? Every day proves to me more and more that this American world was not made for me."

Three years later, Hamilton himself was killed in a duel with his longtime political foe Aaron Burr. On Saturday, July 14, his adopted home, New York City, turned out to mourn him. The funeral procession moved slowly as a band of uniformed soldiers, followed by artillery, infantry, and militia companies, led the way along Pearl and Beekman streets to Broadway, toward Trinity Church. Next came the Society of Cincinnati, whose members were former Revolutionary War officers, and clergymen from the city's many Protestant denominations. Hamilton's family and relatives followed the coffin. Behind them trailed the long lines of foreign dignitaries; city officials; Columbia College trustees, faculty, and students; and finally officers of the city's major financial institutions, including its banks and chamber of commerce. British and French frigates in the harbor fired their guns, the French sailors perhaps unaware of the irony in honoring this pro-British American on Bastille Day. A despairing Hamilton may have thought that "this American world was not made for me," but his mourners, and history, assure us that Alexander Hamilon played a major role in making that American world.

New York from Brooklyn Heights, John William Hill, 1837. On a high bluff in Brooklyn overlooking the busy East River waterfront, prosperous New York merchants found refuge from the chaos and bustle of the rapidly expanding immigrant city. One contemporary Brooklyn real-estate advertisement boasted that the new residential district combined "all the advantages of the country, with most of the conveniences of the city." The spacious homes of the world's first commuter suburb were just a 15-minute ferry ride from Manhattan's commercial district.

ORDER AND
1825–1865
DISORDER

N ew York is notoriously the largest and least loved of any of our great cities. Why should it be loved as a city? It is never the same city for a dozen years altogether. A man born forty years ago finds nothing, absolutely nothing, of the New York he knew. If he chances to stumble upon a few old houses not yet leveled, he is fortunate. But the landmarks, the objects, which marked the city to him, as a city, are gone.

Harper's Monthly, 1856

Looking north along Broadway, from the corner of Spring Street, 1859. Then as now, the bustling boulevard was the spine of the city's commercial district—"the most showy, the most crowded, and the richest thorough- fare in America," the edi- tor of *Putnam's Monthly* proudly declared. "There is not a street in London," one visiting Englishman acknowledged, "that can be declared . . . even equal." Every day more than 15,000 vehicles streamed past St. Paul's Chapel at the corner of Broadway and Fulton, the site of legendary traffic jams.

BEFORE THE FLOOD

Fewer than 170,000 people lived on the island of Manhattan in 1825. By any modern standard, the largest city in America was still a relatively peaceful place—compact, orderly, even rural.

North of Houston Street—less than two miles from where the Dutch had first settled two centuries before—the close-knit town quickly tapered off into a bucolic tangle of farms, apple orchards, country lanes, and open fields. George Templeton Strong, a native New Yorker born in 1820 as work on the Erie Canal got under way, could easily walk from his father's house down near the Battery up to the old pear tree Peter Stuyvesant had planted on the northern outskirts of town.

Across the river, in the village of Brooklyn—population eleven thousand—Long Island–born Walt Whitman loved to play a new game called baseball in the vacant fields that surrounded the sleepy town. "Brooklyn," Whitman wrote, looking back, "had such a rural character that it was almost one huge farm and garden in comparison with its present appearance."

For all the bustling diversity of the port in 1825, New York was still a relatively homogeneous place. Four out of five New Yorkers were still native-born—the vast majority of them Protestant, Anglo-Saxon, and white. There were fifteen thousand Irish in the city, only a handful of Germans, and fewer than five hundred Jews.

The mayor—a genial ex-auctioneer named Philip Hone, long considered New York's leading citizen—was still appointed by a board of aldermen itself made up almost exclusively of wealthy merchants like Hone himself.

In run-down districts like the Five Points, north of city hall, New York's twelve thousand African American inhabitants struggled to hold on. Though slavery had all but died out in the state, a rigid color barrier still separated them from whites. "The freedom to which we have attained is defective," a black minister named Peter Williams declared after the last slaves in New York were freed on July 4, 1827. "The rights of men are decided by the colour of their skin."

Life in both cities was still strikingly simple, even crude.

There was no regular police force. No professional fire department. No sewage system. No public transportation, and only a handful of public schools. Water was still drawn mostly from pumps in backyards and street corner wells, and garbage collection was performed primarily by pigs, which still roamed the streets unchecked. At night, flickering gas lamps, introduced only two years before, scarcely lit the poorly paved streets, which after sundown were nearly deserted, except for an occasional night watchman or passing carriage.

Never again would life in the city be so simple, or so harmonious. In the years to come, forces that had been gathering for two hundred years would converge on the island of Manhattan—transforming every aspect of life in the city, and bringing every possibility and every problem of the modern age. In the next four decades, New York would be plunged as no city on earth into the fiery crucible of capitalism and democracy—growing as no city had ever grown before, its population rising from 200,000 to almost a million in just thirty years.

No city in America had ever had to feed, clothe, house, heal, police, educate, or bury so many people. No city in the world had ever brought so many different kinds of people together—squeezed onto an island scarcely larger than a medium-sized Kansas farm.

Between 1825 and 1865—as a commercial engine unlike any the world had ever seen pulled hundreds of thousands of people into its orbit—New Yorkers would confront the most daunting question of their entire history. Could they create a new kind of world on the island of Manhattan? Or would the city explode into chaos and violence, and subside into complete anarchy?

THE VORTEX

We are rapidly becoming the London of America. I myself am astonished & this city is the wonder of every stranger.

John Pintard, 1826

No one—not even Alexander Hamilton or De Witt Clinton—could have predicted the magnitude of the explosion that overtook New

Published in 1834, D. H. Burr's *Map of New-York and Its Vicinity* prophetically included all five counties later consolidated to form Greater New York—still almost entirely rural at the time. On Manhattan, New York's northward march had reached only as far as 14th Street, while across the river, the village of Brooklyn—formally chartered as a city that same year—occupied only a tiny corner of King's County, which stretched on for mile after mile of farms and open fields.

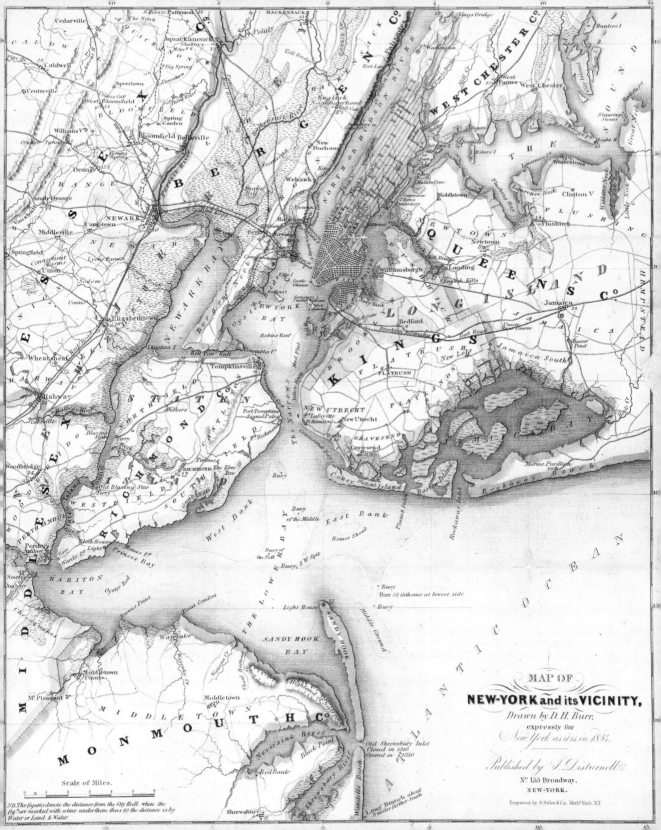

MAP OF
NEW-YORK and its VICINITY,
Drawn by D. H. Burr,
expressly for
New York as it is in 1834.

Published by J. Disturnell,
Nº 155 Broadway,
NEW-YORK.

Engraved by S. Stiles & Co. Merchs Exch. N.Y.

Scale of Miles.

N.B. The figures denote the distance from the City Hall, when the
figs are marked with a line under them thus 10 the distance is by
Water or Land & Water.

Less than a decade after the opening of the Erie Canal, New York had become the largest shipbuilding center in the United States—its designers and builders admired around the world for their trim square-rigged packet ships, said to be the finest vessels afloat. This view of Smith & Dimon's East River shipyard, painted by James Fulton Pringle in 1833, shows the hull of a packet ship being launched, while in the background another vessel is already under way. Eleven years later, the same firm would pioneer an astonishing innovation in ship design by launching the *Rainbow*, the first of the true China clippers—the fastest sailing ships ever built.

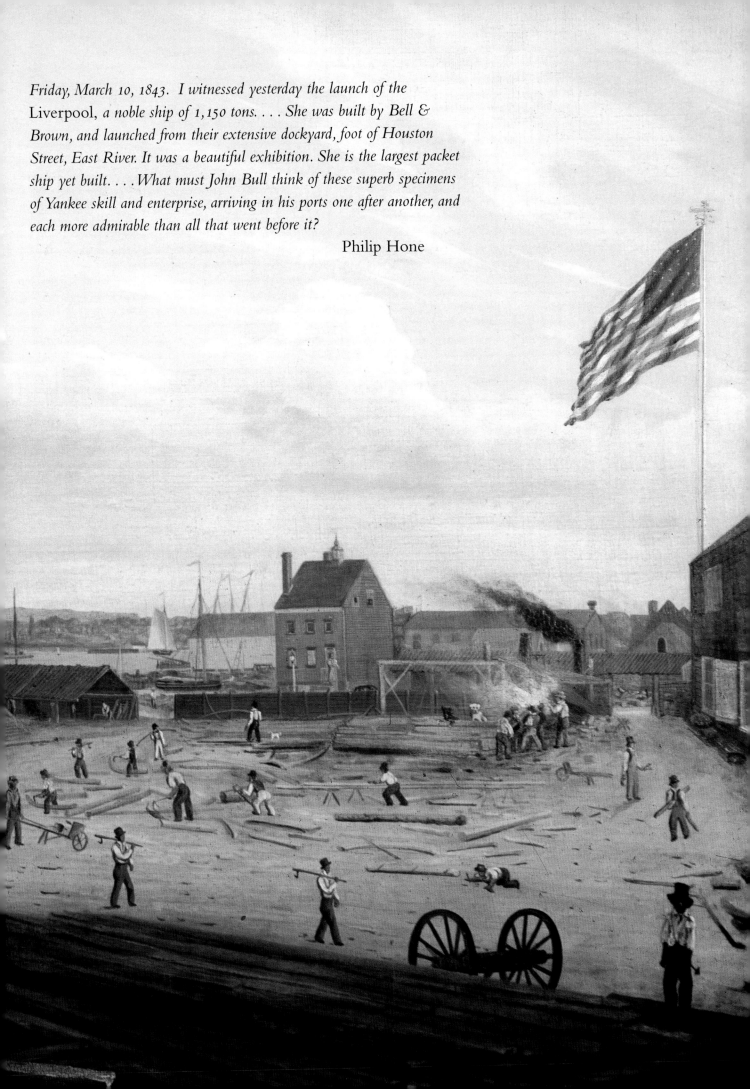

Friday, March 10, 1843. *I witnessed yesterday the launch of the*
Liverpool, *a noble ship of 1,150 tons. . . . She was built by Bell &*
Brown, and launched from their extensive dockyard, foot of Houston
Street, East River. It was a beautiful exhibition. She is the largest packet
ship yet built. . . . What must John Bull think of these superb specimens
of Yankee skill and enterprise, arriving in his ports one after another, and
each more admirable than all that went before it?

Philip Hone

York in the years following the opening of the Erie Canal. Within less than a year, ten new shipping companies had been founded. Thirty-nine new banks had been organized. Five hundred new mercantile houses had opened. More than three thousand new buildings had gone up—and it was just the beginning.

"New York never saw such days as the present since it was a city," the editor of the *Evening Post* declared in the fall of 1825.

Within a decade, a third of all the goods exported from the United States, and *two-thirds* of those imported from abroad, were passing through New York Harbor—including timber from the Northwest, coal from Pennsylvania, grain, flour, and whiskey from the Ohio Valley, cotton from Mississippi, manufactured goods from England—fueling a wave of physical and demographic growth unlike anything ever seen before in the city's history.

"New York has become so enriched," one man wrote, as the city implacably captured the economy of the entire Midwest, "that she may call Ohio her kitchen-garden, Michigan her pastures, and Indiana, Illinois, and Iowa her harvest fields."

In 1828, Philip Hone, who had stepped down as mayor two years before, began to keep track of the bustling town he liked to call "my village"—which even as he wrote was beginning to dissolve before his very eyes.

Monday, May 9th, 1831. The city is now undergoing its usual annual metamorphosis; many stores and houses are being pulled down and others altered, to make every inch of ground productive to its utmost extent. . . . Wednesday, May 1st, 1839. A row of low buildings has been removed to make way for one of those mighty edifices called hotels. The spirit of pulling down and building up is abroad. The whole of New York is rebuilt about once in ten years.

Philip Hone

One by one, the snug, leafy blocks around Wall Street and lower Broadway, where private homes had once coexisted with workshops and countinghouses, were torn down to make way for the imposing stone facades of banks, insurance companies, and brokerages. By 1836, the New York Stock Exchange, which had started

life under a buttonwood tree on Wall Street just four decades before, was awaiting completion of its new home, located in a massive building called the Merchants' Exchange, which could hold three thousand merchants and brokers at a time.

As commerce inexorably crowded everything else out of lower Manhattan, the area around Wall Street and Trinity Church became the first district in the world devoted exclusively to business. In 1836, as the old city broke apart under the centrifugal force of its own growth, Philip Hone sold his brick house on Broadway, right across from city hall—for nearly three times the price he had paid for it just fifteen years before—and joined the exodus of wealthy New Yorkers moving uptown to escape the rising tide of commerce and strangers.

May 1845. The city of New York is so overgrown that we in the upper regions do not know much more of what is passing in the lower, nor the things which are to be seen there, than the inhabitants of Mexico or Cairo.

Philip Hone

With astonishing speed, the outlines of a modern mass metropolis were beginning to emerge on the island of Manhattan—including the first slums and suburbs, the first regular police force, the first public transit system, the first department store, and a vast new waterworks, the massive Croton Aqueduct, on the outskirts of town. By the 1840s, just a decade and a half after the canal opened, New York was moving into uncharted territory—no longer merely a port but a giant vortex, drawing everything in America, and increasingly the world, into its orbit: goods, money, people, ideas—and, increasingly, problems.

For better and for worse, one man wrote, "New York is fast becoming, if she be not already, America."

DEMOCRATIC TURBULENCE

April 7th, 1845. Overturn, overturn, overturn! is the maxim of New York. The very bones of our ancestors are not permitted to lie quiet a quarter of a century, and one generation of men seems studious to remove all relics of those which preceded them.

Philip Hone

In 1828, Philip Hone—a prosperous ex-auctioneer and onetime mayor, said to be on speaking terms with every distinguished citizen of New York—began to keep an extraordinary diary, which by the time of his death in 1851 stretched to 28 notebooks and more than 2 million words. By turns nostalgic, forward-looking, enthusiastic, and skeptical, Hone took deep pride in his city's stunning commercial growth but often questioned the price of progress—from the sweeping destruction of the city's landmarks, to New Yorkers' obsession with speculation and real estate, to the rising influx of immigrant poor, who were rapidly transforming his once-cozy "village" into a sprawling, unfamiliar place.

Friday, June 15th, 1832. The Albany steamboat which came down this afternoon brought the alarming news that the cholera, which has of late been the scourge of the eastern continent, has crossed the Atlantic and made its appearance first in Quebec and from thence travelled with its direful velocity to Montreal. It was brought to the former city in a vessel called the Carricks, *with a cargo of Irish emigrants.*

Philip Hone

In the summer of 1832, the first dark consequence of New York's headlong growth struck with terrifying fury.

On Monday, July 2—after weeks of alarming reports that a deadly cholera epidemic was filtering down from Canada—Philip Hone grimly confirmed that the dread disease had reached Manhattan. "It is quite certain that the cholera now exists in our city," he wrote. "There have been nine cases, of which eight have died. A Mrs. Fitzgerald and her two children died at 75 Cherry Street."

Anyone who could afford to leave quickly departed the city, taking refuge in farms and country houses for 30 miles around. But "large numbers," Walt Whitman observed, "still remain. While fear drove away so many, poverty, quite as strong a force, also compelled many to stay where they were."

In the weeks to come, the virulent disease—carried by Manhattan's contaminated groundwater—circulated with nightmarish speed through the eerily quiet city, from which 100,000 residents had fled. As the number of sick and dying mounted, the city's Board of Health begged the trustees of New York Hospital for help, but the privately owned institution refused to admit any of the stricken.

The city hospital, Bellevue, was soon overwhelmed with victims, the corridors littered with corpses and with dying patients, moaning for water and relief.

By late July, the death rate had reached 100 a day. Hardest hit were new slum districts like the Five Points where—helpless to stop or even slow the epidemic—city officials began distributing coffins to the poor.

It was "melancholy," a merchant named John Pintard observed, walking by St. Patrick's Churchyard on Mulberry Street, "to notice the number of new graves dug to hold three and four coffins, called by their size cholera graves."

Wednesday, Aug. 8—Cholera report: 82 new cases, 21 deaths. The mortality is principally among the wretched population about the Five Points and similar places.

Philip Hone

It took six weeks for the epidemic to run its course. By the time the disease abated at the end of August, 3,513 New Yorkers had died—most of them poor immigrants, who were swiftly blamed for the disaster. "They have brought the cholera this year and they will always bring wretchedness and want," Philip Hone wrote. "The boast that our country is the asylum for the oppressed in other parts of the world is very philanthropic and sentimental, but I fear that we shall before long derive little comfort from being made the almshouse and the place of refuge for the poor of other countries."

Some religious leaders thought they saw a moral lesson in the fearful calamity. The Reverend Gardiner Spring claimed that "the hand of God" had used the disease "to drain off the filth and scum which contaminate and defile human society."

Others placed the blame elsewhere. "It may be heretical," George Henry Evans, publisher of the *Workingman's Advocate*, wrote, "but we firmly believe that the cholera so far from being a scourge of the Almighty is a scourge which mankind have brought upon themselves by their own bad arrangements which produce poverty among many, while abundance is in existence for all."

In the end, New York's own health inspector, Gerritt Forbes, provided the most level-headed explanation for the disaster—though it would take half a century more for the city's political leaders to do anything substantive about it. "Some cause," he wrote, "should be assigned for the increase of deaths . . . [and none] appears so prominent as . . . the crowded and filthy state in which a great proportion of our population live, and . . . we have serious cause to regret that there [are] in our city so many mercenary landlords, who contrive [to] stow the greatest number of human beings in the smallest space."

By the late 1820s, the area known as Five Points, northeast of city hall, had become the most notorious district in the city—famous for its squalid, overcrowded dwellings, its polyglot population—"a race of beings," the *Evening Post* lamented, "of all colours, ages, sexes and nations"—and for its raucous, licentious street life. Originally intended as a middle-class neighborhood with small homes and shops, the area had been hastily built on poorly laid landfill near the Fresh Water Pond. As the houses started to sag, most of the original residents fled—abandoning the area to those who could afford no better.

December 17th, 1835. How shall I record the events of last night, or how attempt to describe the most awful calamity which has ever visited these United States. The greatest loss by fire that has ever been known . . . I am fatigued in body, disturbed in mind, and . . . filled with images of horror which my pen is inadequate to describe.

Philip Hone

Three years after the cholera epidemic, another disaster struck the closely built-up city. On the bitter cold night of December 16, 1835, a fire broke out in a warehouse on Pearl Street. The city's under-manned volunteer fire brigades rushed to the scene, but what little water could be pumped from the nearby hydrants turned to ice in the frigid night air, and the crews—exhausted from fighting a blaze the night before—were soon completely overwhelmed.

As a crowd of onlookers watched in horror, the flames, fanned by a freezing wind, blazed completely out of control, leaping from one building to another, racing through the combustible district of densely packed warehouses, office buildings, and banks.

Along South Street, sailors were ordered to cast their ships away from the docks to spare them from the flames. By midnight, the entire heart of New York's business district was burning. The glow in the sky could be seen in Philadelphia, 110 miles away.

Among the crowd of onlookers was 15-year-old George Templeton Strong, mesmerized by the blaze, but fearful that his father's law office would be destroyed. "Wednesday, December 17th— Very bad news," he wrote in a diary he had begun to keep a few months before. "Papa came in this morning at five and his return woke me up. The Exchange, the office, everything in that quarter is going, and by his account we are in some danger, as the fire is unchecked. . . . The smoke is hanging over all that part of the city. . . . Such a scene of confusion I never witnessed."

It took all night and all the next day to bring the fire under control. "Gunpowder was finally employed," a novelist and journalist named Asa Greene observed. "Several stores were blown up, to occasion a vacancy in the line of buildings where the flames were progressing. To the east, it was arrested only by the river itself."

By the time the flames were out, a *quarter* of the city's business district had been destroyed, including every one of the old Dutch houses that had survived the fires of the Revolution. George Templeton Strong's father's law firm had been spared. But the printing shop where 16-year-old Walt Whitman worked as a typesetter had been destroyed. He was forced to find work outside the city and it would be five years before he returned.

"Nearly one half of the first ward is in ashes," Philip Hone glumly reported the next day. "500 to 700 stores, which with their contents are valued at $20,000,000 to $40,000,000, are now lying in an indistinguishable mass of ruins. . . . The insurance offices are all bankrupt, and every man is his own underwriter."

Hone needn't have worried. To the amazement of all New Yorkers, the Great Fire of 1835 only accelerated the commercial frenzy that had in part brought it on. "Twenty lots in the 'burned district' . . . were sold at auction this day," Hone noted wonderingly just two months

One of the greatest catastrophes in the city's history, the Great Fire of 1835 began in a five-story warehouse on Pearl Street, and raged for more than two days. By the time it was over, 674 buildings—including the stately Merchants' Exchange, at center—had been destroyed. In the aftermath, 23 of New York's 26 fire insurance companies would be forced into bankruptcy and 4,000 clerks thrown out of work. Remarkably, only two people were killed in the conflagration—evidence that the area was already well on its way to becoming the first district in the world devoted entirely to commerce.

Workers laying the huge High Bridge water main across the Harlem River, north of the city. After 200 years of inadequate and foul groundwater the Croton Water Works, completed in 1842, delivered millions of gallons of fresh upstate water to long-suffering New Yorkers. To this day, the city continues to rely on the extraordinary system, which has been upgraded and expanded every few decades. This photograph was taken in 1861.

Fountain was switched on for the first time—sending a jet of water soaring 50 feet into the air above City Hall Park, as a huge crowd of New Yorkers—including Walt Whitman and George Templeton Strong—roared out their approval. "It is for the future even more than for the present," one man wrote, "and will attest . . . that, magnificent as may be the works of conquerors and kings, they have not equaled . . . the noble aqueduct, constructed at their own cost, by the freemen of the single city of New York."

For all the jubilant celebration, a bitter irony marred the city's triumph. Despite the new system, foul water, abysmal sanitation, and life-threatening disease would remain the norm for New York's poorest citizens for decades to come, as landlords in slum districts like the Five Points simply refused to connect their tenants' shabby dwellings to the new water mains.

But for Philip Hone and George Templeton Strong and tens of thousands of middle-class New Yorkers, the waterworks brought an unheard-of luxury—indoor plumbing. "I've led rather an amphibious life for the last week," Strong noted happily, "paddling in the bathing tub every night and constantly making new discoveries in the art and mystery of ablution. Taking a shower bath upside down is the last novelty."

By 1846, row houses being built in Manhattan routinely advertised the availability of hot and cold running water in downstairs kitchens and pantries, and in bathrooms on every floor. By 1852, just ten years after the system's completion, New Yorkers were using more than 30 million gallons of Croton water each day—and could hardly remember what life had been like without it.

later, "at most enormous prices, greater than they would have brought before the fire, when covered with valuable buildings." Despite the astonishing extent of the devastation, one year later the entire burned area had been completely rebuilt—"with more splendor than before," Hone wrote.

By then, the city's fire department had been bolstered and reorganized, building codes had been strengthened, and—spurred into action by the epidemic and Great Fire—New Yorkers had voted to replace their medieval water supply with a brand-new system—the biggest and most modern in the world. When complete, the Croton Water Works would draw upward of 60 million gallons a day from the sparkling Croton River far upstate, and send it streaming along 41 miles of stone tunnels and aqueducts, to a massive, Egyptian-style distributing reservoir at 42nd Street and Fifth Avenue, on the outskirts of town.

"Nothing is talked of . . . in New York but Croton Water," Philip Hone wrote excitedly as work on the system neared completion. "Fountains, aqueducts, hydrants, and hose attract our attention and impede our progress through the streets. . . . Water! Water! is the universal note which is sounded through every part of the city, and infuses joy and exultation into the masses."

Finally, the system was ready. On October 14, 1842, the Croton

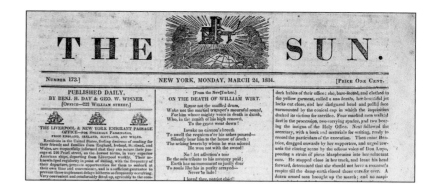

The flight was a bold and perilous one; but here I am, in the great city of New York, safe and sound, without loss of blood or bone. In less than a week after leaving Baltimore, I was walking amid the hurrying throng, and gazing upon the dazzling wonders of Broadway. The dreams of my childhood and the purpose of my manhood were now fulfilled. A free state around me, and a free earth under my feet! What a moment this was to me!

Frederick Douglass, 1838

April, 1842. Who does not know that our city is the great place of the western continent— the heart, the brain, the focus, the main spring— the pinnacle, the extremity, the no more beyond of the New World?

Walt Whitman

In the spring of 1841, Walt Whitman, a twenty-two-year-old printer's apprentice and ex-school-teacher, arrived in Manhattan, looking for work as a writer and reporter. The son of a failed carpenter from Brooklyn, whose own mother thought him "a good boy, but very strange," he was one of the tens of thousands of young men flooding into the city each year from the countryside to find work. The energy of the new metropolis broke over him like a thunderstorm.

"This is the city," he wrote ecstatically, "and I am one of the citizens."

Silence? What can New York—noisy, roaring, rumbling, tumbling, bustling, stormy, turbulent New York—have to do with silence? Amid the universal clatter, the incessant din of business, the all swallowing vortex of the great money whirlpool—who has any, even distant, idea of the profound repose . . . of silence?

Walt Whitman

He took to the city instantly. Settling in a boardinghouse on Centre Street, Whitman soon found work at a paper called the *Aurora*—one of the dozens of daily newspapers springing up all over the island. There had never been anything like them. Sold on the streets for a penny apiece by gangs of ragged boys, the new "penny papers" were filled not with sober shipping reports, like the commercial journals that preceded them, but with eye-catching stories of crime, vice, and sex—often drawn from the streets of the city itself.

Though ordinary New Yorkers took to the new dailies at once, upper-class citizens were appalled by them. "There is a paper published in this city," Philip Hone wrote on February 1, 1841. "I am not in the habit of quoting from it, for I consider it a disgrace . . . nor would I do it now, but to protest against the depraved and vitiated taste of newspaper readers. . . . It is an undeniable fact that this filthy sheet has a wider circulation, not only here but in other cities, than any other."

The most popular and outrageous of all the new papers—and the one Philip Hone could scarcely bring himself to mention—was the *New York Herald*, founded in 1835 by a homely, bombastic Scotsman named James Gordon Bennett, who liked to compare himself in the columns of his own paper to Alexander the Great, Julius Caesar, Homer, Napoleon, Confucius, Shakespeare, and Zoroaster. It was, in many ways, the first modern newspaper: the first to cover the whole city, the first to turn the city itself into front-page news, and the first intended, as Bennett himself declared, "for the great masses of people." Introducing many of the essential features of the modern daily newspaper—including weather reports, sports coverage, and financial columns—Bennett was the first to send reporters out to *uncover* the news—to the docks, the slums, the night courts, to Wall Street, Broadway, the big hotels and theaters, establishing beats that continue to this day.

Attuned to the sensibility of the tens of thousands of ordinary working people flooding into the city each year, the *Herald* was above all the first newspaper to give readers not what they needed but what they wanted. In its first two weeks alone, the paper carried blood-curdling accounts of three suicides, three murders, a fire that killed five people, an accident in which a

When it first appeared in New York in September 1833, the *Sun*—the brainchild of an enterprising young printer named Benjamin Day—was something entirely new in American journalism—small, easy to read, and sold not by subscription to merchants and bankers but on the street, for a penny, to the general reading public. New Yorkers took to it instantly and within months the *Sun* was selling 4,000 copies a day. With the advent of the steam press two years later, the paper's circulation jumped to 22,000 copies—an unheard-of figure and far greater than any other newspaper in the country.

A figure of comically immense "vanity and egotism"—as he himself readily acknowledged— James Gordon Bennett, the brilliant and innovative editor of the *Herald,* would complete the revolution the *Sun* had begun.

alleged to have killed her, the *Herald*'s circulation tripled overnight, to more than twenty thousand.

"What is to prevent a daily newspaper," Bennett thundered later that year, "from being made the greatest organ of social life? Books have had their day—the theatres have had their day—the temple of religion has had its day. A newspaper can be made to take the lead of all of these in the great movements of human thought, and of human civilization. A newspaper can send more souls to heaven, and save more from hell, than all the churches and chapels in New York—besides making money at the same time."

He was right. Year by year, the *Herald*'s circulation surged upward, until it had become the most widely read newspaper in the world and the model for a host of imitators and rivals. By 1841, more than twenty dailies and dozens of weeklies crowded a five-block stretch across from city hall, called Printing House Row—including William Cullen Bryant's *Evening Post*, and Horace Greeley's *Tribune*, which, though it never outsold the *Herald* in the city, soon became the most influential journal in the country. Boasting a national circulation that would rise to more than 200,000 copies a week—and a corps of foreign correspondents that included the young Karl Marx—the *Tribune* helped make New York the center of serious national debate on everything from women's rights and western expansion to the growing conflict over slavery.

With Samuel Morse's brand-new telegraph office about to open just a few steps down Broadway—right next door to Mathew Brady's new Daguerrian Miniature Gallery and Plumbe's National Daguerrian Gallery—the bustling district around City Hall Park had become the undisputed media capital of the entire nation.

> *The pave was filled with an eager and laughing crowd, jostling along and each intent on some scheme of pleasure for the evening. I felt confused for a long time with the universal whirl.*
>
> Walt Whitman

Reporting to work at the offices of the *Aurora* at 162 Nassau Street, Whitman found himself

Nothing would do more to establish the *Herald*'s popularity—or notoriety—than its coverage of the murder of a prostitute named Helen Jewett on the night of April 10, 1836. Day after day, the riveting story of the beautiful girl and the respectable young man accused of murdering her dominated James Gordon Bennett's penny paper—which, by the time the trial was over, had become the most widely read daily in America.

In 1841, Horace Greeley founded the *Tribune*. Greeley's opening issue denounced James Gordon Bennett and the *Herald* as "unprincipled and reckless." Bennett fired back, calling Greeley an "unmitigated blockhead" and insisting that a "galvanized New England squash . . . would make as capable an editor."

man blew his own head off, and an eyewitness account of a guillotine execution in France.

To feed his readers' growing fascination with the private lives of the rich, Bennett sent informants into the homes of the city's elite—once slipping a reporter disguised as a knight into a fancy dress ball attended by Philip Hone himself. "This kind of surveillance is getting to be intolerable," Hone wrote, "and nothing but the force of public opinion will correct the insolence. . . . They find that the more personalities they have in their paper the more papers they sell."

And yet even Hone could not tear himself away from the story Bennett broke in the spring of 1836, when a beautiful prostitute named Helen Jewett was found dead in her rooms on Thomas Street—her head split open with an ax and her bed on fire. When Bennett published excerpts from Jewett's torrid love letters to the well-educated Connecticut jewelry store clerk

Finding it impossible to do anything in the way of heavy business, we took our cane and our hat, and sauntered down Broadway to the Battery. Strangely enough, nobody stared with us in admiration—nobody said, "there goes Whitman of the Aurora!"—nobody ran after us to take a second and better look, nobody wheeled out of our way deferentially—but on we went, swinging our stick in our right hand, with our left hand thrust in its pocket.
Walt Whitman

Few people can have thrown themselves more exuberantly into the life of New York City than Walt Whitman—an ex-schoolteacher and onetime printer's apprentice who in the spring of 1841 returned to Manhattan after an absence of five years to find work in the newspaper business.

Arriving in the midst of one of the greatest periods of change in the history of the city, Whitman "sounded all the experiences of life," a close friend named John Burroughs remembered, "with all their passions, pleasures, and abandonments. He was young, in perfect bodily condition, and had the city of New York and its ample opportunities around him."

Ambitious, but lazy and unreliable, he moved restlessly from one job to another in the eight years to come, working at one time or the other at the *Aurora*, the *Sun*, the *Democrat*, the *Tattler*, the *Statesman*, the *Plebian*, and the *Mirror*. On long afternoons while pretending to work, he wandered the streets of Brooklyn and New York, jotting down scenes of city life in the small green notebook he carried with him everywhere.

He loved to stroll the crowded downtown boulevards, plunging into what he called the "fascinating chaos" of Broadway—"looking in at the shop-windows"—"flatting the flesh of my nose on the thick plate glass"—reveling in "the beautiful ladies, the bustle, the show, the glitter, and even the gaudiness."

He thrilled to the city's vibrant political culture—the "immense processions," he wrote, "with torches, fireworks, noise of wild bands, at the time of elections, the crowds free and abounding"—attending rallies of workingmen in City Hall Park, and auditioning briefly as a political orator at Tammany Hall—an up-and-coming political club on Nassau Street that had been gaining power since 1834, the first year New York's mayor was elected by direct vote.

I know well . . . the real heart of this mighty city—the tens of thousands of young men, the mechanics, the [clerks] . . . In all of them burns, almost with a fierceness, the divine fire which more or less during all ages, has only waited a chance to leap forth and confound the calculations of tyrants. . . . At this moment, New York is the most radical city in America.

At Plumbe's Daguerrian Gallery on Broadway he stared in wonder at the uncanny sea of images—phantom progenies of light and shadow that captured as nothing else before the strangeness and piercing beauty of the real world.

There they stretch from floor to ceiling—hundreds of them. Indeed, it is little else on all sides of you, than a great legion of human faces—human eyes gazing silently but fixedly upon you, and creating the impression of an immense Phantom concourse—speechless and motionless, but yet realities. You are in a new world—a peopled world, although mute as the grave.

Plunging almost every evening into Manhattan's vibrant night life—and using his position as a reporter to gain free admission wherever he could—he took in "everything, high, low, middling"—"absorbing theatres with every pore." He went to the new Astor Place Opera House just off Broadway, where he heard Verdi and Rossini, and to the Bowery Theater, where he saw Edwin Forrest and Junius Brutus Booth perform Shakespeare. Just three blocks east of Broadway's fashionable crowds, but a world apart, he plunged into the raucous workingmen's saloons, dance halls, and minstrel shows along the Bowery, where he saw Irish immigrants and African American performers parodying and mimicking and

The unofficial poet laureate of Brooklyn and New York, Long Island–born Walt Whitman relished having his photograph taken. This portrait, probably made by the photographer John Plumbe in the early 1840s, shows the aspiring journalist soon after his return to New York.

borrowing from each other at every turn. The mixture, he predicted, would one day make "a native grand opera in America."

Everywhere he went, he saw a world in the midst of flux and change—"the pull-down and build-over-again spirit" of the city," and "the rabid feverish itching for change." At a burial ground on Delancey Street, he saw a frantic woman brandishing a revolver, desperately trying to protect the graves of her husband and children from being obliterated by a crew of builders. The "divinity of trade" prevailed in the end, Whitman noted, and the graveyard was torn up to make way for a new row of houses.

Fleshless bones, and ghastly skeletons, and skulls with the hair still attached to them, and the brittle relics of young infants . . . were struck in by the cold steel, and pitched to and fro, as loafers pitch pennies upon the dock.

A cottage in the rural outskirts of Brooklyn, probably built in the 1840s.

at the heart of one of the most dynamic and complex environments on earth. Within a ten-block radius of his office, a world of astonishing contrasts had arisen—from city hall, the center of government, to Wall Street, the center of finance, to the Five Points, the city's worst slum. The streets themselves, and Broadway especially, were teeming with a "fascinating chaos," Whitman said, a "democratic turbulence," all in motion.

In this mighty metropolis, the stranger may . . . perceive the eddying throngs gathering and whirling, scattering and hurrying hither and thither, in the activity of commercial pursuits. He may become confused by the never-ending turbulence and commotion, with the hundreds of mingled notes and noises which are ever rising from the multifarious trades and occupations of its thousands of inhabitants. . . . He here sees that nothing is fixed, nothing is permanently settled—all is moving and removing, organizing and disorganizing, building up and tearing down; the ever active spirit of change

seems to pervade all bodies, all things, and all places in this mighty metropolis.

J. C. Myers, 1849

Here you see Jew and Gentile, Priest and Levite, as well as all other classes—the old and young of all the nations upon the earth, and all the conditions and hues of the genus homo. . . . Chatham-street is a sort of museum or old curiosity shop, and I think Barnum would do well to buy the whole concern, men, women, and goods, and have it in his world of curiosities on the corner of Ann and Broadway.

Glimpses of New-York City, 1852

In the winter of 1841, an extraordinary establishment called the American Museum opened its doors for the first time on the corner of Broadway and Printing House Row—at the very heart of the new metropolis. Its proprietor was a thirty-one-year-old itinerant showman from Connecticut named Phineas T. Barnum, an ex-newspaperman with a genius for self-promotion and an uncanny instinct for

the new mass culture beginning to emerge in New York City.

Part spectacle, part theater, part humbug, the American Museum was like nothing anyone had ever seen before. Eager to exploit the shifting interests—and anxieties—of New York's increasingly diverse citizenry, Barnum programmed something for everyone in the American Museum—including a scale model of Dublin for the growing number of Irish immigrants—and a three-thousand-seat Moral Lecture Room for New York's upright middle-class establishment.

The Museum contains many objects of real interest, particularly to the naturalist and geologist, intermingled with a great deal that is spurious and contemptible. . . . There is a collection of horrors or monstrosities attached, which appears to fascinate the vulgar gaze: a dog with two legs, a cow with four horns, and a calf with six legs.

Isabella Bird

Barnum's most popular attractions included a "mermaid" from Fiji; a knitting machine oper-ated by a dog; a bearded girl named Annie Jones; a twenty-five-inch midget named General Tom Thumb; a pair of Chinese brothers named Chang and Eng, the original Siamese twins; and—playing to the growing national obsession with the question of race and origins—an eighteen-year-old microcephalic black man from Georgia, whom Barnum presented simply as the "What-Is-It?"

The first great impresario of the democratic age—and the spiritual grandfather of the city's distinctive culture of advertisement, public relations, and ballyhoo—Barnum understood that people enjoyed being fooled, as long as they got their money's worth, and that the greatest spectacle he had to offer was the crowd itself. "Now and then someone would cry out 'humbug' and 'charlatan,'" Barnum said, "but so much the better for me. It helped to advertise me, and I was willing to bear the reputation—and I engaged queer curiosities, and even monstrosities, simply to add to the notoriety to the Museum."

Eager to reach as wide an audience as possible, he kept the museum open 365 days a year, from sunrise until long after dark; determined

Looking south down Broadway from the foot of City Hall Park, August Köllner painted the crossroads of the bustling commercial city. By 1848, Barnum's American Museum, festooned with spectacular colored "transparencies," had become the greatest tourist attraction in the country. Across the street, St. Paul's Chapel was one of the last remnants of the colonial city. Next door, the sumptuous block-long Astor House hotel (with gaslight in every room and indoor bathing facilities on every floor), built by John Jacob Astor to handle the more than 70,000 businessmen and tourists now flooding into the city each year, could accommodate 800 guests at a time.

A group portrait (above) of P. T. Barnum's "living curiosities," including three giants, two midgets, two albi-nos, a pair of "Circassian beauties," and a thin man wedded to a fat lady. An inveterate self-promoter and advertising genius, the great showman himself is seen posing (right) with a 22-year-old dancing sensation named Madame Ernestine de Faiber, and (below) with his star attraction, "General" Tom Thumb, whom Barnum helped make one of the most famous men in the world.

The transient attractions of the Museum were constantly diversified, and educated dogs and industrious fleas, automatons, jugglers, ventriloquists, living statuary, tableaux, gipsies, fat boys, giants, dwarfs, rope-dancers, dioramas, panoramas, models of Niagara, Dublin, Paris and Jerusalem the first English Punch and Judy in this country, mechanic figures, fancy glassblowing, dissolving views, and American Indians, who enact their warlike and religious ceremonies on stage—these, among others, were all exceedingly successful.

Phineas T. Barnum

"to turn every possible circumstance to my account"—"to make the Museum the town wonder and town talk"—he festooned the exterior of the building with bright flags and huge color murals visible down Broadway for more than a mile. On the roof, he staged fireworks displays and balloon ascensions, and installed the world's largest searchlight—whose powerful beam, sweeping up and down Broadway each night, was bright enough to read a newspaper by.

The American Museum was a stunning success. In the years to come Barnum would sell 42 million tickets—7 million more than the entire population of the United States. Sooner or later, everyone went to Barnum's—society matrons, children, lawyers on their lunch hours, black porters, Irish day laborers, single women, and tourists, who with each passing year were flocking into New York City in increasing numbers.

Inside, the enormous differences dividing New Yorkers dwindled for a moment, against the backdrop of the freakish human extremes on display.

Outside, on the city streets, however, those differences were becoming more and more troubling with each passing year.

THE FLOOD

For years, the number of immigrants in the city had been on the rise, as the demand for workers spiraled upward. By 1840, New York's immigrant communities were nearly as large as the entire city had been twenty years before—and still the numbers grew.

Forty thousand Germans alone had pushed in, creating an insulated neighborhood of their own called Kleindeutschland—Little Germany. An even greater number had come from Ireland, impoverished farmers and unskilled day laborers mainly, most of whom quickly found work, taking on the worst and toughest jobs in the city—digging sewers, paving streets, building houses, or working as servants, scullery maids, and seamstresses.

"America demands for her development," one newspaper editor said, "an inexhaustible supply of physical energy, and Ireland supplies the most part of it. There are several sorts

June 2nd, 1836. There arrived at this port during the month of May, 15,825 passengers. All Europe is coming across the ocean—all that part at least who cannot make a living at home—and what shall we do with them? They increase our taxes, eat our bread and encumber our streets, and not one in twenty is competent to keep himself.

Philip Hone

of power working at the fabric [of] this Republic—waterpower, steam-power, and Irish-power. The last works hardest of all."

For most, it was better than what they had known. "I must only say that this is a good place," a young Irish girl wrote to her father back home. "Any man or woman without a family are fools that would not venture and come to this plentyful country."

Year by year, the number continued to rise. By 1841, nearly 100,000 Irish Catholic immigrants had flooded into the city—fueling waves of virulent anti-Catholic bigotry among upper-

Hundreds of thousands of Irish and German immigrants were disembarking at the Battery at the foot of Manhattan each year by 1855, when Samuel B. Waugh painted *The Bay and Harbor of New York*. To handle the immense influx of newcomers, Castle Garden, the circular structure on the left— a onetime fort and concert hall originally built in

1811—was converted for use as an immigrant processing station, the first of its kind in the country, and a forerunner of Ellis Island. A number of details—including the crudely lettered inscription "Pat Murfy for Ameriky" scrawled on one newcomer's trunk—betray the widespread anti-Irish bigotry of the time.

class New Yorkers, and the bitter resentment of native-born workers, who feared for their jobs.

That year, Samuel Morse, the inventor of the telegraph, called for an end to Catholic immigration altogether, portraying the influx as a sinister papal conspiracy, aimed at bending American democracy to the will of Rome. "Up! Up! I beseech you," he warned. "Awake! To your posts! Shut the open gates. Your enemies in the guise of friends, many thousands, are at this moment rushing into your ruin through the open portals of naturalization." "If I had the

power," another man declared, "I would erect a gallows at every landing place in the city of New York, and suspend every cursed Irishman as soon as he steps on our shores."

The vice of drunkenness among the lowering laboring classes, is growing to frightful excess, and the multitudes of low Irish Catholics . . . restricted by poverty in their own country run riot in this. . . . As long as we are overwhelmed with Irish emigrants, so long will the evil abound.

John Pintard

Our good city of New York has already arrived at the state of society to be found in the large cities of Europe; overburdened with population, and where the . . . extremes of costly luxury in living, are presented in daily and hourly contrast with squalid misery and hopeless destitution.

Philip Hone, 1847

In their search for affordable shelter, the famine Irish naturally gravitated to the very poorest parts of the city—especially to the old, run-down wards near the East River waterfront.

By 1855, nearly 10,000 Irish immigrants had crowded into a ramshackle district north of city hall, called the Five Points— named for an intersection on the Lower East Side where three shabbily paved streets converged.

As more and more newcomers crowded into the area, profit-hungry landlords—often former

immigrants themselves—divided the old, sagging houses into ever-smaller living spaces, often packing more than six people to a room.

When those were filled, landlords erected crude wooden shacks in what had once been backyards, then began throwing up a new kind of structure—"tenant houses," or tenements—large, hastily built dwellings specifically designed to house as many people as possible under a single roof. One notorious tenement on Goerck Street, called The Barracks, eventually became home to 1,100 people.

"I have noticed blocks of new buildings so slightly built," Philip Hone wrote in 1850, "that they could not stand alone, and, like drunken men, require the support of each other to keep from falling."

Crazy old buildings—crowded rear tenements in filthy yards; dark, damp basements; leaky garrets, shops, outhouses, and

stables converted to dwellings, though scarcely fit to shelter brutes—are the habitations of thousands of fellow citizens in this wealthy city.

R. M. Hartley, Tenement House Report, 1853

By 1850, the Five Points had become the most crowded place in America, and the tenement districts themselves had begun to expand northward—to accommodate yet another wave of foreigners, as tens of thousands of Germans fleeing persecution, unrest, and hunger in their homeland now poured into the city almost as rapidly as the famine Irish. By 1854, so many Germans were crossing the Atlantic that the port of Bremen became known as Der Vorort New-Yorks—"the suburb of New York"—and New York itself had become the third-largest German-speaking city in the world, after Berlin and Vienna.

Sprawling north of the Five

Points, Kleindeutschland, or Little Germany, as the neighborhood was called, was soon home to more than 75,000 people. It was something entirely new in American life—not just a poor district, or a slum, but a city within a city, where American traditions— and English itself—were all but unknown. Older New Yorkers venturing into the district found themselves strangers in their own city, bewildered by the German-language signs everywhere, and by the web of narrow alleyways that led to thousands of small workshops, rear tenements, and beer saloons.

Life in Kleindeutschland is almost the same as in the Old Country. . . . There is not a single business which is not run by Germans. Not only the shoemakers, tailors, barbers, physicians, grocers, and innkeepers are German, but the pastors and priests as well. . . . The resident of Kleindeutschland need not even know English in order to make a living, which is a considerable attraction to the immigrant. The shabby apartments are the only reminder that one is in America.

Karl Theodor Griesinger

In less than three decades, a pocket of poverty once concentrated around the Five Points had expanded more than a mile uptown—past Houston Street, past Tompkins Square, almost all the way to 14th Street—forming a vast area that by the eve of the Civil War was home to more than 300,000 people. "The destiny of all of the east side of the island," the *New York Herald* lamented, "seems to be as an abiding place for the poor." In a single generation, the Lower East Side was born.

By 1859, the Five Points—named for the intersection of three streets northeast of city hall—had become famous around the world as the worst slum in America. Looming above the ramshackle wooden dwellings is a five-story tenant house, or tenement—one of the first ever built in the country and the forerunner of many more. "Where dogs would howl to lie," Charles Dickens wrote after touring the impoverished neighborhood, "women, men, and boys slink off to sleep, forcing the dislodged rats to move away in quest of better lodgings."

This uncharacteristically tranquil view of the Five Points, taken sometime in the 1860s or '70s, gives little hint of the violent brawls and pitched battles that broke out with frightening regularity between rival gangs with names like the Fly Boys, the Bowery Boys, the Plug Uglies, the Roach Guards, and the Dead Rabbits.

Year by year, incidents of ethnic violence increased, as the city split into hostile factions of religion, nationality, race, and class. In the spring of 1842, an angry mob of Protestant workingmen—enraged at the attempts of the city's Irish bishop, John Hughes, to get public funds for Catholic schools—marched down to Mulberry Street and threatened to destroy St. Patrick's Cathedral.

April 13th, 1842. Bishop Hughes' premises were assaulted and other dwellings more or less injured by stones and brickbats. The military were ordered out about nine o'clock in the evening and their presence alone saved the Cathedral and other churches of the Catholics from being destroyed by this mob.

New York Herald

Unrest on the crowded streets of New York had already reached alarming levels by the mid-1840s—when a tragedy of unimaginable proportions in the Irish countryside sent an even larger wave of immigrants streaming toward the city. It began in the summer of 1845, when a mysterious blight spread across the potato fields of Ireland—destroying the only food supply of millions of poor Irish farmers and triggering the greatest disaster of Irish history. By 1846, as disease and famine stalked the countryside, desperate Irish farmers were fleeing their homeland any way they could—the vast majority on cargo ships bound for New York City.

It was the greatest movement of people in world history up to that time. Over the next ten years, 2.5 million people would leave Ireland. Of the 1.5 million that came to America, more than a million would come to New York City. The massive influx would change forever the social and political balance of the city.

The people, the young and old, are dying as fast as they can bury them. The fever is raging here at such a rate that those in health in the morning know not but in the evening they may have taken the infection. There is neither trade nor business of any sort going on. Any person that have the means of going to America is either gone or preparing to go there.

John Nowlan, 1847

By 1847, forty ships a day were arriving in New York Harbor, some with as many as seven hundred immigrants crammed into their dank and reeking cargo holds. So many immigrants died during the grueling, thirty-day crossing that the vessels soon became known as "coffin ships."

"The flood arrives without interruption," an astonished French visitor wrote, watching the daily influx streaming off the piers. "Ireland is no longer where flows the Shannon, but . . . beside the banks of the Hudson."

No city on earth had ever had to contend with such an onslaught of humanity. In 1854 alone, 319,000 immigrants streamed off the piers at South Street and vanished into the backstreets and alleys of Manhattan. To handle the flood tide of impoverished newcomers, Castle Garden—a onetime fort and concert hall at the foot of Manhattan—was pressed into service in 1855. Run by the state, it was the first immigrant processing center ever established in the city—or the country.

It could not have come too soon. By then, there were more Irish in New York City than any other place in the world except Dublin—and still they came on, pushing the congestion in the new slums to more than three hundred people per acre—a level never before seen in an American city—and more than five times the density city fathers had anticipated when laying out the street plan fifty years before.

Hundreds of our people, just cast on shore from the emigrant ships, parade, daily, the streets of New-York as howling beggars. They sleep, in droves . . . in the station houses; the Com-

missioners supplying them with bread. In the morning they wander over the city begging.
Irish American, 1850

As thousands of poor Irish immigrants pushed into the Five Points—one of the only areas in the city where African Americans could afford to live—racial tensions began to mount, as the two groups were thrown into bitter competition for the worst dwellings and lowest-paying jobs.

"Every hour sees us elbowed out of some employment," Frederick Douglass wrote, "to make room perhaps for some newly arrived immigrants, whose hunger and color are thought to give them title to especial favor."

By 1855, most of the black population had been forced out of the Five Points to new slum districts a mile uptown, as the already severe racial restrictions faced by African Americans increased. "Even the noblest black," the abolitionist Gerrit Smith wrote, "is denied that which is free to the vilest white. The omnibus, the [street]car, the ballot-box, the jury box, the halls

All through the 1850s, the appalling filth and overcrowding in the slums triggered one epidemic after another—cholera, typhoid, tuberculosis, diphtheria—and pushed annual mortality rates to the highest in the city's history. By 1856, nearly 1 in 25 adults were dying each year—and nearly 1 in 5 infants—and more New Yorkers were dying annually than were being born. Without the flood of immigrants, one city inspector noted, "the city would in a few years be depopulated."

By the 1850s, thousands of homeless and orphaned children wandered the streets of New York City—which, under a new law, now required that abandoned children between the ages of 5 and 15 be arrested and institutionalized. The Home for the Friendless at right—an orphanage run by the American Female Guardian Society on East 29th Street and Madison Avenue—was one of dozens of private relief organizations attempting to cope with the flood of immigrant poor, including the Society for the Employment and Relief of the Poor, the New York Society for the Reformation of Juvenile Delinquents, the Society for the Relief of Poor Widows with Small Children, the Five Points House of Industry, and the Christian Home for Female Servants. Fearful of the growing numbers of Catholics in New York, Protestant organizations like the Guardian Society openly mixed missionary efforts with charitable work and limited their assistance to what they called the "deserving" poor.

of legislation, the army, the public lands, the school, the church, the lecture room, the social circle, the table, are all either absolutely or virtually denied to him."

Profit-hungry businessmen only made matters worse by hiring Irish laborers instead of blacks, because they would work for even less money, then using blacks as strikebreakers whenever the Irish threatened a walkout for better wages. By 1855, the two groups with the most in common found themselves locked in a life-and-death struggle on the lowest rung of the city's economic ladder—while the Irish themselves confronted a wall of bigotry and hatred no less withering than that faced by the city's blacks.

Ostracized, [the immigrants] soon experience the depressing effects of being strangers in a strange land; ignorant where to look for

support, thousands are cast upon charity for a meagre and uncertain existence. Living with their acquaintance awhile in crowded apartments, in cellars, in crumbling tenements, and narrow courts and streets . . . they are peculiarly exposed to inroads of disease. . . . It is truly surprising how small a space some families can reside in, and how densely they are willing to crowd themselves.

Dr. John H. Griscom

Few groups coming to New York would ever suffer the hardship and misery experienced by the famine Irish—crowded into filthy, vermin-infested housing, and brutally derided by their fellow citizens. Devastating outbreaks of cholera and other diseases routinely swept through the wards they inhabited—where the death rate was often three times higher than that of the rest of the city.

I look upon . . . the size . . . and nature of [New York's] population as a real danger which threatens the security of the democratic republic . . . and I venture to predict that [it] will perish from this . . . unless the government creates an armed force which . . . will be independent of the town population and able to repress its excesses.

Alexis de Tocqueville, 1835

By the late 1840s, the crowded commercial city had become a deeply divided place—its citizens separated into increasingly hostile camps by religion, race, nationality, and class. "Union Square and the Avenues," an Episcopal clergyman named Charles Loring Brace wrote, "know as little of Water Street or Cherry Street as if they were different cities. The poor and the rich are forming almost castes toward one another."

In the spring of 1849, years of smoldering anti-English sentiment, heightened by class antagonism, exploded in one of the strangest and most violent confrontations in the city's history. On the evening of May 10, an angry crowd of 8,000 Irish and American workingmen descended on the Astor Place Opera House, where a performance of *Macbeth* was in progress. Partisans of the popular American actor, Edwin Forrest, they were determined to disrupt the performance—incensed by the appearance in the title role of Forrest's great rival, an aristocratic English actor named William C. Macready. City police and units of the New York State Militia were quickly called out to maintain order. When the unruly mob outside the theater refused to disperse, militiamen fired directly into the crowd, killing 22 people, and wounding more than 150 others.

May 11th, 1849. Row last night at the Opera House, whereof I was a spectator. Mob fired upon, some twelve or fifteen killed and four times as many wounded, a real battle, for the b'hoys fought well and charged up to the line of infantry after they had been fired upon. Prospect of a repetition of the performances tonight on a larger scale, for the blackguards swear they'll have vengeance. . . . I'm going up now to clean my pistols.

George Templeton Strong

For three days the city remained under martial law. Astor Place, one newspaper editor suggested, should be renamed DisAster Place.

In the aftermath of the riot, worried New Yorkers like Philip Hone took some comfort in the brutal efficiency with which the mob was put down. "Although the lesson has been dearly bought," he wrote, "the fact has been established that law and order can be maintained under a Republican form of government."

The editor of the Philadelphia *Public Ledger* saw things differently. "It leaves behind it a feeling to which this community has hitherto been a stranger," he wrote a week after the terrible event. "There is now, in our country, in New York City, what every good patriot has hitherto felt it his duty to deny—a *high* class and a *low* class."

The bloody climax of the Astor Place Riots was captured in a Currier & Ives lithograph widely reprinted around the country.

"Infants and children die in fearful ratios," one worried observer noted. And yet even as the concern of middle-class reformers mounted, most New Yorkers blamed the newcomers themselves for their condition.

These immigrants are destitute, sick, ignorant, abject . . . they demand immediate food, garb, shelter, and permanent means of obtaining these necessities. They swarm in filthy localities, engendering disease, and enduring every species of suffering. . . . They are often habitual sots, diseased and reckless, living precariously, considering themselves outcasts, and careless of any change in their condition.

Report on the Condition
of Tenant Houses in New York
and Brooklyn, 1857

You have no idea . . . what an immense vat of misery and crime and filth this great city is. I realize it more and more. Think of ten thousand children growing up almost sure to be prostitutes and rogues.

Charles Loring Brace

Fearing for the future of the city, Protestant missionaries and reformers invaded the slums, hoping to turn the Irish into respectable Americans before it was too late. In 1853, an Episcopal clergyman named Charles Loring Brace started the Children's Aid Society, where for seventeen cents a night, orphans could get a warm bed and bath, a hot supper of pork and beans, and Protestant religious instruction.

But it was not nearly enough. Brace's lodging houses were soon filled to overflowing with nearly nine thousand abandoned children each year. Brace himself, in a volume called *The Dangerous Classes of New York,* warned his fellow citizens that their city was being overrun by a permanent underclass of illiterate, impoverished, demoralized Irish Catholics.

"Thousands are the children of poor foreigners," Brace wrote, "who have permitted them to grow up without school, education, or religion. All the neglect and bad education and evil example of a poor class tend to form others, who, as they mature, swell the ranks of ruffians and criminals. So, at length, a great multitude of ignorant, untrained, passionate,

The greatest diarist the city has ever seen, George Templeton Strong was the son of a distinguished New York lawyer connected to the best families in the city. A conservative and courteous family man who spent most of his life in a Wall Street law firm at a job he all but despised, he started his journal in the fall of 1835 while a sophomore at Columbia College. Nearly every day for the next 40 years he set down his thoughts about the rapidly changing city around him.

irreligious boys and young men are formed, who become the 'dangerous class' of our city."

By 1854, many feared New York's traditional sources of authority could no longer contain the rising tide of disorder and violence.

The streets at night are infested with ruffians of all descriptions. They hang around corners. . . . They move about in gangs, men and boys together, abusing and sometimes hitting the quiet passerby. . . . There is no security for life or limb in the present disorderly state of things.

New-York Times

Violence of every kind now routinely erupted on the streets of the lower wards. There were working-class riots against the upper class, nativist riots against the foreign born, anti-Irish riots, anti-English riots, and antiblack riots. In the Fifth Ward, and what was now called the Bloody Sixth, rival gangs of Protestants and Catholics vied for control of the streets—striking terror in the hearts of middle-class New Yorkers, who now retreated even farther uptown.

November 13th, 1854. Met a prodigious Know-Nothing procession moving uptown, as I omnibussed down Broadway to the vestry meeting—a most emphatic and truculent demonstration. Solid column, eight or ten abreast and numbering some two or three thousand, mostly young men of the butcher-boy and prentice type. They looked as if they might have designs on St. Patrick's Cathedral, and I think the Celts of Prince and Mott Streets would have found them ugly customers. We may well have a tremendous riot and carnage here at any moment.

George Templeton Strong

For the immigrants—excluded from traditional sources of political power by the city's Protestant ruling elite—the gangs were often the only source of order they recognized or trusted. In the years to come, the informal fraternal organizations—based in saloons, social clubs, and volunteer fire companies—would form the nucleus of an indigenous political order in the city, connecting the turbulent social culture of the streets to rising political structures, like Tammany Hall—a venerable Democratic social club, that now began to reach out to immigrant voters for the first time: helping them through immigration, finding them jobs, and "teaching" them how to vote.

By 1854, the chaos on the streets seemed to reach all the way to city hall. That fall, years of rising tension between New York's old ruling elite and new immigrant constituencies burst into the open, when—to the horror of upper-class New Yorkers—a slippery and corruptible onetime liquor store owner named Fernando Wood swept into the mayor's office on a tide of Irish and German votes, delivered with the help of Tammany Hall. Described as "a brilliant desperado" by one Republican opponent, Wood seemed willing to stop at nothing to stay in power—hiring street gangs to steal ballot boxes, and using the municipal police force as his own private army.

By 1857, New York was on the verge of what George Templeton Strong called "municipal civil war." That spring, Wood's Republican opponents, determined to drive the Democrat from office, had the state legislature rewrite the city charter—stripping the mayor of most of his powers. On June 17, two rival police departments—Wood's Municipals and the state-run Metropolitans—rioted on the steps of city hall,

in the heart of what the *New-York Times* called "the worst governed city in the world."

"We're in a 'state of siege,' " Strong reported grimly, "and if half the stories one hears be true, in something like a state of anarchy."

Surveying the chaos, the editor of *Harper's Monthly* threw up his hands in despair. "Nothing has gone as it was meant to go," he wrote, "nor is anything where, according to map and calculation, it should be."

Mayor Fernando Wood, a flamboyant and mercurial onetime businessman and real-estate speculator, was one of the first politicians in New York to woo immigrant voters with the promise of jobs and patronage—laying the groundwork for later Tammany Hall chieftains like Boss Tweed. Innovative, shrewd, and almost compulsively corrupt, Wood served two terms in office, periods marred by one scandal after another. "Wood is a man of great energy, ambition, and perseverance," George Templeton Strong acknowledged in 1857. "Pity he's a scoundrel."

City hall around 1860, during Fernando Wood's second term as mayor.

The view north along Chatham Street in 1853, left, culminating at the far end in Chatham Square—the foot of the Bowery. From the endless rows of shops and stalls that lined the streets off Chatham Square, immigrant merchants from Germany, Ireland, Italy, and Central Europe sold old hardware, secondhand clothes, groceries, tobacco, flowers, window shades, and candy.

For years, a view of the north side of the Battery (above) was thought to be the oldest surviving photograph of New York. Printed from a wax-paper negative taken by Victor Provost in 1853, it shows a row of shipping companies along Battery Place—including the headquarters of Cornelius Vanderbilt's steamship company, located at number 10, the third entrance from the left. The view below, however—showing street work on Broadway between Franklin and Leonard streets—has recently been traced via contemporary newspaper accounts to May 1850—making it the earliest known photograph of the city.

July 7th, 1857. Yesterday morning I was spectator of a strange, weird, painful scene. Certain houses . . . are to be erected on the north west corner of this street and Fourth Avenue, and the deep excavations are therefore in progress. Seeing a crowd on the corner, I stopped and made my way to a front place. The earth had caved in a few minutes before and crushed the breath out of a pair of ill-starred Celtic laborers. Around them were a few men who had got them out, I suppose, and fifteen or twenty Irish women, wives, kinfolk, or friends, who had got down there in some inexplicable way. The men were listless and inert enough, but not so the women. I suppose they were "keening"; all together were raising a wild, unearthly cry, half shriek and half song, wailing as a score of daylight Banshees, clapping their hands and gesticulating passionately. Now and then one of them would throw herself down on one of the corpses, or wipe some trace of defilement from the face of the dead man with her apron, slowly and carefully, and then resume her lament. It was an uncanny sound to hear, quite new to me. . . . Our Celtic fellow citizens are almost as remote from us in temperament and constitution as the Chinese.

George Templeton Strong

THE CRYSTAL PALACE

October 27th, 1850. Sunday. How this city marches northward! The progress of 1835 and 1836 was nothing to the luxuriant rank growth of this year. Streets are springing up, whole strata of sandstone have transferred themselves from their ancient resting-places to look down on bustling thoroughfares for long years to come. Wealth is rushing in upon us like a freshet.

George Templeton Strong

Despite the turmoil, New York continued to grow—hurtling into the future at breakneck speed—at once richer and poorer, faster growing and more chaotic, than any other place in America. The city and country were connected now as never before by ribbons of iron and wire. In 1851, the New York and Erie Railroad had been completed, retracing the route of the Erie Canal with what one man called "a ligature of iron." By then, telegraph lines from around the country were converging on lower Manhattan, carrying a ceaseless flow of infor-

The streets are alive with business, retail and wholesale, and present an aspect of universal bustle. Flags are to be seen in every direction, the tall masts of ships appear above the houses . . . hosts of omnibuses, hacks, drays and railway cars at full speed, ringing bells, terrify unaccustomed foot-passengers. There are stores of the magnitude of bazaars, "daguerrean galleries" by hundreds . . . huge hotels, coffee-houses, and places of amusement; while the pavements present men of every land and colour, red, black, yellow and white, in every variety of costume and beard, and ladies, beautiful and ugly, richly dressed. Then there are mud huts, and palatial residences. . . . Waggons discharging goods across the pavements . . . railway whistles and steamboat bells, telegraph wires, eight and ten to a post, all converging towards Wall Street . . . groups of emigrants bewildered and amazed, emaciated with dysentery and sea-sickness, looking in at the shop-windows; representatives of every nation under heaven, speaking in all earth's Babel languages.   Isabella Bird, 1854

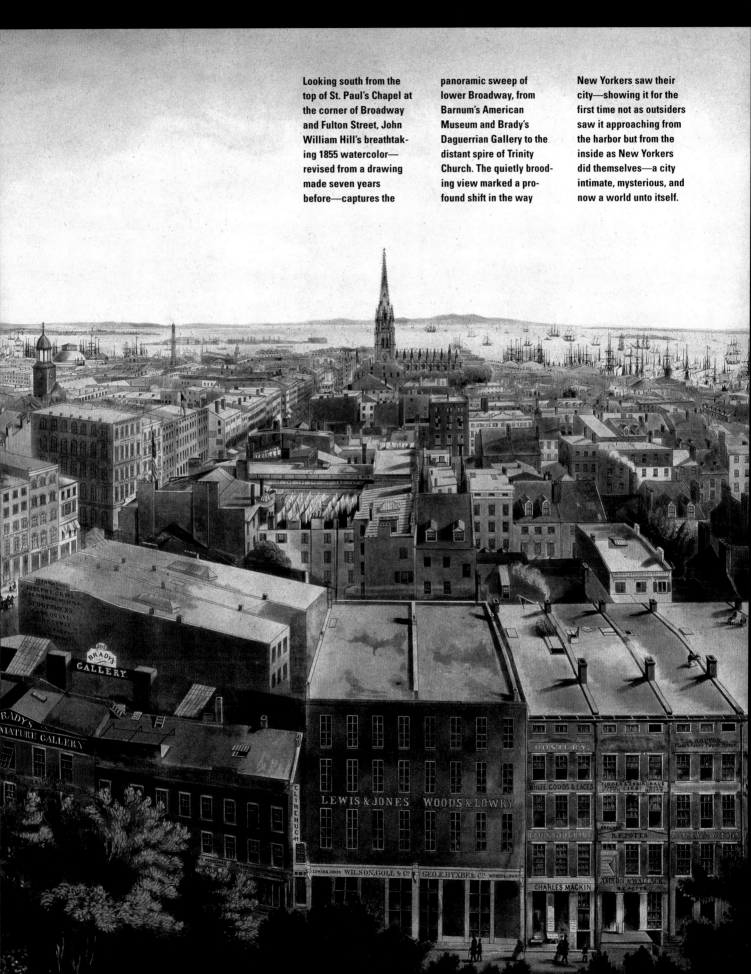

Looking south from the top of St. Paul's Chapel at the corner of Broadway and Fulton Street, John William Hill's breathtaking 1855 watercolor—revised from a drawing made seven years before—captures the panoramic sweep of lower Broadway, from Barnum's American Museum and Brady's Daguerrian Gallery to the distant spire of Trinity Church. The quietly brooding view marked a profound shift in the way New Yorkers saw their city—showing it for the first time not as outsiders saw it approaching from the harbor but from the inside as New Yorkers did themselves—a city intimate, mysterious, and now a world unto itself.

In 1852, a group of wealthy New York merchants—their patriotism fired by rising secessionist sentiment in the South—commissioned the sculptor Henry Kirke Brown to create this bronze equestrian statue of George Washington. Based on a well-known work by the French artist Jean-Jacques Houdon, it still stands just north of 14th Street at the south end of Union Square.

THE OUTRAGEOUS
CONDUCT OF A HACKMAN

August 4th, 1853. At 6:30 yesterday afternoon, the wife and sister of Judge Woodward, of Yonkers, hired a hack from a livery stable at the corner of Lexington and Twenty-third St., contracting to pay $1 per hour . . . to drive them to the Hudson River Railroad Depot. . . . The driver promised acquiescence with their instructions, instead of which he took a roundabout way, and arrived at the depot sometime after the train had left. Here he refused to permit them to get out of the carriage unless they paid him $4. This, as they had not used the vehicle more than one hour and a half, they refused to do. Whereupon he began to use the most vile and abusive language to them, and was about to drive off with them to some other part of the city, when the bystanders interfered, and were ready to have almost torn him in pieces, so grossly had he abused the ladies when Police Officer Sanford Porter arrested him, and took him to the office of the chief of police.
                    New York Daily Tribune

By 1848, the city's wealthier citizens had all but completed their northward migration, leaving behind the noise and tumult and immigrant crowds of lower Manhattan for fashionable new districts uptown (seen in this aerial view by C. Bachmann, looking south from Union Square). "New blocks of houses, capacious and stately, are springing up with surprising celerity," the *Mirror* had reported nine years before. "Fourteenth Street will doubtless be considered the heart rather than the extremity of the town in the course of a few years." By 1848, the prediction was coming to pass, as several of the city's most important new institutions made their home in the area—including Grace Church, at Broadway and 10th Street, and New York University, whose marble-fronted main building stood on the northeast corner of Washington Square.

mation to the city's financial markets—and to the offices of the world's first wire service, the Associated Press, located on Printing House Row, where it was edited, rewritten, and sent out again across the nation.

"The diverse races of men," George Templeton Strong wrote in his diary, "seem tending toward development into a living organic unit with railroads and steam-packets for a circulating system, telegraph wires for nerves, and the *London Times* and *New York Herald* for a brain."

New York is essentially national in interest, position, pursuits. No one thinks of the place as belonging to a particular state, but to the United States.

James Fenimore Cooper, 1851

With each passing year, the city consolidated its hold on the nation's economy—to the growing dismay of politicians around the country. "The great city of New York," Senator Willis A. Gorman of Indiana complained in 1851, "wields more of the destinies of this great nation than five times the population of any other portion of the country. . . . [Warn the] people of the west, the south, southeast and northwest, what they must expect from the absorbing might and increasing strength of the city. The city of New York controls at the present time, with its immense monetary power, the commercial destinies of the Union."

By 1853, every tension in the increasingly divided nation could be felt on the streets of New York, which had become the meeting point not only of the nation's commerce but of its conflicts as well: a cauldron of immigrant energy and of anti-immigrant rancor; the center of the movement to abolish slavery, and of the powerful Southern cotton interests in the North.

From the pulpit of Plymouth Congregational Church in Brooklyn, the Reverend Henry Ward Beecher, renowned for his passionate opposition to slavery, mocked the city's divided loyalties. "It is a dreadful state of things here in New York," he thundered scornfully, "where we feed upon Cotton, and have our very living in the smiles and favor of the South, to be hurting their feelings by talking so much about liberty."

And yet, year by year, as tensions around the country continued to rise, a river of wealth con-

Looking west down Wall Street from the spire of Trinity Church, top. On the right side of the street stands the domed Merchants' Exchange—the massive, $1.1 million granite structure which had risen from the ashes of its predecessor in the aftermath of the Great Fire of 1835. The old brick residences had given way, the *Herald* observed, to a commercial "street of palaces . . . great, gaudy, splendid, Corinthian, scheming, magnificent, and full of all kinds of roguery."

Looking north on Broadway from the foot of City Hall Park, bottom. On weekdays, an endless stream of private carriages, stagecoaches, and horse-drawn streetcars jammed Broadway—one-way south during the morning rush hours, then one-way north in the late afternoon. "There is a perpetual jam and lock of vehicles for nearly two miles along the chief thoroughfare," the *London Times* observed.

tinued to pour into the city—cotton from Mississippi, gold from California, grain from Illinois, cloth from England—fueling an economic boom that by 1853 had stretched into its thirteenth year.

By 1854, lower Broadway had become the busiest boulevard in the world and, with its high, elaborate facades of cast iron and stone, one of the most impressive—with nineteen grand hotels and a fleet of glittering new clothing stores, including Brooks Brothers, Lord & Taylor, and A. T. Stewart's Marble Palace. "Extravagance in living, extravagance in style, extravagance in habitations, extravagance in everything prevail in New York," James Gordon Bennett observed in the *New York Herald*.

And yet, for all the wealth of the downtown streets, nothing could compare to the city's expansion uptown. "The growth of the city in the upper wards is astonishing," Bennett wrote as the boom got under way. "Whole streets of magnificent dwelling houses have been erected in the vicinity of Union Square within the last year. Fifth Avenue is rapidly filling up, and in the course of a few years will be one of the finest streets on the continent."

Uptown, *Putnam's Monthly* reported in 1853, a "new city" had "risen up like enchantment, telling of new times, a new people, new tastes, and new habits." In the summer of 1853, a vast glass-and-iron exhibition space arose—far out on Sixth Avenue from Fortieth to Forty-second streets, at the very outskirts of town.

Erected in the shadow of the giant Croton Reservoir, the structure was like nothing ever built before in America—a soaring pavilion

made of eighteen hundred tons of iron and fifteen thousand panes of glass, enclosing four acres of interior space. Called the Crystal Palace, it was at once a celebration of the astonishing material progress of the city, and a dazzling glimpse of the future.

Beneath its immense 123-foot-high dome—the highest ever constructed in America—were arrayed the proud engines of the industrial age, including steam-powered rotary presses, daguerreotype cameras, sewing machines, experimental electric lamps, high-powered artillery, and newfangled cotton gins. One popular exhibit displayed a twelve-foot section of the two-thousand-mile-long telegraph cable about

to be laid beneath the Atlantic Ocean, connecting New York and London. Twice a day from a tower outside, a local engineer named Elisha Graves Otis demonstrated his daring new invention, called the elevator.

The Crystal Palace was an enormous popular success, often drawing six thousand people a day on weekends for more than two years. Walt Whitman was among the huge milling crowds on opening day, and in the months to come he returned to the exhibit as often as he could—wandering amid the chaotic profusion of people and things, where he thought he could feel the outlines of a new kind of culture arising.

On October 5, 1858, fire broke out inside the Crystal Palace and raced across the combustible prairie of wooden floorboards. The searing heat melted the iron framework, sending thousands of panes of glass crashing into the fiery interior. Within half an hour, all that remained was a smoldering heap of twisted metal and fused glass—which a Mrs. Richardson promptly cut into small pieces and sold as curios.

Walt Whitman (above) in 1854, during the composition of *Leaves of Grass*; and (below) the anonymous cover and illustrated frontispiece of the first edition of Whitman's masterpiece. "The worst thing about this," the poet said of the illustration, "is that I look so damned flamboyant—as if I was hurling bolts at somebody—full of mad oaths—saying defiantly, to hell with you!" He came to like the portrait in the end—"because it is natural, honest, easy: as spontaneous as you are, as I am, this instant, as we talk together."

DEMOCRATIC VISTAS

Mannahatta! How fit a name for America's great democratic island city! The word itself, how beautiful! how aboriginal! how it seems to rise with tall spires, glistening in sunshine, with such New World atmosphere, vista and action!

You will hardly know who I am or what I mean. But I shall be good health to you nevertheless . . . these heated, torn, distracted ages are to be compacted and made whole.

Walt Whitman

On July 5, 1855, a slim volume of poetry, bound in green cloth and embossed in gold, went on sale in the city's bookstores. Though his name appeared nowhere on the front cover, the author was Walt Whitman, now thirty-six years old and living with his mother on Ryerson Street in Brooklyn, doing odd jobs as a printer and builder. "The book," Whitman said, "arose out of my life in Brooklyn and New York, absorbing a million people, for fifteen years, with an intimacy, an eagerness, an abandon, probably never equalled."

It was called *Leaves of Grass*. A hymn to the city, and to the boundless possibilities of the modern world, the astonishingly prophetic work was like nothing ever written before in the English language.

"Wherever one goes in New York," the critic Lewis Mumford would write nearly a century later, "whether one knows it or not, one walks in the steps of Walt Whitman."

The twelve poems the book contained, and the dozens more Whitman added in the years to come, were composed during the most turbulent years in the life of New York, as the forces of growth and expansion threatened to pull the city apart. Yet they projected an astonishing vision of what a modern democratic metropolis could be. Embracing the entire human landscape of New York, Whitman hoped to show his fellow citizens what brought them together, rather than what drove them apart.

The job of the poet, he wrote, was to "resolve all tongues into his own . . . The poet is the joiner . . . he sees how they join."

. . . Nested in nests of water-bays, superb,
Rich, hemm'd thick all around with sailships
*   and steamships, an island sixteen miles long,*
*   solid-founded,*
Numberless crowded streets, high growths of
*   iron, slender, strong, light, splendidly uprising*
*   toward clear skies. . . .*
The countless masts, the white shore-steamers,
*   the lighters, the ferry-boats, the black sea-*
*   steamers well model'd,*
The down-town streets . . . the houses of
*   business, of the ship-merchants and money-*
*   brokers, the river-streets. . . .*
Immigrants arriving, fifteen or twenty thousand
*   a week,*
The carts hauling goods, the manly race of
*   drivers of horses, the brown-faced sailors . . .*
Trottoirs throng'd, vehicles, Broadway, the
*   women, the shops and shows,*
A million people—manners free and superb—
*   open voices—hospitality—the most*
*   courageous and friendly young men,*
City of hurried and sparkling waters! city of
*   spires and masts!*
City nested in bays! my city!

Walt Whitman, "Mannahatta"

Walking the same streets as other New Yorkers, Whitman glimpsed a new kind of city being born—a great democratic vista that as yet only he could see. Where some saw a crowd of alien strangers, he saw an endless river of people, each pursuing his or her own destiny. Where some saw the clash of races, classes, religions, and nationalities, he saw a *daily sharing*, and reveled in the dissonant chorus of New Yorkers, calling it "the glorious jam." Where some saw

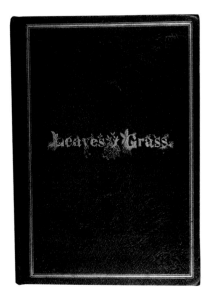

tumult and unrest, he felt the thrilling excitement of city life, and the rising of a new kind of culture, based on curiosity, fantasy, and desire.

> *City of orgies, walks and joys,*
> *City whom that I have lived and sung in your*
> *   midst will one day make you illustrious,*
> *Not the pageants of you, not your shifting*
> *   tableaus, your spectacles repay me,*
> *Nor the interminable rows of your houses, nor*
> *   the ships at the wharves,*
> *Nor the processions in the streets, nor the bright*
> *   windows with goods in them,*
> *Nor to converse with learn'd persons, or bear*
> *   my share in the soiree or feast;*
> *Not those, but as I pass by O Manhattan,*
> *   your frequent and swift flash of eyes offering*
> *   me love,*
> *Offering response to my own—these repay me,*
> *Lovers, continual lovers, only repay me.*
> Walt Whitman, "City of Orgies"

"The proof of the poet," Whitman declared, "is that his country absorbs him as affectionately as he has absorbed them."

To bolster sales, he mailed in anonymous reviews of his own work to literary journals—including one calling it "the most glorious of triumphs in the known history of literature," and another lauding the author's refusal to "separate the learned from the unlearned, the northerner from the southerner, the white from the black, or the native from the immigrant just landed at the wharf." But though Whitman hoped his book would take the country by storm, most readers were shocked by his unconventional style and by the frank sexuality of the poems. *Leaves of Grass* did not sell well.

And yet even in the difficult times to come, Whitman continued to hope that his countrymen would make the immense democratic promise he had seen on the streets of New York a concrete reality—speaking urgently in his greatest poems, like "Crossing Brooklyn Ferry," not only to the men and women of his own generation but to those of generations yet to come.

> *Flood tide below me! I see you face to face! . . .*
> *On the ferry boats the hundreds and hundreds*
> *   that cross, returning home, are more curious*
> *   to me than you suppose,*
> *And you that shall cross from shore to shore*
> *   years hence are more to me, and more in my*
> *   meditations, than you might suppose . . .*
> *It avails not, time nor place—distance*
> *   avails not,*
> *I am with you, you men and women of*
> *   a generation, or ever so many generations*
> *   hence,*
> *Just as you feel when you look on the river*
> *   and the sky, so I felt,*
> *Just as any of you is one of a living crowd,*
> *   I was one of a crowd,*
> *Just as you are refresh'd by the gladness of the*
> *   river and the bright flow, I was refresh'd,*
> *Just as you stand and lean on the rail, yet*
> *   hurry with the swift current, I stood yet*
> *   was hurried,*
> *Just as you look on the numberless masts*
> *   of ships and the thick-stemmed pipes of*
> *   steamboats, I look'd. . . .*
> *These and all else were to me the same as*
> *   they are to you.*
> Walt Whitman,
"Crossing Brooklyn Ferry"

For all its rapid growth uptown, the city Walt Whitman celebrated remained intimately linked with the rivers and bay from which it had arisen. Every workday, thousands of commuters traveled to work on one of the dozens of ferry lines that connected Manhattan Island to Brooklyn, Staten Island, and New Jersey. From the Atlantic Avenue ferry slip in Brooklyn (left), lower Manhattan can be seen in the distance. From the Battery in Manhattan (center) crowds gathered on the Fourth of July to watch an annual regatta. A steam launch (right) shuttles immigrants from the ship at anchor to Castle Garden, the immigrant processing station at the foot of the island.

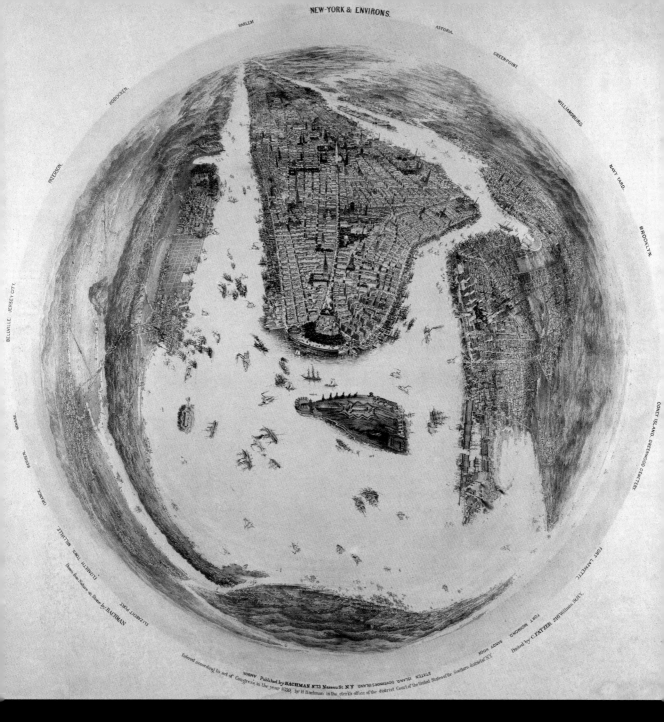

NEW-YORK & ENVIRONS.

Published by BACHMAN N°73 Nassau St. N.Y.

Printed by C. PATZER, 216 William St. N.Y.

Emboldened by New York's increasingly central place in American life, the artist John Bachmann rendered this view of the city as the center of the world in 1859. The vertiginous vantage from high above the foot of Manhattan looks directly down on Governor's Island and the Battery. To the north the spire of Trinity Church rises on the west side of Broadway, and above that, the green triangle of City Hall Park. To the east, south, west, and north, respectively, Brooklyn, Staten Island, New Jersey, and the Bronx curve over the horizon into infinity.

City of the World! (for all races are here,
All the lands of the earth make contributions here;)
Proud and passionate city—mettlesome, mad, extravagant city!
Spring up, O city—not for peace alone, but be indeed
yourself, warlike!
Fear not—submit to no models but your own O city!

Walt Whitman

PANIC

September 1st, 1857. Very bright, beautiful weather, but clouds and thick darkness rule in "The Street"... Panic very sore—and spreading... There have been several pretty serious failures among the stock operators. This may be the beginning of terrible trouble, for the specie in our banks is a ridiculously minute percentage of their circulation.

George Templeton Strong

In the summer of 1857, Whitman's hopes for his democratic island city were dealt a grievous blow. In the last weeks of August, nearly twenty years of frenzied speculation on Wall Street came to a sudden end when panic swept through the financial district. Triggered by the failure of the New York branch of the Ohio Life Insurance and Trust Company, the panic rapidly blossomed into the severest economic crisis in the nation's history.

As the failures on Wall Street multiplied, and brokers, banks, and railroads around the country were plunged into bankruptcy, resentment that had been festering for years burst into the open. New York, the editor of the *New Orleans Crescent* wrote, was "the center of reckless speculation, unflinching fraud and downright robbery, [whose] rotten bankruptcies [are] permeating and injuring almost every solvent community in the Union."

For the country's growing population of city dwellers—dependent for their livelihood on factories as never before—the panic was nothing less than a disaster. Walt Whitman estimated that 25,000 people in New York alone were soon out of work—and 100,000 more facing hardship and even starvation. Hardest hit were those with the fewest resources: the immigrant poor and the city's beleaguered black population. By the end of 1857, an army of hungry, homeless people had joined the gangs of young men roaming the congested streets, adding to the chaos.

From his law office on Wall Street, George Templeton Strong looked on in horror as the crisis deepened, week by week:

September 28th, 1857. Panic is very dreadful in Wall Street... failures are multiplying, and

The oldest extant photograph of Wall Street, taken in the 1850s, looks west from the East River to Trinity Church. By the time of the Civil War, the half-mile-long lane—built where the old Dutch wall had once stood—was the undisputed financial capital of the nation, home to 60 commercial banks, 120 insurance companies, hundreds of brokerage houses, and dozens of speculative exchanges. Among the newest businesses were those created to speed the movement of money itself—including the New York Clearing House and the American Express Company, which carried much of the $175 million in bullion and gold dust that poured into the city during the California Gold Rush.

The scene on Wall Street as the panic of 1857 took hold was captured in James H. Cafferty and Charles G. Rosenberg's painting, *Half Past Two O'clock, October 13, 1857*—the moment when the announcement was made that all but one of the city's banks had suspended cash outlays indefinitely. Steamship magnate Cornelius Vanderbilt is at the far right. A notorious stock manipulator named Jacob Little—known as "the Great Bear"—stands at center in a light gray topcoat, stunned by the news. Normal banking operations were not resumed until December 12, 1857.

no one knows on whom he can depend, or on what. Every security is distrusted. . . . October 8th. Bluer and darker every day. Monday's rally followed by collapse. Failures many and important. . . . October 10th. We seem [to be] foundering. Affairs are worse than ever today, and a period of general insolvency seems close upon us. . . . People's faces in Wall Street look fearfully gaunt and desperate. . . . October 22nd. . . . We are a very sick people just now. The outward and visible signs of disease . . . are many. Walking down Broadway you pass great $200,000 buildings begun last spring or summer that have gone up two stories and stopped, and may stand unfinished and desolate for years. . . . November 10th—This financial crisis has thrown thousands of the working class out of employment and made it a difficult matter enough to maintain peace and order in the city through the winter.

George Templeton Strong

In the fall of 1857—as banks failed, and businesses closed, and thousands of unemployed New Yorkers wandered the city streets, homeless—the state authorities now in control of New York embarked upon one of the greatest public works projects ever undertaken in an American city. It would be the most ambitious attempt yet to make Whitman's "democratic island city" a concrete reality.

PARK

Circumambulate the city on a dreamy Sabbath afternoon. What do you see?—Posted like silent sentinels all around the town, stand thousands upon thousands of mortal men . . . some leaning against the spiles, some seated in the pier heads, some looking over the bulwarks of ships. These are all landsmen; of weekdays pent up in lath and plaster—tied to counters, nailed to benches, clinched to desks. How then is this? Are the green fields gone?

Herman Melville, *Moby-Dick*

Of all the deficiencies of the grid plan of Manhattan, none had become more glaring by 1857 than the failure to provide enough park space for New York's overworked and overcrowded citizens. The metropolis—as De Witt Clinton's commissioners had envisioned it back in 1811—was to have been an orderly paradise of single family row houses, each with its own backyard. The island's endless shoreline, it was assumed, would provide more than enough space for play and recreation.

By mid-century, however, five decades of explosive industrial growth had transformed much of lower Manhattan into a congested wasteland of factories, warehouses, boardinghouses, and tenements—with more than half a million people packed into the area below Twenty-third Street, in buildings seldom more than five stories tall.

For poor New Yorkers there was simply no escape. What few backyard spaces remained in the slums had been all but obliterated by foul-smelling privies and shabby "rear tenements," while access to the shoreline had been almost completely cut off by a tangled belt of shipyards and muddy docks.

"Commerce," William Cullen Bryant wrote in the *Evening Post*, "is devouring inch by inch the coast of the island, and if we would rescue any part of it for health and recreation, it must be done now."

There is no place within the city limits in which it is pleasant to walk, or ride, or drive, or stroll; no place for skating, no water in which it is safe to row; no field for baseball or cricket, no pleasant garden where one can sit with and chat with a friend, or listen to the music of a good band.

Clarence C. Cook

In 1844, Bryant challenged the city to set aside a large tract of undeveloped land north of the city limits—one last piece of nature for public use, on what was rapidly becoming the most built-up piece of real estate in the world. "What are called parks in New York are not even apologies for the thing," a landscape gardener named Andrew Jackson Downing declared, "they are only squares or paddocks." "New York is sadly deficient of parks," another writer lamented. "Without these safety valves, to vitalize the dense city with its teeming throngs . . . the wonder is that we do not suffer collapse sooner than we do."

Year by year, the park movement grew—despite fierce opposition from business leaders and real estate developers, loath to place any kind of limit on property development in Manhattan. "There is no need of turning one-half of the island into a permanent forest for the accommodation of loafers," the editor of the *Journal of Commerce* declared. "The grand park scheme is humbug and the sooner it is abandoned the better." By way of reply, Bryant pointed to Green-Wood Cemetery in Brooklyn—where each Sunday thousands of families, desperate for open space, were forced to picnic within sight of freshly dug graves.

In 1857—after years of acrimonious debate, and with unemployment and homelessness compounding the miseries of the crowded industrial city—New York finally embarked upon the greatest physical transformation of Manhattan since the grid. That fall, the city finished purchasing a vast tract of sparsely populated land north of the city limits for $5 million—then issued eviction notices to the sixteen hundred black, Irish, and German settlers living on it.

Two weeks later, Mayor Fernando Wood announced a special design competition for what was called simply "the central park." Six months later, the winner was announced: entry number thirty-three, called Greensward, by Calvert Vaux and Frederick Law Olmsted.

In some ways, they were an unlikely choice for the job. Vaux, a respected English architect, had never designed a public park before. Olmsted, a frail and melancholy thirty-five-year-old writer, had never designed anything at all—flitting so often from one passion to another that his own father called him "a truant." But both Vaux and Olmsted were acutely aware what the driving commercial city was doing to its people—breeding physical congestion, social disorder, and spiritual unrest.

The park they proposed would be an entirely new kind of public space—a man-made nature that would soften the harsh social and economic

"In the absence of public gardens," the landscape gardener Andrew Jackson Downing observed in 1849, "cemeteries in a certain degree [supply] their place. But does not this general interest, manifested in these cemeteries, prove that public gardens, established in a liberal and suitable manner near our large cities, would be equally successful?" Within a few years of its opening in 1838, Green-Wood Cemetery—a lush oasis on the southern outskirts of Brooklyn—was drawing more than 60,000 people a year to its 478 acres of landscaped grounds. Visitors strolling its winding paths or relaxing by the banks of picturesque ponds like Silver Lake (above), did their best to overlook the somber gravestones and marble monuments that were never entirely out of sight (bottom).

The prime movers behind Central Park, photographed, opposite, in 1862 atop Willowdell Arch. From left to right: Andrew Haswell Green, a well-connected lawyer, was president of the Park Commission—and father, 30 years later, of the effort to consolidate New York and Brooklyn into a single giant metropolis. George Waring, the brilliant young sanitary engineer who laid out the park's innovative drainage system, would as sanitation commissioner lead a revolutionary effort to clean up the city streets.

The vast majority of the workers were unskilled Irish and German day laborers—often paid only a dollar a day, and drawn, Olmsted said, from the "poorest, or what is generally considered the most dangerous, class of the great city's population." To prevent any trouble with the Irish, African Americans were excluded from the workforce entirely.

My office was regularly surrounded by an organized mob carrying a banner inscribed "Blood or Bread." This mob sent in to me a list of 10,000 names of men alleged to have starving families, demanding that they should be immediately put to work.

Frederick Law Olmsted

Each afternoon, tremendous explosions rocked the northern outskirts of the city, as the crews blasted and excavated 2.5 million cubic yards of stone and earth.

It was grueling, sometimes dangerous work. The first casualty was a laborer named Luke Flynn, killed by an explosion. Timothy McNamara was "instantly killed by being struck in the head with a large stone thrown from a blast" five hundred feet away.

Once the terrain had been prepared, workmen installed ninety-five miles of underground pipe, creating an artificial drainage system— itself a masterpiece of sanitary engineering— then set to work relandscaping the entire site with 6 million bricks, 65,000 cubic yards of gravel, 25,000 trees, and a quarter of a million shrubs. "Every foot of the park," Olmsted proudly declared, "every tree and bush, every arch, roadway and walk, has been fixed where it is *with a purpose.*"

June 11th, 1859. Improved the day by leaving Wall Street early and set off to explore the Central Park, which will be a feature of the city within five years and a lovely place in A.D. 1900, when its trees will have acquired dignity and appreciable diameters. Perhaps the city itself will perish before then, by growing too big to live under faulty institutions corruptly administered. Reached the park a little before four, just as the red flag was hoisted—the signal for the blasts of the day. They were all around us for some twenty minutes, now booming far off to the north, now quite near, now distant again, like a desultory "affair" between two great

Calvert Vaux, an English architect and the park's codesigner, was responsible for its thousands of structures, bridges, terraces, arches, stairways, fountains, benches, fences, gates, walls, and lampposts. Ignaz Anton Pilat, a Viennese landscape gardener and the park's master horticulturalist, supervised the planting of more than 240,000 trees and shrubs. Jacob Wrey Mould, a stylish English architect considered "the greatest ornamentist of modern times," created much of the exquisite detail that graced the finished terraces, bridges, and structures of the park. Frederick Law Olmsted, the chief creative force and visionary codesigner of Central Park, was superintendent during much of its construction.

divisions of the industrial metropolis and provide relief from the unrelenting commercial intensity. As New Yorkers of every class entered the park, they would leave behind the constant reminders of their differences and, it was hoped, rediscover their common humanity.

[New Yorkers display] a remarkable quickness of apprehension [along with] a peculiarly hard sort of selfishness. Every day of their lives they have seen thousands of their fellow-men, have met them face to face, have brushed against them, and yet have had no experience of anything in common with them. . . . There need to be places and times for re-unions [where] the rich and poor, the cultivated and the self-made, shall be attracted together and encouraged to assimilate.

Frederick Law Olmsted

With their hand-picked team of architects, artisans and engineers, Olmsted and Vaux set to work—"translating democratic ideas," as Vaux himself wrote, "into trees and dirt." By the spring of 1858, more than three thousand men were busy dredging, clearing, grading, and planting— laboriously remodeling every feature of the rugged landscape. There were German gardeners, Italian stonecutters, and an army of masons, carpenters, blacksmiths and road-building teams.

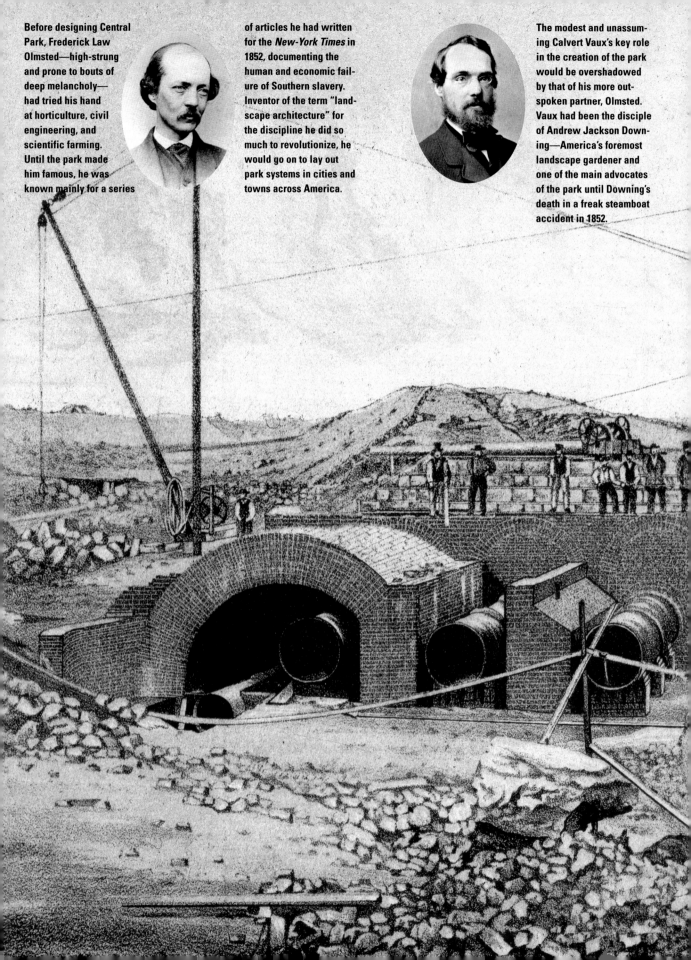

Before designing Central Park, Frederick Law Olmsted—high-strung and prone to bouts of deep melancholy— had tried his hand at horticulture, civil engineering, and scientific farming. Until the park made him famous, he was known mainly for a series of articles he had written for the *New-York Times* in 1852, documenting the human and economic failure of Southern slavery. Inventor of the term "landscape architecture" for the discipline he did so much to revolutionize, he would go on to lay out park systems in cities and towns across America.

The modest and unassuming Calvert Vaux's key role in the creation of the park would be overshadowed by that of his more outspoken partner, Olmsted. Vaux had been the disciple of Andrew Jackson Downing—America's foremost landscape gardener and one of the main advocates of the park until Downing's death in a freak steamboat accident in 1852.

Even as work on Central Park continued, another mammoth project got under way within its boundaries: the expansion of the Croton Water Works. When complete, the huge reservoir located in the heart of Central Park would be three times as large as the original receiving reservoir. This 1862 view of workmen constructing the southern gatehouse shows a cross-section of the system's gigantic hydraulics—including cast-iron water mains as tall as a man.

CENTRAL PARK.

armies. . . . *It promises very well. So does all the lower park, though now in most ragged condition: long lines of incomplete macadamization, "lakes" without water, mounds of compost, piles of blasted stone, acres of what may be greensward hereafter but is now mere brown earth. . . . Celts, caravans of dirt carts, derricks, steam engines, these are the elements out of which our future Pleasaunce is rapidly developing. The work seems pushed with vigor and system. A broad avenue, exceptionally straight. . . . with quadruple rows of Elms, will look Versailles-y by A.D. 1950.*

George Templeton Strong

In the spring of 1859, an inventor named Thaddeus Lowe sailed high above the construction site in his brand-new hydrogen-filled observation balloon, called *The City of New York,* from which he could see the first completed sections of the park. He was stunned by what he saw.

Sprawling across 843 acres, *eighty times* the size of the next largest park in the city, stretched an endless labyrinth of cunningly composed vistas and scenes—the largest public space of its kind ever constructed in America. When complete, there would be something for everyone—a sheep meadow and a wild ramble, secluded groves and sparkling lakes, bridges and castles, winding streams and hidden ponds—the whole artfully arranged so that visitors might lose themselves amid an endless wandering tapestry of nature.

It was the most astonishingly farsighted urban vision since the Commissioners' Plan itself.

Nothing about Central Park—seen in an 1863 bird's-eye view by John Bachmann—was more extraordinary, or forward-looking, than its complex, interwoven system of circulation. There were miles of winding paths for strolling pedestrians, serpentine scenic drives for carriages, a bridle path for horses and riders, and—tucked ingeniously below the rest of the park's landscape—four "transverse roadways" that allowed commercial traffic to flow inconspicuously across the park, between the Upper East and West sides of Manhattan.

Glimpes of the new park: Right top, a view of the lake; below, a winding pathway. By 1860, it was clear that Central Park was everything the city's elite had hoped it would be—a vast pleasure garden, with places for boating and horseback riding, for lawn tennis and bird-watching, for open-air concerts and terrace dining.

In 1859, Professor Thaddeus Lowe's hydrogen-filled balloon, *The City of New York*, rose above the southern edge of Central Park, at 59th Street and Sixth Avenue. The contraption never made the ambitious journey across the Atlantic for which it had been designed, but within two years, its inventor had found a more immediate use for his lighter-than-air vehicles—as Union army observation balloons, tracking Confederate troop movements during the Civil War.

Then, city fathers had proposed placing a man-made grid on the natural topography of the island. Now, on top of that artifice, Olmsted and Vaux were placing an artificial nature—a "central park" built not in the middle of what the city was but in the middle of what the city would one day become.

"The time will come," Olmsted confidently predicted, "when New York will be built up, when all the grading and filling will be done, and when the picturesequely varied, rocky formations of the Island will have been converted into rows of monotonous straight streets and piles of erect buildings. There will be no suggestion left of its present varied surface, with the single exception of the Park. Then the priceless value of the present picturesque outlines of

the ground will be perceived, and its adaptability for its purpose more fully recognized."

"The Park, if one can believe its name," one French visitor remarked, "will one day be in the center of the city. Nothing is more American than this ambitious name, given at first sight to wild terrain situated beyond the suburbs."

The park should be an antithesis to its bustling, paved, rectangular, walled-in streets. The chief effect [should be] like that of music, [which] goes back of thought and cannot be fully given the form of words.

Frederick Law Olmsted

But what no one was prepared for was the extraordinary aesthetic experience of the park itself. It was, one man later said, "nineteenth-century America's greatest work of art."

Entering the park at Fifth Avenue and Fifty-ninth Street, visitors were led slowly out of the city along a regal tree-lined mall—a street of nature—skewed away from the city's rigid street plan and penetrating ever deeper into the park. At the far northern end, the scene suddenly widened to reveal a breathtaking vista. In the middle of what the city would one day be, Olmsted and Vaux had created the illusion of an open space that went on forever—an image of the unspoiled continent America had once been, now transformed into an urban paradise and permanently preserved.

May 1859. The whole place presents its very best appearance this month—the full flush of trees, the plentiful white and pink of the flowering shrubs, the emerald green of the grass spreading everywhere, yellow dotted still with dandelions—the specialty of the plentiful gray rocks cropping out, miles and miles—and over all the beauty and purity of our summer skies.

Walt Whitman

October 1st, 1859. Who is not proud that, in a day of swindling in politics, and of cast-iron in building, such grand works can be achieved in rugged honesty and solid stone? It silences forever the clatter of skeptics of the democratic principle as inimical to vast public works.

Harper's Weekly

Aesthetically, Central Park was a triumph from the start. But to Vaux and Olmsted's dis-

Though slavery had finally ended in New York State in 1827, African Americans struggled to hold on in the rapidly changing city—hemmed in by racial prejudice and legal discrimination at every turn. Freed from actual bondage, they were still denied many of the basic rights of citizenship—including the most fundamental of all, the right to vote. The 1821 Constitutional Convention that had brought about univeral white male suffrage had imposed harsh property requirements on potential black voters—limiting suffrage to that tiny fraction of African American men who owned $250 or more in taxable property.

For some, opportunity lay not *in* the city but just outside it, in self-sustaining communities on the out-skirts of town. In the 1830s, African Americans founded the neighboring farm villages of Weeksville and Carrville, on the eastern edge of Brooklyn, near present-day Bedford-Stuyvesant.

By then, a handful of African American farmers and day laborers had begun to put down roots in a rock-strewn area of upper Manhattan, many building their own houses and acquiring sufficient property to vote. Year after year, the little hamlet flourished, until by 1853, "Seneca Village," as it was then known, had grown into a thriving interracial community of 250 people—two-thirds black, one-third Irish—with two schools, three cemeteries, and three churches, including the all-black A.M.E. Zion Church and a racially mixed Episcopalian congregation called All Angels'.

August 5th, 1853. The cornerstone of the First African Methodist Episcopal Church of Yorkville was laid yesterday afternoon. . . . The sermon on the occasion was preached by Rev. Christopher Rush, Superintendent of the African Churches. . . . Built of wood, and painted white, [its] basement . . . will be a school-room for the education of colored children. Toward fifty colored families reside in the neighborhood of this Church. There are thirty members in this Society, and the congregation usually numbers about 100 persons.
New York Daily Tribune

By 1853, Seneca Village's days were numbered. That year, whether its inhabitants knew it or not, the land it stood on—just east of Eighth Avenue, between 82nd and 86th streets—was set aside by city officials for a vast public improvement project. Three years later, as preliminary work on "the central park" began, the city moved swiftly to condemn the area and prepare it for reconstruction. Residents of Seneca Village who owned land were paid a modest sum for the homes they had worked so hard to secure, then evicted. By October 1, 1857, every house and church in the little town had been torn down and hauled away, and its inhabitants had disappeared without a trace.

Skaters on the pond in Central Park, in the winter of 1859–60. A line of wooden shanties and houses can be seen in the background just outside the boundaries of the new park, on the south side of 59th Street between Fifth and Seventh avenues.

Central Park in the 1860s: Above, women under the Wisteria Arbor just east of the Mall. At center, a view of the Lake from the Terrace. Below, the Marble Arch, Stairs, and Grotto. As early visitors discovered to their delight, the environment that Olmsted and Vaux had created was less a single landscape than an unfolding *series* of landscapes, seamlessly compressed within the park's boundaries, where every movement or turn seemed to offer a new, carefully composed view.

"On a bright moonlit night in the summer," the guidebook author James D. McCabe, Jr. wrote a few years later, "the scene to be witnessed on the lake is brilliant. The clear waters gleam like polished steel in the moonlight, and are dotted in every direction with pleasure boats . . . the swans sail majestically up and down in groups; on every side is heard the dash of oars, and the sound of laughter and happy voices; and the air is heavily laden with the perfume of the flowers along the shore. No sight or sound of the great city is at hand to disturb you, and you may lie back in your boat with half-shut eyes, and think yourself in fairyland."

appointment it proved more popular with wealthier New Yorkers than with the city's working poor—who needed it most but found it hardest to reach. On Sunday afternoons, its long sweeping drives streamed with elegant car-

riages that fewer than one in twenty New Yorkers could afford—while commercial vehicles were barred entirely. For working-class families, meanwhile, often struggling to survive on a dollar a day, traveling to the remote pleasure ground from the congested tenement districts far downtown meant an hour-long journey by omnibus or horse car—at the prohibitive cost of five cents per person each way.

The Irish and German day laborers who had helped build the park found themselves further discouraged from using it by the long list of rules Olmsted had drawn up for its use. "A large part of the people of New York," he wrote, "are ignorant of a park. They will need to be trained to the proper use of it, to be restrained in the abuse of it."

There were signs posted everywhere, prohibiting group picnics, walking on the grass, and "strenuous activity" of any kind. Schoolboys were forbidden from playing baseball in the park, unless they had a note from their principal.

With the experience of riots and gang violence still vivid in the minds of city officials, Olmsted's park police constantly patrolled the grounds, to stop any trouble before it started.

May 9th, 1860. The admirable order which prevails on the Central Park is of itself a moral lesson and encouragement . . . in the midst of the official corruption and general municipal disarray of the times. . . . Give us at Albany, at the City Hall, at the Federal Capital, the same honest energy and discipline which have rule in the affairs of the Park, and it would soon be found that Americans are no more insensible than other people to the charms of decency and the advantages of order.

New-York Times

By 1860, the main features of Central Park were nearing completion. But Olmsted and Vaux's masterpiece had done little to ease tensions in the congested city—and by then, few New Yorkers, and few Americans, were thinking about parks, anyway.

Unrest that had been building for half a century in the city was about to be overtaken by the worst crisis in American history. In the conflict to come, New York City would play a role more eventful and strange than anyone could have imagined.

THE GREATEST MAN SINCE ST. PAUL

At 11:30 on the morning of Saturday, February 25, 1860, a tall, gangling man in an ill-fitting black coat and battered beaverskin hat stepped off the Cortlandt Street ferry in lower Manhattan. A lawyer and ex-congressman little known outside his home state of Illinois, he had come to New York hoping to bolster his slim chances of winning the Republican presidential nomination.

When no one met him at the ferry, Abraham Lincoln made his way alone to the Astor House hotel across from City Hall Park—the main watering place for politicians, journalists, and visiting celebrities. Within hours, word of the candidate's arrival had circulated through the newsrooms of Printing House Row, and reporters had been dispatched to cover the westerner's visit to the metropolis.

On Sunday, Lincoln took in the sights, boarding the East River ferry to Brooklyn to hear the Reverend Henry Ward Beecher deliver a thundering sermon against slavery. Back in Manhattan that afternoon, he toured the Five Points and attended a minstrel show on the Bowery—roaring with delight at a new hit tune, written in New York the year before, called "Dixie." "Let's have it again!" Lincoln bellowed out when the performance was over. "Let's have it again!"

But the candidate had not come to New York to see the sights. The visit would be the only real chance he had to capture the attention of the American public—and everything was riding on the speech he was to give at a workingmen's college called the Cooper Institute on Monday night. That afternoon, in a cold, pouring rain, Lincoln stopped by Knox's Hat Store on Broadway, and traded in his old beaverskin for a shiny silk top hat—then crossed over to Mathew Brady's Daguerrian Gallery to sit for a formal portrait.

As evening came, and the rain turned to snow, Lincoln's worries mounted. But New York's publicity engine had done its work, and by seven-thirty, more than fifteen hundred people had filled the Great Hall of the Cooper Institute to capacity. Stifled laughter rippled through the hall as the odd-looking westerner with a high, nasal voice began to speak. But the crowd grew quiet as he warmed to his theme—imploring his listeners with passionate logic to restrict

the spread of slavery—though not to abolish it completely. No one who was there would ever forget the power of Lincoln's words, or the force of his character.

Pretty soon he began to get into his subject; his face lighted with an inward fire; the whole man was transfigured. I forgot his clothes, his appearance and his peculiarities. Presently, forgetting myself, I was on my feet with the rest, yelling like a wild Indian, cheering this wonderful man. . . When I came out of the hall . . . a friend with his eyes aglow, asked me what I thought of Abe Lincoln, the rail split-

ter. I said: "He's the greatest man since St. Paul." And I think so yet.

An Audience Member,
as Reported to Noah Brooks

The next morning, Lincoln awoke to find himself a national celebrity. "No man ever before made such an impression on his first appeal to a New York audience," Horace Greeley wrote in the *Tribune*'s national edition, in an editorial that would eventually be read by more than a quarter of a million readers. By then, Lincoln's speech had been reprinted in full in four major newspapers, and in pamphlets that were already making their way across the country, together with reproductions of Mathew Brady's photograph.

Looking back, Lincoln never forgot what his three-day sojourn in New York City had done for him. "Brady and the Cooper Institute," he said simply, "made me President."

OMENS, AUGURIES, AND PORTENTS DIRE

On November 15, 1860, one week after Lincoln's election, a giant meteor could be seen illuminating the skies above the city. "Omens, auguries, and portents dire," the *New-York Times* reported gloomily. Lincoln's startling rise confirmed the worst Southern fears: the North, with its rapidly expanding cities, was going to destroy the Southern way of life.

Within days of the election, South Carolina had called for a special session of the state legislature to consider seceding from the Union.

In New York, merchants and bankers fretted over the $200 million owed them by Southern cotton brokers—a debt that would be all but uncollectible in the event of war.

Wednesday, November 13th, 1860. Stocks have fallen heavily today, and I think they will fall much lower before this game is played out. . . . Southern securities are waste paper in Wall Street. Not a dollar can be raised on them. Who wants to buy paper that must be collected by suit in the courts of South Carolina and Georgia?

George Templeton Strong

As the contagion George Templeton Strong called "secessionitus" spread from one Southern state to another, tension in the city grew. By the winter of 1861, no place in America was

more divided than New York, which had become a microcosm of the troubled country at large—at once fiercely pro-Union and yet, with its powerful business ties to the South, a hotbed of pro-Southern sentiment.

On January 21—fearing that war would destroy the cotton trade and cripple the city's economy—Mayor Fernando Wood proposed to the city's Common Council that New York itself secede from the Union. On February 19, Abraham Lincoln passed through the troubled city again, on his way to Washington to be inaugurated. From an omnibus on Broadway, Walt Whitman caught his first glimpse of the man on whom the fate of the Union now hung—and feared for the president-elect's life. "Many an assassin's knife and pistol," he worried, "lurk'd in hip or breast pocket there, ready, as soon as break and riot came."

George Templeton Strong was also in the crowd. Like Whitman, he had voted for the westerner, despite grave doubts about his ability to lead; yet something about the president-elect's aspect reassured him. "The great rail-splitter's face was visible to me for an instant," he noted in his diary, "and seemed a keen, clear, honest face, not so ugly as his portraits." Less than two months later, Strong recorded a fateful entry in his diary. "This morning's papers," he wrote, on Saturday, April 13, 1861, "confirmed last night's news; viz., that the rebels opened fire at Sumter yesterday morning. . . . So Civil War is inaugurated at last. God defend the Right."

The shocking news galvanized pro-Union sentiment in the city. "There is but one feeling now," a merchant wrote, "and that is to sustain our flag and government at all costs." On April 20, in response to Lincoln's call for 75,000 recruits, a quarter of a million merchants, clerks, and workingmen jammed Union Square for a rally in support of the Northern cause. It was, the *Tribune* said, "the greatest popular demonstration ever known in America."

April 20th, 1861. Walked uptown at two. Broadway crowded and more crowded as one approached Union Square. Large companies of recruits parading up and down, cheered and cheering. . . . Every other man, woman and

Mathew Brady's "Cooper Union portrait" of Lincoln: With a large mole on his right cheek and prominent Adam's apple, the newcomer from Springfield, Illinois, posed a special challenge to the New York photographer, who had "great trouble," he later recalled, "in making a natural picture." Brady had the little-known candidate lift his collar to hide his throat, then ordered his assistants to retouch the negative to soften the westerner's harsh facial features. The resulting likeness—reprinted in thousands of copies, including engravings in the *Tribune* and other New York papers—became the candidate's official campaign portrait, and the first in a series of photographs by Brady that would forever fix the image of the twelfth president of the United States in the public imagination.

*child bearing a flag or decorated with a cock-
ade. The city seems to have gone suddenly wild
and crazy.*

George Templeton Strong

The city and the country went to war. Before
the terrible conflict was over, more than a hundred and fifty thousand New Yorkers—including fifty thousand Irishmen, tens of thousands

of Germans, and two thousand blacks—would
fight for the Union cause.

Frederick Law Olmsted quickly resigned
from his post at Central Park to run the U.S.
Sanitary Commission. He would soon be
responsible for the health and medical treatment of hundreds of thousands of Union soldiers. Walt Whitman went south, too, as a
volunteer in the crowded Washington hospi-

tals. George Templeton Strong, too old at forty-one for active duty, helped train a brigade of sharpshooters, called the New York Rifles.

Outside the hastily pitched recruiting tents in City Hall Park, young men lined up in droves to answer Lincoln's call. Within days, more than six thousand Irishmen had applied for admission to the Sixty-ninth New York Regiment, and within two weeks of the attack on Fort Sumter, a thousand raw recruits were on their way to defend Washington.

With its four thousand factories, ninety thousand workers, and a manufacturing output almost equal to that of the entire Confederacy, the nation's largest industrial city would play a pivotal role in the world's first industrialized conflict. Supercharged by the demands of war, New York's factories, mills, foundries, and ship-yards simply exploded, churning out rifles, ammunition, blankets, tents, uniforms, shoes, hardtack, foodstuffs, wagons, engines, furnaces, boilers, gun turrets, and artillery pieces to feed the insatiable Union war machine.

Garment manufacturers—called upon to produce tens of thousands of uniforms for soldiers they would never see—pioneered the use of standard clothing sizes, while Brooks Brothers manufactured dress uniforms for officers, and Tiffany's turned out swords, medals, and insignia.

At the Brooklyn Navy Yard, six thousand men were soon at work, turning out dozens of massive wooden warships, along with a strange new one, clad entirely of iron. Brooklyn pharmaceutical makers like Edward Squibb and Charles Pfizer would soon be producing thousands of bandages, splints, and vials of surgical ether—and, as the war dragged on, artificial eyes and limbs.

To help pay for it all, Wall Street bankers sold nearly $2 billion in government bonds—making the city, in the process, the clearing-house for a truly national economy.

March 1863. Things here . . . are in a great state of prosperity. You can have no idea of it. The large amount expended by the government has given activity to everything and but for the daily news of the War in the papers and the crowds of soldiers you see about in the streets you would have no idea of the war. Our streets are crowded, hotels full, and manufacturers of

all kinds except cotton were never doing so well and business generally is active.

William Dodge

And yet—while industrialists and business-men grew rich off the war, and profiteers made huge fortunes selling overpriced and often shoddily made supplies to the War Department—tens of thousands of ordinary New Yorkers and the working poor suffered, as rents and inflation soared, and the standard of living plummeted.

In the years to come, the Civil War would test more than any other event in the city's history whether New York could address the immense human problems of the industrial age or subside into chaos and anarchy. It would also bring to a tragic climax tensions that had been rising for years—between rich and poor, native-born and immigrant, Protestant and Catholic, black and white. All those tensions would come to a head in the long, hot summer of 1863, and when the trouble came it would begin with the most desperate of the city's beleaguered citizens.

THE DEVIL'S OWN WORK

February 5, 1863. These be dark blue days. . . . We are in a fearful scrape, and I see no way out of it. Recognition of the Confederacy is impossible. So is vigorous prosecution of the war twelve months longer. We are in a . . . deadlock of contradiction, I fear; the North cannot be defeated and the South cannot be conquered.

George Templeton Strong

By 1863, opposition to the war had been growing for more than a year, especially among the Irish. As one Union defeat followed another, and the horrifying casualty lists grew longer, anger toward the government intensified. Abraham Lincoln's Emancipation Proclamation, which had taken effect on the first of the year, and which asked whites to fight and die for the freedom of blacks, only made matters worse.

But it was the passage of the Conscription Act in the spring of 1863—the first federal draft in American history—that aroused the most fury. It authorized the government to draft hundreds of thousands of men into the army against their will. Anyone with $300 to spare, meanwhile—nearly a year's wages for most work-ingmen—could buy his way out.

For the Irish—already convinced that Emancipation would result in hordes of freed slaves coming north to take their jobs—it was the last straw. "The draft would compel the white laborer to leave his family destitute and unprotected," Fernando Wood's brother, Benjamin, declared in the pages of the *New York Daily News*, a fiercely antiwar newspaper he himself edited, "while he goes forth to free the negro, who being free, will compete with him for labor."

The reality, of course, was somewhat different. African Americans—next to the Dutch themselves, the oldest ethnic group in the city—had for years been driven from their jobs by Irish immigrants willing to work for less money. But the fear among many of the Irish was that blacks would take their jobs—while they fought and died in a war only the rich could avoid fighting.

In June, as resentment among the immigrant poor festered, Confederate forces under Robert E. Lee invaded the North, spreading

terror throughout the Union, and threatening Harrisburg, Philadelphia, even New York itself.

As the July date set for the city's draft lottery approached, rumors of a mass protest, and even armed uprising, began to circulate about the city, and antiwar feelings began to seethe out of control—fanned by Democratic politicians eager to exploit the rising anti-Republican sentiment.

"Remember this," Governor Horace Seymour warned ominously—in a speech decrying Lincoln's "extremist" war measures—"that the bloody, and treasonable, and revolutionary doctrine of public necessity, can be proclaimed by a mob as well as by a Government."

On the Fourth of July, word reached New York City by telegraph that more than fifty thousand men had fallen outside a tiny town in Pennsylvania, only 150 miles away, called Gettysburg.

The Sixty-ninth New York Regiment, composed almost entirely of Irish immigrants, had suffered such grievous casualties it could scarcely be said to exist any longer as a fighting unit.

One week later, on Saturday, July 11, 1863, drawings began at the uptown draft office on Third Avenue near Forty-sixth Street. The first to be called was a man named Jones. By six that night, more than twelve hundred names had been pulled from the drum. The next day, the list of unlucky ones was published in the Sunday papers.

"Draft has begun here," George Templeton Strong noted apprehensively in his diary, "and was in progress in Boston last week ... we shall have trouble before we are through. The critical time will be when de-faulting conscripts are hauled out of their houses, as many will be. . . . This draft will be the *experimentum crucis* to decide whether we have a government among us."

Sunday, July 12, dawned sullen and hot in New York City, without a breath of wind. With every shop and office closed until Monday, people began drifting out of the stifling tenements and into taverns, and began to drink, and talk. With almost every able-bodied soldier in the area still at Gettysburg, the city's militia was woefully undermanned, but there was still no cause for alarm.

Sometime during the night, the mood changed. By dawn, disturbing reports began filtering in to police headquarters on Mulberry Street, of gangs of angry, drunken men roaming the streets.

Not long after sunrise, on July 13, 1863, waves of angry men—the vast majority of them Irish immigrants—began spilling out of the Lower East Side, moving west across Broadway, and heading uptown toward the draft office, armed with iron bars, brickbats, and bludgeons, and growing all the time.

At 8:30 a.m. an urgent dispatch went out from police headquarters. "Trouble brewing. Telegraph lines cut. Rush large force." In the next few hours, with terrifying speed, decades of mounting resentment among the city's immigrant poor—so often maligned by nativists and missionized by reformers, and now bearing the economic brunt of a war they had come to despise—would explode on the streets of New York in the worst episode of civil unrest in the nation's history.

"It was a strangely weaponed, ragged, coatless army as it heaved tumultuously toward Third Avenue," a telegraph operator named Charles Chapin later remembered. "The mob," one black eyewitness recalled, "was composed of the lowest and most degraded of the foreign population, (mainly Irish), raked from the filthy cellars and dens of the city. . . . Calling at places where large bodies of men were at work, and pressing them in, their numbers rapidly increased to thousands."

On the first morning of the July riot, one or two of the gangs of workmen employed on the Central Park left their work, and marched down[town], forcing or inducing the other gangs to leave their work also and follow them, and the whole body then proceeded to take part in the business of murder and rapine then going on in the City, and continued engaging in it during two entire days, furnishing by far the best organized, and, therefore, most dangerous and destructive of the bands.

New-York Times

By nine o'clock, the unruly, disorganized crowd had grown to five thousand. By the time it reached the draft office at 677 Third Avenue, it had swelled to fifteen thousand—and then the violence began. The enraged mob beat through the scanty police guard, smashed and burned the draft office, then turned their fury on a detachment of thirty-two militiamen, beating and kicking one soldier to death, then turning on another. The mob "grabbed him," the *Tribune* reported, "and taking him to the top of the rocks stripped his uniform off him, and after beating him almost to a jelly, threw him over a precipice some twenty feet high on the hard rocks beneath."

By eleven-thirty Monday morning, the federal draft had been officially suspended in New York, and the city itself was in a state of siege. In desperation, civic leaders implored the archbishop of New York, John Hughes, to do something—anything—to help restore calm. But there was little Hughes, or anyone, could do.

> *The beastly ruffians were masters of the situation and of the city. After a while sporadic paving stones began to fly at windows. . . . Then men and small boys . . . began smashing the sashes and the blinds and shied out light articles, such as books and crockery, and dropped chairs and mirrors into the back yard. At last a light smoke began to float out of the windows.*
>
> George Templeton Strong

> *The scene on Third Avenue at this time was appalling. It was now noon but the hot July sun was obscured by heavy clouds which cast dark shadows over the city. . . . As one glanced among the dense mass of men and women the eye rested upon huge columns of smoke rising from burning buildings—for the mob had now begun to plunder and burn—giving a wild and terrifying aspect to the scene.*
>
> Charles Chapin

The eight hundred men of the Metropolitan Police fought bravely where they could, but even reinforced by militia from around the harbor, they were outnumbered fifteen to one. All day, marauding mobs rampaged up and down the island—ripping down telegraph poles and wires, destroying streetcar and train tracks, looting and burning the armory on Twenty-first Street, Brooks Brothers on Fifth Avenue, the Harlem Temperance Room, and the Magdalen Asylum for aged prostitutes, as well as the homes

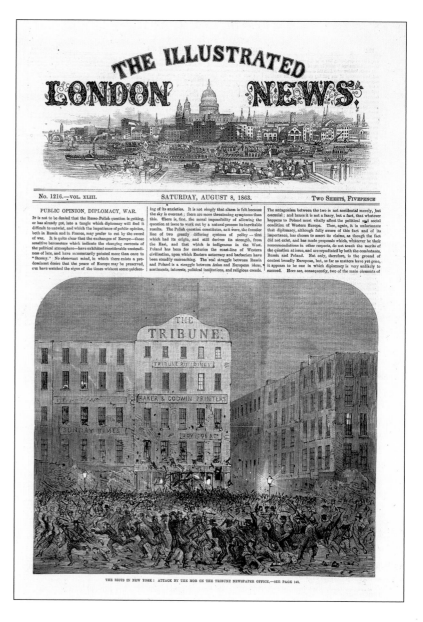

THE RIOTS IN NEW YORK : ATTACK BY THE MOB ON THE TRIBUNE NEWSPAPER OFFICE.—SEE PAGE 143.

of police officials, prominent Republicans, politicians of any kind, and the rich.

Institutions that openly supported the party of Lincoln, and the Union cause, were especially vulnerable. On Printing House Row, the owners of the *Evening Post* and the *New-York Times*—bitterly resented for their staunch support of the war—had to barricade their entrances to keep out the mob, and station men with Gatling guns facing City Hall Park. On Wall Street, banks and brokerage houses placed office workers on their roofs, armed with pots of boiling oil, while navy gunboats took up position out in the East River, ready if necessary to fire onto the mob.

But the crowd's greatest fury was reserved for blacks, whom they blamed for all their woes.

Enraged by the imposition of the first federal draft in American history, angry crowds exploded onto the streets of New York in July 1863. Descending on Printing House Square, the mob started to attack the offices of the *New-York Times,* then fell back, put off by the sight of Gatling guns bristling from the upper windows. They turned instead to the well-barricaded but unarmed offices of the *Tribune,* next door—before being pushed back by units of police rushed over from Brooklyn.

On Good Friday in the spring of 1861—a few days before the start of the Civil War—children from the Colored Orphan Asylum posed in the backyard of the private institution that was their home, on Fifth Avenue and 43rd Street (below). Two years later, on the afternoon of July 13, 1863, the orphans were forced to flee for their lives as a mob broke through the front entrance, smashed and looted the asylum's furniture, then set the building on fire, attacking firemen as they tried to put out the flames (above). As the mob pelted him with rocks, a young Irishman named Paddy McCaffrey escorted the last two dozen children to the safety of the Twentieth Precinct.

At two-thirty, an infuriated mob screaming "burn the nigger's nest" surrounded the Colored Orphan Asylum at Fifth Avenue and Forty-third Street, home to more than two hundred African American children under the age of twelve. All of the terrified children managed to escape out a back door, the older ones carrying the younger ones on their backs, before the mob broke in, hacked apart furniture and toys with axes, then set the building on fire. A ten-year-old girl watching from the street was killed when a dresser heaved from a window struck her in the head.

July 13th, 1863. The Colored Half Orphan Asylum on Fifth Avenue is burned. "Tribune office to be burned tonight." Railroad rails torn up, telegraph wires cut, and so on. If a quarter of what one hears be true, this is an organized insurrection in the interest of the rebellion and Jefferson Davis rules New York today.

George Templeton Strong

Late on the first night of draft riots, an African American cartman named William Jones—trying to defend his wife and child and save his home from being burned—was set upon by a large mob and lynched from a chestnut tree near the corner of Clarkson and Hudson streets in Greenwich Village. Afterward, the crowd built a fire under him and danced around his burning body.

By the end of the first day of rioting, the wealthiest and most important city in the nation lay in a state of anarchy all but complete. As darkness fell, an ominous pall of smoke shrouded New York City. Toward midnight stabs of lightning, and lashing sheets of rain, broke over the town.

> *No sleep. The sultriness pervades the air,*
> *And binds the brain—a dense oppression . . .*
> *Beneath the stars the roof desert spreads*
> *vacant as Libya.*
> *All is hushed near by.*
> *Yet fitfully from far breaks . . .the Atheist roar*
> *of riot . . .*
> *The town is taken by its rats—ship-rats,*
> *And rats of the wharves . . .*
> *And man rebounds whole aeons back in nature.*
> Herman Melville, "The House-Top"

> *July 14th. Eleven p.m. Fire bells clanking, as they have clanked at intervals throughout the evening. . . . There have been sundry collisions between the rabble and the authorities, civil and military. . . . Many details come in of yesterday's brutal, cowardly ruffianism and plunder. Shops were cleaned out and a black man hanged in Carmine Street, for no offence but that of Negritude.*
> George Templeton Strong

On Tuesday, the second day of rioting, the atrocities against African Americans grew worse. On Eighth Avenue, a mob went house to house, searching for black families and interracial couples to hang and burn. On Wednesday, the hottest day of the year, a black shoemaker named James Costello was beaten, kicked, stoned, trampled, and then hanged. A few hours later, a mob of Irish laborers pulled a crippled twenty-two-year-old black coachman named Abraham Franklin from his lodging house. He was tortured, lynched, burned, and mutilated, then dragged through the streets by his genitals.

> *Having been taught by the leaders of the Democratic party to hate the negro, this infuriated band of drunken men, women and children paid special visits to all localities inhabited by the blacks, and murdered all they could lay their hands on. . . . Blacks were chased to the docks, thrown into the river and drowned; while some, after being murdered, were hung to lamp-posts. Between forty and fifty colored persons were killed, and nearly as many maimed for life.*
> An Anonymous Black Eyewitness

Around ten o'clock on Wednesday night—after three full days of anarchy and violence—the first Union troops—the Sixty-fifth New York Regiment—began arriving by ferry from

For nearly four days, New York belonged to the mob. Only after Lincoln sent in Union troops fresh from the fields of Gettysburg was the rebellion put down. Here, soldiers from G Company of New York's Seventh Regiment stand at ease on a street near the Five Points—a handful of the nearly 6,000 troops that had occupied the city by the evening of Thursday, July 16.

Gettysburg. The Seventh Regiment arrived the next morning, and the tide of battle quickly turned. "We soon cleared the streets," Captain H. R. Putnam of the Twelfth U.S. Infantry reported, "and then commenced searching the houses, killed those within that resisted, and took the remainder prisoners. Some of them fought like incarnate fiends, and would not surrender. All such were shot on the spot. The fight lasted about forty minutes. The mob being entirely dispersed, we returned to head-quarters."

The exhausted, sunburned troops Lincoln had sent were almost all local boys, and like the New York police themselves, many were from Irish and German families with strict orders to disperse the immigrant mob and, if necessary, to shoot to kill. Though some Protestant New Yorkers feared the Irish would never fire on their own, in the end the police and soldiers acquitted themselves heroically, fighting and often dying to protect the beleaguered citizens of their town.

It must be remembered . . . that in many wards of the city, the Irish were during the late riot staunch friends of law and order; that Irishmen helped to rescue the colored orphans in the asylum from the hands of the rioters; that a large proportion of the police who behaved throughout the riot with the most exemplary gallantry, are Irishmen; and that the Roman Catholic priesthood to a man used their influence on the side of the law.

Harper's Weekly, August 1863

By Friday, New York had been completely occupied by six thousand federal troops. Except for a few scattered outbursts, calm had been restored. But the city lay shattered. Hundreds of buildings had been burned or destroyed, and $5 million in property ruined. Thousands of black families had lost their homes.

Over three thousand are to-day homeless and destitute, without means of support for their families. It is truly a day of distress to our race. . . . The Irish have become so brutish, that it is unsafe for families to live near them, and while I write there are many now in the stations and country hiding from violence.

Christian Recorder

"A gloom of infamy and shame will hang over New York for centuries," the editor of the black-owned *Christian Recorder* wrote. The loss of life had been appalling. So many bodies were thrown in the river the exact number would never be known. But at least 119 people had been killed, including 11 blacks, 16 soldiers, and 89 rioters, most of them Irish, in the worst instance of civil unrest in American history.

"Nothing delights us more greatly," the *Charleston Daily Courier* declared, "as to hear of Yankees burning, destroying and killing Yankee buildings, Yankee property, and Yankee men."

From Washington, Walt Whitman had followed the nightmarish unfolding of events with horror and disbelief. It had been, he wrote, "the devil's own work all through." In an anguished letter to his mother in Brooklyn, he struggled to make sense of what had happened to his city, and his people: "So the mob has risen at last in New York. It seems the passions of the people were only sleeping, & have burst forth with a terrible fury—I do not feel it in my heart to abuse the poor people, or call for rope or bullets for them—we are in the midst of strange and terrible times—one is pulled a dozen different ways in his mind, and hardly knows what to think or do."

The city's African American population dropped by several thousand in the aftermath of the Draft Riots as hundreds of families left the city, never to return.

It would take decades for New Yorkers to come to terms with what had happened on their own city streets. In the weeks and months following the riots, efforts were made to make restitution to the city's black population. But it was too little, too late.

"The loss of life and property make only a small part of the damage," wrote an African American minister named Dr. J. W. C. Pennington, who had spent his career fighting for the rights of black New Yorkers. "The breaking up of families; the blasting of hopes just dawning; the confidence destroyed; . . . and lastly, the gross insult offered to our character as a people. Relief, and damage money, is well enough. But it cannot atone, fully, for evils done by riots. It cannot bring back our murdered dead. It cannot remove the insults we feel; and . . . it gives us no proof that the people have really changed their minds for the better towards us."

In increasing numbers blacks left the city. As late as 1900, fewer than sixty thousand African Americans made their home in Manhattan—out of a population of almost 2 million.

The draft riots were a defining moment in the history of New York—and a harrowing sign that the city had become a world-class metropolis. Paris and London had had tremendous social explosions in the late eighteenth and early nineteenth centuries. Now Gotham, too, had been marked by blood and come of age. The riots also marked a crucial turning point in the life of New York City, as New York's leaders, shocked by the magnitude of the violence and disorder, vowed never to let it happen again.

Within a year, the first comprehensive public health survey of New York's tenements had been conducted—a mammoth undertaking without precedent in American cities that would lead to the establishment of the Metropolitan Board of Health in 1866, and the first laws regulating housing a year after that. In the decades to come, the city's Metropolitan Police would be transformed into the first modern police force in the country.

The political ramifications of the calamity would in the end prove even more momentous. It was clear now to almost everyone that the city's huge population of immigrant poor could no longer be ignored. The very year of the riots, a forty-year-old local politician named

William M. Tweed, with close ties to the city's immigrant Irish population, was made Grand Sachem of Tammany Hall. One of his first acts was to push through a special low-interest loan program that enabled poor New Yorkers as well as rich to buy their way out of the draft.

THE END COMES

Slowly but surely, the Civil War came to a close, as the industrial might of the urban North inexorably wore the Confederacy down. In New York itself, the war ended as it had begun, with an outpouring in the streets.

On the morning of April 3, 1865, telegraph offices on Wall Street posted the news that Richmond had fallen. As businessmen and clerks spilled out of their offices and workshops and filled the streets in celebration, George Templeton Strong—so often reserved at moments of public emotion—threw himself headlong into the joyous throng of New Yorkers.

An enormous crowd blocked . . . Wall Street. . . . The cheers . . . were spontaneous and involuntary and of vast "magnetizing" power. . . . I think I shall never lose the impressions made by this rude, many-voiced chorale. It [seemed] a revelation of profound national feeling, underlying all our vulgarisms and corruptions, vouchsafed for us in their very focus and centre, Wall Street itself. Men embraced each other and hugged each other; kissed each other, retreated into doorways to dry their eyes and came out again to flourish their hats and hurrah. There will be many sore throats in New York tomorrow.

George Templeton Strong

Less than two weeks later, on Saturday, April 15, church bells began tolling all over Brooklyn and New York. The morning papers carried staggering news: President Abraham Lincoln had been assassinated the night before.

On Portland Avenue in Brooklyn, Walt Whitman and his mother silently passed the morning papers back and forth, too stunned to eat or talk. Late in the afternoon, he took the ferry to Manhattan and walked up Broadway under a darkening sky. The normally bustling thoroughfare was quiet, the storefronts shuttered and hung with black. Here and there people huddled in doorways to escape the steady rain. "Black clouds driving overhead," Whitman wrote in his notebook. "Lincoln's death—black, black, black—as you look toward the sky—long broad black like great serpents undulating in every direction."

Ten days later, a funeral train brought Lincoln's body to New York. Hundreds of thousands of grieving New Yorkers silently lined the streets of Manhattan, as the president's body was borne slowly down Broadway toward city hall, where it lay in state for two days. African Americans were barred from the ceremonies at first, then allowed to march at the last minute, at the very end of the parade. Scalpers sold choice positions along the route for eight dollars apiece. From the second floor of his family's house on East Twenty-eighth Street, seven-year-old Theodore Roosevelt and his brother looked on.

"Parties for the moment do not exist," the *New-York Times* wrote, "while all men of whatever religious faith, of whatever political creed . . . are united perhaps for the first time in the history of the republic in love for the departed, in sympathy with the bereaved. . . . Touching evidence of the firm seat occupied in the popular heart by our lamented President, is the almost universal exhibition by the poor, the very poor people of this city and the adjoining city of Brooklyn."

The war's end, and Lincoln's death, brought New Yorkers together in a rare display of civic harmony. But in the restless, turbulent decades to come, as New York led America into a new age, crucial questions remained. Would it be possible to bridge the enormous chasms dividing Americans, and make the union an enduring reality?

On April 24, 1865, Lincoln's funeral train stopped in New York on its way home from Washington to Springfield, Illinois. After lying in state overnight in city hall, the president's casket was borne up Broadway in a solemn four-hour-long procession—seen here passing Astor Place—that drew nearly a million mourners.

Page 130: Approximately 120,000 New Yorkers paid their last respects to the fallen president at city hall, where Lincoln's casket lay at the head of the staircase in the rotunda.

THE NATION MOURNS.

"THE LOCOMOTIVE
OF THESE
UNITED STATES"

MIKE WALLACE

In the mid-1850s, New York was charging into the future—and cavalierly erasing its past. Businesses were spreading "with such astounding rapidity over the whole lower part of the city," *Putnam's Magazine* fretted in 1853, that they were "prostrating and utterly obliterating every thing that is old and venerable, and leaving not a single land-mark, in token of the former position of the dwelling-places of our ancestors." So thoroughgoing was the razing and rebuilding that some New Yorkers, gripped by unaccustomed nostalgia, fostered efforts at commemoration. The city's yearly *Manuals* began including romanticized prints of "little olde New York," portraying a cozy, drowsy village—a delightful contrast to the mid-century metropolis, all whoosh and whirl.

But back in the early 1800s, whoosh and whirl had been precisely what the town's cozy burghers yearned for. They had known all too well that picturesque somnolence presaged only disaster for Manhattan and its surrounds. Accordingly they had plunged ahead with spectacular energy and imagination, launching one modernizing project after another, each building on the last, each generating exciting new possibilities, until in little more than three decades they succeeded in transforming Washington Irving's sleepy little hamlet into Walt Whitman's booming metropolis.

The indispensable initiative had been the Erie Canal. The great public works project, by providing an inexpensive water route from the Great Lakes to the Hudson River, set midwesterners to plowing canals toward their inland seas. Produce and timber that had once rafted southward along the Ohio and Mississippi rivers to New Orleans now reversed course and headed toward New York. Within a decade, distant agricultural hinterlands had been pulled into Manhattan's orbit—Ohio by 1830, Indiana by 1835, Michigan by 1836—and the seaport at the Hudson's mouth emerged as America's preeminent entrepôt.

Rival coastal cities, facing catastrophe, tried to build their own canals, but frenzied ditchdigging availed them little. Boston was just too far from the western wheat fields and Philadelphia lacked New York's break in the Appalachians. Baltimore, however, was closer to the fertile West, and when a canal proved prohibitively costly, its citizens, with the daring of desperation, decided to build a railroad. By 1830 the Baltimore and Ohio had begun snaking its way west.

Responding to the threat to the city's canal-based primacy, Manhattanites jumped into railroading, though it would take two decades for the biggest projects to come to fruition. By the early 1850s, passengers on the Hudson River Rail Road could scoot north along the riverbank 144 miles to Albany in less than four hours, then ride interconnecting roads west to Buffalo. Alternatively they could board the New York and Erie line and spear diagonally across the state 447 miles to the shores of Lake Erie. As Erie director and ironmonger William E. Dodge jubilantly exclaimed: "The Empire City and the great West, the Atlantic Ocean and inland seas, are by this ligature of iron made one!"

If New Yorkers excelled at gathering the nation's goods into their harbor, they proved equally adept at moving them out again onto the sea lanes to Europe. Since the Black Ball line's success had demonstrated the appeal of regularly scheduled service to Liverpool, competitors had been thronging into the business. By the 1830s, the city could offer shippers an average of three sailings a week to Liverpool and Le Havre, with an average transit time of thirty-nine days. New York's shipbuilders then enhanced the port's appeal by turning out boats of ever greater agility, size, and speed. By the 1850s the East River yards were famed for their great clippers—slender, heavily sparred and canvased vessels, with bows that cut rather than butted the waves.

New York had also pioneered the introduction of steam to navigation with Robert Fulton's breakthrough in 1807. Soon vessels built by his successors were plying coastal and inland waterways in ever growing numbers, greatly facilitating the flow of goods into the port. No steam-powered ship dared an Atlantic crossing, however, until April 23, 1838, when the future hove into view just before noon. The *Sirius*, a small paddle-wheel steam packet nineteen days out of Cork, limped across the Upper Bay, its coal supply all but exhausted, and made landfall to the cheers of a great crowd gathered at the Battery. Most steamers that followed would continue to be of English or European provenance, a function of their governments' willingness to subsidize the new technology (a hundred years later, as a result, most great transatlantic liners would have names like *Queen Mary* and *Normandie*). Nevertheless, the decision of foreign steamers to make Manhattan their primary port of call, along with the spectacular efflorescence of New York's sailing fleet, guaranteed that the city would remain the nation's principal link to Europe.

New York merchants reached out elsewhere on the planet, too. With Latin American markets newly accessible in the wake of anticolonial revolutions, ships arrived in Manhattan from Central and South America with their holds stuffed with Brazilian coffee, Argentine hides, and Mexican silver, then headed back south laden with cargoes of flour, domestic textiles, furniture, carriages, horses, and machinery for sugar mills. The city came to dominate American trade with China, too, and great companies like the House of Low commissioned clipper ships to shave weeks off the voyage to Canton. The new vessels, in turn, left China traders perfectly positioned to cash in on the discovery of gold in California. The tens of thousands of prospectors arriving in San Francisco after 1849 drove the price of necessities sky-high. When a barrel of flour worth $6 back in Manhattan fetched $200 in the gold fields, China traders rerouted their outbound clippers west around South America, rather than east around Africa, and made a stopover in California to maximize returns.

Despite Californian, Chinese, and Latin American initiatives, the European connection remained decisive in determining New York's future. Having adroitly inserted itself between three of the most dynamic regions of the early nineteenth-century global economy—England's manufacturing Midlands, the cotton-producing slave South, and the agricultural Midwest—New York would prosper by shipping cotton and wheat east, by funneling manufactures, cultural goods, labor, and capital west, and by capitalizing on the manifold advantages that accrued to it as the mediator between Europe and the American continent.

COMMERCE AND ITS CORRELATIVES

Ramifications of the city's new status rippled out in all directions from ground zero—the riverfront docks where land and sea converged. Mercantile activities brought an unprecedented multitude of ships into the harbor. On a single day in 1836, 921 vessels lined the East River bulkhead, their bowsprits and carved figureheads looming over South Street, while another 320 bobbed along the Hudson. By 1849 the volume of shipping had tripled, and the vessels that sailed or steamed into the harbor from more than 150 foreign ports carried with them half the nation's imports and departed with nearly one-third of its exports. In the Gold Rush decade (1849–59), ship tonnage through the port jumped by another 60 percent. The result was a cacophonous harbor, with pilots and crews jockeying for berths, while schools of sloops and lighters darted in and out among canal boats, schooners, yachts, barges, ferries, and two-thousand-ton steamers that plowed along at speeds approaching twenty miles per hour.

By 1850 a collar of piers, docks, and slips circled Manhattan below Fourteenth Street—sixty on the East River (favored by sleek Liverpool packets and great square-rigged clippers) and another fifty or more on the Hudson (preferred by deeper-draw coastal and transatlantic steamships). Offshore chaos generated onshore mayhem, as goods were transferred to a profusion of conveyances. In 1857, 598 licensed hacks, 4,500 carts, and 190 express wagons competed to tote bales and barrels around the city. The din was terrific, what with hundreds of iron horseshoes striking cobblestone pavements, boxes rattling, drivers cursing and fighting. The throng and rush along waterfront thoroughfares and on Broadway itself was so enormous—on an average weekday fifteen thousand vehicles rumbled by St. Paul's—that movement was often choked off altogether. Clotted conditions in Man-

hattan prompted promoters on Brooklyn's side of the East River to fill in tidal marshes, build breakwaters, and throw up blocks of docks and warehouses. One of the largest such projects transformed forty acres of Red Hook marshlands into the Atlantic Basin, a massive holding bin capable of sheltering one hundred ships at a time.

With increased traffic came important changes in the scale, organization, and tempo of the city's commercial life. Premier commercial houses grew ever more specialized—concentrating on single commodities, like silks or metals. They grew ever larger, too, erecting five- and six-story warehouses, many handsomely designed in the latest Italianate mode with white marble or brownstone facades. The new structures were difficult to shoehorn into narrow dockside lanes until the Great Fire of 1835, by burning down 674 buildings, allowed the transformation of crooked seventeenth-century alleys into broader, gaslighted thoroughfares.

Metamorphosis was not limited to the mercantile sector. The number of commercial banks flourished—twenty-seven new ones were organized between 1851 and 1853 alone—and by 1857 they had a colossal $40 million out in loans (a good many of them ill-advised, as became clear during the panic of that year). There were new *kinds* of banks, too. Savings institutions accepted deposits primarily from working people, and were allowed to invest only in government-backed securities, like those of the Erie Canal. The canal also spurred development of investment banks. Firms like Prime, Ward & King bought up securities and resold them to wealthy individuals or institutional investors seeking safe and steady dividend income. As many of their clients were London banking houses like the Baring Brothers, New York's investment bankers in effect imported European capital as their mercantile counterparts imported commodities.

As banking emerged from its former status as a mere rib of commerce, becoming a distinct business enterprise with a profit motive all its own, so too did stockbrokering take off in these years. So many millions of dollars poured through the doors of the old Tontine Coffee House in pursuit of canal stocks—trading in which was managed by the New York Stock & Exchange Board (1817)—that by 1830 New York had overtaken Philadelphia as the nation's premier money market. Manhattan solidified its position by assuming the lead role in railroad financing in the 1830s to 1850s.

Flocking to Wall Street along with solid investors came speculative wheeler-dealers who cared little about a company's real world prospects, preferring to manipulate the virtual world of the market itself. Warring cliques of bulls and bears routinely drove prices up and down, using underhanded maneuvers that were not only legal but were widely admired for their daring. By the late 1850s, hundreds of new brokerage houses—sober and speculative alike—had appeared in the city, and the massive volume of trades in

The piers of South Street, at Wall Street, 1865.

shares of railroads, banks, canals, and coal mines had made New York one of the largest and most sophisticated capital markets in the world.

The swelling financial sector, which also included credit reporting firms, and fire, maritime, and life insurance companies, engaged (as had the mercantile firms) in a burst of architectural assertiveness. No longer satisfied with quarters in renovated private residences along Wall Street, some dating from before the Revolution, prosperous bankers and brokers demanded proper offices of suitable scale and grandeur in the regnant fashion—with Greek Revival tem-

ples of the 1830s giving way to brownstone Italianate palazzos in the 1850s.

RETAIL PLEASURES

The tremendous momentum of the wholesale mercantile economy spilled over into a booming retail sector. Jewelers and watchmakers, bookstores and confectioners, tailors and hatters first clustered in profusion around fashionable lower Broadway and then spread northward up the thoroughfare. By the early 1830s, many shops were brilliantly aglow with the new gaslight and, in staying open as late as those of London and Paris, gave New York a lively night-time appearance in marked contrast to Philadelphia's.

Local retailers adopted radically new marketing techniques to increase the volume and velocity of sales. In 1846, dry goods merchant Alexander T. Stewart opened a cavernous new store on the east side of Broadway between Chambers and Reade streets. The magnificent Renaissance palazzo, five stories tall and sheathed in dazzling white Tuckahoe marble, with a street-level facade boasting fifteen huge plate-glass windows, soon won the popular sobriquet of Marble Palace. But the real innovations were indoors, where Stewart encouraged customers to stroll at leisure, inspecting wares laid out on polished mahogany counters and marble shelves, everything clearly tagged with a set price and organized into separate departments. Stewart's emporium was a sensational success. Outside, private carriages jammed Broadway. Competitors like Brooks Brothers set up shop nearby in the 1850s, as did specialized stores like Tiffany & Company. Throngs of window shoppers now promenaded up and down Broadway—smartly dressed women, all ribbons and silks and Parisian fashions, and dandified males with kid gloves, thin trouser legs, and patent leather shoes. At night gas lamps and illuminated store windows captured the streams of pedestrians in their glow, and the colored lamps on carriages and omnibuses transformed Broadway into a river of light.

With New York now established as both a center of wholesale bargains and a point of entry for the latest European fashions, commercial travelers and tourists alike descended on Manhattan. Every spring and fall, thousands of prosperous and adventuresome storekeepers converged on the city, prowling its countinghouses and auction rooms in search of bargains. Tourists flocked to Stewart's and the other great emporia, and to myriad other wonders, such as P. T. Barnum's American Museum and the burgeoning number of theaters and pleasure gardens.

To deal with the clamor for space, old private homes were converted to boardinghouses, and builders and investors flung up new hotels. John Jacob Astor's six-story, three-hundred-room Park Hotel (soon renamed the Astor House) opened on Broadway in 1836 and remained the nation's most prestigious hostelry until the 1850s. Then, when a new flood of tourists and visiting businessmen poured in on the new rail lines, drawn by up-to-date wonders like the Crystal Palace (a rival to London's), the crush nourished a new spate of hotel construction. Nineteen deluxe establishments appeared on Broadway alone between 1850 and 1854, paced by the six-story, six-hundred-room St. Nicholas Hotel (1853), soon famous for its white marble facade, walnut wainscoting, frescoed ceilings, and technological wonders such as gaslight chandeliers, hot running water, central heating, and its telegraph in the lobby. In 1859 it was in turn outclassed by the Fifth Avenue Hotel at the corner of Twenty-third

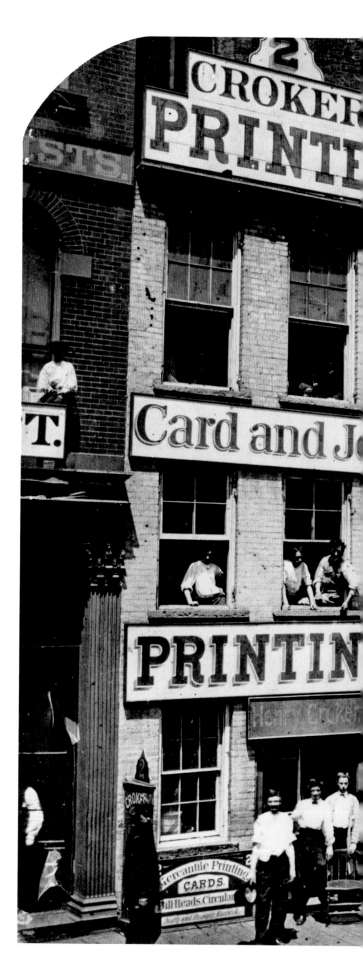

View of the west side of Hudson Street, between Chambers and Reade streets, in August 1865.

Civil War victory parade marching up Fifth Avenue, spring 1865.

Street. Hailed by a correspondent for the *London Times* as "a larger and handsomer building than Buckingham Palace," the Fifth Avenue offered an unprecedented extravagance: a passenger elevator, described variously as a "perpendicular railway intersecting each story" or "a little parlour going up by machinery."

MACHINE SHOP AND MANUFACTORY

Elevators—produced by Elisha Graves Otis, who first displayed his crucial safety device before Crystal Palace crowds—were yet another spinoff of the great commercial boom. Indeed, it was in these decades that New York emerged as the nation's leading manufacturing center—and one of the fastest-growing industrial areas in the world.

Much manufacturing was a direct offshoot of commerce. A great shipbuilding complex sprang up along the shores of the East River to turn out sturdy packets for the Black Ball line, clippers for the China trade, swift slavers that could

outrun naval patrols, and vessels for the Russian and Italian navies.

Production of steamboats—and then railroads—in turn galvanized New York's iron foundries and machine shops to meet the need for the thirty-ton marine engines, the enormous bedplates on which a ship's machinery rested, and for locomotives, tracks, and boilers. Ironworks rose along the East and Hudson river waterfronts, growing steadily larger in extent and employment rolls. Largest of the lot, an acknowledged wonder of the age, was the sprawling Novelty Iron Works on the East River shore at the foot of Twelfth Street, a five-acre maze of buildings that employed as many as twelve hundred workers by the early 1850s.

The iron industry also benefitted from the growth of wholesale warehouses and retail stores, especially after inventor James Bogardus developed and patented a method for mass producing cast-iron building elements. Bogardus and his emulators prefabricated columns, panels, and arches, packed them in straw, loaded them on horse-drawn drays, and shipped them to construction sites, where they were raised and bolted into place, ready for painting and the installation of plate-glass windows. New York had commenced a love affair with metal-frame structures that would culminate in its passion for skyscrapers later in the century.

Architectural ironworks were also kept busy turning out large multistory factories, themselves the product of a momentous transformation in manufacturing. In trade after trade, small workshops were giving way to huge production units. Printing and book publishing were among the pioneers, encouraged by the brisk growth of a national market for reading matter, the easy access to western readers afforded by railroads and the Erie Canal, and the yoking of steam power to printing. Robert Hoe imported the country's first Napier cylinder press and improved it, and soon Harper & Brothers was using the new machine in a four-story plant on Cliff Street. By 1853, when its workforce of five hundred issued more than 4.5 million volumes, Harper was among the largest employers in New York City. When its Cliff Street plant burned down that year, the firm immediately set James Bogardus to building two splendid cast-iron, five-story structures—a half-acre complex on Franklin Square that secured Harper's position as largest of the 112 publishers in New York City, and one of the largest in the world.

There were, however, drawbacks to erecting giant industrial plants in Manhattan. Overcrowded streets, jammed docks, and a rapid rise in the price of land led some big manufacturers, like the piano firm of Steinway & Sons, to seek a more satisfactory perch on the northern edge of built-up Manhattan or across the East River—thus Frederick C. Havemeyer built his million-dollar sugar refinery on the Williamsburg waterfront.

Yet despite the exodus of larger companies to an industrial belt engirdling Manhattan, New York City remained the country's number one manufacturing city because the great bulk of production took place not in king-sized ironworks, factories, and refineries but in small frame or brick houses near the waterfront, without steam power or other elaborate equipment, and typically involved the production of light consumer goods—shoes, furniture, and clothing for wholesalers or auction houses. These manufacturers stayed in Manhattan in part because it was easiest there to get information about, and ship to, distant markets; because New York was itself a tremendous market; because the city provided access to other manufacturers, who produced components they needed; and above all because New York was awash in cheap labor. Irish peasants, German craftsmen, and English factory hands flooded into New York because it was the principal western terminus of transatlantic traffic. In 1854 alone, the United States accepted 428,000 immi-

grants, of whom roughly 319,000 descended on Manhattan—more than the entire population of the city in 1840.

The new arrivals helped make Manhattan a manufacturing powerhouse, but the surge in productivity and profits was accompanied by a sharp drop in quality of life for many in the city's working population. The old artisanal universe collapsed, taking paternalist institutions like apprenticeship down with it, leaving workers to fend for themselves. Master craftsmen evolved into entrepreneurial contractors who, lashed by competition, were impelled to depress wages to ever lower levels. The process was particularly quick and brutal in the men's clothing trade. New York wholesalers, auctioneers, and jobbers presided over the creation of a huge new national market in mens' ready-mades—"Negro cottons" for slaves, dungarees for farmers and miners, and "slop" clothing for the urban working classes. Manufacturers stepped up production by expanding the number of women employed—paying them less than half what men received—by turning to child labor, and by hiring immigrants off the boat.

Plummeting wages led to formation of the first labor unions, though the new organizations found it hard to establish a permanent footing amid the abundant oversupply of workers. There would be still other unfortunate aspects of the great commercial boom, among them downward lurches of a newly arrived business cycle, conflict between ethnic and religious groups for access to jobs and housing, racial conflict between insecure whites and newly freed blacks, and a startling increase in the numbers of people (particularly women) who found themselves relegated to the city's poorhouse or penal institutions.

The plight of workers and the growing number of destitute didn't make it into the large number of prideful, self-congratulatory guidebooks that appeared during the boom years, however. Despite the miniboom in nostalgia for the good olde days, New York's prosperous classes were in general delighted by their city's emerging metropolitan status and not shy about trumpeting its virtues. Addressing a national, indeed an international, audience, the guidebooks—many of which were underwritten by the new monster hotels or prepared for visitors to the Crystal Palace—proclaimed the city's civic grandeur, its commercial entrepôts, its palaces of pleasure, its charitable and educational institutions. In Bunyanesque prose they boasted of the sheer scale of it all: their city had the greatest concentration of wealth and energy and people in America, it was the largest market in America. They saw themselves as the vanguard of American development, and applauded the boast of George Francis Train in 1857 that New York was "the locomotive of these United States," pulling the rest of the nation faster and faster into the future: "twenty miles an hour—thirty—forty!"

Though manufacturing and finance would increasingly dominate New York's economy in the years after the Civil War, the city's commercial cornerstone—shipping and trade—would continue to expand at an astonishing rate. By 1868, when this bird's-eye view of the Upper Bay was painted by George Deegan, more than 30,000 ships a year were passing through the Narrows, carrying more than half of the entire nation's foreign trade—nearly half a billion dollars' worth of goods in all.

SUNSHINE

1865–1898

AND SHADOW

The shapes arise!
Shapes of factories, arsenals, foundries,
   markets,
Shapes of the two-threaded tracks of
   railroads,
Shapes of the sleepers of bridges, vast
   frameworks, girders, arches. . . .
The main shapes arise!
Shapes of Democracy total, result
   of centuries,
Shapes ever projecting other shapes.
Shapes of turbulent manly cities. . . .
Shapes bracing the earth and braced with
   the whole earth.
                    Walt Whitman
                    "Song of the Broad-Axe," 1867

The Brooklyn Bridge, 1881. Even before completion, the great bridge brought an entirely new scale to the city. This view—taken two years before the opening of the span— shows the floor beams of the roadway being suspended from the web of hanging steel cables. The two men in the foreground (probably engineers surveying the work) stand on a temporary footbridge set up to allow workmen to install the main cables.

THE ANGEL OF THE WATERS

In the summer of 1865, as four long years of Civil War came to an end, Frederick Law Olmsted returned to New York, and with his old partner, Calvert Vaux, resumed work on Central Park.

During his work for the U.S. Sanitary Commission, Olmsted had seen more of the horrors of war than he cared to remember. Now he had come home, to try and heal the wounds the city and country had inflicted on themselves.

That year, as finishing work on the park continued, the sculptress Emma Stebbins—sister of park board president Henry G. Stebbins—completed drawings for a special memorial to the Union naval dead, to be located on the park's main terrace.

Eight years later the statue was complete—the first major public work in New York executed by a woman. Crowning the incomparable Bethesda Fountain at the very heart of the park and of the immense city already beginning to grow up around it, Stebbins had set a simple life-size bronze figure—the *Angel of the Waters*, drawn from the Gospel of St. John, symbol of the healing power of nature.

Central Park was finished at last.

Ordinary New Yorkers took to Stebbins's masterpiece at once—though many critics did not, outraged by the statue's cost, and by the statue itself, which looked, one writer said, like "a servant girl executing a polka." But despite her homespun appearance, or perhaps because of it, visitors were moved by the unassuming beauty of Stebbins's angel: by the simple power of her gesture—one arm upraised as if to bless, or simply touch, the restless tide of humanity endlessly ebbing and flowing about her—and by the soothing circumference of water around her, which seemed to open a quiet parenthesis in the center of the bustling city.

In the years to come, Olmsted would extend his remarkable vision to cities across America: from Prospect Park across the East River in Brooklyn—which he and Vaux considered their true masterpiece—to green spaces in Boston, Chicago, St. Louis, and Detroit.

Central Park itself would finally become the democratic meeting ground Vaux and Olmsted had always dreamed of—if not always in ways they had envisioned—as new forms of public

Looking south across
Central Park Lake, 1896.
The designers Frederick
Law Olmsted and Calvert
Vaux returned to New
York after the Civil War to
put the finishing touches
on their great park pro-
ject, including the centerpiece of the entire design:
the Bethesda Terrace,
whose central fountain
culminated in a hauntingly
beautiful bronze figure,
the *Angel of the Waters*,
by the sculptress Emma
Stebbins. Vaux considered
the Terrace to be the
"drawing room" of the
park, while Olmsted noted
that its expansive views
"invite . . . observers to
leisurely contemplation."
By the 1870s, the broad
plaza had become
one of the most popular
gathering places in the
city, especially on
Sundays.

For 200 years, this venerable pear tree, right, stood at the corner of Third Avenue and 13th Street, where Peter Stuyvesant himself had planted it back in 1667. Stuyvesant's estate had long since disappeared, along with the rest of the old Dutch farms—the lots carved up, then paved over and built upon with streets, stores, and houses. In February 1867, after a massive winter storm, the scarred and withered veteran finally succumbed to the ravages of time and the city and was pulled down—severing the last living connection to the old Dutch settlement.

B. Quackinbush & Son, Druggists, 703 Greenwich Street, near Amos Street (today's West Tenth Street), in 1880, opposite. The proprietors and staff of a Greenwich Village pharmacy pose proudly in front of their shop, whose trade is revealed not only by a large painted sign but by the carved wooden mortar-and-pestle symbols, placed atop the canopy supports at the curb.

closely together, poor and rich, young and old, Jew and Gentile. I have seen a hundred thousand thus congregated. Is it doubtful that it does men good to come together in this way in pure air and under the light of heaven?

      Frederick Law Olmsted

Inscribed in Central Park was an extraordinary vision of what a great democratic metropolis might be.

Yet beyond its borders, tremendous tensions remained. The park itself would soon be embroiled in a bitter struggle over who controlled the city's future: middle-class reformers, robber barons and financiers, a shrewd new class of professional politicians, or the people themselves.

In 1870, Olmsted would be driven from his post by the Grand Sachem of Tammany Hall, Boss William M. Tweed—who saw the park's potential not for spiritual uplift but for political patronage and lucrative commercial concessions.

In the decades to come—as the forces unleashed by the Civil War brought a stunning new scale to the city and the country—two powerful impulses would vie for supremacy in the soul of the metropolis: the hunger for wealth, and the search for something higher; the yearning for community, and unfettered greed.

Between 1865 and 1898, as the city grew, building dazzling new structures of commerce and trade, New York would be caught uneasily between two worlds.

During that time it would become home to the greatest concentration of wealth in human history. It would also become home to the greatest concentration of poverty, and to the greatest division of rich and poor, not one city but two: one dazzling and one benighted—one virtuous and one vice ridden—one city of sunshine, as guidebooks frequently pointed out, and another of shadow.

Year after year, as the city grew and the immense chasms haunting it grew wider, a crucial question remained.

Would it be possible to bridge the two cities and make New York whole?

Whoever writes of New York truly, will do so in lines of light and gloom. Life here is more intense; crime is more vivid and daring; the votaries of fashions and pleasure more pas-

transportation, like the Metropolitan Elevated Railway, soon brought poor New Yorkers as well as rich up to the park on weekends, and then carried the city itself northward into new residential districts that soon flanked the park.

By 1869, more than 8.5 million people a year were visiting Central Park—which had become, the *New-York Times* declared, "a majestic breathing space for the life of the city."

In winter, night skating on the lake drew twenty thousand people at a time—the immense crowds illuminated by great calcium flares—while in summer forty thousand people gathered on the mall for free band concerts.

"When one is inclined to despair of the country," the editor of the *New York Herald* observed, "let him go to the Central Park on a Saturday, and spend a few hours there looking at the people—not those who come in gorgeous carriages, but those who arrive on foot, or in those exceedingly democratic conveyances, the streetcars."

[Here are] all classes, represented with common purpose, competitive with none, disposing of jealousy toward none, each adding by his mere presence to the pleasure of all the others; all helping to the greater happiness of each. You may often see vast numbers of persons brought

sionate and open. Great cities must ever be cen-
ters of light and darkness, the home of the best
and worst of our race; holding within them-
selves the highest talent for good and evil.

The Reverend Matthew Hale Smith,
1868, *Sunshine and Shadow in New York*

THE GILDED AGE

In February 1867, Samuel Clemens—a thirty-two-year-old journalist and travel writer from Missouri, not yet famous as Mark Twain—returned to New York after an absence of almost thirteen years.

He was struck with wonder by the changes since his last visit—by the extraordinary growth that had, he wrote, "increased the population [by] a quarter of a million souls," and covered "her waste places with acres upon acres of costly buildings"; and by the ever-widening extremes, that had "made five thousand men wealthy," while a million others found it "a matter of the closest kind of scratching to get along."

In the coming months, Clemens would finish reinventing himself as Mark Twain, and with the help of New York's publishing and publicity machine, finish launching a brilliant literary career.

But though fascinated by the gaudy spectacle of the metropolis, he never felt at home in the restless, sprawling city—which by the time of his visit was rapidly becoming the capital of what he himself would call "the Gilded Age."

June 1867. I have at last, after several months'
experience, made up my mind that [New York]
is a splendid desert—a domed and steepled soli-
tude, where a stranger is lonely in the midst of
a million of his race. . . . Every man seems to
feel that he has got the duties of two lifetimes
to accomplish in one, and so he rushes, rushes,
rushes, and never has time to be companion-
able—never has any time at his disposal to fool
away on matters which do not involve dollars
and duty and business. . . . The natural result
is . . . the serene indifference of the New Yorker
to everybody and everything without the pale
of his private and individual circle.

Mark Twain

As Twain could see, New York City—more than any other place in America—had won the Civil War.

Looking north along Broadway from Trinity Church, 1865. The sprawling industrial city did not favorably impress visitors familiar with the grandeur of European capitals. "The first impression of New York," a young French traveler named Ernest Duvergier de Hauranne wrote in 1864, "is that it is repulsive and vulgar. The broken pavements, the muddy streets, the squares overrun with grass and underbrush, the disreputable horse cars, and the irregular houses plastered with huge handbills have the careless ugliness of an open-air bazaar. The old cities of Europe all have character; this has nothing but commonplaces."

One of the most desirable residential blocks in the city, Lafayette Place (now Lafayette Street)—seen here in an 1866 view looking south from Great Jones Street—had been originally laid out by the millionaire real-estate magnate John Jacob Astor, who joined several of its properties to create a site for the first public library in the city, the Astor Library, whose building would later become home to the Public Theater.

In 1866, at the urging of a hatter named Genin—whose shop was located on the west side of Broadway—this $14,000 cast-iron footbridge was erected at Fulton Street to ease the movement of shoppers across the traffic-choked thorough-fare. From the moment it opened, however, merchants on the *east* side of Broadway—notably Genin's rival, Knox Hats—complained that it blocked the sun from their storefronts and, within a year, had succeeded in having the structure taken down.

Four years of brutal warfare had proved once and for all that the nation's future lay in the city—as Hamilton had predicted—not in the countryside—as Jefferson would have preferred.

It had also unleashed the city's industrial capacity as nothing else had.

Supercharged by the insatiable demands of war, the factories and shipyards of Brooklyn and New York had exploded, doubling their productive output in just four years, and churning out an endless supply of guns and ironclads, hardtack and medical supplies, uniforms and shoes.

To pay for it all, Wall Street bankers had arranged for $2.5 billion in financing for the federal government, and Congress, in turn, had restructured the banking system of the entire nation around New York—making it

the "Central Reserve City" of America and the undisputed financial clearinghouse of the United States.

As a river of silver and gold bullion poured into Manhattan, a host of new exchanges sprang up—in petroleum, mining, cotton, corn, dry goods, produce, and gold—while older ones were consolidated and expanded. "The ascendancy of dollars," the English novelist Anthony Trollope observed while the war still raged, "is written on every paving stone along Fifth Avenue, down Broadway, and up Wall Street."

By 1865, the New York Stock Exchange, which had started life under a buttonwood tree on Wall Street less than a century before, was trading nearly $3 billion a year in securities from its massive new headquarters on Broad Street.

Painted by William Holbrook Beard in 1879, *The Bulls and Bears in the Market* captures the spirit of unfettered competition on Wall Street in the years after the Civil War, transforming the market's two figurative "breeds"— bulls, who foresee prices rising, and bears, who believe prices are about to fall—into actual animals, locked in a life-or-death struggle. Beard framed his fanciful vision of the street's daily life with a careful depiction of the street itself— precisely rendering the facades of the new Stock Exchange and Custom House (the templelike structure at right, built in 1842 on the site of the old Federal Hall), as well as subtle details such as the letters "W.U."—Western Union—inscribed on the wooden telegraph pole at far left.

No one embodied the shift in the city's economy after the Civil War more than Commodore Cornelius Vanderbilt, opposite, the onetime ferryboat operator from Staten Island who by the 1850s had become the owner of the largest steamship line in the world. During the war years, Vanderbilt sold off most of his fleet to buy up a series of short-line railroads and consolidate them into the first national system, the New York Central—extending New York's centrality from shipping and canals to the networks of steel track that were now linking the continent together. By the time of his death in 1877, Vanderbilt's fortune was estimated to exceed $100 million—making him the richest man in America.

Almost overnight, New York had become the second largest financial center in the world after London.

"Not Byzantium, nor London, nor Paris, nor Moscow," one New Yorker proudly declared, "can now surpass the future certainties of this thirteen-mile-long island of Manhattan."

And there was more. Four years of bloody warfare and strife had unleashed a tremendous urge for union in America—along with the means of achieving it for the first time on a truly continental scale: the railroads.

In the years to come, nothing would change New York—or the country—more than the unimaginably vast enterprise.

The railroads required, Henry Adams later wrote, "the energies of a generation . . . to be created—capital, banks, mines, furnaces, shops, power-houses, technical knowledge, mechanical population, together with a steady remodeling of social and political habits, ideas, and institutions to fit the new scale and suit the new conditions. The generation between 1865 and 1895 was already mortgaged to the railways, and no one knew it better than the generation itself."

[I am living] in the noonday glory of the Great Civilization, a witness of its gaunt power, sordid splendour and mean ambitions. . . . Wonderful in scientific marvels . . . in material inflation which it calls progress . . . it is a civilization which has destroyed the simplicity and repose of life; replaced its contentment, its poetry . . . with money fever.

Mark Twain

On Wall Street, there was money to be made as never before, as the booming bull market begun during the war accelerated almost out of control—fueled by the tremendous burst of railroad construction already reshaping the city and the country.

As the age of ships gave way to the age of rail and steam, seventy-five-year-old Cornelius Vanderbilt—"the Commodore"—sold off much of his vast shipping empire and reinvested in railroads, ruthlessly consolidating seventeen smaller lines to form a single giant system, called the New York Central: the first national railroad in America.

When the line was complete, passengers could board one of Vanderbilt's trains in Chicago and not step off until they reached Manhattan, nearly a thousand miles away. On arrival, they entered the city through a gateway unlike anything they had ever seen. The Grand Central Depot, two hundred feet wide, a hundred feet tall, and more than four city blocks long, could hold nearly a hundred trains and fifteen thousand people at a time under a vast roof of iron and glass—the largest interior space on the North American continent.

By 1865, when this view of its new Broad Street headquarters was taken, the New York Stock Exchange boasted more than a thousand members—ten times the number of just a decade before. Though much larger than the exchange's earlier quarters, the new building soon proved inadequate for the city's exploding financial markets, and officials found it necessary to expand the structure in 1871—just six years after it was completed—and again in 1879, when the size of the central trading floor was more than doubled.

What the Erie Canal had done with water and the telegraph with wire, the New York Central did with track—reshaping the geography of the continent around New York.

It also made Commodore Vanderbilt the richest man in America, by far. An eccentric autocrat, utterly indifferent to public opinion, the old man traveled everywhere he could now in his private red-and-yellow railway car, routinely terrorized competitors, and—despite a personal fortune that exceeded $100 million—almost never gave to charity, on principle. "Let others do what I have done," he said, "and they need not be around here begging."

Year after year, the boom went on.

In 1866, the Atlantic telegraph cable went into service, directly linking New York and London for the first time, and speeding the flow of European capital to new investment opportunities in the American West, made possible by the railroads.

By 1869, foreign investors held $1.5 billion in American securities—a quarter of a billion in railroad stock alone—and New York had become a financial funnel between the money centers of Europe and the rapidly industrializing West.

"A strange craziness is abroad in the land," the editor of *The Round Table* observed uneasily, as money poured into Wall Street. "Some mysterious spirit of evil has led our people into the blindest, wildest infatuation. Wild and foolish speculation . . . At least half the people are living beyond their means."

"The light of Mammon gleams on nearly every face in Broadway and Wall Street," another

After gaining control of the Harlem, Hudson, and New Haven railroads in the 1860s, Commodore Vanderbilt expanded service and extended existing lines, which in turn encouraged the growth of new commuter suburbs across upper Manhattan, the Bronx, and Westchester. In 1874, he built this temporary rail trestle, located at 100th Street and Fourth Avenue (today's Park Avenue), to maintain service on the Harlem line while a permanent viaduct was constructed. At the time the view was taken, most of the surrounding area remained rural, but new rows of brownstones—their construction spurred by the expansion of the railroad itself—can already be seen rising in the distance.

Upon its completion in 1871, Commodore Vanderbilt's Grand Central Depot, left, at 42nd Street and Fourth Avenue, became the city's prime gateway and a tourist attraction in its own right. Built to disperse the smoke and steam of locomotives, the station's iron-and-glass train shed—100 feet tall, 200 feet wide, and stretching four city blocks long—was the largest interior space on the North American continent, spacious enough to hold 15,000 people and nearly 100 trains at one time.

The steam-powered locomotives and wooden cars of the Metropolitan Elevated Railway (quickly nicknamed the El) flashed along at 15 miles an hour, on tracks raised 30 feet above the street—running "so near the houses," novelist William Dean Howells wrote, "that you might shake hands with the inhabitants and see what they had for dinner." The first line opened on Greenwich Street in 1872 (above left), with trains running every two minutes; soon new lines were being extended up the length of Manhattan (the view below shows iron framework being installed at Ninth Avenue and 65th Street). By 1880, four separate elevated lines were transporting 200,000 people a day (the view above right shows the serpentine stretch called the "snake curve" at Coenties Slip in lower Manhattan). "Ephemeral, precipitate, hurried," an amazed English visitor wrote after riding one of the new trains, "we seemed to be running at full speed on nothing through the air."

The station and tunnel entrance of Alfred Ely Beach's Pneumatic Railway, in a view taken soon after the opening of the line in 1870. One of the system's ornate fittings is visible on the left—a gilded statue, supporting a gaslight chandelier.

By 1865, lower Manhattan had become one of the most dangerously congested places on earth. The commercial advantages of its compact geography had created an economic monster all but choking on its own explosive growth.

North of the Wall Street financial district, block after block of tall, dark factories—tanneries, chemical and paint manufacturers, iron foundries and textile companies—spewed noxious fumes into the air, and an unending river of raw materials and finished goods into the already jammed streets. Along Broadway, horse-drawn trolleys and horse-drawn streetcars—now carrying *35 million passengers a year*—vied with an endless stream of wagons, trucks, vans, carriages, and hackney cabs.

"In going to and from my meals," Mark Twain complained on a visit before the war, "I go by the way of Broadway—and to *cross* Broadway is the rub—but once across, it is *the* rub for two or three squares. My plan—and how could I choose another, when there *is* no other—is to get into the crowd; and when I get in, I am borne, and rubbed, and crowded along, and need scarcely trouble myself about using my own legs; and when I get out, it seems like I had been pulled to pieces and very badly put together again."

Something, everyone agreed, had to be done. In 1867, as plans for the Metropolitan Elevated Railway got under way, Alfred Ely Beach—the enterprising editor of *Scientific American*, and a sometime inventor—came up with a novel idea. Certain that the future of public transportation lay not above the congested streets but below them, Beach proposed building an "underground pneumatic railway"—a subsurface train propelled by blasts of compressed air.

Setting out to win city support for his farsighted system, Beach ran headlong into Boss Tweed, who saw no reason to jeopardize the success of the new elevated lines (in which he had a large financial interest) by allowing a competing system to proceed. Undaunted, Beach went ahead anyway—in secret. Obtaining permission to build an underground postal tube for the transportation of mail, he instructed his crew to make the tunnel nine feet wide—large enough to carry passengers.

For two months, Beach's men burrowed in secret beneath lower Broadway, working by candlelight so close to the surface they could hear the sound of traffic rumbling overhead. At one point along the route, they ran into the wall of an old Dutch fortification, and had to take it out stone by stone.

Finally, on February 26, 1870, Beach unveiled his experimental system. "Fashionable Reception Held in the Bowels of the Earth!" the *New York Herald* declared, as crowds of curious New Yorkers went underground to explore the city's first subway. Beach had appointed the single station of his system with frescoes, chandeliers, a grand piano, and a bubbling fountain. The "train" itself—a single cylindrical car outfitted with richly upholstered seats for twenty-two people—was driven through the 312-foot tunnel by an immense fan. When the car reached the end of its abbreviated run, the fan was reversed—sucking the car back the other way.

Though 400,000 people rode Beach's line during its first year of operation, the Panic of 1873 extinguished all hope for additional financing. One year later, Beach was forced to close the line. For a time, he rented the tunnel out as a wine cellar, then as a shooting gallery. It was eventually sealed up and forgotten.

In February 1912—nearly a decade after the city had been linked by a massive subway system able to carry millions of passengers a day—workmen digging a new line near City Hall Park broke through a wall of rock and stumbled upon the ghostly system Alfred Ely Beach had built 40 years before. Except for some rotted wood, the lavish station looked much as it had the day Beach closed it in 1874, with its cut-glass chandeliers and ornate fountain, dry now, but still intact. The tiny railroad car still sat on the tracks in the middle of the station, patiently waiting for its next load of passengers—which never came.

The remnants of Beach's Pneumatic Railway, after being uncovered by subway construction workers in 1912.

onlooker agreed, as the frenzy of speculation—unconstrained by regulation of any kind—brought a brazen new class of sharp-eyed financiers to the fore.

There was Daniel Drew, the unscrupulous, nearly illiterate treasurer of the Erie Railroad, who happily destroyed the stock value of his own company to realize a quick profit.

There was James Fisk, a flamboyant financier and ladies' man, who routinely bribed judges, arranged for the arrest of business rivals, and once hired forty thugs to impersonate the stockholders of the Albany and Susquehanna Railroad.

And there was Jay Gould, a dapper, swarthy financial wizard known as "Mephistopheles," beneath whose prim and deaconlike manner lurked an insatiable appetite for making money by whatever means possible.

On Friday, September 24, 1869, Gould and Fisk conspired to corner the market in American gold, using money Gould had embezzled from the stockholders of the Erie Railroad. The outrageous scheme failed, but not before the two men had driven one broker to suicide, destroyed several other stockbroking houses, and briefly paralyzed the entire American economy on what was forever after known as "Black Friday."

"The genuine aristocracy of the city," Mark Twain wrote, "stand stunned and helpless under the new order of things. They find themselves supplanted by upstart princes of shoddy. . . . They move into remote new streets up town, and talk feelingly of the crash which is to come when the props are knocked from under this flimsy edifice of prosperity."

Money is made easily by many in New York; fortunes are acquired in a day, families go from a shanty on a back street to a brown-stone front in upper New York, but they carry with them their vulgar habits and disgust those who from social position are compelled to invite them to their houses.

The Reverend Matthew Hale Smith

And still, the juggernaut of speculation rolled on—powering a burst of physical growth unlike anything the city had yet seen.

By 1869, the same steam and steel revolution unifying the continent was transforming Manhattan itself with astonishing speed—bringing vast upper reaches of the island within easy commuting distance of the congested commercial districts downtown.

In little more than a decade, four elevated railroad lines—soon known as the El—had been built the length of Manhattan, and the Upper East and Upper West sides had exploded in a frenzy of construction, as block after block was filled with middle-class row houses and working-class tenements, at the rate of more than two thousand new buildings a year.

Once, transit lines had *followed* patterns of growth. Now they helped create them. "Put the road there," Commodore Vanderbilt declared, "and people will go there to live." By 1870, Vanderbilt's commuter lines had extended across the Harlem River to the Bronx, where open countryside would soon be annexed in anticipation of still more development.

Year by year, isolated farmlands in the far-flung Bronx—along with tiny hamlets in the county of Queens, and old Dutch estates on Staten Island—were pulled into the orbit of the rapidly growing metropolis, which in the next thirty years would expand to *fifteen* times its prewar size.

Even New Yorkers like George Templeton Strong, who had witnessed the boom following the Erie Canal, were amazed by the rapidity of the city's growth.

March 18th, 1865. Crossed at Wall Street ferry, and explored sundry new districts of Brooklyn. . . . I hereby prophesy that in 1900 A.D. Brooklyn will be the city and New York will be the suburb. It is inevitable if both go on growing as they have grown for the last forty years. Brooklyn has room to spread and New York has not.

George Templeton Strong

Across the East River, the once quiet residential paradise Walt Whitman had called the "city of homes and churches," was growing at an even more impressive rate than its sister city on Manhattan.

By 1867, there were 352 churches in Brooklyn, which had become a major manufacturing center in its own right, and—with 400,000 residents of its own—America's third largest city.

From Olmsted and Vaux's newly completed Prospect Park, blocks of elegant row houses

[The city of Brooklyn] which, in 1834, had hardly one and a half square miles of closely built houses, now has about 34 miles of densely populated houses and factories, with numerous churches, school-houses, theaters, halls and vast warehouses. [And it] is pushing forward with more energy than ever before to occupy those lands whose virgin soil is yet unbroken.
Henry Stiles

radiated out along wide, tree-lined parkways—also designed by the two men—that pushed east into the open lands of Long Island, and south toward the ocean—a suburban haven for businessmen and their families weary of the high cost and hubbub of Manhattan.

And yet, even as Brooklyn's elite shrank away from their city's rude, sprawling cousin across the East River, Brooklyn itself was becoming "a kind of sleeping place for New York," as the English novelist Charles Dickens remarked—and the first commuter suburb in the nation.

By 1867, more than a third of Brooklyn's working population went to jobs in Manhattan every day, and five ferry lines ran back and forth between the two cities, carrying 50 million passengers a year.

"Brooklyn works for New York," the journalist Julian Ralph wrote, "and is paid off like a shop-girl on Saturday nights."

It is a vast aggregation of streets and houses and buildings, with a government of its own. Yet many things it has not got—things which many a little town could put it to blush. [It] has no hotels worthy of its size. It has not one morning newspaper. It has no vicious section or houses of evil savor, no gambling dens, no speculative exchanges. New York supplies all these things for it.

Harper's Weekly

By 1867, only one obstacle seemed to stand in the way of the restlessly expanding cities—the treacherous half-mile-wide tidal strait dividing New York from Brooklyn.

When the East River froze solid during the frigid winter of 1867, locking the ferries in ice and crippling commerce between the two cities for weeks, a daring idea took hold.

It so happens that the work which is likely to be our most durable monument, and which is likely to convey some knowledge of us to the most remote posterity, is a work of bare utility; not a shrine, not a fortress, not a palace, but a bridge.

Montgomery Schuyler

By 1870, when this view of Brooklyn Heights was taken, the settlement across the East River had become America's third largest city, home now to more than 400,000 people. Sprawling 34 square miles across Long Island, the city of Brooklyn was already larger than Manhattan Island, and had endless room to grow—a fact that helped to keep its property costs relatively low. "It is possible for a clerk to own a house in Brooklyn," *Harper's Weekly* observed a few years later. "It is easier for a clerk to fly than own one in New York."

Numbers 16 and 18 High Street, Brooklyn, 1872, home of the National Shades Company. Though its inhabitants prided themselves on the residential character of their city, by the 1870s Brooklyn had emerged as one of the largest and fastest-growing industrial centers in the nation, with more than a thousand factories turning out glassware, steel, chemicals, books, whiskey, beer, oil, glue, refined sugar, and scores of other products. Within ten years, the number of plants in the city would increase to more than 5,000.

THE BRIDGE

Nothing expressed the spirit of the age—its vaulting ambition, obsession with progress and size, and yearning to connect—more than the extraordinary project that got off the ground in the spring of 1867.

For years, people had been dreaming of a structure that could span the turbulent expanse of water—a gigantic bridge that would free transportation from the tyranny of the weather and unite the two great cities.

Before the ice had thawed that spring, a group of businessmen, politicians, and real-estate developers had incorporated the New York Bridge Company—and charged it with the task of finding someone capable of building such a structure.

The very thing that made the bridge so cru-

cial made it all but impossible to build. The East River was the busiest stretch of water in the world, filled with ferries, steamers, clipper ships, launches. Nothing could be allowed to interfere with the constant traffic.

"If there is to be a bridge," one skeptic wrote, "it must take one grand flying leap from shore to shore over the masts of ships. There can be no piers or drawbridge. There must be only one great arch all the way across."

There was probably only one man in the world who could build such a bridge: an intense sixty-one-year-old German-born engineer and inventor named John A. Roebling, who had already made a fortune pioneering the manufacture of wire rope, and was widely considered the premier bridge builder in the United States, if not the world.

An enigmatic, iron-willed archrationalist—who nevertheless believed in hydropathy and the spirit world—he had studied with the great German philosopher Hegel, who called him "my favorite pupil."

Now, with his thirty-year-old son, Washington, a former colonel in the Army Corps of Engineers, Roebling drew up plans for a structure unlike any ever before attempted.

"The completed work," he wrote, "will not only be the greatest bridge in existence, but it will be the greatest engineering work of the continent, and of the age. . . . As a great work of art, and as a successful specimen of advanced bridge engineering, this structure will forever testify to the energy, enterprise and wealth of that community which shall secure its erection."

Its central span would be 1,595 feet long—half again as long as any bridge in existence—and its towers 276 feet tall—*seven times higher* than the four-story skyline of Manhattan.

By the summer of 1869, work on the giant structure had begun.

On June 28, Roebling himself was surveying the foundation for the Brooklyn tower, when a ferry rammed the pier on which he was standing, crushing his right foot. Lockjaw set in, and after three weeks of unbearable agony, during which Roebling refused all medication, he died—leaving responsibility for the most ambitious engineering project of the age on the shoulders of his son, Washington.

In the end, building the immense bridge would prove far more difficult, and take far longer, than anyone had expected. Before it was over, the twin cities it connected would have to descend into a maelstrom of political and financial chaos—and then rise again.

GRAND SACHEM

To be a citizen of New York is a disgrace. The New Yorker belongs to a community worse governed by lower and baser blackguard scum than any city in Western Christendom.

George Templeton Strong

In the summer of 1871—as the Brooklyn Bridge struggled to get off the ground—New York exploded in the biggest political scandal in its history.

At the center of the storm stood another structure, only a hundred yards away from the New York entrance of the bridge—an unfinished stone courthouse that by 1871 was entering its twelfth year of construction, with no end in sight.

The revelations about to emerge from it would immortalize one man above all as the most corrupt urban politician in American history—Boss William M. Tweed.

They would also reveal the shadowy inner workings of one of the most extraordinary polit-

ical organizations ever created in America—
Tammany Hall.

The Society of Saint Tammany, as it was originally known, had risen with the city itself—
taking its name from a venerable social club on
Nassau Street, organized in 1789. Since the
opening of the canal in 1825—and especially
since the advent of popular sovereignty in
1834—much of its power had come from the
Lower East Side, and from the growing number of impoverished newcomers flooding into
the city with each passing year.

The men who ran it had no grand political
platform, few illusions, and even fewer ideals.
What they had was a shrewd grasp of the political opportunities in the rapidly expanding city
of immigrants.

Reaching out to the city's despised Irish and
German settlers, Tammany alone offered them
comfort and a voice in the system—knowing
that on election day they would reap the gratitude of the new immigrant voters.

It was something entirely new in politics:
not charity, or philanthropy, or noblesse oblige—
but politics *as a business*—a frank exchange of
services for power.

In return for unswerving loyalty at the polls,
Tammany's leaders offered help—modest to
be sure, but often the only help immigrants
could find. In a city with no safety net for the
poor—no social security, medical or accident
insurance, workmen's compensation or unemployment relief—the Tammany ward boss was
often a lifeline, providing jobs for the unemployed, shelter for families in trouble, food and
coal for the needy at Christmas.

*The morning of the election was a busy time
at the Alm's House. Officers hurrying to and
fro—getting together inmates of the establishment, clad in their new clothes—distributing
to them tickets to vote and tickets for grog—
putting into their hands nice pieces of silver
coin, that they might solace themselves after
the arduous labor of depositing their ballots.*

Report to the Board of
Aldermen from the Commissioners
of the Alm's House, 1845

Year by year, Tammany's power grew. New
York's largely Anglo-Saxon and Protestant ruling class did everything they could to check its

advance—horrified by the onslaught of Irish
Catholic invaders—and by the rampant corruption of Tammany's leaders, who distributed
jobs to loyal followers, sold off franchises for
ferry and streetcar lines, and routinely rigged
local elections.

But there was little the old guard could do.
By 1851, more than half of the city's voters were
foreign-born, and Tammany's Democratic organization was buying, bullying, and sometimes
fabricating new voters by the thousands. That
year, for the first time, Tammany officials gained
control of the Board of Aldermen—a beach-
head they exploited with a binge of corruption
so brazen it was quickly dubbed "the Forty
Thieves."

But it was the harrowing draft riots of 1863
that propelled Tammany to the forefront of city
politics. In the aftermath of the terrible conflagration, even conservative New Yorkers were
willing to concede that Tammany was the only
organization even remotely capable of channeling New York's seething immigrant energies.

The year of the riots, a genial ex-fireman
from Cherry Street was made Grand Sachem
of Tammany Hall. His name was William M.
Tweed, and in the years to come, he would transform Tammany into the most potent political
force in the city's history.

In many ways, the two had grown up
together. The son of a chairmaker from the
Lower East Side, Tweed at twenty-six had
formed his own volunteer fire brigade, the
Americus Engine Company. Recruited by Tammany that same year, he had risen swiftly through
the ranks, serving as alderman, congressman,
and state senator before being sworn in as Grand
Sachem in 1863.

Once in office, he moved swiftly to consolidate his power, welding the society's rival factions for the first time into a unified political
organization, whose trademark—a snarling red
tiger—would be drawn from the insignia of
Tweed's old fire brigade.

There had never been anyone quite like him
in New York politics. He had, an English visitor remarked, "an abounding vitality, free and
easy manners, plenty of humor, though of a
coarse kind, and a jovial, swaggering way."

Caricatured by Republican opponents as a
vulgar, hard-drinking Irishman, he was in fact

John Augustus Roebling (opposite top), considered the greatest bridge designer in America, if
not the world, had been dreaming of a span over
the East River ever since the winter day in 1852,
when, icebound for hours on a Brooklyn ferry, he
had traced in his mind's eye a single sweeping
arc from shore to shore. In 1869, working side
by side with his son, Washington (opposite
bottom)—a superb engineer in his own
right—Roebling drew up detailed plans for a
suspension bridge of unprecedented size (upper
left). Spanning nearly a third of a mile, the projected structure would be far more daring
than anything anyone had attempted before—
including Roebling himself, whose famed
iron-cabled bridge across the Ohio River in Cincinnati was scarcely two-thirds the length. To carry
its loads across so vast a distance, the proposed
East River span would be suspended not by
iron but by steel—a new metal, the elder
Roebling pronounced, for a new age.

a fourth-generation Scots Protestant, unfailingly courteous and nearly teetotal, and despite his imposing height and immense girth—he weighed nearly three hundred pounds—surprisingly nimble and graceful on his feet.

He was also a superb politician, who inspired fierce loyalty in his largely Irish Catholic constituency—providing jobs, building almshouses, hospitals, and orphanages, and channeling public funds to parochial schools and charities. Tweed's standing in New York's immigrant communities rose still higher when, in 1866, he persuaded the state legislature to relax the city's rigid blue laws, making it legal to buy liquor on Sundays.

In the end, the legendary corruption scandal that overtook Tweed's regime would obscure the real nature of his achievement. But the achievement was real. Harnessing the political energy of New York's immigrant communities as no one before him, Tweed was among the first American politicians to grasp the power of mass politics.

No one before him had ever mobilized so large or so diverse an urban constituency. Nor had anyone ever used that power to steal so much money, or so many elections, in so short a period of time.

"The fact is," as Tweed himself later testified with striking candor, "that New York politics were always dishonest, long before my time. There never was a time when you couldn't buy the Board of Aldermen. A politician coming forward takes things as they are. This population is too hopelessly split up into races and factions to govern it under universal suffrage, except by the bribery of patronage or corruption . . . I don't think there is ever a fair or honest election in the city of New York."

It was not merely Tweed's corruption that set him apart from his predecessors but—like so much else in the postwar city—its breathtaking scale. Previous Tammany chieftains had expanded voter rolls by a few hundred immigrants a month. At the height of Tweed's power, Tammany magistrates were manufacturing *two thousand* new American citizens *a day*—more than three new voters a minute—faster, the editor of the *New York Tribune* calculated, than a Cincinnati packinghouse turned pigs into pork.

Under Tweed's deft supervision, Tammany Hall gained control of the city's political apparatus as never before, then used it to set in motion vast public works—parks, streets, bridges, hospitals, and schools—knowing there were huge dividends in money and power to be reaped along the way.

There were lucrative building contracts for grateful contractors, who happily paid Tammany's leaders enormous cash kickbacks to get them. There were thousands of jobs for Tammany's loyal constituents—who gratefully voted Tammany's leaders back in power. New York's upper classes, meanwhile, professed to be appalled by Tammany but quietly looked the other way as real-estate values in Manhattan skyrocketed.

It all worked like a machine: *a political machine.* And no one knew how that machine worked better than Tweed, who by 1870 had concentrated more power in himself than anyone in the city's history—simultaneously holding positions as school commissioner, assistant street commissioner, president of the Board of Super-

In 1868, with its coffers swelling and its power growing, the Tammany Society moved uptown from its old home on Nassau Street to a lavish new headquarters (known in Tammany parlance as the Wigwam) on the north side of 14th Street, between Irving Place and Third Avenue. Always open to the opportunity for extra income, Tammany leaders installed a variety theater—later run by the showman Tony Pastor—on the ground floor of their imposing clubhouse. In the niche above the building's cornice stands a large-than-life statue of the Indian chief, Tammany, from whom the organization had taken its name in 1789.

Boss William M. Tweed, about 1870. The most notoriously corrupt figure in the history of American cities was a complex and contradictory man: a superb politician whose boundless appetite for money and power was matched by his genuine commitment to the city's growth and his careful attention to the needs of his working-class, largely immigrant constituency. Shrewd and charming, a man who for all his 300 pounds was strikingly nimble on his feet, Tweed would do more than anyone before him to extend popular democracy in New York—even as he and his partners systematically raided the city treasury of tens of millions of dollars.

visors, chairman of the New York County Democratic Committee, state senator—and Grand Sachem of Tammany Hall.

The zenith of Tweed's power came in the spring of 1870, when he bribed the New York State Legislature to rewrite the city charter—abolishing the state commissions that had run the city for thirteen years, returning home rule to Manhattan, and granting to himself complete control over every aspect of New York's government.

With his hands now on the reins of twelve thousand city jobs—and every cent the city paid out in public services—Tweed took off. Accelerating the city's already explosive growth still further, he pushed forward the construction of mile after mile of elevated railways and street-level rail lines in upper Manhattan: winning praise from progressive businessmen—from middle-class New Yorkers, who were soon commuting from spacious new districts far uptown—and from tens of thousands of engineers and ordinary workmen, for whom Tweed had found jobs building sewer, water, and gas lines beneath the raw new streets of the Upper East and West sides.

Month after month, eyebrows rose higher, as rumors of graft and corruption flew. But Tweed's detractors, one Tammany man claimed, were merely "rich old men who cannot realize that New York is no longer a series of straggling villages."

Meanwhile, as the frenzy of building went on, Tweed and his associates were brazenly siphoning off staggering sums of money from the projects under their control—and helping shady investors like Jay Gould and Jim Fisk make off with still more—speculating in real estate with the incalculable advantage of knowing in advance where the new streets and transit lines were to go.

By the end of 1870, the onetime fireman from the Lower East Side had become one of the largest landowners in the city, with gold-plated harnesses on his carriage horses, a private steam yacht, and a mansion on Fifth Avenue. When his daughter, Mary Amelia, was married at Trinity Church in the winter of 1871, her dazzling trousseau was spangled with diamonds—while Tweed himself, one newspaper reported, "wore a diamond like a planet in his shirt front."

As indignant reformers began questioning where Tweed's lavish fortune came from, all eyes turned to the still uncompleted county courthouse on Chambers Street—a special project of Tweed's. Begun in 1858, it was supposed to have cost $350,000, including furnishings. But after twelve years of construction, the price tag had reached $13 million and kept right on rising.

The building, critics complained, had already taken twice as long to build as the Erie Canal—and cost more than the entire Houses of Parliament, and twice as much as Alaska.

It was a level of corruption astonishing even by New York's standards. In three years under Tweed's rule, the city debt had increased more than $30 million, and taxes had more than doubled. "People begin to tire of holding their noses," George Templeton Strong wrote, "and are looking about in a helpless way for some remedy."

As the tide of official malfeasance rose, even Walt Whitman's bright vision of the city's prospects began to darken. "The spectacle is appalling," he wrote in 1871. "The official services of America ... are saturated in corruption, bribery, falsehood, maladministration. ... The great cities reek with respectable as much as non-respectable robbery and scoundrelism."

When immigrant riots again erupted in the summer of 1871, Tweed's public support began to crumble.

Day after day, the ultrarespectable *New-York Times* railed against his excesses. "No Caliph, Khan or Caesar has risen to power or opulence more rapidly than Tweed [the First]. Ten years ago this monarch was pursuing the humble occupation of a chairmaker. ... He now rules the State as Napoleon ruled France. ... There is absolutely nothing—nothing in the city which is beyond the reach of the insatiable gang who have obtained possession of it."

But in the end, it was a German-born artist named Thomas Nast, with close ties to the Republican party, who brought Tweed down, with an extraordinary series of political cartoons. Week after week, Nast savaged what he called the Tammany "Ring" in the pages of *Harper's Weekly*.

There was Peter "Brains" Sweeny, the brooding, shadowy lawyer who served as city treasurer—Richard "Slippery Dick" Connolly, the rotund, pompous city comptroller—and Mayor Abraham Oakey Hall, Tweed's debonair, smooth-talking puppet in city hall, whom Nast liked to call "The Elegant Oakey" and "Mayor Haul." Finally, there was Boss Tweed himself, whom Nast depicted as a licentious, balding, overfed monster, literally devouring the city.

"I don't care a straw for your newspaper articles," Tweed declared, as public sentiment against him mounted. "My constituents don't know how to read. But they can't help seeing them damned pictures."

On July 8, 1871, the *New-York Times* delivered the killing blow—publishing excerpts from secret courthouse records, obtained from a disgruntled city official Tweed had cheated out of thousands of dollars in kickbacks.

The figures were incredible. Eleven thermometers had been purchased for $7,500, dust brooms for $41,000, windows for $8,000 apiece. One contractor had been paid $5.5 million for window shades, carpets, and furniture. The bill for three chairs and forty tables had come to $179,792.

It would never be clear how much Tweed's corruption had been exaggerated by the press; the *Times* put the final tally at almost $200 million. But in the end, it didn't matter. New York needed a villain equal in scale to its giant park and giant bridge, and Tweed fit the bill—largely because he looked the part.

On December 15, 1871, Boss Tweed was indicted on 3 counts of fraud and grand larceny, and, two months later, 220 misdemeanor charges. He was sentenced to twelve years in prison, and though the convictions were later

In 1858, the architect John Kellum drew up designs for a new county courthouse on Chambers Street that was to cost $350,000. But by 1863, construction had scarcely progressed past the first floor (top). The following year an additional $800,000 was authorized for the project—the start of an eventual $13 *million* in appropriations that would be poured into the building.

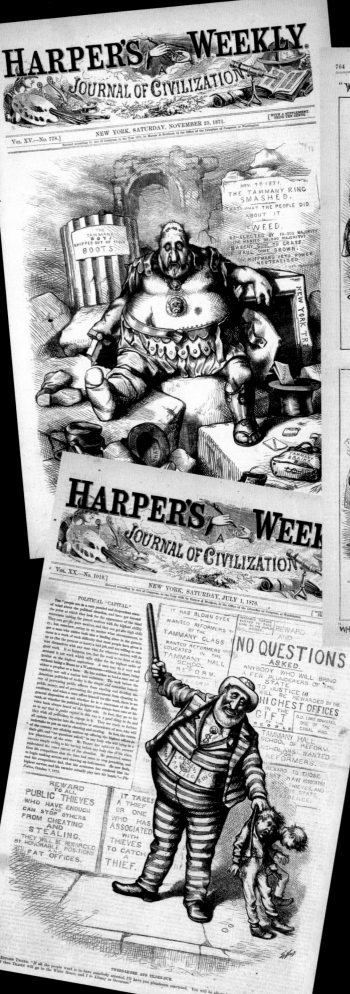

Thomas Nast's *Harper's Weekly* cartoons of Boss Tweed and his "Ring"—a term Nast himself originated—so infuriated the Tammany leader that in 1871 he offered the German-born artist half a million dollars to drop the campaign and leave the country. Nast refused and continued to caricature the corrupt boss week after week in a series of drawings that not only helped to bring Tweed down, but forever engraved in the American imagination the image of the big-city boss as a florid, gluttonous, and rapacious figure.

When he came into the great dining room at dinner time, and looked at all the tables thronged with members of the Legislature and the lobby, he had a benignant, paternal expression, as of a patriarch pleased to see his retainers happy. And he never doubted that he could buy every man in the room if he were willing to pay the price. George William Curtis

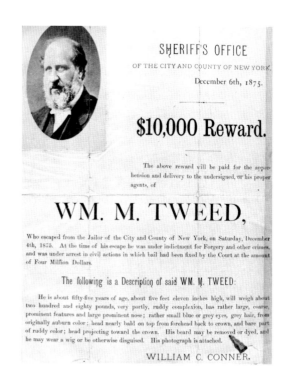

SHERIFF'S OFFICE

OF THE CITY AND COUNTY OF NEW YORK.

December 6th, 1875.

$10,000 Reward.

The above reward will be paid for the apprehension and delivery to the undersigned, or his proper agents, of

WM. M. TWEED,

Who escaped from the Jailor of the City and County of New York, on Saturday, December 4th, 1875. At the time of his escape he was under indictment for Forgery and other crimes, and was under arrest in civil actions in which bail had been fixed by the Court at the amount of Four Million Dollars.

The following is a Description of said WM. M. TWEED:

He is about fifty-five years of age, about five feet eleven inches high, will weigh about two hundred and eighty pounds, very portly, ruddy complexion, has rather large, coarse, prominent features and large prominent nose; rather small blue or grey eyes, grey hair, from originally auburn color; head nearly bald on top from forehead back to crown, and bare part of ruddy color; head projecting toward the crown. His beard may be removed or dyed, and he may wear a wig or be otherwise disguised. His photograph is attached.

WILLIAM C. CONNER.

overturned, a civil suit stripped him of his assets and forced him into debtor's prison. By then, all the members of Tweed's Ring were in exile or disgrace, except for Jay Gould and his Wall Street partners, who had emerged from the scandal unscathed, and richer than ever.

In the winter of 1875, he somehow slipped past his guards, and escaped to Spain, but the Spanish police recognized him from one of Thomas Nast's cartoons, and he was quickly recaptured and returned to prison.

Gaunt and ailing, Tweed eked out his last years in jail. On April 12, 1878, he died of pneumonia in his cell in the Ludlow Street Jail he himself had built, penniless and broken.

"A villain of more brains would have had a modest dwelling and guzzled in secret," the editor of *The Nation* wrote. "His successors here . . . will not imitate him in this, but that he will have successors there is no doubt."

THE POOR

Let us remember that [Tweed] fell without loss of reputation among the bulk of his supporters. The bulk of poorer voters of this city to-day revere his memory, and look on him as the victim of rich men's malice; as, in short, a friend to the needy who applied public funds, with as little waste as was possible under the circumstances, to the purposes which they ought to be

applied—and that is to the making of work for the working man.

E. L. Godkin, *The Nation*

Lost in the uproar of the Tweed scandal were the needs of New York's poor—which Tammany alone had been addressing, however imperfectly.

Though some steps had been taken in the aftermath of the draft riots to alleviate the worst suffering in the slums, the constantly rising tide of new immigrants continued to outstrip the city's social services.

By 1873, the problem of the poor had reached epidemic proportions in New York.

"If some potent magician," Walt Whitman wrote, "could lift the veil which shrouds, in alleys, dark streets, garrets and a thousand other habitations of want, the miseries that are everyday going on among us, how would the spectacle distress and terrify the beholder?"

Almost nothing protected most working people from the brutal realities of the marketplace.

Even in the best of times there was no minimum wage—no limit to the number of hours or days that factory workers could be forced to labor each week—no medical help or insurance for those injured or crippled on the job

After his fall from power, Tweed was sued in civil court, stripped of his assets, and sentenced to prison. Yet he was still allowed the privilege of an occasional outing, and on December 1875, on a visit home to his wife and son, he managed to slip past his guard and escape to a boat waiting on the Hudson, which ferried him to New Jersey and freedom. Embarrassed officials offered a handsome reward for his capture, and within a year, the disgraced boss had been apprehended in Spain and returned to the Ludlow Street Jail.

The Five Points Mission (shown here around 1875) was an early version of urban renewal—one of a series of privately sponsored attempts to improve Manhattan's most infamous slum. The mission had been built in 1852 on the site of the Old Brewery, a huge, hulking onetime factory that had later become notorious as the rowdiest tenement in the city. In place of what it called a "pest house of sin," the Methodist Episcopal Church established this "school of virtue"— which included a chapel, classrooms, bathrooms, and twenty dwellings for the poor.

Baxter Street in the Five Points, about 1873 (opposite). Though no longer as raucous and dangerous as it had been before the Civil War, the Five Points area remained the city's worst slum, filled with rotting wooden houses—now a half century old—and tall brick tenements, crammed with poor families. By the 1870s, the area— dominated before the Civil War by the Irish—was being colonized by newer waves of impoverished immigrants, including Italians and Chinese. (See page 88 for an earlier view of the same street.)

—and no relief for those too sick or feeble to work.

For the tens of thousands of unfortunate people who fell by the wayside each year, the only recourse was Blackwell's Island—a forbidding cluster of stone fortresses out in the East River, where the city's most desperate and dangerous people were confined.

The island's stark facilities—the penitentiary, the workhouse, the lunatic asylum, the Hospital for Incurables—were routinely filled to capacity, its two dismal almshouses, one man wrote, crowded with "broken down and decrepit men and women, and old chronic cases, sent there to die."

On Manhattan itself, meanwhile, harrowing symptoms of poverty were visible everywhere. City officials estimated that more than 100,000 working-class children between the ages of five and fourteen toiled in factories— twelve hours a day, six days a week—making envelopes, paper boxes, twine, artificial flowers, cigars.

Less fortunate still were the thousands of abandoned children and orphans forced to fend for themselves.

"There are ten thousand children living on the streets of New York," an Episcopal minister and guidebook author named James D. McCabe, Jr. estimated, "gaining their bread by blacking boots, by selling newspapers, watches, pins, etc., and by stealing. Some are thrust onto the streets by dissolute parents, some are orphans, some are voluntary outcasts, others drift here from the surrounding country. Wherever they may come from, or however they may get here, they are here, and they are nearly all leading a vagrant life."

On the main commercial avenues, visitors were often shocked by the scores of hungry, ill-clad newsboys hawking their wares. "Climbing onto a streetcar," one man wrote, "they will offer you their papers in such an earnest, appealing way that nine times out of ten, you buy from sheer pity for the boy."

In June 1870, a twenty-one-year-old Danish immigrant named Jacob Augustus Riis arrived in New York with forty dollars in his pocket. He had brought with him high hopes but no real profession, and when his money ran out, he learned firsthand what immigrant life in the city could be like.

I joined the great army of tramps, wandering the streets in daytime with the one aim of somehow stilling the hunger that gnawed at my vitals, and fighting at night with vagrant curs or outcasts as miserable as myself for the protection of some sheltering ash-bin or doorway. I was finally and utterly alone in the city, with

*the winter approaching and every shivering
night in the streets, reminding me that a time
was rapidly coming when such a life as I led
could no longer be endured.*

One cold, rainy night, soaked to the bone
on a deserted pier above the dark waters of the
Hudson, he came close to jumping in. Instead,
he drifted over to the Five Points to catch a few
hours' sleep on the filthy floor of a police lodging house, before getting up to tramp the streets
again the next day, trying to find some kind of
work, more dismayed than ever by the misery
he saw all around him.

In the years to come, Riis would find work,
and somehow he put himself back on his feet.

But though he never again came so close to
destitution, he would never forget the suffering he had seen on the streets of New York
City—or the appalling indifference of his fellow citizens to the plight of the poor.

"Poverty is a terrible misfortune in any city,"
one reformer wrote darkly, the year after Riis
arrived. "In New York, it is frequently regarded
as a crime."

In the money-mad atmosphere of the gilded
age, most wealthy New Yorkers blamed the poor
themselves for their condition, subscribing to
the wisdom of the noted preacher Russell H.
Conwell in his celebrated "Acres of Diamonds"
sermon.

> *The opportunity to get rich, to attain unto great
> wealth, is within the reach of almost every man
> and woman. . . . Let us remember there is not
> a poor person in the United States who was
> not made poor by his own shortcomings. . . .
> It is all wrong to be poor anyhow.*
>
> The Reverend Russell H. Conwell

AL SMITH

In the end, the impetus to transform the darkest consequences of the industrial city would
arise from the mean streets of the Lower East
Side themselves—which in the last decades of
the nineteenth century became a breeding
ground of political energy and social reform.

In 1873—the same year Boss Tweed began
his jail term—one of the most influential political figures in the history of New York was born
in a back room of his parents' tenement apartment overlooking the East River waterfront.

All New York went into making Alfred
Emanuel Smith. Descended from German, Italian, and Irish immigrants, he grew up on South
Street, across from the docks where his mother's
family had arrived from Ireland three decades
before. His father, a genial self-employed team-
ster with a big booming voice, was fiercely
proud of keeping his family a notch above the
poverty level.

As a boy, he loved to play amid the maze of
shipmasts, bowsprits, and rigging along the busy
waterfront, plunging with friends on hot summer days into the turbid, surging waters of the
East River. From the windows of his family's
third-floor apartment, he liked to watch the
sweeping expanse of the river itself—the traffic of horses and people on South Street, and
the gigantic bridge that slowly filled the sky
above the harbor.

"The bridge and I grew up together," Smith
later recalled. "I have never lost the memory of
the admiration and envy I felt for the men
swarming up, stringing the cables, putting in
the roadways as the bridge took shape."

One wintry Sunday, he and his father
stole into the construction site, and walked across
the rough wooden planking of the still-uncom-
pleted span. Years later, Smith would recall, his
father liked to say that he and his boy had been
the first New Yorkers ever to use the Brooklyn
Bridge.

At the time the portrait
above was taken in 1890,
Al Smith—a future
governor, presidential
nominee, and the man
destined to change the
political landscape of
twentieth-century New
York—was still an
ordinary day laborer,
supporting his mother and
sister with the $12 a week
he brought in from his job
at the Fulton Fish Market,
where he spent 13 hours a
day rolling barrels and
wrapping fish. Years later,
Smith—who had quit
school at the age of 13,
three years before this
view was made—would
say proudly that he
possessed only one
degree: "F.F.M."

At left, Smith stands in the
background of a family
portrait made four years
later; his mother,
Catherine, sits in the front
row, left, and his future
wife, Catherine Dunn, in
the second row, far right.

PANIC

The greatest economic catastrophe of the nineteenth century struck in the fall of 1873.

Reckless investment in North American railroads had already strained European bond markets to their limits, when, in early September, the troubled Northern Pacific line went under, triggering a financial crisis of global proportions.

As foreign banks called in their loans and the flow of overseas capital slowed to a trickle, New York's overextended bond market began to collapse with terrifying swiftness. At noon on September 18, to the stunned disbelief of onlookers, Jay Cooke & Company—the brokerage that had underwritten the bankrupt railroad—closed its doors forever, sending prices plummeting on the New York Stock Exchange.

"The whole world has become a city," Baron Rothschild gloomily observed, as one world capital after another fell to the panic.

Day by day, as the crisis deepened, George Templeton Strong kept track of events in his diary.

September 19th, 1873. Panic grows on Wall Street, "the hubbub multiplies," and indications are graver than any crisis since 1857. . . . Many notable speculators have suspended, among them Fisk & Hatch, reputed impregnably strong. . . . All this may be a mere flurry, or may be much more.

On September 20—with the entire market in free fall—the New York Stock Exchange closed the trading floor for the first time in its eighty-one-year history, hoping to stem the tide.

It didn't work. Within weeks, as shock waves of the panic swept across the country, five thousand commercial firms, fifty-seven brokerage houses, and eighty-nine railroads had gone bankrupt.

As hundreds of factories and mills around the country shut down, hundreds of thousands of people were thrown out of work—and the nation plunged into an economic crisis more damaging and far-reaching than any before it.

October 27th. Wall Street continues in feverish, nervous malaise. Its pulse keeps going up to 120 under hourly rumors of defalcation in this or that great corporation, railroad, or others. Faith in financial agents is gone. . . . Every treasurer and cashier is "suspect," and no wonder, after the recent epidemic of fraud. . . . Factories and employers throughout the country are discharging hands, working half time, or reducing wages. . . . October 29th . . . Prospects for the coming winter look darker and darker.

George Templeton Strong

Nowhere were the effects felt worse than in New York City. By the winter of 1874, ninety thousand unemployed and homeless people—many on the verge of starvation—were sleeping on the filthy, vermin-ridden floors of the city's police stations.

On the morning of January 13, 1874, seven thousand workingmen and their families gathered in Tompkins Square, despite the bitter cold, to protest the appalling conditions and to call on the city for emergency relief.

The official response was swift and brutal. Battalions of mounted policemen rode the demonstrators down in the street, beating them with nightsticks, and placing scores under arrest.

"It was the most glorious sight I ever saw," New York's police commissioner wrote, "the way the police broke and drove that crowd. Their order was perfect as they charged with their clubs uplifted."

In March, unwilling to sustain even minimal efforts to help the homeless, New York City suspended its programs for "outdoor relief" entirely.

By December 1874, *Harper's Weekly* reported, nine hundred New Yorkers had starved to death. Three thousand infants had been abandoned on doorsteps, and the corpses of a hundred more discovered in ash barrels, areaways, and refuse dumps.

There had never been anything like it. It had taken less than a year for the city to recover from the panic of 1857. Now, as month after month went by with few signs of recovery, it began to be clear that something far worse had gone wrong.

Sparked by the panic of 1873, the first prolonged downturn in the history of the modern global economy—*a depression*—had begun.

"Farewell 1874," George Templeton Strong wrote glumly, on the last day of the year. "May 1875 be more prosperous and more fruitful of good works."

Overleaf: As a child growing up on the Lower East Side, Al Smith found his recreation along the busy piers of South Street, swimming on hot summer days in the filthy waters of the East River. This view, taken in 1892 (when Smith was nineteen), shows a group of young boys preparing to dive off the floating docks behind the Fulton Fish Market, while a laborer in the foreground drags a barrel of fish toward the market—the same job that Smith himself held at the time.

THE END OF AN ERA

For Strong himself, that was not to be. By 1875, he had finally retired from the law firm his father had started half a century before.

Day after day, for more than thirty-four years, he had dutifully gone to the office at 68 Wall Street—grimly attending, he said, to "the weary work of running that venerable machine."

Now it was over. "It seems like a dream," Strong wrote, "that I should be free to keep away from Wall Street without an uneasy conscience."

Hardly a week went by now without the passing of an old friend, or a business partner, or an acquaintance from the war years. He worried more, often struggled with bouts of deep melancholia, and was plagued with dyspepsia and "sick headaches."

June 12th, 1875. Saturday. I tried for a drive in the park with Ellie; but the vile pavement of Fifth Avenue caused me such pain that I had to turn about, and I got home feeling faint and prostrate.

June 25th. Friday. I have been improving the wrong way, like bad fish in warm weather. One day last week, I had a woeful day of headache, nausea, and malaise, which left me as weak as a sea anemone at low water. Since then, there has been no improvement.

It was the last entry he ever made in the diary he had kept for more than forty years. On July 21, 1875, George Templeton Strong died at his home in Gramercy Park and was buried two days later in Trinity Churchyard. He was fifty-five years old.

PHOENIX

Year after year, the city sank further into uncertainty and economic gloom.

Signs of depression were visible everywhere. Up and down Broadway, bankrupt businesses sold off goods at auction, and dwindling crowds of shoppers hurried past empty storefronts. "Vacant shops, stores and manufactures," the mayor reported, "stare at us in every street."

One bleak February morning, as the depression stretched into its fourth year, the giant amputated hand of a woman appeared on Madison Square. Part of a towering statue the French hoped to present as a gift to the American peo-

ple, it was to stand in the middle of New York Harbor—if New Yorkers would only pay for the pedestal.

But New Yorkers had refused. "No true patriot," the *New-York Times* declared, "can support expenditures for a bronze female in the present state of our finances."

Year after year, the huge upraised hand stood on Fifth Avenue—"an embarrassment," one

In 1876, to aid fund-raising efforts for the statue's pedestal, Liberty's right hand and torch were brought to New York and installed on the west side of Madison Square. There they would remain for four years, startling visitors and passersby.

Not until 1872, nearly three years after work on the Brooklyn Bridge began, was the arduous—and to the public, almost invisible—work on the foundations completed, allowing the massive towers to begin their slow rise into the sky (above, the New York tower under construction). It was another five years until the towers were completed and the first temporary footbridge strung between them (below, a group of bridge company trustees stand near the Brooklyn end, in 1877). Built of solid masonry and weighing 120 million pounds each, the towers were by far the most massive structures on the continent.

SAFE FOR ONLY 25 MEN AT ONE TIME. DO NOT WALK CLOSE TOGETHER. NOR RUN, JUMP, OR TROT. BREAK STEP! W.A. Roebling. *Engr in Chief*

Commuting by ferry between Brooklyn and Manhattan, the photographer Joshua H. Beal was mesmerized by the sight of the great bridge rising slowly above the river. In 1876, he ascended the Brooklyn tower to prepare this extraordinary panorama—for which he exposed five negatives to create a composite photograph nearly seven feet long.

The view reveals a predominantly low-rise city whose tallest peak remains the spire of Trinity Church, at left. But it also hints at the city's skyward destiny—not only in the pier of the bridge but, to its left, the cluster of early office towers around City Hall Park, including the nine-story headquarters of the *New York Tribune,* completed that year.

enth year, with no end in sight—battered by financial troubles, strikes, political corruption, and a series of nightmarish accidents.

Supervising work on the foundations, in the highly compressed atmosphere of the watertight caissons deep beneath the riverbed, Washington Roebling himself had been stricken by a mysterious new affliction—called caisson disease, or the bends—and hadn't been seen at the site for years.

And yet somehow the work went on, the ailing chief engineer monitoring progress through binoculars from his bedroom window, and relaying instructions to the site through his wife, Emily, who now assumed day-to-day command of the mammoth project.

Slowly, the gaunt stone towers rose above the harbor—bringing an entirely new scale to the two cities. Rising above the rooftops like visitors from another planet, the 120-million-pound structures were the most massive manmade objects on the North American continent.

On a cold windy morning in January 1876, in the very depths of the depression, a photographer named Joshua H. Beal wrestled his cumbersome equipment up thirty flights of stairs, then stepped out onto an open platform atop the recently completed Brooklyn tower, and set to work—carefully exposing five glass-plate negatives to form a single giant photograph, more than seven feet long.

The stunning panoramic image showed New Yorkers the city as they had never seen it before: a city that, for all its problems, had grown like no city in history, becoming too vast to be grasped or understood in conventional terms—no longer simply a city but a teeming, unknowable metropolis.

"Far as the eye can reach it stretches away," an astonished French visitor named Paul Bourget would write only a few years later, looking out on the same extraordinary view. "This is not even a city in the sense in which we understand the word, we who have grown up amid the charm of irregular cities which grew as the trees do, slowly, with the variety, the picturesque character of natural things. This is a table of contents of unique character, arranged for convenient handling. Seen from here it is so colossal, it encloses so formidable an accumulation of

newspaper complained, to passing nannies and governesses, unable to explain to their youthful charges what the surreal sculpture was doing there, with its eight-foot index finger and twelve-inch nails.

As interest in the monument waned, one newspaper proposed that the giant figure might become a novel kind of "serial statue," its parts distributed as they were finished to different parks around the city.

Down along the East River, meanwhile, work on the Brooklyn Bridge ground on into its sev-

In 1877, New Yorkers watched in amazement as the two towers of the Brooklyn Bridge were connected by a sweeping arc of four steel "working ropes" from which the bridge's suspension cables would be laid. When complete, more than a year and a half later, each of the four cables would contain more than 3,500 miles of steel wire.

human efforts, as to overpass the bounds of imagination."

And so the city rose, and fell, and rose again. From the anxiety and gloom of depression, New York began to come back to life, and as it did, the outlines of a new kind of metropolis began to emerge.

In the fall of 1878, one of the world's first telephone exchanges commenced service, in lower Manhattan—followed six months later by the city's first telephone directory, a tiny, double-sided card that listed just 252 names.

A tangled skein of telephone lines now joined the shroud of telegraph wires fretting the sky above the downtown streets—"a perfect maze of . . . wires," an English visitor named Walter G. Marshall observed in 1879, "crossing and recrossing each other from the tops of houses. The sky, indeed, is blackened with them; it is as though you were looking through the meshes of a net."

A few years later, New Yorkers were astonished by an even greater innovation—one that would change the look and feel of city life forever.

For months, a team of workers led by the inventor Thomas Alva Edison had labored round the clock to assemble the world's first commercial electrical generating plant at 257 Pearl Street.

On the afternoon of September 4, 1882, at 3:00 p.m. precisely, an electrician named John Lieb threw the master switch. As the powerful current surged through cables, three thousand new incandescent lamps began to glow throughout the half-square-mile area of lower Manhattan that Edison had designated District One.

The era of gaslight was over.

"The effect of the light . . . can scarcely be described," a British journalist named W. E. Adams wrote, "so weird and so beautiful it is."

September 5th, 1882. In the stores and business places throughout the lower quarter of the city there was a strange glow last night. The dim flicker of gas . . . was supplanted by a steady glare, bright and mellow, which illuminated interiors and shone through windows, fixed and unwavering.

New York Herald

Even as the electric lights came on for the first time, another even vaster transformation was under way—one that would have unimaginably far-reaching consequences for the city and the nation.

Edison himself was not at Pearl Street when the switch was pulled, but in the office of his principal financial backer—an imperious, forty-five-year-old Wall Street banker, who at that very moment was orchestrating almost single-

"It is the desire of every American to see New York," one guidebook author wrote in 1872, "the largest and most wonderful city in the Union." For most visitors the first stop in New York was Broadway—the dazzling commercial spine of the city. From the hotel district at Madison Square, the sweep of daytime traffic carried visitors south toward a fleet of enormous commercial buildings, stretching from 23rd Street down to 14th Street. It was called the Ladies' Mile, and by the 1870s it had become the epicenter of a new kind of consumer culture in America—and the greatest shopping district in the world.

"Go into Broadway," the editor of the *New York Independent* declared in 1878, " and we will show you what is meant by the word 'extravagance.'"

At the heart of the district was an extraordinary new retail establishment—pioneered in New York a few decades before—the department store. Up until 1846, New Yorkers had shopped like everyone else—in specialty stores, each stocked with a single kind of merchandise. That year, a Scots-Irish merchant named Alexander Turney Stewart opened a huge five-story emporium on Broadway and Chambers Street that gathered dozens of different shops or "departments" beneath a single roof. Called the Marble Palace, it was the first department store in America.

It looks like some fair palace of ancient story, white parapets extended against the evening sky and innumerable windows full of lights. . . . Broadway is transformed into a beautiful fable, a dream.
Cincinnatti Commercial

"[It is] spacious and magnificent," Philip Hone wrote, "beyond anything of the kind in the New World, or the Old either, as far as I know." In 1862, Stewart opened an even larger cast-iron edifice on Broadway and Tenth Street, which

R. H. Macy's occupied this cast-iron building at the corner of 14th Street and Sixth Avenue until 1902, when the store moved to its present-day location at 34th Street and Broadway.

stunned shoppers with its sheer scale—with 5,000 feet of counter space on the first floor alone, a rotunda 80 feet high, and room for 50,000 customers a day. Among its entranced patrons was Mary Todd Lincoln, who incurred her husband's wrath in 1864 by running up more than $5,000 of bills during shopping sprees.

A few blocks away, meanwhile, Stewart's chief rival, a onetime

ship captain named Rowland H. Macy, was already widening the concept of the department store. A marketing genius, Macy enormously expanded the selection of merchandise at his 14th Street emporium, boosted the volume of customers with clearance sales, and, in 1874, almost single-handedly invented the Christmas shopping season—keeping the store open late, filling the win-

dows with dolls and toys, and arranging for an employee to dress as Santa Claus.

By 1879, more than 20 great department stores and countless specialty shops—including B. Altman, Lord & Taylor, Brooks Brothers, and Tiffany—lined Broadway and spilled over to 23rd Street and Sixth Avenue. Swept along the bustling pavements, past gleaming show windows of plate

Bargain counter, Siegel-Cooper Department Store, 1897. Located at 18th Street and Sixth Avenue, in the heart of the Ladies' Mile, Siegel-Cooper was the largest department store in the city, with more than 18 acres of interior floor space. On opening day in 1896, a crowd of more than 150,000 people gathered at the entrance to the building, waiting to get in.

glass that were themselves an innovation, visitors were dazzled by the overwhelming abundance of things to buy: window after window, store after store, block after block, for nearly a mile. "If in some way the rest of the city should be demolished," the editor of *Harper's Monthly* declared, "Broadway could supply the survivors with every necessity and luxury of life, from dinners at Delmonico's to marmoset monkeys, from Cashmere shawls to house-hold furniture, from colossal bronzes to silk stockings, from cigarettes to refined lard."

Out on the bustling pavements, horse-drawn trolleys vied with hundreds of private carriages and endless throngs of well-dressed, fast-moving shoppers. But even more remarkable to many observers was the fact that this extraordinary new public space had been created primarily for women. Visitors were amazed by the number of women moving unescorted about the stores and streets—thousands of working "shopgirls," mingling with wealthier women customers, and often dressed, confusingly enough, in cheaper versions of the same

stylish clothes, which the explosion of retail jobs and consumer goods had allowed them to buy.

"Buying and selling," one man wrote, "serving and being served—women. On every floor, in every aisle, at every counter, women . . . At every cashier's desk, at the wrappers' desk, running back and forth with parcels and change, short-skirted women. Filling the aisles, a constantly moving and departing throng of shoppers, women. Simply a moving, seeking, hurrying mass of femininity, in the midst of which the occasional man shopper, man clerk, and man supervisor looks lost and out of place."

"New York," another observer agreed, "is a paradise for women."

In the beginning . . . this vast and complex . . . mechanism did with enormous effort what the one store of the remote wilderness did easily—supplied the wants of its constituency. But the department store of the city does more. It creates appetites and caprices in order that it may wax great in satisfying them.
Anne O'Hagan

Eager to draw still more customers, the department stores soon supplemented their merchandise with tea rooms, writing rooms, cooking lectures, free concerts—anything to keep visitors in the building and in the mood to buy. A new phrase—*window shopping*—came to describe the pastime of strolling up and down Broadway, vicariously enjoying the goods on display.

"It is a perfect bazaar," an English visitor named Iza Duffus Hardy wrote. "Not only is there a brilliant display in the windows of everything good to look at, from exotic flowers to encaustic tiles, and everything one can possibly wear, from Paris imported bonnets to pink-satin boots, but the sidewalk is fringed with open-air stalls, heaped high with pretty things, many of them absurdly cheap."

For some, the temptation was too much. In the 1870s, an epidemic of middle-class kleptomania swept the Ladies' Mile. "Women of respectable position," the guidebook author James D. McCabe, Jr., wrote, "led on by their mad passion for dress, have been detected in taking small but costly articles,

such as laces, handkerchiefs, etc. from some of the principal houses. Such matters have usually been 'hushed up' through the influence of the friends of the offender."

What hurrying human tides, or day or night,

What passions, winnings, losses, ardors, swim thy waters!

What whirls of evil, bliss and sorrow, stem thee!

What curious questioning glances—glints of love!

Leer, envy, scorn, contempt, hope, aspiration!

Thou portal—thou arena—thou of the myriad long-drawn lines and groups.

(Could but thy flagstones, curbs, facades, tell their inimitable tales;

Thy windows rich, and huge hotels—thy sidewalks wide;)

Thou of the endless, sliding, mincing, shuffling feet!

Thou, like the parti-colored world itself—like infinite, teeming mocking life!

Thou visor'd, vast, and unspeakable show and lesson!
Walt Whitman,
"Broadway," 1888

handedly the rebirth of the entire American economy.

His name was John Pierpont Morgan. No one since Hamilton himself had so transcendent a belief in the possibilities of American capitalism.

No one in the history of the United States would ever wield more power.

More than six feet tall, barrel-chested and broad-shouldered, he was, one admirer said, "a perfectly huge man [with] a voice like a bull," who radiated an air of extraordinary personal authority.

"Facing his gaze," the photographer Edward Steichen later agreed, was "like facing the headlights of an oncoming train."

The son of a wealthy New England banker with close ties to the financial capital of London, Morgan had made his mark on Wall Street during the wild and woolly days of the postwar boom.

But—like Peter Stuyvesant before him—Morgan had an almost holy passion for discipline and order and—unlike so many of his contemporaries—he was appalled by the chaotic free-for-all of the Gilded Age, with its unregulated markets, ruinous competition, and wasteful overbuilding.

For the market to work, he believed, there had to be rules, as well as strict compliance with them.

"We do not want financial convulsions," he declared, "and have one thing one day and another thing the next." The panic, he was sure, had proved him right and, having cleared the field of most of his competitors, had given him the chance to do something about it.

From his offices at number 23 Wall—the first in the city to be lit by Edison's new system—he went right to work, turning all of his immense power to restructuring the way Wall Street did business.

First, he forced the railroads to stop undercutting one another, putting his own partners on the board of every company he bailed out, to ensure financial discipline. Then, he began buying up railroads himself, eliminating redundancies and reorganizing smaller lines into ever-larger ones—headquartered increasingly in New York.

It was called "morganizing." Soon, J. P. Morgan owned one-sixth of all the railroad track in the country—33,000 miles in all—and the era of cowboy capitalism and unfettered speculation was coming to an end.

By 1883, thanks in large part to Morgan, the depression was a thing of the past, and the panic a receding memory. New York was once again awash in money and power.

Night after night, one man later recalled, "the lights at 23 Wall Street shone far into the night, when all else was dark over New York." It was Morgan and his partners, charting a course into the giddiest heights of capitalism, and on into the future.

He lives in a world of his own, but he cares for this world. . . . That's his distinction from his peers. He sees that we must not kill the geese that lay the golden eggs. Not much to see? No, but very few of us see that; very few; and whenever he and the rest of us have nearly killed the birds . . . Morgan calls a halt. And we halt.

A Wall Street Broker, as Reported by Lincoln Steffens

THE PEOPLE'S DAY

By the spring of 1883—seven full years after the completion of the towers and fourteen years after work had first begun—the Brooklyn Bridge was nearly complete.

It had taken three times longer and cost nearly twice as much as John Roebling had estimated. More than five thousand workingmen, mainly Irish, German, and Italian immigrants, had toiled for as little as two dollars a day to build it, stone by stone, wire after wire, foot by foot.

Erecting the great towers had been impressive enough. But what came after was even more astonishing. Fourteen thousand miles of wire rope had been spun back and forth across the river and draped over the towers in four giant cables.

From them an avenue wider than Broadway had been suspended across a span nearly a third of a mile long. From below, the roadway seemed to float on air as it soared gracefully across the sky, supported without visible effort by its gossamer web of steel.

Lo, Soul! Sees thou not God's purpose from the first?
The earth to be spann'd, connected by network . . . ,
The oceans to be cross'd, the distant brought near,
The lands to be welded together.

Walt Whitman,
"Passage to India," 1871; 1881

On the evening of May 23, 1883, the day-long celebration of the opening of the Brooklyn Bridge came to a climax with the greatest display of fireworks in the city's history. For more than an hour, 10,000 pieces—14 tons in all—exploded without stop above the river, while hundreds more shells burst in the skies over New York and Brooklyn. After a giant finale—500 rockets, all fired at once—the hundreds of thousands of celebrants were treated to one last and unexpected spectacle. "Hardly had the last falling spark died out," the editor of the *Tribune* wrote, "when the moon rose slowly over the further tower and sent a broad beam of benediction across the river."

Now, with the official opening set for May 24, all that remained were the finishing touches.

Five days before the opening ceremonies, electricians finished installing seventy electric arc lamps along the suspenders. Near midnight, the dynamos were switched on for the first time, to test that the lights were working. Commuters on the last ferries to Brooklyn looked up in amazement as the majestic bridge shone out of the darkness in the blue-and-white glow.

Whether they knew it or not, one historian later said, they were seeing the future: electricity and steel.

May 24, 1883—officially renamed The People's Day in honor of the bridge—dawned fair and mild, without a cloud in the sky. By noon, virtually every business in town had shut its doors. As tens of thousands of cheering New Yorkers looked on, President Chester A. Arthur and Governor Grover Cleveland led the gala procession down Broadway, and up and over the great bridge.

They were greeted on the other side by Brooklyn's mayor, Seth Low—and Emily Roebling, standing in for her husband, Washington, who had begged off, claiming he was still too weak to attend.

Later, the president and the governor called on the chief engineer at his home in Brooklyn Heights. Roebling was honored by the visit but questioned the need for all the fuss and ceremony. "Why can't they just put up a sign saying, The Bridge Is Open," he said.

One after another, the reigning dignitaries of New York and Brooklyn extolled the wonders of the extraordinary bridge.

"The beautiful and stately structure," Mayor Low declared, "fulfills the fondest hope. The impression upon the visitor is one of astonishment that grows with every visit. No one who has been upon it can ever forget it. Not one shall see it and not feel prouder to be a man."

Henry C. Murphy—Low's predecessor, and one of the bridge's earliest and most ardent champions—saw the inevitable political consequences of the great roadway. "It requires no spirit of prophecy," he said, "to foretell the union of New York and Brooklyn. The river which divides them will soon cease to be a line of separation, and, bestrode by the colossus of commerce, will prove a link which will bind them together."

All afternoon, while the speeches dragged on, thousands of New Yorkers and Brooklynites ventured out onto the bridge for the first time—overwhelmed by the beauty of the structure, and by the glorious view, and by being so high above a river.

At dusk, the bridge was cleared, and the greatest fireworks display in the city's history began. For more than an hour, fourteen tons of fireworks streamed skyward from the bridge itself, from boats below, and from both shores; while still more were launched from gas balloons. At the stunning finale, five hundred rockets were touched off simultaneously, blossoming in the night sky above the gorgeous structure.

When the perfected East River bridge shall permanently and uninterruptedly connect the two cities, the daily thousands who cross it will consider it a sort of natural and inevitable phenomenon, such as the rising and setting of the sun, and they will unconsciously overlook the preliminary difficulties surmounted before the structure spanned the stream, and will perhaps undervalue the indomitable courage, the absolute faith, the consummate genius which assured the engineer's triumph.

Thomas Kinsella, *Brooklyn Daily Eagle*

"F.F.M."

New Yorkers and Brooklynites took to the bridge at once, as if no one could remember what life had been like without it.

On its first full day of traffic, nearly 2,000 vehicles, and more than 150,000 pedestrians, streamed between the two cities.

Then, on May 31, Memorial Day—only a week after the new structure was opened to the public—disaster struck.

Twenty thousand people were out on the bridge enjoying the pristine spring weather, when a woman tripped on a narrow staircase packed with people. Someone screamed that the bridge was falling, and panic ripped through the dense, surging crowd. In the confusion and terror that followed, twelve people were crushed to death on the packed stairway, and hundreds more trampled in the deadly stampede.

Among the horrified onlookers was ten-

It was the inspiration of the bridge's designer, John Roebling, to include what he called an "elevated promenade"—a walkway reserved for pedestrians and raised above the level of the roadway and streetcar tracks. The unique feature, he said, would "allow people of leisure, and old and young invalids, to promenade over the bridge on fine days, in order to enjoy the beautiful views and fine air.... In a crowded commercial city, [it] will be of incalculable value." On the first full day the bridge was open, 150,000 people crossed on foot to enjoy the extraordinary views of the city and harbor—as millions more would do in the decades to come.

year-old Al Smith, whose ailing father had worked as a watchman on the bridge during construction. He and a group of friends were playing below the Manhattan tower when a dark cloud of coats, hats, parasols, and pocket-books began to rain down upon them from the roadway above. "That was my first view of a great calamity," he later recalled. "I did not sleep for nights."

It was only one of a number of searing child-hood memories that would stay with Smith all his life. Three years later, his father—worn down by a lifetime of overwork and a linger-ing illness that had drained the family's sav-ings—died at the age of forty-five, leaving his wife and two children, Al and Mary, with no means of support.

It was the turning point of Smith's life. Walk-ing back from the funeral, he recalled, the heart-broken family was filled with dread—haunted by the specter of deepening poverty and by the shadow of future partings, since by New York law widows unable to support their children often had them taken by the state.

"I don't know where to turn," Smith's mother admitted to her children in despair. "I don't know where to turn."

It was then that her thirteen-year-old son spoke up. "I'm here—I can take care of you," Al declared—and it was soon apparent he meant every word he said.

Within the space of a few months, he had quit school for good and gone to work—first as the assistant to a truck dispatcher, then as a day laborer at the Fulton Fish Market just up the street, rolling heavy barrels of fish up and down the ramps, thirteen hours a day, six days a week, from four in the morning to five in the afternoon—except on Fridays, when the work began at three.

Years later, the self-educated politician was fond of saying that he had only one degree—"F.F.M.," for Fulton Fish Market—but it was one that he was fiercely proud of. Though the hours were long, at twelve dollars a week the job paid enough to keep the family together, and soon Smith had begun to rise within the tight-knit community of New York's Fourth Ward—befriending members of the Downtown Tammany Club and running errands for a pop-ular district leader named Tom Foley.

In the evenings, he sang old Irish favorites in a local saloon owned by Foley himself. Sit-ting in the audience, some of the older Tam-many bosses began to take notice of the energetic and affable young man—whose strong, distinctive voice, they said, might one day make him a good candidate for office.

PROGRESS AND POVERTY

It is only a matter of three miles from Madi-son Square to Hester Street, but who would dream, who had not seen it, that the same town held within so short a distance scenes and peo-ple so contrasted?

E. S. Martin, *Harper's Monthly*, 1898

Though the great bridge was finished, other chasms remained—which, in the years to come, would grow wider, and deeper, and more dif-ficult to span.

On Memorial Day, May 31, 1883, one week to the day after the Brooklyn Bridge opened to the public, 20,000 people were out on the walkway when a woman at the top of a staircase at the New York end lost her footing, screamed, and set off a panic in the dense throng. As hundreds of terrified people tried to shove their way through the crowd, 12 were trampled to death and dozens more injured. A week later, *Harper's Weekly* published this lithograph, based on eyewitness reports.

For businessmen such as the oil tycoon John D. Rockefeller (top) or the steel magnate Andrew Carnegie (bottom)—from Cleveland and Pittsburgh, respectively—relocating to the city offered crucial access to investment capital as well as a professional network of lawyers, accounting firms, engineers, and advertising agencies. For socially ambitious wives, a move to New York offered the possibility of joining the rarefied upper stratum of American society, whose lavish formal events were reported on across the country. At one of the greatest of these, the Vanderbilt ball in May 1883, Alice Vanderbilt—presumably inspired by Edison's triumphant lighting of lower Manhattan six months earlier—came dressed as "Electric Light" (right).

With the city's industrial engine roaring at full throttle, immigrants as never before were pouring into New York from around the world—fueling the most dynamic economy on earth.

Even as they did, another migration was under way—of millionaires—as one by one, the nation's industrial titans converged on Manhattan, which by the 1880s had become the mecca of all who sought power and prestige in America.

From Pittsburgh came the steel magnates, Andrew Carnegie and Henry Frick—from Chicago, Philip Armour, the millionaire meatpacker—from Cleveland, the world's richest oil tycoon, John D. Rockefeller.

By 1892, nearly half the country's millionaires—eighteen hundred in all—had taken up residence in New York City and its suburbs.

"The movement in this direction is obvious," the social commentator Herbert Croly wrote a few years later, as the pilgrimage continued. "New York is steadily attracting . . . the

best business ability in the country, not only as a matter of convenience, but . . . because of the exceptional opportunity it offers its favored inhabitants of making and spending money. [Wall Street] is as much filled with corporations which conduct business in other parts of the country, as Fifth Avenue is filled with the residences of capitalists who made their money in the West."

The West was yielding tremendous riches . . . steel barons, coal lords, dukes of wheat and beef, of mines and railways, had sprung up from obscurity. Absolute in their own territories, they longed for fresh worlds to conquer. Newspaper accounts of New York Society pictured this organization in colors that thrilled the newly rich of the West. In a great glittering caravan the multi-millionaires of the midlands moved up against the city and by wealth and sheer weight of numbers broke through the archaic barriers.

Marina Van Rennselaer

As the new industrial millionaires poured into the city, they brought with them a scale of public extravagance startling even by the standards of New York.

Along Fifth Avenue, once lined with somber brownstones, a parade of ornate mansions, palaces, castles, and villas soon stretched for two and a half miles—a mind-boggling display of wealth and opulence like nothing seen before or since.

"The interminable succession of luxurious mansions," one observer wrote, "proclaims [a] mad abundance. This avenue has visibly been willed and created by sheer force of millions . . . which has left not an inch of ground untouched."

The transformation had begun in 1883, when Alva Vanderbilt and her husband, William—heir to the commodore's vast fortune—had a fashionable architect named Richard Morris Hunt build them an immense, thirty-seven-room French chateau on the corner of Fifth Avenue and Fifty-second Street.

Before it was done, the extraordinary marble edifice had cost more than $3 million—an unheard-of sum. "The Vanderbilts have come nobly forward," one man wrote, "and showed the world how millionaires ought to live."

This 1883 view, north from St. Patrick's, shows the lower end of what was becoming the most opulent thoroughfare in the world: Fifth Avenue, which would soon be lined for more than two miles with an astonishing succession of palaces, villas, and mansions. In the foreground is the home of William K. Vanderbilt, completed that year by the architect Richard Morris Hunt. Built of imported marble and shaped like a fifteenth-century French chateau, the structure gleamed brilliantly against the austere brownstone of New York's residential districts, establishing a new style and scale for the homes of the city's rich.

To celebrate its completion, the Vanderbilts spent a quarter of a million dollars more on the most elaborate fancy dress ball the city had ever seen. Preparations, the *New York Times* reported, "disturbed the sleep and occupied the waking hours of social butterflies . . . for over six weeks."

On March 26, 1883, all New York turned out for the Vanderbilt ball. Alva's sister came as "Electric Light," wearing a brilliant white satin gown embroidered with diamonds. Alva herself came as a Venetian princess, surrounded by a fluttering flock of real doves.

Even Mrs. Caroline Schermerhorn Astor—the undisputed arbiter of New York's insular high society—made an appearance, thus admitting into her tightly guarded circle a family once dismissed as "railroad money."

"Up to this time," Mrs. Astor's discriminating social secretary, Ward McAllister, observed, "to be worth a million dollars was to be rated as a man of fortune, but now, bygones must be bygones. New York's ideas as to values, when fortune is concerned, leaped boldly up to the ten millions, fifty millions, one hundred millions, and the necessities and luxuries followed suit."

Never . . . has civilization beheld greater lavishness than that which our metropolitan plutocracy displays. More ornate than the swirl of London and more resplendent than that of Paris, only royalty can vie with it, and not always with success. There is many a palace in Europe that would hide its diminished roof beside the sheer luxury of Fifth Avenue homes.
Edgar Saltus

And still the flood of millionaires came on—along with the flood of immigrants—each growing larger with each passing year.

Though the gap between them grew wider, rich and poor alike were greeted now as they came into the harbor by a remarkable sight, rising like an apparition from the Upper Bay.

On October 28, 1886, the gift the French had been trying to give for seventeen years was finally unveiled—its massive stone pedestal designed by Richard Morris Hunt but paid for in the end by the nickels and dimes of hundreds of thousands of ordinary citizens.

Thousands of New Yorkers turned out once again for the opening celebration—though only the city's elite were invited to the formal unveil-

Unlike the exquisite weather that had accompanied the opening of the Brooklyn Bridge three years before, there were leaden, overcast skies for the ceremonial unveiling of the Statue of Liberty on October 28, 1886. The tens of thousands of hardy New Yorkers who lined the shoreline or watched the event from boats in the harbor were further frustrated when a naval artillery salute, fired to welcome President Grover Cleveland onto Bedloe's Island, threw up a shroud of smoke that almost obscured the statue.

The most famous statue in the world—destined to be permanently linked in the public imagination with the very idea of America and New York—was not built by New Yorkers, not wanted by most Americans, and almost never got built at all.

The idea had been born in France, during the tumultuous years following the American Civil War, at a time of deep despair for French liberals. The republican values and love of liberty that both nations shared—and that, tested by fire, had just reemerged in America stronger than ever before—were being trampled on by Napoléon III.

In 1865, hoping to rekindle at home the stability and liberty they so admired in America, a group of French diplomats and businessmen hit upon a novel idea. To commemorate the hundredth anniversary of the Declaration of Independence, the people of France would give the people of America a huge statue, far larger than anything built since antiquity, dedicated to liberty and to the long friendship between the two nations.

Six years later, Frédéric-Auguste Bartholdi, the remarkable 32-year-old painter and sculptor chosen to design the extraordinary monument, set sail for New York to find a suitable site for the project and convince Americans to help build it. Sailing through the

Narrows for the first time on June 21, 1871, he was overwhelmed by the bustle and beauty of the Upper Bay and knew instantly he had found the perfect spot for his statue: a sea-washed outcropping of rock on the western edge of the harbor called Bedloe's Island, once a pauper's grave, and now home to an abandoned fort.

"I have made a little drawing of the work as it would look when emplaced there," Bartholdi wrote. "The island belongs to the government—just opposite the Narrows, which are, so to speak, the gateway to America." Larger than the legendary Colossus of Rhodes built 22 centuries before, the immense classical figure he had in mind would be called *Liberty Enlightening the World.*

"If I myself felt that spirit here," he reasoned, "then it is certainly here that my statue must rise; here where people get their first view of the New World, and where liberty casts her rays on both worlds."

Finding the right spot was one thing, however. Finding "a few people," as Bartholdi himself wrote, "who have enthusiasm for something other than themselves, and the Almighty Dollar," would be another. In the end, it would take more than fifteen years to complete the mammoth undertaking.

At heart, the plan was a simple

one and—as the French thought—Gallically generous: the statue would be paid for not by the government but by private subscription, and if Americans would provide the pedestal, the French themselves would bear the huge costs of building the statue.

Work began on the French side almost immediately. By the end of 1875, the colossal form was taking shape in the immense workshops of Gaget and Gauthier in the rue de Chazelle in Paris.

The logistics alone of building the 151-foot-high sculpture were mind-boggling. Starting from a plaster model just four feet high, the figure had to be painstakingly scaled up 16 times, section by section, from one successively larger model to another. Liberty's eyes would be two and a half feet in diameter; the book she held, inscribed with the date of the Declaration of Independence, taller than a two-story house. To keep from collapsing under its own weight, Liberty would have to be hollow, her outer skin made of thin sheets of hammered copper, less than an eighth of an inch thick, carefully beaten into shape inside immense wooden molds.

The body, it was later said, had been modeled on Bartholdi's mistress, while the features of the face itself were said to resemble those of the sculptor's strong-willed mother.

Once completed, each copper section was bolted separately to a flexible metal armature—itself attached to a rigid iron framework almost 100 feet high. The fantastically strong, superbly light skeleton was the work of an engineering genius named Gustave Eiffel, whose most famous structure was yet to come.

Exposed to the high winds and corrosive sea air of the harbor, the completed statue would have to be not just an artistic but an engineering triumph—able to expand and contract in the heat and cold, and breathe with the changing weather.

Sculptor Frédéric-Auguste Bartholdi, creator of the Statue of Liberty.

By 1876, a section of the right arm was complete, and it was sent to the United States to help with the fund-raising efforts for the pedestal. By 1878, the head and shoulders had been finished, and two years after that, the last French funds were in hand: 600,000 francs in all, raised in subscription drives in towns and villages across the nation.

On July 4, 1884, the completed statue was officially handed over to the American ambassador, Levi P. Morton, then dismantled for the long voyage to New York—where, to Bartholdi's horror, the fund-raising effort had ground to a complete halt.

For three years, the American Committee for the Statue of Liberty had done what it could to raise money for the foundation and for the elegant, 114-foot granite pedestal it would stand on, designed by the architect Richard Morris Hunt. By 1883, some money had trickled in, but from the very start, Bartholdi's project had met with skepticism and indifference in the United States. One newspaper editor thought the idea "an oddity too fantastic and too poetic to be realized." It was somehow too abstract—too artistic—too French. Others resented paying anything at all for what was supposed to be a gift, and few politicians were willing to divert American taxes for a cause so inherently frivolous.

The Statue of Liberty's toes and the base of her torch, Bedloe's Island, 1885.

In March 1885, news hit the papers that funds had all but run out—$100,000 short of the goal.

March 15th, 1885. Money must be raised to complete the pedestal for the Bartholdi statue. It would be an irrevocable disgrace to New York City and the American Republic to have France send us this splendid gift without our having provided even so much as a landing place for it..
    Joseph Pulitzer

Joseph Pulitzer was a red-haired, manically energetic 38-year-old Hungarian immigrant who had come to America 20 years before without a penny in his pocket. Throwing himself into the newspaper business, he had personally pioneered a new kind of illustrated daily newspaper that appealed to the millions of new working-class immigrants in America, for whom English was scarcely even a second language.

In 1883, he moved to New York and took over a struggling daily paper called the *New York World*—then looked around for a cause to help boost circulation. He soon found one.

We must raise the money! The World *is the people's paper, and it now appeals to the people to come forward and raise the money. . . . The statue . . . was paid [for] by the masses of the French people— by the workingmen, the tradesmen, the shop girls, the artisans—by all, irrespective of class or condition. Let us respond in like manner. Let us not wait for the millionaires to give this money. It is not a gift from the millionaires of France to the millionaires of America, but a gift of the whole people of France to the whole people of America. Take this appeal to yourself personally. . . . Let us hear from the people.*
    Joseph Pulitzer

The campaign was a spectacular success. Day after day, the *World* excoriated New York's rich, while exhorting the people to join the cause—printing the name of every loyal citizen willing to make any contribution to the pedestal.

The donations poured in. In five months, more than 120,000 people, mostly working people and school-children, contributed more than $100,000, sometimes in sums as small as a nickel.

"The people have done their work well," Pulitzer declared. "Their liberality has saved the great Republic from disgrace." It had also made Pulitzer's name a household word.

In the spring of 1886, the last stone of Hunt's exquisite pedestal was set in place, and soon the great statue itself—which had been slumbering on Bedloe's Island in 200 wooden crates for almost a year—finally began to rise above the harbor. When complete, perched high atop her massive Egyptianate base, the statue soared 305 feet above the water—higher even than the towers of the recently completed Brooklyn Bridge—the tallest structure in the New World.

On the rainy, windswept afternoon of October 28, 1886, huge crowds surged down to lower Manhattan and lined the shorefront around the harbor to catch a glimpse of the elaborate opening ceremony. "Not a square centimeter of the streets was clear," one foreign journalist wrote. "The Brooklyn Bridge groans under its load of humanity. Sidewalks, portals, balconies, penthouses, were covered by a happy throng."

Ships of every kind jammed the bay and circled Bedloe's Island. Shortly after one in the afternoon President Grover Cleveland stepped ashore for the unveiling ceremony, and the harbor exploded in a deafening roar, as steam whistles blew, cannon boomed, and sirens wailed from ships and buildings on shore.

Bartholdi, the undisputed hero of the day, climbed up into the statue's head to officially unveil Liberty's face. President Cleveland—who as governor of New York had vetoed funds for the project two years before— delivered the keynote address.

Instead of grasping in her hand thunderbolts of terror and death, she holds aloft the light which illumines the way to man's enfranchisement. There it shall gleam upon the shore of our sister republic in the East. Reflected and joined with answering rays, a stream of light shall pierce the darkness of ignorance . . . until liberty enlightens the world.

Night came, and the crowds went home. Out in the harbor ships moved back and forth across the darkening bay: freighters bound for every port in the world; barges filled with oil and coal; big ocean-going steamships, packed to the rails with tourists, businessmen returning from abroad—and thousands upon thousands of immigrants.

Passing the dimly glowing statue that first night, the boatloads of new immigrants knew nothing of its French sponsors or their lofty ideals. And yet the meaning of the statue seemed obvious enough. At the very edge of the New World, Americans had placed a giant statue of a woman with a torch to welcome them as they arrived, as if to confirm that they had made the right choice, after all, in coming.

The Statue of Liberty rising in the Paris workyard of Gaget and Gauthier, about 1883.

ing, where President Grover Cleveland thanked the French for so nobly upholding the highest republican ideals.

On November 2, 1886, five days after the Statue of Liberty was unveiled, New Yorkers went to the polls.

On the ballot was a brilliant social theorist named Henry George, whose book, *Progress and Poverty*, had already made him one of the most celebrated political thinkers in America.

More than any other campaign in the city's history, the election would prove to be a dramatic referendum on the city's glaring disparities of poverty and wealth.

"Where . . . material progress [is] most fully realized," George declared, "we find the deepest poverty."

The promised land flies before us like the mirage. . . . Material progress does not merely fail to relieve poverty—it actually produces it. . . . This association of progress with poverty is the great enigma of our times. It is the central fact from which spring industrial, social and political difficulties that perplex the world, and with which statesmanship and philanthropy and education grapple in vain. It is the riddle

which the Sphinx of Fate puts to our civilization, which not to answer is to be destroyed.
Henry George, *Progress and Poverty*

"Why should there be such abject poverty in this city?" George thundered. "We are toiling, perhaps, for Mrs. Astor . . . [or] the heirs of some dead Dutchman."

Running as an independent candidate, George called for a uniform land tax that would subsidize public transportation and improve housing and working conditions throughout the city.

Though bitterly attacked by both the Republican party and Tammany Hall, George drew support from a surprising coalition of German socialists, Irish labor union leaders, garment workers, schoolteachers, merchants, doctors, clergyman, lawyers, and reformers.

It was in many ways the closest New Yorkers ever came to adopting a radical alternative to capitalism—but in the end Henry George was no match for Tammany, which had arisen from the Tweed scandals stronger than ever before.

Frightened by the strength of George's support, Tammany's bosses threw their support

Mrs. Almond lived much farther up town, on an embryonic street, with a high number—a region where the extension of the city began to assume a theoretic air, where poplars grew beside the pavement (where there was one) and mingled their shade with the steep roofs of desultory Dutch homes, and where pigs and chickens disported themselves in the gutter.

> Henry James,
> *Washington Square*

For years, visitors and residents alike had been struck by the contrast between the lower end of Manhattan—one of the most densely built-up settlements in the world—and the miles of sparsely populated farmland farther up the island. In the decades following the Civil War, as the city pushed north of 59th Street and swept around Central Park, the juxtaposition of city and country grew stranger than ever on the island of Manhattan—a landscape eerily poised now between a fading rural past and an advancing urban future.

We are out of town now; the numbers of the streets are running up into the hundreds, and the streets themselves are little more than numbers— mere rows of vacant lots where houses are to be. A horde of dwellings, from the mere mud hovel to the neat little wooden cottage, have sprung up, straggling anyhow and everywhere. Garments of all kinds are flapping in the breeze to dry; geese and fowls, gaunt pigs and bare-footed children, all run wild together. Squatters all, having no claim upon the land they occupy, to be turned out someday—but meanwhile, "someday" is far off.

> Mary Duffus Hardy, 1881

The census of 1870 disclosed that nearly 10,000 Irish, German, and African American settlers were living in the upper wards of Manhattan Island (a number that increased dramatically after the Panic of 1873, as hundreds of newly unemployed New Yorkers, unable to afford even the cheapest quarters in the city itself, rented shacks or hovels in the exurban sprawl north of the metropolis, or simply squatted on other people's property). A decade after the Civil War, the northern half of Manhattan remained a largely undeveloped expanse of open fields and subsistence farms, interrupted here and there by isolated settlements, some dating back to the colonial era—including Harsenville, a rural village on the Upper

Cows grazing on a pasture at 45th Street and Lexington Avenue, about 1872. In the distance looms the northern end of the vast iron-and-glass train shed of Grand Central Depot (see page 150).

West 54th Street, just off Fifth Avenue, 1866. Fifteen years after this view was taken, this brownstone mansion was purchased by John D. Rockefeller, who preferred the relative peacefulness of its side-street location to the ostentation and bustle of Fifth Avenue itself. The property would later be donated by the Rockefeller family to the Museum of Modern Art, and eventually became the site of the museum's sculpture garden.

Looking south from the Dakota apartment house at 72nd Street and Central Park West, about 1890. The completed landscape of the park and the rectangular grid of city streets made for a dramatic contrast with the run-down shanties and subsistence farms of an earlier era.

A subsistence farm on the west side of Columbus Avenue, between 78th and 79th Streets, taken in 1892 by the Brooklyn photographer Julius Wilcox (see page 197).

West Side—Manhattanville, a thriving industrial hamlet near 125th Street and Broadway— and Harlem, a sprawling farming community north of Central Park founded by the Dutch in 1640. Though Harlem's big colonial estates had long ago been subdivided into smaller properties, several eighteenth-century houses still survived. On Sundays, middle-class New Yorkers enjoyed taking carriage rides along the leafy lanes first laid out by Dutch and English colonists, which still meandered through the area. Boys fishing in Harlem Creek sometimes pulled up a button from the uniform of a Revolutionary War soldier.

By 1880, however, the rumble of the approaching city could be heard all across upper Manhattan— including the earsplitting reports of black-powder explosions, as demolition teams blasted their way through granite outcroppings 20 feet tall or more, clearing the way for new streets and avenues.

(The deafening explosions sent enormous missiles of flying stone hurtling through the air—and occasionally through the roofs of nearby shacks and houses.) After the demolition crews came teams of surveyors and builders, installing water, sewer, and gas lines beneath the streets, then laying out the streets themselves in strict accordance with the 1811 Commissioners' Plan, now more than half a century old but still governing the city's growth. The result was a strange vision of paved streets and bluestone sidewalks, neatly defining the rectilinear blocks of a city which did not yet exist.

Then at last the city itself arrived, as substantial dwellings began to rise on the empty lots. In the vanguard were New York's newest rich, anxious for the prestige of a Fifth Avenue address but unable to obtain properties farther south. Along a narrow corridor lining the park's eastern edge, elaborate mansions of limestone and granite began rising amid the poultry farms and wooden shacks. The pouring of tea in the first-floor salon of an ornate new mansion might well be interrupted by the sound of a chicken being slaughtered on the farm next door.

"It was her habit to sit in a window of her sitting room on the ground floor," the novelist Edith Wharton wrote of one such wealthy pioneer, "as if watching calmly for life and fashion to flow northward to her solitary doors. She seemed in no hurry to have them come, for her patience was equalled by her confidence. She was sure that presently . . . the quarries, the one-time saloons, the wooden greenhouses in ragged gardens, and the rocks from which goats surveyed the scene, would vanish before the advance of residences as stately as her own . . . even statelier; and that the cobblestones over which the old clattering omnibuses bumped would be replaced by smooth asphalt, such as people reported having seen in Paris."

behind Abram S. Hewitt, a moderate Democratic businessman who had been a key supporter of the Brooklyn Bridge.

Thanks to Tammany's machinations, on election day George was defeated by one of the largest margins in the city's history.

But though in the years to come the gulf he had hoped to bridge grew wider, his campaign had revealed an extraordinary fact about New York City.

The most capitalist place in America was beginning to generate the most vibrant alternatives to capitalism itself—and the most radical urban culture in the country.

OUT OF THE SHADOWS

February 12th, 1888. With their way illuminated by spasmodic flashes, as bright and brief as those of lightning itself, a mysterious party has lately been startling the town. Denizens of the dives, tramps and bummers in their lodgings, and all the wild variety of New York night life have marveled at the phenomenon. What they saw was three or four figures in the gloom, a ghostly tripod, some weird and uncanny move-ments, the blinding flash, and then they heard the patter of retreating footsteps and the mysterious visitors were gone.

Jacob Riis, *New York Sun*

In October 1890, a groundbreaking publication appeared in the bookstores of New York City.

Featuring printed text side by side with half-tone photographs for the first time in a published manuscript, it was called *How the Other Half Lives*.

In the years to come, it would change forever the way people thought about the city.

Its author was a forty-one-year-old Danish immigrant named Jacob Riis, who had come to the city twenty years before. After suffering months of grueling poverty on the streets of New York, Riis had eventually found work at the *New York Tribune*, and spent the next eleven years exploring the wretched slums of the Lower East Side as a police reporter.

"The sights," he later said, "gripped my heart until I felt that I must tell of them or burst."

Determined to show the world what he had seen, he began publishing magazine articles, but they "seemed to make no impression," he wrote.

Once an Irish district but now almost entirely Italian, the angled stretch called Mulberry Bend (right) was "the foul core" of the slums, according to the photographer and reformer Jacob Riis (above), who knew the area from his years as a police reporter, working out of a press office at 301 Mulberry, across from police headquarters. "In the twenty years of my acquaintance," he wrote, "I do not believe there was a week in which [the Bend] was not heard from in police reports, generally in connection with a crime of violence.... So between the vendetta, the Mafia, the ordinary neighborhood feuds and the Bend itself, always picturesque, outrageously dirty, it was not hard to keep it in the foreground." After years of tireless campaigning by Riis, city officials agreed to demolish the block on the left and, in 1897, opened a landscaped park on its site.

He thought of taking pictures, but the tenements were too dark for the photographs to come out.

Then, in 1887, he read of a dramatic breakthrough in photographic technology—a special magnesium powder that ignited while the camera's shutter was open, flooding even the darkest scenes with a brilliant flash of light.

"There it was," Riis later wrote, "the thing I had been looking for all those years. A way had been discovered to take pictures by flashlight. The darkest corner might be photographed that way."

Armed with the new equipment, Riis and his colleagues set out into the New York night.

It was dirty, exhausting, dangerous work. The explosive powder was tricky to use and could be hazardous. Riis twice set fire to houses he was investigating, once set his own clothes on fire, and once nearly blinded himself.

But the results were worth it. The images Riis and his colleagues brought back were like nothing anyone had ever seen before—and brought New Yorkers face-to-face with a reality most had long sought to avoid: their city, one of the wealthiest in the world, had become home to hundreds of thousands of desperately poor people, living in conditions of unspeakable deprivation.

He took his camera everywhere—down obscure courtyards and back ways known by names like Rag Picker's Row, Blind Man's Alley, and Bottle Alley.

In a place called Bandits' Roost, he photographed a dozen men, all wanted for murder, he said.

He was especially moved by the plight of the young—the "street arabs" who sold newspapers by day and slept in alleys by night, the child laborers who worked long hours, sometimes seven days a week, in stifling factories and sweatshops, the abandoned children who had been left by their parents to fend for themselves.

But his main focus was the wretched tenements themselves—where by 1890 more than *two-thirds* of New York's 1.5 million citizens were forced to dwell.

"I went up the dark stairs in one of those tenements," Riis wrote of one expedition into a rear tenement, "and there I trod upon a baby. It is the regular means of introduction in the old dark houses, but I never was able to get used to it. I . . . photographed [the] baby standing with its back against the public sink in a pool of filth that overflowed on the floor. I do not marvel . . . that one in five children in the rear tenement, into which the sunlight never comes, was killed by the house. It seemed strange, rather, that any survived."

The worst buildings were the oldest, built without regulations of any kind. On narrow city lots originally intended for single-family row houses, landlords had thrown up buildings seven stories high and often more than ninety feet deep.

Packed side to side and back to back, they entombed their tenants in thousands of coffin-like rooms, most without access to air or light.

More recent structures were hardly any better. In 1879, an ill-conceived effort at housing reform had given rise to a new generation of almost equally dismal structures. Built on the notorious "dumbbell" plan, the cramped new buildings were pinched in the middle to provide shallow airshafts on each side—too narrow, at two and half feet, to provide anything more than a gloomy half-light to the apartment interiors.

Over the next ten years, more than twenty thousand of the dark, grim, poorly ventilated structures were built—not only in the Lower East Side, but all along the eastern and western edges of Manhattan.

"Where are the tenements of to-day?" Riis wrote. "Say rather: where are they not? In fifty years they have crept up . . . the whole length of the island. . . . Crowding all the lower wards, wherever business leaves a foot of ground unclaimed; strung along both rivers, like ball and chain tied to the foot of every street. . . . The tenements to-day *are* New York."

In the end, the most shocking thing about the tenements was their sheer crowding.

One district in the Eleventh Ward contained nearly six hundred people per acre—easily surpassing its closest rivals, the Black Hole of Calcutta and the slums of Bombay.

Ill fed and ill clothed, packed into buildings with few sinks or toilets and sometimes with no plumbing at all, tenement dwellers were prey to every kind of disease: diphtheria, influenza, typhoid, pneumonia. Worst of all was the dis-

Baxter Street Court, 22 Baxter Street, 1890. In an effort to reform the city's housing laws, Riis took his camera to the yards behind the tenements—narrow, leftover areas which provided the only open space, other than the teeming streets, available in the slums. "I counted the other day the little ones, up to ten years old, in a . . . tenement that for a yard has a . . . space in the center with sides fourteen or fifteen feet long, just enough for a row of ill-smelling [water] closets . . . and a hydrant. . . . There was about as much light in this 'yard' as in the average cellar. . . . I had counted one hundred twenty eight in forty families."

For his 1892 book, *Children of the Slums*, Riis interviewed dozens of young tenement dwellers, including this girl, Katie (top), who lived on West 49th Street. "'What kind of work do you do?' I asked," he wrote. "'I scrubs,' she replied promptly, and her look guaranteed that what she scrubbed came out clean. . . . On the top floor of a tenement she was keeping house for her older sister and two brothers, all of whom worked. She scrubbed and swept and went to school all as a matter of course and ran the house with an occasional lift from the neighbors, who were poorer than they. . . ."

Home of an Italian ragpicker, Jersey Street, about 1889 (bottom).

Bandits' Roost, 1895. From his days as a crime reporter, Riis came to know the secluded haunts of the city's slums—such as this narrow alley just off Mulberry Street known as Bandits' Roost. "It has borne this name these many years," he wrote, "and though there have been entire changes of occupants in that time, each succeeding batch seems to be calculated in appearance and character to keep up the appropriateness of that name."

ease called the white plague—tuberculosis. Every year, twenty thousand new cases were reported. Every year, eight thousand people died of the disease.

How the Other Half Lives was a call to arms—awakening New Yorkers to the condition of the poor as nothing else had.

Riis's photographic polemic was a new way of seeing the world—a *modern* way—and he used it not only to underscore his outrage but to spur people to action. The slums were not inevitable, he insisted. They had been built by men and women, and men and women could change them.

Not long after the book was published, New York's energetic young civil service commissioner, Theodore Roosevelt, called on Riis at his office on Printing House Row. The writer was out, but Roosevelt left his calling card, with a note on the back.

"I have read your book," the message said, "and I have come to help."

July and August spell death to the army of little ones whom the doctor's skill is powerless to save. Sleepless mothers walk the street in the gray of the early dawn, trying to stir a cooling breeze to fan the brow of the sick baby. There is no sadder sight than this patient devotion against fearfully hopeless odds. Little coffins are stacked mountains-high on the decks of the Charity Commissioners' boat when it makes its semi-weekly trip to the city cemetery.

Jacob Riis

Potter's Field on Hart Island, photographed by Jacob Riis, 1889. On an isolated spot of land in Long Island Sound, tens of thousands of New Yorkers unable to afford a private burial were interred by the city, in coffins stacked three deep in mass, unmarked graves. The field remains in use to this day.

Although he did not seek the larger social impact of Jacob Riis, the Brooklyn photographer Julius Wilcox was also moved to carry his camera and flash to the lesser-known corners of the city. Above, a workingmen's saloon called Silver Dollar Smith's, photographed near midnight in 1892; below left, a view of four corpses in "the cooler" at the city morgue; below right, a row of holding cells—known as the "ten-day pen"—in the Tombs, the city's main jail, located on Centre Street in lower Manhattan.

By 1879, New York's Metropolitan Police had grown to a force of more than 2,100 men—the largest and best organized law enforcement agency in the country. Along the way, its responsibilities had expanded enormously. To a startling degree, it fell to the city's patrolmen to keep the complex metropolis in running order—reporting water breaks and broken streetlamps, curbing rabid animals, inspecting steam boilers to prevent explosions. A special force of 109 men patrolled the harbor, while hundreds more were assigned the daunting task called "protection of interior communications"—or traffic duty—dispersing crowds, regulating parades, and preventing horses and carriages from racing through the streets.

Yet despite it all, the department remained riddled with corruption and brutality. "There is more law at the end of a police-man's nightstick than in all the decisions of the Supreme Court," the notorious precinct captain Alexander "Clubber" Williams was said to have declared proudly. Williams had gained his nickname the first day on the job, when he picked a fight with two thugs, beat them senseless with his club, then threw them both through a shop window.

During his career, he would be brought up on brutality charges 358 times—and forced to pay 224 fines. He would also be remembered for giving the city's red-light district its name—the Tenderloin. "I've been eating chuck steak ever since I've been on the force," he said, on hearing he was to be assigned to the area. "Now I'm going to have a bit of the tenderloin."

In 1880, the public's imagination was captured by another law enforcement official—a 37-year-old Irish-born police inspector who had just been promoted to chief of detectives, after solving a daring robbery of $3 million from the Manhattan Bank. Dynamic, zealous, and ruthlessly efficient, Inspector Thomas F. Byrnes would do more than anyone else to bring New York's police department into the modern age.

He was a "czar," Jacob Riis later wrote, "with all the autocrat's irresponsible powers. But he made the detective service great." Behind closed doors, Byrnes himself could be astonishingly brutal—employing a long, harsh questioning technique that he called the "third degree." But unlike his predecessors, Byrnes was careful to hide any trace of violence—or corruption—from public view. Disguising his native Irish brogue under an elaborate English vocabulary, he presented himself as "a smooth and skilled man . . . of system and method," and from the day he took over he began to modernize the way the city's police went about their jobs.

He began by creating the first "mug books"—photographic images of 7,000 known criminals—with copies kept at headquarters and local precincts and, in some cases, passed along to police in other cities. He reorganized the Detective Bureau, weeding out the most openly corrupt men and installing in their place a handpicked group of younger officers—many of whom, one astonished journalist reported, "were college bred, and could pass muster in the best society."

A natural politician, Byrnes shrewdly focused most of his crime-fighting resources on the Wall Street financial district, where tens of millions of dollars in banknotes, bonds, stock certificates, and precious metals were carried daily around the streets by hand—and were being stolen with dismaying regularity. "Skilled thieves," one reporter wrote, "prized it as the richest of their hunting grounds."

Unlike his contemporaries, who looked to the brothels and saloons of the Tenderloin for payoffs, Byrnes realized that the gratitude of Wall Street's brokers and bankers would dwarf anything a local saloonkeeper could provide. On March 11, 1880, Byrnes announced—with all the fanfare of a natural-born public relations man—that the northern boundary of lower Manhattan's financial district, Fulton Street, would henceforth be considered a "dead line," below which any known swindler or criminal would be arrested on sight, whether they had committed a crime or not.

"They may view afar," *Harper's Magazine* noted approvingly, "but they may not enter. Any thief found below a line drawn across the city through Fulton Street is seized at once and compelled to account for himself. If the explanation be not satisfactory, the grip of the law tightens around the culprit, and the familiar jail again becomes his home."

The edict was draconian—and by later standards, almost certainly unconstitutional—but it worked. Looking back in 1887, Byrnes boasted that "from the 12th of March 1880, until today, they have not lost a ten-cent stamp in Wall Street by a professional thief—not a penny, not a cent."

As Wall Street became the financial center of the country, Byrnes efficiently immunized it from the rest of the struggling immigrant city. The city's financiers—now guaranteed a secure place in which to transact their business—joined the chorus of praise for the chief detective, and as Byrnes had hoped, some expressed their gratitude in quieter but more tangible ways. In 1894, when a group of reformers called the Lexow Committee began a sweeping investigation of police corruption in New York, Byrnes abruptly decided it was time to leave public service. He went on to spend the last 14 years of his life in comfortable retirement—living off a personal fortune of $350,000 that he had somehow amassed on an annual salary of just $2,000.

Policeman directing a stranger, Fulton Street and Broadway, about 1895.

115 116 117

ELLEN CLEGG,
ALIAS ELLEN LEE,
SHOP LIFTER AND PICKPOCKET

MARY HOLLBROOK
ALIAS MOLLY HOEY,
PICKPOCKET

MARGRET BROWN,
ALIAS OLD MOTHER HUBBARD,
PICKPOCKET AND SATCHEL WORKER

118 119 120

CHRISTENE MAYER,
ALIAS KID GLOVE ROSEY,
SHOP LIFTER

LENA KLEINSCHMIDT,
ALIAS RICE and BLACK LENA,
SHOP LIFTER

Among the innovations made by Thomas F. Byrnes, chief inspector of the New York Police Department (left), was the extensive use of photography to identify professional criminals—such as the six women, far left, shown in a page from his "rogues gallery," the first mug book. Above, convicted prisoners assembling in the snow, in the yard of the penitentiary on Blackwell's Island—now called Roosevelt Island—in the middle of the East River.

A detective manhandling a suspect into a cell at the Tombs, about 1895.

Sunday, March 11, 1888, dawned warm and unseasonably mild, with a scent of spring in the air. The day before, the *New York Herald* had published a poem by Walt Whitman about the first flower of spring, and with the trees already in bud in Central Park the mildest winter in 17 years was coming to a close with a bout of rainy, temperate weather.

From the eight-story Equitable Building on lower Broadway, the U.S. Weather Bureau released its evening forecast: "Cloudy, followed by light rain and clearing."

Toward sunset, the gentle rain turned to a downpour, and the temperature started to plummet.

At 10 o'clock, Al Smith's mother instructed her 14-year-old son to fasten the shutters on the family's candy store on Dover Street and come back inside. Around midnight, the rain turned to snow, driven by a fierce, rising wind. As two gigantic storm systems converged on New York City, the Blizzard of 1888—the greatest winter storm of the nineteenth century—had begun.

The wind howled, whistled, banged, roared and moaned as it rushed along. It fell upon the house sides in fearful gusts, it strained great plate glass windows, rocked the frame houses, pressed against the doors so that it was almost too dangerous to open them. It was a visible, substantial wind, so freighted was it with snow.
  Julian Ralph, New York Sun

Sign boards were stripped from the fronts of stores and hurled through the storm clouds. Hats were picked up and carried out of sight . . . men and women were blown flat on the ground or picked up into the air and thrown against buildings. Hundreds of pedestrians were cut and bruised. Many were run over. . . .

Looking up New Street in lower Manhattan, after the blizzard of 1888.

It seemed as if a million devils were loose in the air.
  New York Herald

No one could remember anything like it. One man saw a "veritable rain of sparrows falling dead from the eaves of nearby buildings." By Monday, train service in and out of the city had been suspended, and ships were no longer able to enter or leave the port. Thirty-foot drifts blocked storefronts and building entrances, rendering travel by horse cars all but impossible.

Despite the raging storm, tens of thousands of working-class New Yorkers, unable to afford the loss of a day's wages, set out for work on foot or aboard the few elevated trains that were still running. By noon, the last of these had gone out of service, stranding 15,000 people high above the streets in unheated coaches that tottered frighteningly in the wind. Enterprising boys propped ladders against the tracks, and escorted anxious passengers to safety, for a 25-cent fee.

For more than two days, the city huddled against the strange white seige. Every bed in every hotel room in New York City was taken, and stranded visitors spilled out into the lobbies, where they slept on sofas, billiard tables, and the floor. At Macy's, shopgirls bedded down for the night on display room mattresses, and hundreds of people with nowhere else to go retreated to the relative warmth of the city's jails.

Hardest hit by the lethal storm were the wretched tenement districts of the Lower East Side, where by Monday night conditions had become appalling. At 10:00 p.m. the gas jets were closed down, plunging frightened tenants into complete darkness. With the temperature hovering near zero, coal supplies ran out and stoves went cold, forcing tenement dwellers to huddle together for warmth.

On Wednesday, after 54 hours, the snow finally stopped, and the city began digging out. Rescue parties wading through the huge drifts found bodies buried beneath the snow. In all, more than a dozen New Yorkers had frozen to death. Property damage was estimated at more than $20 million.

Though rural areas had been hit far harder than New York, it was in the city itself that the blizzard's impact became a legend. Dependent now upon intricate lines of gas, water, telephone, and electricity, New Yorkers found themselves vulnerable in new modern ways: two-thirds of Manhattan's telephone and electric poles had come down, completely disrupting service. "It is our own advantages," wrote one New Yorker, "that have gone back on us."

Having been reminded by the elemental force of nature of their common humanity, New Yorkers quickly resolved never to let it happen again. Within months, by mayoral decree, the unsightly tangle of utility lines had begun to be buried safely beneath the city streets. That same year, the *New York Times* published a detailed proposal for an entirely new kind of public transportation system, one that would be invulnerable to the weather. Powered by electricity, it would run the length of Manhattan—entirely underground.

GREATER NEW YORK

After an absence, I am now again in New York City and Brooklyn, on a few weeks' vacation. The splendor, and oceanic amplitude and rush of these great cities . . . the endless ships, the tumultuous streets, Broadway, the heavy, low, musical roar, hardly ever intermitted, even at night; . . . More and more, I realize that not Nature alone is great in her fields of freedom and the open air, but in the Artificial, the work of man too is equally great—in this profusion of teeming humanity—in these ingenuities, streets, goods, houses, ships—these hurrying, feverish, electric crowds of men . . . and all this mighty, many-threaded wealth and industry concentrated here.

Walt Whitman

In January 1892, Walt Whitman sent an announcement to the *New York Herald*, notifying his readers that *Leaves of Grass*, the revolutionary book of poems he had lovingly rewritten for almost forty years, was now complete.

Two months later, on March 26, 1892, the most visionary poet the city had ever seen died.

"I bequeath myself to the dirt to grow from the grass I love," he wrote, in lines that were placed on his grave. "If you want me again look for me under your boot-soles."

I did feel that there was a tingling beneath this huge city of ours; a restlessness that promised we knew not what. We could literally see New York expanding, growing, reaching out.

Charles Hanson Towne

Designed by the firm of McKim, Mead and White, and built in 1890 at a cost of $3 million, Madison Square Garden was an elegant civic playground for New York's social elite, and the largest building in America devoted entirely to entertainment. Covering a full block, the structure included a 5,000-seat amphitheater (big enough for horse shows, national political conventions, or Barnum's circus), a small opera house, a ballroom, a restaurant, and a rooftop cabaret where light musical shows were staged on summer evenings. When Augustus St. Gaudens's nude statue of the goddess Diana was installed atop the tower, New Yorkers were scandalized—as they would be again, sixteen years later, when the structure's architect, Stanford White, was shot to death by a jealous husband, Harry Thaw, as he sat watching a performance of *Mam'selle Champagne* in the rooftop cabaret.

By then, the city that Whitman had helped imagine—and that men like Olmsted, Roebling, Tweed, and Morgan had done so much to transform—had changed beyond recognition.

No longer the "straggling, unfinished" place visitors had disparaged in 1865, New York now covered virtually all of Manhattan Island, with a staggering ninety thousand residential buildings and twenty-five thousand commercial structures.

During that time its population had swelled from 900,000 to almost 2 million.

Its 575 miles of paved streets were served by 444 miles of sewer line, 685 miles of water mains, and over twenty-eight thousand streetlamps—almost all of them electrified.

On the eve of the Civil War, there had been 600 textile factories in New York. Now, there were 10,000. In all, there were more than twenty-five thousand industries in the city, producing 299 types of products, worth $750 million a year.

More than 350,000 New Yorkers now spent their days in factories and shops—building sewing machines, making pianos, brewing beer, rolling tobacco, printing books. Others refined sugar, tanned leather, milled lumber, processed chemicals. Still others hauled coal, slaughtered cattle, or sorted rags and refuse.

Five hundred workers in the city made coffins. Five thousand made artificial flowers. A hundred fifty thousand made clothing.

By the last decade of the nineteenth century, the transformation of New York from merchant city to industrial metropolis was complete.

But even greater changes lay in store.

Four decades before, Frederick Law Olmsted and Calvert Vaux had imagined the sylvan grandeur of Central Park as an antidote and spiritual respite to the unrelenting commercial city.

Now a new generation of New Yorkers—for whom the accumulation of personal wealth no longer seemed an end in itself—proposed that the city aspire to the highest ideals of culture, beauty, and repose.

Nothing expressed the imperial aspirations of the new metropolis more obviously than the elaborate ceremonial structures built to honor Admiral George Dewey for his 1898 naval victory against the Spanish in Manila Bay. Erected at 23rd Street and Fifth Avenue, the Roman-style triumphal arch and colonnade—built entirely of wood and plaster—were carefully aligned with the Washington Arch, fifteen blocks to the south, turning the entire length of lower Fifth Avenue into a grand processional setting for the admiral's victory parade. The structures were dismantled within a year.

"Today conditions are rapidly changing," a critic named Arthur Hoeber declared. "We have emerged from the primitive state. We are heaping up unprecedented wealth. [But] it does not suffice to roll up an enormous bank account; there is something else in this life of ours."

In little more than ten years—in an astonishing burst of philanthropy, cultural ambition, vanity, and civic pride, unlike anything ever seen in America before or since—New Yorkers made unspeakably rich during the Gilded Age began to use their wealth to create a series of extraordinary public institutions. They were eager to show the world that New York was now the cultural equal of London, Paris, and Rome—and to show themselves, perhaps, that their grasping commercial metropolis was capable of creating something that transcended commerce.

It would be the greatest flowering of civic culture in the history of America.

In 1890, an extraordinary entertainment complex arose on Madison Square—called Madison Square Garden—its ornate 304-foot-tall tower modeled on the Giralda of Seville.

One year later, the largest concert hall in the country, Carnegie Hall, opened its doors for the first time on Seventh Avenue and Fifty-seventh Street, with an inaugural concert by the New York Philharmonic, conducted by the great Tchaikovsky himself.

In 1892, an elegant neoclassical plaza, called Columbus Circle, was finished at Fifty-ninth Street and Central Park West, timed to celebrate the four hundredth anniversary of the discovery of the new world.

Farther uptown, meanwhile, work had begun on the largest cathedral on earth, the Cathedral of St. John the Divine.

With astounding speed the outlines of a new metropolis—an Apollonian dream city—were beginning to emerge.

Inspired in part by the gleaming White City of the World's Columbian Exposition, which opened in Chicago in 1893—architectural geniuses like the partners Charles McKim, William Mead, and Stanford White were beginning to call forth from within the confines of their own blackened metropolis a new kind of city—a more unified, orderly, and majestic city,

The quality of being metropolitan is not merely a matter of population. A city must possess other claims to superiority. It must not only reflect national tendencies, but must sum them up and transform them. It must not only mirror typical American ways of thought and action, but it must anticipate, define, and realize national ideals.

Herbert Croly

Riverside Drive, looking north toward Grant's Tomb, 1897. Just before his death in 1885, former president Ulysses S. Grant, who had spent the last years of his life in New York, indicated a desire to be buried in the city. By 1897, a vast neoclassical structure—the largest mausoleum in America, its interior modeled on the tomb of Napoléon Bonaparte in Paris—had arisen at the edge of Morningside Heights, overlooking the Hudson, and swiftly become a popular destination for carriages making pleasure trips along Riverside Drive.

whose architecture and public institutions befitted the imperial capital New York was becoming.

In 1893, Columbia University decided to abandon its cramped midtown quarters for a magnificent neoclassical campus on Morningside Heights, high above the Hudson River, that was soon being called the Acropolis of America.

One year later, New York University opened its own fifty-acre campus across the Harlem River in the Bronx—and by then work had begun on magnificent new homes for the Brooklyn Museum, the American Museum of Natural History, and the Metropolitan Museum of Art.

"The rage of Wall Street is to convert all baser things into gold," Joseph Choate, one of the Metropolitan's founding trustees, declared when the museum's massive Fifth Avenue wing opened in 1895. "But ours is the higher ambition to convert your useless gold into things of living beauty that shall be a joy to a whole people for a thousand years."

And still the amazing renaissance went on—with the most moving edifice of them all yet to come.

In the spring of 1897, at the corner of Forty-second Street and Fifth Avenue—where the massive Croton Reservoir had once stood—construction began on an extraordinary new institution—the New York Public Library, formed from the consolidation of three smaller collections.

Built by private funds and—unlike any comparable institution in the world—open free of charge to the general public, it would become the greatest municipal library in the world.

"What London is to the Continent, what Rome in its imperial day was to the Empire," a Wall Street financier proudly declared, surveying what the city achieved in less than ten years, "New York is to the immense domain of the American republic, a natural stage . . . for the great drama of civilization on this Continent."

"Old New York has been torn down," another critic agreed, "and another city has arisen on its site."

And there was one last consolidation to come before the century came to an end—more breathtaking than anything that had come before.

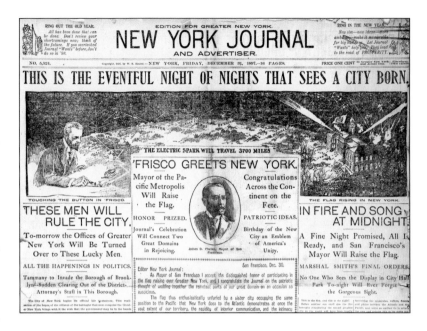

At the stroke of midnight, December 31, 1897, the cities of New York and Brooklyn, together with 38 towns and villages in Queens, the Bronx, and Staten Island, were politically consolidated into a single five-borough metropolis called Greater New York. With 327 square miles and nearly 3.5 million people, New York overnight became the second largest city in the world, after London.

Unlike many Brooklynites, who were proud of their city's independence and angered by its loss through consolidation, the editors of the *Brooklyn Daily Eagle* welcomed the creation of Greater New York, choosing to symbolize the new five-borough city with an image of five women, joining their torches to create a light of massed brilliance.

Since just after the Civil War, civic leaders led by a visionary city planner named Andrew Haswell Green had been calling for the city to expand its borders beyond the confines of Manhattan Island—fearful of being overtaken by New York's younger rival, Chicago, and mindful that the manifest destiny of any great metropolis was to grow.

On January 1, 1898, the wave of corporate mergers and cultural consolidations sweeping

New York came to an astonishing climax, when the city itself was reinvented virtually overnight—on a scale unlike anything that has ever happened to an American city before or since.

After three decades of intense political maneuvering, the largest city in America resolved to fling back its boundaries—merging with Brooklyn, itself the third largest city in America, and thirty-eight towns and villages in Queens, Staten Island, and the Bronx, to create a gigantic five-borough metropolis, now called Greater New York.

As midnight approached on December 31, 1897, 100,000 people crowded into City Hall Park in the rain to celebrate the birth of the new city.

It was, the *Tribune* said, "the biggest, noisiest, and most hilarious New Year's Eve celebration that Manhattan Island had ever known."

With the crash of cannon and the roar of exploding bombs, the flag of "Greater New York" was officially unfurled over City Hall at midnight—and the second city of the world came into existence.

New York Times, January 2, 1898

The sun will rise this morning on the greatest experiment in municipal government that the world has ever known.

New York Tribune, January 1, 1898

Manhattanites had voted enthusiastically for the idea, in a nonbinding public referendum conducted four years before.

So had the sparsely populated communities in outlying areas of Queens, Staten Island, and the Bronx, which stood to gain enormously from city services and capital improvements they could not otherwise afford: schools, roads, port facilities, transit systems, water and sewer lines.

Only Brooklyn had held out—ever mistrustful of the crowded immigrant city just across the river. In the end, the vote on consolidation won there by only 277 votes out of 129,211 cast.

Afterward, some residents draped black crêpe from their shops and house windows in mourning. For decades to come, consolidation would be known as the Great Mistake in the new borough of Brooklyn.

But whether its new citizens liked it or not, New York had with the stroke of a pen become the second largest metropolis in the world.

It now encompassed 327 square miles and nearly 3.5 million people—more than twice the population of Chicago, its closest American rival. It was now bigger than Berlin, Paris, and Moscow—bigger than any city in the world except London.

At the rate it was now growing, London itself would soon be eclipsed.

"The imagination," Mayor Abram Hewitt had written a few years before, "can place no bounds to the future growth of this city in business, wealth, and the blessings of civilization. [New York's] imperial destiny as the greatest city in the world is assured by natural causes, which cannot be thwarted, except by the folly and neglect of its inhabitants."

At the dawn of what would soon be called the American Century, New York—which only 125 years before held fewer than five thousand citizens—prepared to take its place at the very vanguard of world cities.

SUNSHINE AND SHADOW

Today there are no new worlds to find. Upon us is the responsibility never before laid on a people—building the world's capital for all time to come. What we do well will serve mankind forever; what we do ill will be a stumbling block until it is remedied. To none before us have been given such opportunities—to be used or wasted.

John DeWitt Warner, March 1898

The rise of New York, the philosopher Oswald Spengler later wrote, had been "the most pregnant event of the nineteenth century."

And yet, for all that the city had accomplished in its breathtaking, meteoric rise, as the century came to a close, the most urgent issues facing New Yorkers remained almost completely unresolved.

Immense wealth had been created, immense populations gathered, and immense chasms spanned.

And yet the disparities between rich and poor remained as great as ever—and indeed grew wider with each passing year.

Reflecting on that stark division, thoughtful citizens like the Reverend Lyman Abbott—pastor of Plymouth Church in Brooklyn—could not help but grow sober as the dizzying century came to an end.

The city presents in microcosm all the contrasts of our modern life—its worst and its best aspects. Here are the broad avenues . . . the beautiful parks where landscape gardening has done its best, and here the fetid streets whose festering filth pollutes the atmosphere; here palaces on which selfish extravagance has lavished every artifice for luxury and display, and here tenements where, in defiance of every law, moral and sanitary, men, women, and children are crowded together like maggots in a cheese. Here are the greatest universities, equipping men for the noblest intellectual work, and here the grossest illiteracy and the most absolute ignorance of the simplest and plainest laws of life. . . . Here are the noblest men and women putting forth the most consecrated energies in self-sacrificing labors for the redemption of their fellow-men, appalled, but not discouraged, by the immensity of the problem which confronts them; and here the most hopeless specimens of degraded humanity, in whom, so far as human sight can see, the last spark of divinity has been quenched forever. What shall we do with our great cities? What will our great cities do with us? These are the two problems which confront every thoughtful American.

The Reverend Lyman Abbott,
Plymouth Church, Brooklyn

Lower Manhattan, looking north to the Brooklyn Bridge.

THE SECRETS
OF THE
GREAT CITY

DANIEL CZITROM

New York is a great secret, not only to those who have never seen it, but to the majority of its own citizens. Few living in the great city have any idea of the terrible romance and hard reality of the lives of two-thirds of the inhabitants. . . . No matter how clever a man may be in his own town or city, he is a child in the hands of the sharpers and villains of this community, and his only safety lies in avoiding them. His curiosity can be satisfied in these pages, and he can know the Great City from them, without incurring the danger attending an effort to see it.

Edward Winslow Martin,
The Secrets of the Great City, 1868

As New York expanded at an unprecedented pace in the mid-nineteenth century, a curious new genre of guidebooks came to the fore. Revolving around the literary axis of shocking contrast, they were an obvious reflection of the economic, social, and architectural extremes visible everywhere on New York's streets, and ingeniously exploited the public's growing fascination with the newly foreboding—and titillating—urban spaces of the city. Touting the importance of understanding urban vice while assuring the reader that knowledge alone could not corrupt, the new guidebooks promised to reveal dark secrets while providing a kind of prophylactic against the depravity they described. Worn, dog-eared copies of these guides are still easy to find in small-town used bookshops and tag sales, suggesting their lingering role in shaping the out-of-towners' imagination of "the Great City."

Guides to New York's "secrets" did not emerge in a vacuum. English antecedents, dating back to the early eighteenth century, had accompanied the metropolitan growth of London. Closer to home, the guidebooks emerged in tandem with the penny press—newspapers like James Gordon Bennett's *New York Herald* and Benjamin Day's *Sun*, which were filled with detailed accounts not only of trade and commerce but of street doings, court proceedings, and the exotic trivia of the burgeoning city. Like the penny papers, the guidebooks offered a compressed version of city life, a dizzying array of subjects randomly pushed up against one another.

But unlike the penny papers—intended for New Yorkers themselves—the guidebooks contained an explicit appeal to strangers in the city, and to their imagination of metropolitan life—frankly acknowledging the centrality of

Bowery at Night, about 1895, by W. Louis Sonntag.

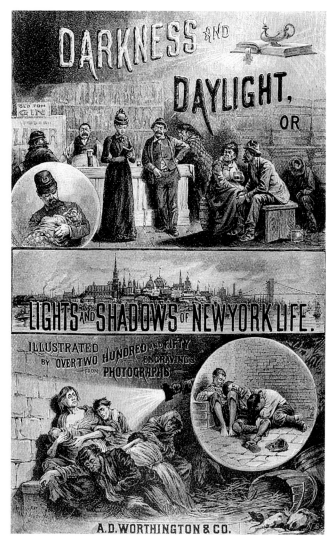

The frontispiece of *Darkness and Daylight, or Lights and Shadows of New York Life,* by Helen Campbell, 1899.

for the *New York Tribune*, and was soon expanding and collecting his daily pieces into book form. Familiar with the city from his journalistic tramps, Foster invited his readers to accompany him and enjoy the urban anonymity that allowed one to "do any and everything you please—stay as long as you like, go when it suits you, at any hour of the day or night, and no questions asked nor observations made." His hyperrealistic tone promised to rip off masks, to shine lights in dark corners, to figuratively undress the city. Yet his invocation of truth, justice, and philanthropy put him squarely in the line of journalists who identified their commercial success with the republican principle of serving the public good by providing objective and useful information to all. From its first paragraph, the book promised both to tantalize and inform:

> *New York by Gas-Light! What a task we have undertaken! To penetrate beneath the thick veil of night and lay bare the fearful mysteries of darkness in the metropolis—the festivities of prostitution, the orgies of pauperism, the haunts of theft and murder, the scenes of drunkenness and beastly debauch, and all the sad realities that go to make up the lower stratum—the underground story—of life in New York! What may have been our motive for invading these dismal realms and thus wrenching from them their terrible secrets? Go with us, and see. The duty of the present age is to discover the real facts of the actual condition of the wicked and wretched classes—so that Philanthropy and Justice may plant their blow aright.*

As no American writer before him, Foster elaborated the "sunshine and shadow" metaphor as a way of seeing New York—insisting that in the modern city, one could not have one without the other. But he challenged American pretensions to superior civilization by emphasizing the extreme inequalities ever more visible on the city's streets. "Thousands of men, women, and children, he reported, "live in daily danger of starvation and perishing; and it is my positive belief that a great proportion of the petty crimes and of the immoralities of the lower class of society proceed directly from the dire urgency of cold and hunger." Foster had little use for moralists and ministers who year after year "preached against the terrible vices of theft, and robbery, and prostitution, which spring directly from want," and insisted instead on a republican analysis and cure: "it is the imperative duty of the community itself to provide for the comfort of every one of its members, and then to hold them responsible for the faithful performance of their duties in the respect due to the rights and properties of others." New York, he argued, needed to expand its public culture, with "public galleries, public libraries and reading rooms, public dramatic and musical entertainments, public lectures, and the more attractive branches of public education."

visitors to the success of all of New York's commercial entertainments, from Barnum's American Museum to the city's better-known theaters. Authors borrowed freely from one another for their descriptions and endlessly recycled woodcut illustrations. Books were written, rewritten, cobbled together, plagiarized, cut and pasted, until, by the 1870s, one could have written a "guidebook" without ever having seen the city. Some of the guidebooks were written by journalists and were secular in tone; others were composed by Protestant ministers and evangelical reformers and were overtly religious in spirit. Yet whatever their inflections or accents, the nineteenth-century guidebooks reflected both real changes in New York life and the nation's uneasy fascination with its first metropolis.

George Foster's *New York by Gas-Light*, published in 1849, provided the extremely popular prototype for the secular guidebook, selling 200,000 copies around the country. A onetime printer and newspaper journalist, in 1848 Foster had written a notable series entitled "New York in Slices"

After the Civil War, guidebook authors largely abandoned Foster's republican slant, assuming that the yawning economic and social gaps among New Yorkers were a permanent and even natural state of affairs. They also devoted more attention to the growing publicness of the city's vice economy, especially prostitution, gambling, the sale of liquor, sexually expressive theater, counterfeiting, and street-based confidence games. The war itself had brought a tremendous upsurge in the number of male visitors to the city, spurring the growth of new "concert saloons" along stretches of the Bowery and lower Broadway—establishments that advertised "pretty waiter girls" who might perform musical numbers onstage, service male customers in private rooms, or both. There was nothing new about the use of females to attract customers; waterfront dance houses had done this for decades. What made the postwar concert saloon new was its combination of a liquor bar, women performers/waiters, and variety shows within the same space—operating openly in the city's main business districts, and prominently—not to say garishly—advertised with newspaper ads, street signs, and banners. What made these places "extremely dangerous to public morals," one grand jury investigation concluded, was their tendency to break down established class boundaries, especially among young men. "Apprentice boys, clerks, idle sons of the virtuous and the rich, strangers, the numerous class of young and old . . . are thus drawn into these open and accessible retreats of sensuality and vice, often to the irretrievable ruin of character and hopes."

The "secrets of the great city" were no longer so secret. A new, more public vice economy in the post–Civil War years reinforced fears of the city as a place that unmoored visitors from their usual routines and moral sense. Guidebooks now highlighted "the traps and pitfalls of the great metropolis, especially to those, who, coming upon the sights and sounds of the huge city for the first time, are confused by them and forget for a moment those maxims of prudence by which they have previously regulated their conduct." As an 1865 book called The Rogues and Rogueries of New York warned, though some visitors to the city were swindled through ignorance and innocence, many more were "snared with the help of their own greed for unearned gain or unlawful pleasure."

Evangelical writers of this era retained the guidebook's essential form—a relentless compression and condensation of urban experience—with chapters organized randomly, designed to be dipped into rather than read from cover to cover. But they emphasized the city as fertile ground for saving souls, a "paradise for preachers." The most popular of these, the Reverend Matthew Hale Smith's Sunshine and Shadow in New York, published in 1866, sold an astonishing 300,000 copies, thus inspiring a raft of imitators. Unlike Foster's reportorial accounts, Smith's book offered second-hand descriptions of the city's dance halls, gambling houses, cheap theaters, prostitutes, saloons, and criminals. Lurid sections on "Black Mailing as an Art," "The Five Points," and "Low Class Gambling Houses" were interspersed with high-minded profiles of Cornelius Vanderbilt, John Jacob Astor, and Ulysses S. Grant. Prejudiced accounts of the city's Catholic, Jewish, and working-class populations pushed up against paeans to leading Protestant divines or histories of Wall Street. Smith acknowledged the enormous gulf between rich and poor but emphasized the charity work of the former. "In no other city is mission-work, Sunday-School labor, the visiting of prisons, hospitals, penitentiaries, performed by the wealthy as it is in New York." And this despite the fact that "a worse population than can be found in New York does not inhabit the globe."

Variations on the guidebook continued to appear in the 1870s and 1880s. The Nether Side of New York, published in 1872 by the New-York Times police reporter Edward Crapsey, linked the rise in lawlessness, public vice, and pauperism to the recently exposed frauds of the Tweed Ring. For Crapsey, the "nether side" was not a permanent or structural feature of metropolitan life but a measure of the city's recent decline. "With its middle classes in large part self-exiled, its laboring population brutalized in tenements, and its citizens of the highest class indifferent to the commonweal, New York drifted from bad to worse, and became the prey of thieves, ruffians and political jugglers." Crapsey deployed an array of statistical data to make his case, which, even if exaggerated, reflected a real and growing sentiment among the city's business and professional classes. Other books played both sides of the street in their desire to "guide." Snares of New York, or Tricks and Traps of the Great Metropolis promised to protect its readers visiting New York—but its detailed descriptions of con games may have also provided pointers for aspiring crooks, thieves, and sharpers trying to earn their living in "the Great headquarters of Swindledom." In 1888, the celebrated criminal defense attorneys William Howe and Abraham Hummel wrote (or had ghostwritten for them) In Danger, or Life in New York—a book that often reads like an advertisement for their services. Chapters on criminals and their haunts and the history of city gangs offer sympathetic, inside knowledge of how the city's underworld operated. Elaborate accounts of sensational love scandals involving prominent citizens sought to establish the two attorneys as the men to see if nasty publicity surrounding New York adventures threatened to sully a gentleman's reputation.

In 1890, the "secrets of the great city" tradition came to both a climax and turning point when the veteran police reporter Jacob Riis published his landmark study of the city's poor, How the Other Half Lives—a work that effectively combined the genre's reportorial and evangelical strains. Certainly Riis's publisher looked to exploit his connection to the guidebook genre, as is evident in the book's advertising copy:

The reader feels that he is being guided through the dirt and crime, tatters and rags, the byways and alleys of nether New York by an experienced cicerone….No work yet published—certainly not the official reports of the charity societies—show so vividly the complexion and countenance of the "Downtown Back Alleys," "The Bend," "Chinatown," "Jewtown," "the Cheap Lodging-Houses," the haunts of the negro, the Italian, the bohemian poor, or gives such a veracious picture of the toughs, the tramps, the waifs, the drunkards, paupers, gamins, and the generally gruesome population of this centre of civilization.

But if Riis looked backward to the older nineteenth-century ways of seeing New York, he also pointed ahead to innovative new ways of understanding the city. *How the Other Half Lives* included an impressive array of statistics on New York's public health, along with a concise history of its tenement housing. In truth, Riis's "other half" really described the other two-thirds: of New York's 1.6 million residents in 1890, 1.1 million lived in tenement houses—most of them terrible places to live. In the years to come, Riis's social-scientific spirit of careful observation and collection of data would become a hallmark of the Progressive movement, embodied in groups like the Bureau of Municipal Research, founded in 1907. And if Riis made use of racist stereotypes and sentimental human interest stories, his book was also suffused with genuine compassion and a zeal to better the city. An entire generation of young reformers—from Frances Perkins to Fiorello La Guardia—would find themselves seared and transformed by the book. The older "secrets of the great city" tradition had largely ignored New York's middle class, except as an implied audience. Riis insisted that middle-class New Yorkers ignored the poor at their own peril and, by appealing to both self-interest and Christian duty, succeeded in inspiring a great number of them to take up the cause of reform.

The "secrets of the great city" would remain a powerful means of explaining the city well into the twentieth century—translated now into new means of communications, from movies to tabloid newspapers. Many of the early story films produced by New York's infant motion picture industry depicted street scenes of public sexuality, "slumming" parties, city night life, and urban crime—all centered on voyeuristic representations of the city's underside. Movies such as *How They Do Things on the Bowery* (Edison, 1902) and *The Deceived Slumming Party* (Biograph, 1908) recycled or parodied "the secrets of the great city" for urban moviegoers. By 1912, D. W. Griffith's crime drama *The Musketeers of Pig Alley* offered an amalgam of social realism, cynicism toward city politics, multiethnic street games, and shocking violence that recalled the sensibility of Riis, while anticipating the gangster cycle of the sound era.

New York's new tabloid newspapers, which would revolutionize city journalism in the years after World War I, would also borrow from and extend the "secrets of the great city." In theme and format, the tabloids resembled nothing so much as the nineteenth-century guidebooks adapted to the needs of modern urban journalism—relentlessly condensing urban experience within a half-size format for convenient reading on subways and buses, employing a terse, lively reporting style, and devoting a large proportion of their space to photographs and drawings. With their intensive coverage of murder and divorce, show business and sports, sex and scandal, vice and crime, the tabloids insisted on exploring and exposing the hidden connections between the underside and the respectable realms of politics and society. The most popular—and ultimately influential—tabloid feature proved to be the gossip column, invented by Walter Winchell at the *Evening Graphic*, which chronicled the secret lives of public figures with a distinctive urban argot—connecting high society, show business, politics, and the underworld. He mapped these relations as they existed not only on the streets but, more important, in the new mass media of the 1920s: press, radio, and motion pictures.

In the decades to come, it would prove more difficult to separate the intertwined strands of reform and spectacle, analysis and sensationalism, empathy and tourism in representations of New York and its place in American life. For New York historians, the guidebook tradition would continue to cast a long and troubling shadow over their efforts to create a more accurate vision of the past. Some of the most widely read and influential histories of New York, most notably Herbert Asbury's 1928 *The Gangs of New York*, plainly owe more to the "secrets of the great city" tradition than to scholarly standards. For many readers, these books *are* the history of New York. While the attractions of the books are obvious—narrative verve, an eye for colorful detail, vivid character portraits—so are their weaknesses: an overreliance on newspaper accounts, invented dialogue, a dearth of notes and bibliography, and a fundamentally uncritical attitude toward historical sources. Most recently, Luc Sante's best-selling *Low Life: Lures and Snares of Old New York*, published in 1991, offered readers not an "academic history," its author wrote, but "an attempt at a mythology of New York." Sante's deeply felt, lively, sometimes hallucinatory prose shamelessly recycles much of the "secrets of the great city" style and content in an entertaining way. But when Sante describes his book as an effort "to extract some essence of New Yorkness not tied to commerce or public relations but resident in the accumulated myth of

Italian concert hall on the Bowery, 1890.

the city itself," he reveals—perhaps unintentionally—the danger of conflating history with myth. It is difficult to find a story or source in the book that is *not* entangled with commerce or public relations.

What is important, finally, is that New York's history not be reduced to the "secrets of the great city." It is easy to forget how much those "secrets" have been both rooted in and contributors to the deep antiurban currents in American politics and culture. And these in turn have too often

provided flimsy cover for prejudice, parochialism, or reactionary fear. By largely ignoring the city's middle and skilled working classes, the guidebook tradition presented a sharply distorted version of New York. For much of the past two centuries Americans have readily confused representations of New York with the reality of big-city life. The quest for a truer, more human, more complex history of New York is a part of the continuing struggle to gain a rightful place for *the urban* in American politics and culture.

Immigrants waiting to be ferried from Ellis Island to lower Manhattan, October 30, 1912. Of the 12 million newcomers who entered the harbor between 1892 and 1924, 4 million remained in the city and its vicinity.

"We all went down and got on the ferryboat," an immigrant named Donald Roberts later recalled, "and the ferryboat ran to the Battery. And then we just walked off, just like letting the birds out of the cage."

THE POWER AND

1898-1919

THE PEOPLE

Gigantic, colossal, enormous,
daring, there are no words—words
are inadequate to this apparition, this landscape, in which the
vast river serves as frame for
the display of still vaster human energy.
Reaching such a pitch of collective
effort, this energy has become a force
of nature itself. It is the poetry of
Democracy, an immense concert. This
is not the Parthenon—that little temple
on a little hill . . . it is the obscure
and tremendous poetry of the modern
world, and it gives you a tragic
shudder, there is in it so much of mad
and wilful humanity.

Paul Bourget, 1893

No structure better sym-
bolized New York's
relentless drive into the
sky than the ill-fated
Gillender Building, which
stood at the northwest
corner of Wall and
Nassau streets, in the very
heart of the financial
district. Upon its completion in 1897, the 19-story
tower was one of the
tallest buildings in the
city, but by 1910, its underlying real estate had
grown so valuable—
worth more than $700 a
square foot—that it was
torn down to make way
for the Bankers' Trust
Building—at 37 stories
nearly twice as high.
The Gillender Building's
13-year lifespan was the
shortest of any skyscraper
in the city's history.

CITY IN MOTION

At two o'clock on the afternoon of May 11, 1896, a photographer named William Heise hoisted a cumbersome device up onto a tripod at the southern end of Herald Square at Thirty-third Street and Broadway. Passersby assumed he was about to expose a glass-plate negative of the scene, but the strange-looking apparatus—the latest invention of Heise's employer, Thomas Alva Edison—did not take still pictures.

Instead, the extraordinary device—which exposed one frame after another, each just an instant apart from the next, sixteen times a second—was capable of capturing for the first time the speed and vitality of urban life. The motion picture had been born.

Mesmerized by the kinetic energy of New York, the first movie cameramen carried their equipment everywhere, shooting short films they called "actualities." Real-life views of actual events and places, most had no plots, no characters, and lasted only a minute or two. But audiences everywhere flocked to see them—enthralled by the spectacle of the city itself, which, as Edison and his competitors quickly realized, had become the greatest show on earth.

By 1896, New York had the nation's busiest harbor, the world's biggest ships and longest bridges, the densest slums and grandest mansions. It had a statue fifteen stories tall and a park 840 acres in size. It had trains that ran a hundred feet above the ground and leaped across rivers. And it had people by the millions, filling its streets and sidewalks and open spaces.

Though the cameras sometimes captured civic ceremonies and grand public events, the most engaging films were of ordinary daily life—children delivering newspapers, shoppers crowding bargain stores, immigrants first touching American soil at the Battery. Capturing the most evanescent and elusive moments—a windy day, a trolley passing down the street, a woman's smile—the cameras heralded a new and distinctively modern sensibility: ephemeral, fragmentary, rapidly changing, and above all, urban. Their hypnotic movement drew upon, and ultimately celebrated, the very congestion and density that nineteenth-century observers had found so frightening.

And yet, even as motion and change became a way of life in Manhattan, an even greater transformation was under way. For all that had come before in the city's extraordinary history, nothing could have prepared New Yorkers for what was about to happen in the first decade of the new century.

In the years following the consolidation of Greater New York, the potential the old Dutch explorers had sensed three hundred years before would come to a tremendous crescendo.

In the decades to come, the entire world would arrive on the city's doorstep as America finished assembling itself as the first global nation. As the city spilled out across the immense canvas that consolidation had given it, the two great forces of modern life—capitalism and democracy—would give rise to an entirely new kind of city, more awesome and more intricately interconnected than any city on earth.

Propelled by the tidal wave of newcomers, virtually every aspect of life in New York would be transformed. And yet, in the end, nothing would be more moving, or prove to have more lasting consequence for New York or for the nation, than the changes the people themselves would bring to the political life of the city.

In little more than twenty years, the twentieth century itself would be born on the streets of New York.

A VAST AND ENDLESS ARMY

Now one can stand in any district town of Hungary, Poland or Italy and see, coming down the mountains or passing along the highways and byways of the plains . . . groups of peasants, not all picturesquely clad, passing in a never ending stream, on, towards a new world. The stream is growing larger each day, and the source seems inexhaustible.

Edward Steiner, 1906

It began in the 1880s, spurred on by poverty and persecution, by financial panic and political upheaval, by family strife and personal woe. They came not from northern Europe this time, from Germany and Ireland, but from the east and from the south: Italians, Jews, Greeks, and Poles; Russians, Hungarians, Ukrainians, Armenians, and Turks.

Above, immigrants being ferried to Ellis Island, 1908. After arriving at the Hudson River piers, first- and second-class steamship passengers were given a cursory inspection on board and allowed to disembark immediately. Steerage passengers were then herded onto crowded ferries for the trip downriver to Ellis Island. In the busy season, several ferries packed with immigrants might be lined up at the island's slip for hours, waiting to discharge their human cargo.

Right, immigrants on an ocean liner, 1907. By the start of the twentieth century, the sailing ships that had once carried Irish and German newcomers across the Atlantic had been replaced by enormous steel-hulled ocean liners, built to transport as many immigrants as possible. British and German vessels such as the *Mauretania*, the *Olympic*, and the *Vaterland* could carry 2,000 to 3,000 steerage passengers in a single crossing.

"Out of the remote and little-known reaches of Europe," one awestruck observer wrote as the numbers grew, "marches a vast and endless army." Enmeshed in an increasingly global economy, many of those streaming across the Atlantic shipping lanes arrived by dint of curious reversals. When wheat grown in Kansas began being shipped to the Baltic, generating surpluses in the peasant population there, the people turned around and came flooding back toward America.

For some, like the country people of Sicily and southern Italy, the voyage was a flight from crushing poverty and generations of slavelike servitude, made worse by economic depression and natural catastrophes that were destroying

In early December 1883, a 34-year-old Jewish poet named Emma Lazarus, appalled by the recent upsurge of anti-Semitic violence in Russia, submitted a 14-line poem to help the faltering fund-raising campaign for the pedestal of the Statue of Liberty.

The precocious, well-educated daughter of a prosperous New York sugar refiner, she had hesitated at first—reluctant to write "on order," she said, and intimidated by the fact that more celebrated writers, including Walt Whitman and Mark Twain, had also been asked to

make contributions. But something about the immense statue the French hoped to raise in the harbor fired her imagination, and—hoping it might somehow help her distressed and harried people— she sketched out a sonnet called "The New Colossus."

The liberty the short poem celebrated had nothing to do with the abstract political ideals the French had originally intended. It was liberty as a beacon of hope shining out to oppressed peoples around the world, the future reaching out to the present to unchain humanity from the shackles of the past. In time, the hundreds of thousands and then millions of immigrants passing through New York Harbor would see in the statue what Lazarus had seen—and associate it with their own deepest hopes and dreams in coming to America.

Lazarus herself never saw the statue her poem so movingly commemorated or the epic human tide it foretold. While on vacation in Europe during the final months of the statue's construction, she was diagnosed with Hodgkin's disease and, in the harbor, on her way home in the summer of 1887, she was too ill and weak even to come up on deck. She died in her home in Manhattan, four months later, at the age of 38. None of the obituaries mentioned "The New Colossus," which by now had been all but forgotten.

Fifteen years later, on May 6, 1903—after the tireless efforts of a friend and admirer named Georgina Schuyler to save the poem from obscurity—a bronze plaque inscribed with Emma Lazarus's stirring words was finally affixed to the base of the statue. It would take decades more for Americans to realize the full meaning of the gift the French had given them.

Above, the poet Emma Lazarus, about 1883, the year in which she wrote "The New Colossus." Below, immigrants arriving in New York Harbor on the *Olympic* in 1910, catching sight of the Statue of Liberty. "The first time I saw the Statue of Liberty," an immigrant named Elizabeth Phillips recalled, "all the people were rushing to the side of the boat. 'Look at her, look at her,' and in all kinds of tongues. 'There she is, there she is,' like it was somebody who was greeting them."

> Not like the brazen giant of
>   Greek fame,
> With conquering limbs astride
>   from land to land;
> Here at our sea-washed,
>   sunset gates shall stand
> A mighty woman with a torch,
>   whose flame
> Is the imprisoned lightning,
>   and her name
> Mother of Exiles. From her
>   beacon-hand
> Glows world-wide welcome;
>   her mild eyes command
> The air-bridged harbor that
>   twin cities frame.
> "Keep, ancient lands, your
>   storied pomp!" cries she
> With silent lips. "Give me your
>   tired, your poor,
> Your huddled masses yearning
>   to breathe free,
> The wretched refuse of your
>   teeming shore.
> Send these, the homeless,
>   tempest-tost to me,
> I lift my lamp beside the
>   golden door!"

> *The entrance into our political, social and industrial life, of such vast masses of peasantry, degraded below our utmost conceptions, is a matter which no intelligent patriot can look upon without the gravest . . . alarm. These people . . . have none of the inherited instincts . . . which made it comparatively easy to deal with immigration in olden times. They are beaten men from beaten races; representative of the worst failures in the struggle for existence.*
> Professor Francis Walker,
> Yale University

the wheat and grapevines on which their lives depended. "We plant and we reap wheat but never do we eat white bread," one embittered Italian peasant said. "We cultivate the grape but we drink no red wine. We raise animals for food but we eat no meat. We are clothed in rags. . . . You counsel us not to abandon our country. But is that land, where one cannot live by toil, one's country?"

For others, it was an escape from military conscription or persecution or the violence and barbarism of the pogroms sweeping Eastern Europe. Before the great floodtide of immigration was over, more than one-third of the Jewish population of Europe would leave their homes—most of them bound for the United States.

Together with a number of families, my wife and children and I are cowering under a storm of bullets over our head. We remain powerless, useless, paralyzed. . . . Before our eyes and in the eyes of the whole world, [the Russian soldiers] helped to smash windows, break down doors, break locks and to put booty in their pockets. Before our eyes and in the eyes of our children, they beat Jews grievously—men, women, and children—and they shouted, "Money, give us your money." Before our eyes women were hurled from windows and children thrown to the cobblestones. . . . What shall we do? No place to hide. Gentiles will not give shelter to Jews. . . . My people are being consumed.

Sholom Aleichem

One way or the other most people had heard the same thing. There was freedom and opportunity in America, for anyone willing to work, and the place with the most jobs was the sprawling, unfathomably large port city of New York. Between 1880 and 1919—just thirty-nine years—5.5 million European immigrants settled permanently in the city. The largest groups by far were the Italians and the Jews—tens of thousands, then hundreds of thousands, of southern Italians and Russian Jews. Of the 1.2 million people arriving in New York in 1907, 289,000 of them came from Italy, and 256,000 more from Russia.

For most, it meant leaving everything familiar behind.

"The day I left home," a Lithuanian immigrant named Julia Goniprow remembered, "my mother came with me to the railroad station. When we said goodbye, she said it was like seeing me go into my casket. I never saw her again."

For decades, immigrants to New York had come through Castle Garden—a ramshackle state-run depot at the foot of Manhattan, where the first Dutch settlers had landed. By 1890, the antiquated facility had been all but overwhelmed by the tidal wave of new immigrants. That year, the federal government began work on a new processing station, far out in the harbor, on an abandoned ammunition dump called Ellis Island.

Opened in 1892, then rebuilt in 1900, the massive complex of brick, stone, and steel was, when complete, an island city unto itself, with thirty-four buildings in all, including its own

After disembarking from the ferries, immigrants waiting to enter the complex were lined up under a canopy in front of the main building. At the baggage room on the building's first floor, new arrivals could arrange to have their bags and bundles forwarded to their final destination—but many, fearful of losing all their worldly possessions, kept their baggage with them through the entire inspection process.

power station, a 125-bed hospital, police and fire departments, and laundries, dormitories, and kitchens. Built to accommodate half a million people a year, it would soon be handling twice that number. Touring the sprawling complex in 1906, the English novelist H. G. Wells was staggered by the sheer magnitude of the logistical challenge involved in the immense operation—as one ocean liner after another discharged its human cargo.

> *"Look there," said the Commissioner, taking me by the arm and pointing, and I saw a monster steamship far away, and already a big bulk looming up the Narrows. "It's the* Kaiser Wilhelm der Grosse. *She's got . . . eight hundred and fifty-three more for us. She'll have to keep them until Friday at the earliest. And there's more behind her, and more strung out all across the Atlantic."*

For the immigrants themselves, the arrival in New York was both an ending and a beginning—the midway point in a voyage of transformation that had begun thousands of miles away. In the years to come, the experience of these newcomers would be woven into the myth of America and no one would ever forget the day they arrived.

It was, one man said, like a second birth.

After anywhere from eight to fourteen dank and miserable days at sea—packed like cattle in poorly ventilated steerage compartments at the bottom of huge iron-hulled ships—immigrants were often moved to tears simply by the magnificence of the vast and tranquil harbor—and by the extraordinary sight off the port side of the ship of a giant woman, her arm stretched thirty stories in the air, bearing a torch of welcome.

"About four or five o'clock in the morning we all got up," an immigrant named Sarah Asher recalled. "The whole boat bent toward her because everybody went out—everybody. She was beautiful with the sunshine so bright—and so big, and everybody was crying. The captain came and said, please everybody, we should move a little bit to the center, but nobody would move."

Once past Liberty Island, however, anticipation turned to unease, as the domes and minarets of Ellis Island loomed into view. "The thrill

was unbelievable," an Italian immigrant named Joseph Talese recalled. "But always the fear . . . because you have to go through Ellis Island. I heard all kinds of things that they would tell you on the boat. 'My God,' I said, 'I hope they're not going to send me back.'"

An English journalist named Stephen Graham, observing the epic tide of immigrants in 1913, could see the fear in people's faces. "All were thinking, shall I get through?" he wrote. "Have I enough money? Shall I pass the doctor?"

> *It was like the House of Babel: so many languages, and so many people and so full of fear.*
> Barbara Barondess

Year by year, the number of arrivals kept rising: eight thousand a day, then ten thousand. By the spring of 1907, more than eleven thousand men, women, and children were sometimes passing through the complex in a single day.

On disembarking, the pilgrims entered a vast, bewildering, and impersonal machine—an assembly line for processing immigrants. With numbered tags pinned to their clothes, they were swiftly herded into long lines, then ush-

By far the most feared part of the inspection process on Ellis Island was the eye examination, in which doctors pulled up the newcomers' eyelids with a buttonhook to check for an incurable and highly infectious disease called trachoma. Anyone found infected was sent back. "Let no one think [entering Ellis Island] is a pleasant experience," the clergyman Edward Steiner wrote in 1906. "It is a hard, harsh fact surrounded by the grinding machinery of the law, which sifts, picks, and chooses; admitting the fit, and excluding the weak and helpless."

ered inside the main building, while harried officials barked orders at them in a babel of tongues.

Visiting the island in the summer of its peak year, 1907, the novelist Henry James was moved and disconcerted by the ceaseless flow. "Before this door," he wrote, "which opens to them only with a hundred forms and ceremonies, grindings and grumblings of the key, they stand, appealing, and waiting, marshalled, herded, divided, subdivided, sorted, sifted, searched, fumigated, for longer or shorter periods. It is a drama that goes on without a pause, day by day and year by year . . . [a] clock that never, never stops. . . ."

Inside the main building, the new arrivals

were forced to run a frightening, dehumanizing, brutally efficient gauntlet. Immigration officials were required by law to turn back polygamists, paupers, criminals, and the mentally ill, as well as anyone with a heart condition, or a physical disability, or a contagious disease. The inspections were brusque, irreversible, and carried out with remarkable speed; on the busiest days, the examiners had less than six seconds to detect any one of sixty conditions.

The unlucky ones were swiftly removed from the line without explanation and sent to special examination rooms, with chalk letters hastily scrawled on their coats—*L* for lameness, *EC* for eye problems, *H* for heart problems, *X* for

Though most immigrants passed through the inspection process in three to five hours, approximately one in five was detained for further examination. In a special room, these men—suspected by officials of mental illness or impairment (as indicated by the letter *X* chalked onto their coats)—are awaiting additional testing.

Registry Room, Ellis Island, 1907. From the medical examination immigrants were directed to the Registry Room for a final inspection. Shunted into long lines divided by high metal railings—which invariably reminded observers of cattle pens—the newcomers waited hours for their names to be called. "Every so often somebody called out names of immigrants . . . to be questioned," a newcomer named William Chase later recalled. "I was very nervous because it was so noisy. I couldn't hear the names and I was afraid that I would miss my name and remain there forever."

suspected insanity. No part of the ordeal was more traumatizing than the examination for trachoma, an incurable disease of the eye. Anyone infected was sent back—regardless of their age or family situation.

"It was harrowing to see families separated," wrote a twenty-five-year-old interpreter named Fiorello La Guardia. Fluent in five languages, including German, Italian, Yiddish, and Croatian, La Guardia was often called upon to relay the terrible news. "Sometimes, if it was a young child who suffered from trachoma, one of the parents had to return to the native country with the rejected member of the family. When they learned their fate, they were stunned. They had never felt ill. They had never heard the word trachoma. They could see all right, and they had no homes to return to. . . . I never managed during the three years I worked there to become callous to the mental anguish, the disappointment and the despair I witnessed almost daily."

Once they passed the medical examiner—as most immigrants successfully did—the last hurdle was the high-ceilinged Registry Room, where the final interrogation was held. "It was,"

Though the majority of immigrants passing through Ellis Island in the first years of the century came from southern and Eastern Europe—such as the Russian-Jewish family in the 1900 view at bottom—the facility received hopefuls from all over the world. Top, a group of newcomers from the Caribbean, about 1908.

one observer said, "the nearest earthly likeness to the final Day of Judgement." In rapid succession, each was asked to state his or her name, place of birth, destination, and occupation; how much money he or she had, whether he or she had ever been in jail, or had ever been an anarchist.

Contrary to popular opinion, no immigrant's name was ever known to have been changed by the inspectors at Ellis Island, who merely confirmed information already before them in the ship's manifest. And in the end, despite the ordeal, less than 2 percent of the immigrants were denied entrance to the United States.

"On they go," H. G. Wells wrote, watching from a balcony above, "from this pen to that, pen by pen, towards a desk at a little metal wicket—the gate of America. Through [it] drips the immigration stream—all day long, every two or three seconds an immigrant, with valise or bundle, passes the little desk and goes on . . . into a new world. . . . All day and every day, constantly replenished . . . till the units mount to hundreds and the hundreds of thousands."

Between 1892 and 1919, more than 12 million men, women, and children would funnel through its maze of corridors, waiting rooms, and inspection halls. For most, the experience was over in four or five hours, when without ceremony or congratulations, they were curtly waved down a flight of stairs toward the exit— and out into the New World.

Following signs marked "New England," and "West," most of the immigrants quickly dispersed to distant towns and cities around the country. But for one in four of the new arrivals, the final destination was a fifteen-minute ferry ride away, on an island many of them would never leave again.

On board the ferry, approaching the Battery, they stood in wonder at the last and most extraordinary sight of all—the gleaming white skyline of New York—a vision that seemed to corroborate everything they hoped the New World might be.

"Everybody was looking at Manhattan," one Italian immigrant recalled. "And I must admit, that sight I don't think I will ever forget."

"I thought I was in heaven," another agreed. "My God—was this a city on earth, or a city in heaven?"

INTO THE SKY

Newcomers approaching Manhattan as the century came to a close were greeted by an astonishing sight. Down at the tip of the island, from the narrow lanes the Dutch had laid out three centuries before, the city had begun to soar straight up into the sky.

Not since the advent of the great Gothic cathedrals eight hundred years before had there been such a revolution in the way men built. Summoned from the earth by titanic forces that had been converging on Manhattan for years, the gigantic new shapes were a stunning expression of the creative power of the modern world.

Skyscrapers under construction in lower Manhattan, about 1900. "The skyline of New York is changing so rapidly," the journalist Lincoln Steffens wrote a few years later, "that the American traveller who goes abroad can recognize with more certainty the profiles of the foreign cities he approaches than that of his own metropolis as he sees it from the deck of the steamer on his return."

Street, drawn by the tremendous concentration of resources that had been Manhattan's advantage since the time of the Dutch.

By 1901, the corporate consolidation movement J. P. Morgan had started a quarter of a century before had reached critical mass in lower Manhattan. Sixty-nine of the nation's two hundred largest companies now made their homes in New York—including Standard Oil, General Electric, American Tobacco, and U.S. Steel—the world's first billion-dollar corporation, assembled that year by Morgan himself from the steel interests of Rockefeller and Carnegie.

As the number and size of corporations in lower Manhattan increased, each requiring huge staffs with which to direct increasingly far-flung operations, the demand for office space grew dramatically, and with it the urge to defy gravity.

"Confined on all sides, the only way *out* was *up*," the journalist Lincoln Steffens wrote. "Limited as to the ground, business [sought] the air. It had to be done, but how? To pile more stories on the sixth was useless, since no one would climb up to them; the young brokers and lawyers might be willing to do it, but their customers would not follow."

Two things were needed to make tall buildings possible—the elevator and steel-frame construction. The first had arrived fifty years before, when in 1853 an engineer named Elisha Graves Otis demonstrated the first "safety elevator" to gasping crowds outside the Crystal Palace, who marveled at the ingenious device that stopped cars from plummeting even after the cables had broken.

New York's rise into the heavens had begun. In 1869, the Equitable Life Insurance Company, the first office building ever equipped with an elevator, rose an impressive seven stories, only to be surpassed by the new nine-story headquarters of the *Tribune*, and then by the Western Union Building, which reached ten stories.

"One might believe that the chief end of the present crop of buildings," the *American Builder* declared, "is the observation of comets." Yet, as builders themselves well knew, the effective height limit had now been reached for brick and stone buildings. "Masonry structures of ten stories . . . demanded walls of such fortresslike

"It is as if some mighty force were astir beneath the ground, hour by hour," *Harpers Weekly* declared in 1902, "pushing up structures that a dozen years ago would have been inconceivable."

"It is not an architectural vision," the architecture critic Montgomery Schuyler declared archly, "but it does, most tremendously, look like business."

The giant structures had been called into being by the phenomenal economic forces gathering in New York in the second half of the nineteenth century. For years, companies from across the country had been gravitating to Wall

thickness and sparse window[s]," the engineer William A. Starrett later explained, "that the ground floor space, most valuable of all, was devoured and the sunlight all but excluded."

Then, in the mid-1880s, architects in Chicago and New York, influenced in part by bridge builders like John and Washington Roebling, began to develop a revolutionary form of steel construction that would allow them to build towers fifteen stories high—twenty stories high—theoretically any height at all.

The architect, seeing [the engineer] spinning his suspension bridge, called him down to consultation. . . . The engineer suggested that iron could be made to carry the floors. The architect, blocked by the widening base of his brick walls, was taught that a slender pillar of iron could carry as much as his fattest mound. The next step was a brilliant one: why not let the frame that had carried the floors so easily take also the weight of the walls? The steel cage assumed the whole burden. The walls became a veneer, panels to protect the tenants from weather. An architect recently began at the top, and put his walls in succession downwards to show that it could be done. . . .
Lincoln Steffens

With the advent of steel-frame construction and electrically powered elevators, New York's skyline rose with remarkable speed, starting with the Tower Building in 1889. An eleven-story "steel bridge stood on end," its designer, Bradford Lee Gilbert proudly declared, it was quickly dubbed the Idiotic Building by skeptical New Yorkers, who gathered at a safe distance as construction went on, expecting to see it collapse.

It did not, and less than a year after it opened, it was surpassed by the World Building, which climbed to the unthinkable height of eighteen stories. Stepping off on the top floor, one awestruck visitor loudly called out, "Is God in?"

"When Americans find themselves a little crowded," a Scottish journalist named William Archer observed in 1899, "they simply tilt a street on end, and call it a skyscraper." The word itself, aptly enough, was an old nautical term, used to describe the topmost sail of the big three-masted ships that once plied the Atlantic between Liverpool and New York.

METROPOLITAN TOWER AT NIGHT, NEW YORK.

Flat Iron Building, Broadway and 23 rd. Street, New York.

Opposite, the Flatiron Building under construction, 1901. Unlike traditional buildings, skyscrapers were not supported by their outer walls but by an interior framework of steel or iron columns and beams. As shown here, the building's facade—hung from each floor like a curtain—could be installed on the structure's upper stories, even if the floors below it were incomplete.

When completed in 1909, the 693-foot Metropolitan Life Insurance Company tower, above left, was the tallest building in the world, with clock faces larger than those of Big Ben, and, at its peak, a powerful searchlight that signaled weather conditions to ships out at sea. The wedgelike mass of the Flatiron Building, above right, rising straight up from the busy intersection of Fifth Avenue and Broadway, created a sensation upon its opening in 1902. "There is scarcely an hour when a staring wayfarer doesn't by his example collect a big crowd of other staring people," the *New York Tribune* observed that year. "No wonder people stare! A building 307 feet high presenting an edge almost as sharp as the bow of a ship . . . is well worth looking at."

Year by year, the city pushed ever higher into the sky—"shooting up," one man said, "with startling abruptness." In 1902, the twenty-one-story Fuller Building went up, quickly called the Flatiron for its unusual triangular shape. "It appeared to be moving toward me like the bow of a monster ocean steamer," a young photographer named Alfred Stieglitz wrote, mesmerized by the towering structure, which he photographed again and again, calling it "a picture of new America still in the making."

Five years later, the elegant tower of the Singer Building soared forty-seven stories into the air above Broadway. At 612 feet, it was twice as high as the Flatiron—and the world's tallest building, by far. "This new height sets a standard which cannot forever remain unchallenged," one reporter wrote, and he was right. Within a year, the Metropolitan Life Insurance Company completed a dizzying tower above Madison Square. Standing almost seven hundred feet high, it was now the tallest structure on earth.

The skyscraper . . . gathers into a single edifice an extraordinary number of activities, which

On April 23, 1896, at Koster and Bial's Music Hall, on West 34th Street, New Yorkers got their first glimpse of an astonishing new form of entertainment. As the audience watched in disbelief, a screen mounted on the stage suddenly came alive with a series of moving photographic images: waves crashing on a shore, a train approaching the station, two dancers performing a Highland fling. Up in the balcony, the inventor Thomas Edison—whose company had produced the films in his laboratory in West Orange, New Jersey—modestly acknowledged the audience's cheers. It was the first movie show in America.

Within months, a new industry had sprung up to produce films commercially—and from the very start, it was located in the heart of New York City. That spring, Edison's company opened a workshop on West 28th Street in Manhattan, while his main rival, the American Mutoscope and Biograph Company,

established itself on the sixth floor of a loft building at 13th Street and Broadway. A third company, Vitagraph, opened for business a year later on Nassau Street, downtown. Searching for a convenient outdoor space in which to shoot their earliest films—of vaudeville acts, circus performers, magic tricks—the fledgling companies looked to the roofs of their buildings, where, high atop the city, they constructed open-air stages that could rotate to track the sun as it moved across the sky.

But from the start, filmmakers realized that one of most compelling of all subjects lay right at their doorstep—the city itself. Soon, cameramen such as Edison's Edwin S. Porter and Biograph's G. W. "Billy" Bitzer were fanning out across New York to produce what were known as actualities—short, documentary-type films, without plot or characters, that simply offered a glimpse of the city and its life. They took their cameras everywhere, from the poorest tenement streets to the grand avenues of the rich, from the bucolic landscapes of the city's outskirts to the crowded urban vistas of its central business districts. They were especially drawn to the workings of the city itself, from the heroic exploits of its policemen and firemen to the construction and operation of its engineering marvels—the new suspension bridges and railroad

terminals and subway system that were transforming the shape of the city—and to the constantly changing spectacle of the lower Manhattan skyline.

Though audience interest in the actualities began to flag around 1906, the intense fascination with the changing city continued, and helped to shape the first "story" films that were now taking their place. Several scenes in *The Skyscrapers*, a 1906 Biograph melodrama about a pair of rival construction workers, were actually shot on the steel skeleton of a new office building rising on Broadway and 13th Street (below left), while another Biograph film made that same year, *The Tunnel Workers,* was set amid the construction of the Pennsylvania Railroad's new tunnel under the Hudson River.

By then, however, New York's film companies were swiftly outgrowing their Manhattan quarters, having discovered that the complex needs of film production—sets, wardrobe, editing, distribution, booking, as well as the shooting stages themselves—called for more space than could be found economically in the middle of town. In 1905, Vitagraph decamped to Flatbush Avenue in Brooklyn, opening what was arguably the first true film studio in America; in 1906, Edison moved to Decatur Avenue and 176th Street in the Bronx, where Biograph joined them a year later. Within a few years, most of the city's smaller

film companies had left Manhattan, many relocating across the Hudson River to the sleepy town of Fort Lee, New Jersey, which in the years between 1910 and 1919 became a major production center for American films.

Though several major studios would later be built in the city—including Paramount's massive facility in Astoria, Queens, which opened in 1920—the growing need for inexpensive open land and near-constant sunshine would ultimately push most feature film production out of the city entirely, to sprawling studio lots in and around Los Angeles. Yet in the decades to come, the American film industry would be crucially linked to New York, which would remain its financial and administrative headquarters, provide a major source of its talent, and, as it had since the start, offer one of the greatest settings and subjects for the movies themselves.

Thomas Edison's studio on Decatur Avenue in the Bronx, soon after its completion in 1908, with frames from two early films. Above, *The Skyscrapers*, 1906, a film shot on the skeleton of an office building under construction on 12th Street and Broadway. Top right, *The European Rest Cure*, 1904, showing the skyline of lower Manhattan from the Hudson River.

Wall Street, looking west from William Street, about 1910. For decades the financial center of the nation, by 1910 lower Manhattan had become headquarters to America's new corporate economy as well. Companies like Standard Oil, Western Union, and American Telephone and Telegraph built towering office buildings to house their fast-growing clerical workforces, which (as can be seen in this lunchtime view) now included significant numbers of women as well as men.

other-wise would be widely separated. Each building is almost a complete city, often comprising within its walls banks and insurance offices, post office and telegraph office, business exchanges, restaurants, clubrooms, and shops. The business man can provide himself with clothes, shoes, cigars, stationery, and baths; receive and dispatch his mail and his telegrams; speculate; consult his lawyer and his architect in their offices; and transact his own business, all without leaving the building in which his office is located. The express elevator which shoots

The development of the apartment house is entirely a New York idea. The old capitals of Europe have absolutely nothing to offer by way of comparison. In Paris, Vienna and Berlin the elevator is a rumor, and steam heating a possibility for the future.

Everett N. Blanke, 1893

One of the greatest revolutions in American urban life began in New York City in 1869, when an unusual five-story building opened its doors on East 18th Street, near Irving Place.

Called The Stuyvesant, the novel structure had been built on the site of Peter Stuyvesant's old fruit farm by Rutherfurd Stuyvesant—a 29-year-old descendant of New Amsterdam's legendary director general. Designed by the architect Richard Morris Hunt to house 20 families under a single roof at the same time—in spacious living quarters, served by a common hallway, staircase, and lobby—it was the first apartment house ever constructed in America.

The early occupants of the building included a curious assortment of celebrated iconoclasts willing to risk the opprobrium attached to so unconventional a lifestyle—among them the free-thinking publisher George Putnam; Lavinia Booth, the mother of the actor Edwin Booth and his brother, John Wilkes Booth, the assassin; and Libby Custer, who moved into the building in the fall of 1876 after her husband was killed at the Battle of Little Big Horn.

From the very start, the new structures generated controversy. One resident of the Upper East Side voiced the opinion of many prosperous New Yorkers—nearly all of whom still lived in private row houses—when he declared that, "Gentlemen will never consent to live on mere shelves under a common roof."

But to their builders, the logic of the communal houses was obvious. Gathered together in one large structure that allowed them to share amenities, middle-class families could enjoy space and service they might not otherwise be able to afford. "There are but few persons who are princely enough to wish to occupy an entire palace," a real-estate developer named Edward Severin Clark observed, "but there are many who would like to occupy a portion of a great building, which would be more perfect in its arrangement than any palace in Europe."

In 1880, Clark proposed building the world's largest apartment house on Central Park West and 72nd Street, in a sea of wooden shacks and small farms so far north that one of his partners was said to have asked, "Why don't you go a few blocks more and build it in the Dakotas?" Sure of the neighborhood's future, Clark cheerfully named his building The Dakota, then had the head of an Indian sculpted into the facade.

Determined to draw tenants to the new frontier, Clark poured everything he had into the Dakota. Many of the apartments were comparable in size to large single-family row houses, with anywhere from 12 to 20 rooms. There were hotel-style rooms for out-of-town guests, attic rooms for servants, an in-house laundry service, an in-house restaurant with its own wine cellar, a ballroom for parties, and a landscaped roof garden with views for 20 miles in all directions. Determined to create the most modern building in the world, Clark installed 4,000 electric lights in the building—along with 300 electric bells that connected every apartment with a private stable, messenger service, telegraph office, and florist.

The very fact that a hundred families can dwell together in harmony under one roof should be inspiring to the nineteenth century architect. He should seize the idea of their unity, of their solidarity, and express it in stone and bricks and iron. He should build tremendous stairs

When it opened in 1884 in the remote precincts of 72nd Street and Central Park West, the Dakota, top, was the city's most luxurious apartment house. The Central Park Apartments, bottom, at 59th Street and Seventh Avenue, completed in 1883, remained the largest apartment building in Manhattan for the next two decades.

for his brave one hundred; splendid cities with pillars and arches; front doors as wide as those of a cathedral . . . he should provide marble pavements, frescoed halls, gardens full of statuary and fountains. The system will engender a new sentiment— the apartment house sentiment, which will take the place of civic pride, of family feeling, perhaps even of patriotism.

Real Estate Record

The earliest apartment houses, like the Stuyvesant and the Dakota, were built of stone and brick. By the 1890s, however, apartment buildings began to be built with the same steel skeletons used in skyscrapers downtown—and with elevators that allowed tenants to reach higher floors with ease. As

the buildings shot up, upper floor apartments, and the utilitarian structures known as "penthouses," acquired cachet among city dwellers, because of the superior views they afforded.

If structurally apartment houses now resembled skyscrapers, legally they were still classified as tenement houses. Anxious to differentiate their buildings from those inhabited by the poor, real-estate agents took to calling them French flats, hoping to conjure up visions of sophisticated Parisian urbanity. The term, however, only reinforced the reputation apartment houses already had as motley, not quite respectable, places—home, one man said, to "con men, clergy men, heiresses, actresses, fast people, slow people, good people, bad people; people you know, people you'd like

In the years after 1900, the stretch of upper Broadway known as the Boulevard (seen here looking north from 70th Street, in 1904) quickly filled with apartment houses and hotels, including the ornate Dorilton, at right, built in 1901, and, in the distance, the 17-story turreted Ansonia, which upon its completion in 1904 was the largest apartment hotel in the world.

to know, people you don't want to know—but all of them interesting to look at, to think about."

And yet little by little, the idea of apartment living caught on, until, by the turn of the century, a wave of construction had begun to sweep across upper Manhattan, especially on the underdeveloped Upper West Side. The grandest of the new buildings was the Ansonia, at 73rd Street and Broadway, which, when completed in 1904, boasted 2,500 rooms, 350 enormous apartments, an immense fountain in the lobby that sported live seals, and the largest indoor pool in the world. From the start, the building appealed especially to tenants in show business and the arts. Musicians in particular loved its thick, soundproof walls, and in time the building would become home to Enrico Caruso, Arturo Toscanini, Igor Stravinsky, and Yehudi Menuhin. The impresario Florenz Ziegfeld lived on the twelfth floor with his wife, the French actress

Anna Held—while keeping an apartment on the tenth floor for his mistress, Lillian Lorraine.

In the next eight years more than 4,000 apartment buildings were built across the Upper East and Upper West sides of Manhattan—each home to 100 people or more. Many were quickly filled with Jewish and Italian immigrant families who, as their fortunes rose, fled the old tenement districts for more spacious areas uptown. Dr. S. Josephine Baker sketched the classic path of immigrant success up the island: "While [their son] was being educated [at law or medical school]," she wrote, "the whole family worked like mad under sweat-shop conditions and skimped incredibly on food, clothes, and rent, not to mention soap and sunlight. Then when the chosen son started making money, they moved out and followed his rising fortunes uptown; first to Lexington Avenue . . . then to

Riverside Drive, and sometimes finally to Park Avenue or the Upper East Fifties or Sixties. That was as regular a progression as spring, summer, autumn, winter."

To distance themselves from the stream of new arrivals, upper-class New Yorkers began to establish what were first called home clubs and later cooperatives—buildings whose apartments were not rented but collectively owned by the tenants, who could admit or refuse newcomers as they wished. "Unless the cooperators unite to constitute themselves a vigilance committee," the *Architectural Record* warned in euphemistic but plainly anti-Semitic language, "someday there will elude the vigilance of the janitor or the real estate agent a hook-nosed tenant, of the kind of hook-nose you know and apprehend."

By 1910, when the first apartment house rose on Fifth Avenue—998 Fifth, a luxurious 12-story

structure designed by McKim, Mead and White, with one enormous apartment per floor—even the very wealthiest New Yorkers had begun to desert their old mansions and row houses for apartment buildings. "A family who would require from four to eight servants in an ordinary dwelling," Chas. F. Wingate explained in the pages of *Building*, "can easily get along with half that number in an apartment house." When in 1913, for the first time since the Civil War, the federal government imposed a tax on personal income, the trend toward apartments gathered even more momentum. From that year on, no new mansion would ever rise again along Fifth Avenue, and even the building of ordinary row houses began to slow. Soon almost everyone in New York—rich and poor and everyone in between—was living in the same kind of house: an apartment house.

him up to the sixteenth story or drops him with breathless speed to the basement is a product of this same American haste and economy. . . .

A. D. F. Hamlin, 1897

"The great function of the office building," one New York building manager observed, "is to make it possible for the businesses that deal with one another to be close together."

By 1902, no fewer than sixty-six skyscrapers had risen above lower Manhattan—most grouped within a few blocks of one another around Wall Street, where real estate prices now spiraled into the stratosphere, making land beneath the big towers the most valuable pieces of property on earth.

By 1910, frontage along Wall Street was selling for $25,000 a foot—spurring owners to throw up even bigger buildings, with even more rentable floor space—pushing land prices higher still and starting the cycle all over again.

Valuable as they were as property, skyscrapers in New York quickly acquired another function, often prized even more highly by the companies that owned them. "The first towers actually were erected as super billboards," a real-estate agent named Earle Schultz later wrote. "Immediately the towers took on prestige and glamor and became fantastically successful advertisements for their owners." A distinctive architectural form began to emerge, which would distinguish tall buildings in New York from those in Chicago or elsewhere: the slender free-standing tower soaring above a massive base—and often culminating at the top in an impractical but memorable form—a Babylonian ziggurat, a French mansard roof, a neo-Gothic steeple, that instantly registered its company's trademark in the sky.

Within a few years, the breathtaking towers clustered together at the southern tip of Manhattan had begun to compose the distinctive modern profile of New York, exploiting to maximum advantage the already dramatic prospect of the island city, as seen from the decks of ships entering or leaving the harbor. As "cathedrals of commerce" replaced the church spire as the dominant forms on the city's horizon, a new urban image was born—the *skyline*—an unforgettable symbol of the immense secular power of the vast commercial metropolis.

In the early years of the twentieth century—on the old, narrow streets that had once comprised New Amsterdam—the world's first skyscraper district began to rise. In the aerial view, above, the old shoreline of the Dutch colony is traced by the dark, sinuous line of the elevated railroad tracks—now several blocks inland—while the dense cluster of towers reveals the drive for proximity that helped to propel the new buildings into the sky. The 1907 view, left, looking north on Broad Street, shows the same forest of towers from street level, rising around the focal point of the district—the New York Stock Exchange, which in 1903 replaced its earlier headquarters (see page 148) with a towering neo-classical structure faced entirely in marble.

Money and greed may have produced it; but the thousands who lift their eyes to it daily, from ferry-boats and trains and bridges, are not thinking of the money behind it when they admire, rising out of the broken glitter of busy water at its base, the huge chain of buildings. The mass is beautiful. The commercial is lost in the esthetic.

Mildred Stapley

THE NEW COSMOPOLIS

If I had a friend who was desirous of seeing certain European cities—Vienna, Prague, St. Petersburg, Warsaw, Cracow, even Berlin and Naples—I would invite him for a week's cruise on our East Side. There is no necessity of going across the water to hear foreign tongues or see odd costumes. They are all on view every day and night in New York, the only New Cosmopolis on the globe. Every nation is represented: each has its own café, its newspaper, its church, its theatre. Optimism rules.

James Huneker

Since the time of the Dutch, New York City had been the most cosmopolitan, heteroge-neous place in America, if not the world. And yet nothing could have prepared it for the diversity and sheer volume of humanity with which it now had to contend, or for the baffling complexity of the human ecology that would arise within its borders between 1890 and 1910.

Every day, hundreds of immigrants stepped off the Ellis Island ferry at the Battery in lower Manhattan and took their first hesitant steps in the New World.

Still dressed in peasant clothes and carrying their belongings in big, unwieldy bundles, the bewildered newcomers walked up Broadway—overwhelmed by the new towers looming up on all sides—and buffeted by the busy crowds and rushing traffic of the financial district. Most had spent their entire lives in towns and villages so small that every inhabitant, every building, every path was familiar. Nothing had prepared them for the noise, the crowds, the traffic—or their own anonymity.

"Trolleys rushed through the streets with terrible force," a Polish immigrant named David Ignatow remembered. "Waves of people pounded the streets, their faces like foam. It was all wild, all inconceivable . . . this unimaginable city."

"Where were we to go?" a Jewish immigrant named Abraham Cahan later wrote, remembering his first day in New York City. "What were we to do?

A voice hailed us in Yiddish. Facing about we beheld a middle-aged man. . . . Prosperity was written all over his shaven face, but he was unmistakably one of our people. It was like coming across a human being in the jungle. "You have no trade, have you? . . . Well, don't worry. You will be all right. If a fellow isn't lazy or a fool he has no reason to be sorry he came to America." When we reached the General Post Office, our guide . . . slipped a silver quarter into my hand and bid me good-bye. "Walk straight ahead," he said to me, waving his hand, "just keep walking until you see a lot of Jewish people."

Confronted by the onslaught of hundreds of thousands, and then millions of impoverished European immigrants, many native New Yorkers were—as many native New Yorkers had

By 1900, when this view of Hester and Essex
streets was taken, the streets of the Lower East Side
had become a vast marketplace lined with hundreds of shops, saloons,
bakeries, and groceries—along with thousands of pushcarts
selling fruits, vegetables, crockery, clothing, eyeglasses, buttons,
stationery, scissors, underwear, remnants of fabric, and hundreds
of other items. "Every conceivable thing," one man said, "is for sale."

always been—deeply mistrustful and sometimes openly hostile toward the new arrivals.

"This alien flood," Richard Williams wrote in the *Wall Street Journal*, is "the poorest, the most vicious, the most wholly undesirable peoples that have ever come to American shores." The editor of one New York newspaper put it more simply. "The floodgates are open," he wrote. "The dam is washed away. The sewer is unchoked. Europe is vomiting!"

And yet, whether they knew it or not, each and every one of the new arrivals—like each and every native New Yorker—was taking part in an extraordinary, and indeed almost unprecedented, experiment: to determine what kind of world they would be able to make for themselves—and what kind of unity, if any, it would be possible to fashion from such a bewildering and sometimes deeply disconcerting diversity.

For older New Yorkers, no less than for the new, the challenges to be faced and the distances to be traversed were daunting—not only geographical distances but cultural, political, and psychic ones. Even to begin to close them would require the construction of immense new structures unlike any built before: new physical structures, new structures of feeling and thought, and in the end, new political ones.

As for the new immigrants themselves, coming to New York had launched them on one of the most extraordinary journeys in history—a voyage through time as well as space—not only crossing an ocean but exchanging an ancient way of life for the most modern and frenetic environment on earth, one that many immigrants found almost incomprehensibly alien and estranging.

Even when the courtyards within New York's slum blocks were relatively large (like those shown above), they were usually subdivided by fences and walls into small plots, rendering them useless for outdoor recreation or most other activities except the drying of laundry on clotheslines.

This 1908 view of Mott Street (below) shows an altar to Our Lady of Help—one of the elaborate shrines created for the feasts held annually to honor the patron saint of each Italian community. "To the homesick peasant who hangs about the Mott-street café for hours," Jacob Riis observed, "the [patron] saint means home and kindred, neighborly friendship in a strange land, and the old communal ties which, if anything, are tightened by distance and homesickness."

The old village might have been "wretched," the writer Irving Howe later observed, "but it was a thoroughly known place, where one's ancestors lay buried. It did not loom up to terrifying heights before one's eyes, it required no special knowledge of machines in shops or on trolleys, and it seldom had much to do with the rigors of the clock."

All the immigrants coming to New York would somehow have to bridge the enormous chasms that opened up almost immediately upon arrival—between expectations and actualities, between what was lost and what was gained, between the tantalizing allure of the new world all around them, and the claims of the old world they had left behind.

The voyage, as most new immigrants discovered, only began upon arrival at Ellis Island—which was the starting point for a long process of acclimation and transformation that, in the end, would change the city and the country even more than it changed them.

CITY OF NATIONS

By 1907, the entire world seemed to be reassembling itself on the streets of Manhattan.

"Every four years," the writer Edwin Hill later said, "New York adds to itself a city the size of Boston or St. Louis. It is the largest Jewish city in the world, the largest Irish city, one of the largest German cities. More than 700,000 Russians call it home, and it houses more Italians than Rome. New York is the great whirlpool of the races."

There were now more Italians living in New York than in Genoa, Venice, and Florence combined. Block by block—sometimes house by house—entire Italian towns and villages were being re-created on the Lower East Side, as immigrants remapped the social structures and religious customs of the Old World onto the New.

No less than the Italian republic itself, New York's Little Italy was a loose assemblage of provinces, each commanding its own loyalties. Neapolitans centered around Mulberry Street, then spilled over to Mott Street. Western Sicilians settled on Prince and Elizabeth Streets; those from east Sicily, on Catherine and Monroe. Calabrians gathered on Mott between Broome and Grand Streets, the Genoese on Bleecker and Baxter, the Pugliesi on Hester.

On some blocks the mapping was finer still, as families from an Italian or Sicilian settlement occupied adjoining apartments in the same building—an ancient hill town or farming village reconstituted within a single New York tenement.

"In Elizabeth Street," Jacob Riis remarked, as "in Mulberry, Mott, and Thompson streets downtown, and in the numbered streets of Little Italy uptown, almost every block has its own village of mountain or lowland, and with the village its patron saint, in whose worship or celebration—call it what you will—the particular camp makes reply to the question, 'Who is my neighbor?'"

Nothing symbolized the transfer of the old ways to the new city more than the religious festivals, or feasts—over twenty in all—celebrated every year in New York's Italian communities. Dedicated to the patron saint of each neighborhood or block, the colorful processions, once held in tiny rural villages, now passed between the high, narrow tenement streets of the city—church officials, marching bands,

crowds of children and adults, and, in the middle of it all, an enormous painting or towering statue of the local saint.

The patron saint of Mulberry Street, in the very heart of Little Italy, was San Rocco, whose feast came every year on August 16.

Mulberry Street was on holiday: from the windows of the Italian houses hung tapestries, flags,

The Grand Theater on the Bowery, 1908. The most artistically ambitious of New York's 20 Yiddish theaters, the Grand had been founded by the celebrated actor and director Jacob P. Adler, who promised the public "only beautiful musical operas and dramas giving truthful and serious portrayals of life." Around the time of World War I, the peak years of the city's Yiddish theater, more than 1,000 performances a year—from broad comedies and coarse melodramas to sophisticated adaptations of Shakespeare's plays—were presented to more than 2 million patrons.

and three-coloured lanterns, and everywhere were garlands of light bulbs. . . . In the street, the crowd was happy and noisy: women . . . wore their holiday dresses and brought the gay note of gaudy colours amid the dark suits of the men and uniforms of the military societies. San Rocco was being celebrated, and the Italians of Mulberry wanted to do things properly. Towards 11 a.m., the call of the trumpets was heard and in the distance flags and banners appeared. . . . A squad of policemen headed the procession followed by the Conterno Band, and right after by a banner on which San Rocco was painted in oil, with all his wounds and his dog. Two flags, one Italian, one American, flapped at the banner's sides, thus placing the saint under double protection.

Bernardino Ciambelli, 1893

And yet as large as Little Italy had become, larger still was the vast, seemingly endless agglomeration of Jewish immigrants, the largest single immigrant group in the city. By 1907, more than 1 million Jews lived in New York—more than 400,000 on the Lower East Side alone.

"It is a seething human sea," Abraham Cahan wrote, "fed by streams of immigrations flowing from all the Yiddish speaking centres of Europe. . . . Jews from every nook and corner of Russia, Poland, Galicia, Hungary, Rumania; Lithuanian Jews . . . south Russian Jews, Bessarabian Jews; Jews crowded out of the 'Pale of Settlement'; Jews expelled from Moscow, St. Petersberg, Kiev; Jewish runaways from justice; students shut out of the Russian universities, artisans, merchants, teachers, rabbis, artists, beggars—all come in search of fortune."

Hungarian Jews occupied the blocks at the district's northern edge that had once been part of Kleindeutschland. Russian Jews spread out to the south along East Broadway, the commercial spine of the district. In between—"in the very thick of the battle for breath," one man said—were Jews from Galicia and Romania, and the newest arrivals, Levantine Jews from the Middle East.

Across the district entire industries arose to meet the needs of the vast Jewish population. Five hundred bakeries produced black bread, bagels, and matzoh. Another hundred plants bottled seltzer and soda water, sometimes called

For the vast majority of immigrants streaming into New York at the turn of the century, the path from Ellis Island led straight to the Lower East Side. By 1900, its 450 blocks had become the most densely crowded place on earth—home to more than half a million people already, with thousands more arriving every month. A decade before, Jacob Riis had been stunned to find 500 and sometimes 600 people jammed onto each acre in the crowded slum. Now there were more than 1,000 people per acre—sometimes more than 3,000 on a single city block—a concentration of humanity unlike anything ever experienced in world history, before or since.

In the years to come, the sheer mass of people on the Lower East Side, together with the energies generated on its teeming streets and the dreams incubated within its narrow tenement walls, would propel an extraordinary transformation in American culture, and be knit into the myth of America.

The streets swarmed with immigrants. . . . The scurry and hustle of the people was not merely overwhelmingly greater, in volume and intensity, than my native town. The swing and step of the pedestrians, the voices and manners of the street peddlers, and a hundred and one other things seemed to testify to more self-confidence and energy, to larger ambitions and wider hopes, than the crowds in my birthplace.

Abraham Cahan

In time, the very dwellings in which the newcomers first settled would become the stuff of legend. Built originally as cheap temporary housing for German and Irish immigrants, most of whom had now moved on, the tenements were taken over by new waves of Italians, Russians, Poles, Greeks, Hungarians, Armenians, and a half dozen other nationalities, who could afford to live nowhere else in the city.

With 20 or more people sometimes crammed into a single apartment, children were frequently sandwiched four and five to a bed, while adults themselves were sometimes forced to sleep in shifts. Families unable to meet the rent—about ten dollars a month—took in paying boarders, who slept on mattresses laid wall to wall in bedroom alcoves and kitchens. When the mattresses ran out, chairs were used with a board placed between them.

On hot and humid nights, tenement dwellers fled the stifling, unventilated rooms and climbed out onto the fire escapes, or up onto the roofs. "What a mélange in the starlight!" the novelist Michael Gold wrote. "Mothers, graybeards . . . exhausted sweatshop fathers, young consumptive coughers and spitters, all of us snored and groaned there side by side, on newspapers or mattresses. We slept in pants and undershirt, heaped like corpses. The city reared about us."

With space in the tenements at a premium, life spilled out onto the city streets, which became the focus and main arena of daily activity—at once playground, workspace, safety valve, social club, classroom, school, and theater. Block after block, from long before dawn until long after dark, the streets were one vast, raucous open-air bazaar, swarming with peddlers and vendors of every kind, hawking their wares from the sidewalks or from pushcarts rented out for ten cents a day.

By 1900, there were more than 25,000 pushcarts on the streets of the Lower East Side, selling everything from fruits and vegetables to pots and pans, shoelaces, ribbons, bolts of cloth, tools and crockery, books and stationery, eyeglasses for 35 cents a pair, old coats, and hats for a quarter.

In the poorest wards, peddlers sold goods in minute quantities: a single candle, the wing of a chicken, one egg, or just the yolk of one egg. For recent arrivals, peddling offered a start in the New World. "You need no more than to know the English names of a few items," one man said, "and be blessed with a special gift— shamelessness, so that you don't become depressed when you are turned away or taunted by strangers." A successful peddler could earn as much as 15 or 20 dollars a week—enough perhaps to start a small shop or business of his own.

Forget your past, your customs, your ideals. Select a goal and pursue it with all your might. No matter what happens to you, hold on. You will experience a bad time but sooner or later you will achieve your goal. . . . A bit of advice for you: Do not take a moment's rest. Run, do, work and keep your own good in mind. A final virtue is needed in America—called cheek. . . . Do not say, "I cannot; I do not know."

G. M. Price

I came to understand that it was not the land of fun. It was a Land of Hurry-Up. There was no gold to be dug in the streets here. . . . Nu, so I worked. I worked with my hands, liver and sides. I worked!

Michael Gold

A Lower East Side tenement interior, 1905, photographed by Jessie Tarbox Beals.

A drawing of the excursion boat *General Slocum* sailing up the East River with 1,300 passengers, as she looked on the morning of June 15, 1904, moments before a devastating fire broke out on board. Despite her shipshape appearance, the vessel proved a deathtrap, equipped with malfunctioning fire hoses, unusable lifeboats, and crumbling life jackets.

At 9:40 on the bright, clear morning of Wednesday, June 15, 1904, an excursion steamer named the *General Slocum* cast off from the Third Street pier and headed north up the East River for a day trip to Long Island.

Most of the 1,300 people aboard were women and children—the families of German immigrant workingmen—who had signed up for a midweek outing that had been sponsored by a German Lutheran church called St. Mark's, located on the Lower East Side near Tompkins Square.

Less than 20 minutes out, the pleasure excursion turned into a horrifying nightmare.

As the *General Slocum* approached a treacherous stretch of water called the Hell Gate, a fire broke out in a forward storeroom and began to spread out of control. Instead of beaching the vessel at the nearest shoreline, the captain tried to make a run for it, hoping to reach a small dock at North Brother Island, a few miles to the north. It was a fatal error. As the steamer throttled up to full speed, the quickening breeze fanned the flames into a blazing inferno that rapidly engulfed all three passenger decks, as horrified spectators looked on from shore.

It took only ten minutes for the *General Slocum* to reach North Brother Island, but by the time the charred and limping ship had docked, 1,021 people were dead. Dozens of women and children had been overcome by the smoke and flames. Hundreds more had jumped into the swirling, swiftly moving current of the East River and drowned.

The disaster left a permanent scar on New York's German immigrant population. In the months to

For days after the fire, the bodies of the *Slocum*'s victims washed up on the shores of North Brother Island.

come, hundreds of families, too emotionally devastated and heartbroken to remain in their old neighborhood downtown, began a mass exodus from Tompkins Square to an Upper East Side area, near 86th Street, known as

Yorkville. Within a matter of years, the uptown district had all but replaced Kleindeutschland as the center of German American life in New York—a role it would fulfill for most of the century to come.

"the workers' Champagne." The Tenth Ward alone contained 140 groceries, 131 butcher shops, 36 bakeries, 30 dairy stores, and 62 candy stores, along with fish shops, fruit stores, cigar stores, herring stands, tea shops—and 15 stores that carried nothing but sacramental wine for the Sabbath dinner on Friday night.

Every day, the sound of Hebrew could be heard in more than five hundred synagogues and religious schools—but it was Yiddish, the language of everyday Jewish life, that created a sense of community in the enclaves of the Lower East Side. Yiddish was the common language of the Romanian and Polish, Russian and Hungarian Jews—spoken around the pushcarts, in the shops and markets, and in the local cafés and coffee-and-cake parlors where religion, culture, and politics were debated long into the night.

By the turn of the century, six Yiddish newspapers were published daily in New York, boasting a combined circulation of nearly half a million. Meanwhile, along a ten-block stretch on the Bowery called the Jewish Rialto, more than twenty theaters were drawing 2 million visitors a year with Yiddish-language performances of everything from tawdry melodramas to Shakespearean dramas, modernized and transposed into contemporary Jewish settings. Audiences thrilled to the performances of tragedians such as Boris Thomashvski and Jacob Adler. "The Lear of Adler," the *New York Times* declared, "is . . . a modernized comedy of manners into which the old patriarch and his three daughters are transported with surpassing dramatic effect."

Like the Italian feasts, the Yiddish theaters of New York offered a vital and powerful link between the immigrants' European past and their American present. On their stages, New York's Jews could see reflected the entire story of their struggle: the uprooting, the arrival in a new and strange place, and, at last, the adaptation and carrying on with life.

From all over the world they are pouring into New York, Greeks from Athens . . . Sparta and Macedonia, living six, seven, eight, nine, ten, eleven, twelve, in one room, sleeping on the floors and dressing and eating and entertaining themselves God knows how. Jews from Russia, Poland, Hungary, the Balkans, crowd-

ing the East Side and the inlying sections of Brooklyn, and huddling together in thick, gummy streets . . . ; Italians from Sicily and the warmer vales of the South, crowding into great sections of their own, all hungry for a taste of New York; Hungarians, French, Polish, Swedish, Armenians, all with sections of their own and alive to the joys of the city, and how eager to live—great gold and scarlet streets throbbing with them!

Theodore Dreiser

Dotted in and around the large Jewish and Italian districts lay a bewildering array of smaller enclaves—neighborhoods of Greeks, Armenians, Turks, Poles, Czechs, Swedes, Norwegians, Syrians, Lebanese, and more than a dozen other groups from around the globe. By 1900, an eight-block area just north of Chatham Square had become home to more than six thousand Chinese-born immigrants—the second largest Chinatown in America, after San Francisco. "A map of the city, colored to designate nationalities," Jacob Riis observed, "would show more stripes than on the skin of a zebra, and more colors than any rainbow."

However much they differed from one another, the maze of immigrant neighborhoods in New York served the same purpose. Each was an intimate zone of familiarity, carved from the enormous and unfamiliar city around it, filled with the sights, sounds, and smells of home. Insular and self-contained, each was a haven where newcomers could find everything they needed, and which, in fact, they rarely if ever had to leave.

"Though I was in America," a Jewish immigrant named Rose Cohen remembered, "I lived in practically the same environment which we brought from home. Of course, there was a difference in our joys, in our sorrows, in our hardships . . . but on the whole we were still in our village." Italian women who had lived in the city for years, one parish priest reported, used the expression " 'I have been down to America today,' meaning they had gone a few blocks outside the district of the Italian colony."

"Riding in street cars was expensive and nickels were too scarce to be squandered on such extravagance," a young immigrant named Marie Ganz observed. "So it was little we really knew of the strange world that lay just beyond

Syrian children in New York. Though Russian Jews and southern Italians formed the city's largest immigrant communities, by 1900 Manhattan and Brooklyn were dotted with dozens of smaller ethnic districts—including Little Syria, where several thousand immigrants from the Ottoman Empire had settled just north of the Battery on Washington and Rector streets in the years after 1878, working mostly as peddlers, factory workers, and small businessmen.

Following pages: children playing on the Lower East Side outside a new public school on the corner of East Houston and Lewis streets. After the 1898 consolidation, New York City embarked on a massive school construction program to meet the influx of newcomers, and put up hundreds of new school buildings across the five boroughs. By 1909, more than half a million students—70 percent of them foreign-born—were attending public school in New York City.

our own domain—of the region that lay before us dim and mysterious in the distance on summer nights as we stood on the house-tops."

One day, a friendly carriage driver making his rounds took the young girl on a tour of the upper reaches of Fifth Avenue and Central Park—places she had heard about, but never actually seen.

In almost no time we were flying along what had been the western edge of the world for me, the Bowery, the jumping off place into the unknown. Then on and on to streets that were strange and wonderful . . . where there were no pushcarts . . . where even the faces were different. . . . No tenements now, with fire escapes hung with bedding . . . but stately buildings that almost reached the sky and bore no sign of family life. . . . Gorgeous carriages passed by with men in gaily colored uniforms . . . and inside surely princes and princesses, women and men and children dressed most wonderfully, even the children dressed with furs. Far behind now were the cloud-piercing buildings. On one side were beautiful trees, a forest of trees decked in autumn colors; on the other, palaces of brownstone and marble, solemn, mysterious, forbidding. . . . It is growing dark. Great white lights are throwing a magic glare over streets and buildings. All the windows of the palaces and

great buildings glow with light. Mysterious shadows come and go. Nothing seems real. Am I awake or am I dreaming?

Marie Ganz

TRANSFORMATIONS

We have to be Americans. We shall be. We shall learn English. We shall accommodate ourselves to the laws and organization of the country. . . . We shall love America and help to build America. We shall accomplish in the New World a hundred times more that we could in the Old. But you will not be able to erase the old home from your heart. The heart will be drawn elsewhere. And in your solitude, images will rise up and stare in your faces with eternal sorrow.

Abraham Cahan

Viewed through the eyes of a stranger the Lower East Side was an unimaginably crowded and squalid place. Yet to the immigrants themselves the district was a way station along the road to a better life.

Never had a city been the means of change for so many people on so vast a scale, in so short a time. In less than a single generation—in just ten years, on average—most families on the Lower East Side moved up or on.

The process of change began almost immediately, with the young. "An [immigrant] father delivers his children to the public school," one man wrote, "as if it were an act of consecration."

In 1901, for the first time in a major American city, school attendance in New York became mandatory for all children up to the age of twelve. Inside the crowded classrooms, teachers—themselves often the sons and daughters of immigrants—looked out upon an astonishing mix of faces. By 1909, more than 70 percent of the city's 550,000 schoolchildren had been born abroad.

"No other municipality," a journalist named Adele Marie Shaw declared, "had ever to meet a problem so difficult, so peculiar, and at the same time so all-embracing . . . [the city's] salvation is dependent upon the conversion of Russians, Turks, Austro-Hungarians, Sicilians, Greeks, Arabs, into good Americans."

Public education in New York had once been a local matter, supervised by trustees from each ward. But in 1896, after a fierce debate, officials reorganized the public schools into a single city-wide system, with a standard curriculum set by a central Board of Education. "[Local control] is not a good thing in a city . . . so largely impregnated with foreign influences, languages, and ideas," an aide to Mayor William L. Strong declared, "for in many localities the influences . . . would be unquestionably un-American. The best interests of the city demand

that the children of such population be brought under American influence and instruction."

In what would become a model for the nation, New York public schools sought to Americanize immigrant children as fast as they could, suppressing in their pupils all traces of the Old Country. Teachers stressed English grammar, American history, lessons in hygiene, and manners. "We were 'Americanized,' one man recalled, "about as gently as horses are broken in."

By 1907, the public schools were part of an educational system like nothing else in the nation—or the world. Every weekday evening, over a hundred thousand working people—including forty thousand women—attended night school in New York, studying everything from basic English and simple arithmetic to advanced accounting, law, and medicine. Thousands more went to the city's industrial training schools or attended one of its extraordinary public colleges—City College, Hunter College, and, a few years later, Brooklyn College—whose degree programs were available free of charge to any qualified New Yorker.

Children and adults alike flocked to the city's thirty-seven free branch libraries—jewel-like treasure houses sprinkled across Manhattan and the Bronx, paid for by Andrew Carnegie. "Long lines of children reaching down two flights of stairs and into the street," the *New York Evening Post* reported, "may not infrequently be seen at the Chatham Square branch of the New York Public Library . . . drawing books in English at the rate of 1,000 a day."

Nor were the forces of change limited to public institutions. Fearing that their established position was being threatened by the waves of poor, "alien" Jews pouring in from Russia and

New York public school, around 1910. In addition to teaching English, history, arithmetic, and spelling, schools sought to Americanize immigrant children through classes in manners, hygiene, and the fundamentals of democracy. Each classroom, New York School Superintendent William H. Maxwell declared in 1911, "is the melting pot which converts the children of the immigrants . . . into sturdy, independent American citizens."

Poland, New York's German Jews took it upon themselves to speed the process of assimilation, sponsoring classes and publications on how to be an American, and founding a towering cultural center called the Educational Alliance, in the very heart of the Lower East Side.

"I recall a large cool room . . . and a big class of bright-eyed Jewish children, boys and girls," H. G. Wells wrote in 1906 after a visit to the alliance. "Some of them had been in America a month, some much longer, but here they were— under the auspices of the wealthy Hebrews of New York . . . being Americanized. They sang of America—'sweet land of liberty'; they stood up and drilled with the little bright pretty flags; swish they crossed and swish they waved back, a waving froth of flags and flushed children's faces."

But the largest classroom of all was the city itself. "The streets were ours," Irving Howe later recalled. "We would roam through the city tasting the delights of freedom, discovering possibilities far beyond the reach of our parents. The streets taught us the deceits of commerce, introduced us to the excitements of sex, schooled us in strategies of survival and gave us our first clear idea of what life in America was going to be like. . . . [The street] drew Jewish boys and girls like a magnet, offering them qualities in short supply at home: the charms of the spontaneous and unpredictable. . . . To go beyond Cherry Street on the south, where the Irish lived, or west of the Bowery, where the Italians were settling, was to explore the world of the gentiles—dangerous, since one risked a punch in the face, but tempting, since for an East Side boy the idea of *the others,* so steadily drilled into his mind by every agency of his culture, was bound to incite curiosity."

And yet, even as the children turned toward the New World, their parents were haunted by the Old. "The parents remain foreign," an educator named Julia Richman wrote, while "the children become American. There is . . . an almost unbridgeable gap between the two."

In immigrant families, it was often the children—whom Jacob Riis called "go-betweens" —who translated citizenship forms, apartment leases, or medical records for their Yiddish- or Italian-speaking parents. "I became a sort of junior father," one man said. The parents themselves, meanwhile, looked on as their children became increasingly Americanized, and they felt mingled pride and sorrow.

During the years [my daughter] was here without us she became a regular Yankee and forgot how to talk Yiddish. . . . She says it is not nice to talk Yiddish and that I am a greenhorn. . . . Once I saw her standing on the stoop with a boy so I went up to her and asked her when she would come up. . . . She did not reply, and later when she came up she screamed at me because I had called her by her Jewish name. But I cannot call her differently. I cannot call her by her new name.

A Mother

For the children of immigrants, the divisions were inescapable, and often painful. "I'm wandering between worlds at once too old and too new," the immigrant writer Anzia Yezierska said. "I can't live with the old world and I'm yet too green for the new. I don't belong to those who gave me birth or to those with whom I was educated."

And yet, in the end, the tide of change was irreversible, as children fought and played with children from other backgrounds; as men and women pushed ever farther beyond the borders of the neighborhoods, taking streetcars or the new subway to destinations all across the

A class in a New York public school. Observers in the 1900s were struck not only by the size but the startling diversity of the city's immigrant population. In a single school district on the Lower East Side, officials counted students from 25 countries, including Denmark, Greece, Holland, Finland, France, Hungary, Norway, Poland, Sweden, Syria, and Romania.

city; as the sons and daughters of immigrant families began to mingle, socialize, and, eventually, intermarry. Even in the heart of the Lower East Side, tenements once occupied by people from the same local village began taking in strangers from all over the world.

"The tenants in our building were from Palermo, Naples, Minsk, Bucharest, and Warsaw," recalled Milton Catapano, the son of an Italian-born immigrant. "How did we communicate? In Yiddish, partly. . . . My father, a tailor, mastered conversational Yiddish in the needle trades; conversed in Italian with his compatriots; and spoke English at home. My [American-born] mother spoke enough Italian and Yiddish to shop and communicate with in-laws and neighbors."

By 1908, the most remarkable thing about the city's immigrant districts—and the immigrants themselves—was not their insularity but the speed with which they were mixing.

What is a New Yorker? Is he Jew or Irish? Is he English or German? Is he Russian or Polish? He may be something of all these, and yet he is wholly none of them. Something has been added which he had not before. He is quicker in his movement, less trammeled in his judgement. Though he may lose wisdom in sharpening his wit, the change is unmistakable. New York, indeed, resembles a magic cauldron. Those cast into it are born again.

Charles Whibley, 1907

On October 5, 1908, a new phrase entered the language with the premiere of a four-act stage play by a London-based writer named Israel Zangwill. It was called *The Melting Pot*, and it told the story of a young Russian Jewish musician who dreams of composing an epic symphony capable of embracing the composite American he sees rising from New York's amalgamation of cultures—the breathtaking symphony of cultures arising from the streets of New York City.

"There she lies," the musician exclaims, looking out on the city from a Manhattan rooftop, "the great Melting Pot—listen! Can't you hear the roaring and the bubbling? There gapes her mouth—the harbor where a thousand mammoth feeders come from the ends of the world to pour in their human freight. Celt and Latin,

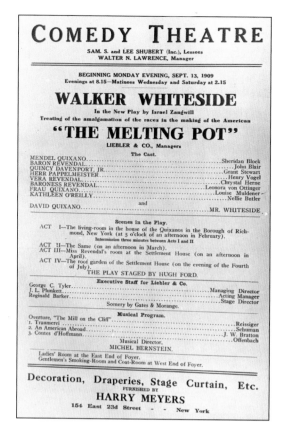

A program for Israel Zangwill's 1908 play, *The Melting Pot*. Unlike such New York immigrant writers as Abraham Cahan and Anzia Yezierska—who wrote movingly of the conflicts of newcomers still struggling with the pull of tradition, Zangwill—writing from London—saw New York as a crucible in which all traces of the Old World would melt away, bringing forth from the city's diverse population a new composite breed of American.

Slav and Teuton, Greek and Syrian—black and yellow—Jew and Gentile. . . . How the great Alchemist melts and fuses them with his purging flame."

Zangwill's play was dismissed by the *New York Times* as "romantic claptrap." But its title took hold instantly in the public imagination. Though they might disagree about its meaning or desirability, almost everyone agreed that a powerful, almost chemical, transformation was under way in New York, one that would change forever the city—and ultimately the nation.

This great city of ours, with its diversities of race, of religion, of social, political and personal ideals—has a unity which the country has as yet failed to recognize, a genius which belongs to the future rather than to the past, and which, because it is of the future, is slow to reveal itself. We forget that New York is not only one of the first cities of modern birth . . . but also a city of a new type. Its very diversities are creating here a kind of city which men have not seen before; in which a unity of a more inclusive . . . [o]rder is slowly forming itself; a city . . . which has the light of prophecy in it.

Hamilton Wright Mabie, 1904

HOLE IN THE GROUND

By 1900, New York's huge immigrant population was propelling a transformation in the city's physical infrastructure on a scale that staggered the imagination, even by the standards the city itself had set.

Two years before, consolidation had redrawn the city's political boundaries, incorporating hundreds of square miles into five immense boroughs to form the outlines of modern New York. Now, over the next decade and a half, New Yorkers would fill those lines in, connecting the far-flung reaches of the city, and pioneering the most advanced and efficient metropolis on earth.

Along the way, they would make the political consolidation of Greater New York a breathtaking reality.

Like much of Brooklyn and nearly all of Staten Island and Queens, the Bronx in 1900 was still a rural duchy of fields and farms and country towns. The highest structures on the horizon were grain elevators, and the main link to Manhattan, a horse-drawn trolley, ran so slowly that commuters could hop off, pick a pail of wild huckleberries, and get back on the same car.

Yet the borough's pastoral days were already numbered, though few people realized how fast the end would come. By late 1900, city surveyors could be seen laying out the route for a vast new public transit system. Powered by electricity and built almost entirely underground, it would link the remotest reaches of the outer boroughs to the bustling heart of Manhattan and unify the city as never before.

There had been talk of a subway for decades. Champions of the idea pointed to London, Paris, and half a dozen other European cities where trains were already running underground. Though skeptics dismissed the entire idea as ludicrous—one financier confidently asserted that "New Yorkers will never go into a hole in the ground"—by 1900 the city had let out a contract for construction and work had begun in earnest.

Operated by a private firm called the Interborough Rapid Transit Company, the mammoth project was under the direction of a financier named August Belmont, one of the richest men in New York.

In four years, Belmont's army of 7,700 men, most of them Irish and Italian immigrants, con-

Looking east across the Bronx from 179th Street and Bryant Avenue, 1904. Although a cluster of factories, breweries, and coalyards crowded its southern end, in 1904 most of the Bronx's 43 square miles remained rural—a series of small villages scattered among open lots, planted fields, orchards, and meadows. But that same year the first IRT subway line would bring an explosion of urban growth, swelling the population of the borough from less than 90,000 to nearly half a million people in just two decades.

structed more than twenty miles of subway line through the densely congested city—a mind-boggling rate of construction made possible by an ingeniously efficient method called cut and cover. Instead of boring tunnels through bedrock far below the surface, workers dug a trench right down the middle of the city's streets. Deftly threading their way through a tangle of underground pipes and conduits, the crews built walls, laid tracks and platforms, then covered it all over with a metal lid that served as a platform for the streets and sidewalk above.

Just four and a half years after construction began, the IRT—the most modern transportation system in the world—was ready for service.

On October 27, 1904, in an exquisitely tiled station thirty feet beneath city hall, Mayor George B. McClellan, the son of the famous Civil War general, was presented a ceremonial silver motorman's handle, along with the honor of starting up the train for its first official run.

SUBWAY STATION, N. Y. CITY.

Best wishes Your Brother.

As worried engineers looked on, the mayor quickly throttled the eight-car train up to full power, rocketing north through the Bleecker Street station at forty-five miles an hour. When the chief engineer, his hand nervously poised above the emergency brake, suggested he relinquish the controls, the exhilarated mayor roared back, "I'm running this train!" and pushed on to 103rd Street, seven miles to the north.

Finally, at seven that evening, after an endless series of ceremonial rides and an hour-long safety inspection, the chief engineer gave the signal, and the subway was opened to the public.

The fare was a nickel.

For the first time in his life, Father Knickerbocker went underground yesterday, to the number of 150,000, amid the tooting and whistles and the firing of salutes. . . . The official train made its run exactly on time, arriving at One Hundred and Forty-Sixth Street in exactly twenty-six minutes, and all along the way, crowds of excited New Yorkers were collected around the little entrances talking about the trains that they knew were dashing below and waiting eagerly for the first passengers to emerge from the underground passageways at their feet.
New York Herald

New Yorkers fell over one another to ride the underground rails, which they called "doing the subway." On the system's first Sunday in operation, nearly 1 million people tried to use the train, many carrying picnic baskets, braving long lines that often went on for blocks.

Rich New Yorkers went, too, venturing down in furs and jewels to explore the underground marvel. A lucky few got to tour the system in August Belmont's private car, the Mineola, which had been fitted out with mahogany trim, gleaming picture windows, and a dozen leather chairs. "A private [subway] car," Belmont's wife told reporters, "is not an acquired taste. One takes to it immediately."

But in the end, it was the lives of countless ordinary New Yorkers that would never be the same. The IRT would prove to be nothing less than a democratic revolution in mass transportation. Men and women once forced to live within walking distance of their jobs could now commute the length of Manhattan in less than half an hour. Traveling from one end of the sprawling metropolis to the other, people soon forgot what life had been like without it.

Within four years, nearly a million people a day were riding the subway and the city had embarked upon a massive expansion program, adding six hundred miles of track in ten years, giving New York the largest transit system in the world and opening the vast reaches of the

Brooklyn terminal of the Brooklyn Bridge, 1900. The new subway system was added to a public transportation network that was already the largest and most complex in the world, including hundreds of miles of elevated train lines and thousands of electric streetcars, such as those seen crossing the bridge.

The Brooklyn Subway, New York.

Above, newly completed subway tunnel and train. Below, near City Hall Park rush-hour passengers prepare to return to Brooklyn.

By 1905, Coney Island, a spit of land at the foot of Brooklyn, had become the most famous amusement center on earth—"an enchanted, story-book land," one man wrote, "a world removed—shut away from the sordid clatter and turmoil of the streets." Each year, the resort drew more than 20 million visitors, drawn by its sparkling sands and salt air (above), its hotels and dance halls, but above all by its three major parks—Steeplechase, Luna Park (top), and Dreamland (right). At night, Luna Park's 250,000 incandescent bulbs, enhanced by Dreamland's 1 million lights, created a dazzling spectacle known as "the Electric Eden," visible 30 miles out to sea. "It is," one immigrant girl declared, "just like what I dream of when I dream of heaven."

consolidated city to all New Yorkers—for a nickel.

As distant, undeveloped stretches of Brooklyn and the Bronx were brought within minutes of Manhattan's factories and offices, the greatest real-estate boom in New York's history got under way.

Nailed against a fine and ancient tree, in the midst of desolate waste, I saw a board with these words: "a new subway station will be erected on this corner."

Arnold Bennett, 1912

The boom began. Lots leaped from five hundred dollars to five thousand dollars literally overnight. Farms were dismembered; the Lydig estate, at West Farms, was almost torn apart by bidders. Streets sprang out, twisting like the tendrils of some quick-growing plant. . . . Householders went mad, sold lots on one street and bought on the next: won, lost. . . . It was nothing to sell off a hundred acres in an hour, to turn over a profit of a hundred and fifty thousand dollars in an afternoon.

Robert M. Coates

In the years to come, tens of thousands of immigrants would use the subway to escape the Lower East Side for a new way of life in the outer boroughs. The Bronx, which just years before had been a rural district of 60,000 people, exploded almost overnight into a metropolis of 430,000—the sixth largest city in the United States.

District after district from one end of the borough to the other was rapidly filled with block after block of tenements and six-story apartment houses—some featuring canvas canopies, wood-lined elevators, and landscaped gardens with fountains and statuary. Soon, nothing would remain of the old farm villages but their names—Fordham, West Farms, Tremont, Belmont, Crotona.

I was urgently invited to see how the folk lived in the Bronx. I was led to [an area] where five years previously there had been six families, and where there are now over two thousand. This is the newest New York. . . . A stout lady inducted me into a flat of four rooms. She enjoyed the advantages of central heating, gas, and electricity; a refrigerator and kitchen

range . . . such amenities for the "little people" simply do not exist in Europe; they do not even exist for the wealthy in Europe. And now I began to be struck by the splendour and the cleanliness of the marble halls, tesselated landings and stairs . . . the whole producing a gorgeous effect. The people showed no trace of the influence of those older civilizations that seem to pervade the internationalism of the [Lower] East Side. The Bronx is different. The Bronx is beginning again, and beginning better.

Arnold Bennett, 1912

Less than a decade after opening, the New York subway system was transporting nearly a billion passengers a year—whisking people to jobs and classrooms, and bringing the far-flung wonders of the sprawling five-borough city within the reach of all New Yorkers—from the woods of Van Cortlandt Park at the edge of Westchester to the dazzling lights of Coney Island by the shores of the Atlantic—from the uptown campus of City College, with its free summer symphonies at Lewisohn Stadium, to the bohemian nightclubs and tea shops down in Greenwich Village.

More than just an easy way of getting around the metropolis, the subway was an engine of

By 1909, when this view of Prospect Avenue in the Bronx was taken, much of the borough had been transformed—seemingly overnight—into an endless urban landscape of small apartment houses, better-quality tenements, and low commercial buildings. The freshly planted trees and smooth, unblemished sidewalks reveal the recent vintage of the district's construction while the absence of traffic around the central grassy mall suggests the relatively spacious and tranquil atmosphere that first attracted newcomers from Manhattan's teeming immigrant districts. The horse-drawn wagon on the left side of the street is tipping back to deliver heating coal into the cellar of a tenement— a ritual that would continue throughout the city for decades.

democracy and social transformation. As never before immigrant and working-class New Yorkers could now explore the riches of their city—the museums and libraries and parks and concert halls. As new worlds of intellectual and cultural possibility were opened to all New Yorkers, a new kind of cosmopolitanism, and a democratic worldliness, began to develop, that would become one of the hallmarks of the twentieth-century city.

MERCURY

While work on the subway continued below street level, an equally dazzling change was taking place aboveground. Between 1901 and 1913, the same electric-powered revolution transforming travel within the city would tie New York by rail to the rest of the country as never before.

In little more than a decade, the tremendous drive to consolidate and connect that had defined the city since the time of the Erie Canal would come to an extraordinary crescendo, as the island of Manhattan was physically linked for the first time since the ice age to the mainland of the North American continent.

For nearly a century, trains traveling from the west had been forced to stop on the New Jersey side of the Hudson, where passengers disembarked and proceeded by ferry to Manhattan. Even if there had been a tunnel under the great river, smoke-belching steam engines were unable to travel under the long stretch of riverbed—leaving New York without a direct rail link to the rest of the country.

The advent of electricity and electric-powered engines changed everything. In little more than a decade, the two greatest railways in America—the Pennsylvania Railroad and the New York Central—drove a massive system of tunnels under the Hudson and East Rivers, up into the heart of midtown Manhattan, then across the width and length of the island via a complex network of viaducts, tunnels, and

Pennsylvania Station under construction, about 1908. Designed by the noted firm of McKim, Mead and White, Pennsylvania Station covered nearly eight acres, and sat atop an even larger network of underground platforms and tracks. Though the classically inspired building was faced with granite on the exterior and travertine marble inside, its interior structure—as this view reveals—relied on the same modern steel-framing system used by the city's skyscrapers.

The main waiting room in Pennsylvania Station, right, was modeled on the ancient Roman baths of Caracalla—then scaled up 20 percent to meet the needs of the new metropolis. "The conditions of modern American life," the architect William Symmes Richardson wrote, "in which undertakings of great magnitude and scale are carried through, involving interests in all parts of the world, are more nearly akin to the life of the Roman Empire than that of any other known civilization." From the waiting room, departing passengers entered the main concourse (above and below) where an immense volume of interior space sat under an airy canopy of iron and glass 100 feet high.

One does not rush to catch a Pennsylvania train—one proceeds to it in orderly but expeditious manner. It is only when looking down into the great waiting-room from the head of one of the four staircases that one realizes that he is gazing into a space as large as the nave of St. Peter's, the largest church in Christendom.

Charles Moore

An estimated 100,000 sightseers thronged Pennsylvania Station on opening day, Sunday, November 27, 1910. "In thousands they flooded the acres of its floor space," one New York newspaper reported, "gazed like awestruck pygmies at the vaulted ceilings far above them, inspected curiously the tiny details of the place, so beautifully finished . . . and pressed like caged creatures against the grill which looked down upon subterranean tracks, trains and platforms. . . . There was no letup all day."

bridges that connected the largest metropolis in the country to New Jersey to the west, Long Island to the east, and New England to the north.

It was one of the greatest moments in the life of the city—or in the life of any city, anywhere, anytime. To crown the arrival of the two giant railways, twin stations—the most imposing ever built in the world—now rose twelve blocks apart from each other in the middle of Manhattan.

The first to be completed was Pennsylvania Station, at Thirty-third Street and Seventh Avenue, which opened its doors to the public for the first time in September 1910. Designed by the firm of McKim, Mead and White, it was larger than the ancient Roman baths of Caracalla on which it had been modeled. Its magnificent waiting room alone soared fifteen stories into the sky—a monumental entryway to an even grander interior space: the main concourse—an immense, ethereal volume of air and light held within an intricate mesh of iron and glass like nothing ever seen before in America.

It was, the *New York Times* declared, "The largest and handsomest [station] in the world"—built to last for all time, and proof, one awestruck observer said, that the city itself had come of age.

The station . . . was murmurous with the immense and distant sound of time. Great, slanted beams of moted light fell ponderously athwart the station's floor and the calm voice of time hovered along the walls and ceiling of that mighty room, distilled out of the voices and movements of the people who swarmed beneath. It had the murmur of a distant sea, the languorous lapse and flow of waters on a beach. . . . Few buildings are vast enough to hold the sound of time, and . . . there was a superb fitness in the fact that the one that held it better than all the others should be a railroad station. Here, as nowhere else on earth, men were brought together for a moment at the beginning or end of their innumerable journeys, here one saw their greetings and farewells, here, in a single instant, one got the entire picture of human destiny. Men came and went, they passed and vanished, all were moving through the moments of their lives . . . but the voice of time remained aloof and unperturbed, a drowsy and eternal murmur below the immense and distant roof.

Thomas Wolfe

The new Grand Central Terminal, completed in 1913, replaced Commodore Vanderbilt's 1871 iron-and-glass shed (see page 150) with a completely modern facility, served by two levels of underground railroad tracks. At the heart of the complex was the main concourse, right, one of the grandest rooms ever built in America: 120 feet wide, 375 feet long, surmounted by a vaulted ceiling stretching 125 feet high, and decorated with the artist Paul Helleu's mural of the constellations—complete with 60 twinkling stars lighted by electric bulbs.

Less than three years after the completion of Penn Station, Grand Central Terminal opened its doors just twelve blocks away. At the intersection of Forty-second Street and Park Avenue, Commodore Vanderbilt's old glass-and-iron shed—at one time the largest interior space in North America—had been completely demolished to make way for an even grander edifice.

Less colossal in scale than its rival across town, the new station was even more visionary—the centerpiece of a sprawling, futuristic complex of hotels, clubs, shops, apartment houses, and office buildings, built atop tracks running beneath the street and linked by an elaborate network of concourses, ramps, passageways, and viaducts.

North of the new station, along what had once been Fourth Avenue, the open tracks of the New York Central line would eventually be covered by a sweeping avenue of elegant, landscaped malls that went on for two miles, called Park Avenue, which would become one of the most luxurious boulevards in the world. Anchoring the new district was the magnificent Grand Central Terminal itself—a mythic urban crossroads and mighty gateway, from whose immense vaulted ceiling, studded with

electric stars, glittered all the constellations of the night sky.

Outside, crowning the monumental south facade, soared a forty-foot-tall statue of Mercury, the winged god of speed.

Everything that machinery can do to make life easy and comfortable is done, and done thoroughly: mechanical conveniences undreamed of in London—the electric streetcars, the elevated railroads, the telephones, the elevators. The latest invention comes red-hot from the Patent Office and spreads over the city while you sleep. In London, one draws the blind in the morning to see if it has stopped raining; in New York, to find out whether a service of flying-machines has not been organized overnight. The abashed Englishman, as he looks on the contrast, can only wonder what sort of prehistoric country he hails from; and in the first flush he will argue that no town that cannot take hold of a man and shoot him up a twenty-story building like a torpedo from its tube, or whirl him along an elevated railroad on a line with somebody's second-floor parlor, can possibly be worth living in.

Charles Whibley, 1908

The south facade of Grand Central Terminal, 1914. Recognizing that the railway station had become the primary entrance to the modern American city, Grand Central's architects laid out the terminal's facade around three monumental arches, evoking the triumphal gateways of ancient Roman cities. Above the central arch—and the 15-foot-wide clock—stood Jules Guerin's 40-foot-tall statue of Mercury, the god of speed. The Pershing Square Bridge, which allowed Park Avenue's traffic to be lifted above and around the terminal on a pair of raised "circumferential drives," was yet to be constructed when this view was taken.

Wall Street is not merely a street; neither is it [a] local financial district. . . . Wall Street is a national institution. It is to American business what Washington, D.C. is to national politics . . . [and] it ramifies all over the United States. . . . It is enormous; and it is growing . . . the most vital, the most perfect, and the most powerful part of the organized life of human society in America, not excepting the United States Government.

Lincoln Steffens

In the first week of October 1907—for the sixth time in 70 years—Wall Street's overextended financial markets began to break apart with terrifying speed after a group of trust companies was hit with a sudden downturn in the market and failed to meet their obligations. As word spread, thousands of frightened depositors lined up to withdraw their funds, driving several of the trusts into bankruptcy, and one company president, Charles Barney, to suicide.

By Monday, October 22, with stock prices tumbling precipitously, it was clear to most people that a full-fledged crisis was at hand. Businessmen with memories of the terrible panics of 1873 and 1893 feared the worst—months of financial chaos, followed by years of economic depression. In desperation, the city's bankers and brokers now turned to the one person who could possibly come to their rescue—the aging financier at 23 Wall Street, who by 1907 had become an almost mythic figure in American economic life.

The journalist Lincoln Steffens called him the country's "personal sovereign" and "the boss of the United States." On Wall Street, he was frequently referred to as Jupiter. When a newspaper quoted him as saying "America is good

enough for me," one midwestern politician replied, "Whenever he doesn't like it, he can give it back."

In the course of nearly a half century on Wall Street, John Pierpont Morgan had assembled more power and influence than any other private citizen in American history—acting, in an era before government regulation of finance and before the creation of the Federal Reserve—as the de facto comptroller of the American economy. Controlling "the wealth of a nation," one newspaper declared, "rather than that of a mere man," he ran what was in effect the unofficial central bank of the United States—the House of Morgan, a commercial institution that had helped to fix the country's monetary policy and exchange rates, and often represented the United States itself in financial negotiations with foreign countries.

Morgan was not in New York when the panic struck, but in Richmond, Virginia, attending a convention for high-ranking Episcopalian laymen. Retired now from the day-to-day operations of the House of Morgan, the 69-year-old banker had been suffering in recent weeks from a serious head cold and a bout of melancholia. But the crisis revived him, and racing back to the city in his

private railroad car, he set right to work.

By Tuesday night, using all the authority at his command, he had obtained an interest-free loan of $25 million from the secretary of the treasury, George B. Cortelyou, to help shore up the trust companies. By Wednesday, he had secured another $3 million in private funds.

But the market continued to plummet, and at noon on Thursday, the president of the New York Stock Exchange, Ransom H. Thomas, strode grimly across Broad Street to the House of Morgan to inform Pierpont that without an immediate infusion of cash, fifty brokerage houses were sure to fail that same afternoon and trigger complete economic collapse.

It was a moment of truth for Morgan, and the defining moment of his extraordinary career. Springing into action, he gathered all of the city's bank presidents at the offices of the New York Clearing House at Cedar and Nassau streets, where—through a sheer act of will and the force of his personality—he raised another $13 million in 16 minutes. Half an hour later he was racing back to his office, anxious to inform the exchange and get back to work.

No one who saw him would ever forget the image of the most powerful man in the history of Wall Street, at the very moment of his greatest influence, making his way through the busy sidewalks of the financial district. "He walked fast down Nassau Street," the stockbroker Herbert Satterlee wrote. "His flat-topped black derby hat was set firmly down on his head. . . . His eyes were fixed straight ahead. He swung his arms as he walked and took no notice of anyone. . . . Everyone knew him, and people made way for him, except some who were equally intent on their own affairs; and

these he brushed aside. . . . He was the embodiment of power and purpose. Not more than two minutes after he disappeared into his office, the cheering on the floor of the Stock Exchange could be heard out on Broad Street."

For three weeks, the Panic of 1907 ran its course, lurching from one crisis to the next. In the end, it took one final extraordinary all-night meeting—held that Saturday in Morgan's private library on 36th Street—to bring the crisis under control. Placing bank presidents in one room and trust company presidents in another, the great financier simply locked the doors and refused to let anyone out, until, at nearly five in the morning, a solution had been hammered out.

It was Morgan's greatest triumph. No one else, his rival Jacob Schiff acknowledged, "could have got the banks to act together, and to join hands in the work." "Where there had been many principalities," one man later wrote, "there was now one kingdom, and it was Morgan's."

It was also his last hurrah. Morgan had saved the economy, but there were no guarantees his successors would act as effectively or, on the whole, as honorably. "We may not always have Pierpont Morgan with us," Senator Nelson W. Aldrich pointed out, "to meet a crisis." Within weeks of the panic, Congress was calling for ways to ensure financial stability without relying on the character and resources of a single financier.

In the coming years, Morgan himself would help craft legislation that would eventually put federal regulators in Washington, not private bankers in New York, in control of the nation's economic fortunes. But it took two decades more and another crisis—far more severe—before power truly began to shift away from the bankers and brokers who ruled Wall Street.

J. Pierpont Morgan, left. By 1907, the time of the panic, the great banker had largely retired from business, and spent less time on Wall Street than in his library—a Roman-style palace on East 36th Street designed by Charles McKim—or on his yacht, a 300-foot-long black-hulled sloop called the *Corsair.* Traveling extensively in Europe, he now collected art and antiques with the same single-minded intensity he had focused on finance. His vast collection included paintings by Rembrandt, Raphael, Vermeer, and Rubens, an altarpiece by Fra Filippo Lippi, Napoleon Bonaparte's watch, Leonardo da Vinci's notebooks, Catherine the Great's snuffbox, Shakespeare's first folios, and most of the jewelry of the Medici family.

The Washington Square Arch, lighted for the 1909 Hudson-Fulton Celebration, right. Held over ten days in late September and early October, the festival commemorated two key events in the city's history—Henry Hudson's discovery of the Hudson River in 1609 and Robert Fulton's launching of the world's first steamboat service on that same river in 1807. The event's climax came on October 2, 1909, when more than a million incandescent bulbs were switched on to illuminate bridges, skyscrapers, ships, civic buildings, and monuments all across the city.

CITY OF FIRE

By 1909, the concentration of human and economic forces in New York City was reaching an all-time peak.

Decade after decade, the accumulation of corporate and financial power in lower Manhattan had ensured that New York, not Washington, remained the effective capital of the nation.

Two years before, in the fall of 1907, J. P. Morgan—whom Lincoln Steffens now called "the boss of the United States"—had mobilized all of his power and influence to staunch a massive panic on Wall Street, almost single-handedly saving the American economy.

In April that year, Ellis Island had experienced the busiest single day in its history, when in one twelve-hour period, 11,747 newcomers were admitted to the country.

Out in the harbor, immense new ocean liners—eight stories tall and eight hundred feet long, capable of transporting three thousand people at a time, mostly in steerage—now berthed where Henry Hudson's ship, the *Half Moon,* had once ridden at anchor.

In the fall of 1909—three hundred years after Hudson first sailed into New York bay, and a century after Robert Fulton launched his steamboat off the west side of Manhattan—New York held the greatest birthday party in its history. Called the Hudson-Fulton Celebration, it was a triumphant salute to the remarkable metropolis that in less than three centuries had risen so spectacularly from the sea.

For ten days, hundreds of thousands of New Yorkers lined the waterfront to watch an immense procession of naval ships streaming in and out of the harbor, and to catch their first glimpse of an airplane—piloted by Wilbur Wright himself—circling within twenty-five feet of the Statue of Liberty.

The climax came on a brilliantly clear autumn night in early October, when a million incandescent lights provided by the Edison

Company turned the bridges, ships and tall towers of Manhattan into a glittering city of fire.

The city was one long banner of light that sparkled and scintillated in the crisp night air, paling even to insignificance a moon of harvest splendor. There were electric wonders for all to gape at, tall buildings enough to send their shafts of molten splendor where all might see, and searchlights enough to streak the sky wherever crowds were gathered.

New York Times

Never again would the fires of capitalism burn so brightly—or rage so unchecked—in New York City. Never again would so many people be gathered together on the slender island of Manhattan, which in less than a year would reach its all-time peak population of 2.3 million people.

Six weeks after the Hudson-Fulton Celebration ended, tens of thousands of New Yorkers again took to the streets—not in celebration this time but to protest the appalling suffering, terrible poverty, and stunning inequalities that had haunted the city for almost a century.

The extraordinary political transformation about to sweep New York would involve every player in the sprawling metropolis in an effort vastly greater than that required to build bridges, skyscrapers, and railroads.

Before it was over, the most harrowing tragedy of the industrial age would sear the conscience of the city. But it would change life in New York—and America—forever, extending the bounty of the modern world to the men and women creating it, and making the city for the first time a true home to all its people.

THE CHILDREN OF JACOB RIIS

Year after year, the pressure for change had been slowly mounting, driven by a band of determined young reformers who were, to a striking degree, Jacob Riis's spiritual sons and daughters.

In the years following the publication of his groundbreaking book, *How the Other Half Lives*, Riis himself had lobbied tirelessly to change the appalling conditions in the slums—his efforts joined by a growing movement of reformers, progressive politicians, social workers, and muckraking journalists.

But after nearly a decade, almost nothing had changed. Though ten thousand infants died each summer in the city's wretched tenements, thousands of dark, airless buildings were put up each year, all perfectly legal. Tammany Hall, meanwhile—the only force in the city capable of changing the law, did nothing—fearful of offending the city's powerfully entrenched real-estate interests.

The first ray of light came in the fall of 1898, when Jacob Riis's old friend and ally, Theodore Roosevelt, was elected governor, and threw himself into the struggle, mobilizing public support with the help of one of Riis's most brilliant young disciples.

Though just twenty-six, Lawrence Veiller was already an acknowledged expert on hous-

The East River bridges lighted for the 1909 Hudson-Fulton Celebration. The event was intended not only as a historic commemoration but as a celebration of the city's recent progress, demonstrated by its remarkable burst of physical improvement and construction. In less than ten years, the city had repeated its first span across the East River, the Brooklyn Bridge (right), three more times—with the 1903 Williamsburg Bridge (left), the 1909 Manhattan Bridge (center), and the Queensborough Bridge at 59th Street (not visible in this view), also completed in 1909.

ing and the poor. Galvanized by Roosevelt's campaign pledge to alter conditions in the slums, the politically astute young reformer mounted an elaborate exhibition on housing in New York—hoping to highlight the tragic cost of the burgeoning slums.

When it opened in February 1900, the stunning exhibit, in which Veiller indicted New York as "the City of Living Death," swayed public opinion as nothing else had—drawing ten thousand visitors, Veiller proudly wrote, "from the millionaire to the poorest unskilled laborer." Roosevelt himself, deeply moved by Veiller's exhibit, knew the time was ripe to press for legislation. "Tell me what you want," he said "and I will help you get it."

In a matter of weeks, Veiller had drafted the language of a revolutionary new housing law. It would require landlords to equip new buildings with fireproof construction, interior fire stairs, bathrooms in every apartment, and windows in every bedroom—and to improve older ones by installing sinks in every kitchen and toilets on every floor.

With Roosevelt's backing, Veiller's bill was rushed with record speed through the New York State Legislature—bypassing Tammany completely—and on April 18, 1900, was signed into law by Roosevelt's successor, Benjamin Odell. It was the first comprehensive housing legislation in American history.

Permanently altering the condition of housing in New York, it would become a model for cities across the country.

The horrible dumbbell tenement is now a thing of the past. At one stroke it was wiped out of existence. In its place is the new-law tenement, with large courts providing adequate light and ventilation for every room. What this one change means to the future welfare of the city cannot be overstated.

Lawrence Veiller

Wretched housing was not the only problem being ignored by Tammany Hall. Year after year, while the fight for tenement reform went forward, workers of every kind were fanning out across the city.

By 1900, the sight of uniformed young women clambering over the rooftops from one tenement to another had become a familiar one to slum dwellers. New York's pioneering visiting nurse service had been started seven years before by a blithe and energetic German Jew-

Visiting nurse on a tenement rooftop, 1908. Making the rounds of tenement apartments in their starched blue uniforms, Lillian Wald's visiting nurses quickly learned to avoid climbing up six flights of tenement stairs by using the rooftop as a shortcut between buildings. By 1908, Wald's service was sending out scores of trained nurses on tens of thousands of visits a year.

Brooklyn slum children on a privately sponsored "fresh-air outing," 1913. By 1913, dozens of private organizations had been founded in the city to improve the lives of New York's residents and the workings of its government, including the Reform Club, the Social Reform Club, the Women's Municipal League, the Outdoor Recreation League, the Kindergarten Association, the Public Education Association, the Association for Improving the Condition of the Poor, the City Improvement Society, the City Vigilance League, the Legal Aid Society, the Charity Organization Society, and the Municipal Art Society.

ish nurse named Lillian Wald, who had moved into a top-floor apartment on Jefferson Street in the Lower East Side, determined to bring health care to the poor, single-handedly if necessary.

Read each figure a human being. Read that every wretched unlighted tenement described is a home for people—men and women, old and young, with the strengths and weaknesses, the good and bad, the appetites and wants common to us all. . . . Reading of these things must bring a sense of fairness outraged, the disquieting feeling that something is wrong. . . . Say to yourself, Is there a wrong in our midst, what can I do? Do I owe a reparation?

Lillian Wald, 1896

Determined to raise money for her program, Wald turned to an unusual ally—Betty Loeb, the mother-in-law of Jacob Schiff, the Wall Street banker second only to J. P. Morgan in power and prestige.

"An extraordinary young woman has called upon me," Mrs. Loeb wrote to her daughter, Nina. "I don't know whether she is a genius or is mad. . . . I prefer to think she is a genius, so I am going to ask Jacob to help give this woman a chance."

Schiff—who believed that New York's prosperous German Jews had a special responsibility to help the poor Russian Jews flooding into the city—agreed to provide Wald with money for a six-month test, on the condition that she provide him with a daily record of her work.

Night after night, after long grueling days in the tenements, Wald bent over her desk, carefully documenting the rounds she had made.

Meyer P. . . . age five years, injured his hip. He lay for seven months in the Orthopedic Hospital . . . was discharged as incurable . . . the cripple is in pain and cries to be carried. . . . [Meyer's family] had no rooms of their own, but paid $3 to Hannah H. . . . who allowed the family to sleep on the floor.

By 1909, Dr. S. Josephine Baker—the 28-year-old founder of the city's Bureau of Child Hygiene—had become a recognized leader in the field of public health and a leading force behind innovative programs credited with saving the lives of thousands of slum children in the city.

Yet only two years before, as a young medical inspector with the Department of Health, she had undergone trial by fire in the most notorious case in the annals of public health history.

It began when a sanitary engineer named George Soper, puzzled by a sudden outbreak of typhoid across the New York area, discovered that all of the affected households had one thing in common. Each had employed a fastidious and highly competent 40-year-old Irish cook named Mary Mallon, who—though she showed no symptoms of the disease herself—must have been carrying the deadly typhus germ from one home to another.

Assigned to bring Mallon in for tests, Baker tracked her down to her latest employer on Park Avenue but was brusquely turned away at the kitchen door. Under strict orders to apprehend the suspected carrier—if necessary, by force—Baker returned the next day with three policemen in tow. This time the resourceful, hot-tempered cook was waiting for them, and, flinging back the kitchen door, lunged at Baker with a huge kitchen fork, then disappeared down a back alley. After a three-hour search, a policeman spotted a telltale swatch of calico peeking from a service door nearby, hidden behind some ashcans.

"The ashcans were removed," Baker wrote, "and there was Mary. . . . She came out fighting and swearing, both of which she could do with appalling efficiency and vigor. . . . The policemen lifted her into the ambulance and I literally sat on her all the way to the hospital; it was like being in a cage with an angry lion." Mallon's test results, Baker said, revealed "a living culture of typhoid bacilli." In screaming headlines, the city's newspapers nicknamed the cook Typhoid Mary.

Mallon was placed in quarantine—but released within a few years, after solemnly promising never to work as a cook again. Five years later, when two dozen cases of typhoid broke out in a Manhattan maternity hospital, Baker discovered Mallon busy at work in the hospital kitchen, infecting every dish she touched. She was quarantined again—this time indefinitely—on a remote spot in the middle of the East River called North Brother Island.

In the years to come, Dr. Baker would advance from one triumph to another in New York—licensing midwives, requiring that milk be pasteurized, and building dozens of health stations where babies could be cared for—and mothers given what she called "cheerily disguised lessons" in child care. Her pioneering programs would transform the health of slum children in New York, then become a model for cities across the country.

As for Mary Mallon, she lived for 23 years in a small cottage on North Brother Island, accompanied only by a English bulldog, until her death from a stroke in 1938.

Above, Doctor S. Josephine Baker at her desk at the Bureau of Child Hygiene. Below, Mary Mallon—better known as Typhoid Mary—sits fourth from the right, among a group of inmates quarantined on an isolated island in the Long Island Sound.

Wald's spare and eloquent accounts of misery and suffering so touched Jacob Schiff that the financier agreed to fund the expansion of her nursing service—as well as another project of Wald's—the Henry Street Settlement house. When it opened a year later, the "House on Henry Street" provided free classes on child-rearing, hygiene and housekeeping, and, in back, something no one had ever before seen in America—a children's playground.

> A good beginning has been made in New York toward the realization of the better American social ideas. In no city in the country have reformers had more cunning and stubborn enemies; and in no city has their success, temporary though it may be, been more fairly deserved. This work must be done in large cities, and it is encouraging that New York is taking the lead in doing it.
>
> Herbert Croly

Within little more than a decade, Lillian Wald had become a force to contend with in city life—supervising seven settlement houses, sending out ninety-two nurses on more than 200,000 visits a year, and making Henry Street the center of a worldwide network of reformers and social workers.

By 1909, New York stood in the vanguard of a revolution in public health. In the slums, once dreaded diseases—cholera, diphtheria, typhoid, and yellow fever—had been virtually wiped out through the heroic efforts of the city's Health Department. That summer alone, Dr. S. Josephine Baker, a pioneer in the field of preventative medicine, saved twelve hundred infants in a single tenement district—the first of an estimated *ninety thousand* slum children whose lives she would save in the course of her career.

But though change had come, it had been limited in the main to the fields of health and housing, affecting the places people lived, not the places in which they worked. No force of change, it seemed, could penetrate the core of the city's industrial machine—the thirty thousand factory floors and sweatshops, where each year 612,000 workers, most of them immigrants, were now turning out nearly a tenth of the industrial output of the entire United States.

And yet nowhere was change more essential, or more urgently needed, especially in New York's fiercely competitive garment industry, where a quarter of a million men, women, and children were producing half of the men's clothes in America, and three-quarters of the women's—laboring eleven hours a day, six days a week under brutal, dehumanizing, and often dangerous conditions.

THE GREAT UPRISING

> There were three endless tables running almost through the entire length of the loft in parallel lines. Each table was dotted with a row of machines, and in front of these sat the operatives like prisoners chained to their posts. Men and women they were, collarless, disheveled, bent into irregular curves; palpitating, twitching, as if they were so many pistons and levers in some huge, monstrous engine. . . . The intermittent whirring of wheels, the gasping and sucking of the power engine (somewhere out of sight), the dull murmur of voices, heightened the oppressive effect.
>
> Marcus Ravage

By 1909, conditions in New York's eleven thousand garment factories had become nightmarish.

Though the International Ladies' Garment Workers Union had been founded nine years before, it remained a small and relatively powerless organization—whose every effort to effect change was thwarted by the intense pressures of the industry. Thousands of the so-called factories were in reality little more than makeshift spaces in lofts or brownstones, casually rented out to immigrant entrepreneurs—many of them former garment workers themselves—who required employees to bring their own sewing machines to the workplace. Faced with furious competition, the owners routinely underbid each other to win contracts from the city's large manufacturers and big department stores—and then, to stay afloat, were forced to wring as much work as they could, for as little as possible, from their hapless employees.

Year after year, as the competition pressures spiraled upward, life on the unregulated factory floors grew more appalling—not only in the small shops but at big firms like Leiserson's and the Triangle Waist Company, where hundreds of young immigrant women turned out fashionable lightweight cotton blouses called shirt-

By 1909, 256,000 garment workers in New York were turning out nearly two-thirds of the clothing produced in the United States. Though the industry was still dominated by thousands of small sweatshops (see page 280), newer manufacturers were more often located in large industrial buildings, on floors crowded with long rows of sewing machines and cutting tables (above). There conditions were generally less primitive than in the older shops, but employees in the big plants were subject to different pressures, such as the relentless drive to increase output through speed-ups, which required every worker to match the output of the fastest employees.

waists. For sixty-six hours of grueling work, seamstresses often received less than five dollars a week—from which owners deducted a fee for the use of a sewing machine, along with a fee for electricity, a fee for needles and thread, and a fee for machine oil.

To increase productivity, shop foremen set brutal quotas, as well as firing employees at whim, docking the pay of anyone caught talking or humming on the job, and often locking the fire exits—to prevent theft and keep the women focused on their jobs.

"Yes, the doors ought to be open," one fire safety consultant admitted, "but . . . practically it can't be done! Why, if you had doors open so that the girls could come and go, they might get away with a lot of stuff. The doors have to be locked. Haven't you got to protect the manufacturer?"

At seven o'clock we all sit down to our machines and the boss brings to each one the pile of work that he or she is to finish during the day. . . . The machines go like mad all day, because the faster you work the more money you get. Sometimes in my haste I get my finger caught and the needle goes right through it. . . . I bind the finger up with a piece of cotton and go on working. We all have accidents like that. . . . All

the time we are working the boss walks around examining the finished garments and making us do them over again if they are not just right. So we have to be careful as well as swift.

Sadie Frowne

When change started to come, it would begin with the most powerless of New York's long-suffering workforce—the army of young immigrant women toiling in the dismal shirtwaist factories.

All through the summer of 1909, anger and frustration had been building among the shirtwaist workers. When a series of small strikes against individual manufacturers failed to make headway, the idea of a *general* strike—aimed not just at one manufacturer but at the industry as a whole—began to take hold.

On the evening of November 22, 1909, three thousand women—most of them immigrants, and many still in their teens—showed up for a mass meeting at the Great Hall of Cooper Union, where fifty years before Abraham Lincoln had delivered the speech that propelled him to the White House. When the time came to consider a general action, most of the major labor leaders hesitated. There had been no general strike within New York City in living memory. Even well-established unions,

The November 22, 1909, mass meeting in the Great Hall of Cooper Union, right, marked a turning point for the city labor movement. One after another, such established leaders as Samuel Gompers, the president of the American Federation of Labor (on the podium), cautiously encouraged the overflow crowd of mostly female shirtwaist makers, who were considering a motion to strike. But it was the passionate, unscheduled speech by a fiery 23-year-old garment worker named Clara Lemlich (above, center) that electrified the group—and forced the motion to the floor. Described by one reporter as a "pint of trouble for the bosses," the Russian-born Lemlich was an intense, fiercely committed union organizer and Socialist activist who just two months before the meeting had suffered six broken ribs during a picket-line brawl.

Thousands and thousands left the factories from every side, all of them walking down toward Union Square. It was November, the cold winter was just around the corner, we had no fur coats to keep warm, and yet there was the spirit that led us on and on until we got to some hall. I can see the young people, mostly women, walking down and not caring what might happen . . . the hunger, cold, loneliness. . . . They just didn't care on that particular day; that was their day.

Pauline Newman

like the plumbers or steamfitters, quailed before the combined power of the factory owners and Tammany Hall, which typically sent the police in to deal with striking labor unions. Even Samuel Gompers, the powerful head of the American Federation of Labor, counseled caution and offered only encouraging platitudes to the increasingly restless crowd of women.

Then, as yet another labor leader launched into his speech, a member of the audience came forward and asked to say a few words. She was Clara Lemlich—a frail twenty-three-year-old seamstress and union activist, so battered from a recent brawl on a picket line that she had to be helped to the platform. But once before the crowd, her eyes flashed, her voice rose, and she spoke with mesmerizing fervor. "I am a working girl," she said, in a rush of words that no

one present would ever forget, "one of those who are on strike against intolerable conditions. I am tired of listening to speakers who talk in general terms. What we are here for is to decide whether we shall or shall not strike. I move that we go on a general strike—now!"

The response was overwhelming. As Jewish workers translated the young woman's Yiddish speech into Italian and English, the hall exploded in cheers and applause, and her motion was resoundingly endorsed. The next morning, fifteen thousand shirtwaist workers left their machines and manned the picket lines. Within a few days, they had been joined by five thousand more.

Nothing like it had ever been seen in New York before. It is "a conflict between employer and employees not only unprecedented in its development," one newspaper wrote, "but also

New York sweatshop, about 1900. Thousands of the city's garment "factories" were actually small, makeshift spaces in lofts, warehouses, or brownstones, rented by entrepreneurs— often garment workers themselves—who required workers to supply their own sewing machines. In these cramped, unsanitary, and often dangerous spaces, workers and bosses alike put in ten to thirteen hours a day, six days a week.

Women on the picket lines during the shirtwaist makers' strike of 1909. "In spite of being underfed and thinly clad," one reporter wrote, "the girls took [it] upon themselves . . . to patrol the streets in midwinter with the temperature low and with snow on the ground, some days freezing and some days melting. It takes uncommon courage to endure such physical exposure, but these striking girls underwent as well the nervous strain of imminent arrest, the harsh treatment of the police, insults, threats, and even actual assaults from the rough men who stood around the factory doors."

the largest strike of women ever known in the United States."

"Never before," William Mailly wrote in the *Independent*, "have so many working women quit work at one time and place, and with such spontaneity and unanimity. . . . They have carried their sisters along with them by the very force of their own determination and the spirit of resistance to the general conditions prevailing."

Week after week, the extraordinary action went on—despite the intransigence of the factory owners, the hostility of Tammany Hall, and increasingly bitter winter weather. "There was never anything like it," one union official said. "An equal number of men would never hold together under what these girls are enduring."

Every day, ill-clad young women stood shivering in the freezing rain and cold, huddling together for warmth. Again and again, gangs of

thugs hired by the owners charged the ragged protestors—followed by squads of policemen, sent by Tammany to arrest the strikers for "disorderly conduct." One picket line, led by Clara Lemlich herself, was attacked as a reporter from the *Sun* looked on.

"Stand fast, girls," called Clara, and then the thugs rushed the line, knocking Clara to her knees, striking at the pickets. There was a confused melee of scratching, screaming girls and fist-swinging men and then a patrol wagon arrived. The thugs ran off as the cops pushed Clara and two other badly beaten girls into the wagon.

McAlister Coleman

Somehow, the picket lines held. But by the third week of December, the union's financial resources had been all but exhausted, and the strike itself was on the point of collapse—when

help arrived from an unexpected quarter, as the flame of protest now leaped from the ragged band of immigrant women to the wives and daughters of some of the richest men in the city.

Working through a reform organization called the Women's Trade Union League, socialites like Anne Morgan, the daughter of the powerful financier, rushed to the aid of the strikers. Mocked in the newspapers as the Mink Brigade, the society women did everything they could to keep the strike alive, raising money for the strike funds, guarding the picket lines, and bailing out jailed protesters, as part of advancing another cause—the right of women to vote.

On December 21, 1909, Alva Belmont—who had once been married to a Vanderbilt—staged a novel automobile parade through the canyons of lower Manhattan: fifteen limousines plastered with signs demanding shorter work days and the right to vote for women. Inside, the wives of millionaires sat next to the thin, hungry strikers—most of whom had never ridden in a private car before.

In the end, the "uprising of the twenty thousand"—the first great strike of the modern labor movement in New York—was doomed to failure, as dwindling resources and bitter cold took their toll. By the end of February, most of the strikers had returned to work, having wrested only minor concessions from the owners—and having failed, once again, to win recognition for their union.

But what Clara Lemlich and her fellow workers had started could never be undone. Public awareness about conditions in the factories had been aroused, an alliance had been forged between upper-class reformers and working-class unions, and the workers themselves had learned an invaluable lesson.

They now knew how to strike.

Three months later, when the cloak makers' union went out, the strike was planned carefully in advance, set for the late spring, and supported by ample funds. This time not twenty but *sixty* thousand workers joined the picket lines in what was called the Great Revolt. For the first time in history, an entire industry in New York was shut down and its owners forced to the bargaining table. The resulting settlement—called the Protocol of Peace—was a watershed for the labor movement, requiring

Both the diversity of New York's immigrant workforce and the international orientation of the city's garment unions are reflected in this view of English, Yiddish, Italian, and Russian picket signs at a 1913 clothing workers' strike in lower Manhattan.

recognition by the owners of the cloak makers' union, creating a board of arbitration, limiting the work week to fifty hours, and providing double pay for overtime.

Everywhere men and women, old and young, embraced and congratulated each other on the victory. It was early [the next] morning, Saturday, September 3rd, before the streets were emptied of the masses of humanity. . . . Saturday afternoon, trucks decorated with flags, with bands of music, and carrying crowds of cloakmakers drove through the streets, announcing the strike had been settled.

Abraham Rosenberg

The strikes of 1909 and 1910 had been a breakthrough, firmly establishing the principles of trade unionism in New York City. In practice, however, the new protections for workers proved difficult to enforce.

Real improvement in the appalling working conditions had yet to be wrung from the recalcitrant factory owners—while some of the largest firms, like the big Triangle Waist Company on the east side of Washington Square,

simply refused to sign the Protocol of Peace altogether.

Despite all the garment workers' union had accomplished, there was still no law regulating conditions in New York's factories, which by the spring of 1911 remained as brutal, unsanitary—and dangerous—as ever.

In the past year alone, four small fires had broken out in the building occupied by the Triangle factory. The owners still did nothing, pointing out that, under the city code, their building was technically "fireproof."

INFERNO

Mounting the stairs of the [shirt]waist factory, one is aware of heavy vibrations. The roar and whir of the machines increases as the door opens, and one sees in a long loft . . . rows and rows of girls with heads bent and eyes intent on the flashing needles. They are all intensely absorbed; for if they be paid by the piece they hurry from ambition, and if they be paid by the week they are "speeded up" by the foreman to a pace set by the swiftest workers.

McClure's, November 1910

A labor rally on the Lower East Side during the cloak makers' strike of 1910. Built on the fervor from the shirtwaist makers' strike but carefully planned in advance, the cloak makers' strike in the summer of 1910 surpassed any union action before it—drawing 60,000 workers to the picket lines, shutting down the entire industry, and for the first time forcing owners to bargain in earnest. "The two strikes came to be thought of as prologue and principal act," the writer Louis Levine later observed. "The shirtwaist makers' strike was an 'uprising.' The cloak makers' strike was 'the great revolt.'"

On the afternoon of March 25, 1911, a fire swept through the Triangle shirtwaist factory

It was late on the afternoon of Saturday, March 25, 1911, and the five hundred employees of the Triangle Waist Company—teenage girls, for the most part—were racing to fill their quotas, eager to finish up, collect their pay, and plunge into the mild spring evening.

Around 4:45 p.m., with just fifteen minutes left in the workday, someone on the eighth floor dropped a match or burning cigarette into a heap of discarded fabric that littered the shop floor.

Within seconds, the combustible scraps of cloth had burst into flames, and wafted burning across the shop floor. Before anyone could stop it, the fire had spread with startling speed from one stack of fabric to another, engulfing rack after rack of finished shirtwaists, before reaching the big discard bins, which were filled with thousands of pounds of cotton remnants.

Within minutes, the fire had swelled to an inferno. As cries of alarm went up, panicked workers scrambled for the exits—which to the horror of the desperate women had been locked from the outside.

> *I heard somebody cry "Fire!" I ran for the door on the Washington Place side. The door was locked and immediately there was a great jam of girls before it. [The bosses] had the doors locked all the time. The fire had started on our floor, and quick as I had been in getting to the door, the flames were already blazing and spreading fast. If we didn't get out we would be roasted alive. Some girls were screaming, some were beating the door with their fists, some were trying to tear it open.*
>
> Rosie Safran

Somehow, workers on the top floor of the building—the tenth—managed to escape, helped to safety across an adjoining rooftop by students from New York University. Hundreds more made it down by elevator, thirty people at a time jammed into cars meant to hold half that number.

But by 4:55, the last of the elevators had been forced out of service, and the fire had begun to spread from the eighth floor to the ninth. For the nearly two hundred women still trapped inside, the Triangle shirtwaist factory became a scene of unimaginable horror.

On the eighth floor, workers had tried bravely to stop the fire, but the flames were too quick, and the water pressure in the fire hoses failed them. As the searing heat and smoke intensified, the factory floor became an incinerator, bodies piled up in front of the locked main exit. Those who still could raced for a fire escape on the far western end of the building. Fewer than twenty women managed to escape before the rusted metal supports gave way, send-

Crowds gathering in Washington Square, a block from the Triangle shirtwaist factory. As word of the fire spread, more than 10,000 people—including hundreds of desperate husbands, parents, and children—raced to the site of the disaster to try to locate their loved ones.

ing several workers plunging to their deaths—and cutting off the last means of escape for all the others.

With a wall of fire advancing on them, the terrified women moved to the open windows.

The girls behind us were screaming and crying. Several of them, as the flames crept closer, ran into the smoke, and we heard them scream as the flames caught their clothes. One little girl, who worked at the machine opposite me, cried out in Italian, "Good-bye, good-bye."

Tessa Banani

Outside on the street below, a huge crowd had gathered.

Within minutes of the call, the New York Fire Department had swung into action, rushing thirty-five vehicles to the scene, many of which carried the most modern firefighting equipment in the country. But even the tallest ladder could reach no farther than the sixth story—two floors below the burning factory floor, where tongues of flame could already be seen curling out of the windows.

At 5:05, a laborer named Dominick Cardiane, pushing his wheelbarrow down Greene Street, heard a muffled explosion, followed by the sound of breaking glass. Glancing up, he saw what he thought were dark bales of cloth, sailing from an eighth-floor window. As they hit the sidewalk, he realized they were not bundles of clothes but women.

A reformer, Martha Bensley Bruère, was walking through Washington Square when two young women rushed up. "They were white and shaking as they caught me by the arm," she wrote. " 'Oh,' shrieked one of them, 'they are jumping! Jumping from ten stories up! They are going through the air like bundles of clothes and the firemen can't stop them and the policemen can't stop them and nobody can help them at all!' "

By now, dozens of women could be seen standing at the eighth- and ninth-floor windows, all but engulfed by the inferno of fire. As those below watched in horror, groups of women, three and four at a time, grabbed each other by the hand, closed their eyes—and stepped out into oblivion.

Frances Perkins, a thirty-one-year-old advocate with the Consumers' League, stood with her hand at her throat, helpless to stop the unfolding tragedy. "The nets were broken," she wrote. "The firemen kept shouting for them not to jump. But they had no choice; the flames were right behind them for by this time the fire was far gone."

William Shepherd, a reporter for the United Press International, called the story in to the city desk, as he watched from a pay phone at the scene.

The evening of the Triangle fire, a temporary morgue was set up at the 26th Street pier on the East River, where family members attempted to identify the remains of the victims, a process that required three full days.

Bodies of several women workers lie on the sidewalk while police and onlookers watch the progress of the fire above. In all, 146 people died in the worst industrial catastrophe in the history of New York.

I learned a new sound—a more horrible sound than description can picture. It was the thud of a speeding, living body on a stone sidewalk. Thud—dead, thud—dead, thud—dead, thud—dead. There was plenty of chance to watch them as they came down. The height was eighty feet. The first ten thuds—deads shocked me. I looked up, saw that there were scores of girls at the windows. The flames from the floor below were beating in their faces. Somehow I knew that they, too, must come down. . . . I even watched one girl falling. Waving her arms, trying to keep her body upright until the very instant she struck the sidewalk. Then came the thud—then a silent, unmoving pile of clothing and twisted, broken limbs.

"They hit the pavement just like rain," a stunned fireman named Edward Worth later testified.

By 5:15, the scene on the street outside the Triangle shirtwaist factory had become a surreal bedlam, as thousands of workers poured out of nearby factories and pressed against the barricades. Fire-engine horses reared at the strong smell of blood; police tried without success to control the crowd. "What can policemen do against a whole quarter mad with terror at seeing its sisters and daughters burned before its eyes?" wrote Martha Bruère. "Can you quiet a man who thinks that the charred mass over which a blanket has been thrown is his newly married wife?"

It was over in less than half an hour.

"The floods of water from the firemen's hose that ran into the gutter were actually stained red with blood," William Shepherd wrote. "I looked upon the heap of dead bodies and I remembered these girls were shirtwaist makers. I remembered their great strike of last year in which these same girls had demanded more sanitary conditions and more safety precautions in these shops. These dead bodies were the answer."

Firemen inspecting the burned floors the next day found dozens of bodies—charred, headless trunks, some still bent over the sewing machines. Among the remains, the inspectors found eleven engagement rings. In all, 146 people—teenagers for the most part, immigrant girls, some as young as fourteen—had died in the greatest industrial disaster in the city's history.

At a temporary morgue on an East River pier, relatives lined up to identify the corpses, a ghastly process that took three full days. In the end, seven bodies remained unidentified, and on April 5, 1911, a mass funeral was held for the anonymous victims. Despite a heavy rain, 120,000 people joined in the procession, while 400,000 more watched silently from the sidewalk.

"A mass emotion of sorrow and despair was felt everywhere that day," a garment worker named Louis Waldman wrote. "But in the weeks that followed, these emotions gave way to angry questioning and a determination that a similar tragedy must never take place in New York again."

In the wake of the fire, however, New Yorkers were stunned still further to discover that no laws existed to prevent such a tragedy from recurring.

In the months to come, the owners of the Triangle Waist Company, Isaac Harris and Max Blanck—who had, after all, locked their employees in—were put on trial for manslaughter. But to the shocked disbelief of the victims' families, and of most New Yorkers, the two men were acquitted. The prosecution had been unable to prove that either man had actually known that the exit doors were locked at the exact time of the fire.

Within weeks, the Triangle factory had reopened in a nearby building. Visiting the new plant, fire inspectors found the exit door blocked by rows of sewing machines.

PHOENIX

But now something extraordinary began to occur. Stunned by the horror and magnitude of the tragedy and by the innocence of its victims, groups of New Yorkers that had never before found common ground began to come together in an outpouring of grief and call for change.

"The greatest monument we can raise to the memory of our 146 dead," one man declared at a vast rally held at the Metropolitan Opera House a week after the fire, "is a system of legislation that will make such deaths hereafter impossible."

From the ashes of the Triangle Company fire began to rise one of the most dramatic and far-reaching political transformations in American history—one that would set into motion a process of change that would eventually rede-

fine forever the role government played in the lives of ordinary people.

The coalition that now came together to make that possible reflected every conceivable group in the complex political universe of the city—immigrant workers and patrician lawyers, union activists and Wall Street bankers, socialists and socialites, rabbis and priests, safety experts, and progressive reformers. At the center of it all, however, to the amazement of almost everyone, would be the calculating, hard-eyed leaders of Tammany Hall, who for more than fifty years had resisted the forces of reform in New York.

Within days of the meeting at the Metropolitan Opera, socialites from the Women's Trade Union League had persuaded some of the most powerful businessmen in New York—Wall Street financiers and corporate attorneys, far removed from the gritty workings of the immigrant garment industry—to petition Albany formally for new factory laws.

As everyone knew, the key to change lay with the New York State Legislature. The key to the legislature, however, lay in the pocket of "Silent Charlie" Murphy, the taciturn,

Laconic, shrewd, and immensely effective, Charles Francis Murphy— Silent Charlie—was the boss of Tammany Hall for 22 years, longer than anyone else in its history. Some claimed it was because he hardly ever spoke a word. "Most of the troubles of the world could be avoided," he once remarked, "if men opened their minds instead of their mouths." In the aftermath of the Triangle fire, Murphy would do more than anyone else to transform Tammany into a positive force for social change, appointing his two closest protégés—Robert Wagner and Al Smith—to the Factory Investigating Commission, then backing their efforts to turn the panel's recommendations into law.

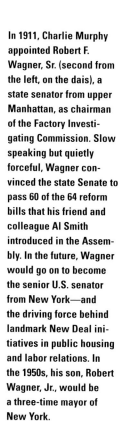

In 1911, Charlie Murphy appointed Robert F. Wagner, Sr. (second from the left, on the dais), a state senator from upper Manhattan, as chairman of the Factory Investigating Commission. Slow speaking but quietly forceful, Wagner convinced the state Senate to pass 60 of the 64 reform bills that his friend and colleague Al Smith introduced in the Assembly. In the future, Wagner would go on to become the senior U.S. senator from New York—and the driving force behind landmark New Deal initiatives in public housing and labor relations. In the 1950s, his son, Robert Wagner, Jr., would be a three-time mayor of New York.

inscrutable boss of Tammany Hall—and the last man in New York from whom reformers could expect any help.

But Charlie Murphy had a problem. For years, Tammany's leaders had looked on with concern as New York's population changed and its constituency dwindled. Many of the Irish and German immigrants who had once formed the backbone of its support had started to move up and out, while many of the new immigrant groups coming into the city looked elsewhere for solace and support. For many Jews and Italians, in particular, the traditional Tammany perquisites—the Christmas turkey, the sack of coal, and the Sunday picnic—were not enough. In growing numbers, immigrants in New York were turning for support to rival organizations—to the Socialist party, progressive Republicans, the settlement movement, and a variety of reform groups—all of which could point, as Tammany could not, to genuine accomplishments that had improved the lives of ordinary people.

Realistic, shrewd, and utterly unsentimental, Silent Charlie understood that something had to be done, if Tammany were to stay in power. As the clamor for change swelled in the aftermath of the Triangle factory disaster, he made a fateful decision. Embracing the aims of the radical reform movement, Tammany itself would now not only cease resisting change but take the lead in an extraordinary effort to make government answerable to the needs of the people.

Murphy went right to work as skeptical reformers looked on in suspicion. His first act was to support the formation of a statewide Factory Investigating Commission, intended to lay the groundwork for new laws governing the workplace. He then placed his two closest protégés—Robert F. Wagner and Alfred E. Smith, whom Murphy liked to call "my fair-haired boys"—in charge of the new commission, which counted among its members almost every distinguished labor leader and reform activist in New York State, including the great labor leader Samuel Gompers, and Frances Perkins, the young consumer advocate who had watched the Triangle women jump to their deaths.

Neither Smith nor Wagner inspired much confidence in their reform-minded colleagues on the commission. Wagner, the dapper well-educated leader of the New York State Senate, was considered Tammany's most reliable man in Albany. Smith, who had risen from the streets of the Lower East Side to become majority leader of the New York State Assembly, raised even more eyebrows. With his bright red face, gold-capped teeth, loud suits, and omnipresent cigar, he was the very image of the hardbitten Tammany pol—condemned by reformers only a year before as "one of the most dangerous men in Albany" and reviled as Silent Charlie's "brilliant henchman."

Then the Factory Investigating Commission began its work, and life in New York would

During his three years as vice chairman of the Factory Investigating Commission, Al Smith, left—the majority leader of the New York State Legislature, and a politician once reviled by reformers as Tammany's "henchman" in Albany—underwent a profound political transformation, emerging as a forceful voice for workers' rights and the unexpected champion of the labor and reform movements in New York.

In March 1911, Frances Perkins, an idealistic young advocate for the Consumers' League, had stood horrified on the sidewalk as the women of the Triangle Waist Company jumped to their deaths. Later that year, she volunteered as executive secretary for the Factory Investigating Commission, took the stand herself to provide crucial testimony on working conditions in the state, and helped draft recommendations for dozens of new laws regulating factory life. In 1933, she would be appointed by Franklin Roosevelt as secretary of labor—the first female cabinet member in the nation's history.

never be the same. Week after week, month after month, the commission ground on—taking testimony from fire inspectors, sanitation experts, health officials, and labor leaders—calling in its first year alone more than two hundred witnesses and recording more than two thousand pages of grim and sobering testimony about the horrific conditions in many New York factories. Almost inevitably, members of the commission missed some of the testimony—but not Al Smith, who could always be seen up on the dais, listening intently. When the commission, in an unprecedented move, left the hearing room to tour the state, Smith never missed a trip—visiting scores of dank, grim, and dangerous factories around the state, where parents and young children toiled side by side seven days a week. In one factory in which the commissioners had been assured no children were working, he and his colleagues stumbled across a dozen young boys and girls hidden in an elevator that had been stopped between floors.

Smith never forgot what he saw and heard in the factories and sweatshops of New York. Along the way, Smith deeply impressed his once skeptical colleagues, who could see in his face

how powerfully affected he was by the visits. When the commission's work was done and the time came to draft legislation, Smith, like an avenging angel, took the lead. Painfully aware of his own lack of formal education, he turned to the staff of faithful reformers whose admiration he had now won and said simply, "You make the proposals. I'll fight for them."

It was the turning point. For decades, reformers had trooped up to Albany, trying and failing again and again to get laws passed regulating child labor, women's labor, factory conditions, disability insurance, workmen's compensation. Now, in three historic sessions of the New York State Legislature between 1912 and 1914, reformers looked on from the galleries as Al Smith—a man they had once despised—pushed one reform bill after another through the Assembly, then sent them on to the state Senate, where his old Albany roommate, Robert Wagner, made sure they became law.

The results, one man later said, were "epoch-making"—a flood of legislation affecting every aspect of factory life. Plant owners would now be required to provide enclosed staircases, fire sprinklers, and adequate lighting, ventilation, washrooms, and first aid. Dangerous machin-

It was, Al Smith later acknowledged, "probably one of the longest days of my life up to that time."

On election night, November 5, 1918, the 44-year-old hero of the labor reform movement in New York sat anxiously in the ballroom of the Hotel Biltmore in New York watching the returns come in. The early returns from the city itself gave the Democratic candidate for governor of New York State a commanding lead over the wealthy Republican incumbent, Charles S. Whitman. But as the upstate vote came in overnight, it soon became clear that the election was too close to call.

It took two days in all for the votes to be tallied, and in the end, one of the most historic elections in the history of New York had to be decided by the absentee ballots of thousands of New York soldiers still fighting overseas. But by Thursday night, it was clear they had pushed the red-faced, cigar-chewing champion of the working-man over the top with a slender majority of 15,000 votes. Suspicious of the outcome, Whitman demanded a recount in a number of New York City districts, where the results had been particularly lopsided—including one in Smith's own Fourth Ward, where the vote had run 387 to 2 against the Republican—but no irregularities appeared. For his part, Smith professed to be amazed that Whitman had done so well in the old district.

However narrow the margin of victory, it was a triumph for the immigrant experience in New York—and a particularly gratifying personal one for Al Smith himself, marking as it did the sixteenth time he had run for public office and the sixteenth time he had won. Somehow, the loud-mouthed, back-slapping uneducated boy from the Lower East Side had reached the highest office of the most populous and most important state in the Union—becoming, along the way, the first Irish Catholic ever to be elected governor in the history of the United States.

New York's working classes could not believe their good fortune. On the Lower East Side, jubilant immigrant voters, Irish and non-Irish alike, danced in the streets, while down in the Fourth Ward housewives tied brooms to the railings of their tenement stoops—the old Tammany symbol for a "clean sweep."

On December 31, 1918, the night before Al Smith's inauguration, thousands of Irish American New Yorkers took the train up to Albany, marching till dawn through the streets of the capital, singing chorus after chorus of Smith's campaign song—the lilting two-step called "The Sidewalks of New York." The song, an old favorite, had been written in 1894 by a Manhattan hat salesman named James W. Blake, who had transformed the memory of his old East Side block into a hymn to the immigrant city:

> *Down in front of Casey's*
> *Old brown wooden stoop,*
> *On a summer's e'ening,*
> *We formed a merry group.*
> *Boys and girls together,*
> *We would sing and waltz,*
> *While Ginnie played the organ,*
> *On the sidewalks of New York.*
>
> *East side, west side,*
> *All around the town.*
> *The tots sang Ring-a-Rosie,*
> *London Bridge is falling down.*
> *Boys and girls together.*
> *Me and Mamie O'Rourke,*
> *Tripped the light fantastic,*
> *On the sidewalks of New York.*
> James W. Blake and
> Charles B. Lawlor,
> "The Sidewalks of New York"

Smith himself spent the evening inside the cavernous State Armory, the guest of honor at the inaugural ball—an event which soon "took on the flavor," one man later said, "of a Lower East Side block party," as hundreds of Smith's friends and supporters from downtown Manhattan mixed incongruously with the aristocratic elite of Albany society. Mrs. William Bayard Van Rensselaer found herself being greeted by "Silent Charlie" Murphy and his daughter Mabel, while a beaming Tom Foley, the local saloonkeeper and Tammany district leader who had discovered Smith, pumped the hand of every patrician in sight, whether proffered or not.

Up in the family box, Smith's mother, Catherine, took out a card she had been holding on to for 16 years and passed it around. When he had first moved to Albany in 1904 as a newly elected state assemblyman, Smith had sent her a picture postcard of the Executive Mansion. "Dear Mother," he had written on the back. "This is a picture of the governor's residence. I'm going to work hard and stick to the ideals you taught me and some day—maybe—I'll occupy this house."

ery would be regulated by law. Women would not be allowed to work more than fifty-four hours a week. Children under fourteen would not be allowed to work in factories at all.

Business interests were outraged. "To own a factory in New York is now a calamity," the head of the Real Estate Board of New York declared. But nothing could stop the momentum of the campaign that Smith was now leading with evangelical fervor. Of the sixty recommendations made by the Factory Investigating Commission, fifty-four were passed into law. By the end of 1913, New York had the most advanced factory law in the United States.

In the end the carnage of the Triangle shirtwaist factory fire would prove to have been one of the most transforming events in American political history. As the members of the Factory Investigating Commission—reformers, labor leaders, and Democratic politicians—moved into positions of power in city hall, in Albany, and eventually in Washington, the remarkable alliance would become an unstoppable coalition for change, not only in New York but across the nation.

As the subway had brought New Yorkers together physically, so the grief and horror of the Triangle fire had united them emotionally, spiritually, and finally politically. "We banded ourselves together," Frances Perkins later recalled, "moved by a sense of stricken guilt . . . to prevent this kind of disaster from ever happening again."

Looking back, Perkins—appointed by Franklin D. Roosevelt as secretary of labor, and the first woman cabinet member in American history—would say simply that the New Deal itself had begun "in that terrible fire, on March 25th, 1911."

THE CROSSROADS OF THE WORLD

At 7:30 precisely on the evening of April 24, 1913, President Woodrow Wilson pressed an electric switch in the White House. Two hundred miles to the north, on the corner of Broadway and Park Row in New York, the eighty thousand lights of a brand-new skyscraper—the Woolworth Building—blazed out brilliantly across the city.

It looked, one man said, like "an immense ball of fire, giving the effect of a gorgeous jewel

resplendent in its setting of rich gold, and [visible to] mariners forty miles out to sea." Rising sixty stories and nearly eight hundred feet into the sky, the tallest building in the world by far was immediately called the Cathedral of Commerce.

[Is] New York the most beautiful city in the world? It is not far from it. No urban nights are like the nights there. I have looked down across the city from high windows. It is then that the great buildings lose reality and take on magical powers. Squares and squares of flame, set and cut into the ether. Here is our poetry, for we have pulled down the stars to our will.

Ezra Pound, 1913

By 1913, anything seemed possible in New York.

The kinetic, constantly shifting forms of the metropolis represented an entirely new kind of human construct—"shapes ever projecting other shapes," as Walt Whitman had predicted, so many years before, city blocks tilted up on end to form giant skyscrapers, then laid back down again and put to sea as great ocean liners, which resembled nothing so much as massive floating models of Manhattan—the greatest ocean liner of them all—now completely man-made, electrified and interconnected, and filled from one end to the other with a teeming mass of humanity.

And now that metropolis had a new center—high up on Broadway, north of Forty-second Street. For years, the focus of the city had been migrating north from the canyons of lower Broadway—up toward a place called Long Acre Square, an area on the west side of town that only ten years before had been a sleepy district of carriage shops and livery stables.

Adolph Ochs, the visionary new publisher of the *New York Times*, had led the way—abandoning the paper's old offices down near city hall for a brand-new twenty-two-story skyscraper that by 1904 soared above the district the city had renamed Times Square in the paper's honor.

Less than ten years later, subways from every part of the city were converging on the hourglass-shaped intersection—bringing men and women, young and old, immigrant and native-born, into the great democratic hub that was rapidly becoming known as the crossroads of the world.

By 1913, Times Square had emerged as the center of theater, vaudeville, music publishing, motion pictures, and nightlife in America—the undisputed capital of the nation's entertainment and the laboratory of a new kind of popular culture.

By day, the district hummed with the business of show business—its sidewalks filled with thousands of performers, directors, designers, songwriters, managers, and musicians circulating in and out of thousands of theaters, rehearsal spaces, scenery shops, booking agencies, press offices, and restaurants.

By night, it was transformed into an urban gathering place without rival or precedent— the focal point not of civic authority but of the city's great democratic pleasure-seeking crowds. Each evening, tens of thousands of New Yorkers poured into Times Square—drawn to the

musical comedies, to the revues and vaudeville shows, to the dance halls and lobster palaces, and to the magical roof gardens, high atop the grand hotels and theaters that seemed to float above the city and under the stars.

And yet, with literally hundreds of plays, movies, vaudeville acts, sideshows, concerts, and musical revues to choose from, the single greatest attraction was Times Square itself—which every night blazed into life. From its immense signboards millions of brilliant incandescent bulbs seemed to bathe the entire district in a streaming, flickering electric glow, as if New York itself had somehow taken on the mutable, dreamlike character of a motion picture.

One September evening, the French novelist Pierre Loti stood on a Broadway sidewalk transfixed by the spectacle of the future itself coming to life on the streets of New York City.

When it opened in 1882 at the corner of Broadway and 39th Street, the luxurious Casino Theater (right) had been located at the northern edge of the city's theater district—an eight-block stretch of Broadway above Herald Square and 34th Street, popularly known as the Rialto. The theater's heyday came in the late 1890s, when it was celebrated for its lavish musicals featuring stars such as the voluptuous Lillian Russell and the sextette of beautiful chorus girls known as the Floradora Girls—every one of whom, it was said, had been pursued by a millionaire admirer. By the time this view was taken in 1915, the entertainment district's move to Times Square had left the Casino behind, and the theater's glamour had begun to fade. It was demolished in 1930.

A view of Times Square about 1914. Broadway's first electric sign had been installed in 1897; in 1906 the Knickerbocker Theatre advertised a play called *The Red Mill* with a lighted windmill whose arms seemed to turn—the first moving sign. By 1913, Times Square was dazzlingly illuminated each evening with more than a million incandescent bulbs, whose intense glow gave the district its nickname: the Great White Way.

"The Great White Way." New York.

It appeals to the business-man, tired and worn, who drops in for half an hour on his way home; to the person who has an hour or two before a train goes . . . ; to the woman who is wearied of shopping; to the children who love animals and acrobats; to the man with his sweetheart or sister; . . . to the American of all grades and kinds who wants a great deal for his money. . . . It may be a kind of lunch-counter art, but then art is so vague and lunch is so real.

      Edwin Milton Royle, 1899

Children in front of theatrical billboards on a Manhattan street corner. Just above the group of children is a poster for the "Matchless Show" of Tony Pastor, the New York impresario and manager credited with inventing vaudeville.

Nothing captured the human and cultural complexity of the new metropolis more than the vital, raucous, hugely popular form of entertainment called vaudeville. Though it would eventually stretch to every corner of the nation, vaudeville's commercial heart and creative wellspring would always remain in New York, where it was born one day in October 1881— and where 51 years later it would be declared officially dead on another October day.

It started when an enterprising theater owner named Tony Pastor opened a new concert saloon on 14th Street and sought to expand his potential audience by replacing the old, licentious variety shows with a new kind of entertainment— so respectable and wholesome, one man said, "that children could take their parents to it." Called vaudeville—a name drawn, some said, from the French *voix de ville*, or "voice of the city"—the new entertainment proved wildly popular with working-class audiences and was soon being replicated in theaters across New York.

Running two or three times a day, each vaudeville bill presented a colorful parade of mingled performances—eight separate acts, including balladeers, acrobats, jugglers, female impersonators, animal acts, dancers, magicians, ventriloquists, strongmen, opera singers—"every nook and corner of show business," the comedian Billy Glason observed,

including "dramatics, comedy, timing, pacing, personality."

Relying heavily on ethnic caricature and stereotype, the wide variety of acts offered a bright, garish reflection of the city's diversity. There were Jewish comedians like Eddie Cantor—who had been raised, he said, "on the sidewalks of New York, with an occasional fall into the gutter"— and singers like Sophie Tucker, whose performance of "My Yid-dishe Mama" brought tears to the eyes of audiences who spoke not a word of Yiddish. There were "Dutch" knockabout comics like Joe Weber and Lew Fields, who performed in broad German accents. There were Irish song-and-dance teams like the Four Cohans—whose young son, George M. Cohan, was already stealing the show with catchy tunes he himself had written. Some vaudevillians preferred to mimic the style or accent of other nationalities, or to mix disparate traditions together. "I'm the human dialect cocktail," the German-born

singer Emma Carus explained. "A little Scotch, considerable Irish, a dash of Dutch and a great deal of Negro, together with a bit of British."

> *I don't have to make a sightseeing tour to get my types. I was born in New York right among them. . . . When I sing an Italian or Irish or Yiddish song, I have a definite character in mind that I've known for years.*
>   Belle Baker

Yet while drawing from a variety of immigrant traditions, vaudeville itself looked to the American mainstream. Its theaters were usually located on the city's main commercial streets, and most of its acts were, however heavily accented, in English—to appeal to a wide range of customers. In its audiences, Irish, Jewish, Italian, and German immigrants mixed indiscriminately, laughing and crying at one another's traditions and experiences, even as rendered in the broadest strokes of cari-

cature and burlesque. Though its instincts were strictly commercial, vaudeville helped to foster a new sense of common identity—as Americans and New Yorkers— among the city's diverse immigrant groups.

Ironically, that shared experience often came at the expense of another group. African Americans, who as customers were segregated into balconies (or excluded entirely), were frequently caricatured onstage by white performers in blackface, an old minstrel tradition, updated by vaudeville. Not only white but African American performers were required by managers to apply the crude makeup and adopt the strutting or shuffling caricature of plantation slaves. "Nothing seems more absurd," wrote the black comedian George Walker, one of the few who refused outright, "than to see a colored man making himself ridiculous, in order to portray himself." Yet Walker's own partner, the incomparable singer and comedian Bert Williams, delighted black and white audiences alike with his subtle and complex black-face performances—and eventually transcended vaudeville altogether to appear as a headliner in Florenz Ziegfeld's lavish Follies.

Originally a local phenomenon, vaudeville was revolutionized in 1900 through a commercial innovation that transformed New York's place in the world of American entertainment. That year, two showmen named Benjamin F. Keith and Edward F. Albee began booking vaudeville acts into cities across the country—creating the first of many nationwide circuits that eventually linked 2,000 theaters from New York to San Francisco. It was the first national system of entertainment in American history, and New York—where the acts were auditioned, produced, and booked—became the nation's undisputed head-quarters of show business. No less than Morgan or Vanderbilt before them, Keith and Albee used their centralized power to ride over the interests of smaller businessmen—local theater owners who now found themselves consolidated, whether they liked it or not, into the New York–based circuits.

Aspiring vaudevillians soon converged on the city from around the country, hoping to catch the eye of the big circuit producers and bookers whose offices were clustered around Times Square. Performers everywhere dreamed of appearing at the Palace—the luxurious 1,800-seat theater on Broadway and 46th Street considered the pinnacle of vaudeville ambition. "All the years of playing the hick towns," the columnist and onetime vaude-villian Walter Winchell would later recall, "getting the rebuffs and the humiliations, and hoping someday that you'll play the Palace. It's difficult for people who weren't part of vaudeville . . . to under-stand. But for me, playing the Palace was better than being elected to the White House."

New York's own performers, meanwhile, left behind the city's familiar confines to spend months in what they called the sticks— a perhaps not entirely flattering reference to the endless rows of telegraph poles marching across the American hinterland. "We had to brazen our way into strange towns in the Midwest and down South," a Manhattan-born

vaudevillian named Harpo Marx later recalled, "where we knew we had three strikes against us. One: we were stage folks. Two: we were Jewish. Three: we had New York accents. And, well—strike four: we weren't very good." In towns and cities across the coun-try, audiences soon grew familiar with the distinctive accent and fast-paced speech patterns of immigrant New Yorkers, which were becoming the sound of American popular culture.

Yet new rivals were already challenging vaudeville's primacy within that culture. Borrowing Keith and Albee's booking system, motion picture companies— themselves based on Times Square—assembled nationwide chains of theaters in the years before the First World War, anchored by enormous flagship movie houses on Broadway, all within a few blocks of the Palace: the Strand in 1914, the Rialto in 1916, the Rivoli in 1917, the Capitol in 1919—"cathedrals," the comedian Fred Allen said, "that made the vaudeville houses look like privies."

With the advent of talking pictures in late 1927, vaudeville's

era came to a close with stunning swiftness. One by one, vaudeville theaters across the country switched to showing films, until only the Palace itself held out. Finally, on October 16, 1932, the Palace replaced its traditional evening bill with a program of short live shows, running five times a day, interspersed with the showing of films. Thirty-two blocks and a half century from where it had been born, vaudeville was declared dead.

Yet vaudeville's influence would be felt for the rest of the century, as young performers like Al Jolson, Buster Keaton, George Jessel, Eddie Cantor, Fanny Brice, Jack Benny, George Burns, Gracie Allen, Cary Grant, Mae West, Milton Berle, Bill Robinson, Fred Astaire, Jimmy Cagney, and Jimmy Durante carried its rich traditions to musical comedies, theatrical revues, feature films, radio shows and, eventually, television programs. "An academy of the streets" as one critic later called it, vaudeville was the crucible of a new kind of American popular art, risen from the immigrant districts of the city to spread across the country and around the world.

A New York theatrical production, about 1902. Like many vaudeville acts, this skit was set in the city itself—a typical Manhattan street corner, complete with an Irish saloon and a German grocery store.

The opulent shops, with their immense show-windows, remind one of our own boulevards; but the electricity which flows in rivers, and dominates everything, is a thousand times more aggressive than it is with us. Everything seems to vibrate, to crackle, under the influence of these innumerable currents which dispense power and light. One is himself electrified almost to the point of quivering under the stimulus. . . . When I return from here, Paris will seem just a quiet, old-fashioned little town, with tiny, low houses; nor will any of its Fourteenth of July illuminations approach in brilliancy the phantasmagoric display that one may see in New York on any night of the year. Everywhere multicolored lights change and sparkle, forming letters, and then dissolving them again. They fall in cascades from top to bottom of the houses, or in the distance seem to stretch in banners across the street. But it is up in the air that one chiefly gazes for up there, on the tops of buildings, are signs that move, operated by ingenious mechanisms, visions that dance. . . . The apparitions flash out, move, fade away, quickly, very quickly—so quickly, indeed, that the eye barely follows them. From time to time, some enormous advertisement perched on top of a dark sky-scraper, almost invisible in the murky atmosphere, breaks out into red flame, like a constellation, hammers some name in your memory, and then as quickly vanishes.

Pierre Loti

This composite panorama, made in 1911, shows the basic elements of Times Square taking shape—commercial buildings and theaters, covered with billboards and surmounted by large electric signs on metal frameworks. Unprepossessing by day, the district came alive by night, when the girdered supports disappeared and the giant signs seemed to float above the city.

By election night, 1916, when this view was taken, Times Square had become the central gathering place for the city's population. "It is the forum," Gerald W. Johnson wrote a few years later, "the market place in which the people rush under stress of any great emotion. . . . There every four years they gather a million strong to hear the news of their own decision as to their own government. There on the last night of the year they gather again, straining their eyes toward the luminous white ball at the top of the flagstaff to catch the first hint of its movement at the tick of midnight; each wishing to be first to hail his neighbors with greeting for the New Year which is always to be happier than the last."

WHERE THE MODERN WORLD TOOK SHAPE, 1898—1929

KENNETH T. JACKSON

In the three decades between the 1898 consolidation of the five boroughs into one enormous municipality and the stock market crash in 1929, New York became a city unlike any the world had ever before seen. To be sure, in earlier centuries other urban centers had grown to significant size and influence, but Gotham was almost as different from Istanbul, Venice, Tokyo, London, and Paris as those historic capitals were from their own provincial towns. In part New York's unusual character was a function of size. By 1930, the city alone had almost 7 million residents, and the surrounding suburbs added another 4 million. At the time, no other metropolitan region anywhere comprised 11 million people. New York was also unusual in terms of diversity and density. In 1930, for example, the city contained more than 2 million foreign-born persons (including 517,000 Russians and 430,000 Italians) and had the largest immigrant labor force on earth.

But Gotham's true distinctiveness has always been less in its size and more in its way of life. Although it was not the national capital, New York assumed a cultural dominance early in the century that equaled its role in finance and industry. The hub of communications, Manhattan swept past Boston late in the nineteenth century as the center of book and magazine publishing. Broadway emerged as the focus of American theater, while the Metropolitan Musuem of Art and the Metropolitan Opera set a standard of excellence matched only in Europe. Artists, many of whom repudiated traditional values, congregated in Greenwich Village, and America's foremost writers often made their homes in one or another of the city's hundreds of neighborhoods.

New York was also a leader in building the infrastructure, creating the institutions, and celebrating the diversity that would define metropolitan life for decades to come. Dozens of technological, managerial, and sociological changes made Gotham the home of modernity in the first three decades of the twentieth century. Five developments in particular had a strong influence on the region: new residential patterns that allowed for both low-density suburbs and tall apartment buildings; new commercial and retailing structures, especially the office skyscraper and the grand department store; new forms of communication, especially mass-market newspapers and extensive radio networks; new forms of leisure, especially restaurants, amusement parks, and spectator sports; and new forms of transportation, especially a subway system of unprecedented size and complexity.

NEW RESIDENTIAL PATTERNS

More than half of the residents of New York City in 1900 lived in tenements, usually of the "dumbbell" variety, that stood six stories high, contained eighty-four small rooms, and housed approximately 150 persons. So many New Yorkers were forced to crowd into the airless and dimly lit dwellings that in 1914, one-sixth of the city's total population lived on the teeming Lower East Side, where the *average* density was 260,000 people per square mile in 1900, the most intense concentration of humanity the planet had ever seen. At that density, New York City could have housed 78 million residents. The dumbbell was hailed by contemporaries for the light and ventilation provided by the air shaft and for the seemingly adequate toilet facilities (twelve in the whole building). But such structures only exacerbated crowding and misery.

In 1901, reformers finally managed to pass legislation that prohibited the construction of any more dumbbell units. Commonly called the New Law, the Tenement House Act of 1901 became the most significant municipal housing statute in American history and the most significant housing measure of any kind other than the Federal Housing Administration and the public housing program. It set the standard for cities around the nation, and its provisions remain the basis for the regulation of low-rise housing design in New York City. In effect, the New Law radically improved the quality of tenement housing, and it established design controls that were effective and enforceable.

Beyond the tenements, the New York region was creating two other residential types that would have more enduring influence. The first—perhaps surprisingly for the country's greatest urban center—was the suburban house. The ideal of semirural living dates back for centuries, but its realization on a large scale dates only to 1817, when Robert Fulton established regular steam ferry service from Brooklyn Heights to the business district in lower Manhattan. For the first time, businessmen could move their families to a bucolic retreat safely removed from the presumably dangerous and polyglot streets of New York and yet be within a fifteen-minute commute to their offices or countinghouses. The experiment worked, and by the middle of the century, Walt Whitman, whose office at the *Brooklyn Daily Eagle* overlooked the Fulton Ferry slip, was frequently commenting on the suburb's phenomenal growth. In Brooklyn, he said, "men of moderate means may find homes at a moderate rent, whereas in New York City there is no median between a palatial mansion and a dilapidated hovel."

Helped along by an extensive rail network, New York continued to spread out through the early decades of the twentieth century, and a residential tide of huge proportions engulfed thousands of square miles in Westchester County—to the north of the city—as well as in Nassau County—on Long Island, to the east—and Hudson, Essex, and Bergen counties in New Jersey. Meanwhile, the row house that was common in the first suburbs, like Brooklyn Heights, was replaced in the middle-class imagination by the classic single-family house on its own plot of land. This cottage ideal quickly caught on in other cities as well, although then or now no other metropolis had so extensive a suburban population and network as New York.

Despite suburbanization, Gotham remained both in fact and in the popular imagination a city of big residential buildings. The most important change in the half century after the Civil War was the increasing respectability of apartment house life. Before 1870, the guardians of middle-class morality thought it scandalous to place two unrelated families in the same building or even to put a bedroom on the same floor as a parlor. That Parisians had been doing exactly that for decades simply proved their point. The first New York structure to challenge this assumption was the Stuyvesant on East Eighteenth Street, designed in 1869 by Richard Morris Hunt, an architect trained appropriately in Paris. Other grand buildings followed, including the Dakota, built in 1884 at Seventy-second Street and Central Park West, and by 1900, the large apartment house was replacing the brownstone as the residence of choice for the Manhattan upper class. In order to attract such people, the early apartments had to somehow re-create on a single floor all the amenities of a row house—maid's rooms and pantries and a careful separation of family and servant spaces—in order to satisfy families who had previously enjoyed a kind of upstairs-downstairs style of existence in a five-story row house.

As apartment living became acceptable to the rich, middle-class families in Brooklyn, the Bronx, and the upper regions of Manhattan looked with more favor on the multi-story buildings that awaited them in ordinary neighborhoods. Such structures soon became ubiquitous, especially on the Upper East and West sides, where they were often exceptionally large. Between 1904 and 1908, for example, three new residential buildings on Broadway were successively crowned as the world's biggest: the Ansonia at Seventy-third Street, the Apthorp at Seventy-ninth Street, and the Belnord at Eighty-sixth Street. This last structure, a twelve-story palazzo with an interior court, occupied the entire square block between Broadway and Amsterdam Avenue. It offered full concierge service, pneumatic mail delivery, and 175 apartments, arranged in suites of eight to fourteen rooms.

The most prolific builder of tall apartment buildings in the early decades of this century was the architect Emery Roth, whose first major creation in New York, the Belleclaire Hotel on Broadway at Seventy-seventh Street, opened in 1903. Over the next three decades no other person so dominated luxury apartment construction in the city. From his drawing boards came the San Remo and Beresford apartments on Central Park West, the Ritz Tower on Park Avenue, the Normandy apartments on Riverside Drive, and the venerable 417 Park Avenue, completed in 1911. In all of them, Roth managed to adapt Renaissance and classical details to modern building forms, and he succeeded in convincing his clients, most of whom could easily have chosen to move to the suburbs, that high-rise living combined elegance and sophistication with convenience and ease.

NEW COMMERCIAL FORMS

By 1900, New York was the home of the greatest concentration of corporate officials, industrial designers, consulting engineers, lawyers, bankers, and architects in North America. By that time, the Wall Street law firm had become a national institution, and investment bankers like J. P. Morgan, Jacob Schiff, the Seligman brothers, and August Belmont had become legendary figures. And as national corporations emerged from once small firms, Gotham became the headquarters city for American industry.

As much as anything else, two new kinds of commercial structures—the skyscraper and the grand department store—symbolized the new style of metropolitan life. Typically, the tall office building has been considered largely an engineering and architectural achievement. Equally important, however, was the way in which such a structure required a new way of working. By the 1910s, hundreds of thousands of white-collar clerical employees in New York were riding elevators to work in artificially lit rooms where hundreds of other people were engaged in similar routines. In some respects, the office building was a kind of giant filing cabinet, with separate drawers and compartments for the minutiae of the modern white-collar workplace.

The department store defined the modern city as much as the office skyscraper. This new form of retailing was born in 1846, when Alexander T. Stewart, a Scottish immigrant, opened a huge new emporium at Broadway and Chambers Street in lower Manhattan. Previously, a person wishing to buy a dress or a pair of shoes went to a specialized and small establishment, often a dry goods store, to purchase a bolt of cloth or to make arrangements for a one-of-a-kind fitting. Stewart, along with John Wanamaker in Philadelphia, changed all this. Dividing his store into departments, he offered his customers a matchless selection of goods, and over time he introduced new concepts, like large-scale advertising and money-back guarantees, that revolutionized the trade. By 1862, he had opened an even grander establishment at Broadway and Tenth Street. Along with selection and price, it had a central rotunda, a double staircase, and continuous organ music.

If A. T. Stewart revolutionized commerce by introducing new merchandising concepts to centuries-old retailing practice, the city itself was responsible for creating an unprecedented concentration of department stores in a small area. By 1900, the term Ladies' Mile referred to a stretch along Broadway and Sixth Avenue, roughly from Tenth Street to Twenty-third Street, in which there were more great stores than anywhere else on earth. The Siegel-Cooper Company was one such place. It opened its enormous brick-and-terracotta building on Ladies' Mile in 1896 and immediately advertised itself as selling "everything under the sun." Indeed, it was the largest department store in the world at the time, and it featured a lavish interior and a trademark fountain just inside the main door. "Meet me at the fountain" became a popular expression of the day. And people around the city swapped stories about how the managers at Siegel-Cooper would go to any length to satisfy a serious customer. When one such person indicated, as a secret joke, his desire to purchase a live elephant, he was surprised several weeks later to receive a telegram: "Steamship *Van Dam* arriving from Ceylon tomorrow with white elephant. What are your instructions?"

The grand brick, stone, and cast-iron buildings of Ladies' Mile were important not just for their architecture. They also represented the "feminization" of the central business district. Before the department store era, women generally shopped near their residences; the working part of the city was a mostly male preserve. The retailing revolution brought on by the rise of the department store changed all that. While making money took most of the energy of middle-class husbands, their wives sought to realize their growing expectations through the purchase of ready-to-wear clothes, items for the home, and toys for the children. The central business district, and in New York especially the department stores, began to cater to the female half of the population. By the early years of the twentieth century, when huge retail establishments typically displayed a large variety of goods in an impressive building, offered guarantees on all purchases, and advertised extensively in the daily newspapers, shopping had become almost the exclusive preserve of women. And because of the department store, women found their way into the heart of the city, a district previously dominated by the business activities of men only.

In typical New York fashion, just as the Ladies' Mile was becoming famous, the big retail emporiums followed their customers and moved northward. R. H. Macy was the first to shift farther uptown. Nathan Straus and his brother Isidor (who later went down on the *Titanic*), bought the company

in 1888, and in 1902 they relocated the store from Fourteenth Street to a gargantuan structure at Thirty-fourth Street and Broadway. Macy's thus became the first large store north of Twenty-third Street. Soon afterward, B. Altman began work on a twelve-story structure between Thirty-fourth and Thirty-fifth streets and Madison and Fifth avenues. Built of French limestone in the Italian Renaissance style, it had broad aisles, high ceilings, crystal chandeliers, and parquet floors, and it was especially well known for its elaborate window displays during the Christmas holidays.

Anchored by Altman's and Macy's, two great new shopping districts, Fifth Avenue and Herald Square, arose in midtown with modern new structures and locations for Gimbel's, Arnold Constable, Saks Fifth Avenue, Lord and Taylor, Bonwit Teller, and a dozen others. Taken together, they offered more retail floor space than any group of similar stores on the planet.

NEW FORMS OF COMMUNICATION

Although Gotham had long been the newspaper and information capital of the nation, the city's journalism industry expanded dramatically in the decades before World War I. For example, ten years after buying the *World* in 1883, the publisher Joseph Pulitzer introduced color printing and color comics, and along the way he pioneered the modern format of the city newspaper and won the largest Sunday circulation in the nation. Meanwhile, William Randolph Hearst arrived in 1895 from San Francisco and purchased the *New York Journal*. He soon took advantage of new types of high-speed rotary presses to increase readership by the hundreds of thousands. Named yellow journalism by critics, the bellicose editorial policies of Pulitzer and Hearst helped push the United States to war with Spain in 1898, even as they attracted such well-known reporters as Nelly Bly, Lincoln Steffens, and Stephen Crane.

The first three decades of the twentieth century were even better for New York newspapers. Dozens of specialized publications, like the *Jewish Daily Forward* (1897), the African American *Amsterdam News* (1909), and the Communist *Daily Worker* (1927) were established, as well as news services, like the Associated Press (created in 1848 and strengthened after 1900), the United Press (1909), and the International News Service (1909). Similarly, the 1920s saw the development of tabloid newspapers, which were characterized by huge circulations, large photographs, and wild headlines. The most notable was the *Illustrated Daily News* (1919), soon renamed the *Daily News*, the circulation of which reached almost 2 million per day by 1930, making it the most widely read newspaper in the world.

But the most important journalistic development in the early twentieth century was the emergence of the *New York Times* as the world's most powerful and prestigious newspaper. Founded in 1851, it was floundering in the 1890s and had a circulation of only 9,000 in 1896, compared to the *World*'s 200,000, the *Journal*'s 300,000, the *Herald*'s 140,000, and the *Sun*'s 70,000. In 1896, however, Adolph S. Ochs purchased the *Times* and its building on Park Row, and he immediately raised its prestige, primarily by seeking readers who wanted a paper that was dependable, that focused on the news, and that did not overemphasize crime and sex. In the next two decades it became the paper of record in the United States, in part by reporting in depth on such scientific events as Robert Peary's exploration of the North Pole and Albert Einstein's discoveries, and in part by gearing its coverage to the strengths of the city—especially financial news and the growth of the retailing and fashion industries. The *Times* soon won critical recognition, especially for its coverage of the sinking of the *Titanic* and the carnage of World War I, when managing editor Carr Van Anda's uncanny journalistic instincts occasionally enabled his reporters to reach battle sites before combat began.

When newspapers were threatened by the new science of telecommunications in the 1920s, New York again led the way to a new journalistic paradigm. Wireless telegraphy, the forerunner of radio, was introduced to the United States in 1899, when James Gordon Bennett, owner of the *New York Herald*, broadcast an America's Cup yacht race in New York Harbor to a station at Thirty-fourth Street. KDKA in Pittsburgh was the nation's first commercial station, but Manhattan soon became the center of radio programming and management. The first network, the National Broadcasting Company (NBC), led by David Sarnoff, began in the city in 1926. The rival Columbia Broadcasting System (CBS), also headquartered in New York, began operating in 1927, as did the Blue Network, later to be called the American Broadcasting Company (ABC). Together, the growing radio networks brought such New York star performers as Fred Allen, Jack Benny, Al Jolson, George Burns, and Gracie Allen to a national audience.

NEW FORMS OF LEISURE

Another way for ordinary citizens to escape the monotony of the workplace and the home was to partake of the new types of fun that became available in the half century after 1880. Three kinds of establishments typify these new opportunities: restaurants and nightclubs, amusement parks, and spectator sports arenas.

Going out to eat—even to McDonald's—has become such a common activity at the turn of the millennium that it is hard to imagine a time when most families took all of their meals at home. Yet this was the common experience of most households in the United States until after World War II. Cities were the places where this enormous shift in living patterns first occurred. In New York, the trend toward dining out began in 1831, when two Swiss brothers opened Delmonico's on William Street in lower Manhattan. Based on the Parisian model, the beautifully supervised establishment set the pattern for all restaurants in the United States. By the time of the Civil War it was the nation's most famous restaurant, a mecca for gourmets and celebrities, constantly enlarging and moving through a dozen lavish locations, including Broadway at Bowling Green, where Jenny Lind and Louis Napoleon dined, and Fifth Avenue and Fourteenth Street, where Samuel F. B. Morse sent the first cablegram across the Atlantic Ocean while seated at his regular table.

During its long history (1831–1923), Delmonico's created or popularized such dishes as lobster Newburg, pie à la mode, Delmonico steak, and chicken à la king.

After the Civil War, when competitors like Rector's, Maison D'Orée, and Louis Sherry's opened, and especially after 1900, when the city's selection of restaurants was enriched by the arrival of hundreds of thousands of new immigrants, New York became the undisputed food capital of the nation. Barbetta, which opened in 1906 on Thirty-ninth Street and moved to West Forty-sixth Street in 1925, brought Piedmontese cuisine to the theater district, as did Mamma Leone's, which also began in 1906. Lüchow's became the city's best-known German establishment, and the expanding Jewish population introduced a new-style, combination grocery-restaurant, called a delicatessen, that offered everything from salmon to pickles to cream soda. In 1899, the Café Martin introduced banquet seating, and at about the same time many dozens of Chinese restaurants began to introduce New Yorkers to chop suey, egg foo young, and chow mein.

After dining out, the next step toward modernity was the creation of the nightclub, a kind of establishment that helped make New York—as much as Madrid and Barcelona—a stay-up-late kind of town. The new trend began about 1911, the year of the fox-trot and the year the Bustanoby brothers introduced dancing with dinner to their popular restaurant. Other establishments, like Rector's and Reisenweber's soon followed suit, so that drinking, dining, and dancing were no longer separate endeavors but essential parts of a sophisticated evening spent in the company of the opposite sex. Prohibition put a temporary crimp in the late-night revelries of New Yorkers, but the city's entrepreneurs soon developed a new phenomenon—the speakeasy—to appeal to essentially the same audience. And after the Volstead Act was repealed in 1933, a whole series of new nightclubs, like El Morocco, the Stork Club, and the Copacabana, would set new standards for spectacle and opulence.

If the nightclub was the preserve of the fashionable and the comfortable, the amusement park was the special home of the working classes. And no amusement park anywhere could compare to the one at Coney Island. It started slowly. At the time of the Civil War, Coney Island was simply a secluded seaside retreat with a few hotels. By the late 1870s, however, no fewer than six railroads connected Manhattan to various points along the beach. And by the late 1880s, new hotels dotted the area, and horse racing and prize-fighting were attracting tourists by the thousands.

But the real changes at Coney Island came at the turn of the century. In 1897, George Tilyou opened Steeplechase Park, named for the exciting mechanical racetrack that ringed its borders. In 1903, Frederic Thompson and Elmer Dundy created Luna Park, which featured Venetian gondoliers, a Japanese garden, an Eskimo village, a Dutch windmill, a Chinese theater, and an elevated promenade. And Luna's 250,000 lightbulbs made twenty-four-hour entertainment possible. Finally, in 1904, William Reynolds, a politician, opened Dreamland across the street from Luna Park. It lit the night sky and its white buildings with 1 million lightbulbs.

There was nothing like Coney Island anywhere, although Blackpool and Brighton in England had provided earlier models. And when the subway reached Coney Island in 1920, at a cost of only a nickel, millions of people could experience thrill rides, freak shows, wax museums, and more lights and excitement than they could ever have imagined. The price of hot dogs and rides soon also dropped to five cents so that families could budget for a spectacular weekend at the amusement park and the adjacent beach and boardwalk. Until Disneyland opened in southern California in 1955, Coney Island was the best-known and most heavily patronized amusement park in the world.

As the nation's largest and richest city, New York also provided opportunity for every kind of spectator sport. A variety of racetracks offered ample opportunity for wagering on the horses, and the metropolis became the nation's most important venue for boxing matches in the first half of the twentieth century. Notable bouts included Jim Jeffries's defeat in twenty-two rounds of James J. Corbett for the world heavyweight championship on May 11, 1900, and Jack Dempsey's victory over Luis Firpo on September 14, 1923, which attracted 82,000 spectators to the Polo Grounds. Meanwhile, in 1920, the New York State Legislature legalized prizefighting and set up a state athletic commission to supervise it. Two weeks after the law was passed, the promoter Tex Rickard, with the aid of circus impresario John Ringling, obtained the financial backing to lease Madison Square Garden. Under his astute management, the Garden, which had not been particularly successful under previous managers, became the most famous indoor arena in the United States. Rickard offered a variety of attractions unequaled by any other entertainment palace on earth, including boxing, wrestling, rodeos, ice hockey, basketball, circuses, and horse shows.

But baseball was the peculiar "American pastime," and New York not only gave birth to the sport (Cooperstown was much later) but remained its spiritual home. It is the only city in American history to have had three major league teams at the same time—the New York Giants, the New York Yankees, and the Brooklyn Dodgers—and all of them had a devoted fan base. The Yankees of course became the most storied franchise in the nation, largely because of the ability and personality of one man—Babe Ruth. Nicknamed the Sultan of Swat and the Bambino, he began playing for the team in 1920 and was soon hitting so many home runs that he changed the way baseball was played. He led the Bronx Bombers to seven pennants and four world championships, and Yankee Stadium, whose 67,000 seats made it the biggest sports facility in the world at the time, came to be known as the House That Ruth Built because it was made large enough to seat Babe Ruth's many fans. Meanwhile, going out to a ball game meant more than just cheering for a favorite team. Instead, in a summer setting reminiscent of rural life, baseball introduced immigrants unfamiliar with the rules of their new society to the concept of limits and restraints.

NEW FORMS OF TRANSPORTATION

New York's skyscrapers, apartment buildings, department stores, amusement parks, and sports palaces—in short, its residential, commercial, communications, and recreational infrastructure—could not have succeeded had it not been for a transportation network so extraordinary that it could overcome the region's unusual geography to become the most extensive system on earth. Virtually an archipelago, with only the Bronx attached to the mainland of the United States, New York has more than five hundred miles of shoreline. And its rivers and bays are wide, unlike the small, charming, and easily spanned waterways that flow through London, Paris, Berlin, and Rome. Thus, Gotham's challenge was to find a way to put tracks and roads over and under great waterways and dozens of other obstacles in order to link a huge and divided metropolis and transform it into a kind of organic whole.

The solution was to build bridges and tunnels and railroads and subways and controlled-access highways—and to build more of them than any other place. The Brooklyn Bridge, completed in 1883, was only the most famous of seventy-six bridges that ultimately crossed New York's waterways, most of them constructed in the first three decades of the twentieth century. In one remarkable six-year span, for example, the Williamsburg (1903), Manhattan (1905), and Queensborough (1909) bridges were all constructed over the East River. Eight other bridges were thrown across

the Harlem River between 1889 and 1910, by which time other bridges also spanned Dutch Kills, Newtown Creek, and the Gowanus Canal.

New York also put together a spidery web of tunnels that was as extensive as those anywhere. Gotham's first underwater tube was begun in 1874. Intended for steam railroad use and connecting Cortlandt Street in Manhattan to Exchange Place in Jersey City, it did not open until 1908. Soon thereafter, the various subways, which initially were privately operated, built many tunnels under the East and Harlem rivers, while the Pennsylvania Railroad was building two tubes for its own trains. Finally, in 1927, the Holland Tunnel became the world's first underwater vehicular roadway. Its ventilation system soon became a model for similar tunnels around the world.

Tunnels and bridges were necessary but not sufficient. More important in connecting the various parts of the metropolis were the steam railroads, the above- and below-ground rapid transit lines, and the electric streetcars. Together, they gave the metropolitan region a public transportation system without equal in the world in the first half of the century—whether measured by route miles, track miles, capital investment, rides per capita, or total ridership.

The subway in particular became New York's signature, the physical manifestation of a new kind of city, a place of unparalleled concentrated human, commercial, and economic activity. Manhattan's first underground route opened in 1904, long after London (1863) and shortly after Glasgow (1886), Budapest (1896), Boston (1897), Paris (1900), and Berlin (1902). But New York's subway was more important than its European and American predecessors for two reasons. First, until after World War II it had about twice the size (308 route miles and 722 track miles) and twice the ridership (more than 4 million per day, exclusive of buses and streetcars) of any other system on earth. Second, as designed by William Barclay Parsons, its chief engineer, the New York subway became a technological pacesetter. It was the first in the world with a fully integrated system of express and local trains, and it pioneered the cut-and-cover method of digging, which was cheaper and more efficient than boring through the ground.

New York's immense and interconnected transportation system changed the way that people lived. Because a ride on the subways, elevated trains, streetcars, and buses cost only five cents as late as 1948, the city's inhabitants were able to see more than their immediate neighborhood and to experience more than their particular ethnic group. Some indication of the significance of the system can be deduced from the fact that the Interborough Rapid Transit Company's (IRT) first line was carrying 600,000 passengers *per day* within one year of its opening, a number that had doubled by 1914. And in 1925, an amazing 86 percent of New

York's population lived in the ninety-seven square miles served by subways or elevated trains. The remaining 14 percent of the population lived on 70 percent of the city's land area. The Bronx, for example, was completely transformed by the new transportation options. There, the Third Avenue El reached 177th Street in 1891, Fordham Road in 1901, and Gun Hill Road in 1920, each time creating a building boom along the Third Avenue corridor. Meanwhile, trolley lines, which mostly ran east and west to connect with the subways, replaced the old horsecar routes. And the subway first reached the Bronx in 1905, running under 149th Street to Third Avenue, where it turned north until reaching 241st Street and White Plains Road. Before these routes opened, the Bronx was mostly fields and farms. By the 1920s, it was one of the fastest-growing counties in the United States.

Almost as important as the ubiquitous subways and elevateds were the railroads that came into the city from the surrounding countryside. First introduced in the 1830s, they served a mostly suburban clientele. They reached the middle of Westchester and Nassau counties long before the Civil War, and they stimulated an early exodus to rural cottages in places like New Rochelle and Mount Vernon. With the introduction of electric locomotives early in the twentieth century this mode became even more viable. By 1900, about one thousand trains per day were rolling into Manhattan, a level of long-distance commuting that no city anywhere could match. From the west, New Jersey trains discharged passengers at Hoboken, where commuters then took ferries across the Hudson River into the city. From the east, locomotives brought suburbanites to Atlantic Avenue in Brooklyn, where they were close to the Wall Street financial district. And from the north, just the three passenger lines running along the Hudson River, the Harlem River, and Long Island Sound were alone bringing 118,000 commuters per day into Grand Central Terminal. Meanwhile, much of the region's outlying development was encouraged by the railroads, which developed communities, promoted the advantages of suburban living, and offered discounts for regular travelers.

The success of railroad commuting soon necessitated the building of two grand passenger terminals. The first was Pennsylvania Station, a transportation complex of unprecedented proportions that rose from a two-block hole between Thirty-first and Thirty-third streets between 1904 and 1910. And just a few years later, the almost equally elegant and gargantuan Grand Central Terminal was enlarged and made more efficient by dividing its sixty-seven tracks between two underground levels and by electrifying most of the trains using the hub.

New York, the quintessential subway and railroad commuting city, even led the world in the building of controlled access roads, or expressways. William K. Vanderbilt's Long Island Motor Parkway (1906–1911) was the world's first thoroughfare restricted solely to the passenger automobile, and especially designed for its needs. More significant was the bucolic and meandering Bronx River Parkway, which ran sixteen miles from Bruckner Boulevard in the Bronx to White Plains in Westchester County. Begun in 1906 and completed in 1923, it ran through a valley and thus could be bridged without massive earthwork. The result was a beautifully landscaped road that stimulated automobile commuting from such places as Scarsdale, Mount Vernon, Bronxville, and New Rochelle. Within ten years, the metropolitan region also witnessed the construction of the Hutchinson River Parkway (1928), the Saw Mill River Parkway (1929), and the Cross County Parkway (1931). To this day, among American cities, New York, not Los Angeles, has the largest total of highway miles within its borders.

CONCLUSION

New York was not the only city to build apartment buildings, subways, or office towers. But it was perhaps the one place in the world where the hand of man shaped the environment as much as the hand of God. The metropolis at the mouth of the Hudson River was not only a big city but a new kind of city, a place where stone, glass, pavement, tracks, sidewalks, and bridges dominated the landscape. Nowhere else were the symbols of modernity so abundant and so obvious. The apartment buildings, the skyscrapers, the department stores, the baseball stadiums, and the subway tracks were not the only manifestations of a new age, but they were obvious to every resident and to every visitor. More important, they changed the daily experience of ordinary citizens. The rise of the big-circulation newspaper, for example, was tied to large-scale advertising by department stores, which was itself tied to the expanding transportation network. Thus, a housewife in Brooklyn or the Bronx or the Lower East Side might read in a tabloid newspaper of a particular bargain. She could take the subway for a nickel to Herald Square at Thirty-fourth Street and find there in any of several stores almost all the consumer products of the world's most productive economy. The result, then, was not just a new city of stone and glass but a new city of ordinary experience—a modern city for the modern world.

By the 1920s, the mile-long stretch of Fifth Avenue north of 34th Street had become the greatest shopping street in the world, lined with scores of specialty shops and dozens of major department stores, including B. Altman's, Lord and Taylor, Saks, Best and Co., Bergdorf Goodman, and Bonwit Teller. In this 1926 view, looking north from 42nd Street, the noontime crowds of pedestrians, a sea of cars and taxis, and Fifth Avenue's special double-decker buses swarm past one of New York's first traffic towers, installed in 1922.

COSMOPOLIS

1919–1931

"**W**hat floor, please?" said the elevator man.
"Any floor," said Mr. In.
"Top floor," said Mr. Out.
"This is the top floor," said the elevator man.
"Have another floor put on," said Mr. Out.
"Higher," said Mr. In.
"Heaven," said Mr. Out.

F. Scott Fitzgerald,
"May Day," 1920

Ironworker with the Chrysler Building, photographed from the upper floors of the Empire State Building, September 29, 1930. Photographers were as dazzled by the nerve and skill of New York's "high steel" ironworkers as they were by the extraordinary towers they were constructing. From his vantage point atop the tallest building in the world, the worker mocks the relatively small size of the Chrysler Building—which only a few months earlier had itself been the tallest building in the world.

HOMECOMING

All through the spring and summer of 1919, the streets of New York were filled with parades and troops of marching men returning in victory from the grim and distant battlefields in Europe.

For months, every hotel and boardinghouse in the city was filled to capacity—including two new giants in midtown, the Hotel Commodore on Forty-second Street and the Pennsylvania on Seventh Avenue, each with two thousand rooms—as more than 3 million people from around the country converged on Manhattan to take part in the delirious victory celebration.

> *There had been a war fought and won, and the great city of the conquering people was crossed with triumphal arches and vivid with thrown flowers of white, red and rose. All through the long spring days the returning soldiers marched up the chief highway behind the strump of drums and the joyous, resonant wind of the brasses, while merchants and clerks left their bickerings and, crowding to the windows, turned their white-bunched faces gravely upon the passing battalions.*
>
> F. Scott Fitzgerald

Week after week, crowds lined the streets to cheer the victorious regiments as they swung up Fifth Avenue—past the hundred-foot-high victory arch at Twenty-third Street—past the solemn memorial in front of the New York Public Library at Forty-second Street—and up to the spectacular "curtain of jewels" at Fifty-ninth Street and Central Park—nine thousand shimmering crystal prisms sewn together and flooded by two dozen blazing searchlights.

The first regiment to be honored was the 369th—an all-black regiment from Harlem to which the French had given their highest honor, the Croix de Guerre, along with the nickname Hellfighters, for their legendary valor under fire. On February 17, 1919, they marched proudly up Fifth Avenue, past the reviewing stand of newly elected Governor Alfred E. Smith and his wife, to the rousing music of James Reese Europe, who had dazzled nightclub audiences all across the continent with his syncopated ragtime dance tunes—and who now led two thousand battle-hardened troops up Lenox Avenue

Crowds line Fifth Avenue to greet returning World War I troops, 1919. Millions of Americans from around the country descended on New York in 1919 to welcome the war-weary veterans back from Europe. The victory parades began in late February and continued for nearly a year, with visitors sometimes arriving as early as 6:00 a.m. to secure choice spots along the five-mile-long route—which ran up Fifth Avenue from Eighth Street in Greenwich Village to the foot of Harlem, at 110th Street.

and home, to the strains of "Here Comes My Daddy."

"The multitude went wild with joy," the *New York Times* reported the next day. "The sidewalks were packed like a subway train at the rush hour, the windows were filled with faces, and the roofs were held in force. . . . Each person in the throng seemed to be shouting to a particular soldier . . . until the unison of voices became a mighty roar such as Harlem had never heard."

To most New Yorkers, the horizon seemed limitless that spring and summer. On August 26, 1919, the Nineteenth Amendment to the Constitution had taken effect. After decades of passionate struggle, American women had finally won the right to vote. In January, Alfred E. Smith—a poor boy from the Lower East Side, who had become the hero of the labor reform movement—had been sworn in as the first Irish American governor in America—a triumph for the immigrant experience in New York City.

"Everything is possible," a twenty-three-year-old midwesterner from St. Paul, Minnesota, named F. Scott Fitzgerald wrote to the girl of his dreams, Zelda Sayre, the day he arrived in February 1919. "I am in the land of ambition and success."

> *New York had all the iridescence of the beginning of the world. The returning troops marched up Fifth Avenue and girls were instinctively drawn east and north toward them—this was the greatest nation and there was gala in the air.*
>
> F. Scott Fitzgerald

In the decade to come, nothing would go as people planned—not for Scott and Zelda Fitzgerald, not for Al Smith, not for the immigrants who had transformed the city, not for the residents of Harlem. What few could see, in the heady days following the First World War, was how deep a chasm had opened up between the past and present—how dramatically the city and country had already changed in just five years, and how dramatically they would change again in the months to come.

The war itself had already caused one of the most momentous changes in New York's history, though only a few yet grasped its significance. For over half a century, European capital had flooded into New York, underwriting much of America's spectacular industrial growth and westward expansion. But the war in Europe had changed everything. In desperate need of funds to sustain their vast military campaigns, the Europeans had been forced to sell off their sixty-year accumulation of foreign investments—and then, in a remarkable shift in fortunes, were forced to borrow directly from the United States. The United States, which had gone into the war $3 billion in debt, emerged from the conflict a $3 billion creditor. The House of Morgan and other major Wall Street firms—once agents for European investment in America—now became prime lenders to Europe itself.

"Three years ago, New York's light was the brightest in the Western World," the essayist Edwin C. Hill wrote in 1917. "The war has made New York the lighthouse of the whole world." By 1919, New York had displaced its last and greatest rival, London, as the investment capital of the world, and money was flowing into the city, one British observer remarked, "as water flows downhill." "Only by careful and constant extravagance," one New Yorker replied impertinently, "can we keep it from bursting the banks!"

> *The borrowers of America and all the world turn to New York....It is to the quotations on the New York Stock Exchange that men of affairs from Penobscot to Honolulu turn each morning to find how beats the pulse of prosperity and enterprise. It is to New York that the Government of France turns frantically for help when the franc takes a headlong plunge toward oblivion and from New York it receives sustenance and strength.*
>
> Charles A. Beard, 1924

Yet even as the city leaped to the center of the global economy, the nation itself was recoiling from its recent foreign entanglement—reflexively isolating itself from a European world that, despite the coming of peace, was still racked with social and political upheaval, including workers' uprisings in England, France, Italy, and Germany, and—most frighteningly of all—a full-fledged revolution in Russia.

"The poison of revolt," President Woodrow Wilson declared grimly, "has forced its way into the veins of this free people."

> *The Bolshevik revolution was managed by a small clique of outcasts from the East Side of New York. . . . Because a disreputable alien, Leon Bronstein, the man who now calls himself Trotsky—can inaugurate a reign of terror from his throne room in the Kremlin—because this lowest of all types known to New York can sleep in the Czar's bed . . . should America be swayed by such doctrines?*
>
> U.S. Attorney General
> A. Mitchell Palmer

As a wave of political reaction began sweeping the nation, groups in New York that had enjoyed triumphant success only a few years before—immigrant workers, progressive reformers, radical politicians, and union organizers—found themselves on the run.

In the fall of 1919, just six months after the triumphant parades up Fifth Avenue, U.S. Attorney General A. Mitchell Palmer ordered a series of brutal raids on hundreds of suspected radical groups in New York and around the country. In early December, 250 outspoken activists, including the famed anarchist Emma Goldman, were rounded up on suspicion of treason and transported to Ellis Island. There, in the same rooms where millions of hopeful newcomers had once been received into the country, the political outcasts spent weeks in confinement, unsure of their fate. Finally, in the early morning of December 19, they were herded onto an old troop ship chartered by the War Department and deported to Russia.

Driven by the fierce wave of xenophobia and isolationism—and by fears of a horde of postwar refugees flooding the country—the golden door now began to close. Two years after the war, Congress passed an emergency quota act to curtail immigration from southern and Eastern Europe. The next year, Ellis Island, which had seen a million newcomers a year pass through its maze of corridors only a decade before, welcomed fewer than 150,000, and, when the restrictions became permanent three years later, the number dropped to half that. "America must be kept American," President Calvin Coolidge declared, as the greatest movement of human beings in history came to an end.

The myth of the melting pot has been discredited. The United States is our land. . . . We intend it to remain so. The day of unalloyed welcome to all peoples, of indiscriminate acceptance of all races, has definitely ended.

Congressman Albert Johnson,
Washington State

Emma Goldman, left, delivering a speech about birth control at Union Square, 1916. The best-known anarchist in the country and a leader of New York's radical community for nearly thirty years, Goldman was harassed, censored, and arrested for her unpopular views, and in 1919 was deported to Russia for speaking out against America's entry into World War I. Unlike many of her fellow radicals, Goldman remained wary of Russia's Bolshevik regime, and upon her deportation reportedly remarked, "I never wanted a revolution where the people aren't allowed to dance."

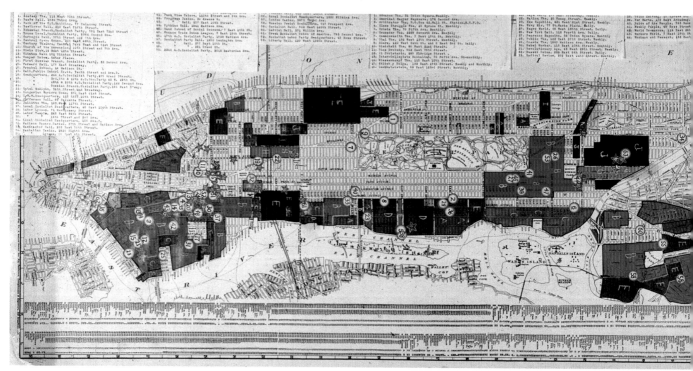

As the fear of foreigners increased, the anxiety many Americans felt toward their own sprawling, immigrant-filled cities found expression in the Volstead Act—a federal law intended to enforce the controversial Eighteenth Amendment, which prohibited the sale of alcohol. "The Noble Experiment," a young congressman named Fiorello La Guardia warned, would "require a police force of 250,000 men, and a force of 250,000 men to police the police." But Prohibition passed anyway, with the overwhelming support of rural voters in the South and Midwest—who feared the rising tide of immorality and lawlessness they thought they saw sweeping America's cities.

By 1921, the era of immigration was coming to an end; political protest had been driven underground; the sale of alcohol in America had been prohibited; and forces of business were in the ascendant in New York as never before.

Though no one could have known it, the curtain was about to rise on the most spectacular act in the city's astonishing three-century history, as 130 years of relentless commercial growth now moved to its highest crescendo. In the decade to come, as the city and the country kicked themselves free of the past and rose into a seemingly limitless future, New York would become the most commercially and culturally creative place on earth—committed as never before or since to the intoxicating dreams of capitalism and commerce.

Before the decade came to an end, a new kind of culture—a mass culture—and a new kind of city—a city of desires and dreams—would be brought into existence on the island of Manhattan. As it was, New York would soar upward in a frenzy of speculation, rising higher and higher, and then falling lower, than it ever would again.

It is a European city no longer. It is American. It is itself. Imperial New York. Plenty of time yet. Men and machines. We are all so young yet. Wait and see. Wait and see what New York will do.

Sherwood Anderson

PARADISE

One of the first signs of what the decade held in store came in the spring of 1920, when F. Scott Fitzgerald—the young Minnesotan who had come east to reinvent himself—found his entire life turned upside down.

For months after his arrival in the winter of 1919, the intense and hopelessly self-absorbed young writer with intoxicating dreams of fame and glory had tried to make a go of it—writing jingles for an advertising agency and sending back increasingly anxious love letters to his beloved Zelda in Alabama.

Nothing came of it. By June, he had collected 122 rejection slips from publishing houses, which he pinned to the walls of his dark and drab apartment on Claremont Avenue—"one room," he wrote, "in a high horrible apartment house in the middle of nowhere."

When Zelda—fearful of his faltering prospects—broke off the engagement in June, he went on a three-week drinking binge, then sobered up and with remarkable discipline rewrote the manuscript of the rejected novel that he had tentatively entitled *The Romantic Egoist.*

Within two weeks, Scribners had agreed to publish it. By the end of the year, Zelda had relented, too, and when on March 26, 1920, the book appeared—under a new title, *This Side of Paradise*—the critical and popular response was overwhelming. The book, the writer A. Scott Berg later said, "unfurled like a banner, over the entire age." Its author became an instant sensation, thrown into a whirlwind of attention and fame. Within weeks, the blond midwesterner—with the eerily ravishing looks, one man said, of an archangel—had became a national celebrity, and the most poignantly meteoric career in the history of American letters had begun.

"To my bewilderment," Fitzgerald later said, "I was adopted, not as a Middle Westerner, not even as detached observer, but as the archetype of what New York wanted." Both to their contemporaries and to posterity, Scott and Zelda seemed to embody the wanton spirit of the city—"a homeland of the uprooted," one man said, "where everybody you met came from another town and tried to forget it; where nobody seemed to have parents or a past more distant than last night's party."

From the confusion of the year 1920, I remember riding on top of a taxi-cab along deserted Fifth Avenue on a hot Sunday night, and a luncheon in the cool Japanese gardens at the Ritz . . . and writing all night again and again . . . then out into the freshly bewitched city, through strange doors into strange apartments with intermittent swings along in taxis through the soft nights. . . . Lastly from that period I remember riding in a taxi one afternoon between very tall buildings under a mauve and rosy sky; I began to bawl because I had everything I wanted and knew I would never be so happy again.

F. Scott Fitzgerald

Fitzgerald's dazzling career was launched as the city itself began its giddy upward climb. In the years to come, no one would chronicle more eloquently—or embody more movingly—the

In the early 1920s, F. Scott and Zelda Fitzgerald became instant celebrities—the subject of countless interviews and stories in fashionable new magazines such as *Vanity Fair*, *Smart Set*, and *Metropolitan*, as well as in hundreds of syndicated newspaper columns. The vivacious, free-spirited Zelda, widely considered a model of the "new American woman," gave interviews and penned columns of advice for young women, while Scott was quizzed about his newfound success, which had propelled his literary earnings from less than $900 in 1919 to nearly $19,000 in 1920.

Just days after the Volstead Act took effect, a man named Perkins created an illegal bar in the basement of a midtown brownstone—the first speakeasy in New York. By the early 1920s, police estimated there were 32,000 speakeasies in the city—twice the number of legal saloons before Prohibition. The best known was the establishment at 21 West 52nd Street, called Jack and Charlie's, or Club "21," or simply "21" (left), which featured two bars and a restaurant, and contained a secret chute down which bottles could be tossed during a raid. More business was done there daily, one man said, than at the Stock Exchange. "Behind grilled doors," one man wrote of the place, "lovely little debutantes, the intelligentsia of Wall Street, Broadway and Fashion Avenue foregather at any hour to discuss the news of the town. The speakeasy has become the coffee-house of the age."

By the 1920s, the skyscraper skyline of New York had become one of the greatest pictorial challenges for modern artists and photographers. The Italian-born painter Joseph Stella returned to New York from a stint in Europe deeply influenced by Picasso and the artists of the Italian futurist movement, and sought to use the multiple vantage points of cubism to render the modern city's dynamic sense of motion in his five-panel 1922 masterpiece, *New York Interpreted*. At right, the center panel of the series, entitled *Skyscrapers*.

mesmerizing arc of the city's dark and shining trajectory across the decade of the 1920s.

The whole golden boom was in the air—its splendid generosities, its outrageous corruptions and the torturous death struggle of the old America. There seemed little doubt about what was going to happen—America was going on the greatest, gaudiest spree in history and there was going to be plenty to tell about it.

F. Scott Fitzgerald

EXPLOSION

Wednesday, September 16, 1920, dawned partly cloudy and pleasantly warm in New York City.

The morning papers brought welcome news that a brief subway strike in Brooklyn had been settled. In less than twenty years the vast network had become the city's circulatory system, carrying 5 million passengers a day over nearly six hundred miles of track, welding Manhattan, Brooklyn, the Bronx, and Queens into a single metropolitan unit. Only Staten Island—a sleepy landscape of rolling farmland and country estates accessible only by ferry—remained a world apart.

In the Bronx that morning, services were held for seven people, killed when their car skidded off an elevated roadway in the rain. The nineteenth-century city was coming to an end. Only a decade before, there had been 128,000 horses in New York, outnumbering cars a hundred to one. Now there were scarcely half that many and in the next ten years the number would be cut in half again, as the number of automobiles on the city streets exploded to nearly 800,000.

As the morning rush hour got under way, nearly 3 million people—more than the entire population of Chicago—converged on the southern half of Manhattan to work in its fifteen thousand factories and warehouses, hundreds of department stores and specialty shops, and scores of skyscrapers in midtown and Wall Street—where fully a third of the city's workforce were now employed in white-collar jobs.

It was a good day on the New York Stock Exchange, with prices rising slowly but steadily all morning. Across the street, at number 23 Wall, business purred on at the House of Morgan, a low-slung building with thick limestone

Looking west on Wall Street, on September 16, 1920, minutes after a massive explosion killed 38 people and wounded hundreds of others. The bomb, hidden in a horse-drawn wagon, exploded moments before noon; had it gone off a few minutes later, after lunch-hour crowds had filled the streets, the death toll would almost certainly have been far higher.

shattering windows a half mile away, sending a pillar of fire shooting high into the air and a deadly hail of iron shrapnel hurtling into the unsuspecting lunchtime crowds on Wall Street.

A block away, the financier Joseph P. Kennedy was hurled to the ground by the power of the immense explosion, which turned Wall Street into a scene out of Dante's *Inferno*, with torn and mangled bodies and body parts strewn everywhere amid a blackened wreckage of twisted steel, broken glass, and smoking debris. The wagon itself was vaporized instantly, along with the horse—whose hooves came clattering to the pavement up near Trinity Church. All that was found of a millionaire named Edward Sweet was a finger with the ring still on it.

In all, thirty-eight people were killed in the deadly attack on the House of Morgan, and three hundred more injured. There had been only two fatalities inside the bank itself, including a young clerk named William Joyce, who had been sitting at the window closest to the explosion. Junius Morgan, whose desk on Broad Street faced away from the blast, suffered only minor injuries to his hand.

Almost a century later, the deep scars gouged in the building's limestone facade that morning would still be visible—the "stigmata of capitalism," as the historian John Steele Gordon has remarked.

Bolshevik groups and radical anarchists were immediately suspected of perpetrating the dastardly crime, but no evidence to support the accusations was ever found. The wagon driver was never identified. No one was ever brought to trial.

That evening, lights were strung to allow hastily assembled work crews to repair the damage. "By one o'clock," the *New York Times* reported the next morning, "it was evident that all of Wall Street and the financial district, with most of the necessary repair work virtually completed, would go on with business as usual today."

On Thursday, September 17, 1920, the House of Morgan opened for business with its shattered windows boarded over. That morning, to everyone's amazement, the market continued its upward trend without a bump.

The Roaring Twenties had begun.

walls and the air of an elegant fortress. J. P. Morgan himself was long gone now—having died on the eve of the great war at the age of seventy-five—and his son, J. P., Jr., known since boyhood as Jack, now ruled in his place. A less imposing figure than his autocratic father, he was currently traveling in Scotland, and had left his son, Junius Spencer Morgan, to mind the affairs of the mighty bank.

As the lunch hour approached, office workers began spilling out of the skyscrapers clustered around the intersection of Wall Street and Broad. A few minutes before noon, a horse-drawn wagon covered with a canvas tarpaulin pulled to a stop on the north side of Wall Street, just across from the House of Morgan. No one paid any attention to the driver as he stepped away from the vehicle and vanished into the lunchtime crowds.

Then, a few seconds before noon, all hell broke loose.

Without any warning, the wagon—which had been filled to the brim with dynamite and iron sash weights—exploded with a blinding flash of light and deafening roar that ricocheted through the canyons of the financial district,

HARLEM

I, too, sing America
I am the darker brother.
They send me to eat in the kitchen
When company comes.
But I laugh,
And eat well,
And grow strong.

Tomorrow I'll sit at the table
When company comes
Nobody'll dare
Say to me,
"Eat in the kitchen" then.

Besides, they'll see how beautiful I am
And be ashamed, —
I, too, am America.
            Langston Hughes, "I, Too"

Nowhere in New York would the hope and excitement and heartbreaking promise of the extraordinary decade be felt more keenly than in a fifty-block area of upper Manhattan that by 1921 had become one of the largest black communities in the world—and the undisputed capital of black America.

"In nearly every city in the country," the writer James Weldon Johnson observed in 1927, "the Negro section is a nest situated somewhere on the border. In New York it is entirely different. Negro Harlem is not a fringe, nor a slum nor a 'quarter' consisting of dilapidated tenements. It is a section of new-law apartment houses and handsome dwellings, with streets as well paved, as well lighted and as well kept as any other part of the city. It is a black city, located in the heart of white Manhattan, and containing more Negroes to the square mile than any other spot on earth. It strikes the uninformed observer as a phenomenon, a miracle straight out of the skies."

> *Harlem has attracted the African, the West Indian, the Negro American; has brought together the Negro of the North and the Negro of the South; the man from the city and the man from the town and village; the peasant, the student, the business man, the professional man, artist, poet, musician, adventurer and worker, preacher and criminal, exploiter and social outcast. Each group has come with its own separate motives and for its own special ends, but their greatest experience has been the finding of one another.*
>
>   Alain Locke, 1925

Less than two decades before, there had been no black faces at all in Harlem, a row-house district north of Central Park originally developed as a commuter suburb for middle-class whites. Indeed, for three hundred years, New York's second oldest ethnic population (after the Dutch) had not had a space they could call their own on the island of Manhattan—pushed progressively north from one area to another by successive waves of white immigration and commercial development: from the Five Points area north of city hall, to Thompson Street in Greenwich Village, to a tenement district on Seventh Avenue around Thirty-third Street known as Little Africa, which by 1903 was being

To a startling degree, the rise of Harlem as the capital of black America was the work of one man—an enterprising real-estate agent named Philip A. Payton, who in less than four years at the turn of the century won for his people what they had never had: a sanctuary of their own in the sprawling city.

For decades, an implacable wall of racial prejudice had barred most blacks from any but the poorest neighborhoods in the city. "The Czar of all Russias," Jacob Riis wrote in 1890, "is not more absolute upon his own soil than the New York landlord in his dealings with colored tenants. Where he permits them to live, they go; where he shuts the door, stay out."

Indeed, for most of its venerable history, Harlem itself had not been one of the places landlords permitted blacks to live. First settled as a Dutch farming village in the 1650s, it became in the 1870s, following the construction of the El, a commuter district for middle-class Germans—then, two decades later a safety valve for Jewish and Italian immigrants eager to escape the crowded tenements of the Lower East Side. (Some German landlords, eager to halt the exodus, put up rental signs reading KEINE JUDEN, UND KEINE HUNDE: "No Jews, and No Dogs.")

In the end, it was the subway that set the stage for change—in ways no one could have anticipated. In 1900, when city officials announced that the new IRT line would run up Lenox Avenue to 145th Street, Harlem exploded in a frenzy of speculation and construction. "The great subway proposition permeated the air," the developer John M. Royall remembered. "Real estate operators and speculators [imagined] becoming millionaires, and bought freely in the West Harlem district in and about the proposed subway stations. Men bought property on thirty and sixty day contracts, and sold their contracts . . . and made substantial profits. On they went, buying, buying. . . ."

Then, just four years later, the boom collapsed as quickly as it had begun, as rival districts on the Upper West Side drew away prospective tenants. Block after block of brand-new apartment houses and new-law tenements stood all but empty in Harlem, whose desperate white landlords were now practically begging for tenants.

Enter Philip A. Payton, Jr., an eagle-eyed real-estate speculator with the air of a minister and the instincts of a professional gambler, who knew a good business opportunity when he saw one. A graduate of Livingston College in North Carolina, he had moved to the city in 1899 brimming with ambition but could find work only as a janitor in a white real-estate firm. When the subway was announced and whispers of a boom began, he lit out on his own and by 1904 he had become the most successful black real-estate agent in the city. That year, as the boom went bust, Payton approached Harlem's landlords with a daring proposition. His firm, the Afro-American Realty Company, would rent empty apartments to select black tenants—above market value and with a monthly guarantee.

Under any other circumstances, Payton knew, the landlords would have refused outright, and even now, many capitulated only reluctantly. But "economic necessity," James Weldon Johnson wrote, "usually discounts race prejudice—or any other kind of prejudice, so the landlords with empty houses whom Mr. Payton approached accepted his proposal, and one or two houses on 134th Street were taken over and filled with colored tenants. Gradually other houses were filled."

It was a stunning breakthrough for blacks in New York City. Though Payton's clients paid a premium—at least $5 more a month than white families paid for equivalent dwellings—after nearly three centuries on Manhattan Island, African Americans could finally enjoy well-built, well-maintained homes in a stable, established community.

By opening for colored tenants first a house on one block, and then a house in another I have finally succeeded in securing . . . over two hundred and fifty first-class flats and private dwellings. . . . The fight that I am making has got to be made sooner or later and I see no better time than now. . . .
Philip A. Payton, Jr., General Manager, Afro-American Realty Company

In the end, Philip Payton's insatiable need to speculate and scheme carried his own company under. But inroads had been made and others soon stepped in—including two of his former salesmen, John E. Nail and Henry C. Parker, who by 1911 were opening up not only tenements and row houses but luxurious apartment buildings to new black tenants.

"Those of the race who desire to live in grand style," the Urban League declared, "with elevator, telephone and hall boy service, can now realize their cherished ambitions." As building after building opened its doors to black tenants, newcomers began streaming into Harlem from all over the country—to the dismay of white landlords on the west side of Seventh Avenue, who in 1911 launched a counteroffensive to keep blacks out.

"When will the people of Harlem wake up," the editors of the white-run *Harlem Home News* thundered in August of that year, "to the fact that they must organize and maintain a powerful anti-invasion movement if they want to check the progress of the black hordes that are gradually eating their way through the very heart of Harlem?"

But it was too late. The tide could not be checked. "Although organizations to prevent the settling of colored citizens in certain sections of Harlem mushroom overnight," the editors of the black-owned *New York Age* calmly replied, "the colored invasion goes merrily along." By 1914, the black population of Harlem passed 50,000. "The colored [people] are in Harlem to stay," John M. Royall declared that same year, "and they are coming each year by the thousands."

"When Negro New Yorkers evaluate the benefactors of their own race," James Weldon Johnson wrote in 1930, "they must find that not many have done more than Phil Payton. . . . Harlem has provided Negroes with better, cleaner, more modern, more airy, more sunny houses than they ever lived in before. And this is due to the efforts made first by Mr. Payton."

Harlem, 1905. The sign reads RESPECTABLE HOUSING FOR COLORED FAMILIES ONLY.

dismantled to make way for the Pennsylvania Railroad, as once again, black New Yorkers were on the run. Four decades after the harrowing white-on-black violence during the draft riots of 1863, the African American presence in New York remained startlingly small—comprising, as late as 1900, less than 2 percent of the city's population of 3.5 million.

But then, in the opening years of the twentieth century, the most fateful migration in American history had begun—coming not from outside the country this time but from within, as tens of thousands, then hundreds of thousands of American blacks streamed north from the rural South, looking for work and sanctuary and a new way of life. At the very same moment, the new subway system in New York spurred a frenzy of overbuilding in upper Manhattan—bringing together a people in desperate search of decent housing with housing now in desperate search of people.

Black Harlem was born.

If I were to offer a symbol of what Harlem has come to mean in the short span of 20 years, it would be another statue of Liberty on the landward side of New York. Harlem has become the greatest Negro community the world has known without counterpart in the South or in Africa. But beyond this, Harlem represents the Negro's latest thrust towards Democracy.

Alain Locke, 1925

In the fall of 1921, an ambitious nineteen-year-old poet from Cleveland, Ohio, arrived in New York and took the subway uptown to Harlem. Emerging from the station at 135th Street and Lenox Avenue, the young Langston Hughes could scarcely believe his eyes. "I exulted at the sight of so many fellow Negroes," he said. "I wanted to shake hands with them all."

Let me tell you one of the things that meant so much to people. There was this big black giant of a policeman, Lacy, at 125th Street and Seventh Avenue, directing traffic, making white folks stop and go at his bidding. Where I came from, there was no black authority figure who commanded respect. To see him pull over a car full of white people and saunter . . . and say, "As big and black as I am, you mean to tell me you can't see my hand in the air?" This [was] something that we had not seen before. It was impressive.

Elton Fax

Year after year, the exodus continued, accelerated by the availability of work in the North, anti-black violence in the South, and the coming of the First World War. By 1919, nearly a hundred thousand African Americans had settled in Harlem, making it the largest enclave of African Americans in the country—and, despite the numbing poverty of many of its inhabitants, a beacon of hope and refuge from the frenzy of racial violence gripping the nation in the wake of the European war.

That summer—known forever afterward as the red summer—lynchings claimed the lives of seventy blacks across the South, including veterans just back from Europe, while angry white mobs in cities across the North, enraged by the influx of African Americans, rampaged through black communities.

Amid it all, Harlem alone remained quiet—its size, stability, and permanence making it a bastion of safety in the rising storm—and increasing the influx of newcomers still more. "I'd rather be a lamppost in Harlem," one black saying went, "than governor of Georgia."

A blue haze descended at night and with it strings of fairy lights on the broad avenues . . . From the window of an apartment on Fifth Avenue and 129th Street I looked over the rooftops of Negrodom and tried to believe my eyes. What a city! What a world!

Arna Bontemps

By 1921, the thriving black mecca had become a city within a city, with sixty churches, a YMCA and YWCA, branches for the Elks, Masons, and Pythians, and two respected newspapers, the *New York Age* and the *Amsterdam News.*

It was also a cauldron of political activism and ferment, with its own chapter of the Democratic party, and the Republican party, as well as one of the founding branches of the National Association for the Advancement of Colored People, which urged blacks to join the mainstream of American life, and the headquarters of Marcus Garvey's Universal Negro Improvement Association, which urged them

to turn away from white America and return to Africa.

Though most of its residents were working people of modest income, Harlem boasted levels of prosperity without equal in African American history. Scores of black lawyers, doctors, ministers, and businessmen lived in elegant apartment houses along the stretch of Edgecombe Avenue known as Sugar Hill, or in stone-fronted row houses purchased outright. A generation before, scarcely half a dozen blacks had owned land in Manhattan; now African Americans accounted for more than $60 million of Harlem real estate. "Buying property," one man said, "became a contagious fever."

On Sundays, Harlem residents strolled the wide boulevards of the district after church, dressed in their best. "Even Fifth Avenue was never like this," one man said. "Harlem boasts fifty-two Easters a year."

Although it had been brought into being in no small part by the harsh racial restrictions of the era—which forced blacks to concentrate, willingly or not, in a single uptown community—Harlem by 1921 had become an indisputable source of power and pride: a meeting ground and crossroads for African Americans from across the country, and a true metropolitan capital for a population that until recently had been largely dispersed.

Throughout New York City itself—like the rest of the country still rigidly segregated by

Among the more than 100,000 African Americans who migrated to Harlem during the 1920s were some of the country's greatest writers, artists, and musicians. Langston Hughes (opposite), the son of a prosperous lawyer, arrived in New York from Cleveland in 1921 to attend Columbia University. "More than Paris, or the Shakespeare country, or Berlin, or the Alps," he later wrote, "I wanted to see Harlem, the greatest Negro city in the world." Put off by the casual racism he found at Columbia, Hughes plunged instead into the artistic whirlwind of Harlem, soon becoming one of the leading figures of its literary renaissance. The view above, taken at a party honoring Hughes about 1926, shows several other prominent Harlem writers of the era, including (from left to right) Hughes, Charles Johnson, E. Franklin Frazier, Rudolph Fisher, and Hubert Delaney.

David Levering Lewis later wrote, "had been laid down regarding a place in the arts. Here was a small crack in the wall of racism, a fissure that was worth trying to widen."

And widen it did. Year after year, writers, musicians, artists, poets, and intellectuals from around the country poured into Harlem, fired by the dream of forging a new black culture in America.

The younger generation comes, bringing its gifts. They are the first fruits of the Negro Renaissance. Youth speaks, and the voice of the New Negro is heard . . . with arresting visions and vibrating prophecies; forecasting in the mirror of art what we must see in the streets of reality tomorrow, foretelling in new notes and accents the maturing speech of full racial utterance.

Alain Locke

Harlem, the writer Wallace Thurman declared, "is almost a Negro Greenwich Village. . . . Every other person you meet is writing a novel, a poem, or a drama." As a growing stream of essays, monographs, plays, poems, and novels came flowing out of Harlem, an extraordinary cultural interaction began to occur, quite unlike anything that had ever taken place in America before.

New York's publishing establishment began to take notice. Something about the new black literature struck a deep and resonant chord, not only among African Americans but among white Americans as well, for whom it seemed refreshingly unfettered by the hackneyed conventions of white culture.

By 1925, the African American literature pouring out of Harlem had become the rage of literary New York, and "the Negro," as Langston Hughes dryly remarked, "was in vogue."

On May 1, 1925, a magazine called *Opportunity: A Journal of Negro Life* hosted a special awards banquet at the elegant Fifth Avenue Restaurant to showcase Harlem's new talent. The cream of literary New York turned out for the glittering event, applauding enthusiastically as the jury—including literary lions like Robert Benchley and Alexander Woollcott—announced the names of the all-black winners, including the twenty-three-year-old poet Langston Hughes.

race—blacks were restricted from all but the worst jobs, denied access to good housing and schools, and forced to sit in the upper balcony of theaters and to endure a thousand other daily indignities.

And yet, with the decade to come, the blocks north of Central Park would become one of the most artistically creative places on earth and the epicenter of an astonishing cultural revolution.

The canyons of Wall Street and most union jobs may have been closed to African Americans, but "no exclusionary rules," the historian

Afterward, an elegantly dressed blond man came up to greet Hughes. His name was Carl Van Vechten, and he was one of the most well-connected literary figures in New York. Fascinated by the energy and engagement of the new black literature, he would do everything he could to further Hughes's career. "Now is the psychological moment," he wrote to the young poet, "when everything chic is Negro."

"Why were we seen as so special?" the poet Arna Bontemps asked, looking back. "One of our advocates on Park Avenue made an interesting suggestion. Primitive man, she said, had contacts with the infinite which civilization had broken. The 'New Negro' was to recapture this dim quality in poetry, painting and song. By this means he must transmit it to all America. Through us, no less, America would regain a certain value that civilization has destroyed."

However complex or ambiguous the motives, one thing was clear. Never before had black and white intellectuals mingled so indiscriminately in New York. Black writers like Hughes, Wallace Thurman, Alain Locke, Zora Neale Hurston, and Countee Cullen—the only Harlem writer actually raised in Harlem—found themselves swept up in a whirlwind of fashionable parties and literary events. "I am just running wild in every direction," Hurston said, "trying to see everything at once."

"When we were not too busy having fun," Bontemps said, "we were shown off and exhibited in scores of places, to all kinds of people. And we heard their sighs of wonder and amazement when it was whispered or announced that here was one of the 'New Negroes.' Nothing could have been sweeter to young people who only a few weeks or months earlier had been regarded as anything but remarkable. . . . We were heralds of a dawning day . . . first born of the dark renaissance."

Fragile as it was—and in the end heartbreakingly brief—the Harlem Renaissance marked a fateful breakthrough. Here was a powerful confirmation from the sophisticated center of American high culture that what defined America at its very soul was not its purity but its constant intermingling of peoples—black and white, native-born and immigrant, male and female, high and low—a never-ending

Women promenading on Seventh Avenue and 124th Street, 1927. Harlem in the 1920s was celebrated for its elegant boulevard life. Every Sunday, after church, prosperous Harlemites strolled up and down the wide sidewalks of Seventh Avenue between 125th and 138th streets—the women wearing full-length furs with parasols, the men in checkered suits and white spats, bowler hats and silk handkerchiefs.

process of migration, crossing, and transplantation that had been going on in New York City for almost three hundred years.

> *It's Harlem—and anything goes. Harlem, the new playground of New York! Harlem—the colored city in the greatest metropolis of the white man! Harlem—the capital of miscegenation! Harlem—the gay musical, Parisian home of vice!*
>
> Edward Doherty

By 1925, as Harlem's high cultural renaissance went on, an even more far-reaching explosion in popular culture was taking place, also centered in Harlem.

Nothing embodied the intoxicating spirit of the age—or the spirit of the cosmopolitan city that was its capital—more than the amazing new music pouring from Harlem's nightclubs and speakeasies.

What F. Scott Fitzgerald called the Jazz Age had begun.

> *It was New York that filled our imagination. We were awed by the never-ending roll of great talents there . . . in society music and blues, in vaudeville and songwriting, in jazz and theater, in dancing and comedy. Harlem, in our mind, did indeed have the world's most glamorous atmosphere. We had to go there.*
>
> Duke Ellington

It was the culmination of a process that had begun long before. Ever since the opening of the Erie Canal, New York had served as the clearinghouse of American popular culture—the one place where all the disparate elements of American entertainment flowed together and converged.

But the increasing concentration of cultural production in New York, together with the new forms of media starting to emerge—phonograph records, radio, moving pictures—now began to extend New York's reach to infinity, drawing along the way artists from every part of the country and transforming a regional folk art into the anthem of an entire nation.

Like the city itself, jazz owed its form to the convergence of many sources, from field hollers and black church music to ragtime and German marches. It had begun in the hinterlands of America, along the Mississippi in New

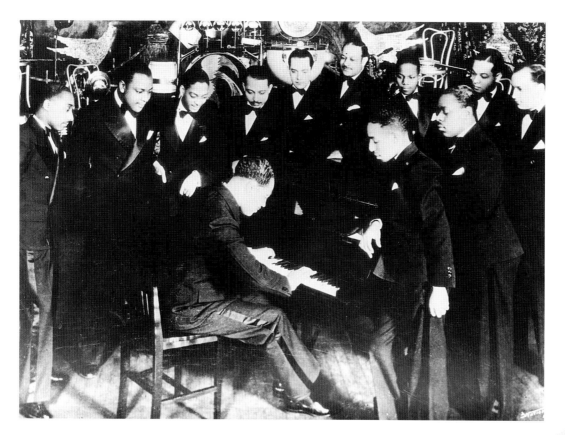

Orleans, then migrated north to St. Louis, Kansas City, Chicago. But it was in New York, Duke Ellington later said, that the new music "converged . . . and blended together." And as it had before, the giant city on the Hudson would soon steal the thunder of its rivals.

In 1921, Ethel Waters, a slender, twenty-five-year-old blues singer from Chester, Pennsylvania, who had already made a name for herself on Broadway, cut a record for a faltering black-owned recording company called Black Swan. Backed by a little-known arranger and band-leader named Fletcher Henderson, Waters's rendition of "Down Home Blues" sold more than half a million copies to black and white audiences across the country.

Two years later, Bessie Smith, a blues singer from Chattanooga, Tennessee, arrived in Harlem, and made her first recording. In less than six months in 1923, Smith's rendition of "Down Hearted Blues" sold more than 780,000 copies—lifting its label, Columbia Records, from near bankruptcy and making Smith an international celebrity.

The stampede was on. "Negro stock is going up," the novelist Rudolph Fisher wrote, "and everybody's buying."

Colored singing and playing artists are riding to fame and fortune with the current popular demand for "blues" disk recordings and because of the recognized fact that only a Negro can do justice to the native indigo ditties such artists are in great demand.

Variety, July 26, 1923

The watershed year was 1924—the annus mirabilis of the Jazz Age. In February, Edward Kennedy Ellington—a sideman from Washington who had arrived in New York several months earlier—became the leader of his own jazz band. Two months later, a cornetist from New Orleans named Louis Armstrong moved to the city from Chicago to play in Fletcher Henderson's band at the Roseland Ballroom. In the months and years to come, Louis Armstrong's unique sound and improvisational flair and Duke Ellington's ravishing, elegant arrangements would take the city and country by storm.

By 1925, *Harlem* had become synonymous around the world with the exhilarating vitality of American culture—and the ultimate expression of the urban age. Every strand and stream of American life seemed to converge in the new music, which, like the grid of Manhattan itself, was a unique blend of the improvisatory and the highly disciplined, at once intricate and chaotic, and tuned as nothing before it to the shifting rhythms of the metropolis—the very sound and soul of city life.

"Jazz time," the black music critic J. A. Rogers wrote, "is faster and more complex than African music. It bears all the marks of a nerve-strung, strident, mechanized civilization. It is a thing of the jungles—modern, man-made jungles."

Hot jazz . . . like the skyscrapers is an event . . . represent[ing] the forces of today. The jazz is more advanced than the architecture. If architecture were at the point reached by jazz, it would be an incredible spectacle. . . . Manhattan is hot jazz in stone and steel.

Le Corbusier

"The legend of Harlem by night," the writer Lloyd Morris declared, "crossed the continent and the ocean." In 1924, when the modernist French composer Darius Milhaud was asked on a visit to New York which American music

Baljeunesse, a 1927 watercolor by the Harlem artist Palmer Hayden, captures the excitement of the dance revolution that accompanied the jazz explosion of 1920s Harlem. New steps like the Charleston, the turkey trot, the shim sham, and the boogie-woogie quickly made their way from the nightclubs of Harlem to dance halls across the country, adopted by millions of young white Americans who preferred the looser and more frankly sexual movements of black dances to the formality of the waltz and other traditional steps. Dozens of Harlemites found steady work in the 1920s as dance coaches, teaching the latest moves and steps to white New Yorkers.

A visit to Harlem at night—the principal streets never deserted, gay crowds skipping from one place of amusement to another, lines of taxicabs and limousines standing under the sparkling lights of the entrances to the famous nightclubs, the subway kiosks swallowing and disgorging crowds all night long—gives the impression that Harlem never sleeps and that the inhabitants thereof jazz through existence.

James Weldon Johnson, 1930

The fascination of white New Yorkers with Harlem is revealed in this 1929 view of a floor show at Small's Paradise Club (left)—an establishment that seated more than 1,500 customers and was patronized by a mixed audience of blacks and whites (at far left, an African American performer has donned blackface as part of the show). The January 1928 cover of *Vanity Fair* presents a stylized rendition of Harlem musicians and dancers, revealing in its layout the identification of the new African American culture with artistic modernity.

had the largest influence in Europe, he startled reporters by answering, "Jazz."

"Maybe these Nordics at last have tuned in on our wave-length," Wallace Thurman mused.

Let's listen to Louis Armstrong . . . the black Titan of the cry, of the apostrophe, of the burst of laughter, of thunder. He sings, he guffaws, he makes his silver trumpet spurt. He is mathematics, equilibrium on a tightrope. He is Shakespearean! Why not?

Le Corbusier

"To call yourself a New Yorker," Thurman declared, "you must have been to Harlem at least once. Every up-to-date person knows Harlem." By 1924, white New Yorkers were pouring up to Harlem, which had become "the nightclub capital of the world," one man said, with more than 125 licensed cabarets and clubs and at least three hundred more operating outside the law.

At Small's Paradise Club on 135th Street, Fats Waller played piano and Ethel Waters sang the blues while waiters danced the Charleston or roller-skated their way through the crowded dining room, spinning their loaded trays without missing a beat. At Pod and Jerry's nearby, the attraction was Willie "the Lion" Smith and his infectious stride piano riffs. The vast Savoy Ballroom—"the home of happy feet"—could hold four thousand people and was built with a bandstand at either end to allow "battles" between bandleaders Fletcher Henderson and King Oliver.

At the Cotton Club, which catered especially to whites, seven hundred customers sat in a room filled with African masks, artificial palm trees, and bongo drums, and watched the chorus line of young, light-skinned performers dance to the music of Duke Ellington or Cab Calloway. On any given night, Charlie Chaplin might be seen there, or Harold Lloyd, or the financier Otto Kahn, or the heiress Gertrude Vanderbilt Whitney and Lady Mountbatten. "To [white] Americans," one observer said, "the Negro is not a human being but a concept."

Beneath the bright surface of Harlem's nightlife, however, the harsh realities for black New Yorkers remained in force. "It was a glam-orous atmosphere," the dancer Fayard Nicholson acknowledged dryly. "The only problem was my people couldn't get in."

When Carl Van Vechten arrived at the Cotton Club one night with a group of black friends, he was politely informed that mixed parties were not admitted, and that—except as performers or waiters—almost no blacks were allowed to enter the establishment. W. C. Handy, the composer called the father of the blues, was once denied entrance to the Cotton Club. Standing outside, he could hear one of his own songs playing within.

Every nightclub in Harlem was owned by whites, as was every major store on 125th Street, Harlem's principal shopping district, where African Americans were barred from working even as salespeople.

And Harlem's growth was bringing problems of its own. Apartment rents, always higher for black New Yorkers, soared as Harlem's population doubled in the course of a decade to nearly 200,000. Rent parties became a Harlem tradition. When even that was not enough, tenants began doubling up, cordoning off rooms with sheets, or placing sleeping cots in dining rooms. By the end of the decade, Harlem would rival the Lower East Side as the most crowded district in New York.

And yet, something had changed. "If my race can make Harlem," one man said, "Good Lord—what can't it do?" An extraordinary cultural outpouring was occurring in Harlem, a creative force so powerful that all New York, indeed the entire world, was forced to acknowledge it. Once relegated by whites to the periphery of American life, blacks—at least for the moment—stood at the very center of the dizzying, modern culture that New York was pioneering.

Harlem is more than the Negro capital of the nation. It is the Negro capital of the world. And as New York is the most glorious experiment on earth of different races of divers groups of humanity struggling and scrambling to live together, so Harlem is the most interesting sample of black humanity marching along with white humanity.

Claude McKay

Greenwich Village is to me a spiritual zone of mind. . . . The city which hasn't a Greenwich Village is to be pitied. It has no life, no illusion, no art.
Hippolyte Havel

By the 1920s, a hundred blocks south of Harlem, a second city-within-a-city had emerged in Manhattan: Greenwich Village—which, having defiantly detached itself from the city's mainstream a decade before, was now struggling to maintain its fragile independence against the powerful commercial forces of the era.

In some ways, the Village had always seemed a world apart. Laid out in the colonial era and developed as a row-house suburb in the 1820s and '30s, the area had entered the twentieth century as an urban backwater, isolated from the rest of the city by its confusing maze of oddly shaped blocks and narrow streets. "The streets have run crazy and broken themselves . . . into strange angles and curves," the writer O. Henry observed. "One street crosses *itself* a time or two." Lined with old, dormered brick houses—most now cut into small, cheap apartments—along with tea shops, taverns, and inexpensive restaurants, the neighborhood's low-rise blocks offered a striking contrast to the rushing city around it. "There was quietness and quaintness," one resident recalled, "there were neighbors who knew each other, there was sauntering in the streets."

But by 1911 "something was in the air," the critic Floyd Dell wrote, "something was happening, about to happen." Within a few years, the quiet, insular district became America's first genuine bohemia— "a hotbed of circles, clubs and cliques," one man said, whose citizens were in favor of "socialism, sex, poetry, conversation, dawn-greeting—anything so long as it was taboo in the Midwest." The early pioneers, drawn by the area's cheap rents and picturesque streets, included writers like John Reed, Edna St. Vincent Millay, Lincoln Steffens, and Eugene O'Neill; artists like John Sloan, Robert Henri, and Edward Hopper; and political activists like Emma Goldman, the celebrated anarchist; Big Bill Haywood, the fiery, charismatic head of the International Workers of the World; and Margaret Sanger, the outspoken advocate for birth control and family planning.

The unlikely epicenter of the chaotic alternative universe emerging in the Village was an elegant high-ceilinged apartment at 23 Fifth Avenue—the home of Mabel Dodge, an iconoclastic art patron and heiress who convened a regular Thursday-night salon, she said, "to get people together, so that they can tell each other what

The City from Greenwich Village, by John Sloan.

Patchin Place in Greenwich Village, photographed by
Jessie Tarbox Beals, 1916.

they think." In the spring of 1913,
Dodge's lively soirees gave rise to
two extraordinary events in the
cultural life of the city: the Armory
Show, a controversial exhibition
that introduced Americans for the
first time to the provocative modern
art coming out of Europe; and the
Paterson Pageant—an innovative
work of political theater held at
Madison Square Garden, intended
to raise funds for striking textile
workers in Paterson, New Jersey.

By then, the Village had
become a cauldron of political
radicalism and artistic experimentation.

"Everywhere," the critic
Malcolm Cowley later wrote, "new
institutions were being founded,
magazines, clubs, little theaters,
art or free-love or single-tax
colonies, experimental schools,
picture galleries. Everywhere
was a sense of comradeship
and immense potentialities for
change." That year, an extraordinary new magazine named

The Masses hit the newsstands,
electrifying readers. Edited by
John Reed, Floyd Dell, and a former
philosophy instructor from Columbia named Max Eastman, the
new journal brought together all
the currents flowing through the
Village: Marxism, anarchism, birth
control, free love, cubism, futurism,
Freudianism, feminism, the new
theater. "It is the recording
secretary for the Revolution in the
making," the poet and activist
Arturo Giovannitti wrote, "an
earnest and living thing, a battle
call, a shout of defiance, a blazing
torch running madly through the
night to set afire the powder
magazines of the world."

On the night of January 23,
1917, the painter John Sloan and a
group of friends descended on
Washington Square to make the
revolution official. Climbing to the
top of the Arch, they lit candles and
convened a midnight picnic,
decorating the monument with
balloons and declaring that the

area known as Greenwich Village
had seceded from the United
States, and was to be known thereafter as the Free and Independent
Republic of Washington Square.

*When I think of Greenwich
Village, it is almost with tears.
For there this battered battalion
dress their guns against the
whole nation. From the darkest
corners of the country they
have fled for comfort and
asylum. You may think them
feeble and ridiculous—but
feebleness is always relative.
It may require as much force of
character and independent
thought for one of these to
leave his Kansas home and
espouse the opinions of Freud
as for Wagner to achieve new
harmonies, or Einstein to
conceive a finite universe.*
Edmund Wilson

Just six months later—with the
country now at war—federal
officials moved swiftly to crush
any illusions of political autonomy.
In July 1917, under the provisions
of the newly passed Espionage Act,
the U.S. Post Office declared *The
Masses* seditious and denied the
publication mailing privileges,
forcing it to fold. In November, the
Justice Department charged
Eastman, Reed, and Dell with
conspiracy for their editorials
denouncing American intervention
in the war. A chill came over the
once buoyant community, which
soon came to feel "like a conquered country," Malcolm Cowley
wrote, whose "inhabitants were
discouraged and drank joylessly."

That same year, city officials
shattered the Village's physical
isolation by driving an extension of
Seventh Avenue south of 14th
Street—complete with a new IRT
subway line beneath the street.
The new thoroughfare not only
divided the district in two, but,
along with the new subway,
encouraged a flood of outsiders to
enter the area.

*I went to the old places. I saw
no one I had ever known, and
all was changed. The village—
our village—was dead and*

*gone. Here were young people,
as young as we once had been,
as gay and eager. They were
the new Greenwich Villagers.
They did not mind the changes,
because they had never seen
our village. Doubtless they
already knew all the things we
had so painfully learned. I saw
ourselves, in retrospect, as
touched with a miraculous
naïveté, a Late Victorian
credulousness, a faith, happy
and absurd, in the goodness
and beauty of this chaotic
universe. The young people
knew better. Well, it was their
village now; let them have it,
and make of it what they
chose!*
Floyd Dell, 1924

In the early 1920s, the Village
was reinvigorated by a stream of
new arrivals—many of them
veterans like Cowley, embarking
on what he called "the Long
Furlough." "After the war," he
wrote, "most of us drifted . . . to
the crooked streets south of
Fourteenth. . . . We came because
the living was cheap, because
friends of ours had come already
(and written us letters full of
enchantment), because it seemed
that New York was the only city
where a young writer could be
published." Though many of the
prewar Villagers were gone—dead
or exiled or simply living elsewhere—newcomers such as the
poet e. e. cummings, the critic
Edmund Wilson, and the novelist
John Dos Passos were doing their
best to uphold the community's
reputation as what one man called
"the cradle of modern American
culture." The same year *The
Masses* was shut down, the *Little
Review* moved to New York from
Chicago, the first of the self-styled
"little magazines" that would
eventually include the *Dial, The
New Masses,* and *Partisan Review*
and would make lower Manhattan
the crossroads of intellectual
debate in America for much of the
century to come.

Yet something had changed.
Floating on the tide of 1920s
prosperity, the Village was known

less for its radical politics now than for its free-spirited, bohemian way of life. Newcomers to the district threw elaborate balls—called bacchanals or pagan romps—that began at Webster Hall (also known as the Devil's Playhouse), then spilled onto the streets until early morning. A new breed of "professional Villagers" emerged, such as the Baroness Elsa von Freytag-Loringhoven, a flamboyant character known for shaving her head, painting her face, and wearing a coal scuttle, upside down, for a hat. In the Village, one magazine insisted, visitors could be sure of seeing "ladies with short hair and long fingernails, and men with long hair and short bank accounts."

To the horror of its older residents, the once insular and self-contained colony was rapidly becoming not only a caricature of itself but a popular tourist attraction. Guidebooks offered tantalizing accounts of the

district's heady philosophy of "free love," referring to the area as the Latin Quarter and Greenwich Thrillage. Tour guides, confirming outsiders' expectations with their artist's smocks and open-toed sandals, directed groups around the picturesque streets, often steering them to shops and cafés owned by friends. To cater to the flood of tourists, dozens of self-consciously picturesque tearooms sprang up, with names that suggested, one man said, a "tinted zoology"—the Black Parrot, the Purple Pup, the Green Witch, the Vermillion Hound, along with wildly decorated cabarets like the Bandit's Cave, the Nut Club, and Don Dickerman's Pirate's Den, where a coffin served as a signboard, and all the waiters dressed as buccaneers. "If you stumble and fall in the Village," one guidebook noted, "you are sure to land in a restaurant."

By the end of the decade, thanks in part to the influx of

visitors, Greenwich Village had become one of the best-known communities on earth—its very name, like Harlem's, familiar to people around the globe. But long-time residents now spoke nostalgically of the years when the Village had stood for something more than just an exotic style of life, and mourned the genuine bohemian community that seemed to be dead, or dying.

The lines between art and commerce that had helped to define the Village—so clear before the war—were now growing blurred, as the media culture arising in midtown transformed bohemia's cherished axioms of living into ingenious marketing strategies.

Thus, self-expression *and* paganism *encouraged a demand for all sorts of products—modern furniture, beach pajamas, cosmetics, colored bathrooms with toilet*

paper to match. Living for the moment *meant buying an automobile, radio, or house, using it now and paying for it tomorrow.* Female equality *was capable of doubling the consumption of products— cigarettes, for example—that had formerly been used by men alone. . . . Everything fitted into the business picture.*
Malcolm Cowley

"If the Village was really dying," Cowley recognized, "it was dying of success. It was dying because it became so popular that too many people insisted on living there. It was dying because women smoked cigarettes on the streets of the Bronx, drank gin cocktails in Omaha and had perfectly swell parties in Seattle and Middletown—in other words, because American business and the whole of middle-class America had been going Greenwich Village."

Polly's, a popular restaurant in MacDougal Alley in Greenwich Village, photographed by Jessie Tarbox Beals, 1916.

MIDTOWN

Wonder was the grace of the country. Any action could be justified by that—the wonder it was rooted in. Period followed period, and finally the wonder was that things could be built so big. Bridges, skyscrapers, fortunes, all having a life first in the marketplace, still drew on the force of wonder. But then a moment's quiet. What was it now that was built so big? Only the marketplace itself. Could there be wonder in that? The size of the con?

George W. S. Trow

Extraordinary as it was, the cultural explosion coming out of Harlem was only a part of a much vaster commercial and cultural transformation overtaking New York City in the 1920s. An economic boom unlike anything ever experienced before in American history was sweeping the nation, ushering in an era of unparalleled prosperity and propelling a massive shift in American culture.

By the end of the First World War—and thanks in part to the war itself—the problems of mass production had been largely solved. By 1919, American manufacturers had learned how to make things faster, cheaper, and in greater number than ever before.

As a flood of new consumer products came within reach of middle-income and working-class American families for the first time—refrigerators, telephones, automobiles, washing machines, vacuum cleaners, household appliances—a second Industrial Revolution got under way, a profound transformation not only in the kinds of goods being manufactured but in the way things were made, and perhaps above all, in the way they were marketed and sold.

Formerly the task was to supply the things that men wanted; the new necessity is to make men want the things which machinery must turn out if this civilization is not to perish . . . the problem before us today is not how to produce the goods, but how to produce the customers.

Samuel Strauss, 1924

Almost inevitably, the epicenter of that transformation was located in New York—in a new center of gravity called midtown, where, by 1923, the twentieth century itself was rising into the sky, and the most astonishingly creative half decade in the history of American capitalism had started to unfold.

For nearly a century, since the days of James Gordon Bennett and Horace Greeley, New York had been the undisputed center of information and communications for the entire nation. Now, supercharged by the postwar surge in prosperity, it was rapidly becoming the command center of a new kind of culture—one based not on

The elegant department stores and specialty shops that now filled midtown—such as the I. Miller shoe shop, above, at 562 Fifth Avenue—not only satisfied consumer needs but sought to generate desires with their extravagant window displays, seminars on the newest styles, and lavish advertising campaigns. I. Miller, which presented the work of Italian designers such as Andrea Perugia, further lured customers by providing free tea service every afternoon and offering women cigarettes on the house.

By the 1920s, more than 600 magazines were being published in New York, with new ones being started every month, including the *Reader's Digest*, founded in 1922 in a Greenwich Village basement by DeWitt and Lila Acheson Wallace, and *Time*, begun the following year in midtown by a pair of Yale graduates named Henry Luce and Britton Hadden. But the urbane tone of the era—what F. Scott Fitzgerald called "the Metropolitan Spirit"—was set by upscale publications such as Condé Nast's *Vogue* (right), and its new magazine, *Vanity Fair*. Bringing together glamorous photographs, society news and comment, reports from fashionable resorts and foreign capitals, and essays and articles by writers such as Dorothy Parker, Robert Benchley, Sherwood Anderson, and Aldous Huxley, the "smart" magazines aimed themselves not only at the upper classes but at those who emulated them—mainly middle-class women who aspired to the fashions and lifestyles displayed within. In 1925, a new weekly, *The New Yorker*, promised from the start to be "a reflection in words and pictures of metropolitan life, full of gaiety, wit and satire." "It expects a considerable national publication," its editor Harold Ross declared, "but this will come from people who have a metropolitan interest. It is not edited for the old lady in Dubuque."

production but on consumption, not on need but on desire—at once fed by and feeding the fantasies and dreams of an entire nation, and accelerated to infinity by the power of the new media.

One by one, the elements of a modern mass culture were being assembled in a twenty-block area of midtown Manhattan—a frankly sexualized and relentlessly commercial culture that as never before would blur the distinctions between fantasy and reality, private and public, high culture and low—extending far wider and penetrating far deeper than ever before into the conscious and unconscious dreams of the body politic of American life.

In little more than half a decade—for better or for worse—it would finish stitching together the disparate pieces of American life to form a truly national culture.

It would also make midtown, which for years had been competing with Wall Street for hegemony within the commercial universe of New York, the new center of life in Manhattan, as with remarkable speed an intricate, ultramodern nexus of office buildings, department stores, apartment houses, and hotels sprang up around the visionary transportation complex of Grand Central Terminal to service the city's new clean industries, including advertising, communica-

tions, public relations, retailing, and mass-market entertainment.

The Illustrated Daily News *is going to be your newspaper. . . . We shall give you, every day, the best and newest pictures of the interesting things that are happening in the world. . . . The story that is told by a picture can be grasped instantly.*
Daily News *editorial, June 1919*

It began with a revolution in daily journalism.

On June 29, 1919, the first issue of the *Illustrated Daily News*—its name soon shortened to the *Daily News*—hit the city's newsstands. The first tabloid newspaper in America, it was unlike anything ever seen before in New York—half the size of a traditional daily and designed to be read not over morning coffee at home but standing up on the subway or the streetcar. With its big, stark images, screaming headlines, and sensational coverage, it was designed to reach a wider audience than any paper before it, and within a matter of years, its circulation had shot up to more than a million copies a day—heralding a new and, to some, powerfully threatening force in American journalism.

Distort the world, until its news is all murder, divorce, crime, passion and chicanery. To the struggling poor present the places above as tenanted by witless millionaires and shallow adventuresses, contemptible yet glorious in their spending. Sentimentalize everything, with cynicism just beneath. In place of the full life, or the good life, or the hard life of experience, fill the mind with a phantasmagoria where easy wealth, sordid luxury, scandal, degeneracy, and drunken folly swirl through the pages in an intoxicating vulgarity.
Saturday Review of Literature

The success of the *Daily News* launched an avalanche of competitors and imitators. By 1924, seventeen daily newspapers and dozens of weeklies were pouring out of Manhattan. None of them, however, compared to the *New York Evening Graphic*, an outrageously inventive and shockingly scurrilous tabloid, begun that year by Bernarr Macfadden, an eccentric health faddist who liked to walk each day to work from his home on Central Park West—barefoot, and often carrying a forty-pound bag of sand on his back.

There had never been anything quite like the *Graphic*. *Time* magazine, founded in New York only the year before, called it "the country's outstanding example of sleazy, vulgar journalism"—an opinion with which one of the *Graphic*'s own editors readily concurred. "It is the Frankenstein monster of the newspaper world," he wrote, "a riotous, red-hot rampaging scandal sheet" that stopped at nothing to grab and hold its readers' attention. Quickly dubbed the *New York Porno-Graphic* for the relentless diet of sex, mayhem, and scandal it dished up, the *Graphic* rapidly became one of the most popular daily newspapers in America—often boosting circulation on a slow news day by simply manufacturing events.

The *Graphic*'s greatest single attraction was its star columnist, Walter Winchell, who began writing for the paper in 1924. A fast-talking ex-vaudevillian and native New Yorker who had never quite succeeded as an entertainer, Winchell made the switch to journalism in the 1920s, and in the pages of the *Graphic* almost single-handedly invented the modern gossip column. Like nothing before it, Winchell's short, telegraphic items brought together in the democratizing space of a single column all the disparate characters of big-city life: gangsters, gamblers, and bootleggers; judges, senators, and socialites; actors, singers, and movie stars; baseball players, politicians, millionaires, and their divorced wives.

Winchell wrote, the reporter and screenwriter Ben Hecht said, "like a man honking in a traffic jam." Every afternoon, he gave his readers the inside scoop in a language all his own. A new baby was a "blessed event." A wild society girl was called a "debutramp." A quick trip to Nevada for a divorce was called "Reno-vating."

What former dramatic critic and his frau tiffed audibly at 43th St. and 7th Avenue Thursday at 8:37? . . . The latest shipment of whoopee water is only fair. . . . Helen Hayes . . . Helen Hayes . . . Helen Hayes and Helen Hayes. . . . Dorothy Dilley will be divorced from her tonsils this week. . . . Fannie Brice has forty negligees. . . . Who tried to throw acid at Edna Leedom when she was at the hospital? . . . They say the recent Barrymore-

Selznick tiff started over a crack at the heebs . . . Whitney Bolton's new supply of bvd's are silky pink and orchid green things! . . . A not very reliable source reports that Scott Fitzgerald is on the water wagon. . . .

Walter Winchell

It was said that Walter Winchell did for the Great White Way what Mark Twain had done for the Mississippi River. Year after year, his power and influence grew, as his irresistible mix of gossip and scandal reached an ever widening audience, not only in New York but in cities across the country, where his column—one of the first to be nationally syndicated—was avidly followed by hundreds of thousands, and eventually millions, of readers eager to keep up with the latest juicy tidbit from the nightclubs, theaters, and speakeasies of Broadway and Times Square.

Even hardened Broadway producers like Florenz Ziegfeld, David Belasco, and the Shubert brothers lived in fear of the power of Winchell's column, which he used to make and break reputations all over town. When the Shuberts tried to ban him from their theaters, Winchell replied, "If they won't let me come to their openings, I'll wait five days and come to their closings."

Okay, America! Good evening, Mr. and Mrs. North America and all ships at sea. Let's go to press. . . .

Walter Winchell radio broadcast

Within a few years, Winchell's staccato, rapid-fire delivery was not only being read but heard—and by an audience many times greater than that reached by the printed page. As powerful as the new tabloids were, nothing would extend the awesome reach and penetrating power of the media in New York more than the stunning invention already radiating invisibly from the tops of several midtown skyscrapers. In the years to come, radio would perfect New York's already immense hold on the American consciousness—reaching not hundreds of thousands but tens of millions of people at a time, not only on the streets but in the intimacy and privacy of their own homes.

Drawing upon and pulling together every strand of cultural and commercial power in New York from Broadway to Harlem to Wall

By the 1920s, American journalism had been transformed by the advent of New York tabloids such as the *New York Evening Graphic* (opposite, left and right)—whose most popular feature was Walter Winchell's daily gossip column (lower left). When Winchell left the *Evening Graphic* in 1929 for its rival, the *Daily Mirror*, the *Graphic*'s circulation dropped by 200,000, while the *Mirror*'s increased by the same number. In May 1930, Winchell grew even more famous—and powerful—when he began broadcasting his column on national radio (lower right), delivering his breathless, telegraphic accounts of New York nightlife to tens of millions of listeners in towns and villages across the country.

Street to the new advertising industries arrayed around Madison Avenue, radio fused as never before three of the most powerful industries in the city—commerce, culture, and communications—to create an instrument of mass marketing more powerful by far than anything ever conceived.

The immense selling potential of radio was revealed in the summer of 1922, just two years after the first program went on the air, when on August 22, the New York radio station WEAF ran the first paid commercial in broadcasting history—a ten-minute advertisement lauding the virtues of new cooperative garden apartments in a semisuburban community in Queens called Jackson Heights. The response was overwhelming. The advertiser—which had paid fifty dollars for the air time—quickly sold $150,000 worth of apartments, and commercial broadcasting was born, built around its ability to deliver to advertisers a mass audience of consumers, far larger than any ever gathered before.

In 1926, the power of the new medium increased exponentially when a Russian-Jewish immigrant New Yorker named David Sarnoff, a visionary thirty-six-year-old entrepreneur working for the Radio Corporation of America, came up with the idea of linking more than a hundred local stations into a single national system—a *network*—capable of blanketing most of the country at once.

In November of that year, Sarnoff's National Broadcasting Company was launched with great fanfare from the ballroom of the Waldorf-Astoria. One year later, the rival Columbia Broadcasting System was founded by William S. Paley, the son of a wealthy Philadelphia cigar manufacturer. Like NBC, the new network would be headquartered in midtown Manhattan, where it could tap directly into the city's endless pools of talent, from the popular comedians and singers of vaudeville and Broadway to the classical musicians of the New York Philharmonic and the Metropolitan Opera.

Through newspapers and magazines, advertisers had been able to reach tens of thousands of people; through radio, they could now reach tens of *millions*. By the end of the decade, a top-rated radio show on NBC drew more than 40 million listeners, more than half the adults in the country.

The first radio network broadcast in history began at 8:00 p.m. on November 15, 1926, with the inaugural program of the National Broadcasting Company (NBC). The concept of linking local stations into a national chain had been the inspiration of David Sarnoff, a New York radio entrepreneur (above right, on the night of the broadcast, standing at the far left), who became the head of the new network. Twenty-five stations in 21 cities carried the program, which included performances by the Metropolitan Opera, the New York Philharmonic, and the vaudeville team of Weber and Fields. At left, a broadcast booth at the rival Columbia Broadcasting System (CBS), whose main studios, like NBC's, were located in midtown Manhattan.

Driven by the vast new scale of radio audiences, the advertising industry in New York exploded, as for the first time products could be marketed and sold to the entire nation at once. Madison Avenue, a commercial boulevard in midtown Manhattan, soon became synonymous with the constellation of commercial enterprises rapidly concentrating there, from advertising itself to marketing, public relations, and the new science of demographics.

Sell them their dreams. Sell them what they longed for and hoped for and almost despaired of having. . . . Sell them this hope and you won't have to worry about selling them goods.
Helen Landon Cass

By 1926, nothing seemed out of reach of the creative and commercial powers spiraling out of midtown Manhattan.

With business in the ascendant as never before, New York was leading the country into what Wall Street economists confidently called an "era of permanent prosperity."

Edward Bernays, Sigmund Freud's nephew and the father of public relations, sought to convince Americans that industrialists and businessmen stood on the very highest rung of the evolutionary ladder. The year before, Bruce Barton, the son of a preacher and senior partner of BBD&O, now one of the most powerful advertising agencies in New York, published a book that argued that Christ himself was a forerunner of the Madison Avenue ad man. "He would," Barton wrote, "be a national advertiser today, I am sure, as he was the great advertiser of his own day."

That movement, from wonder to the wonder that a country should be so big, to the wonder that a building could be so big, to the last, small wonder, that a marketplace could be so big—that was the movement of history. Then there was a change. The direction of the movement paused, sat silent for a moment, and reversed. From that moment, vastness was the start not the finish. The movement now began with the fact of two hundred million, and the movement was toward a unit of one alone. Groups of more than one were now united not by a common history but by common characteristics. History became the history of demographics, the history of no history.

George W. S. Trow

Who shall paint New York? Who? New York, grandiose and glittering—the modern Wonder City of dynamic pulses, wireless, magnetism, electricity and tempered steel. . . . There she stands, matchless and overwhelming. This to modern artists is the task that beckons with the fatalistic fascination of the unattainable.

Henry Tyrell

"Americans have come over to us," a Parisian art critic observed in 1915. "Now we are coming over to you." In the years following the First World War, the European painters and sculptors who had pioneered modern art began crossing the Atlantic in increasing numbers—eager to experience for themselves the city that had become the supreme modernist creation in the world.

What they found amazed them. New York, the painter Francis Picabia wrote, was "the Cubist city . . . the Futurist city." On his first visit, Henri Matisse was "in complete ecstasy . . . truly electrified." Marcel Duchamp boasted of not having painted a single picture since he had arrived. "New York itself," he said, "is already a complete work of art."

It gushes up. I cannot forget New York, a vertical city, now that I have had the happiness of seeing it, raised in the sky. [It is] the first place in the world on the scale of the new times, the work yard of our era.

Le Corbusier

The Europeans were not alone in their enchantment, as American artists of every kind responded powerfully to what many felt was their country's most exalted creation. "My city, my beloved, my white!" Ezra Pound wrote. "Listen to me, and I will breathe into thee a soul / And thou shalt live forever."

By the early 1920s, American modernists like Stuart Davis, Arthur Dove, Joseph Stella, and Charles Demuth were converging on the city, thrilled by the infinitely

plastic, constantly changing landscape of Manhattan—and by the challenge of translating the powerful dynamism of its man-made geometry to canvas. In 1924, the painter Charles Sheeler and the photographer Paul Strand—certain the kinetic energy of the city could never be captured by traditional forms—turned to film. The result was their mesmerizing eight-minute cinematic portrait of New York, inspired by Walt Whitman and entitled—in homage to the great poet of becoming—"Manhatta."

Even as Strand and Sheeler's cameras rolled, the stunning New York skyline was changing shape again as, propelled by the great real estate boom of the '20s, a breathtaking metamorphosis was under way. "The twenty-story skyscrapers which impressed the European visitor in 1910," the architect Harvey Wiley Corbett wrote in 1925, "have either been demolished or else completely overshadowed in American architecture's skyward race. Each month sees an old landmark tumbled into ruins and in its place a lean steel skeleton ascending toward new heights."

The new round of construction was not only the greatest building boom in the city's history, but the first to be shaped by a new factor in American life—zoning. Until 1915, no law in New York—or any American city—had limited the height or size of new buildings. That year, however, the new Equitable Life Insurance Company headquarters on lower Broadway had risen 40 stories straight up from the sidewalk—casting a shadow four blocks long, plunging 24 neighboring buildings into semi-permanent gloom, and reducing the value of adjacent properties.

Within a year, New York City officials had passed the first zoning law in the United States, a landmark measure that required that buildings narrow as they rose—stepping back according to a formula that varied with the width of the street, to preserve a

From the Shelton Looking North, photographed by Alfred Stieglitz, 1927.

measure of daylight for the sidewalks and structures below. Once a structure pulled back to 25 percent of its building site, however, it was allowed to soar as high as engineering could take it.

The results were nothing less than breathtaking. Powered by the tremendous building boom of the '20s—at once limited and set free by the invisible sculpting hand of the 1916 zoning law—the skyline of New York simply took flight, acquiring a disciplined grandeur, stylized consistency, and sheer height unlike anything that had come before.

As each new developer laid out his building to the maximum shape and size allowed, the new law began to bring a dazzling new symmetry to the skies above Manhattan. Along the great avenues of the Upper East and West sides long lines of majestic apartment houses soon marched to the horizon—residential canyons as regular and grand as any found in Paris, only twice as high. To the south, the requirement that buildings set

back as they rose was turning midtown into a sublime urban landscape of giant staircases, mountainlike towers and slender peaks. "The zoning law has resulted in an unforeseen revolution," one critic wrote, "a city whose streets are lined with terraced cliffs of Gothic and Renaissance workmanship, the terraces abloom with flowers and shrubs and trees; a city of a multitude of hanging gardens."

Significantly, the towers now rising in midtown included not only office buildings but sleek new apartment houses and residential hotels, which lured tenants with the promise of a uniquely modern way of life—at once located in the heart of the city's bustle, yet floating serenely above it.

To [its] high-perched denizen the city sounds become somewhat softened . . . he sees his environment not as a nearby limiting wall, but as a series of distant diminishing silhouettes and perspectives;

he receives the sun's first rays long before they penetrate into the city's canyons, and all day long he gets the bright radiance of an unobstructed and unafflicted sky. He can breakfast looking down on a wilderness of human habitations, and dine looking off on a firmament of lights. [He] commands by day a view . . . of extraordinary interest and variety, and by night of beauty and mystery, for then the harsh jazz of the jagged skylines is muted by a velvet curtain of darkness painted with a silver river and bespangled with innumerable points of lights.
Claude Bragdon

By 1925, the towering man-made landscape of midtown Manhattan had come to seem like God's own work on the eighth day of creation.

That year, Alfred Stieglitz—at 61, the most famous photographer in the world—and his wife, a little-known 37-year-old Wisconsin-born painter and commercial artist named Georgia O'Keeffe, moved from their brownstone on lower Fifth Avenue to an apartment on the 28th floor of the Shelton Hotel, at Lexington and 49th Street, in the heart of midtown.

New York is madder than ever. . . . Georgia and I somehow don't seem to be of New York—nor of anywhere. We live high up in the Shelton Hotel. . . . We feel as if we were out at midocean—All so quiet except for the wind—& the trembling shaking hulk of steel in which we live—It's a wonderful place.
Alfred Stieglitz

The couple's new home would exert a profound influence on their work. For a quarter of a century, Stieglitz had been urging American photographers—Edward Steichen, Paul Strand, and others—to break away from genteel European pictorial traditions and meet the American city on its own terms, in what he called the Photo-Secession. His own images had

East River from the Shelton, by Georgia O'Keeffe, 1927–28.

captured New York's soaring towers as nothing else had—though like most views of the skyline, they had been taken from the street or river, tilted up to capture the spires looming above. Now, from his 28th-floor eyrie, Stieglitz sought to capture the skyward thrust of Manhattan not from below but eye to eye—from a vantage that was itself often lost in low-flying clouds.

O'Keeffe herself was no less mesmerized by the shapes arising outside her window. "I had never lived so high before," she said, "and was so excited that I began talking about trying to paint New York. Of course, I was told that it

was an impossible idea—even the men hadn't done too well with it." Recalling the struggle of the modern artists to render the skyline's complex and ever changing shape, Stieglitz and his friends suggested that O'Keeffe choose a more congenial and less daunting subject—flowers, perhaps.

Stung to the quick, O'Keeffe took up the challenge and in 1925 began an astonishing series of urban views—soaring vertical images of Manhattan's newest skyscrapers, including views of the Shelton itself, and broad panoramas of the city as seen from her midtown perch. Reveling in the city's exquisite Jazz Age

modernity, she sensed at the same time a certain timelessness, and sought to render as a kind of natural landscape the peaks and canyons of midtown, spangled by sunspots and full moons, the plains of industrial Queens spreading to the east beneath its own atmosphere of polluted air.

In 1926, the couple decided to take another apartment at the Shelton, on the thirtieth floor, two floors above. In a letter telling her sister of the move, O'Keeffe declared, "I am going to live as high as I can this year."

BROADWAY

It was three years before we saw New York again. As the ship glided up the river, the city burst thunderously upon us in the early dusk—the white glacier of lower New York swooping down like a strand of a bridge to rise into uptown New York, a miracle of foamy light suspended by the stars. A band started to play on deck, but the majesty of the city made the march trivial and tinkling. From that moment I knew that New York, however often I might leave it, was home.

F. Scott Fitzgerald, 1927

By 1927, New York City held sway over the culture and economy of the United States as never before. Never had the power of the metropolis extended so widely—or penetrated so deeply—into the conscious and unconscious life of the nation. Never before had the city's cultural and economic forces been so intertwined and transfused.

The creative ferment of places like Harlem, where art was aspiring to the condition of commerce, was now reaching every corner of America propelled by the explosion of media in midtown, where commerce was now aspiring to the condition of art.

"Old American music and dances," the automobile magnate Henry Ford complained, "are being rapidly swamped into oblivion by the commercially promoted jazz music emanating from New York."

Everything came together on Broadway, where by 1927 the city's immense artistic and commercial forces had been fused into one dazzling incandescent glow.

As the most creative decade in the history of Broadway came to a stunning crescendo, the values of the relentlessly commercial and democratic metropolis would find expression in an extraordinary musical form, invented in late-nineteenth-century New York.

Witnessing the medley of cultural styles converging on the Bowery almost a century before, Walt Whitman had predicted that they would one day give rise to a "native grand opera in America." Now, in the Roaring Twenties, that opera would finish being born, as the Broadway musical came of age and one of the greatest flowerings of musical culture in American history began.

Everything that was best about the sprawling commercial city came together in the Broadway musical, which could only have arisen in New York. The culmination of a long tradition stretching from minstrelsy and vaudeville to Tin Pan Alley, it drew upon and blended together the extraordinary range of musical forms that had been gathering in the city for decades: the ragtime of Scott Joplin and blues of W. C. Handy, the Viennese operetta of Victor Herbert, the Irish American show songs of George M. Cohan, and above all, the syncopated dance numbers of an immigrant Russian Jew named Israel Baline, who had changed his name to Irving Berlin and, in the years just before World War I, helped to pioneer the modern popular song.

Forged in the teeming cultural cauldron of the city—and arising to a remarkable degree from a group of worldly, culturally ambitious New York Jews—it celebrated the never-ending process of transaction, transformation, and exchange that was the heart and soul of city life.

In little more than a decade, one of the most extraordinary constellations of musical talent ever assembled on the planet would come together on Broadway, including Irving Berlin,

No pair of men did more to transform American popular music than George Gershwin (left) and Irving Berlin (right), seen together in this 1928 view. Born Israel Baline in Russia in 1888, Berlin had grown up on the Lower East Side and worked as a singer and piano player in cheap Chinatown saloons before writing his first hit, "Alexander's Ragtime Band," in 1911. In later years he would become the country's most successful songwriter, producing many of the anthems of American life, including "God Bless America," "White Christmas," and "Easter Parade." ("Berlin," one rival complained, "has used up all the holidays.") Gershwin, eleven years younger than Berlin, deeply admired the older songwriter, to whom he once applied—unsuccessfully—for a job as an assistant. A product of the Lower East Side like Berlin, Gershwin shared many of his idol's influences—notably the syncopated rhythms of African American ragtime—and would build upon Berlin's innovations in his own work even while adapting them to complex new musical forms. "George Gershwin," Berlin later acknowledged, "is the only songwriter I know who became a composer."

Jerome Kern, Richard Rodgers, Lorenz Hart, Oscar Hammerstein II, George and Ira Gershwin, and Cole Porter, the lone WASP from Indiana. Dedicated not to the purity of a single style but to the exhilarating possibilities of many cultures coming together, the music they created would bring together as never before the mainstream and the marginal in American life, knitting city and country, immigrant and native-born, black culture and white, high culture and low into a quintessentially American form.

> We'll have Manhattan
> The Bronx and Staten
> Island too.
> It's lovely going through
> The Zoo.
> It's very fancy
> On old Delancey
> Street, you know.
> The subway charms us so,
> When balmy breezes blow
> To and fro.
> And tell me what street
> Compares with Mott Street
> In July?
> Sweet pushcarts gently gliding by.
> The great big city's a wond'rous toy,
> Just made for a girl and boy,
> We'll turn Manhattan
> Into an isle of joy.
> Lorenz Hart, "Manhattan," 1925

Built around often intoxicatingly lyrical songs that combined sophisticated wordplay with common slang and merged the rhythms and melodies of three continents, the message of the new Broadway musicals was clear. Being American meant being mixed—crossing over—borrowing and commingling to create new forms. The essence of America, in short, lay in New York.

No one in the '20s would explore New York's musical culture more daringly—or attempt more passionately to fuse its myriad strands into one transcendent whole—than the dashing, prodigiously gifted boy from the Lower East Side: George Gershwin.

The son of Russian Jewish immigrants who had moved twenty-eight times in his youth, he had grown up "in the heart of noise," his friend and colleague John Green said. "He hears that

noise and finds music in it." Absorbing every musical current in the city from the time he was six—from ragtime and the blues to marching bands and opera—he had his first show on Broadway in 1919, at the age of twenty, and never looked back.

> New York is a meeting place, a rendezvous of the nations. I'd like to catch the rhythm of these interfusing peoples, to show them clashing and blending. I'd like to write of the melting pot, of New York City itself, with its blend of native and immigrant strains . . . its many kinds of music, black and white, Eastern and Western.
> George Gershwin

Over the next ten years an unending river of music poured from him—including nine musicals and hundreds of songs, many written side by side with his bookish older brother, Ira, a superb lyricist in his own right. In 1924, Gershwin's hit show *Lady, Be Good*—which included the song "Fascinating Rhythm"—featured his childhood friend Fred Astaire and Astaire's sister Adele, and it took the city by storm. Another hit show, *Girl Crazy*, launched the career of a onetime stenographer named Ethel Merman—who could hold a note longer, one man said, than the Chase National Bank, and who belted out the showstopping tune "I Got Rhythm" with a power that left audiences stunned.

> Shortly after half past seven, arrivals from every direction seem to spring from the very ground itself. By eight o'clock the street is full, and notwithstanding a hundred thousand enter the theaters and other places of amusement, [while] additional arrivals take their place and mix in with the surging strollers. Barnum in his palmiest days could never draw such hosts as assemble on the Great White Way every clear evening.
> W. Parker Chase

"New York," the humorist James Thurber said, "is first and foremost a city of theatergoers." Year after year, the popular appeal and democratic reach of the Broadway musical spiraled upward. In 1924 alone, twelve new theaters went up on the blocks around Times Square to meet the growing demand. By 1926, no fewer than sixty-six Broadway theaters were active, along with hundreds more vaudeville houses, music halls, burlesque houses and movie

As soon as dusk falls, Broadway bursts into a scintillation which has no equal anywhere in the world. [It] is the apotheosis of electricity. It makes your head reel; it flares, flows, writhes, rolls, blinks, winks, flickers, changes color, vanishes and sparkles again. Red, white, green, yellow, blue, orange, purple, they urge, solicit, press, command you to go somewhere and buy something. Bottles of beer appear and transform themselves into dwarfs drinking; showers of gold peanuts fall from the skies, dragons breathing smoke become a film title; cigarettes are ignited, automobiles materialize. Mountains, towns, lamaseries, men with top hats, nude women with teeth, spring into existence and are wiped off into oblivion.

Odette Keun

Opening Night, Ziegfeld Follies, 1926, by Howard A. Thain, depicts the scene of pandemonium outside the premiere of **No Foolin',** the 1926 edition of the Ziegfeld Follies, at the Globe Theater on Broadway and 46th Street. Since 1907, the celebrated producer and impresario Florenz Ziegfeld had presented his annual Follies—spectacular musical revues featuring lavish sets, hit songs, comedy routines, and an array of statuesque, barely clad Ziegfeld Girls. Combining elements of burlesque and vaudeville with performances by the biggest stars in show business—Eddie Cantor, Al Jolson, W. C. Fields, Will Rogers, Fanny Brice—Ziegfeld's shows were regularly among the most popular theatrical attractions in the city. At left, newsreel cameras record the bedlamlike scene for the benefit of movie audiences across the country.

Times Square, looking north from 46th Street, 1927. By the 1920s, Times Square had become the undisputed headquarters of an empire of popular entertainment that stretched from coast to coast and included theater, vaudeville, burlesque, movies, music publishing, and radio broadcasting. Each season, more than 200 plays were presented in the district's 66 theaters, including new dramas by Eugene O'Neill, Maxwell Anderson, Robert Sherwood, Edna Ferber, and Elmer Rice, and comedies by George S. Kaufman, Marc Connelly, Ben Hecht, and Charlie MacArthur.

theaters. Each night, a quarter million people flooded Times Square, looking for entertainment and diversion.

In 1927, Broadway's peak year, 264 new plays and musicals opened, including new musicals by Irving Berlin, the Gershwins, and Rodgers and Hart. The day after Christmas that year, eleven new plays opened *in one night*—straining the city's supply of regular theater critics to the limit, and forcing desperate newspaper editors to send out sportswriters in their stead—"not that anyone noticed," the lyricist Alan Jay Lerner remarked.

The next day, December 27, only two shows opened, but one of them—*Show Boat*, by Jerome Kern and Oscar Hammerstein II—would change musical theater forever.

It was like nothing ever seen before on Broadway, a daring and darkly romantic musical saga, set on a nineteenth-century Mississippi riverboat, that took as its subject the mixing of the races and the subjugation of blacks in American life. At its heart was a wrenching story of forbidden love between a white riverboat gambler and the mysterious actress he marries— who turns out to be part African American. In the shocking climax of the first act, as a sheriff arrives to arrest the woman for the crime of miscegenation, the gambler grabs his wife's hand, cuts and sucks the blood from her finger, then declares that he, too, has black blood within him.

Show Boat was a stunning success from the start, touring Europe and America, and running for 572 performances on Broadway—the third longest running show of the era.

It also marked a critical breakthrough in American culture. Its most powerful philosophical message was placed in the mouth of a black stevedore named Joe, who in the haunting, hypnotic song "Ol' Man River," sang of the abiding continuities of life that, like a great river, unite all people.

A parable of racial division in America—created by Jewish New Yorkers for a middle-class American audience—*Show Boat* made explicit the themes of racial and cultural mixing that underlay the musical theater itself. Even more daringly, it suggested to Americans that what made their nation unique was not its purity but its constant intermingling—a never-ending

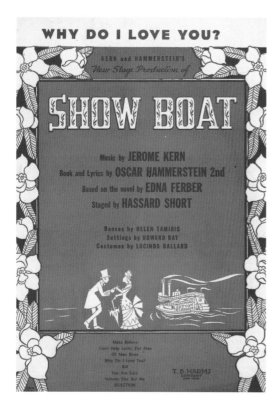

WHY DO I LOVE YOU?

KERN and HAMMERSTEIN'S
New Stage Production of

SHOW BOAT

Music by JEROME KERN
Book and Lyrics by OSCAR HAMMERSTEIN 2nd
Based on the novel by EDNA FERBER
Staged by HASSARD SHORT

Dances by HELEN TAMIRIS
Settings by HOWARD BAY
Costumes by LUCINDA BALLARD

Make Believe
Can't Help Lovin' Dat Man
Ol' Man River
Why Do I Love You?
Bill
You Are Love
Nobody Else But Me
SELECTION

T. B. HARMS
COMPANY
NEW YORK

process of migration, crossing, and transplantation that had been going on in New York for almost three hundred years.

> *Every race in every age, has picked out some one street, one square, one Acropolis mount or Waterloo bridge, to celebrate its most glowing literature. Let it be known to the Americanologist of three thousand a.d. that we New Yorkers idolized a strange, boomerang-shaped, nightly fiery thoroughfare of broken hearts and blessed events, which we called Broadway. That will explain us.*
>
> Gilbert W. Gabriel,
> *New York American*

Show Boat would set the pattern for the great American musicals of the decades to come, not only integrating story and song into a coherent whole for the first time but bringing the marginal into the mainstream of American popular culture as never before. The celebrated shows of the Gershwins, Porter, Berlin, and Rodgers and Hammerstein to come would expand and transcend the mainstream mass culture they also helped define, forging an image of the common ground and higher unity toward which that culture, at its best, might aspire.

RHAPSODY

> *Having been born in New York and grown up among New Yorkers, I have heard the voice of [America's] soul. It spoke to me on the streets, in school, at the theater. In the chorus of city sounds I heard it. . . . Strains from the latest concert, the cracked tones of the hurdy gurdy, the wail of a street singer, the obbligato of a broken violin . . . old music and new music, forgotten melodies and the craze of the moment, bits of opera, Russian folks songs, Spanish ballads, chansons, ragtime ditties combined in a mighty chorus in my inner ear. And through and over it all I heard, faint at first, loud at last, the soul of . . . America.*
>
> George Gershwin

In the end, the most transcendent musical expression of the age did not occur on the Broadway stage but in a revolutionary work first performed in a classical concert hall on Forty-second Street and Sixth Avenue.

In early January 1924, George Gershwin was surprised to read an article in the *Tribune* that described him as hard at work on a new "jazz concerto," to be performed by the bandleader Paul Whiteman. A few months before, he had absentmindedly promised to deliver the piece for Whiteman's concert "An Experiment in

Sheet music for Jerome Kern and Oscar Hammerstein II's "Why Do I Love You," from *Show Boat*, 1927. Though rivaled now by new entertainment forms like radio and phonograph records, music publishing remained an enormous industry in New York, selling as many as 2 billion copies of sheet music a year. For decades, the home of the industry—known as Tin Pan Alley—had been a block of 28th Street between Sixth Avenue and Broadway, where the city's biggest publishers were clustered side by side. Walking past the open windows and hearing a dozen songwriters all plugging their work at once, the composer Morris Rosenfeld had compared the din to "the crash of tin pans." The name stuck—even after the publishers relocated to Times Square in the early years of the century.

George Gershwin in the Whitehall Hotel on Broadway and 100th Street, 1925. No show-business party in 1920s New York was complete without George Gershwin sitting at the piano, showing off his latest compositions. "I've never seen a man happier, more bursting with the sheer joy of living," the publisher Bennett Cerf said, "than George was when he was playing his songs." "George's music gets around so much before an opening," the playwright George S. Kaufman quipped, "that the first night audience think it's a revival."

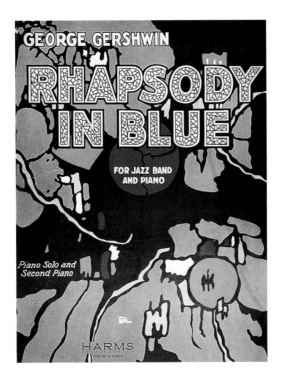

Sheet music for *Rhapsody in Blue*, 1924. "In the *Rhapsody*," Gershwin said later, "I tried to express our manner of living, the tempo of our modern life with its speed and chaos and vitality." The sheet music for *Rhapsody in Blue*, considered a difficult piece to play, sold remarkably well, earning Gershwin about a quarter million dollars during its first ten years.

When the last thunderous chord died away, the audience burst into tumultuous applause. Critics from some of the New York papers were less than flattering, calling the melodies trite, feeble, lifeless, derivative, stale, and inexpressive. But one writer called it "greater than Stravinsky's *Rite of Spring*," and the public itself never had any doubts. In 1924 alone, there would be eighty-four performances of Gershwin's *Rhapsody in Blue*, and when the piece was released as a record in June, sales quickly topped a million and kept right on rising.

THE STEEPLE

Its magazines go everywhere, standardizing ideas; its slang invades the remotest recesses, standardizing speech; its melodies are in every home, standardizing entertainment; the very thought of Broadway, the Main Street of all America, thrills millions who are scattered far and wide.

Collinson Owen

Modern Music," then quickly forgotten all about it.

Now, with just thirty-six days to go, he raced to prepare what he called *An American Rhapsody*. "I heard it as a sort of a musical kaleidoscope," he later said, "of our vast melting pot, . . . of our blues, our metropolitan madness." It was his brother, Ira, who gave the piece its name—*Rhapsody in Blue*.

On February 12, 1924, the cream of New York's musical establishment—including Jascha Heifetz, Igor Stravinsky, Leopold Stokowski, and Sergei Rachmaninoff—gathered at the Aeolian Hall on Forty-second Street for the premiere performance.

It lasted just twenty minutes. Gershwin himself performed several of the bewilderingly intricate piano cadenzas from memory; in the last-minute rush, there had been no time to transcribe them all.

Then stepped upon the stage, sheepishly, a lank and dark young man—George Gershwin. He was to play the piano part in the first public performance of his Rhapsody in Blue *for piano and orchestra. This composition shows extraordinary talent, just as it also shows a young composer with aims that go far beyond those of his ilk, struggling with a form of which he is far from being master. . . .*

Olin Downes

Since the dawn of civilization, every society had had to construct for its members a sense of the collective, of what the larger group they belonged to was. By 1927, New York had become not merely the capital of American culture but the place where the very idea of what it meant to be an American was forged, then beamed out to the rest of the nation and the world.

Half a millennium before, inhabitants of a medieval village, wandering in the countryside outside of town, knew where they came from by pointing to the steeple rising up above the tree line. Now New York had become the steeple rising above the skyline of American culture, the place to which Americans looked, for better and for worse, to understand who they were and where they came from.

Gazing on that image, many people were attracted by what they saw, and many others frightened and appalled. But few could ignore it or take their eyes off it for long.

What, indeed, is New York? Throughout the land it is the target for the scorn, suspicion, and antipathy of the villager or provincial. At the same time it is his pride and boast . . . and with or without his cognizance the arbiter of his manners and thoughts. It designs his clothes, it supplies his music, in large part his books and magazines—even his newspaper has New York's imprimatur on all but the local news. He may berate it as the temple of Mammon, as a hotbed of vice and iniquity, as foreign, continental, un-American. But he projects his local hotel on the model of its great caravansaries. Its Woolworth and Flatiron Buildings are national monuments to him. Its Broadway is reproduced in the "gay white way" of his own town. Its business axioms become his own, its speed, its "pep," its magnificence, its idolatry of success his constant admiration and inspiration.

Ernest Gruening, 1922

And there was something more. The 1920 census had revealed that for the first time in history, more Americans lived in the city than in the countryside. In the coming decade, the move from farm to city would accelerate still more, as the nation's urban population increased by another 17 million.

"Every town dreams of becoming a city," Sherwood Anderson wrote in 1921. "In America, every impulse is toward bigness. Few want to remain small, take life as it is. The movies call. The lighted streets call."

By the early 1920s, two thousand young men and women from around the country were pouring into New York each week, as the great railway stations of midtown replaced Ellis Island as the major portal to the metropolis.

All the country, the ambitious and the eager, the want-to-be wealthy and the would-be smart, have their eyes on Manhattan Island—the mecca and model for the continent. If people must be judged by what they want as well as by what they are, then at least half the residents of the United States are New Yorkers.

The Nation

You can identify the boys and girls, if you stand in Grand Central or Pennsylvania Station and watch their behavior as they step from the train. They hesitate a moment, oblivious to the crowds, looking upward, gripping their bags and bundles, hearing New York, sensing it. They seldom go back.

National Geographic

CELEBRITY

By 1927, the tempo of the city had changed sharply. The uncertainties of 1920 were drowned in a steady golden roar and many of our friends had grown wealthy. But the restlessness of New York in 1927 approached hysteria. The parties were bigger; the shows were broader, the buildings were higher, the morals were looser and the liquor was cheaper; but all these benefits did not really minister to much delight. Young people wore out early—they were hard and languid at twenty-one . . . and none of them contributed anything new. . . . Many people who were not alcoholics were lit up four days out of seven, and frayed nerves were strewn everywhere. . . . Most of my friends drank too much—the more they were in tune with the times the more they drank.

F. Scott Fitzgerald

Looking back, no one could ever quite remember when things started spinning out of control.

By 1927, as the great boom of the '20s moved into its fifth consecutive year, and the city continued its dizzying upward climb, an air of unreality began to take hold. Drunk on the intoxicating promises of the decade, many had come to believe that anything was possible—and little of what they saw around them encouraged them to abandon that dream.

In the skies over Manhattan, buildings and airplanes now soared to dizzying heights, in apparent defiance of the laws of gravity, while invisible bundles of sound, propagated from the tops of the tallest towers, traveled everywhere in the blink of an eye—defying the limits of time and space—and transforming, almost instantaneously, ordinary mortals into national celebrities.

What skyscrapers were to the city streets, fame was to the city's people, and as the desire to get up higher grew stronger, the hunger for celebrity increased, fed by the first culture in the world to be completely saturated by the media, whose massive reach pandered to the dream that anyone might become—like an airplane or skyscraper—larger than life, seen from afar, and looked up to in awe by the masses.

Every yearning of the age came together on May 20, 1927, when an obscure twenty-five-

The June 13, 1927, parade for Charles Lindbergh after his solo transatlantic flight was one of the largest celebrations in the city's history, with as many as 4 million people turning out for the event. The practice of blanketing the skies of lower Manhattan with ticker tape had begun back in 1886 during the parade up Broadway following the dedication of the Statue of Liberty. Someone got the idea of tossing out the long strands of paper that gathered at the foot of the office stock tickers all day long, and a new tradition was born. During Lindbergh's parade, an estimated 3.5 million pounds of paper were sent twirling down to the streets. "New York is yours, Colonel Lindbergh," Mayor Jimmy Walker told the young pilot after giving him the keys to the city on the steps of city hall. "I don't give it to you. You won it. . . . Before you go," he added, "will you provide us with a new street-cleaning department to clean up the mess?"

year-old airmail pilot from Little Falls, Minnesota, took off from a muddy airfield called Roosevelt Field, just east of New York, on the first solo flight across the Atlantic—and flew straight into the heart of the city's deepest dreams of ethereal transcendence.

In the spring of '27, something bright and alien flashed across the sky. A young Minnesotan who seemed to have had nothing to do with his generation did a heroic thing, and for a moment people set down their glasses in country clubs and speakeasies and thought of their old best dreams. Maybe there was a way out by flying, maybe our restless blood could find frontiers in the illimitable air. But by that time we were all pretty well committed; and the Jazz Age continued; we would all have one more.

F. Scott Fitzgerald

On his return to New York three weeks later, Charles Lindbergh was greeted by the biggest and most delirious ticker-tape parade the city had ever seen. Four million people jammed the canyons of lower Broadway to cheer the conquering hero and to strew his path with an estimated 3.5 million pounds of ticker tape—ten times more than was showered on veterans returning in 1919.

"Everywhere within the bounds of this metropolis," the *Daily News* reported, "all eyes are bent upon Lindbergh."

Even the normally restrained *New York Times* compared Lindbergh's achievement to the landing of Noah's Ark and the discovery of Moses in the bulrushes. A *New York Evening World* editorial called it "the greatest feat of a solitary man in the records of the human race."

People told me that the New York reception would be the biggest of all but I had no idea it was going to be so much more overwhelming than all the others. As a general rule I am a fairly calm sort of fellow, but when the Macom *reached Battery Park and I saw the crowd I admit I was moved. Only New York could have produced such a welcome. It beat a snowstorm all to pieces.*

Charles Lindbergh

The publicity machine . . . [scanning] the horizon constantly . . . for the event which may become the next nine days' wonder . . . is an engine that does not flood the world with light. On the contrary it is like the beam of a powerful lantern which plays . . . capriciously upon the course of events, throwing now this and now that into brilliant relief, but leaving the rest in comparative darkness.

Walter Lippmann

By 1927, the craving for celebrity had reached fever pitch in New York—and to feed the public's increasingly insatiable appetite for sensation, the city's immense publicity engine seemed to have fused into a single, continuously operating machine—and the city itself to have become a giant stage for one mass-media frenzy after another.

Begun in New York decades before, the ticker-tape parade had now become a numbingly routine publicity event, overseen by the city's "official greeter," a handsome and exquisitely dapper department store executive named Grover Whalen, whose job it was to escort visiting dignitaries and celebrities from the Battery to the steps of city hall.

Up lower Broadway an open car moves slowly through the yelling throng and on its pulled-back hood, laughing, waving into the snowstorm that flutters thickly downward from high-up windows, sits a returned aviator, explorer, movie actor, champion chess player, the first man to walk the length of Manhattan backwards.

WPA Guide to New York City

The middle distance fell away, so the grids (from small to large) that had supported the middle distance fell into disuse and ceased to be understandable. Two grids remained. The grid of two hundred million and the grid of intimacy. Everything else fell into disuse. There was a national life—a shimmer of national life—and intimate life. The distance between these two grids was very great. The distance was very frightening. People did not want to measure it. People began to lose a sense of what distance was and of what the usefulness of distance might be.

George W. S. Trow

Bombarded by the new mass media with the details—real and imaginary—of the private lives of strangers, people sometimes felt closer to movie stars than to their own kith and kin.

When the ravishingly handsome film star, Rudolph Valentino—the greatest idol of the age—died suddenly at thirty-one at the very peak of his career, thirty thousand desperate fans tried to storm Frank Campbell's funeral parlor on Sixty-sixth Street and Broadway, breaking plate-glass windows and ripping buttons from clothing on the film star's corpse.

Mounted police rode in, but the mob fought back, leaving more than a hundred injured. When order was finally restored, the line waiting in the pouring rain to file past Valentino's now closed casket stretched eleven blocks, including mourners from every class and social station.

Al Smith's wife came to pay her last respects. So did Mrs. Angeline Celestina, a twenty-two-year-old mother of two, who after the funeral returned to her tenement on Cherry Street, drank iodine, shot herself twice, and bled to death lying on a pile of Valentino's pictures.

In March 1927, the press and public went wild again when a middle-class housewife from Queens Village named Ruth Snyder—a chilly blond, as the reporter Damon Runyon put it, alleged to be having a "hot love affair" with a corset salesman named Henry Judd Grey—

bludgeoned her husband to death in his sleep with a sash weight.

With its circulation now approaching 1.5 million readers a day—and *3 million* on Sundays—the *Daily News* exploded in an orgy of coverage, printing every lurid detail of the case from Snyder's arrest, through her trial, sentencing, and execution—at the last minute sneaking a photographer into the execution chamber with a miniature camera strapped to his leg, to capture the exact moment of death of the first woman ever sent to the electric chair.

"She was, as the *News* hinted deliciously to gourmets, about 'to cook, *and sizzle*, AND FRY!' in the electric chair," Scott Fitzgerald dryly remarked.

We can transmit sound over great distances. We can transmit photographs, we can make moving pictures that talk. These inventions combined with the great news-gathering organizations have created an engine of publicity such as the world has never known before. But this engine has an important peculiarity. Once the machine is running in high, it evokes a kind of circular intoxication in which the excitement about the object is made more furious by fresh excitement about the excitement itself.
Walter Lippmann

The city, *The New Yorker* magazine declared, had become a "gymnasium of celebrities."

Everyone was a celebrity now: movie stars, journalists, politicians, policemen, gangsters, murderers, nightclub owners, writers, and baseball players.

At the Algonquin Hotel in midtown, a group of young critics and columnists—including George S. Kaufman, Alexander Woollcott, Robert Benchley, Dorothy Parker, and Franklin P. Adams—transformed themselves into celebrities on the strength of their lunchtime conversation, an endless stream of witticisms and wisecracks, reported almost instantly to the public in the columns of the newspapers and magazines they worked for.

In the speakeasies and nightclubs off Times Square, underworld figures who had once lurked in the city's shadows now basked in its spotlight—gangsters and bootleggers whose distinctive nicknames became as familiar to New Yorkers as those of any entertainer or socialite:

Front page of the *New York Evening Graphic*, August 26, 1926. The sudden death of the film star Rudolph Valentino at the age of 31 sparked an orgy of publicity. The moment the news of the actor's death became public, the *Graphic*'s publisher, Bernarr Macfadden, slipped a photographer and a model into Frank Campbell's funeral parlor at 66th Street and Broadway. The model climbed into a coffin and the reporter snapped the picture. That afternoon, with Valentino's body still in the hospital, a ghastly—and utterly fictitious—front-page portrait of the "Great Lover" lying in state hit the streets of New York. The *Graphic* was forced to run its high-speed presses all night to meet the demand for more papers. The coverage whipped up such a public frenzy that on the day of the funeral, 30,000 distraught men and women stormed Campbell's establishment, smashing windows and fighting off the mounted police sent in to restore order—giving the *Evening Graphic* still more news to cover.

MY LIFE—*Rudolph Valentino*
(Written exclusively for the Macfadden Publications, Inc., before his death.) See Page 4

NEW YORK
EVENING GRAPHIC
Afternoon Edition

NEW YORK, THURSDAY, AUGUST 26, 1926

FEAR RIOT FOR RUDY
Story on Page 3

FIRST WIFE SOBS AT BIER

HUNDREDS MIRACULOUSLY ESCAPE

HAIL "NEW MESSIAH."

A line of women fans wait outside the gates at Yankee Stadium for admission to the first game of the 1926 World Series. After the Yankees' owner, Jacob Ruppert, brought Babe Ruth to New York in 1920, annual attendance doubled, to more than 1.3 million. In 1923, to accommodate the crowds coming out to see Ruth play, Ruppert constructed the largest sports facility in the world: Yankee Stadium, a 67,000-seat, $2.5 million structure on River Avenue in the Bronx that one man called a "skyscraper among ball parks." By the 1926 season, Ruth had been joined on the starting lineup by a spectacular young first baseman named Lou Gehrig, and the Yankees had become a national phenomenon.

Lepke, Bugsy, Lucky, Kid Twist, Mad Dog, Icepick Willie. One gangster named Arthur Flegenheimer, worried that his name was too long to fit in the headlines of the *Daily News*, changed it to Dutch Schultz.

Not to be outdone, a pair of Prohibition agents, Isidore Einstein and Moe Smith—better known as Izzy and Moe—soon made themselves as well known as the gangsters. Taking advantage of Izzy's uncanny gift for languages and Moe's mastery of costume and makeup, the two policemen impersonated tourists, farmers, cattle ranchers, longshoremen, street cleaners, gas meter inspectors, firemen, and gravediggers to infiltrate the underworld and confiscate thousands of bottles of illegal liquor. Their colorful exploits made them "as famous in New York as the Woolworth Building," the columnist O. O. MacIntyre observed—thanks in part to their careful habit of notifying the tabloids before an impending raid.

Up in the Bronx, meanwhile, in the huge, three-tiered baseball stadium that had been built around him, the Yankees home-run-hitting left fielder, Babe Ruth—known in the press as the Behemoth of Bust, the Sultan of Swat, the Colossus of Clout, the Bambino, and the Slambino—was rapidly becoming the biggest celebrity of them all and, with the help of his publicist, Christy Walsh, the first sports figure in history to be packaged like a product. Licensing his name and face to sell everything from candy bars to automobiles, the affable ballplayer with the voracious appetites was soon making twice as much money off the field as on it.

By 1927, the culture of celebrity had permeated every aspect of life in New York, from Harlem to Madison Avenue, from Times Square to city hall—where two years before New Yorkers had installed their own celebrity mayor—a dapper, debonair, and irresistibly charming ex–vaudeville performer and Tammany man named James J. Walker.

He was the perfect mayor for the Jazz Age. A onetime songwriter who had written the 1908 hit tune "Will You Love Me in December As You Do in May?" he was part politician and part showman—a figure "created," one reporter said, "for a time of brass bands, waving flags, parades and bright lights."

The son of an Irish immigrant who had swept into power on a tide of more than half a million votes, he had run on the promise to interfere with the good times as little as possible. "The least government," he declared, "is the best government. Ninety-eight percent of the people want only to be let alone to enjoy freedom in safety. Give me the writing of a nation's songs and I care not who makes its laws."

Even his admirers found his approach to government breathtakingly cavalier. During his two terms in city hall, "he was usually elsewhere," one man said, and so often late for appointments that he was referred to as "the late Mayor Walker."

"He is incapable of sustained effort," a young state parks commissioner named Robert Moses said. "If Walker is given a two-page memo, he reads the first page and then his attention wanders." He rarely rose before noon—insisting,

"Babe Ruth," one man wrote, "was made for New York." The greatest celebrity in a city of celebrities, Ruth delighted the public not only with his extraordinary performance on the field but with his boisterous behavior in the off-season, which was covered no less fully by the city's tabloids. Living out of an eleven-room suite in the Ansonia Hotel, he ran through a succession of expensive automobiles, frequented the city's best nightclubs, and spent riotous evenings in the company of gamblers and movie stars. "Ruth," one man said, "is our national exaggeration."

he said, that the greatest of all sins was going to bed the same day you got up—visited his office only a few hours a day, and seldom more than a few days a week. He had other chores to attend to: greeting visiting celebrities and dignitaries on the steps of city hall—where in six years he gave away nearly three hundred keys to the city—speeding around town in his $17,000 Dusenberg, attending prize fights and Broadway premieres, and living up to the nicknames his indulgent constituents loved to give him—the Jazz Mayor, the Dream Prince, the Night Mayor, or simply Beau James.

He honestly loves life. Not only does he love life, but he also loves a brand of life only to be found on Manhattan Island. Jimmy is a brilliant example of a city man who is happy: who indulges in metropolitan pleasures to the sweet and utter fulfillment of his personality . . . his speech, thought, actions, desires harmoniously adjusted to the rhythm of city life. "My city," he has been quoted as saying, "but right or wrong, my city."

Clare Boothe

During Walker's two terms in city hall, virtually everything was for sale. Ten thousand dollars bought a judgeship; fifty thousand the

exclusive lease for a pier big enough to dock an ocean liner. In six years, Walker personally accepted nearly a million dollars in bribes—which he called beneficences—from companies doing business with the city, and—at a time when New York's public infrastructure of parks, piers, and roadways was beginning to crumble badly—diverted a half million dollars to build a lavish nightclub called the Casino in Central Park, which he used to entertain celebrity friends and his mistress, the actress Betty Compton.

But, in the end, few New Yorkers cared—in part, because he knew what they wanted, and fit the times, and because they saw in him a parable of themselves—the immigrant boy who had shed his past and made a name for himself in the glittering city.

He had also come to understand the fleeting dynamics of celebrity as well as anyone in the Jazz Age. On Charles Lindbergh's last night in New York, Walker was among the celebrity guests at a private party held in the airman's honor at the Warwick Hotel. Just before the celebrated pilot arrived, Walker startled his companions by suggesting they refrain from any loud cheers or applause.

"Ever since that young man returned to America," Walker said, "he's had nothing but acclaim. But as much as I love the people of our glorious nation, this is a dangerous place in which to be a hero. A hero always runs into a time when there are no cheers. Let a man, however popular, make one little misstep that is contrary to the style of the moment and he is criticized, vilified, ignored and then forgotten." Walker's proposal was ignored, but the future would show how prophetic he had been. The man who had made himself famous with a song called "Will You Love Me in December As You Do in May?" knew how fickle fame could be—and that men who rose like meteors could plunge just as quickly into obscurity. There could be no foundations, no grounding, in the empire of air.

By the fall of 1927, politics and show business had become almost completely indistinguishable in New York. One October evening, theatergoers were delighted, but not surprised, when Jimmy Walker rose from his seat at the Ziegfeld Follies, one of the biggest hits on Broadway, to banter with the comedian Eddie Cantor—whose act featured a mocking impres-

"If the honorable James, in these past four years, has done a great deal of decorating and practically no work," the journalist Elmer Davis wrote in *Harper's Monthly* in 1929, "it is not because he could not work if he wanted to. He has worked hard and well in other jobs, when he was driven to it. But he is a shrewd person who knows what the people want. They want some work, of course, but there are plenty of minor officials who are able and willing to do it. They also, and more especially, want a show; and nobody can give them so good a show as Joyful James."

sion of the mayor himself, frantically giving out keys to the city.

Jimmy! We simply had to fall one and all for
Jimmy,
And now we're singing of him 'cause we love him.
Who told Broadway not to be gay?
Who gets his picture taken three times a day?
Jimmy!

We're very glad to show that we all know
That Jimmy is doing fine.
Can't you hear those old New Yorkers
hollering:
Gimme-gimme-gimme Jimmy for mine!
Irving Berlin

Within a few weeks of Walker's big night on Broadway, a fateful event took place only a

yes, we are. . . . We're gonna move up in the Bronx. A lot of nice green grass up there. A whole lot of people you know. There's the Gins-bergs, the Guttenbergs and the Goldbergs. Oh, a lot of bergs. I don't know them all.

Al Jolson, in *The Jazz Singer*

Torn between the claims of his Jewish ances-try and the bright lights of Broadway, the singer comes to understand that the God of his father has been subsumed and transcended by the God of the American dream. Turning his face to the crowd, he consecrates his life to the secular reli-gion of success and the god of infinite rising.

The message of the maudlin talkie was clear: within the transforming luminance of the new mass media, the concrete particulars of the immi-grant experience could be dissolved—at once annulled, transcended, and reconstituted into the body politic of America.

TWILIGHT

By this time contemporaries of mine had begun to disappear into the dark maw of violence. A classmate killed his wife and himself on Long Island, another tumbled "accidentally" from a skyscraper in Philadelphia, another purposely from a skyscraper in New York. One was killed in a speak-easy in Chicago; another was beaten to death in a speak-easy in New York and crawled home to the Princeton Club to die. . . . These things happened not during the depression but during the boom.

F. Scott Fitzgerald

By 1927, the decade was beginning to take its toll on Scott and Zelda Fitzgerald.

The fame he had craved and won had become first an addiction, then a curse, and finally a force of destruction. Two years before, his greatest novel, *The Great Gatsby*, published to critical acclaim but indifferent sales, had cap-tured as nothing else the romance, wonder, and heartbreaking tragedy of the metropolis.

But now Zelda, always unstable, had begun to slide into mental illness, and Fitzgerald him-self, woefully alcoholic, was becoming increas-ingly self-destructive. The ugly drunkenness and fights provoked with strangers had long since lost their charm. Perhaps he had flown too high in the first wild rush of success ever to fly so high again. Perhaps it was true, as Fitzgerald

The marquee for *The Jazz Singer* at the Warners' Theatre on Broadway and 51st Street, October 1927. Based on a play by Sam-son Raphaelson, the story of *The Jazz Singer* closely resembled the life of its star, Al Jolson, who was born Asa Yoelson in St. Petersburg, Russia, in 1886. *The Jazz Singer* was actually Warners's third sound film, but its extra-ordinary popular success in New York and other major cities effectively marked the end of the silent era.

few blocks away—the screening of a film that would define the gaudy era and signal the begin-ning of the end.

Called *The Jazz Singer*, and billed as the first talking picture in the history of cinema, it was a drama of assimilation, and a parable of New York in the Roaring Twenties.

Shot in part on the city streets, it chronicled the journey of a young Jewish boy—played by the singer Al Jolson, himself the son of immi-grant Jews—from his obscure beginnings on the Lower East Side to fame and fortune in show business.

Mama, darling—if I'm a success in this show, well, we're gonna move from here. . . . Oh,

himself declared, that there were no second acts in American lives.

And yet, if the city of ambition and success was destroying him, a few things still seemed possible. Asked by a reporter what his ultimate ambition was, Fitzgerald said simply, "To stay in love with Zelda and write the greatest novel in the world."

At the enchanted metropolitan twilight I felt a haunting loneliness sometimes, and felt it in others—poor young clerks in the dusk, wasting the most poignant moments of night and life. . . . Again at eight o'clock, when the dark lanes of the forties were lined five deep with throbbing taxicabs, bound for the theater district, I felt a sinking in my heart. Forms leaned together in the taxis as they waited, and there was laughter from unheard jokes, and lighted cigarettes made unintelligible circles inside. Imagining that I, too, was hurrying toward gaiety and excitement, I wished them well.

F. Scott Fitzgerald

1928

New York City is the most fatally fascinating thing in America. She sits like a great witch at the gate of the country, showing her alluring white face and hiding her crooked hands and feet under the folds of her wide garments—constantly enticing thousands from far within, and tempting those who come from across the seas to go no farther. And all these become the victims of her caprice. Some she at once crushes beneath her cruel feet; others she condemns to a fate like that of galley-slaves; a few she favours and fondles, riding them high on the bubbles of fortune; then with a sudden breath she blows the bubbles out and laughs mockingly as she watches them fall.

James Weldon Johnson

Looking back, some people traced the beginning of the end of the city's wildest and giddiest decade to the summer of 1928—when the governor of New York, Alfred Emanuel Smith, embarked upon his historic race for the highest office in the land.

With the nation enjoying unparalleled prosperity, the odds against a Democratic upset seemed long from the start, but Smith was sure he could win. The overwhelming choice of his party to run against Herbert Hoover, the immensely popular leader of the most powerful state in the union had won twenty of the twenty-one campaigns he had waged and been elected to an unprecedented four terms as governor.

His record in Albany was nothing less than dazzling. In eight years, he had rationalized and restructured the state government, pushed through landmark reform legislation on education, housing, and workers' rights, and initiated a spectacular program of public works—including an astonishing new park and parkway system on Long Island—through his brilliant young parks commissioner, Robert Moses.

By 1928, the onetime altar boy from the Lower East Side had emerged as one of the most remarkable politicians in the country.

The usual writhing and crawling is simply not in him. Cocky, vulgar, even maybe low, he is never cheap. . . . Al came into the campaign with clean hands . . . he seems to be determined to go out of it with clean hands. Somewhere on the sidewalks of New York, without benefit of the moral training on tap in Kansas and Mississippi, he picked up the doctrine that it is better, after all, to be honest than to lie. It is not a popular doctrine in America. It is dangerous baggage in politics. It gets a man suspected and hated. But it has a merit nevertheless: it makes a man comfortable inside.

H. L. Mencken

The very idea had been unthinkable ten years before—an uneducated Irish Catholic boy from the Fourth Ward of New York City running for the nation's highest office.

But there had never been anyone quite like Al Smith, the man young Franklin Roosevelt himself had called just four years before the Happy Warrior.

Confident that he could extend New York's immense commercial and cultural reach to the political arena, he did nothing to disguise who he was or where he came from, adopting once again "The Sidewalks of New York" as the anthem of his campaign.

The election of 1928, Smith had all but insisted, would be a referendum not only on himself but on the city that had allowed him to rise.

Cheering delegates jam the floor of Madison Square Garden during the 1924 Democratic National Convention in New York, moments after Franklin D. Roosevelt nominated Governor Al Smith for president. Roosevelt gave a rousing address, during which he bestowed the nickname the Happy Warrior on Smith, but a large group of anti-Catholic delegates from the South blocked Smith's nomination. Similar, if even more virulent, religious bigotry would play a crucial role in Smith's 1928 presidential campaign.

The campaign got off to a rocky start. Within days of his nomination, Smith chose as his campaign manager a secretive, self-made Wall Street financier named John Jacob Raskob—"a strange little man," one of Smith's advisors said, "almost Machiavellian really"—who had invented buying cars on credit and who had helped assemble the fortunes of Du Pont and General Motors.

Part of a plan to present the populist governor as a friend of big business, the strategy backfired when the diminutive Catholic millionaire was used to paint Smith as an agent of Rome, and Wall Street.

But in the end, Raskob was the least of Smith's problems, as the presidential campaign of 1928 rapidly descended into one of the darkest episodes in American political history. Everything that had made Smith successful in New York now worked against him out in the countryside, where decades of rising antipathy to the city and everything it stood for rose up like a poisonous vapor.

In small towns and rural places across the country, the jaunty ambassador of the city of Walt Whitman and Emma Lazarus was shocked by the tide of hatred he encountered for what one man called the "foreign populated city called New York."

It was in part a matter of style. Rural voters ridiculed Smith for his derby, cigar, and loud suits, which made him appear almost a caricature of the big-city ward heeler. The powerful new medium of radio, which for the first time played an important role in a presidential campaign, caused further trouble for the New Yorker. His nasal voice and strong Lower East Side accent, which transformed "first" into "foist," "hospital" into "orspital," and the word "radio" itself into "raddio," sounded strange and even alien in many areas of the country.

In part, it was the old antagonism between the country and the city. In conservative towns and states across the country, Smith came under fire for his opposition to Prohibition, for his unmistakably liberal views, and for his links to

Tammany Hall, a synonym for corruption in the countryside.

But it was the virulence of the anti-Catholic hatred that shocked and hurt him most—"a campaign of bigotry almost unbelievable in its intensity," one advisor remembered. It would be, his daughter Emily later said, "the deepest shadow in his life—the greatest sorrow, I am sure, that ever came to him."

On the stump in Kansas, farmers greeted Smith's speeches with stony silence. In Oklahoma, Ku Klux Klansmen placed burning crosses along the route of his campaign train. Across the country, Protestant religious leaders attacked him from the pulpit, condemning New York as the "seat of Satan" and insisting, one minister said, that "no subject of the Pope should be President."

"As ambassador of God," the Reverend Billy Sunday thundered, "it is my duty to defy the forces of hell—Al Smith and the rest of them. His male supporters are damnable whiskey politicians, bootleggers, crooks, pimps and businessmen who deal with him. His female supporters are streetwalkers."

Smith kept silent as long as he could—then, in an eloquent speech in Oklahoma City, on September 20, struck back, imploring his audience to reject all bigotry as un-Christian and un-American. The hostility of the crowd was so palpable that Smith's advisors feared for his safety.

The essential issue in America during the next fifty years will be between city men and yokels. The yokels have ruled the Republic since its first days—often, it must be added, very wisely. But now they decay and are challenged, and in the long run they are bound to be overcome.

H. L. Mencken, July 1928

In the end, America was not ready for New York, or at least to put a New Yorker in the White House.

On election night, November 6, 1928, Smith sat stoically with his supporters in the Armory on Park Avenue, an unlit cigar in his mouth, watching the returns come in.

He had done surprisingly well in the big industrial states, winning majorities in America's twelve largest cities. In what would prove to be a historic realignment in American politics, waves of immigrant voters in the cities had begun to flex their electoral power, and in the years to come the Democratic party, once dominated by rural southerners, would be transformed into the vehicle of an ascendant urban North.

But it would be another New Yorker—and not one from the streets of the Lower East Side—who would reap the rewards of the sea change Al Smith had begun. For now, it was clear only that Herbert Hoover had achieved one of the biggest landslides in American history, winning 444 electoral votes to Smith's 87. In the end, the New Yorker lost almost every state in the union—including New York itself, where upstate voters had turned out in droves against him.

In a cruel twist of fate, Smith's aristocratic colleague, forty-six-year-old Franklin Roosevelt, squeaked into the governor's seat by the slenderest of margins. In the years to come, the rising young politician would build upon Smith's innovative vision of government, drawing lessons that he would ultimately extend onto the national stage.

For Smith, it was all over by 9:30 p.m. Around 10:00, he drove to the Biltmore Hotel to concede defeat and speak to a crowd of his loyal supporters. "It's God's will," his wife, Katie, said, with tears in her eyes. "But we'll see more of you now."

His chin was up and his indomitable heart was high. At the sight of his jauntiness in defeat, men and women workers burst into tears. Deeply touched, Smith barked out a few words of thanks to hide his own mounting emotions, clasped hands, and was gone. Perhaps never in political history was there so much distress among the rank and file of the party as there was over his defeat.

James Farley

In the weeks after the election, Smith tried to put a brave face on his crushing defeat—but his long political career was over. In December, he attended a banquet at the Lotos Club in New York, where for the first time in years, he was not the guest of honor. As he watched the new governor-elect basking in the spotlight, the reality of the disaster began to settle over him—a gloom only intensified by the knowledge that he would soon be out of a job for the first time in forty years.

As the banquet wore on, Smith slipped out of the hall and down to the men's room with his close friend Eddie Dowling, a prominent Broadway producer. Standing at the urinal, Smith was worrying aloud about the bleakness of his prospects, Dowling remembered, when a soft voice spoke up behind them.

It was John Jacob Raskob, the governor's inscrutable campaign manager, who had silently followed the two men in and listened intently to Smith's lament. "Don't worry, Al," the financier now said. "I'm going to build a new skyscraper—the biggest in the world—and you're going to be the president of the company."

SKY WARS

By 1929, a culture of pure speculation had taken hold in New York.

For almost two years, the stock market had been spiraling upward, shattering records month by month. Only a few years before, analysts had been stunned when for the first time, 2 million shares were traded in a single day. Now, 5-million-share days had become routine—Hoover's landslide had triggered a buying spree that topped 7 million—and brokers frequently dropped to the floor in exhaustion following the three o'clock gong.

> *Wall Street was pandemonium. The outside brokers—the curb men—were bidding against one another for stocks not quoted on the New York Exchange, and their hoarse cries mingled in a raucous chorus. I stood outside a madhouse staring at lunatics. Surely it was a madhouse, surrounded by other homes for the incurably insane. . . .*
>
> Philip Gibb

By the spring, the stock market had lost all connection with the economy, and with reality. In less than a year, the market's value, soaring upward along with the volume of sales, had almost doubled—the Dow Jones Industrial Average rising from 191 in 1928 to over 350 by the start of the white-hot summer of 1929.

As the values started to double again, John Jacob Raskob—having made himself rich turning millionaires into billionaires—now turned to the very smallest of investors. In the August issue of the *Ladies' Home Journal* he put forward a breathtaking proposition: *Everyone ought*

to be rich. The trick was simple. Just as people of modest means could buy cars on credit, so even the smallest of investors could buy stocks on credit.

As stock prices rose, the initial debt would vanish in thin air, and pure profits follow. If stocks fell, of course, the investor would be ruined. But it was clear now to almost everyone that was no longer a real possibility. The important thing was to borrow and to buy.

> *In my opinion, the wealth of the country is bound to increase at a very rapid rate. The rapidity of the rate will be determined by the increase of consumption, and under wise investment plans the consumption will steadily increase.*
>
> John Jacob Raskob

By 1929, brokers were routinely lending small investors more than two-thirds of the money they needed to buy a stock. Over $8.5 billion was already out on loan—more than the entire amount of currency circulating through the entire United States.

Increasingly, now, analysts began to warn that the boom could not go on indefinitely. Signs that the cycle was coming to an end were there, some said, for people willing to read them. For much of the decade, the market's gains had been plowed back into industrial production, stoking the nation's booming economy still more.

But production and sales had peaked in several key markets in 1927, and as the returns for manufacturing investments diminished, capital was increasingly moving in two dangerously seductive directions—into the paper speculation that was now driving stock prices on Wall Street into the stratosphere, and into the real-estate speculation that was now driving dozens of new office towers high into the air over lower and midtown Manhattan, completely remaking its fabled skyline.

> *The city is in upheaval. . . . In not more than half a dozen years the skyline of midtown Manhattan . . . has been lifted a hundred feet. . . . American vision, daring, restlessness, engineering skill have all been properly read into this marvelous transformation from brownstone to Babylon. . . . As for building for eternity, the need does not exist. Thirty years from now they will be tearing up the city once more.*
>
> *New York Times,* 1926

Month after month, the frantic speculation and growth continued, as the stock market and the skyline soared upward—with increasingly little regard for the reality of what they might be building upon.

Building after building, block by block, New York was racing into the skies. In less than ten years nearly one hundred buildings twenty stories or taller had been added to the skyline, which now bristled from afar with what looked like the spires of an alien planet.

In the first nine months of 1929, plans were filed for 709 new buildings in New York City, at a total cost of $472 million. On a single day in February the Metropolitan Life Insurance Company issued $74 million in building loans. By spring 1929, there were fifteen buildings over five hundred feet tall. And still the boom went on, as the city's most powerful real-estate developers now embarked on an all-out skyscraper war.

For sixteen years, the sixty-story, eight-hundred-foot Woolworth Building had reigned supreme as the tallest building in the world. Now the race was on to top it, and some of the plans seemed to rise so high as to take leave of reality. There was talk of a hundred-story tower on Madison Square—a 1,050-foot tower at Times Square—a 150-story superskyscraper at Broadway and Duane.

None of them got off the ground, but the spectral edifices fired the public imagination almost as much as real ones did. "Towering 1,600 feet above the level of Broadway," the *Herald-Tribune* wrote of one unbuilt structure, "the roof of more than an acre will be employed as a landing field for airplanes. The structure will be three times as high as its famous neighbor, the Woolworth Building."

Everyone seemed to be breathing the same thin, cold, intoxicating air. "The height of a building is nothing at all," the architect Raymond Hood declared. "I got our engineers to figure . . . the theoretical maximum height for a skyscraper. . . . The formulas that the present building laws allow . . . would enable you to build a tower seven thousand feet high." Hood was proposing a structure that would soar a mile and a half into the air—without batting an eye. "The elevator companies are ready," he said.

I came to the conclusion that what my boys ought to have was something to be responsible for. They had grown up in New York and probably would want to live there. They wanted to work, and so the idea of putting up a building was born. Something that I had seen in Paris recurred to me. I said to the architects: "make this building higher than the Eiffel Tower." That was the beginning of the seventy-seven story Chrysler Building.

Walter P. Chrysler

In the spring of 1929, the race into the skies reached fever pitch.

More than 100 new buildings over 20 stories tall were added to the Manhattan skyline during the late 1920s, as the speculative frenzy on Wall Street spilled over to the city's real-estate market and developers raced to build new office towers and apartment buildings across Manhattan. Left, the 64-story Bank of the Manhattan Company, completed on Wall Street in 1929, was one of a group of soaring towers that transformed the lower Manhattan skyline at the end of the 1920s (another was the Irving Trust Building, at 1 Wall Street, seen rising at the far right). At right, a view of Park Avenue, looking north from 34th Street in 1930, shows the Chrysler Building still under construction, along with two other recently completed towers: the Chanin Building, at center, and the New York Central Building, on the left, rising to the north of Grand Central Terminal.

The frenzied competition that now broke out to create the tallest structure in Manhattan would pit midtown against Wall Street—fueled by the towering ambition of two corporate giants and the even more towering egos of two obsessed architects, who had recently dissolved their long-standing partnership and were now bitter enemies.

It had begun the year before, when the Chrysler Corporation announced plans to build a massive new headquarters at Forty-second Street and Lexington Avenue. Walter Chrysler's instructions to the architect, William Van Alen, had been simple, he later said—to design a tower that would be the tallest structure on earth.

Van Alen's initial plan called for a flamboyant chrome-spangled structure that would rise

840 feet into the sky—until his onetime partner and now archrival, H. Craig Severance, broke ground eighty blocks to the south for the Bank of the Manhattan Company's new corporate headquarters at 40 Wall Street.

When Severance announced that his soaring Gothic-inspired structure would be two feet higher than the Chrysler Building, Van Alen raced to the drafting table and immediately added ten floors to his design—and the battle was on.

Month after month, New Yorkers looked up in wonder as the two builders vied for pre-eminence—each altering his plans again and again in midconstruction to stay ahead of the other. On a clear day, workers high up in each tall tower could track the progress of their rivals

The skyscrapers of east midtown, 1931, as seen from the Empire State Building. By the end of the 1920s, the emerging office and hotel district around Grand Central Terminal had established itself as the new center of the city. In the distance, at left, can be seen the twin pinnacles of the new Waldorf-Astoria, still under construction; in 1929 the hotel had moved from its old location on Fifth Avenue and 34th Street, which had become the site of the Empire State itself (see page 377). To the hotel's right is the New York Central Building, with its ornate pyramidal roof, and the slablike tower of the 54-story Lincoln Building. The stylish 51-story Chanin Building sits directly in front of the towering Chrysler Building, while at far right, the stepped mass of the *Daily News* Building, designed by the architects Raymond Hood and John Mead Howells and completed in 1931, portended a new look for the city's towers, with its simple vertical lines, relative lack of ornament, and flat roof.

So unusual, daring and original is this design of the top of the Chrysler Building that one is almost forced to admire it, sparkling in its dazzling sheath of polished chrome steel. Bizarre, fantastic and exotic, it grasps and holds at least for a moment the attention of the passerby below, as well as the amazed interest of the countryside and distant seafarers for miles around.

Architectural Forum

four miles away. When the Bank of the Manhattan Company finally topped out at 927 feet in the fall of 1929, most were sure it had won the war. Severance had added first a lantern, then ten new penthouse floors, and finally a fifty-foot flagpole, to beat out his rival once and for all.

But William Van Alen would not be outdone, and six weeks later, unveiled his secret weapon.

On October 16, 1929, as pedestrians and reporters looked up in wonder, a 185-foot-long steel spire, assembled in secret inside the building's apex, slowly emerged from its chrome cocoon, and was bolted triumphantly into place in less than ninety minutes. The gleaming, silvery spike raised the Chrysler's Building height to 1,046 feet above street level—exactly 117 feet taller than its downtown rival. A personal triumph for Walter Chrysler and his architect, the victory was also a stunning confirmation that midtown had at last displaced Wall Street as Manhattan's primary center of gravity.

With its gleaming Gothic eaves, hubcap friezes, and stainless-steel gargoyles—some shaped like the radiator caps of a 1928 Chrysler—the majestic seventy-seven-story tower was now taller than the Woolworth Building, taller than the Bank of the Manhattan Company, taller than the Eiffel Tower, indisputably the tallest structure in the world—for now.

> *Some think it's a freak; some think it's a stunt; a few think it is positively ugly; others consider it a great feat, a masterpiece, a tour de force.*
> Kenneth Murchison

Within weeks of the Chrysler Building's triumph that fall, two awesome events would overtake New York City at virtually the same time.

The first would send it plunging into the deepest, darkest abyss of its tumultuous history and bring the giddy decade of speculation to a swift and horrifying end.

The other would send it soaring, against all odds, higher than it had ever gone before—an ensign in the sky that would commemorate, perhaps for all time, the city's insatiable will to rise.

THE CRASH

All through the summer of 1929, there had been ominous rumblings. Unemployment had been rising, automobiles sales and department store revenues had fallen off sharply, across the South and West farms were failing in record numbers.

On Wall Street, the delirious optimism continued, undimmed. On August 27, 1929, the Dow Jones Average reached its peak. An army of buyers converged on New York, swamping the hotels, and in some cases trying to sleep in the steets around the stock exchange, desperate not to miss a single day's trading.

With the coming of fall, the mood changed. As the market dipped, then rose, then slid downward again, investors grew increasingly uneasy. In September, an economist named Roger Babson sent a wave of fear rippling through the market when he warned that "Sooner or later, a crash is coming and it may be terrific." Professor Irving Fisher of Yale University brushed away any concerns. "Stock prices," he declared, "have reached what looks like a permanently high plateau."

And then the bottom fell out.

On Wednesday, October 23, 1929, the first waves of panicky selling began to drive down the price of blue chip stocks like Westinghouse and General Electric.

The photographer Margaret Bourke-White in 1934, shooting a skyline view from one of the gargoyles—actually stylized eagles—that sprouted from the 61st floor of the Chrysler Building (those on the lower floors were shaped to resemble the radiator caps of a 1928 Chrysler automobile). The noted photojournalist was the building's only full-time occupant, living and working in a stylishly decorated studio on the 61st floor. Above her, in the distance, rises the soaring mass of the newly completed RCA Building, located in Rockefeller Center.

The following morning, Winston Churchill was among the crowd of horrified onlookers in the gallery of the New York Stock Exchange, when within minutes of the opening bell the fear turned to panic, and brokers began unloading margin accounts at record speed. Stock prices plummeted sickeningly across the board—spurring the rush of sell orders from terrified speculators still more. As anguished shrieks rose up from the floor of the stock exchange, the visitors gallery was cleared.

In less than two hours, nearly $10 billion of paper value was simply wiped out.

Out on the street, crowds had now massed six deep in front of the stock exchange, while hundreds more stood in shocked silence on the steps of Federal Hall. Newspapers would later try to describe the uncanny murmuring sound that echoed off the stone facades of the financial district that morning—a collective moan of horror and grief and stunned disbelief rising up from thousands of ruined, frightened men.

As they had two decades before during the panic of 1907, the biggest crowds gathered outside the House of Morgan, desperately hoping for a miracle. An audible murmur of relief swept through the crowd when the city's four leading bankers strode purposefully up the steps of 23 Wall Street and into the Morgan Bank. Hopes rose still further when the acting president of the exchange, authorized by the banks to pump $240 million into the crumbling market, strode onto the trading floor at half past one and boldly raised the bid on U.S. Steel by ten full points. The crowd of traders and stock brokers burst into cheers as the market began to rally bravely. News spread that, once again, the House of Morgan had come to the rescue.

But the rescue was short-lived. On Friday, with the market apparently stabilized, the banks withdrew their funds.

The following Tuesday—October 29, 1929, known forever after as Black Tuesday—another tidal wave of selling hit the market, and this time no one was able to stop it. Hour after hour, the market continued its descent into chaos and pandemonium as stock prices collapsed under the torrent of panicked selling, and desperate brokers fought and screamed and trampled one another to get out.

Crowds gather in front of the Sub-Treasury building during the stock market crash of October 1929. On the morning of Thursday, October 24—Black Thursday—$9.5 billion in paper value was wiped out in two hours, as brokers shouted themselves hoarse, panic ruled on the floor, and hysterical visitors in the gallery were removed by the police. But even that loss was dwarfed by the disaster on the following Tuesday, October 29, or Black Tuesday—when 16 million shares of stock were dumped, and the United States lost more capital than it had spent in all of World War I.

In the spring of 1921, with funding from the Russell Sage Foundation, a group of the most powerful men in New York—bankers and financiers, railroad and insurance company executives, foundation heads and urban planners, department store owners and real-estate developers—met in private to begin mapping out the most ambitious and far-flung reconception of the city ever undertaken: the Regional Plan of New York and Its Environs.

From the very beginning, extravagant visions and extra-territorial ambition had been knit into the city's soul—from Stuyvesant's schemes for New Amsterdam, to the 1811 Commissioners' Plan for Manhattan, to Andrew Haswell Green's visionary proposal for the consolidation of the five boroughs into Greater New York. But nothing in history had ever matched the sweep and scale of the Regional Plan, whose field of view would encompass the entire five-borough city, its surrounding suburbs, and a huge swath of the encircling countryside—5,528 square miles in all, spread across 22 counties and three states. Once again, New Yorkers looking to the future sought to fling back the city's borders—this time to encompass an area more than 250 times the size of Manhattan Island.

Nothing like it had ever been attempted before—a single comprehensive plan for an area with 436 local and municipal governments—a maze of jurisdictions, the planners argued, that could no longer meet the needs of the increasingly interconnected and interdependent metropolitan region.

"Draw all the lines you like for states and counties," the former senator and Regional Plan committee member Elihu Root insisted, "but a city is a growth, responding to the inherent atoms that make it up, apart from political or govern-mental considerations. The force from which that growth comes is the force of industrial enterprise, desire, movement—the desire for a living, desire for wealth, comfort, society, acting in the hearts and minds of a vast number of units. That is the great force of life and modern civilization, and that is the thing government cannot imitate."

It took eight years and $1.3 million to complete the Regional Plan. But when it was finally released in the spring of 1929—on the eve of the stock market crash—the ten-volume report offered at once an eerily prophetic glimpse of the city's future and the detailed blueprint for making that future come about.

Manhattan, according to the plan, would continue to be the undisputed center of the region. But it was to be a new kind of center, stripped now of its port and manufacturing functions and given over largely to the new "clean" industries arising in midtown and downtown: finance, banking, insurance, law, advertising, communications, and the executive offices of national corporations—the very industries, not coincidentally, who had sponsored the Regional Plan itself. The planners saw Manhattan's coming role to be that of the first postindustrial city, dominated by financial and managerial activities, by shopping and entertainment, and by exclusive residential districts—a modern, radiant city core whose skyscraper office buildings and housing complexes would themselves be rationally conceived and laid out along the most advanced planning principles.

In the real world, Manhattan in the 1920s remained what it had been for more than a century—the largest shipping and manufacturing center in the nation, with more than 420,000 factory jobs on the lower half of the island alone. But the plan concluded that the city's industrial activities would be more efficiently pursued in a belt along the Brooklyn, Queens, and New Jersey waterfronts, where businesses would no longer have to fight their way through crowded streets or be located in outdated yet expensive industrial loft buildings. Nor, after the move, would Manhattan's newer, white-collar population be discomfited by the noisome, gritty workings of traditional blue-collar industries—or the vast working-class population that made them possible.

To some degree, the proposal to separate blue and white collars was the logical extension of trends that had been building for decades—the growth of new manufacturing districts in Brooklyn, Queens, and New Jersey, the shift of the city's population from the center to the periphery, and the transformation of Manhattan itself from a nineteenth-century industrial city to a modern corporate and financial headquarters. But the plan now proposed to accelerate those changes dramatically, through an astonishingly ambitious—and innovative—pair of transportation proposals.

The first was for an expanded and unified railway system, connecting every part of the region. There was to be a new underground tunnel running beneath the harbor to connect Brooklyn to New Jersey, a mammoth railroad bridge across the Hudson River, and a complex system of linkages that would interconnect the region's patchwork of separate, competing rail lines.

The second proposal was still more daring—a comprehensive road system that would give New York the most advanced vehicular network in the world. A series of circumferential roads and river crossings—including what would later be called the Triborough Bridge, the Verrazano–Narrows Bridge, the Cross-Bronx Expressway, the Belt Parkway, and the Bronx-Whitestone Bridge— would allow drivers to pass through and around the region without traveling through the center of the city.

If indisputably visionary, the Regional Plan was also entirely theoretical—sponsored by a private organization with no official power to build any of it. Yet the plan proved to have a decisive and profound effect on the city's future—as much for what was not built as for what was.

The proposed rail scheme went nowhere. New York's intensely competitive railroad companies proved unable to agree on anything, except their fierce opposition to the proposal to interlink their lines. The rail tunnel underneath the bay would remain unbuilt, while the rail links across the Hudson River and Narrows were transformed into strictly vehicular crossings. New York's freight rail service would remain deficient for the rest of the century—with troubling effects on the region's industrial base.

The proposed road system, by contrast, quickly captured the imagination of New York's two greatest builders of public works. On February 25, 1930, in the Grand Ballroom of the Hotel Commodore, Robert Moses—the ambitious and brilliant state parks commissioner who was now completing his pioneering parkway system on Long Island—presented a master plan for the region's transportation future to 500 high-ranking members of New York's civic establishment. The map he unveiled was suggestively similar to the Regional Plan—though its roadways had now been turned into full-fledged highways—and over the next four decades, he would devote extraordinary energy to filling in the dotted lines on the map with concrete, steel, and asphalt. What few gaps remained would be completed by the Port of New York Authority, the powerful bistate agency that in the coming years would shift its focus from shipping-related activities to creating vehicular links between New York and New Jersey—building the George Washington Bridge, the Lincoln Tunnel, and (in partnership with Moses) the Narrows crossing, which was transformed from a tunnel into the longest suspension bridge in the world.

Indeed, in the century to come, much of the Regional Plan would come to pass. After World War II, shipping and industry would migrate out of Manhattan—the port moving to Elizabeth, New Jersey, precisely as the plan proposed—leaving the island to increasingly resemble the gleaming post-industrial center the plan envisioned. The role of the Regional Plan in bringing on those changes—or simply predicting shifts that would have occurred anyway—would remain a matter of debate.

In the end, however, the plan's greatest legacy was indisputably its pioneering road network—the crucial first sketch of the massive system of highways, bridges, and tunnels that in the years to come would not only transform New York and its surroundings but, for better or worse, provide the model for every modern city in the world.

This rendering from the Regional Plan of 1929 shows the planners' extraordinary vision for the rebuilding of lower Manhattan. One of the city's poorest tenement districts—Chrystie and Forsyth streets, in the heart of the Lower East Side—would be replaced by a dazzling new high-rise district of offices, theaters, shops, and apartment houses—complete with an express highway sunk beneath the level of the street, broad local roadways, and widely spaced skyscrapers, separated by low-rise buildings to maximize light and air.

In the worst single day in the history of the New York Stock Exchange, 16 million shares traded hands, and the market lost $14 billion in value, bringing the week's loss to more than $30 billion—ten times more than the entire annual budget of the federal government, and nearly twice the amount the United States had spent during all of World War I.

It would be twenty-five years before the Dow Jones Average surpassed the peak it had reached in the weeks before the crash—and forty years before the stock exchange traded more shares in a single day than it had on Black Tuesday.

It took months for the reality of what had happened to set in. Worst hit, in the short run, were the thousands of small investors who, believing that everyone could be rich, had bought stock on margin, sometimes borrowing as much as 90 percent of its book value. In a matter of hours, in some cases minutes, they had lost everything—their life savings, their houses, and their dreams.

Financiers who had not been wiped out tried to put a good face on things. "Prudent investors are now buying stocks in huge quantities and will profit handsomely when this hysteria is over," Raskob told the *New York Times* the day after Black Tuesday. "The pendulum has swung too far," he insisted. "The list is filled with bargains and my friends and I are all buying stocks." Raskob himself long before had moved his millions to safer assets.

Wednesday, October 30, 1929. Mr. Raskob was asked if he believed that the decline in the stock market would have great effects on business. He answered that he did not believe the effects would be other than temporary, lasting probably two or three months, and that he did not believe that the effects would be drastic in other than luxury industries.

New York Times

But others feared the worst. "The present week," the editor of the *Commercial and Financial Chronicle* declared, "has witnessed the greatest stock market catastrophe of all times." Horrified by Raskob's insouciance, Senator A. R. Robinson immediately charged the financier with being "psychologically" responsible for the disaster.

Scott Fitzgerald was somewhere in North Africa when the end came, and thought he heard a "dull distant crash" echoing to the farthest wastes of the desert. Zelda's condition was worsening. When he finally returned to Manhattan in 1931, he knew instantly that everything had changed.

I can only cry out that I have lost my splendid mirage. Come back, come back, O glittering and white!

F. Scott Fitzgerald

EMPIRE STATE

It was the building that should never have been built—rising in the wrong place, at the wrong time, propelled skyward by the same intoxicating speculative impulse that had just been so thoroughly punished on Wall Street.

And yet up it went in the deafening silence that followed the crash. And when it was through, though no one could tell whether it had been a success or a failure, everyone knew it was the purest and most glorious expression of everything the city stood for.

Front page of *Variety*, Wednesday, October 30, 1929. The famous headline in New York's leading show-business newspaper reflected an awareness that the stock market crash had implications far beyond the borders of the financial district. In the months and years to come, every part of the city's complex economy, from entertainment to shipping to journalism itself, would be damaged or crippled by the market collapse.

Right: The Waldorf-Astoria Hotel, at Fifth Avenue and 34th Street. The hotel's hyphenated name suggested its origins as two buildings—the 11-story Waldorf, built by William Waldorf Astor in 1893, and the 16-story Astoria, built by John Jacob Astor IV in 1897. At the turn of the century, the Waldorf-Astoria—with more than 1,300 rooms—had been the largest and most opulent hotel in New York. By the '20s, however, the grand hostelry was faltering—a victim of Prohibition, of the move uptown by wealthy New Yorkers, and of its own outdated Victorian style. After a public relations campaign failed to revive its popularity, the owners decided to move the hotel to a new skyscraper structure on Park Avenue, just north of Grand Central Terminal. By 1930, the old building had been torn down, to make way for the Empire State Building.

It was probably inevitable that the man behind the scheme to build the tallest skyscraper in the world was the tiny, secretive speculator, John Jacob Raskob. Since long before the night of his fateful promise to Al Smith in the Lotos Club, Raskob had been burning to build a tower that would soar above the rest—in part, to settle an old score with Walter Chrysler and in part, one man remembered, because he had seen the Eiffel Tower, and "it burned him to think that the French had built something higher." All through the spring and summer of 1929, he had been marshaling his forces in total secrecy.

By April, he had settled on a daring site—an immense two-acre property at the corner of Thirty-fourth and Fifth—a full half mile south of the fashionable center of midtown, on the site of the old Waldorf-Astoria Hotel, which was itself about to remove to a more desirable location on Park Avenue, farther uptown.

By June, the financing was in place, along with a construction firm, the famed Starrett Brothers and Eken, and an architect, William

Lamb of Shreve, Lamb and Harmon, to whom he put a simple breathtaking question: "Bill, how high can you make it, so it won't fall down?"

Rumors had been flying for months, when on August 29—just two days after the stock market hit its peak—news of the staggering project was dramatically unveiled by New York's famous favorite son, the bruised but unbowed warrior Al Smith. True to his word, Raskob had made the former governor president and chief spokesman of what was now called the Empire State Building.

Even in the booming decade that had seen a hundred skyscrapers soar into the sky, the announcement made headline news. With no actual plans, and only the sketchiest idea how it might be built and paid for, Smith was presenting to the public a structure of literally staggering proportions. Eighty-five stories and 1,050 feet high, it would hold more than 2 million square feet of office space and a daily population of sixty thousand—more people in a single building than half the counties in the country, Smith dramatically emphasized, ever the showman.

Nothing of that height or scale or financial risk had ever been built before. Raskob and Smith were proposing to build—on total speculation and without a single tenant—the largest office building in the world, in an undesirable location at the very end of a dangerously overextended building boom, hoping that the sheer overwhelming presence of the colossal tower would draw the center of the commercial city to it.

It is a spectacular gesture. If the owners are right they might fix the center of the metropolis. If they are wrong they will have the hooting of the experts in their ears for the rest of their lives.

Fortune

In October 1929, the very month the stock market began its tremendous downward spiral, work on the Empire State Building began, with the demolition of the old Waldorf-Astoria.

One month later, as the economic situation worsened, Smith called a special news conference. Far from scaling back his plans, Raskob had decided to add a massive two-hundred-foot-tall tower to the top of his eighty-five story building to guard against a counterattack from the Chrysler Building. The spire, itself as tall as a twenty-story building, would raise the final height of the structure to a mind-boggling 1,250 feet—an insurmountable 204 feet higher than its gleaming rival ten blocks to the north.

But the final delirious surprise came with the revelation of the tower's function, which Raskob himself had dreamed up.

It would serve, Smith explained to stunned members of the press, as a mooring mast for transatlantic dirigibles arriving from Europe, allowing passengers to dock a quarter of a mile in the sky over midtown Manhattan, speed through immigration and customs on the eighty-sixth floor, then be delivered by express elevators down to Fifth Avenue far below—in less than ten minutes.

Experts instantly dismissed the scheme as impracticable, pointing to the intense updrafts that would buffet airships as they tried to approach the tower, and questioning whether any passenger in his right mind would be willing to creep down an open gangway a thousand feet in the air.

But nobody seemed to care. As Raskob had predicted, the vision of the city's tallest tower serving as a cosmopolitan port of call for airships from around the world fired the public imagination as nothing else had.

Seven weeks later, on January 22, 1930—three months after the stock market crash—work began on the foundations of the mighty building.

When an unemployment crisis becomes so serious that it can no longer be ignored, the custom of officials is to cast doubt on its importance by predicting that it will soon be over. This year has been no exception to the rule.
The New Republic, March 12, 1930

Months passed, winter gave way to spring, and, despite a string of optimistic statements from financial experts and government officials, the anticipated upturn in the stock market failed to materialize. As business slowed and companies began laying off workers, the entire economy—so vibrant only a year before—began to slide into a deep depression.

Men began to appear on the sidewalks of New York trying to peddle apples that had been sold to them on credit by the Apple Shippers Association. With unemployment on the rise and factories beginning to close their doors, once sturdy banks, unable to collect their debts, began to topple.

As the future began to close in, some people found themselves unable to fend off the inexorably encroaching gloom. One Friday night, just ten days after the crash, a wealthy financier named James Riordan—treasurer of Al Smith's ill-fated campaign and president of the now-failing County Trust Savings Bank—took a pistol from the teller's cage at work, returned to his town house on West Twelfth Street, and blew his brains out.

But even as the grip of the Depression tightened around them, New Yorkers were being treated to an astounding sight, as through the spring and summer of 1930 the bare steel girders of Al Smith's building began to rise like an immense metal phoenix in the middle of Manhattan Island, clearing the rooftops of the lower buildings around it and pushing on up into the sky—a symbol of hope in the darkest of times, and a defiant declaration that the city and the country would survive.

In the lowest moment of depression we have a building shooting twelve hundred feet in the air! This at a time when it is madness to put out as much as six inches of new growth.
E. B. White

Nearly half a century of expertise in building skyscrapers on the island of Manhattan would go into the construction of the Empire State Building—a heroic feat of engineering and workmanship by any measure, at any time—let alone in the depths of the worst depression ever to beset the American economy.

The logistics of the mammoth tower's construction—the coordination of millions of building elements and thousands of men according to a carefully orchestrated schedule of manufacture, delivery, assembly, and completion—were nothing less than overwhelming. "Building skyscrapers is the nearest peacetime equivalent of war," Colonel William A. Starrett, the legendary founding partner of Starrett Brothers and Eken, declared. "In fact, the analogy is startling, even to the occasional grim reality of a building accident, where maimed bodies and even death, remind us that we are fighting a war of construction against the forces of nature."

At the peak of construction, in August 1930, 3,439 men were employed on the building, whose fifty thousand massive steel beams and columns—each weighing more than a ton and finished to tolerances of less than an eighth of an inch—were being assembled like a giant, three-dimensional jigsaw puzzle: ordered to exact specification in Pittsburgh, shipped by train to New Jersey, barged across the Hudson, and trucked along precisely choreographed routes in Manhattan to the building site at Thirty-fourth and Fifth—where, just eight hours after leaving the mill in Pennsylvania, nine massive derricks lifted them in place, and workmen fitted them together.

In an age that had perfected the assembly line for manufacturing cars and consumer goods, Starrett Brothers had perfected the first assembly line for manufacturing skyscrapers. The work progressed so rapidly that people could scarcely believe their eyes—the building all but leaping into the sky as workmen added a floor a day on average.

In one extraordinary ten-day period, fourteen new floors were erected.

On each floor, as the steel frame climbed higher, a miniature railroad was built, with switches and cars to carry supplies. A perfect time-table was published each morning. At every minute of the day the builders knew what was going up on each of the elevators, to which height it would rise, and which gang of workers would use it. On each floor, the operators of every one of the small trains of cars knew what was coming up and where it would be needed. Trucks did not wait, derricks and elevators did not swing idle, men did not wait.

Empire State, A Short History, 1931

Sunday, July 27, 1930. The whole effect is of a chase up into the sky, with the steel workers going first and all the others following madly after them.

New York Times

The workday began at 3:30 in the morning and ended at 4:30 in the afternoon. To save time and prevent congestion in the construction elevators, canteens were installed on the twenty-fourth, forty-seventh, and sixty-fourth floors, where for forty cents workmen got two sandwiches, a cup of coffee or milk, and a slice of pie.

The roar of the riveting hammer is heard by people blocks away. The men who hold the air hammer in their hands soon go deaf. We asked a man what is the most dangerous part of your job. "It is not the bolting together of a high corner still suspended by ropes," he reported. "It is not the walking along the planks with the inhospitable pavement 1000 feet below. It's the weather. When it rains everything gets slippery. When it is cold your hands get so stiff that you can't hang onto anything. Now that is bad."

New York Times

For the crowds of onlookers that gathered each day on the streets far below, the real heroes of the operation were the gangs of riveters—thousands of men working in teams of four, laboriously joining the steel framework together piece by piece. Hanging from beams a thousand feet in the sky, the gangs performed their dangerous tasks at high speed with clockwork precision—heating, tossing, catching, and driving home the red-hot rivets of steel—eight hundred rivets for each thirteen-hour day, at $1.92 an hour with a half hour off for lunch.

These are classical heroes in the flesh, outwardly prosaic, incredibly nonchalant, crawling, climbing, walking, swinging, swooping on gigantic steel frames. Hairy chested huskies, strapping youths, clean-limbed and clear-eyed—fusing the iron of their nerves with the steel of the girders they build into modern cities.

London Daily Herald

There is a good deal of strolling on the thin edge of nothingness. A splattering of fiery particles cascades down from the torches that the steel workers use for cutting ten ton girders in half and for lighting their cigarettes.

New York Times

All through the late summer and fall of 1930 the work went on. By October, the steel frame

The construction of the Empire State Building was recorded—and forever preserved—by Lewis Hine, a photographer working in the tradition of Jacob Riis, using his camera to effect social change by documenting the lives and livelihoods of ordinary working people. For six months, the 55-year-old photographer climbed all over the steel frame, balancing on beams, sharing meals with the workers, while taking more than 1,000 photographs. When the building topped out, Hine arranged to be hoisted above the framework, 1,000 feet in the air, so that he could photograph the installation of the final beam.

The Empire State Building at night, by Lewis Hine, 1930. Even before its completion, the new tower dominated the city's skyline, by day and by night. Its solitary location, above one of the highest points of land in midtown Manhattan, further emphasized its visibility. At the time this photograph was taken, the building's main structure was already complete, while work continued on the mooring mast above. Thanks in part to savings brought on by the deepening economic crisis, the building was completed 45 days ahead of schedule and $5 million under budget.

of the building's eighty-five-story main shaft was complete, and work had begun on the mooring mast. The soaring tower's uppermost beams were riveted into place a quarter of a mile in the sky in January 1931, despite howling north winds, freezing rain, and blinding fog.

At exactly 5:42 p.m. on the afternoon of March 18, 1931, the completed mooring mast was topped off, and a few weeks later the last of the interior finishing work was complete.

In the end, John Jacob Raskob and Alfred E. Smith, the great speculator and the great publicist, had triumphed, conjuring from the dwindling oxygen of the extraordinary decade the tallest building in the world, a distinction it would proudly hold for more than forty years—and despite other, taller structures to come—never seem to lose.

In all, six men had died during the construction of the Empire State Building—two laborers, an ironworker, and three carpenters—a startlingly low figure, given the danger of the work itself, the pressure of the construction schedule, and the absence of many now mandatory safety regulations.

One way or another, the heroic work crews—fully aware that the faster they worked the faster they would be joining the burgeoning ranks of the unemployed—managed to hoist 57,000 tons of structural steel into the sky (almost three times the total used in the Chrysler Building) not only higher but faster than anyone had ever dreamed possible.

From start to finish, from the commencement of work on the foundations to the last piece of interior work on the gleaming marble lobby, it had taken their heroic team of engineers and workmen *just eleven months* to erect the tallest building in the world—one of the greatest feats of construction since buildings began.

Opening day, May 1, 1931, dawned bright and clear. Al Smith, the building's official greeter, presided over the gala event held on the brand-new observation deck on the eighty-sixth floor, which was attended by Raskob and his partners, Governor Franklin D. Roosevelt, and Mayor Jimmy Walker. Under investigation now for corruption, and the object of merciless ridicule in the press, Walker gamely thanked the

building's owners for providing, he said, "a place higher, further removed than any in the world, where some public official might like to come and hide."

That evening, as a brilliantly clear twilight descended on New York, President Herbert Hoover pushed a button in the White House, and the great building was illuminated for the first time.

On May 1, 1931, what the *Brooklyn Daily Eagle* called the House that Smith Built opened with a day of ceremony and fanfare (left). Two of Smith's grandchildren cut a red ribbon outside the Fifth Avenue entrance, then used a silver key to open the doors to the marble-lined entrance hall. At exactly 11:30 a.m., President Herbert Hoover pushed a button on his desk at the White House, and the lights went on up and down the structure. The ceremony was broadcast live across the country by the CBS and NBC radio networks. Asked to comment on the building, Smith said simply, "It's a great piece of work."

On opening day, Alfred E. Smith and Governor Franklin Roosevelt took in the view from the 86th-floor observation deck (right). The governor admitted to being a "little awestruck" by the panoramic view from the great tower. "In looking out from this building," he said, "I have got an entirely new conception of things in the city of New York."

The Empire State seemed almost to float, like an enchanted fairy tower, over New York. An edifice so lofty, so serene, so marvelously simple, so luminously beautiful, had never before been imagined. One could look back on a dream well planned.

> Empire State, A Short History, 1931

And so the Roaring Twenties—the haunting, poetic decade of vaunting ambition and furious dreams—came to an end.

One year later, on a cold February morning in 1932—with much of the world locked now in a global depression—Al Smith ushered Winston Churchill out onto the windy observation deck of his skyscraper, a team of newsmen in tow.

"What you see now is from the Empire State Building," Smith said to the visiting British dignitary, as the cameras rolled, "the tallest building in the world." When Churchill remarked stiffly that he had never been so high up before, the four-term governor from the sidewalks of New York, who had failed in his bid to become president of the United States, replied without missing a beat. "I don't suppose I shall ever get any higher myself," he said.

Al Smith never got over his bitter defeat in the campaign of 1928. In the years to come—convinced Franklin Roosevelt had stolen his thunder—the once Happy Warrior would repudiate the New Deal for which his own state programs had been the model, and drifted away from the Democratic party entirely.

For John Jacob Raskob himself, things were never quite the same. Though he, too, had touched the sky, his beloved tower never lived up to his great expectations. All the high spirits of opening day could not disguise the fact that from the very start the Empire State Building was a commercial failure—and an increasing embarrassment to its principal owner.

The skeptics who had issued dire warnings about the building's risky location were proved right. By opening day, Raskob and his partners had managed to rent only 46 percent of the building's office space. Even Al Smith's immense personal charm and public relations wizardry could not persuade corporate tenants to abandon their perches above Wall Street and Grand Central and move to the oddly placed eyrie. Though the owners proudly kept the lights burning throughout the building, most people knew it was empty from the forty-first floor up and only partially rented below. Wits took to calling it the Empty State Building.

Within a year of opening, what was to have been a symbol of the might of American finance seemed to many to have become a monument to the excesses of the 1920s.

After two unsuccessful attempts to dock dirigibles at the top of the Empire State Building, the mooring mast was abandoned.

The Empire State, a lonely dinosaur, rose sadly at midtown, highest tower, tallest mountain, longest road, King Kong's eyrie, meant to moor airships, alas.

> Vincent Scully

Yet despite all the problems, New Yorkers fell in love with the soaring structure, and almost overnight, the Empire State Building became the most romantic and widely recognizable symbol of the city. Visitors from around the country and the world thronged to its thrilling observation deck, which in its first year of operation took in more than a million dollars—as much as its owners made in rent that year—and instantly became the city's most popular tourist attraction.

The mooring mast, unsuitable for airships, soon found its real vocation, as a mighty wand for casting radio, and then television, signals out over the airwaves. Though the building never made Thirty-fourth Street the center of commercial gravity in Manhattan, even that failure would eventually come to seem a kind of triumph: the simple soaring tower forever standing in its splendid isolation—magnificent, proud, visible from afar, and incomparable.

And so it has stood, from that day to this. Summoned from the earth at the end of the 1920s by commercial and cultural forces that had been building for a century, the Empire State Building was the supreme expression of the city's unparalleled power to shape and reshape its own destiny.

Rising as the city and country sank into the worst depression of their history, it marked a mighty culmination and crucial turning point in the life of New York City. Never again would there be such boundless faith in the future or in the unbridled forces of commerce and

The Empire State Building from above. Built to withstand a horizontal pull of 50 tons, the building's 200-foot-tall mooring mast was structurally capable of fulfilling the function for which it had been designed. Strong updraft winds, however, made it almost impossible for lighter-than-air craft to approach the tower near enough to dock. Only two mooring attempts were ever made—one on September 16, 1931, when a private dirigible was able to link up for three minutes to the peak of the mast, and another two weeks later, when, with great difficulty, the Goodyear blimp *Columbia* managed to approach the tower long enough to drop off a stack of newspapers and a letter addressed to Al Smith. No further landings were attempted. The space on the 86th floor that was to be devoted to baggage rooms and customs desks for air travelers arriving from Europe was converted into a soda fountain for sightseers.

capitalism. Never again would the city hold such unrivaled sway over the culture and commerce of the United States.

Nor would the gleaming metropolis ever feel quite so indisputably like the center of the world. New forces were abroad in the land—unleashed in part by the city's very power and in part by its breathtaking profligacy—and in the decades to come those forces would dramatically transform the relationship of the city and the country.

No one sensed those changes more poignantly, or expressed them more lyrically, than the city's brilliant fallen angel, F. Scott Fitzgerald, whose own career was already descending into darkness.

Two years after the crash, in what he called the "dark autumn" of 1931, he returned to New York for the first time in nearly three years. A lifetime before, he had come to a place where everything seemed possible. Now everything had changed, and in a piercing, clear-eyed, melancholy essay called "My Lost City," he struggled to put into words exactly what that was.

> *From the ruins, lonely and inexplicable as the sphinx, rose the Empire State Building and, just as it had been a tradition of mine to climb to the Plaza Roof to take leave of the beautiful city, extending as far as eyes could reach, so now I went to the roof of the last and most magnificent of towers. Then I understood—everything was explained: I had discovered the crowning error of the city, its Pandora's box. Full of vaunting pride the New Yorker had climbed here and seen with dismay what he had never suspected, that the city was not the endless succession of canyons that he had supposed, but that it had limits—from the tallest structure he saw for the first time that it faded out into the country on all sides, into an expanse of green and blue that alone was limitless. And with the awful realization that New York was a city after all and not a universe, the whole shining edifice that he had reared in his imagination came crashing to the ground. That was the rash gift of Alfred E. Smith to the citizens of New York.*
>
> F. Scott Fitzgerald

Flagrant délit, Madelon Vriesendorp.

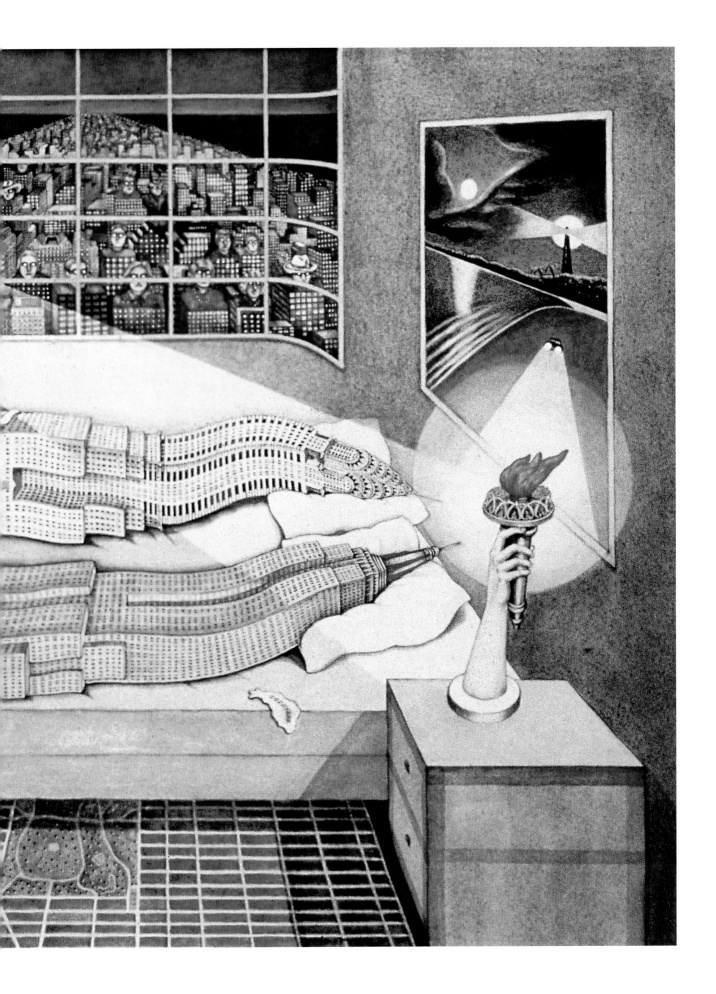

HARLEM RENAISSANCE
DAVID LEVERING LEWIS

How has the African American experience in New York been different from that of other ethnic minorities?

This is a settler nation and knowing what it is to be an American is, of course, terribly important. One way to define what being an American is is negatively—what Americans are not. And increasingly it developed that the definition of Americanness excluded African Americans: not being black is to be a citizen. Not being like them defines what we are. There was a time, in fact, when many whites were not "white." Before 1930 or 1940 there was a hierarchy: the WASP, the Puritan, the German. New ethnic groups were somewhat stigmatized. The Irish were a great danger. The Italians larcenous and felonious. Incredibly enough there was even an official commission that decided the Jews, in the main, were intellectually substandard. And this was, of course, part of the attempt to plank down on this teeming mass of people a notion of Americanness that granted privilege to the earlier Americans. And so Irish weren't really white. Italians were not white. There is much more at work here as well, but one of the phenomena is the distancing of oneself from the African American. And so the African American experience has a kind of double bind, out of poverty, out of an agrarian crucible into the urban situation perhaps a little late. If we had come earlier, we perhaps could have been essential to the formation of labor unions. We come when the main labor union, the American Federation of Labor, is exclusively white. And that combined with this dynamic of distinction makes the African American experience quite different. Not tragic, but a lot harder.

How did Harlem change after World War I?

Very shortly after the war was the "great migration," which is tied up with the turning off of the spigot of European migration and the recruitment of African Americans from the South by large industries and railroads. The magnitude of the population increased: you see estimates of 200,000 African Americans pouring into Harlem from 1917 to about 1925. So Harlem became for African Americans everywhere the chrysalis of the New Negro—of new opportunity. And those people transformed that area of Harlem which in those days—until about the mid-1930s—was West Harlem. Eighth Avenue, which ran straight up the spine of Harlem,

increasingly divided black Harlem from white Harlem. And in terms of proportionality, much of Harlem remained white for a very long time, until after World War II.

What would be the most striking thing for an African American arriving in Harlem in 1925?

I suppose what would impress the newcomer coming out of the subway would be a complex and totally self-sustaining universe that is black. Or, I should say, the *appearance* of it, because as I have written, the Harlem Renaissance took place in rented space. The newcomer would have seen signs indicating that St. Philip's Church owned many blocks of housing. There were African American real-estate concerns. The appearance was of a community that had pooled its resources, as it had, but the reality still was that ownership of Harlem was outside Harlem.

What did Harlem mean for African Americans at that moment?

Certainly an economic opportunity. If you got a job in New York, you made more than you did in the Mississippi Delta or in the Carolinas. In light industry, in domestic service, as a redcap or Pullman porter, work in Harlem meant a considerable augmentation of the quality of life. But on top of that, Harlem became an entity in the *mind*, representing what was called the New Negro, and the opportunities to change the perception of the African American through creativity—which is a very New York story, isn't it? It seems incredible that you would have something that was soon called the Harlem Renaissance—so designated by the *Herald-Tribune*—which came about as a result of a 1925 banquet at a Fifth Avenue restaurant at which were present some of the young Harlem writers. By then, the notion had emerged that the way to combat racism is to create an arts movement—to recruit, from as far as California and the Deep South, people who wrote fiction or poetry or had musical or acting ability—and the National Association for the Advancement of Colored People and the National Urban League in a sense put aside their more obvious mandates and went into the arts business. And soon the fascination, the appeal, the aura of Harlem became transcendental.

How did the Harlem Renaissance affect Harlem itself?

It began as a showcasing of the Talented Tenth, of the New Negro, of what was considered exemplary. And contrary to what a famous participant of the Harlem Renaissance—the poet Sterling Brown—was to say, it *did* percolate. The Harlem Renaissance was appreciated and applauded by the man and woman in the street and in the barber shop and in the beauty parlor. That's what is so fascinating, that you find redcaps and bellhops and postal workers and janitors following the prize-givings at the *Opportunity* magazine banquet or interested in the Guggenheim award that Walter White or Zora Neale Hurston gets. Enthralled by the debates going on about Carl Van Vechten's best-seller, *Nigger Heaven*. It was a curiously participatory time in terms of culture, of using culture as a weapon.

How did Harlem promote the spread of African American culture into the mainstream?

Broadway, to a much larger extent than one might recall, was a creature of Harlem—those early musicals produced by James Weldon Johnson and Rosamond Johnson and by Will Marion Cooke and Bob Cole and, of course, *Shuffle Along* by Miller and Lyles, which was perhaps the most successful Broadway production of its day. All of that got Florenz Ziegfeld going and gave him talent and gave him things to promote or buy at bargain-basement prices to take downtown. So there seems to be a tornado of creativity in these few blocks above Central Park. The success of African American music, in terms of its intrinsic splendors, was great at this time. Even a racist could recognize that Sidney Bechet had one heck of a horn, say, or that Louis Armstrong was a very gifted musician. But of course there was subordination built into the activity. Jazz was far less threatening than a terrific novel by W. E. B. DuBois or by Walter White, and it also benefited from a kind of collaboration of subcultures. There is a definite cooptation of this music as Benny Goodman and Paul Whiteman and others take it on. Then it's safe music.

What was the interaction between Harlem and Greenwich Village?

At opposite ends of Manhattan, they are two countercultures, and both are involved in similar activities—artistic and literary. There's linkage early on, beginning just as World War I is ending with Claude McKay and Jean Toomer moving to the Village. You have Paul Robeson being sculpted by Antonio Seleni, the sculptor whose studio was in the shadow of Washington Square. The difference, though, is that the bohemian artists in the Village were there by election—to make a statement about what was wrong with a culture that they wished to have no part of, until they had transformed it. In Harlem, even though the artists often spoke the same lingo and denounced Mammon and talked about what was wrong with mainstream culture, I think in truth they saw their criticism as a device in order to *enter* the culture. And so although they could understand each other, they often were really talking at cross-purposes. In

Spectators in Harlem windows watch the 1919 victory parade.

other words, the quotient of revolution in the Harlem Renaissance, it seems to me, was distinctly lighter than the articulated quotient of revolution in the Village, thinking of Max Eastman's *Liberator* and its critiques of capitalism. Or the "lyrical left" around *Seven Arts* and other magazines. I think those distinctions—which were not perceived at the time—are useful to bear in mind. But the cross-pollination was of course important, the actual physical interplay as bohemia comes to Harlem, guided by Claude McKay and Jean Toomer, and as Harlem comes to bohemia.

Why did the Harlem Renaissance end?

There is a debate about the termination of the Harlem Renaissance. Some scholars believe that it didn't sputter out. I happen to think it did, because the participants themselves said it had faltered and failed. It failed in the sense that what it initially attempted to accomplish was illusory. Just as with white artists, the transformation of American society through the arts was not going to happen. The arts are important, but there were other forces that certainly precluded that kind of agency. And the African Americans' effort, being more fragile and newer, was that much more vulnerable. It had, in terms of its pool of talent, really quite an incredibly small pool of maybe thirty or forty people. An arts movement launched with about thirty or forty people and so all the more incredible an achievement. But it was not being replenished from below. And one of the reasons it was not replenished from below, at least after 1929, was, of course, the Depression. So you don't have people coming out of Fisk and Howard wanting to get a contract at Knopf. Life became real and earnest. And so at that point, except for the truly gifted artists, the people who would have written had there been no Harlem Renaissance—Langston Hughes, Countee Cullen, Zora Hurston—the others found reasons to withdraw. There is a continuum, to be sure. The Work Progress Administration, in a sense, replaces the NAACP and the Urban League and also the Communist party. But the economic underpinning, taken away with the meltdown of the Depression, I think explains why it becomes a historic achievement—with resonances that will continue, to be sure.

How did Harlem change after the onset of the Depression?

As Gilbert Osofsky has said, it became a slum. It had been a ghetto before, it becomes a real slum afterward. And what's the distinction? The distinction is simply that it had been a place of reasonable viability, of uneven prosperity, but nonetheless some prosperity to keep things ticking along, isolated as it was. After the Depression, rents, evictions,

unemployment, tuberculosis, all sorts of indicia of decay and dysfunction accelerate. But it begins to regenerate in the late 1930s and in the '40s. And one thing that helps it is a political input that Harlem had never had. We've been talking about politics only in terms of the arts and that's because there wasn't politics in terms of politics in Harlem—in large part because the Twenty-first Congressional District, the math of it, precluded African Americans electing someone to represent them as they would have wanted. Around 1944 or so the district is chopped up and recalibrated and that produces Adam Clayton Powell, Jr.—and then we have a new ball game in terms of politics.

Why should we remember the Harlem Renaissance?

If it didn't achieve what it set out to in political or civil-rights terms, it did present the African American as a creative artist, and as an American who knew how to take themes that mattered to Americans and develop them. Institutionally, the influence on Broadway—*Green Pastures* and *All God's Chillun Got Wings* and any number of dramatic breakthroughs, perhaps obsolescent now, at the time said much more about America in general than about African Americans only. Also, it is important because it *is* a legacy. We continue to revisit the Harlem Renaissance and measure what it did and did not accomplish, and that colors our own activities. And I suppose it's also edifying to see the success of a group of people who were recently out of slavery, an institution predicated upon illiteracy. It could only work that way, committing itself to a supremely literate enterprise—writing books and poetry and plays and the rest. As far as New York is concerned, it's just part of that mosaic of heterogeneous activity, some of it more productive, more genuine than others, but all of it an important element in the dynamic of a city.

COSMOPOLITAN CAPITAL: NEW YORK IN THE 1920s

ROBERT A. M. STERN

INTERVIEW

What's distinctive about New York?

New York is the democratic capitalistic capital of the world, and the most modern of cities. It's a city that grew up in the modern period. Very few cities—and almost none outside of the United States—really combine the democratic impulse with the growth of capitalism.

What do you find most moving about New York?

First of all, as an architect, that the city is a physical artifact. Not just buildings but the way buildings influence people's lives. As an architect you could never be bored in the city, because you can always find the history of the place if you can read the buildings. I read the buildings like an archaeologist might read the seven layers of Troy. And when you walk around the city and you read the buildings and go from one place to another, you get an incredible sense of the richness of the place and how it evolved and—despite the fact that we've torn down an awful lot, despite the fact that we don't landmark enough—how much of the history of the city is still pretty much in place. The city streets are a gallery of architecture. The great architecture critic Montgomery Schuyler made that observation around 1900; it is even more true today. To walk the city streets is to walk a great museum of architecture, and one can make up stories about what happened behind each and every one of those facades, in each and every building.

What makes New York's skyscrapers so special?

The incredible office buildings that were built in the city were not just tall buildings. They were something else, a special New York type—the skyscraper. There is lots of confusing discussion about skyscraper construction and so forth, but in my book, a skyscraper is a building that is not only high but sends up a towerlike form above its base that is forever unencumbered by any other building, so it has an iconic presence on what comes to be called a skyline. And that iconic presence, from the 1890s to the 1930s, was concluded with some kind of visible symbol at the top. Gothic tracery in the Woolworth Building. A modern version of Gothic tracery in that spike-like culmination of the Chrysler Building. A kind of phallic who-knows-what at the top of the Empire State Building—but once seen, who can ever forget? The great pyramidal roof of the Bank of the Manhattan Company, 40 Wall Street, on and on. Every one of those buildings becomes a corporate logo. The Bankers Trust Building rises to a stepped pyramid at the top, which is on their stationery and is their corporate logo to this day. So that's another thing that is released, this impulse to make these commercial buildings into civic monuments.

What forces converged to create so many skyscrapers at the foot of Manhattan?

In the early days, it was the shortage of land in lower Manhattan, which had to be maintained as the business district because of all the infrastructure already in place: early telephone, early electricity, the telegraph, the transatlantic cable—it all happened in lower Manhattan. Of course, you needed to have the elevator to allow people to go above five floors comfortably. You needed to electrify the elevator to make it possible for the elevator to go fast and to have all kinds of safety devices. You needed to have a framing system other than bearing-wall masonry to allow people to build at great height without creating such thick walls at the bottom as to render the space at the base of the building virtually uninhabitable. So all those needed to be. But the skyscraper, I think, got an extra kick by the notion that by building great height in a visible site such as Manhattan Island, you have this great advantage. You can get back from it and *see* it. You can take a picture of it. You can show people as they arrive from Europe—not immigrants, they didn't care about them—but all those rich people getting off all those liners, they look up and see lower Manhattan, they say, What's that building? The Bankers Trust Company. What's that building? The Singer Sewing Machine Company. And Singer is an international company.

Why were the early-twentieth-century skyscrapers—the Singer Building, the Woolworth Tower—so distinctive and extraordinary?

The great skyscrapers—the iconic skyscrapers—were built as advertisements. And the idea of advertising and communication through buildings, in advance of communication through other media, was developed in New York. So the reason why lower Manhattan has this great explosion of buildings is because of the great corporations located there, such as Singer and Woolworth. Singer is the most important corporation of the nineteenth century. Every American woman had a sewing machine. It was the way she could survive, creating clothing for her household. So how basic can you get? Then you come to Woolworth, which brings a kind of sophisticated marketing to the average main street of American towns. Frank Woolworth didn't need an office building; he wasn't going to fill sixty stories with people processing bills for his company. He recognized that you build a great skyscraper for advertising value. And he went to his bankers and said he wanted to build this great skyscraper facing City Hall Park. In 1913, there were no tall buildings to rival it nearby, and he had the same front yard that the city government had. So it was a fantastic site. And it was a Broadway location—the main artery of the city, the most identifiable street. All these things pile up. He goes to his bankers and they turn him down. They said, Mr. Woolworth, you don't need this building. We're not even sure this location—slightly outside of Wall Street—is going to rent. So he says, Okay, I'll pay for it myself, cash. Now, that doesn't quite mean he reached into his pocket and took out nickels and dimes, but he basically built it out of his own corporate funds. He paid for the building himself and that was $13 million those days, you have to do some sort of multiplier for today. Even today $13 million is still a lot of money. And he built it.

What made New York so powerful in this era?

All the great industries are capitalized out of New York. All European investment funds—principally from France and England, which are really the bankers of America in the nineteenth century and early twentieth century—pour into New York through Wall Street. J. P. Morgan, who engineers the consolidation of great corporations like U.S. Steel, does it out of Wall Street. All this money is here and Morgan himself, what does he do? He builds this extraordinary library. He gets Charles McKim to lay up the stone as the ancients did. Hardly any mortar in the stone. It's dry stone, like the Parthenon—as if to say, We're not going to screw around in New York, we're going to build something forever, along the same high ideals. Morgan's building of course is a jewel where he keeps his treasures, the great manuscripts. But J. P. Morgan also uses his library as his receiving room for dignitaries. The new Jewish bankers are received there. He forges alliances there, surrounded by all this culture. Culture, God and Mammon, commerce and high cultural ideals are married together in New York in a way that they never were anyplace else in the world. Morgan creates this great environment in which to do business. And he has his office there and then he connects it by an underground tunnel to his house on another corner of the property. Where else does this happen? Nowhere but in New York.

People have often said that the twentieth century did not truly begin until the soldiers returned from the First World War. Do you think this was true in New York?

In the 1920s, New York became for the first time a crossroads of two basically disenfranchised groups. One was very American. It was all the people who'd been living on the farms, who realized that farm life was totally bleak, totally cut off, totally without a future, and they moved to the cities—all these clerks and secretaries and ambitious young writers. Yes, we had them in the 1890s and the 1900s, but by the First World War it was "How are you going to keep 'em down on the farm after they've seen Paree?" Well, you're *not* going to keep them down on the farm. So you have this influx of one disenfranchised group to make their fortune in New York—not as moguls but in the advertising agencies and so forth—even F. Scott Fitzgerald worked for an ad agency in New York after Princeton. You have another group—which was there before, but nobody paid much attention to it—the second wave of immigrants. Suddenly a guy named Izzy Baline becomes Irving Berlin. He rises up from the local bar and writes a song called "Alexander's Ragtime Band." And suddenly everybody's dancing to this work of a Jewish American, Russian-born, New York kid, writing a ragtime associated with African Americans, and high society's dancing to it. And he writes more of them. And then there's George Gershwin and then Italian Americans come in and they're part of a culture, and suddenly popular culture is a part of the world scene. You're seeing Fanny Brice. Who is Fanny Brice? A Jewish American girl from the Lower East Side who speaks with a funny accent, has a hooked nose. She'd never get into a fancy apartment house, but the people who are in the fancy apartment houses are sitting there watching her. And on it goes, a whole new bubbling energy. Jazz music, the vitality of the streets is increased. Motion pictures come into play and they record the city in such a way that it makes it seem even more exciting than it was, and they capture the image of the city in motion. And suddenly people become enthralled with what they were rebelling against in the nineteenth century—traffic itself. Density itself. Then society turns around and gets into its limousines and with its illegal quest for liquor and thrills goes to Harlem, where blacks who had really played not much of a part in mainstream American life are entertaining in white-only clubs. And that's another part of the story.

Why does the Empire State Building occupy such a special place in the heart of this city?

The Empire State Building is the greatest skyscraper of the pure type, ever. It has going for it a number of fantastic things. One is its site—even today it rises virtually unsurrounded by anything high. So there's just the sheer height of it. And then the beautiful massing of the building, symmetrical on every elevation, but stepping back at great scale

Midtown Manhattan, looking northwest from 34th Street and Third Avenue, 1932.

to the top. And then it has this magic terrace where you can look out on the city as though you're almost on the deck of a dirigible. And beyond it has this illuminated lantern—vertical proportioned, phallic if you will—which was supposed to be a landing mast for dirigibles, but who knows what they really had in mind. But what a great culmination—a lantern! It's the great lighthouse for the city. In the ancient world of Egypt or Greece, you had these great lanterns in the harbor. The Statue of Liberty was a great lantern, or lighthouse—"I lift my lamp beside the golden door." Here was the lighthouse of commerce in the middle of midtown where all the buildings were low. And the Empire State Building is not only an incredible icon, it also has the ironic role in this story of coming after the crash of the stock market, like the guest who arrives too late at the party. They had to build the building as quickly as possible in the hopes of getting some tenants in. So the building was built in eleven months, which makes it probably the fastest piece of construction for anything that size. The coordination of men and parts, of the fine materials that went into the building, are stupendous of themselves. And there were these fantastic Lewis Hine photographs of the men out on the girders, the American Indians and others doing stupendous feats—it's beautifully documented.

How did F. Scott Fizgerald recognize the foreboding, the underlying sadness, that encapsulates this period?

You see it in *The Great Gatsby*. You see that sadness amid the champagne gloss. You see in Tom Buchanan, this rich guy living out on the North Shore of Long Island with his sort of trophy wife, they're unhappy. You see the valley of the ashes, which Robert Moses would make so much of because it's the site of Flushing Meadows and the World's Fair; Moses transformed a dump into a fair—from the dump to glory, he would call it. You see it going across the Queensborough Bridge into the glittering heart of midtown Manhattan, where the Plaza Hotel really was the glamorous place. But, of course, a glamorous place that you can't get a drink in. Here you are in the most sophisticated city in the world, and you can't get a drink. So they have to go to a cheap apartment where the girlfriend lives on Riverside Drive. And then there's Gatsby himself, of course, lording it out on Long Island, but is he a bootlegger? Where does he come from? Who are these people in New York? Of course, what's happening in New York is a whole new shadowy class is coming. Fitzgerald is generally very interesting on New York, because he's a writer who really sees the urban frame, he sees the buildings, he sees what they mean. "The diamond as big as the Ritz." Somehow, once you read that phrase, this hotel—a glamorous hotel now gone—is equated in your mind with what it personified, the riches and the jewelry and so forth. He talks about the "first fresh green breast of the republic": what the Dutch settlers must have seen. He is seeing New York as totally cut off from the world of the founding fathers. He is seeing that modern New York has become its own thing and has almost no ties left. Then he goes to the top of the Empire State Building, a new building, higher than man had ever been able to be, and he sees that beyond the edge you can still see green and the real world, and you see his New York as this great self-contained island. So he gives us a vivid picture of the tensions between the city and this continent—and he continues to do so, of course, after the Depression. The bubble has burst. He's sad, his own personal life is kind of screwed up, it's very complicated, but I think that he gives us a wonderful history of the city and its cultural highs and lows. He's a wonderful tour guide to the period.

The Hell Gate crossing of the Triborough Bridge, just after its completion in 1936. Over half a mile in length, the great span was just one of *four* separate bridges that made up the huge Triborough project.

At its center point, the roadway hovered 135 feet above the waters of the Hell Gate, while each of the bridge's towers was taller than a football field standing on end.

THE CITY OF
1931–1939
TOMORROW

New cities have always replaced old cities, by periods. But today it is possible for the city of modern times, the happy city, the radiant city, to be born.

Le Corbusier

The 1939–40 New York World's Fair, seen from the observation deck of the RCA Building in Rockefeller Center. Rising beyond the industrial landscape of Queens are the exposition's unmistakable theme buildings: the futuristic 610-foot- tall tower known as the Trylon, and the 180-foot- diameter Perisphere by its side. Arrayed around the two central structures are the fair's gleaming white pavilions, including the General Motors Futurama, to the right.

THE RADIANT CITY

If F. Scott Fitzgerald had been acute in sensing how severely the Empire State Building rebuked even as it embodied New York's dream of limitless upward growth, he had overlooked another reality—one that, by the fall of 1931, was equally apparent from the observation deck of the mighty tower.

All through the giddy vertical rise of the 1920s, New Yorkers had been pursuing another kind of dream, not upward but out—into the "expanse of green and blue" that, as Fitzgerald had seen, "alone was limitless."

Propelled by the rising prosperity and restlessness of New Yorkers, and by the revolutionary invention that since the turn of the century had become the shining emblem of both—the automobile—this centrifugal movement beyond the boundaries of Greater New York and out into the suburban hinterlands of New Jersey, Long Island, and Westchester County would alter forever the relationship of the city to its surroundings, and pioneer a new way of life in America.

More than any other innovation in the history of the city, the car would transform—and ultimately threaten with extinction—the qualities that had defined New York since the time of the Dutch. For three hundred years, every new breakthrough in transportation and communication, from the packet ship and the Erie Canal to the steamship, telegraph, railroad, and subway, had augmented the city's centrality, increased its density, and enhanced its power, even as the city itself expanded dramatically.

The automobile would be a radical departure from all that. Appearing on the streets of New York in the early years of the century—at the very zenith of the age of rail—the car, and the world that would rise up around it, would challenge all previous assumptions about urban life: replacing the radial patterns of ships and railways that had concentrated forces in the city for centuries with a diffuse grid of roads and highways that dispersed people and resources out across the open countryside.

In the four decades following the crash of '29, as the city moved through the Depression to World War II and beyond, New York would become the arena of a titanic contest between the car and the pedestrian—between the highway and the city block, between the compact if often congested urban neighborhood and the sprawling if often anonymous commuter suburb. Before it was over, that contest would all but tear the city apart and force New Yorkers to confront the most elemental urban questions of all. What is a city? What makes cities work? Why should there be cities at all?

The ironies were many, and stark. Just as the great metropolis arrived at the apogee of its power, the urban ideals it celebrated would be called into question as never before. Much of the theory for this attack would come from European modernists like the Swiss-born architect Le Corbusier, who, at once mesmerized and appalled by New York, assailed the very qualities that made it distinctive—its cramped verticality, congestion, and chaotic human density. "New York is a vertical city," he wrote, "under the sign of the new times. It is a catastrophe with which a too hasty destiny has overwhelmed courageous and confident people." Challenging everything Manhattan stood for, and championing everything it could never hope to be, Le Corbusier proposed a stunning countervision of the modern metropolis: an anti-city that was in essence an anti–New York—dispersed, streamlined, rational, flowing, radiant, pristine, and decentralized—a city built as much around the needs of the automobile as around the needs of people.

"Against New York—" Le Corbusier wrote, "turbulent clamor of the giant adolescent of the machine age—I counteract with horizontal skyscrapers. Paris, city of the straight line and the horizontal, will tame the vertical."

Only time would tell which vision of the metropolis would prevail. In the meantime, as the balance of power shifted dramatically in America between the city and the country, New York would be forced to look outward as it had not since the time of the English and the Dutch, as New Yorkers themselves struggled to come to terms with the confusing, increasingly complex interrelationships between the city and the surrounding region, between the city and the federal government, and between the city and the world.

Our visitors are confronted with so much gaiety in New York, especially where the lights are brightest, that they fall into the literary error of ascribing any metropolitan utilization of voltage to the pursuit of pleasure. And it is difficult to look at the lighted windows . . . [of Manhattan's skyscrapers] and not idealize them into some sort of manifestation of joy and exuberance. But if the writers who thrill so at the sight . . . could . . . be projected along any one of these million beams of fairy light, they would find that it came directly from an office peopled by tired [office workers], each watching the clock as lighting-up time comes, not to start out on a round of merrymaking but to embark on a long subway ride. . . . And this ride will take them on past the haunts that the visitors and their hosts know, past the clubs and theatres and squash courts, to an enormous city . . . where life is, with the exception of a certain congestion in living quarters, exactly the same as life in Muncie, Indiana, or Quincy, Illinois. . . . It is not even picturesque, as the [Lower] East Side is picturesque. It is a melting pot where the ingredients refuse to melt. The people are just as much New Yorkers as those in the Forties, and they outnumber the "typical" New Yorkers to so great an extent that an intramural battle between the two elements could not possibly last for more than twenty minutes, even if the pixies had machine guns.
Robert Benchley, 1928

Even as Manhattan continued its delirious ride through the Roaring Twenties, the outlying boroughs were undergoing a revolution of their own—one that in the space of 10 years would utterly transform the landscape of Greater New York and forever shift the historic balance in population between Manhattan and its surroundings.

As late as 1920, New York's population had been strikingly concentrated on its central island, which was still home to 2.3 million people and—as it had been for three centuries—the most populous part of the entire region. But that same year, the greatest building boom in the city's history got under way—a decade-long burst of construction that, supercharged by the greatest expansion of the transit system ever undertaken, would fill out the vast open spaces of the city's two largest boroughs—Brooklyn and Queens—with breathtaking speed, and drive the most traditionally urban of American cities to pioneer a new kind of environment: the suburb.

It began with a landmark 1913 transit arrangement known as "the dual system" in which the city's two private subway companies agreed not only to interlink their lines but to embark on a joint construction program of unprecedented scope, nearly tripling the size of the system to an incredible total of 619 track miles. In less than a decade, a thick new web of subway lines had been laid across the city, tying Manhattan for the first time to Queens and pushing ever farther into undeveloped areas of the Bronx and Brooklyn.

In Brooklyn—where express lines now extended across the entire length of the borough, all the way to Coney Island and the sea— and in Queens—where huge empty tracts of land were just minutes away from midtown Manhattan— the stage had been set for one of the most remarkable spurts of residential growth in the city's history.

A new city has arisen on the old Sheepshead Bay tract in an incredibly short space of time! It was only five months ago that this magnificent property was broken up into building lots and sold to homeseekers. . . . Today $3,000,000 worth of new homes and stores are under construction. . . . Take advantage of this extraordinary opportunity to buy AT YOUR OWN PRICE. Lots on and near Ocean Avenue, directly in the path of the inevitable expansion of Brooklyn . . . AND ONLY FOUR BLOCKS FROM THE SUBWAY EXPRESS STATION.
Advertisement, *New York World*, January 27, 1924

With more than 2 million residents in 1920, Brooklyn was already a huge city. But most of its population still clustered in the older, solidly built communities in the northwest corner of the borough. Beyond them stretched Brooklyn's southern tier, a vast sandy outwash plain that had remained largely rural—until now. Suddenly, along the path of the newly built subway lines, dozens of new communities began to spring up: Bensonhurst, Midwood, Flatbush, Canarsie, Bushwick, East New York, Sheepshead Bay. By 1922, Brooklyn was leading every other county in the United States in new construction, and every year, thousands of working families in Manhattan—enjoying a modest share of the era's widespread prosperity—were buying or building new homes across the river, a process accelerated by the advent of the installment plan, which allowed new homes to be purchased with only a modest down payment.

"Small tradesmen of the slums, even workingmen, were investing their savings in houses and lots," the editor Abraham Cahan later recalled. "Carpenters, house-painters, bricklayers or peddlers became builders of frame dwellings, real-estate speculators. Deals were being closed and poor men making thousands of dollars in less time than it took them to drink a glass of tea or the sorrel soup over which the transaction took

Greenpoint Park in Brooklyn, after its opening on July 11, 1926

place. Women, too, were ardently dabbling."

Between 1918 and 1929, an astonishing 117,000 new residential buildings were built in Brooklyn—not only multistory apartment buildings but more than 46,000 single-family dwellings, arrayed across "mile after mile of pleasant streets," one man later wrote, "lined with snug, small houses, each having a little grass plot, a porch, a sun-room." As often as not, the new houses also included a small garage, to accommodate a family possession that was quickly becoming as common as the house itself—the automobile. At the far edge of the city, among its fastest-growing communities, New Yorkers were pioneering a new way of life, in which the density and concentration of traditional urban neighborhoods were giving way to a proto-suburban environment of lawns, detached houses—and cars.

By the end of the decade, Brooklyn had gained 540,000 new residents, in districts that now stretched almost the entire length of the borough. "There seems almost no conceivable end to Brooklyn," the critic James Agee wrote a few years later. "[It] seems, on land as flat and huge as Kansas, horizon beyond horizon forever unfolded, an immeasurable proliferation of house on house and street by street; or seems as China does, infinite in time, in patience, and in population as in space."

To the north, meanwhile, the borough of Queens—growing just as quickly—was being transformed even more dramatically, for unlike Brooklyn it had begun the decade not as a city of 2 million but as a sprawling, largely empty landscape of farms, fields, and villages, with only 469,000 people spread across its 114 square miles.

Queens named its communities Forest Hills, Kew Gardens, Elmhurst, Woodside, Sunnyside, Jackson Heights, Corona, Astoria (after the Astors, of all people). The builders built the apartment houses in mock Tudor or Gothic or Colonial and named them The Chateau, The El Dorado, Linsley Hall, the Alhambra. We lived first in the East Gate, then moved to the West Gate, then to Hampton Court. And the lobbies had Chippendale furniture and Aztec fireplaces, and the ele-vators had roman numerals on the buttons. . . . Queens, a comfortable rest stop, a pleasant rung on the ladder of success, a promise we were promised in some secret dream. . . . And isn't Manhattan, each day the skyline growing denser and more crenelated, always looming up there in the distance? The elevated subway, the Flushing line, zooms to it, only fourteen minutes to Grand Central Station.

John Guare

Working in undeveloped areas just minutes from midtown Manhattan, builders in Queens pioneered another suburban ideal: the garden apartment. In Astoria, Sunnyside, and Jackson Heights, large-scale developers such as the Queensboro Corporation put up spacious cooperative apartment complexes, each built around a sweeping central landscape—"the ideal apartment house[s]," their advertisements insisted. "The buildings are set back from the street and the rear yards are treated as a large interior park for rest and recreation."

Covering a full block each, Queensboro's projects offered newcomers from Manhattan an almost unimaginable level of luxury, with playgrounds, community gardens, bowling alleys, tennis courts, and a 12-hole golf course. At the same time, the company insisted that the new arrivals—whose previous home might well have been a tenement—follow strict middle-class standards of decorum. Tenants were forbidden from shaking mops or brooms out of open windows, or hanging clotheslines to dry their wash. The company also helped to reinforce another suburban precedent, insisting that in the name of "common ideals and living standards," and "financial and social compatibility," none of its units be sold to Jews, Italians, or blacks.

By 1929, Queensboro projects stretched 23 blocks across Jackson Heights, and Queens as a whole had gained more than 600,000 inhabitants—transformed almost overnight from a thinly settled collection of villages and farms to a sprawling urban landscape of more than a million people.

Ever since the consolidation of the city in 1898, reformers had dreamed of the day when new forms of mass transportation would allow Manhattan's teeming throngs to disperse themselves across the canvas of the five-borough city. In the single decade of the 1920s, to a remarkable degree, their dream became reality. In 10 years, Manhattan lost half a million people, even as Brooklyn and Queens together gained 1.2 million. For the first time in the city's history, the most populous part of New York was not Manhattan Island but Brooklyn, whose 2.5 million residents made it bigger than any other city in the country except Chicago.

Though Manhattan would always remain the city's commercial and cultural crossroads, New York's residential center of gravity had shifted from the heart of the city to its edge—a change whose impact would grow even more significant in the years to come.

For families moving from cramped Manhattan apartments, the spacious garden apartment complexes in the newly built Queens communities like Jackson Heights (such as Cambridge Court, below) seemed a dream come true. Visiting nearby Sunnyside Gardens in 1925, the journalist Bruce Bliven praised the projects for their "open great lawns, fresh air, sunshine and the chance to participate in a real community."

INTO THE BLUE AND GREEN

The street plan of Manhattan, proud and strong, established in colonial times, a model of wisdom and greatness of vision, is today in mortal danger because of the motorcar.

Le Corbusier, 1937

It seemed an almost comical invention at first—a harmless toy skittering around the surface of Manhattan. Appearing at the turn of the century—just as the newly consolidated city came to a crescendo of rail-based connections, with new underwater links to the mainland, new railway stations in Manhattan, and a massive new subway system that knit the entire city together by rail—the first automobiles were seen less as a serious means of transportation than as the playthings of rich men: expensive, fragile, and rare.

"The ordinary 'horseless carriage,'" the editor of the *Literary Digest* declared in 1899, "is at present a luxury for the wealthy; and altho its price will probably fall in the future, it will never, of course, come into as common use as the bicycle."

And yet from the very start, the car and the pedestrian would engage in a bitter competition for possession of the city streets. Almost immediately, New York's rich—who by 1900 owned half of the eight thousand cars in America—took to racing their noisy new contraptions around Manhattan for sport, wreaking havoc in the lives of ordinary New Yorkers, who had always treated city streets as an extension of the sidewalk.

In the summer of 1901, a two-year-old Italian boy named Louis Camille was killed while playing on the Lower East Side when a chauffeur-driven automobile carrying two Wall Street businessmen ran him over. An angry crowd of immigrants quickly gathered around the car and threatened to hang the well-dressed occupants before the police arrived.

In the next twelve years, nearly a thousand children would be killed by cars on the streets of New York, prompting Woodrow Wilson, the dean of Princeton University, to warn in 1906 that the millionaire's toy was becoming a vehicle of class antagonism.

Less than two years later, an extraordinary breakthrough would occur, which would transform, almost overnight, the "horseless carriage" from a rich man's toy to a machine for the millions—and begin to change city life forever.

I will build a motor car for the great multitude. It will be large enough for the family, but small enough for the individual to run and care for. It will be constructed of the best materials...after the simplest design that modern engineering can devise. But it will be so low in price that no man making a good salary will be unable to own one—and enjoy with his family the blessings of hours of pleasure in God's great open spaces.

Henry Ford, 1909

It began in the spring of 1908, when Henry Ford introduced the Model T—the first mass-produced automobile in history. Sturdy, reliable, and astonishingly affordable—Ford's Tin Lizzie made the automobile available to millions of Americans for the first time. As the price of a new vehicle plummeted to less than three hundred dollars, car ownership soared all across the country. By 1914, there were 125,000 cars on the streets of New York City. Five years later, there were nearly *three times* as many, while the number of horses was falling off dramatically.

The next breakthrough came in 1920, when John Jacob Raskob, the chief financial wizard at Ford's great rival, General Motors, came up with a brilliant marketing innovation that allowed customers to buy cars on credit that they would otherwise not be able to afford. By 1924, there were almost 800,000 cars in New York City—two-thirds of which had been purchased on the installment plan.

Powered by the rising tide of prosperity and the easy availability of credit, New York began to undergo an extraordinary metamorphosis, as for the first time in human history a culture based not only on people's needs but on their desires and dreams began to shape and remodel the contours of the metropolis. For tens of thousands, then hundreds of thousands, of middle- and working-class New Yorkers, upward mobility meant more leisure time, an automobile, and a home of one's own; more and more, moving up meant moving out. Leaving behind the crowded tenement districts of Manhattan, families in increasing numbers took advantage of low-cost mortgages to purchase a semidetached or single-family house in Brooklyn or Queens—which they soon filled with an array of consumer goods, also purchased on credit: radios, refrigerators, dishwashers, toasters—and, tucked away in the garage or standing proudly in the driveway, a new car. A working father might take the subway or streetcar each morning to his job in lower Manhattan or downtown Brooklyn, but the family car was brought out whenever it was time for leisure.

And there *was* leisure time now. By 1920, the seventy-hour work week, standard across the country before the war, had dropped to just sixty hours a week, and, before the decade was over, would plummet still more, to forty-eight. With a half day off on Saturdays already routine, an increasing number of workers were being given the entire weekend to themselves. After five days cooped up in the crowded city, working families increasingly took to their cars and headed out into the countryside, looking for places to relax—open spaces and beaches where they might hike or fish or teach their children to swim, or simply sit for a few hours in the sun. By 1923—the year Alfred Smith returned to the governor's mansion in Albany for the second of his four terms—the vehicle sitting in the driveway of millions of New Yorkers held out the intoxicating promise of freedom, mobility, and escape.

It was, it transpired, an almost completely empty promise. Even with time on their hands and a family car, for most New Yorkers there was simply nowhere to go—and no way to get there even if there were.

Families hoping to get away to the country found that almost without exception the open land around the city was closed to them. North of Manhattan and the Bronx, up along the Hudson, what few recreational areas existed were all but impossible to reach—accessible only by overbooked ferries, or by crowded surface roads choked to a standstill every Sunday afternoon. To the east, out on Long Island, the situation was even worse. Beyond the borders of Brooklyn and Queens, home now to more than 3 million people, stretched eighty-five miles of sparkling beaches, and hundreds of thousands of acres of greenery and open space. But as families setting out to the east soon discovered,

most of the land on Long Island remained firmly in local or private hands. The vast wooded estates along the North Shore were fiercely protected private preserves, whose owners comprised a roll call of America's wealthiest families—the Morgans, Pratts, Phippses, Woolworths, Harknesses, Whitneys, and Vanderbilts. The South Shore, meanwhile, was the province of the notoriously reclusive "baymen"—the local fishermen who for generations had worked the waters of the Great South Bay—and who, distrusting all outsiders, especially those from New York, had reserved almost all oceanfront property for their own use.

And there was another problem. Even if open space *had* been available for the masses of people streaming out from the city, there would have been no convenient way to reach it. At the city border, the broad boulevards of Queens and Brooklyn narrowed into two-lane country roads, intended for strictly local use. Every Saturday and Sunday in good weather, endless lines of cars could be seen crawling their way east, each vehicle filled with frustrated New Yorkers who had set out to find some small patch of land for a picnic or a change of scene. The search could take hours—and, as often as not, led nowhere.

With that impasse, whether New Yorkers realized it or not, the city had arrived at a crucial turning point. For over a century, New York had grown at an astonishing rate by exploiting, and often pioneering, one revolution in transportation after another. Each new breakthrough had solved one problem only to create a new one by its very success in doing so. Innovations like the regularly scheduled packet ship and the Erie Canal had broken through barriers of time and space—only to create in the process the first modern traffic jam, as the number of vehicles and people in lower Manhattan exploded. Subsequent revolutions in steam railways, elevated trains, and suspension bridges opened the city up again—only to create still greater densities on the vaster scales made possible by the new forms of transportation. In the years following the consolidation of Greater New York, electrified railways traveling beneath the rivers and streets had connected the most densely populated city on

The economic boom that followed World War I allowed hundreds of thousands of New Yorkers to leave rented apartments in Manhattan for new homes of their own in Brooklyn, Queens, and the Bronx. Right, a 1920s view of garden apartments and semidetached houses in Forest Hills, Queens, at the outskirts of the developed city (open tracts of land, yet to be built upon, can be seen at the end of the street). The large number of cars parked on the street attests to the growing importance of the automobile in the lives of outer-borough residents.

earth to the country and to itself as never before—increasing circulation, and enhancing the commercial advantages of the city once again—and inexorably drawing in even greater numbers of people, who within an incredibly short space of time would begin to fill out the vast radius of the sprawling five-borough metropolis.

By 1923, the burgeoning twentieth-century city of the car, constrained within the infrastructure of a nineteenth-century city built around trains and horses, awaited the next great transportation breakthrough. Though few New Yorkers knew it, that breakthrough was already taking shape—to a startling degree, in the mind of one man. A hundred years before, as New Yorkers dreamed of the immense wealth that lay locked in the interior of the continent, De Witt Clinton had first envisioned and then built a dazzling artificial waterway to get at it, expanding in the process the city's reach enormously. Now, a modern visionary, as farsighted and commanding as Clinton himself, was about to embark on an even more audacious effort to open the city to the lands beyond its borders, adapting the entire circumference of Greater New York and beyond to the new reality of the automobile. In the years to come, Robert Moses, a driven thirty-five-year-old reformer and urban planner working as an aide to Governor Al Smith, would first envision and then build a system of urban transportation and recreation like nothing created in the history of cities.

In the end, that vision would prove even more fateful to the future of the city—and ultimately the country—than any of the extraordinary transformations that had preceded it. In 1923 and 1924, as George Gershwin scribbled out the score to *Rhapsody in Blue* and F. Scott Fitzgerald finished *The Great Gatsby*, his masterpiece of the American dream stretching from the North Shore of Long Island to the canyons of midtown Manhattan, Robert Moses would begin to compose a different kind of symphony or novel: an exhilarating, brilliantly structured urban rhapsody that would take for its material not notes of music or words on a page but the entire sprawling 2,100-square-mile region that comprised the city of New York and the immense blue-and-green landscape surrounding it.

THE MASTER BUILDER

The new kind of automobile age city, which we are building with an almost frenzied rapidity, requires a new concept of parks and open space . . . as bold and imaginative as the original city park movement of a hundred years ago.

Robert Moses

Robert Moses began to build in 1924, in partnership with Governor Al Smith. By the time Governor Nelson Rockefeller finally drove him from power in 1968, the landscape of New York City and its surroundings had been utterly transformed—to a large extent by Moses himself. During his forty-four years in power, he reshaped the city with a comprehensiveness that dwarfed that of the greatest city builders in history, including Pope Sixtus V in sixteenth-century Rome, and Moses's own idol, Baron Haussmann in nineteenth-century Paris. In a career that spanned five decades, five mayors, six governors, and seven presidents, he would leave almost no aspect of the city untouched, building hundreds of miles of parkways and expressways, hundreds of parks, playgrounds, and public beaches, hundreds of thousands of units of public housing, and an extraordinary system of bridges and tunnels, not to mention Lincoln Center, Shea Stadium, the United Nations, and two world's fairs.

To build on this scale, he would help create an extraordinary new instrument of quasi-governmental power—the public authority—then wield it with a Medicien efficiency and ruthlessness without parallel. The authorities themselves—unique hybrids of public and private power—would in the end be perhaps the most lasting yet least visible aspects of his legacy, and the most striking emblems of a career at once glaringly public and cloaked in secrecy. For five decades, he would be a household name in New York, and yet during that time, the real extent of his power and the actual narrative of his career would remain almost completely obscured.

Indeed, so pervasive was the impact of Robert Moses on the face of modern New York—and yet so little known and so poorly understood was that impact during his own career—that its uncovering in 1974 by Robert A. Caro in *The Power Broker*, the greatest single work of urban history in the twentieth century, would become a defining event in the life of New York and set the terms of debate about city life for a generation. As Moses changed the city itself, Caro's monumental 1,296-page biography would change forever the way Americans understood their own cities and the mechanisms of power that shaped them. The questions it raised, and the troubling, sometimes controversial conclusions it drew, would haunt the city for decades to come, and they remain, on the threshold of the twenty-first century, more pressing than ever before. How are great public works to be built in a sprawling, densely congested urban democracy, and at what cost? What is the impact on the city of the car? How have the politics of race and class been imbedded in the city's physical infrastructure, and with what consequences, and for how long?

These would be the themes to which Caro turned again and again. "Robert Moses," he wrote, "shaped a city and its sprawling suburbs—and, to an extent that would have astonished analysts of urban trends had they measured the implications of his decades of handiwork, influenced the destiny of all the cities of twentieth century America."

PARKS AND PARKWAYS

The city in which the shaping by his hand is most evident is New York, Titan of cities, colossal synthesis of urban hope and urban despair. . . . Would New York have been a better place to live if Robert Moses had never built anything? Would it have been a better city if the man who shaped it had never lived? . . . It is impossible to say. . . . It is is possible to say only that it would have been a different city.
Robert A. Caro

Robert Moses was not an architect, nor was he an engineer. He was not a contractor, an attorney, or an elected official. He was a builder of public works—arguably the greatest in history. Brilliant, arrogant, visionary, ruthless, Moses would remake the city as no one before or since, bending its form to the imperatives of the automobile age.

He had begun his career, the urban historian Gregory F. Gilmartin later said, as "the very flower of New York's reform movement." Born in Connecticut in 1888 to a wealthy German

Jewish family, he was raised from the time he was nine in an elegant row house just off Fifth Avenue in an atmosphere of solid comfort and luxury. Bella Moses, his strong-willed, idealistic mother, had taken an active role in the settlement-house movement, and Moses himself, after graduating with honors from Yale in 1909, chose to dedicate himself to public service, earning graduate degrees in political science from Oxford and Columbia, then going to work in 1914 for the Bureau of Municipal Research, the most influential of the city's "good government" groups.

His first foray into the field of urban reform was a disaster. With a reform mayor in power and the progressive movement swelling to a crescendo in New York, 1914 seemed a propitious moment to effect real change, but the young idealist completely misjudged the power of Tammany Hall. Under the wing of a veteran reformer named Henry Moskowitz, he took on one of the bureau's greatest challenges—rationalizing New York's notoriously corrupt civil service system, a bastion of patronage for Tammany loyalists. Moses's brilliant—and in the end almost comically high-handed—campaign to rate the fitness of New York's fifty thousand municipal employees was stonewalled by the rank and file, then quietly bled to death by the Tammany bosses whose power it threatened.

By the winter of 1918, Tammany had regained control of city hall, the reform movement had been relegated to the sidelines, and Moses himself was all but out of a job. That November, progressives took heart when a new man made it to the governor's mansion in Albany. But Moses, who had met the back-slapping, red-faced Irishman a few years before, dismissed Al Smith as "a typical Tammany politician." "What can you expect," he said, "from a man who wears a brown derby on the side of his head and always has a big cigar in the corner of his mouth?"

Robert Moses himself was startled when, a few weeks after the election, a phone call came from Henry Moskowitz's wife, Belle—a one-time settlement-house worker whose uncanny political instincts had brought her into Smith's innermost circle. The governor-elect, she explained, needed the best reformer he could find to direct the reorganization of the state government, and she had recommended him for the job. Moses jumped at the opportunity, and within a matter of weeks, one of the most fateful partnerships in the city's history had begun.

The new governor soon began taking notice of the bright young man, who, under the firm hand of Belle Moskowitz, now began to temper his idealism with an increasingly shrewd grasp of political reality. When Smith was turned out of office in the Republican landslide of 1920, the two men grew closer still, sharing dinners at Smith's house on Oliver Street and taking long walks around New York. They could not have been more dissimilar—one tall, handsome, and aristocratic, a child of privilege who had enjoyed the finest education in the world; the other short and almost homely, a poor boy from the Lower East Side who had dropped out of St. James' parochial school at the age of thirteen and who had, he said, read only one book in his life from start to finish: *The Life of John L. Sullivan.*

But as Moses soon came to appreciate, Al Smith, far from being a "typical Tammany politician," burned with a desire to transform the lives of New York's ordinary citizens. On their walks, the governor did most of the talking, but not all, as Moses began pouring out a torrent of ideas to the older man. When Smith was swept back into office in November 1922 with one of largest pluralities in the state's history, he brought his fast-rising protégé with him to Albany.

Everything was different now. Moses had power—"executive support"—and while working energetically to carry out the governor's reform agenda, he began to conceive an extraordinary project of his own that would, as never before, put the resources of an entire region at the disposal of the city.

He would build a system of parks—not the local playgrounds and ballfields most people meant by the term but a dazzling archipelago of *state* parks within easy reach of the city—vast beaches and sprawling wilderness areas that would answer New York's crying need for fresh air and open space.

Commuting to Long Island in the summer of 1922, he came across a string of long-forgotten city reservoirs and watershed properties near Hempstead and Valley Stream—more than 2,200 acres, already in public hands, and located just eleven miles from the city line. That same summer, exploring the Great South Bay in a slow-moving motorboat his wife, Mary, had dubbed *The Bob,* he had discovered an all-but-deserted barrier beach just off the South Shore of Long Island. Stepping onto the magnificent empty beach, he realized it lay just twenty-five miles from Times Square. He was standing on what could be the greatest public bathing resort in the world—if he could find a way for New Yorkers to get to it. But he had begun to figure that out, too. Watershed properties already owned by the city could provide some of the right of way for a sweeping network of roads and causeways that could carry people out of the city, east and south across Long Island, then up and over the South Bay and out to the barrier beach.

"I thought of it all in a moment," he would later tell Robert A. Caro. By 1923, when he prepared his *State Park Plan for New York,* that vision had grown vaster still: *fourteen* giant parks stretching the length of Long Island, from just beyond the border of Queens to the eastern tip of Montauk—ten thousand acres in all.

Even more visionary than the parks themselves was his revolutionary proposal for getting the public to them. He would build a network of limited-access, beautifully landscaped

Moses considered his parkways as much a part of the recreational experience as the new parks and lavished a superb eye for detail on their design and landscaping, from the rustic wooden lampposts and guardrails to the overpass bridges—more than 100 in all—that were each faced in stone, and each different in design from the others. Unfolding like a cinematic experience,

roads without intersections, traffic lights, or railway crossings, which would at last unchain the automobile's promise of speed and mobility. The world's first parkway had opened only the year before, running a few miles along the Bronx River. But Robert Moses was proposing to construct on Long Island an entire *system* of sinuous, flowing parkways—124 miles in all—that would become, in effect, the first modern highway system in the world.

Moses was sure it could all be accomplished with a bond issue of $15 million. Smith blanched

at the huge amount. "You want to give the people a fur coat," he told his ambitious protégé, "when what they need is red flannel underwear."

But Moses would not be deterred. Persuading the governor to drive out to Long Island in the dead of winter, he painted a dazzling portrait in words of what the unborn parks would look like in summer, when hundreds of thousands of New Yorkers, released from the crowded confines of the city, came out to enjoy a weekend of picnicking, swimming, hiking, and games.

Smith began to understand. These were his constituents, after all, the sons and daughters of New York's immigrant families, whose hard work and determination had carried them by the millions to the outer boroughs, where they now hoped to enjoy with *their* children a new and better way of life, including a chance to escape the city on weekends for a few hours in a natural environment.

As Smith signaled his approval for Moses's ambitious plans, a chorus of praise rose up from newspapers, women's groups, and reform organizations across the state. The governor began to appreciate the value of parks in blunt political terms. "As long as you're on the side of parks," Moses himself later observed, "you're on the side of the angels. You can't lose."

Smith now threw his full support behind the parks appropriation and, on April 18, 1924, appointed Moses president of the Long Island State Park Commission and arranged for his election as chairman of the State Council of Parks. After decades of dreaming, Robert Moses would finally get a chance to build.

And build he did, with a single-minded drive and ferocity that stunned everyone who came in contact with him. Within weeks, he had set himself up in the old August Belmont mansion near the South Shore—itself to become part of a new state park—and begun the process of acquisition and planning of more than a dozen state parks across Long Island. In the months and years to come, he would assemble lands any way he could, riding ruthlessly over long-entrenched interests, bullying private landowners, and, when necessary, swaying local political bosses by offering inside information on the layout of his proposed roadways.

In 1926, gathering some of the country's best-known architects and landscape designers on the desolate sands of Jones Beach, he took an envelope out of his pocket and began sketching a public recreation facility of a magnitude and on a scale none of his colleagues had ever seen before, or even imagined. It would include two giant bathhouses set a mile apart, each with room for ten thousand lockers—not crude wooden enclosures but vast and elegant structures of brick and sandstone, with Olympic-sized diving pools, wading pools for children, open-air cafés with umbrella tables,

and enclosed restaurants. Connecting the two structures would be a mile-long boardwalk with shipboard games—shuffleboard and quoits, pitch-and-putt golf—and bandstands, he said, so couples could dance under the stars.

The designers simply stared at him. "It was the scale of the thing," one of them later recalled to Caro. "Nothing . . . like this had ever been done in public recreation in America. Here we were on an absolutely deserted sand bar—there was no way even to get there except by boat—and here was this guy . . . talking about bathhouses like palaces and parking lots that held ten thousand cars. Why, I don't think there was a parking lot for ten thousand cars anywhere in America. . . . We thought he was nuts."

As the months passed, Moses pushed himself and his team—a loyal and dedicated cadre of engineers, architects, and designers who were coming to be known as the "Moses men"—to superhuman levels. By the start of 1929, there was a new man in the governor's mansion—Franklin Roosevelt—who, like Smith, swiftly came to understand the sheer political value of parks and, though he personally distrusted Moses, allowed the builder to proceed unimpeded.

That summer, everything came together. In June, Heckscher State Park was dedicated. In July, the Southern State Parkway opened, and on Sunday, August 4, 1929, the jewel of the system, Jones Beach, was formally opened. Both the governor and his predecessor presided over the occasion, Roosevelt commenting in his speech that some critics had called New York's ambitious state park program "socialistic." If so, he noted wryly, "Governor Smith and I are pretty good socialists."

On opening day, twenty-five thousand New Yorkers got in their cars to cross the Wantagh causeway and visit the new park. By the end of the month, 325,000 more had made the journey. Stretching five and a half miles and covering 2,245 acres, Jones Beach State Park was like nothing ever seen in America—a magnificent, exquisitely detailed seaside playground, open to the general public.

"Nothing is too good for the people of the Empire State," Moses was fond of saying, and for all the park's vast size, it was the imagination evident in even the smallest touches that impressed visitors most—the trash baskets shaped like steamship funnels, the water fountains operated by ship's pilot's wheels, the ash receptacles disguised as life preservers. Flagpoles

The construction of Jones Beach State Park on Long Island was a Herculean effort. Forty million cubic yards of sand and gravel were pumped from the bay bottom to enlarge and stabilize the beach, while a million clumps of beach grass were planted on the site to hold the ever-shifting dunes in place. Thousands of men worked around the clock through two freezing winters to complete the work—dredging, digging, and constructing the park's landscape, roads, parking lots, bathhouses, and amenities. Opposite, three snapshots taken by a worker in 1929. Top, laborers from the firm of Johnson-Drake-Piper pouring concrete for a pedestrian underpass. Center, a steady stream of cars and visitors arrive on opening day, August 4, 1929. Bottom, the newly enlarged beach, open for business.

Right, Robert Moses, second from right, partakes of a picnic lunch after the dedication of Heckscher State Park in East Islip, Long Island, in June 1929, flanked by a former and future governor of New York—Al Smith, at far right, and Herbert Lehman, at far left.

sported crow's nests and yardarms, their halyards gaily decked with semaphore signals, while the boardwalk railing made the promenade look like an ocean liner. The very paving that visitors strolled on was adorned with colorful mosaics showing compasses, maps, and the charming little seahorse that Moses had selected as the symbol of the park.

On the ocean side, more than 300,000 people could enjoy the pure white sand and crashing surf of one of the finest beaches in the world. On the bay side, visitors found paddleboats and kayaks, places to moor their motorboats and launches—and, a few seasons later, a marine theater, its stage and seats surrounded by water, where on summer weekends audiences could enjoy a musical show under the stars.

Jones Beach was a triumph from the start, drawing the astonished admiration of designers and park planners from around the world. "This is the finest seashore playground," one English visitor declared simply, "ever given the public anywhere in the world."

And yet in many ways, the project was as striking for what it was not as for what it was. It was certainly not Coney Island, a true working-class resort, accessible by subway, that Moses had long criticized for its overcrowding and commercialism. "There are no concessions, no booths, no bawling hot-dog vendors," one admiring observer wrote. "You won't see any weight-guessers or three-throws-for-a-dime-and-win-a-dolly-alleys or blaring funhouses. For almost the first time in the history of public beaches, this beach is conceived as a spot for recreation, not amusement stimulated by honky-tonk."

Like Frederick Law Olmsted before him, Moses—who shared the great landscape architect's visceral dislike for New York's crowded urban tangle of people, commerce, and traffic— had called forth a serene and orderly middle-class paradise, where commercial pursuits would be subordinated to the elemental pleasures of nature. Like his contemporary, Le Corbusier, he wanted order, predictability, light, and flow— values inscribed in the very structure and program of his parks and parkways, which, as people came increasingly to see, were not universally hospitable to all the city's people.

Easy access to Jones Beach, or indeed to any of Moses's new state parks, required a car, putting the new facilities out of the reach of most of New York's poorer citizens, who depended on subways, trains, and buses. Moses himself had refused to allow the Long Island Rail Road to build a spur line to Jones Beach, and the elegant bridges over his sweeping parkways had— intentionally or not—been built too low for most buses to pass under. In the years to come, Moses's obsession with the automobile, to the exclusion of alternative forms of mass transportation, would strengthen the case of those who saw in the works of the great builder an unsettling disregard for New York's poorer citizens, especially those of color.

But for the one in three New York families that now owned a car, Robert Moses was cheered as a hero, a figure of almost superhuman ability who had given form and shape to Al Smith's promise of a better way of life for the city's masses. For those who just a generation before had been locked in a tenement slum, the Sunday drive along one of the Long Island parkways Moses had built was not just a new recreational activity but a new kind of experi-

The ingenuity and imagination displayed at Jones Beach by Moses and his park designers were boundless—from the water tower, disguised as a stylized Venetian bell tower at the center of the park, to the eighteen-hole miniature golf course, with each hole marked by tiny Long Island landmarks, to the park's directional signs (left), fashioned as fanciful silhouettes and adorned by amusing vignettes.

Previous page, group calisthenics in front of the West Bathhouse, Jones Beach State Park. Built to accommodate 5,400 bathers at a time, the West Bathhouse included refreshment stands, a formal restaurant, terraces, and an open-air area containing a large wading pool for children and an even larger swimming pool for adults, outfitted with an underwater lighting system. Intended to offer an elegant, wholesome, and uncommercial environment for the city's growing middle class, Jones Beach stood in sharp contrast to Coney Island, the Brooklyn beach resort that Moses had long criticized for its relentless commercialism and the raucous, unsavory character of what he called its "mechanical noise-making and amusement devices and side shows."

ence, offering a thrilling sense of modernity, movement, and flow.

Air views show the great sweep of these . . . highways, the beauty of their alignment, the graceful sequence of their curves, but only at the wheel of the automobile could one feel what they really meant—the liberation from unexpected light signals and cross traffic, and the freedom of uninterrupted forward motion, without the inhuman pressure of endlessly straight lines. . . . Confidence was given the driver by the way the road fitted into the earth between its sloping sides . . . yet he was held to a reasonable speed limit by the adaptation of the roadbed to the structure of the country, by its rise and fall, the smooth swing of its curves, its clear open runs before creeping under a cross highway or bridge. Freedom was given to both the driver and the car. Riding up and down the long sweeping grades produced an exhilarating dual feeling, one of being connected with the soil and yet of hovering just above it, a feeling like nothing else so much as sliding swiftly on skis through untouched snow down the sides of high mountains.

Siegfried Giedion

Opened in the summer of 1929, as the stock market reached its all-time high, Jones Beach, like the rest of Moses's park and parkway system, was a stunning success, drawing 1.5 million people in its first year alone, 2.5 million a year later, and more than 3 million the year after that.

Yet even in the glorious summer of its opening, a chill wind was in the air. By 1929, Moses's beloved mentor, Al Smith, had lost his bid for the presidency and been driven permanently from power. When the great crash came that fall, it would knock the props from under the giddy era of prosperity that had made immense projects like Jones Beach seem feasible, and even necessary. By 1931, just two years after the opening of Jones Beach, the city and country lay sunken in the worst depression of their history, and funds for parks and parkways had largely disappeared.

By then, the millions of New Yorkers whose lives Al Smith and Robert Moses had hoped so earnestly to transform were fighting for their very survival. In the difficult years to come, as one catastrophe after another fell on the benighted city, the proud metropolis would be beggared by the Depression, stripped of political autonomy, then humiliated by the worst political scandal since the days of Boss Tweed. As the Depression wore on, and Gotham spiraled ever further down into political and economic chaos, many wondered if anything would ever be built in the city again.

DEPRESSION

Within the greatest anthill of the Western Hemisphere the machinery has slowed down. One out of six New Yorkers depends on the dole. One out of three in the city's working population is without a job.

Isidor Feinstein

By the spring of 1931, it was obvious to everyone that the crash two years before had signaled more than a downturn in the business cycle. Something fundamental, and all but inexplicable, had happened to the American economy.

In 1929, there had been 2.5 million people unemployed in the United States. Now there were 8 million Americans out of work, and by the end of the following year the total would rise to 13 million—one-quarter of the nation's workforce.

At the [Municipal Employment Bureau], the room is almost silent. A slight despairing hum from the job seekers. Waiting. A telephone bell rings. A new job! A dozen men fling themselves at the desk. You are struck by their youth. Here is a boy, seventeen, begging for a job. Here is a skilled mechanic of thirty. Several laborers, none over forty. Two are selected. They dash off hysterically. In the others, hope, faintly flickering, dies to a low black flame.

Louis Stark

In New York, as across the country, every month brought more bad news and the prospect of worse to come. By December 1930, the Bank of United States, one of the nation's largest financial institutions, had gone bankrupt, leaving 400,000 depositors—most of them immigrant workingmen—wiped out overnight.

Of the city's twenty-nine thousand factories, ten thousand had already shut down or would soon be forced to do so. Stocks, meanwhile, had fallen to less than a tenth of their 1929 value.

You turn a corner, and here is a surprising spectacle. There is a line of men, three or sometimes four abreast, a block long, and wedged tightly together—so tightly that no passer-by can break through. For this compactness there is a reason: those at the head of this gray-black human snake will eat tonight; those farther back probably won't.

Bruce Bliven

Years before, Fleischmann's bakery on Broadway had started giving away stale goods at the end of the day to anyone willing to line up. The long queue of men had been dubbed "the breadline." Now there were eighty-two breadlines, all over the city. One cold day in January 1931, 85,000 New Yorkers spent the day waiting for scraps of food. "The bread line," the columnist Heywood Hale Broun wrote, was "the worm that walks like a man."

Some were the shambling hulks that one sees everywhere. . . . But most . . . were just flotsam on the general ruin of the time—honest, decent, middle-aged men with faces seamed by toil and want . . . hungry, defeated, empty, hopeless, restless . . . looking everywhere for work, for the bare crumbs to support their miserable lives, and finding neither work nor crumbs.

Thomas Wolfe

As more than a hundred thousand New Yorkers were evicted from their homes, tens of thousands of people began living in the streets, in parks, or in shantytowns that had sprung up along the East and Hudson rivers, sometimes called Hoovervilles, in ironic tribute to the president. The biggest and best known of the temporary settlements was in the middle of Central Park, where the city had abandoned the demolition of the old Croton Reservoir. Unemployed masons used the stone blocks to build one shanty twenty feet tall, while others lived in the emptied water mains.

The new year brought no improvement. The economy only worsened. Desperation deepened.

"My husband is an ironworker," one woman wrote that year to the City Employment Bureau, "but he's been out of work for eighteen months.

[There's] no money for rent. We've given up applying to employment agencies. I'm wondering how poor, how ragged, and how many children we must have to get help. We can't carry on more than a few weeks longer. This world is only a good place to die in."

By now, the Depression was engulfing not only working people but tens of thousands of managers and professionals who had once considered themselves middle-class. One-third of all doctors in Brooklyn had gone out of business. Thousands of businessmen saw their shiny new automobiles recalled. Brokers and bankers were fired by the hundreds. Six out of seven architects were forced to make ends meet in other ways.

Ashamed of their plight, men left home with empty attaché cases in order to deceive neighbors and friends, then stood on the relief lines with other unemployed men.

There are professional men in the line nowadays—teachers, musicians, . . . doctors, pharmacists, lawyers, expert accountants. Here is one with a fine linen shirt, but no collar or tie; there is one whose clothes were obviously made for him by a good tailor, a long time ago. And while [some] faces are indifferent or sheepish . . . there are others whose gaunt cheeks

At the height of the Depression, nearly one-third of the city's population was out of work, and many who kept their jobs were forced to accept pay cuts or work part-time. Below, scores of men wait to register at the Emergency Unemployment Relief office on East 26th Street in 1931. Though Jimmy Walker's administration made some attempts to address the growing problem through agencies like the Free Employment Bureau, they were dwarfed by the needs of the city's vast unemployed population.

During the Depression, homeless men might keep their few belongings in what they called a Hoover bag, or sleep on a park bench under a Hoover blanket of newspapers, but the most common derisive use of the president's name was for the temporary shantytowns, or Hoovervilles, that sprang up in cities across the country. In New York, the best-known Hooverville was located on the site of the old Central Park Reservoir (above), whose demolition had been halted for lack of funds. By 1931 it had become home to hundreds of unemployed men and been turned into something of a tourist attraction, offering daily performances by an out-of-work tightrope walker.

and staring eyes portray a hell within. One of these men quietly fell forward and died last week, on the steps of an institution devoted to relief. . . . He hadn't known where to go, or else hadn't been willing to go there, until starvation and exhaustion had done their work.

Bruce Bliven

By the end of 1931, there had been ninety-five recorded deaths from starvation in New York. In Central Park, the dwindling flock of animals that had grazed in the Sheep Meadow for decades were moved upstate, for fear that they would be slaughtered for food. That year, the people of Cameroon, Africa, sent the people of New York City a contribution of $3.77 for hunger relief.

The agencies of government in America, meanwhile, at the federal, state, and local level, were now overwhelmed by the magnitude of the disaster. "The temporary bureaucracies of relief thrown up by the crisis," one magazine writer said, "have all the character of a frail expeditionary force sent into a war that is expected to last only three months, and which has become instead a World War. Their theory is still essentially that of charitably helping bums and weaklings over the rough places rather than masses cut down by a kind of economic massacre."

Private charities tried to do what they could to relieve the plight of those without resources. The publisher William Randolph Hearst funded dozens of breadlines. A wealthy New Yorker named Marion Spore Bush paid $1,400 a week to feed three thousand men, earning the nickname Lady Bountiful. Alva Vanderbilt Belmont, who in 1909 had helped support the striking shirtwaist workers, now provided funds to employ more than a thousand single women. In all, private charity provided jobs for thirty-seven thousand New Yorkers.

But it was a drop of relief in an ocean of need. By 1931 there were nearly a million men and women out of work in the city, with few places they could turn for help.

The federal government, for its part, had all but washed its hands of any responsibility for the growing number of destitute Americans.

President Herbert Hoover—now in the final year of his term and almost universally reviled—had been the last in a sequence of three conservative Republican presidents who, with the help of an equally conservative Supreme Court, had dismantled many of the social reforms of the progressive era.

New York State had, to be sure, under Governor Franklin Roosevelt, been among the first states to respond with a large-scale relief program, providing employment or direct aid to hundreds of thousands of New Yorkers. But in the city itself, what relief there was was breaking down. When state money passed through city hall, almost none of it reached the people for whom it was intended, Tammany officials siphoning off most of it and giving much of the rest to party regulars.

New York is colossal, astonishing, fascinating. But politically New York is a failure. As a municipality it is corrupt, and sluttish to the last degree.

Alva Johnson

In a city devastated by economic catastrophe, meanwhile, Jimmy Walker's antics in city hall no longer seemed amusing. By early 1932, New York City's government was moving toward a financial abyss. In a decade and a half of Tammany rule, the municipal budget had nearly tripled, to $620 million—almost a third of which went simply to servicing the city's debt, now growing at the rate of $300,000 a day, nearly equal to the debt of all the states in the Union combined.

During the boom years of the twenties, the city's skyrocketing expenditures had been off-set by fast-rising real-estate tax revenues. With the crash, however, those revenues had plummeted, until by January 1932, Walker's administration faced a reckoning. With municipal

Four months after the stock market crash, on March 6, 1930, New York City experienced its largest and most violent street disturbance in years, when tens of thousands of demonstrators, led by members of the Communist party, gathered in Union Square for International Unemployment Day. The event began peacefully, but when officials refused the group permission to proceed to city hall, the crowd defiantly continued downtown, and police began to break up the march. "Those who had come to see riot had their fill," the *New York World* reported the next day. "Women struck in the face with blackjacks, boys beaten by gangs of seven and eight policemen, and an old man backed into a doorway and knocked down time after time, only to be dragged to his feet and struck down with fist and club. Detectives . . . many wearing no badges, running wildly through the crowd, screaming as they beat and kicked those who looked to them like Communists. Women thrown down by the crowd, and knocked over by the horses. Men, screaming that they were not reds, going down under nightsticks." The artist Peter Hopkins, who witnessed the melee from his studio above the square, painted *Riot at Union Square, March 6, 1930* from memory in 1947.

Right, relief lines run along on both sides of West 18th Street in Manhattan. "The City of New York," the reporter Lorena Hickok wrote in 1931, "with the assistance of the State and Federal governments, is struggling today with the biggest relief job on earth—the biggest job of its kind ever undertaken by a city since the world began. The job consists of trying to feed, clothe, shelter and provide medical care for 1,250,000 men, women and children wholly dependent on public funds for their subsistence."

bankruptcy staring him in the face, and with President Hoover refusing to come to his aid, Walker was compelled to seek emergency bank loans to bail out the city.

In the end, the city's banks agreed to lend him the money, but only if they could audit the city's books, cut city salaries as they saw fit, and direct the city's operations. Humiliated but desperate, Walker had no choice but to accept the terms that New York's bankers dictated to him, which effectively removed the elected mayor of New York from control of the city and its government.

WALKER ON THE RUN

The three things a Tammany leader most dreaded were, in ascending order of repulsiveness, the penitentiary, honest industry . . . and biography.

E. L. Godkin, *The Nation*

Seven months later, Walker himself was gone.

For years, rumors of the breathtaking extent of corruption in his administration had swirled around city hall, but no one seemed to care, as long as the good times went on. Less than a year after the crash, the public mood had changed, and in the spring of 1931, Governor Roosevelt appointed an upright and imposing patrician reformer named Judge Samuel Seabury to lead an investigation into the growing charges. In Seabury, Tammany Hall at last acquired a formidable opponent. The stern judge was said to have nurtured an insatiable hatred of Tammany since childhood, when his family's graveyard in Greenwich Village had been destroyed by a minor Tammany official seeking to line his own pockets in a real-estate deal. Seabury never forgot the name of the official—James J. Walker, Sr.—father of New York's swaggering incumbent mayor.

Seabury leaped into the investigation of Tammany's corruption with the fury of an avenging angel. Over the course of a year he called 175 witnesses, who painted a vivid portrait of city hall under Jimmy Walker's rule as a place where payoffs were common, where inside information and influence were bought and sold, and where virtually every service had a price. The police, witnesses said, were running their own protection racket, hauling respectable women off the streets and threatening them with prostitution charges unless money changed hands.

One witness, Sheriff Thomas Farley—unable to explain how he managed to save nearly $400,000 on an annual salary of $8,500—wanly suggested that the funds had come from a little tin box he kept at home. "Kind of a magic box, wasn't it, Sheriff?" Seabury replied. City bureaucrats and commissioners became known as the tin-box brigade.

Walker himself was the last to be called. "There are only three things in this world a man must do alone," he quipped to a reporter. "Be born, die—and testify."

On the morning of May 25, 1932, the dapper mayor pushed his way through a crowd of five thousand people outside the New York County Courthouse on Foley Square and strode confidently into the courtroom. Once on the witness stand, however, there was little he could do to withstand Seabury's withering attack.

After a year of skunk-flushing in New York City's political woods, Counsel Samuel Seabury bayed resoundingly on the trail of a fox. Never before had the chase come so close to slick little Mayor James John Walker. . . .

Time, May 30, 1932

On the second day of testimony, the wind simply disappeared from Jimmy Walker's sails. "The old gay mayor, he ain't what he used to be," the columnist Franklin P. Adams remarked.

Seabury quickly moved to the heart of his case—evidence of almost a million dollars in kickbacks, which Walker gamely tried to explain away as "benificences." When Seabury charged the mayor the following month with "gross improprieties" and fifteen specific allegations, it was clear to everyone that Jimmy Walker had to go. In late August, Governor Roosevelt dispatched Al Smith himself to deliver the news to his old friend and protégé.

"Jimmy," he said, "you're through."

On September 1, 1932, Walker stepped down, vowing to run again and clear his record, then

On May 25, 1932, Mayor Jimmy Walker (above) arrived at the New York Superior Court to testify before Judge Samuel Seabury on the corruption scandal that had engulfed his administration. Walker was greeted by a mob of cheering supporters, shouting "Good luck, Jimmy!" and "You tell 'em, Jimmy." Despite his popularity with the crowd, the affable ex-vaudevillian knew that the most demanding performance of his life awaited inside the courtroom. "One quip flowed after another, the *New York Times* (right) reported the next day, "as he entered a general denial to all the 'inferences' and 'innuendoes' upon which he charged the case against him was built. Throughout the whole day's session, the Mayor, it seemed, often

27,151. ★★★★+ NEW YORK, THURSDAY, MAY 26, 1932. TWO CENTS

MAYOR ON STAND ANGRILY DEFENDS ACTS AND ACCUSES SEABURY OF PERSECUTION; ADMITS GIFT OF $246,692 STOCK PROFIT

THOUSANDS AT COURTHOUSE

Hot, Partisan and Noisy Crowds Cheer and Hiss Inside and Out.

SCENE LIKE A PRIZE FIGHT

700 Jammed, With Aid of Flying Wedge, Into Space for 300, as Passes Are Ignored.

PARK AVENUE BRINGS LUNCH

Four Women Come Prepared to Stay—Losers in the Rush Give Police All-Day Problem.

MAYOR WALKER ON THE STAND.
His Honor, in a Calm Moment, Undergoing Examination by Samuel Seabury.

Full Text of Walker Testimony Before the Hofstadter Committee

Mayor's Own Version of the Equitable Bus Negotiations, His Financial Affairs and His Trip Abroad as Brought Out in Questioning by Seabury.

PARRIES COUNSEL ALL DAY

Says He Kept Money Won for Him by Publisher in a Safe at Home.

TELLS OF $10,000 CREDIT

Asserts He Put Up $3,000 for Trip—Never Saw Equitable Man Who Bought Letter.

ACCUSES 'TRACTION CROWD'

Charges That Special Interests Ruined Bus Plan—Denies Ever Being Influenced by Hastings.

By F. RAYMOND DANIELL.

---

addressed himself to the crowd out front. Sometimes it was by means of one of the pungent 'wisecracks' for which he is noted. Sometimes it was by a gesture, the raising of an eyebrow or the waggling of a thin finger under Mr. Seabury's nose. Mr. Seabury maintained a detached attitude throughout, seldom engaging in repartee." That night, the mayor addressed a crowd of 18,000 cheering supporters at Madison Square Garden, proclaiming, "I am still mayor of New York!" Within four months he had resigned.

sailed for Europe on board the Italian liner *Conte Grande* with his mistress, the actress Betty Compton. "That dazzling, theatrical, and essentially absurd career has collapsed at last," the *Herald-Tribune* wrote.

"The elimination of Mr. Walker as mayor," Judge Seabury declared, "is a distinct victory for higher standards of public life."

LOOKING FOR A MAYOR

With Walker gone and Tammany Hall on the retreat for the first time in fifteen years, reformers in New York now saw their chance of retaking city hall.

In the aftermath of the Walker scandal, a genuine reform candidate—running on a fusion ticket that combined Republican and Progressive votes—might just win. All they needed was the right man.

When Seabury, ever the idealist, refused even to consider the honor, the choice of the city's reform establishment was obvious: Robert Moses, the renowned creator of the state's public beaches, parks, and parkways. Praised by every

newspaper in the city and widely admired by the general public, Moses was a superb public speaker and had already become known as "the man who could get things done."

City hall, it seemed, was his for the asking.

But Judge Seabury saw something in Moses that made him uneasy—an aloofness that bordered on outright arrogance, and the lack of a common touch. Even more damning, Moses was a protégé of Al Smith's—and Smith, after all, was a product of Tammany, who through Moses might somehow regain control of city hall.

To the dismay of his reform-minded colleagues, Seabury insisted on another man—a short, feisty, fifty-one-year-old Republican ex-congressman named Fiorello La Guardia, who had made a name for himself fighting Tammany and anything else tainted by corruption and foolishness. LaGuardia, Seabury felt, could not only win the election but go on to become one of the greatest mayors in the city's history.

Practically no one agreed. Though widely admired for his fortitude and integrity, La

Guardia was thought to be finished in politics. In the 1929 mayoral election, just four years before, he had gone up against Jimmy Walker himself and been defeated in one of the largest landslides in the city's history. In the most recent election, 1932, he had not even been able to hold on to his congressional seat.

But Seabury saw in La Guardia a remarkable figure—a true man of the people who had lived for years with his wife and daughter in the same tenement apartment in East Harlem—a man of extraordinary conscience and humanity.

Considered the ultimate New Yorker, born in 1882 on Varick Street in lower Manhattan, La Guardia had actually been raised on an army post near Prescott, Arizona, where his father served as bandmaster. Later, the family moved to Italy, where the young Fiorello got his first job, at the American consulate in Trieste. Returning to the United States, the young man had put himself through law school at New York University by working as an interpreter on Ellis Island.

As a lawyer in private practice, La Guardia represented striking workers in the aftermath of the Triangle Shirtwaist fire, then stunned observers in 1916 by winning a congressional seat as a Republican in a heavily Democratic district of lower Manhattan. When the nation entered World War I, he joined the fledgling Army Air Service and flew missions on the Italian front while continuing to carry on congressional business from his briefcase. "I can't take off and I can't land," he acknowledged, "but I sure can fly."

Reelected seven times during the 1920s, La Guardia became a lonely voice of reform during a conservative decade. An idealist who called his own Republican party "the kept woman of big business," he attacked Prohibition and immigrant quotas, and pressed for government intervention in housing and health care. Once, making a speech in Congress about the need to regulate foodstuffs, he waved a slab of raw meat around the House chambers. He was called the Roistering Rebel, the Wild Bull of Manhattan, the Fireball.

Aggressive as a fighting cock, he bears an incongruous Christian name which, translated, means "Little Flower." His friends bury him chin-deep in laudatory adjectives—honest, able, fear-less, and the like. His detractors call him too radical.

Newsweek

For older reformers, the excitable, rabble-rousing La Guardia aroused little but suspicion and distrust. He was, one man said, "Half Wop, half American, half Republican." Again and again the reformers tried to push through the candidacy of Robert Moses—only to be foiled by the redoubtable white-maned Seabury, who at one point stalked out of a meeting with the words, "You've sold out to Tammany Hall. Good-bye."

In the end, recognizing Seabury's power, Moses's supporters retreated. The judge could now anoint the candidate of his choice, and he anointed La Guardia. "He's absolutely honest," Seabury said. "He's a man of great courage. And he can win."

Even in a time of economic crisis, running as a Republican in New York City was an uphill battle. But Fiorello La Guardia brought unique assets to the job. A practicing Episcopalian with an Italian father and a Jewish mother, he was a balanced ticket all by himself, one man said. As a former interpreter, he could give speeches in seven languages, including Italian, Spanish, Hungarian, Croatian, German, and English. When an opponent accused him of anti-Semitism, La Guardia challenged him to a debate—on condition that it be held entirely in Yiddish.

On Election Day, the largest turnout in the city's history—more than 2 million voters—elected La Guardia with a comfortable plurality. At 12:05 a.m. on the morning of January 1, 1934, while the streets filled with thousands of New Yorkers celebrating the repeal of Prohibition, the tiny, pugnacious polyglot politician took the oath of office in the quiet library of Judge Samuel Seabury's East Sixty-fifth Street town house.

Afterward, Seabury shook La Guardia's hand and said, "Now we have a mayor in the City of New York."

LA GUARDIA

January 1, 1934. For the first time in sixteen years the city awakes this morning to find its public destinies in the hands of new men filled with a fresh energy and sense of public respon-

From the moment he was sworn in as mayor on January 1, 1934, Fiorello La Guardia threw himself into the job, working 16 hours a day, seven days a week, and turning his official limousine—equipped with a two-way radio—into a mobile city hall. "It seemed as though the town had been invaded by an army of small, plump men in big hats," one magistrate noted. "He was everywhere." The mayor turned up at murder scenes, car accidents, train wrecks, and fires, often recklessly jumping into the fray next to firemen and emergency workers. But his manic energy took a toll on the 51-year-old politician. Early in his first term he confessed to his old friend Senator Robert F. Wagner, "I am so tired at times I can hardly stand it."

sibility. It is a new year so singular for this community as to be somewhat difficult to take in all at once; its implications may prove so far-reaching in the lives of all residents of the city that no one would attempt to foresee them.

Herald-Tribune

No mayor in the history of New York would have so profound an effect on the city. During his twelve years in office, Fiorello La Guardia would establish the benchmark by which every other mayor in America would be judged for generations to come. And as no one before him or since, he would seek to fulfill the promise of the democratic capitalist city.

He was not without limitations. "I am inconsiderate, arbitrary, authoritative, difficult, complicated, intolerant—and somewhat theatrical," he told one prospective city employee. To another aide he announced, "I invented the low blow." His violent temper could run so hot that more than he once had to be physically restrained from striking other city officials. Slow to give credit to his hardworking staff, he was quick to feel a slight and never missed an opportunity to bully a subordinate. "If you were any dumber," he once screamed at a stenographer, "I'd make you a commissioner!"

He often stuck by his decisions stubbornly, even unpopular ones like his order to clear all Italian organ-grinders from the city streets. But he could also acknowledge his errors. He called his wastebasket "the most important file" in city hall and became known for his line "When I make a mistake, it's a beaut."

Too often, life in New York is merely a squalid succession of days; whereas in fact it can be a great living adventure.

Fiorello La Guardia

As mayor, he was everywhere, racing to fires in a motorcycle sidecar—once rescuing a fireman caught under a girder—and reveling in the limelight, conducting the city orchestra at Carnegie Hall, where he brusquely ordered the stage manager, "No special treatment; just treat me like Toscanini."

His Honor has a few mannerisms as chef d'orchestre. *He beats time occasionally with his left foot. But we like his conducting. He knows what the brasses are for—to be heard. He knows that band music should make the blood tingle.*

Howard Taubman,
Music Critic, *New York Times*

At city hall, he liked to work behind an immense thirty-two-foot-long table so imposing that visitors often didn't notice the little man at the far end. With his glasses shoved high up on his forehead, he worked at a furious pace, anwering letters as fast as they could be read to him, often shaking a fist at absent correspondents, and barking out replies—"Say yes, say no, throw it away, tell him to go to hell"—while two or three stenographers raced to keep up. He was never still, swiveling alarmingly in his chair from one piece of business to the next, peremptorily summoning aides by jabbing one of the six buzzers he had had installed on his desk. The writer John Gunther said he had never seen anyone expend so much energy sitting down. The mayor's staff, weary and limp after their boss left for the evening, often remained at their posts for hours, waiting for calls from the radiophone installed in the mayor's limousine.

When he arrived at city hall on his first day in office, he shook his fist defiantly at the 122-year-old building, and shouted, "*È finita la cuccagna!*"—"No more free lunch!" Skeptical reporters had heard it all before, but La Guardia quickly showed he meant every word he said, cutting tens of thousands of positions traditionally reserved for Tammany loyalists and proposing instead a system of "scientific government," based on expertise and ability, not favoritism and patronage. He had his harried staff scour the country to find the professionals best qualified to run the city government, then threw out dozens of local political favorites and Tammany time-servers, whom he derided as "fat-bellied ex-bartenders." Old hands around city hall were surprised to see more and more Jewish and Italian faces scurrying through the corridors, and even a few African Americans.

All my life I've been hearing about the plight of poor Jews . . . in Russia . . . Poland . . . Armenia . . . now Germany. As I look around the room tonight, I see the Governor here, Herby Lehman. He's Jewish. Take the Mayor, he's half Jewish. The President of the Board of Alderman, my old job, he's Jewish, and so is Sam Levy, Borough President of Manhattan. I'm beginning to wonder if someone shouldn't do something for the poor Irish, here in New York.

Al Smith, 1934

NEW YORK/NEW DEAL

We have a job to do more important than fighting our political enemies. There are real enemies at our door. They are hunger, and squalor, and misery, and disease. They are unemployment, and inefficiency, and dishonesty, and graft. These are our real enemies.

Fiorello La Guardia

It was one thing to root out corruption in city hall and install a nonpartisan government in its place. It was quite another to take on the devastation and suffering wrought by the greatest economic crisis in the city's history. La Guardia himself knew exactly what had to be done and was desperate to get started. The city's physical infrastructure—practically falling down after fifteen years of looting and neglect and mismanagement by Tammany—needed to be entirely rebuilt, expanded, and modernized. Doing so would put tens of thousands of men back to work, provide paychecks for tens of thousands of families, and rebuild the pride and self-respect of New Yorkers. A new New York—progressive, modern, sanitary, and innovative—would arise on the site of the old. "I shall not rest," La Guardia declared, "until my native city is the first not only in population but also in wholesome housing; not only in commerce but also in public health; until it is not only out of debt but abounding in happiness."

But from the start, the little mayor with the big plans had his back to the wall. With few resources, diminished power, and the economic situation deteriorating almost by the month, he had virtually no hope of implementing his glorious vision for New York. Within weeks of his inauguration, the consortium of banks in charge of New York's finances demanded that the new mayor balance the city budget or be cut off without a dime. La Guardia readily complied, cutting back city services, laying off thousands of workers, and beginning the monumental task of repaying the city's mountain of debt. Strapped for funds, with no resources to turn to, he often found himself struggling just to keep the lights on in city hall.

Never had the city's economic prospects seemed so dire. Never had the need to rebuild its crumbling infrastructure been more pressing, and yet never had the traditional resources on which the city had always depended—banks, brokers, real-estate developers, manufacturers, shippers, entrepreneurs of every kind—been more depleted themselves, or more in need of help.

It was all the more extraordinary, then, that—even as the city languished in the depths of the Depression—La Guardia would soon be in a position to embark on the greatest expansion of public services in the city's history, and on one of the most ambitious programs of public works ever undertaken. In an astonishingly short space of time, the little mayor would have at his disposal not millions but *billions* of dollars. Even more astonishingly, New York itself would be

La Guardia's first priority was to shore up the city's deteriorating finances. At right, the mayor argues before a joint legislative committee in Albany, demanding action on his emergency Economy Bill. Dawn after dawn, La Guardia rose to take the early train to the state capital, armed with reams of reports and statistics to win over his entrenched Tammany opposition. After four defeats, the bill was finally passed on April 10, 1934, 100 days after La Guardia took office. Empowered at last to shrink the city government and cut salaries, the mayor began with himself, slashing his own pay from $40,000 to $22,500.

able to take credit for making those funds possible, and thus for leading the city and country out of economic crisis.

In retrospect, the extraordinary revolution in national government that would make it possible for New York to do so would represent perhaps the single greatest accomplishment in the city's history, as well as the single biggest sea change in American government since the early days of the republic. It was called the New Deal, and in many ways it would mark the very zenith of New York's influence over American life—and the beginning of the end of the city's undisputed sway over the nation.

To a remarkable degree the New Deal had been born in New York, constructed on the streets of Manhattan and in the state house at Albany during the first decades of the twentieth century. Now, in the hour of the country's greatest need, the city's progressive political culture would be carried to the corridors of Washington and be given dramatic expression on the national stage.

In 1932—just four years after the American people had resoundingly rejected Al Smith and everything he stood for in the bitterly contested presidential campaign of 1928—another New Yorker had swept into the White House in one

of the greatest landslides in American presidential history. When Franklin Delano Roosevelt arrived in Washington in the spring of 1933, he brought with him a squadron of extraordinary New Yorkers who shared almost two decades of practical experience in New York's unique brand of activist government. Seizing the national government, Roosevelt's army of newcomers would force the federal government to abandon the lassitude of the Hoover years and begin to do at a national level what New York had been doing at the state and city levels since before the time of the Triangle shirtwaist factory fire: that is, use the resources of government to intervene, particularly in times of crisis and danger, in the workings of the American economy and the lives of the American people.

From top to bottom, Roosevelt's administration would be filled with a network of social workers, labor leaders, settlement-house workers, and agency heads, who had tested their ideas on the streets of New York. There was Harry Hopkins, a onetime Manhattan social worker who had directed FDR's state relief programs in Albany and who was now conjuring up an alphabet soup of federal agencies—the CWA, PWA, WPA, CCC, and others—to provide relief

Under the auspices of the federally funded Works Progress Administration, thousands of artists were set to work decorating the city's public buildings with murals and public art. In the Rotunda of the Custom House on Bowling Green in lower Manhattan, Reginald Marsh created a fresco series in the fall of 1937, depicting the arrival of a great ocean liner (loosely based on the French Line's *Normandie*) in New York Harbor, 4 of whose 16 panels are shown here. The first depicts the great ship steaming through the Upper Bay, past the Statue of Liberty and toward the lower Manhattan skyline. The second shows the harbor pilot coming aboard, ready to guide the ship to her berth on the Hudson piers. The third shows the city's newsmen interviewing an arriving movie star, Greta Garbo, on an upper deck. The fourth shows the unloading of some of the ship's precious cargo, including an expensive European sedan. The government paid Marsh and his assistants $1,560 for the work.

and jobs for millions of needy Americans. There was Frances Perkins, veteran of the Factory Investigating Commission, who Roosevelt now made the nation's Secretary of Labor and the first woman cabinet member in American history, and who would soon put in place an innovative workman's insurance program called Social Security. Over on Capitol Hill, Perkins's old colleague on the Factory Commission, Robert F. Wagner—now the senior United States senator from New York—was using his uncanny gift for building political consensus to push through half a billion dollars in funding for Roosevelt's bold relief programs. And, though she held no official title, there was the first lady, Eleanor Roosevelt, who had spent years in the New York settlement-house movement, and who would now act as a kind of ambassador-at-large for the progressive movement in the federal capital.

It was a stunning reversal. By the end of 1934, billions of dollars in federal aid were being funneled through hundreds of new federal agencies to New York and to hard-pressed areas all across the country, affecting almost every aspect of American life. There were funds now for immediate relief programs for the unemployed—for long-term initiatives in health, social security, and labor reform—and, most surprisingly of all in the darkest hour of the Depression, for the large-scale public works programs that Fiorello La Guardia had made one of the centerpieces of his vision for New York City.

In the short run, the New Deal would prove the salvation of the city that had invented it, as money was soon flowing into New York to build schools, hospitals, highways, colleges, health-care centers, and airports. In the long run, however, it would alter forever the city's dominant role in the life of the nation. With the New Deal, New York had, to be sure, exported its ideals to the nation's capital, and from there, out across the country. But in so doing it had helped bring into existence something it had not had since 1804—a genuine rival for economic power: the hugely expanded federal government.

It would take decades for the full implications of that change to make themselves apparent. In the meantime, no one in the country would see more clearly the extraordinary poten-

tial of the New Deal than Fiorello La Guardia—who in the months and years to come would tease astonishing sums from the new federal relief and reconstruction programs.

Washington officials were inclined to help—and not only because the New Deal had begun in La Guardia's, and the president's, hometown. New York, after all, was the symbolic center of the Depression, the financial capital where it had started, and the place where its devastating effects were most keenly felt and, thanks to the media, readily visible. To the world at large, New York *was* America. Both symbolically and in fact, its recovery was deemed an urgent priority.

The city's efforts to win federal aid, moreover, were helped immeasurably by Fiorello La Guardia's personal reputation for probity. In other cities, money had a way of mysteriously disappearing before it reached its destination—in Boston, for example, where the relief administrator had refused federal oversight outright, and in San Francisco, whose mayor acknowledged that registration as a Democrat was necessary to qualify for relief. In New York, of all places, federal funds were actually being spent on the purposes for which they were intended. "New York City," one report concluded, "is remarkably free of political control or influence."

The new mayor had an uncanny instinct for the dramatic gesture. Swearing in the new police commissioner, John F. O'Ryan, with the words "Drive out the racketeers or get out yourself," he declared open war on gangsters and gambling dens, and personally took a sledgehammer to piles of confiscated nickel slot machines as the newsreel cameras rolled (left).

By the time Robert Moses took over the New York City Park Department in January 1934, the Central Park Menagerie had been reduced to 22 rotting shacks. Fearing that some of the larger animals might break free, the previous department heads had stationed men armed with rifles in front of the lion cages, with orders to shoot the animals should a fire break out. Within less than a year, Moses had completely rebuilt and renamed the Central Park Zoo, seen at right on opening day, December 2, 1934. La Guardia, who reveled in the pageantry of opening ceremonies, insisted on personally dedicating nearly all of Moses's park and playground projects—including 60 dedications in 1934, and more than 250 by 1937. Right, the mayor surrounded by children at a city recreation program, 1940.

Above, De Witt Clinton Park under construction, amid the industrial landscape of Manhattan's West Side, at 45th Street and Eleventh Avenue.
Below, men playing checkers in Fort Greene Park, Brooklyn, September 24, 1934.

The effect of La Guardia on New York City has been tremendous. . . . Robert Moses, the Park Commissioner— conservative in his politics and entirely autocratic in his methods—has been a wonder at accomplishment. . . . As for the new parks, the new highways, the new hospital facilities, the new low-cost housing developments, the new sewage-disposal plants, the improvement of transit, the new airport, New York City owes a great deal to largesse from Washington. But not everything: for though the New Deal has poured a neat billion into New York since 1934, the city treasury itself has had to drum up $800 million to get the billion.

John Chamberlain, 1939

And the city enjoyed an additional advantage—in the end, perhaps the most crucial. Despite differences of party, class, and temperament, the new president and the new mayor took enormous delight in each other's company. "The doors of the White House open at his radiant approach," the *Albany Times-Union* reported, "and the President is never too busy to sit down and have a chat with him."

Our Mayor is the most appealing man I know. He comes to Washington and tells me a sad story. The tears run down my cheeks and the tears run down his cheeks and the first thing I know, he has wangled another fifty million dollars out of me.

Franklin Delano Roosevelt

Pioneering the use of the airplane, La Guardia would often fly down to Washington early in the morning and be back at city hall by afternoon, more often than not bringing some new promise of federal assistance. Eager to make his city the municipal exemplar of everything the New Deal stood for, he was, one man said, a "lower-case Frank Roosevelt," and in the end, the relationship flourished because it served both men's purposes. The mayor desperately needed federal funds, which only Roosevelt could provide. The president desperately needed those funds to be spent—constructively, quickly, and above all *visibly*—and knew he could count on La Guardia to do so. Within months, hundreds of millions of dollars had begun to flow from the Potomac to the Hudson—giving La Guardia the resources he needed to fulfill his dream.

Now all he needed was someone to carry it out.

MOSES AND LA GUARDIA

I am in the position of an artist or sculptor. . . . I can see New York as it should be and as it can be, but now I am like the man who has a conception that he wishes to carve or to paint, who has the model before him, who . . . hasn't a chisel or a brush.

Fiorello La Guardia

There was one man above all, La Guardia knew, who could turn New York into what he called a "gigantic laboratory of civic reconstruction"—the miracle worker from Long Island,

who had failed to gain the Republican candidacy for mayor but remained universally known as the man who could "get things done."

Within days of his election, the mayor-elect had asked Robert Moses to become the City Park Commissioner. Moses agreed—but only on several conditions. He wanted all of the old borough park offices to be merged into one citywide department under his direct control. He insisted on keeping all his existing state park posts on Long Island. And he asked for still another job: secretary and chief executive officer of the Triborough Bridge Authority, an immense public works project intended to link Manhattan, the Bronx, and Queens, which had languished so long people had taken to calling it "the bridge to nowhere."

Desperate to get the master builder on board, La Guardia agreed to every one of his demands—overriding the concerns of worried advisors who admired Moses but feared placing so much city and state power in the hands of one man. In the end, Moses himself—whom Al Smith had once called "the best bill drafter in Albany"—wrote the enabling legislation creating his new position, then, on his first day in office, summarily fired all the old borough commissioners and their staffs.

There was, he explained, no time to lose. After a decade and a half of Tammany neglect, the city's playgrounds and open spaces had deteriorated to the point of ruin. "The parks were in disgraceful condition," Moses later recalled. "[T]housands of trees...hacked down to provide firewood for political favorites. The zoos were filthy firetraps...the keepers found with shotguns in their laps to shoot down wild animals in case of fire."

Sending for the crack team of "Moses men" he had used on Long Island, the new city park commissioner swiftly hired six hundred unemployed architects and engineers, then put them to work at drafting tables that had been hastily installed in the garage behind the Park Department's headquarters in Central Park. As men began to leave at the end of their first day on the new job, those with the most pressing projects were told to stay all night—or not come back at all. Every one of them stayed, napping on cots that had been placed in the building's corridors.

One of the most dramatic
and visible of Moses's
early park reclamations
was Bryant Park, a five-
acre green space in the
heart of midtown Manhat-
tan, at 42nd Street and
Sixth Avenue, behind the
New York Public Library.
Originally a potters' field
and later the site of the
Crystal Palace, the space
had been transformed into
a park in 1884 and named
for the poet William
Cullen Bryant, the main
advocate for Central Park.
In 1932, to celebrate the
bicentennial of George
Washington's birth (and
provide make-work for
party regulars), Tammany
Hall erected a hideous
plaster reproduction of
Federal Hall at the west
end of the park, whose
crumbling remains were
quickly swept away
by Moses workmen in
the winter of 1934. Within
months, Moses and his
men (working to the
design of Lusby Simpson,
Aymar Embury II, and
Gilmore D. Clarke) had
fashioned an exquisite
oasis in the middle of the
city—a French-style
formal garden, whose
central lawn was sur-
rounded by 200 London
plane trees, a series of
flagstone walkways, and
an elegant fountain dedi-
cated to the memory of the
nineteenth-century social
reformer Josephine Shaw
Lowell. Rising like a
backdrop behind the park
is the extraordinary
rear facade of the public
library, designed by the
architects John Carrère
and Thomas Hastings.

Left, New Yorkers relaxing at lunchtime in Bryant Park, 1935.

Looking south at the West Side Improvement, right, built by Robert Moses from 1935 to 1937. Tripling the size of Olmsted and Vaux's original Riverside Drive and Riverside Park, (which runs along the edge of apartment houses on the left) Moses transformed a raw industrial waterfront into a six-mile-long landscaped open space combining parkland, recreation facilities, and a limited-access road called the Henry Hudson Parkway. The sprawling yet neatly trimmed city edge that resulted became the builder's distinctive trademark—what the biographer Robert A. Caro would later call "landscape by Moses." "This, then, is the Hudson waterfront," Moses himself wrote. "Tycoons overlook the upper and lower bays and the Jersey piers. Droves of cars zoom or crawl through Riverside Park and down the West Side Highway and view the matchless, unspoiled Palisades. By comparison, the castled Rhine is a mere trickle between vineclad slopes. I wonder whether our people, so obsessed with the seamy interior of Manhattan, deserve the Hudson. What a waterfront! What an island to buy for $24!"

All across the city, meanwhile, Moses's field superintendents—hard-driving Irish foremen known as ramrods—were whipping newly recruited armies of destitute relief workers into a disciplined construction force eighty thousand strong.

We inherited men who were working without plan and without supervision. The plans have now been made, the supervision is being applied, and we expect the men to work.

Robert Moses

The winter of 1934 was one of the coldest in memory, with temperatures in February dropping to an average of eleven and a half degrees Fahrenheit. Desperate to hold on to their jobs, the men in the field persevered. By March and April, triple shifts of workers were carrying on construction twenty-four hours a day.

On Saturday, May 1—the first warm weekend day of the year—New Yorkers venturing out into the parks were astonished by the transformation. Moses's crews had reseeded lawns, painted park structures, reconstructed fences, resurfaced tennis courts. Eleven thousand new trees had been planted; thirty-eight miles of walks had been repaved. In all, seventeen hundred renovation projects had been completed.

And there was more to come. Over the summer, new facilities started opening: ten new golf courses, 240 new tennis courts, fifty-one new baseball diamonds. The construction fence came down around Bryant Park on 42nd Street to reveal an elegant formal garden where a seedy lot had been. A new zoo arose in Central Park, then one in Prospect Park; in the next two summers, seventeen new swimming pools, including ten "million-dollar pools."

The openings were marked by the publication of statistics which seemed to the public all but incredible. The Astoria Pool, for instance, was reported to have accommodations for 6,200 bathers. Nobody had ever heard of anything like that before, but it turned out to be literally true.

Architectural Forum

Moses built new playgrounds by the hundreds, sometimes opening as many as fifteen in a single day, always letting the mayor preside from a lectern designed to hide his short stature. "Okay, kids," La Guardia would conclude each speech, "it's all yours!" "If the children of this city were its electors," Moses wrote, "the mayor could be re-elected by their votes alone."

Along the southeast coast of Queens and the northeast coast of the Bronx, the shoreline was

reshaped and expanded to create two enormous public bathing grounds, Jacob Riis Beach and Orchard Beach—elegant municipal counterparts to Jones Beach. Each could hold more than a quarter million bathers.

In all, Moses would add sixteen thousand acres of new land, and twenty thousand acres of parkland, to the City of New York.

> *Just now in New York City you can see the largest park system in the world in action, you can see it shining and clipped and green from $166,000,000 spent on it in three years. And that is a sight worth all the others put together.*
> Architectural Forum

As he had on Long Island, Moses stretched the definition of parks to include parkways, which, although landscaped, were actually highways. In the coming years, he would build more than a hundred miles of parkways within the city limits—the Henry Hudson, the Grand Central, the Interborough, the Belt—then link them to his Long Island parkways and two new roads in Westchester to create the first arterial highway system of any city in the country. No other American city, meanwhile, had yet built a single mile of arterial highway. While their officials were still reading the fine print on new

federal legislation for public works, Moses had complete plans sitting on agency desks in Washington.

For Moses himself, the most gratifying achievement of all would be the astonishing urban renovation he called the West Side Improvement: covering over the old New York Central tracks and adding 132 acres of landfill to make room for an eleven-mile-long parkway—the Henry Hudson—and a vastly enlarged Riverside Park, filled with dozens of playgrounds, tennis courts, handball courts, basketball courts, baseball fields, and, at Seventy-ninth Street, a public marina where sailboats and yachts could tie up. Dramatically expanding the park space of the city while providing an extraordinary driving experience along the water, the project ingeniously exploited the site's topography to interweave pedestrian traffic and vehicular movement, resulting, the critic Lewis Mumford wrote, in "the finest single piece of large-scale planning since the original development of Central Park."

Less than a year after the election of 1934, Fiorello La Guardia and Robert Moses had begun to transform the landscape of New York—the beginning of an extraordinary epoch of building and renewal that would give the metropolis the most modern urban infrastructure in world. But all the new construction could not disguise the fact that across the city, tremendous human problems and harrowing inequities remained, conflicts that the onset of the Depression had only made worse. One of the oldest and most intractable of these problems would soon explode on the streets and avenues of Harlem, where, in the spring of 1935, more than three decades of relative racial calm in New York came to a tragic, violent end.

THE HARLEM RIOT

Eighty-five times in a hundred, when a Harlem cash register rings, the finger on the key is white. Harlem has no large industries at all, and few small ones in which its residents can find work. Harlem is simply a vast rooming house.

Fortune

More than anywhere else in the city, the Depression had devastated the capital of black America. The Harlem Renaissance, a decade earlier, had been an artistic triumph, not an economic one, and within months of the crash the district's fragile prosperity had begun to disintegrate.

The unemployment rate, always higher in Harlem than anywhere else in the city, soon reached 50 percent. Destitute families, evicted from their homes by the thousands, retreated to any shelter they could find, doubling and tripling up with friends and neighbors, until by 1935 Harlem had surpassed the Lower East Side as the most crowded district in New York. Social workers estimated that some blocks in Harlem were crammed with as many as three thousand residents apiece. One block had four thousand.

As the distress and suffering increased, the pressure on the district's woefully inadequate medical services multiplied. All of Harlem was served by only one hospital—273 beds and 50 bassinets in all, for more than 200,000 black New Yorkers, whose rates of infection by pneumonia and typhoid were twice as high as those of white New Yorkers. Tuberculosis rates, meanwhile, were five times as high.

Exacerbating the misery was the crushing reality of racism. Across New York, as across the country, discrimination in hiring practices was routine, and most companies employed African Americans in menial positions only, if at all. In

On March 19, 1935, a major riot broke out in Harlem, destroying more than 200 white-owned stores. (At right, a view of a black-owned business on 125th Street that had hastily posted signs during the riot, hoping to be spared by the mob.) The disturbance, the Reverend Adam Clayton Powell, Sr., of the Abyssinian Baptist Church, declared, was "an open, unorganized protest against empty stomachs, overcrowded tenements, filthy sanitation, rotten foodstuffs, chiseling landlords and merchants, discrimination in relief, disfranchisement, and against a disinterested administration."

1935, the most progressive city in America had no black telephone operators, no black milkmen, no black employees in hospitals or pharmacies. Twenty-four of the city's trade unions, meanwhile, explicitly banned blacks from membership. The enormous Metropolitan Life Insurance Company, which had more than a hundred thousand policy holders in Harlem, hired no blacks, anywhere, in any capacity.

Even the government programs intended to relieve the suffering caused by the Depression were riddled with racism. White foremen and supervisors at public relief work sites routinely turned away African Americans who applied for positions. To the surprise of practically no one, the new public amenities made possible by the New Deal were not distributed equally across the city. In Riverside Park itself, Robert Moses had built dozens of playgrounds in parts of the park south of 125th Street, the southern border of Harlem. To the north, he had built only one, and that only at La Guardia's fierce insistence. Into the ornamental iron trellis outside its public rest rooms, Moses—legendary for his attention to the small details of material and design—had his workmen fashion iron sculptures of monkeys.

Just eight years after the Harlem riot, during World War II, unrest broke out again, after a white policeman shot and killed a black serviceman. The African American artist William H. Johnson captured the 1943 riot, in which six people were killed, in his painting *Moon over Harlem*, circa 1944.

But for the citizens of Harlem the most enraging bigotry of all was to be found in the heart of their own community. Not a single African American worked as a salesperson in any of the two dozen white-owned shops on 125th Street, the commercial spine of the district.

In 1934, local leaders organized a series of demonstrations outside white-owned businesses on 125th Street that refused to hire black employees. Week after week, protestors paraded in front of the offending stores, carrying signs that read DON'T SHOP WHERE YOU CAN'T WORK! The action came to an end when, to the fury of black New Yorkers, a white judge ruled the peaceful protest illegal and ordered it to cease.

Again and again, black leaders pleaded with La Guardia—one of the few politicians in America who had ever spoken out publicly in favor of civil rights—to intervene, warning that the rising tide of misery and resentment could lead to violence at any time.

But nothing changed, and on the afternoon of March 19, 1935, the violence erupted.

It began with a series of misunderstandings that quickly spiraled out of control, aggravated by the atmosphere of suspicion and mistrust that had poisoned race relations in New York for hundreds of years. At 3:30 p.m., a Puerto Rican boy named Lino Rivera was caught stealing a penknife from the S. H. Kress store on 125th Street, then bit the manager in the scuffle that ensued. As a crowd of curious onlookers began to gather, the shop owner called for help. When a policeman arrived, the manager—hoping to avoid further trouble—asked him to let the boy go. As the officer escorted Rivera toward the shop's back door, a woman shouted out that they were taking "the boy to the basement to beat him up." The arrival of an ambulance, summoned to deal with the manager's bite wound, only increased the suspicion of the crowd. A hearse parked on the street nearby fed rumors that the boy was dead.

As word spread throughout the neighborhood, angry Harlemites converged on 125th Street and laid siege to the white-owned stores. By nightfall, several thousand Harlem residents were rioting, looting stores, attacking pedestrians, and destroying $2 million worth of property. By the time order was restored the following morning, a hundred people were in jail, thirty people were in the hospital, and three people—all black—were dead.

The explosion of March 19th would never have been set off by the trifling incident described had not economic and social forces created a state of emotional tension which sought release upon the slightest provocation.
Commission on Social and Economic
Conditions in Harlem

At the request of Harlem leaders, La Guardia appointed a Commission on Social and Economic Conditions. Its report painted a bleak and discouraging portrait of the city's racial divisions and inequalities. Deeply troubled by the criticism, the mayor refused to release the report publicly.

In the years to come, he worked to expand civil service opportunities for blacks and Puerto Ricans, to integrate city hospitals, and to improve health care, sanitation, and fire and police protection in Harlem. After being assured that the appointment would not raise a furor within the judicial system, he appointed New York's first black magistrate, Myles Paige, a former football star and graduate of Columbia University.

But the mayor—whom the black-owned *Amsterdam News* had praised in 1931 as "one of the most fearless friends the Negro has ever had in or out of Congress"—was not prepared to put racial inequality at the center of his reform agenda. He told one group of black church leaders that he had "no illusion about the difficulties facing your people in New York." But reconciling the disparities brought on by American racism, he felt, was a task beyond even his abilities.

It was an ominous moment for the city. The man who had striven harder and more successfully than anyone in history to make New York a place of justice and equality was admitting that not everyone would fully share the benefits of the effort. Until some future, unspecified date, one group would be left out.

The first race riot in New York was in 1712. The most recent was in 1935. The last is not yet.
Fortune

It is world socialism that I want—for I know this alone can banish the miseries of the world I now live in. It will free the factory slaves, the farm drudges, it will set women free, and restore the Negro race to its human rights. I know that the world will be beautiful soon in the sunlight of proletarian brotherhood; meanwhile, the struggle.

Michael Gold

In the summer of 1937, just as it seemed the Depression might be lifting, the American economy plunged into another slump. Thousands who had finally gotten jobs were thrown out of work again, as the number of unemployed Americans shot back up to 13 million. President Roosevelt and Mayor La Guardia were generally acknowledged to be the best of the system—but by the late 1930s, more and more people were beginning to wonder if the system itself simply didn't work.

We roared our way down and came out into Union Square. The place was boiling, as usual, with crowds lined up at the frankfurter stands, the usual "wobblies," as they called themselves . . . the usual groups in argument before the Automat, the usual thick crowds pouring round and round the square in search of something, anything. . . . There was always a crowd in Union Square; the place itself felt like a crowd through which you had to keep pushing to get anywhere.

Alfred Kazin

New York had long been the center of radical politics in America. But with the advent of what was now being called the Second Depression, the calls for revolutionary change grew louder and more insistent. In Union Square—the center of New York's radical activity—thousands of students and union members gathered each May Day, singing the "Interna-

tionale" and waving bright red banners. In East Harlem, Italian voters elected an outspoken radical named Vito Marcantonio to fill Fiorello La Guardia's old seat in the House of Representatives. In the Garment District, the socialists strengthened their old ties with the city's Jewish labor unions; on 125th Street, Communists sought adherents among African Americans by arguing that revolution was the only hope for equal rights. On Broadway, theatergoers cheered the politically charged plays of the Group Theater, which had been modeled on the Moscow Art Theater and featured directors and performers such as Lee Strasberg, Elia Kazan, John Garfield, Lee J. Cobb, and Sylvia Sidney. Clifford Odets's impassioned play *Waiting For Lefty* re-created a union meeting on a Broadway stage, and ended with the resounding cry of actors planted in the aisles: "Strike! Strike! Strike!"

But nowhere in New York was the spirit of revolution felt more strongly—or argued more passionately—than at the upper Manhattan campus of the City College of New York. Known as the Harvard of the working class, the venerable public college charged no tuition, making it available to even the poorest New Yorkers. But its pick of the brightest graduates of the city's public school system gave the institution one of the most academically accomplished and intellectually charged student bodies in the nation. By the 1930s, City College had become a cauldron of radical sentiment, fueled by the feeling, as one writer later said, "that something had gone terribly wrong." Every left-wing group in the city was represented on the campus, and especially in the cafeteria, where a generation of politically committed students would, as one participant later put it, "argue the world."

The real center of life at City College was in our Alcove 1, one of the ten along the edge of the lunchroom. . . . Here

gathered Trotskyist, Socialist, Lovestonite students with their books, pamphlets, ragged overcoats and cheese sandwiches. You could walk into the thick brown darkness and find a convenient argument about the Popular Front in France, the New Deal in America, the civil war in Spain, the Five Year Plan in Russia. The more versatile among us prided themselves on being able to carry on more than one argument at a time, like chessplayers before two boards. . . .

Irving Howe

Not only in the CCNY lunchroom but throughout the city, radical politics was defined in the 1930s by intense and often bitter factionalism—between socialists who sought to achieve progress through democratic means and Communists who insisted real change would come only with violent revolution—and among Communist party members themselves, between the supporters of Joseph Stalin's regime in the Soviet Union and those who reveled in the insurgency of Leon Trotsky, an exiled Russian leader who sought to regain power in his homeland. "In its excitement and depression the city picked itself up and went to Russia," the critic Lionel Abel later wrote. "Politically New York City . . . became the most interesting part of the Soviet Union. For it became the one part of that country

in which the struggle between Stalin and Trotsky could be openly expressed. And was! And how!"

By 1937, news accounts of what were known as the Moscow trials—in which thousands of political opponents were jailed or executed by Stalin—had made the chasm between the two factions all but unbridgeable. Two years later, reports from Moscow again stunned New York's radical community when it was announced that Stalin had signed a nonagression pact with Russia's ideological archenemy, Nazi Germany. The confusion and uproar that ensued seriously weakened the radical cause—as did America's wartime alliance with Russia, which temporarily muffled the voices of opposition, and the rise of postwar anticommunist sentiment embodied by Senator Joseph McCarthy, which forced many older radicals into retreat.

But the heritage of the 1930s radical movement in New York would continue to cast a long shadow over American life, as the young men and women of City College grew into a major intellectual force in the postwar years, continuing to "argue the world" in influential journals like *Dissent*, *Commentary*, and *Partisan Review*. For decades to come, New York—the undisputed capital of capitalism—would remain the center of debate among those searching for a different way to create and distribute the wealth of the world.

"All the most accomplished philosophers ever born to the New York streets," the literary critic Alfred Kazin would later call his fellow City College students—"tireless virtuosi who threw radical argument at each other morning, noon and night with the same curves and smashes with which they played ping-pong in the college basement." Below, an anti-fascist demonstration on the City College campus, late 1930s.

TRIBOROUGH

*No law, no regulation, no budget stops Bob
Moses in his appointed task.*

Fiorello La Guardia

By 1935, Robert Moses was growing frustrated
by his need to ask for money every time he
wanted to build, especially from La Guardia.
Though they worked together closely and spoke
of each other publicly with only the greatest
admiration, Moses and La Guardia often infuriated each other. After their frequent battles
behind closed doors, Moses would derisively
refer to his boss as "that little organ-grinder"
or, still more viciously, as "that guinea son-of-
a-bitch." To La Guardia, the imperious Moses
was "His Grace." Whenever thwarted, Moses
invariably threatened angrily to resign, leading

the mayor to make up a preprinted resignation
form.

Moses was now determined to establish a
source of funding of his own, one that would
keep him from having to depend on elected
officials ever again. He would find it in the most
ambitious transportation project of all.

The Triborough Bridge was the greatest single challenge that Robert Moses had ever
undertaken. The site alone was stupendous—a
vast tangle of water and land where three of
the city's five boroughs—Manhattan, Queens,
and the Bronx, each as large as a city in itself—
came together. Separating them were the rough
waters of Hell Gate—where the East River,
Harlem River, and Long Island Sound all met—
and two large, isolated tracts of land, Ward's and
Randall's islands. Tens of thousands of years

**Workers laying cable
atop the east tower of
the Triborough Bridge's
suspension span,
June 25, 1935.**

The Triborough is not just a bridge
nor yet a crossing. It is a great
artery, connecting three boroughs
of the city, and reaching out at its
borders into adjacent counties and
states. It is not merely a road for
automobiles and trucks, but a general
city improvement, reclaiming dead
areas and providing for residence
along its borders, esplanades, play
facilities, landscaping and access to
the great new parks.

Robert Moses, 1936

Aerial view of the Triborough Bridge, linking Manhattan (at left), Queens (bottom), and the Bronx
(top). The bridge, with its four spans and two and
a half miles of connecting viaduct, was built atop
two islands—Ward's and Randall's—which Moses
expanded and relandscaped to include parks,
promenades, the 25,000-seat Downing Stadium,
and—tucked beneath the tollbooth area, almost
out of sight—a new headquarters building for himself and his staff.

*The George Washington Bridge over the Hudson is the most beauti-
ful bridge in the world. Made of cables and steel beams, it gleams
in the sky like a reversed arch. It is blessed. It is the only seat
of grace in the disordered city. It is painted an aluminum color and,
between water and sky, you see nothing but the bent cord supported by two steel towers. When your car moves up the ramp the
two towers rise so high that it brings you happiness; their structure is so pure, so resolute, so regular that here, finally, steel architecture seems to laugh. . . . The second tower is very far away;
innumerable vertical cables, gleaming against the sky, are
suspended from the magisterial curve which swings down and
then up. The rose-colored towers of New York appear, a vision
whose harshness is mitigated by distance.*

Le Corbusier

In 1933, four years after the Regional Plan of New York had first been made public, its sponsors issued a progress report on their proposal, which had featured the first comprehensive roadway plan for New York and its surroundings. In the space of just four years, they noted with surprised delight, 555 miles of arterial highway—a *fifth* of their visionary proposal—had been completed or was in construction. In 1936, the plan came another step closer to fruition when the Triborough Bridge opened, allowing drivers to travel for the first time from Upstate New York to Long Island without ever passing through Manhattan. Faster than anyone could have imagined, the once theoretical conception of New York as a vast, interlinked metropolitan region was coming to pass.

Much of the new road network had been built by Robert Moses himself, but not all. Since the late 1920s, the Port of New York Authority had been complementing Moses's efforts with a series of extraordinary new linkages from Manhattan to New Jersey, above and below the Hudson River.

There was the Holland Tunnel —not named, as many thought, for the old Dutch mother country but for Clifford Holland, the brilliant engineer who invented the means

to carry fresh air along its two-mile length. Completed in 1927, it was the first major underwater vehicular tunnel in the world. There was a second Hudson crossing—the Lincoln Tunnel—still under construction, which would be longer still. And there was the George Washington Bridge (right), the greatest suspension bridge in the world, its 3,500-foot span more than twice as long as the Brooklyn Bridge, an engineering feat of such verve and daring that even visionaries like Le Corbusier were amazed. "Here, finally," he said, "steel architecture seems to laugh."

When it had first been proposed, the George Washington Bridge had been intended as a railway crossing. Later it was to carry a mix of cars and trains. But by the time construction began in 1927, the span had been turned over entirely to automobile traffic. By the summer of 1936, when the great "traffic machine" of the Triborough Bridge opened for business, the emerging metropolitan vision had become inextricably bound up with the car, as the men in charge of New York's physical destiny—Robert Moses, Fiorello La Guardia, and the planners of the Port Authority—made the profound and all but irreversible decision to set the future of the region in asphalt, concrete, and steel.

before, the glaciers coming down from the north had torn Long Island from the continental mainland. In attempting to knit the three boroughs back together, Robert Moses would be seeking nothing less than to undo the work of the last ice age.

Accomplishing the job would call for an engineering effort unlike anything even Moses himself had undertaken. Despite its name, Triborough was not really a bridge but four bridges and 13,500 feet of elevated viaduct—"a rendezvous of bridges," in the words of the writer Anson Bailey Cutts, or, in Robert Caro's later description, "a traffic machine, the largest ever built." Its approach roads would require razing apartment buildings by the dozens. Its anchorages would be bigger than the Great Pyramid, its roadway wider than the great highways of imperial Rome. Its cost—$50 million, to be paid for almost entirely by the federal Public Works Administration—nearly equaled the entire amount Robert Moses had spent on all his Long Island projects in the previous decade.

Yet no less significant than the bridge itself was the means by which Moses was going to build and operate it. The concept of a public authority was still a new one in the United States, introduced in 1921 by the Port of New York Authority, the bistate agency founded to build port facilities around the harbor. Like the government, a public authority could issue bonds and condemn property. Yet it could also make contracts like a private corporation, contracts that could be broken or altered by no outsider, including the mayor, the governor, or the president himself.

In theory, public authorities that had been created to construct a single improvement—a bridge, for example—were supposed to go out of business once the structure had been finished and paid for. But, as Caro later revealed, Moses had no intention of ever closing down the Triborough Bridge Authority. He intended to use the millions of coins collected by its token booths to establish a permanent source of income, a continuous stream of revenue upon which he could borrow still more for future projects—a bedrock of power that would place him beyond the interference of the mayor, the governor, or anyone else.

Bob Moses is the greatest engineer in the world!
Bob Moses is the greatest engineer in the world!
Fiorello La Guardia

Work on the massive bridge project was restarted in earnest in the autumn of 1934, with the country still sunk in the Depression. To manufacture the necessary concrete—enough to build a four-lane highway from New York to Philadelphia—contractors reopened cement factories from Maine to the Mississippi. Fifty steel mills in Pennsylvania were opened to turn out the steel for the beams and girders. To make the wood for the forms that would hold the concrete, an entire forest was cut down in Oregon.

In New York, five thousand men worked on the project site, installing and assembling materials that had been produced by tens of thousands more, working in 134 cities in 20 states. In all, 31 million man-hours went into its construction, helping to pump new life into the economies of communities across America.

The completed structure was opened on July 11, 1936, in a ceremony broadcast nationally by radio. President Roosevelt, after first saying he would be unable to make it down from Hyde Park, changed his mind after being assured that Mayor La Guardia, not Robert Moses, would handle the presidential introduction.

We are definitely in the era of building; the best kind of building—the building of great public projects for the benefit of the public and with the definite objective of building human happiness.
Franklin Delano Roosevelt

THE PEOPLE'S MAYOR

[In 1934], it was frankly conceded that my theory of non-political administration for New York was an experiment. I now dare to venture the statement that the experiment has succeeded, and that we have something to offer other American cities. The program that was laid down in January 1934 has been pretty much completed—not in all details, but along broad lines.
Fiorello La Guardia, 1938

Although Moses's parks, parkways, and bridges were the centerpiece of La Guardia's rebuilding program for New York, by the late 1930s the mayor's efforts could be felt almost everywhere in the city. Using tens of millions of dollars in federal money, he had built new municipal markets, three new hospitals, dozens of sewage treatment plants, and hundreds of health clinics and schools. On the Hudson, he built enormous modern piers for the new thousand-foot-long superliners—the *Normandie*, *Rex*, and *Queen Mary*—now beginning to arrive from Europe. He oversaw the completion of the new Independent Subway, then merged it with the private IRT and BMT lines, creating a unified transit system whose 815 track miles carried 7 million people a day. More than three decades after opening, the fare was still a nickel.

The pugnacious mayor even took on the city's oldest and most enduring problem—its slums, which were still home to more than half a million people. In 1934, scorning the powerful private real-estate interests who had long blocked the government from intervening in the housing market, La Guardia had created the New York City Housing Authority, the first of its kind in America. With federal assistance

cloaked as a jobs program and the help of the Astor family, which sold the city a piece of tenement property on the Lower East Side at a bargain rate, the authority created First Houses, the first public housing project ever built in the United States.

On a freezing morning in December 1935, with Eleanor Roosevelt sitting beside him, La Guardia dedicated the project. "They said it would be a cold day before there were houses built with federal aid," he said. "Well, it *is* a cold day—and there are the houses!" For the project's 122 new apartments, fifteen thousand applications were received. Next up were the Harlem River Houses, a handsome courtyard development intended specifically for African American families. Its 576 units drew more than fourteen thousand applications. Over the next five years, the city would build a total of eleven thousand new apartments, for which 115,000 hopefuls would apply.

In November 1937, La Guardia pulled off the simple feat that had eluded every reform mayor before him. He was reelected. The largest plurality in the city's history swept into office a host of new faces, including reform presidents for every borough except the Bronx.

Located on First Avenue and Third Street on the Lower East Side and opened in 1935, First Houses was the first public housing project ever built in the United States. To build it, the fledgling New York City Housing Authority completely reconstructed a row of old-law tenements creating 122 new apartments in a series of four- and five-story walk-up buildings that faced a landscaped courtyard. The project, which was declared a city landmark in 1974, remains in use to this day.

After nearly a century, Tammany's power in the city finally seemed to be crumbling. On election night, boss Christopher Sullivan sat in Tammany Hall, surrounded by only twenty friends.

For La Guardia, the landslide was a mandate to stretch his vision, to take New York somewhere it had never been, without having to spend half his time fighting off narrow-minded bankers or a Tammany-entrenched bureaucracy. "We are going to make the city a real heaven," he said.

Sometimes I see the City of Tomorrow, with marvelous parks and buildings, finer hospitals, safer and more beautiful streets, better schools, more playgrounds, more swimming pools, greater markets. There are fewer prisons, too, because there will be less incentive for crime. I see a city with no slums and little poverty. It will be a reality some day.

Fiorello La Guardia

In the coming years, La Guardia would establish special high schools for science, art, and music, the incubators of generations of gifted students to come. There would be a City Center of Music and Drama, a City Opera, a City Ballet, and a city-owned radio station, WNYC, to promote cultural programs. The city's extraordinary system of free public colleges would be enlarged and expanded with new campuses in Brooklyn and Queens.

And now, at last, the mayor could bring to fruition one of his oldest dreams for the city's future. Once known as "the flying congressman," La Guardia had been among the first to appreciate the coming significance of air travel. "Aviation is established," he declared. "Nothing can stop it." In 1934, to publicize what he took to be the shameful absence of a major airport in New York, the mayor loudly refused to deplane at Newark on a return flight from Chicago, pointing out that his ticket read "Chicago to New York," not New Jersey. With its one passenger, the plane proceeded to the city's lone, hopelessly inadequate public landing strip, Floyd Bennett Field in Brooklyn.

Now, using federal funds, La Guardia vowed to give New York the best airport in America. Set on 550 acres of marshland at the old North Beach field in Queens, the new facility would be the largest WPA-funded project of its kind in the country, with hangars big enough to enclose Madison Square Garden, runways more than a mile long, and the most powerful searchlight in the world. The mayor visited the construction site almost daily, obsessing over every detail, dismissing critics who dubbed the project Fiorello's Folly. La Guardia knew that the city had been at the forefront of every advance in transportation and communication for more than a century—steamboat, canal, railway, telegraph, telephone, parkway, radio—and he was anxious to extend that dominance to the new commercial realm in the sky.

"It is the greatest, the best, the most up to date airport in the U.S.," he proudly wrote President Roosevelt, "'the' airport of the New World." Within a year of its opening in 1939, the field was handling two hundred flights a day and had become the busiest in the world. It needed only one last touch.

We observe that the city of New York is casting about for a name for its new municipal airport. The dynamic mayor's name and works are known from coast to coast. [Name it] "La Guardia Field."

Oklahoma City Times

Of all the mayor's advisors, none was closer than Charles C. Burlingham, the eighty-one-year-old president of the New York Bar and a legendary civic reformer who was known as New York's first citizen. As a young boy, in 1863, he had watched from his bedroom window as the draft riots raged throughout the city. In the seven decades since, he had tracked New York's long and fitful struggle to fulfill the promise of the great "democratic vista" Walt Whitman had glimpsed on its streets so long ago.

Burlingham was as proud as anyone of the extraordinary progress La Guardia had made in transforming New York into what the mayor now called "the world's greatest experiment in social and political democracy." But he had come to fear for the health and well-being of the short, driven man who had taken it upon himself to elevate the city—singlehandedly, if necessary—to new levels of social opportunity, economic prosperity, and human enrichment.

"You are a very tired man, and must get some rest," he wrote in a confidential letter to the mayor. "When I drive through the vast reaches of the Bronx and see the swarming myriads, I say to myself: 'Can it be that one man is responsible for the welfare of these people?'"

THE BARGAIN

All this [public work], of course, would not have been possible even with the enthusiasm, ability and desire that could have been marshalled, were it not that finances were made possible by the Federal Government.

Fiorello La Guardia

In the five years between 1934 and 1939, New York City had received $1.1 billion from federal agencies such as the PWA, CWA, and WPA—a sixth of the entire national budget for public works. Using the torrent of funds, Fiorello La Guardia and Robert Moses had transformed New York—bringing it fully into the twentieth century and making it the most efficient and best-run city in the country, if not the world.

But it had been, in many ways, a Faustian bargain. For more than a century, since the opening of the Erie Canal, New York City had been the unofficial capital of the United States—the source of most of the financing that had built the nation, and the home of the great private enterprises that had guided much of the country's economic destiny. The vast transportation systems and powerful financial institutions built by New Yorkers had, in turn, drawn much of the wealth and resources of the entire continent into the city—so much so that by the late 1930s, the value of the land and buildings in the five boroughs of New York City was greater than that of the entire United States west of a line drawn through the middle of Nebraska.

But the unprecedented catastrophe of the Great Depression had forever altered the equation. Never again would New York—or the United States itself for that matter—rely entirely on private capital for its economic vitality or physical growth. The progressive New Yorkers who had invaded Washington alongside Franklin Roosevelt in the early 1930s had sparked a massive expansion of the federal government into almost every aspect of American life, creating, for the first time in the country's history, a source of governmental power that was at least co-

equal to the traditional commercial power of Manhattan.

Not since 1790, when Alexander Hamilton's fateful deal had sent the federal capital from New York to Washington, had there been so profound a shift in the distribution of economic and political power in America. "For more than a century," the historian Thomas Kessner later wrote, "the imperial municipality had swallowed up outlying regions, annexing them to the greater city. It threw bridges over rivers and tunneled under them, reaching two hundred miles away to bring fresh water, and built an extensive hospital and educational system. It erected the largest subway system in the world and cleared a world class park to adorn its midsection. The colossal city accomplished this and considerably more without federal or state assistance. Indeed, its robust economy produced generous surpluses for Washington and Albany. But modern times had put an end to the self-sufficient city." Depression had come, and to survive the crisis, New York—once the proud financier of all America—had been forced to turn to Washington for help, and in the process lost some of its incomparable sheen. It was, as Fitzgerald had so poignantly seen, the undisputed center of the country no longer; not a universe but a city, one of many, and a hard-pressed city at that, deeply dependent now on the federal government.

And there were other consequences, equally momentous. In the years to come, as Washington extended the largesse of the New Deal to traditionally underdeveloped parts of the country, a seismic shift would begin to occur in the allocation of national resources—away from the mighty cities of the Northeast, to the South and the West, where federal agencies were already undertaking mammoth public works projects—dams, reservoirs, water-supply systems, power plants, electrification grids, and highways. Drawing money from the overdeveloped Northeast to the underdeveloped Southwest, these immense federal projects were the infrastructure of what would eventually become a Sun Belt competitor to New York's economic primacy.

In the decades to come, as the power of the federal government continued to increase, bolstered enormously by the growing importance

This is the Great White Way, theatrical center of America and wonder of the out-of-towner. Here midnight streets are more brilliant than noon, their crowds on ordinary evenings exceeding those of large town carnivals. . . . It is the district of glorified dancing girls and millionaire playboys and, on a different plane, of dime-a-dance hostesses and pleasure-seeking clerks. Here too, in a permanent moralizing tableau, appear the extremes of success and failure characteristic of Broadway's spectacular professions: gangsters and racketeers, panhandlers and derelicts, youthful stage stars and aging burlesque comedians, world heavyweight champions and once-acclaimed beggars. An outer shell of bars and restaurants, electric signs, movie palaces, taxi dance halls, cabarets, chop suey places, and side shows of every description covers the central streets.

The WPA Guide to New York City, 1939

Twenty Cent Movie, by Reginald Marsh, 1936. Known for his gritty, colorful, sometimes grotesque images of city life, Marsh was drawn to the underside of New York—the tawdry amusement parks, raucous burlesque houses, and seedy Bowery flophouses that were the anti-thesis of the orderly, wholesome city that Fiorello La Guardia and Robert Moses—both of whom shared a distinctly puritanical streak—sought to put forth (during the 1930s, La Guardia led a successful campaign to ban the city's burlesque houses). Like many of Marsh's works, *Twenty Cent Movie*—which depicts the entrance to a cheap Times Square movie house—combined elements of reality and fantasy to create a mood of scarcely bridled sexuality, here using invented movie posters for films such as *Joys of the Flesh* and *Stripped Bare*.

of the military, the traditional disparities between New York City and the rest of the country would begin to diminish and fade away. In the end, the imperial city on the Hudson could be said not only to have helped dethrone itself but to have cocreated its own rivals for power.

WORLD OF TOMORROW

Bit by bit the New York of 1920 has rearranged and expanded itself into the New York of 1941. New highways sweep beneath its bold escarpment, new housing and new playgrounds have been carved from its native rock. Giant new bridges soar above its two rivers and new tubes have burrowed beneath the waters. The zoning scheme has opened the blue of heaven to streets which had lived in the shadow. . . . For perhaps the first time in its ruthless, headlong history, some new impulse, something apart from commerce, industry, and finance, has been acting on the town. Some sense of community design and purpose has tempered the obsession with buying and selling. Out of the old demonic energy has come a new ambition to build a city more fit for human use and aspiration.

Clair Price, 1941

By 1939, in just half a decade, Fiorello La Guardia and Robert Moses, backed by hundreds of millions of federal dollars, had succeeded not only in physically transforming the city but in forging a new civic sensibility.

Only a decade before, New York had been the symbol of relentless capitalist drive and profligacy. By the end of the 1930s it had become the showcase for a new economic model, in which ambitious public initiatives would serve to stimulate—and balance—the reckless and often rapacious energies of private enterprise. Within this new dispensation, the city's immense entrepreneurial forces would be harnessed to broader social purposes—the excesses of capitalism tempered in the interests of democracy—and capitalism itself.

As the decade came to an end, this new balance of public and private forces in New York would find expression in two extraordinary undertakings—two astonishing cities within the city. One would be built to last forever; the other would be gone after two summers. Yet, as New York began to emerge from the shock

and despair of the Depression, each in their way would vividly commemorate the emergence in America of a brave new world—whose outlines, though tantalizing, were still far from clear.

THE CITIES OF TOMORROW

Rockefeller Center stands as distinctively for New York as the Louvre stands for Paris.
The WPA Guide to New York City

Begun in 1931, Rockefeller Center had at first seemed the apotheosis of the capitalist city—"the belated culmination," *The WPA Guide to New York City* declared, "of the boom of the 1920s." But by the late 1930s, as the project's full outlines emerged, it became obvious that the twelve-acre complex was something entirely new—"not only a vast skyscraper group," one guidebook observed, "but an organized city."

Unlike the speculative towers of the 1920s, each piling floors on a single plot of land, Rockefeller Center had been conceived from the first as an urban *grouping*—a composition of buildings and open space across three city blocks, maximizing light and air for its occupants, orchestrating the movement of pedestrians, cars, and service vehicles, and creating a sequence of striking, ever-changing vistas from street level. "In a way," one man said, "the Center is an effort to reduce New York to order, still keeping it New York."

From left to right, Robert Moses, Grover Whalen (president of the New York World's Fair), and Mayor La Guardia at the fair's groundbreaking in June 1936. As park commissioner, Moses was given responsibility for preparing the site of the fair, a massive effort that included the removal of the giant ash heap known as the Corona Dump, which F. Scott Fitzgerald had immortalized in *The Great Gatsby* as "a valley of ashes."

Workers atop the 70-story RCA Building in April 1932, the centerpiece of Rockefeller Center. Located on three blocks between Fifth and Sixth avenues, Rockefeller Center included 14 commercial buildings in the heart of midtown, with elegant shops lining Fifth Avenue, an elaborate series of pedestrian promenades and plazas, a network of underground tunnels linking the buildings and providing subway access, and an array of spectacular gardens on the roofs and setbacks of its lower buildings. Though some objected to the appearance of Rockefeller Center—one critic referred to its buildings as "tombstones of capitalism, with windows"—most considered the complex a triumph of modern planning and design.

The newcomer to New York City, American or foreigner, doesn't spend a glance on St. John's on Morningside Heights, or on St. Patrick's on Fifth Avenue, or on the Russian basilica on Fourth Avenue, or thereabouts; but makes for Rockefeller Center where he can get an eyeful worth seeing.
Sean O'Casey

It had begun in 1931, its first buildings rising even as the city and nation sank ever deeper into the Depression. If some had seen it as a beacon of hope for the future, many others thought it was the height of folly—a brand-new set of office towers, going up at a time when the most prestigious buildings in the city were half-empty and begging for tenants.

But by the late 1930s, with most of its elements in place, nearly everyone had come to recognize that Rockefeller Center was a stunning success—not only a viable commercial venture but the very embodiment of the power, style, and self-assurance of twentieth-century New York.

By then, the center had become the undisputed nexus of the city's communications industry, whose power and reach—already enormous in the 1920s—had only grown in the intervening years. At the very heart of the complex stood the RCA Building, a soaring, 70-story skyscraper that was home to NBC's ultramodern broadcast center, popularly known as Radio City. From its 27 studios, the network beamed out everything from Jack Benny's comedy shows to symphonies conducted by Arturo Toscanini, to radio receivers that could now be found in four out of five homes in America. Other buildings in the complex included the offices of RKO Studios, the Associated Press, and Time-Life—the global publishing empire that was perhaps the closest modern equivalent of Horace Greeley's old *New York Tribune*: a font of news

Radio City Music Hall - Rockefeller Center, New York

Though it opened during the depths of the Depression, Rockefeller Center quickly became a popular mecca with New Yorkers and visitors. Radio City Music Hall, above, amazed audiences with its opulent art deco lobby and auditorium, and drew patrons of all classes to its shows, which combined stage performances and feature films.

and information radiating out from Manhattan to blanket the country. Each week, *Time* magazine reached a million people; *Life* magazine, 3 million; the "March of Time" newsreel, 30 million.

The Time-Life Building in Rockefeller Center seemed to me brilliantly alive . . . a slice of the New York feast at its richest and most intoxicating: a brilliant center magnifying everything like the fluorescent tubes in the elevators, which seethed with excessive brightness. At the circular stone counter—the famous "goldfish bowl" where people met to go out to lunch and tourists gapingly followed guides around the concourse—I found myself recharged by the crisp centrality, the splendors of midtown Manhattan. It was impossible to feel oneself less than brilliantly informed and interesting in the Time-Life Building.
Alfred Kazin

More than simply an office complex, Rockefeller Center offered a galaxy of pleasures for the public—restaurants, cafés, and ice-skating, seasonal floral displays and the great Christmas tree, murals and sculpture and elegant retail shops both above and below the street. Nine hundred thousand people a year attended broadcasts at the NBC studios, while tens of thousands more enjoyed the RCA Building's seventieth-floor observation deck, which, if slightly lower than that of the Empire State Building, offered visitors something the taller building could not—a view of the majestic, solitary Empire State itself.

But by far the most popular attraction at Rockefeller Center, if not in New York itself, was Radio City Music Hall, indisputably the greatest movie theater on earth. Everything about the Music Hall was superlative—the world's largest foyer, world's largest screen, world's largest theater

organ, and world's largest auditorium, big enough to hold 6,200 customers at once. On stage, the famous chorus line of 50 "precision dancers"—the Rockettes—executed dazzlingly synchonized kicks and turns. Below, hidden from view, lay another remarkable feature: eight gigantic elevators that could lower the stage floor 40 feet down or lift it 13 feet up. In the late 1930s, U.S. Navy engineers borrowed the design for the giant flight-deck elevators of their newest aircraft carriers.

One last surprise remained, perched at the top of the RCA Building and overlooking the entire city: an enormous nightclub called the Rainbow Room, a place so glamorous and stylish that it seemed to belong less to the real city than to the mythic New York of penthouses, cocktails, and swing music found in contemporary Hollywood movies, such as those of Fred Astaire and Ginger Rogers. The great club was the symbolic epicenter of a dreamy cosmopolitan vision of the city, one that encompassed the twin-towered art deco apartment buildings on Central Park West and the new Waldorf-Astoria hotel on Park Avenue, then stretched over to the Hudson piers, where New Yorkers boarded sleek ocean liners like Cunard's *Queen Mary* or the French Line's *Normandie* for midnight sailings to Europe.

By the time the last of Rockefeller Center's 14 buildings was completed in 1939, it had become not only the city's largest office complex and greatest tourist attraction but had been acknowledged by visitor and native alike as the true center of the modern city. "The Center has the New Yorker's affection," the critic Douglas Haskell acknowledged in 1939. "For it is not only the largest skyscraper aggregation of all, but it gives a good show."

The Rainbow Room, above, catered to the city's elite, who danced to big-band music in its extraordinary dining room, 65 stories above the city. In December 1931, the first winter of the center's construction, a group of workmen put up a Christmas tree, left, to mark the holiday. In years to come, the ceremony would be transformed into a celebrated annual event, with the world's largest Christmas tree placed at the head of the center's skating rink each December, then spectacularly lighted as newsreel cameras—and later live television—captured the moment for a national audience.

Statue of Atlas, Rockefeller Center, New York City   108

Rockefeller Center Buildings at Night

321   New York City   14859

Touring the complex, visitors could see that every aspect of the traditional commercial city had been reconceived, reimagined, and improved. Though some of the buildings were among New York's tallest, several others rose no more than six stories, providing an unprecedented sense of spaciousness in the middle of the city. Large-scale sculpture and murals embellished the entrances to the structures, and in two instances—Paul Manship's gilded *Prometheus* and Lee Lawrie's giant bronze *Atlas*—became familiar New York icons in their own right. Stepping from Fifth Avenue, pedestrians found themselves strolling along an elegant promenade—gently sloped downward to encourage them further—lined with shops, fountains, and lush floral displays that changed with every season. At the center of the complex they came upon a broad sunken plaza—filled with fountains, flowers, and café tables in summer, and with ice-skaters in winter—

around which flew the flags of every state in the nation and every nation in the world. And at the head of the central plaza, each December, the largest Christmas tree in the world made its glittering appearance. "These buildings are not only huge, efficient and comfortable," the author Frederick Lewis Allen wrote in 1938. "They are also gay."

Offering an object lesson in the value of public amenities and comprehensive planning, by the late 1930s the complex had lived up to its name and become the city's true center—the very essence of New York's self-image as an urbane, progressive metropolis, and the most popular tourist attraction in town. At the same time, it proved an impressive financial success, whose ability to fill its buildings with prestigious tenants—even in the worst years of the Depression—confounded skeptics.

Yet even as John D. Rockefeller, Jr., celebrated the completion of the project in 1939

Above left, Lee Lawrie's *Atlas* in the forecourt of the International Building. Right, the RCA Building at night. Visiting New York in 1937, the writer Gertrude Stein observed that "it was the Rockefeller Center building that pleased me the most. . . . Alice Toklas said it is not the way they go into the air but the way they come out of the ground that is the thing. European buildings sit on the ground but American ones come out of the ground."

Sixth Avenue North from Forty-Seventh Street, by John J. Soble, circa 1936. Filled in the foreground with dark tenement buildings, rooftop life, and elevated train tracks, the painting gives way in the distance to Rockefeller Center's soaring masses, rising from the older skyline.

by driving a ceremonial last rivet into its iron-work, New York's other vision of the future had already arisen—not in the center of the city but on its outskirts, at the northern edge of Queens, amid what had been, until 1938, a strange, desolate landscape known as the Corona Dump, a towering ash dump that was the product of thirty years' worth of burnt refuse from Brooklyn's incinerators. A decade before,

in *The Great Gatsby*, F. Scott Fitzgerald had described the unearthly zone as "a valley of ashes."

This is a valley of ashes—a fantastic farm where ashes grow like wheat into ridges and hills and grotesque gardens; where ashes take the forms of houses and chimneys and rising smoke and, finally, with transcendent effort, of ash-gray men who move dimly and already crumbling through the powdery air.

F. Scott Fitzgerald

After two years of arduous work, an army of men under Robert Moses had transformed 1,216 acres of wasteland into the site of the New York World's Fair of 1939–40.

The location was revealing. Placed on the edge of the city, belted by two of Moses's new parkways and surrounded by a suburban landscape of single-family houses, the New York World's Fair inevitably implied a very different destiny than Rockefeller Center, which had sought to enhance the excitement and bustle of the city all around it. According to the World's Fair, the future would not be found in the heart of the city at all but at its edge.

A most cordial welcome to visitors to the World's Fair! We are proud of it! We hope you like it! The theme—"Building the World of Tomorrow"—represents the forward-looking people of the City of New York, and their concern for a better world is evident in the everyday life of this great city.

Fiorello La Guardia

At the center of the fair stood the Trylon and Perisphere—the last of the city's great art deco icons—shimmering in white and presenting a futuristic city, Democracity, inside. All around stood the big pavilions of America's major corporations, each promising a streamlined, chrome-plated future where machines would free housewives from kitchen drudgery.

But the longest lines by far were for General Motors's Futurama, where, once inside, visitors sat in moving chairs and circled a 36,000-square-foot model showing the United States as it would look in the year 1960. They would never forget what they saw there.

America in 1960 would still have cities. But they would be nothing like the New York of 1939. The model's downtown consisted of widely spaced skyscraper towers, bisected by highways fourteen lanes wide on which fifty thousand miniature cars traveled at a hundred miles an hour. Those highways carried people out of the city and into an American landscape where people lived mostly in single-family houses accessible only by car. Subways, streetcars, regional railroads—the mainstays, in other

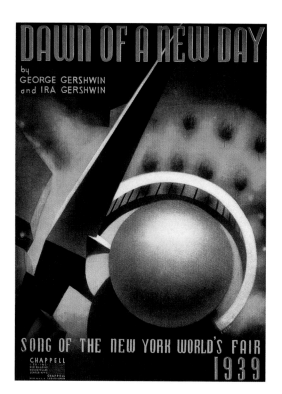

Sheet music of the World's Fair's official theme song, "Dawn of a New Day," by George and Ira Gershwin. After George died unexpectedly of a brain tumor in 1937, his brother, Ira, created the song by adding lyrics to a piece of music he had found in one of George's sketchbooks.

words, of traditional urban transportation—had somehow vanished. According to General Motors, 1960s America would be a world of cars, and of highways, and of suburbs.

In a way, the world presented by the Futurama was the ultimate projection of the new "mixed economy" that Moses and La Guardia had already begun to pioneer, in which vast public efforts—parkways, tunnels, bridges—helped to further the private interests of giant automakers, road builders, real-estate developers, mortgage lenders. But for the city itself, an unsettling subtext could be discerned at the Futurama. In the future, the GM pavilion suggested, public works would be used not to enhance and renew the existing city, as La Guardia and Moses had done, but to fundamentally reshape it around the needs of the car. "General Motors has spent a small fortune," the critic Walter Lippman observed, "to convince the American public that if it wishes to enjoy the full benefit of private enterprise in motor manufacturing, it will have to rebuild its cities and its highways by public enterprise."

At the very center of the park celebrating the city and its achievements, General Motors had a created an eerie blueprint for New York's destruction and for its replacement by a different kind of world entirely.

Crowds gather at Consolidated Edison's City of Light exhibit at the World's Fair. Billed as the world's largest diorama, the exhibition was a three-story-tall, full-block-long animated model of the New York metropolitan area. Visitors witnessed moving subway cars and elevators and factories highlighted by dramatically shifting lights and shadows as a full day passed before their eyes in just 12 minutes, culminating with an afternoon thunderstorm.

This is not a vague dream of a life that might be lived in the far future but one that could be lived tomorrow morning if we willed it so. The great, crushing, all absorbing city of today . . . would no longer be a planless jumble of slum and chimney, built only for gain, but an effective instrument for human activities, to be used for the building of a better world of tomorrow. . . . The relation between these units of stone and steel, highway and green is a symbol of the new life of tomorrow; that life will be based on an understanding of the contributions of all elements to a new and living democracy.

Robert Kohn, Chairman, Committee
on Theme, New York World's Fair

More than 25 million people passed through the gates of the New York World's Fair in the last perfect summer of the 1930s. By night, ravishing fireworks displays and dazzling electric spectacles of light made the temporary buildings seem to glow as in a dream. By day, visitors wandered from region to region in the self-contained universe of the fair, from the ingenious industrial exhibits to the exhilarating amusement area, to the stately international pavilions, where more than three dozen nations, including Russia, France, Poland, England, Italy, and Czechoslovakia, could be seen peacefully coexisting side by side.

Before the first season of the fair was out, however, ominous news came from abroad. On September 1, 1939, word reached New York that Hitler had invaded Poland. Within days, England and France had declared war on Germany, and the battle for Europe had begun. When the World's Fair reopened in the spring of 1940, the Polish pavilion was gone. So was the Czech pavilion, whose sponsoring government had been taken over by the Germans. On May 25, 1940, the tricolor over the French pavilion was lowered to half-staff. France had fallen.

By then, it had become obvious to everyone that the shining image of international harmony the New York World's Fair had projected bore no relation at all to reality. The fair itself would lumber along uncertainly for a few more months before closing in the fall of 1940—with barely enough money left over to demolish the exhibits and clear the land. The three thousand tons of structural steel that made up the Trylon and Perisphere were donated to the United States military.

America itself was still at peace. But it was hard "to block out thought," one man said, "of what might really be in store for the World of Tomorrow."

ROBERT MOSES: THE POWER BROKER

ROBERT A. CARO

INTERVIEW

How can we take the measure of the career of Robert Moses as a public builder?

One measure was its longevity. In a democracy, most people think of power in four-year terms, or eight-year or twelve-year spans. Robert Moses held power over New York and its suburbs for forty-four years, from 1924 to 1968. He held this power through the reigns of six governors: Al Smith, who brought him to power; Franklin Roosevelt, who hated him; Herbert Lehman; Thomas Dewey; Averell Harriman; and Nelson Rockefeller, who finally took his power away. He held this power through the reigns of five mayors: Fiorello La Guardia, William O'Dwyer, Vincent Impellitteri, Robert Wagner, and John Lindsay. Robert Moses held power not for a decade and not for a generation but for almost half a century. And with his power he shaped New York. The story of New York in the twentieth century is inseparable from the story of Robert Moses.

What was his physical legacy?

When you look at New York today, particularly if you're flying in, you see a landscape that was, to a remarkable extent, created by a single human being. If you fly into La Guardia Airport from the north, you will pass over the Triborough Bridge, the Throgs Neck Bridge, the Bronx-Whitestone Bridge, and the Henry Hudson Bridge. Each of those bridges was built by Robert Moses. If you fly into the city from the south, you pass the Verrazano-Narrows Bridge, the Cross Bay Bridge, and the Marine Parkway Bridge. Robert Moses built those bridges, too. The seven major bridges built in New York in the last three-quarters of a century were all the work of this one man. Only one of New York's five boroughs, the Bronx, is on the mainland of the United States, so the city is really a city of islands. It was Robert Moses, more than any other individual, who tied the islands physically together into one city. If you look down at the city, cutting across the rather delicate tracery of the grid of its streets are the heavier lines of the expressways, which carry the city's commerce and its people. With a single exception, the East River Drive, Robert Moses built every one of those roads. He built the Major Deegan Expressway, the Van Wyck Expressway, the Sheridan Expressway, and the Bruckner Expressway. He built the Gowanus Expressway, the Prospect Expressway, the Whitestone Expressway, the Throgs Neck Expressway, and the Clearview

Expressway. He built the Brooklyn-Queens Expressway, the Cross-Bronx Expressway, the Nassau Expressway, the Staten Island Expressway, and the Long Island Expressway. He built the Harlem River Drive and the West Side Highway.

Extending out from the city stretch long ribbons of concrete that are closed to trucks and bordered by parks; these are the parkways. Robert Moses built 416 miles of parkways. When Robert Moses started building them, there were almost no parkways in America, certainly not on the scale he envisioned. Reaching out toward Long Island, he built the Belt Parkway, the Grand Central Parkway, the Laurelton Parkway, the Cross-Island Parkway, the Interborough Parkway. On Long Island he built the Northern State Parkway and the Southern State Parkway, the Wantagh Parkway and the Sagtikos, the Sunken Meadow and the Meadowbrook. Reaching north out of the city, he built the Mosholu Parkway, the Hutchinson River Parkway, the Sawmill River Parkway, the Sprain Brook Parkway, and the Cross-County Parkway. From your plane, you also see a vast expanse of green space. Much of that green was created by Robert Moses. He added twenty thousand acres to the city's parkland, and, for the use of the city's residents but beyond its border, he added another forty thousand acres of parks in the city's Long Island suburbs. He not only tied the city together, he changed its very shape. In his various landfill projects he rammed bulkheads into the water, he filled in the land behind them with rocks and with earth, and on top of the fill he built parkways and parks so that not only the earth and the rock of the shorelines are his but the steel and the concrete of the parkways of that shoreline are his, too. This new land totals sixteen thousand acres, which is twenty-five square miles. All New York City is only 322 square miles. He made twenty-five of those miles. And he was the dominant force behind the creation of many of the most monumental features of the New York landscape—Lincoln Center, the United Nations headquarters, Shea Stadium, the New York Coliseum, the campuses of Fordham and Pratt and Long Island universities—the list could go on and on.

What was his urban vision?

He had the vision of a city shaper. You could not talk to Robert Moses in terms of just one part of New York because he saw the entire city—and its suburbs as well—as interrelated. The Bronx was linked to Staten Island. Jones Beach was linked to Manhattan. I've never talked to an urban planner who could conceive of things in the way that Moses did. He was a visionary on a scale equal to a great city. He saw the city and its suburbs as one unit, and he knew exactly how that city could be. He started laying out the plan when he was a very young man. When he was removed from power decades later, he was still filling in pieces of it.

Is there any other city builder who compares with Moses?

No one in history. We think of Paris to a considerable extent as Baron Haussmann's Paris. And in the central arrondissements, that's true. Haussmann was a great city builder, and what he did is huge and wonderful. But although Haussmann's achievement is certainly comparable in beauty and eloquence to that of Moses, it's not comparable in scope. Today we think of building in terms of the federal government giving billions of dollars. But that's just giving money, it's not building. In terms of dreaming of a public works project, conceiving of it, and carrying it through to completion, no one in history has even come close to Robert Moses. He personally conceived all these projects. He dreamed them starting in 1913, and he was still building them in 1968, fifty-five years later. And he hadn't finished: when you look at a map of New York today, there are gaps that if Moses was still in power he would be filling—with a lower Manhattan expressway, a mid-Manhattan expressway, an upper Manhattan expressway.

Can we think of Robert Moses as a kind of artist?

Absolutely. Robert Moses had an enormous map of New York in his office, and if you saw Moses standing in front of that map, with his pencil going over it in sweeping gestures, you would see the painter in front of his canvas, the dreamer, the visionary, the artist. He saw New York and its suburbs—2,100 square miles, an area in which, when he was building, 12 million people lived—he saw it all as a canvas. He was going to build his roads across it. He was going to build his roads around it. There were going to be parks here and parks there. And then we're going to have public housing here, so we'll shape the park like this and put the road *there*. He saw the whole thing as one huge wonderful mural. You couldn't *not* see him as an artist. You could just see that mind flickering from one thing to another, and it all had a unity, the unity of a single vision. I'm not saying the vision is correct, but it was his vision. And it is the vision to which New York and its suburbs were shaped.

What was Moses like as a young man?

He was an idealist and a dreamer. After college he went to work for an organization trying to reform the civil service system of New York. He lived then with his parents at Seventy-second Street and Central Park West, but in the evenings when he was driven home from his job at the Bureau of Municipal Research he would always tell the taxi driver to take him not to Central Park West but over to Riverside Drive. And he would stand there, this tall, slender, strikingly handsome figure in a white suit, looking down at Riverside Park on the western shoreline of Manhattan Island. It was called Riverside Park but it wasn't a park. It was six and a half miles of muddy wasteland. It's what we see today as the Henry Hudson Parkway and Riverside Park. But then it was only fill, which the city had put in badly decades before, and the water was bubbling up through the earth so that you sank into it when you walked. And along the waterfront were the four tracks of the New York Central Railroad because the city had turned over its entire West Side waterfront to the railroad decades before. On each side of these tracks were rusted barbed-wire fences that cut the city off completely from the waterfront. And down these tracks would come endlessly long trains. They would burn coal and oil in those days—we're now talking about 1913 and 1914—and soot from the engine, a dense gritty cloud of soot, would float up toward the apartment houses on Riverside Drive so the residents would keep the windows closed. If they had to open the windows in the summer, they were kept awake all night by the clang and the coupling of the cars. There were shantytowns in which derelicts lived, and they were considered so dangerous that even the police wouldn't go down into Riverside Park at night. When you stood up on Riverside Drive as night fell you could see the cooking fires of the hobos and the derelicts down there starting to flicker in the darkness. Robert Moses would stand there looking down on this wasteland. One day in 1914, he and a group of friends were on a ferry going to a picnic in New Jersey (of course there were no bridges across the Hudson then). And among the people in the group was his friend Frances Perkins, who later became secretary of labor under Roosevelt, and Perkins recalls Moses suddenly turning to her and looking back at this mud flat covered with dense smog, and saying, "Frances, couldn't this waterfront be the most beautiful waterfront in the world?" He started to talk to her about this great highway that could run up along the water and this beautiful park that could be beside the highway and how the highway and the park would cover the railroad tracks. And the thing that most astonished Frances Perkins was that, in her words, "he had it all figured out." He said you would have to bring the highway around a curve at Seventy-second Street and knock down some buildings there. He saw a marina—it's now the Seventy-ninth Street Marina and Boat Basin—where people could have their sailboats. He wanted tennis courts and bike paths and knew exactly where they should be. Robert Moses was then twenty-four or twenty-five years old, a lower-level employee for a municipal reform bureau. He was talking about an urban public work on a scale unprecedented in America. And he had it all figured out. Often on Sundays, he and Frances Perkins would stroll around the city together and she said, "Bob was burning up with ideas. Just burning up with them. Everything he saw made him think of some way that he could make it better." So he was at this time an idealist and a dreamer and a visionary on a scale really unique in America, in the world.

What was the condition of New York in 1934, when Moses first came to power in the city?

At that time, New York was a city utterly unable to meet the needs of its people. The Tammany machine, which had been in power for years, had been totally corrupt. During Jimmy Walker's mayoralty, the population of New York City had gone from 5.7 million to 6.8 million. That's a 19 percent increase. During that same time, the budget of the City of New York had increased by 250 percent. And this tremendous increase was overwhelmingly due to graft and corruption. The city was strangling on its traffic. For years it had been unable to build a single mile of arterial highway. People had been talking about building the Henry Hudson Bridge but it had not been built. The city had an idea of linking Staten Island to the rest of the city with a tunnel. They had actually begun a Narrows Tube and the holes for the tube were still lying there. The Triborough Bridge had been started and stopped. And there was no hope of initiating these things in any foreseeable future. If you wanted to get out of the city, if you wanted to drive out of Manhattan, all you had was local streets, so you had to creep across Queens or creep across Brooklyn or creep up through the Bronx on local streets. The only route north was over the Broadway drawbridge at 225th Street, which was a narrow bridge and was raised every time a ship came through, so the traffic could back up for hours. And every attempt to free New York from this congestion had absolutely failed, and the city was, in effect, in bankruptcy.

How did Moses's prejudices begin to reflect themselves in his New York City projects?

Robert Moses was an utterly racist man, and his racism was reflected in what he built. For example, during the 1930s Robert Moses built 255 playgrounds in New York City. He built only one playground in Harlem. He built one playground in Bedford-Stuyvesant. There was a large black community in South Jamaica; he built no playgrounds in South Jamaica. So out of 255 playgrounds, he built exactly 2 in areas that black children could use. Harlem was desperate for playgrounds. I remember a letter in Mayor La Guardia's files from a Father Shelton Hale Bishop, who was director of a church on 134th Street in Harlem, and he said, "The children are begging for some place to play. They don't beg out loud. Their need is unexpressed but you know they're begging. There's no place for them to play except in the

Robert Moses standing on a high beam on Roosevelt Island, June 4, 1959, photographed by Arnold Newman.

city streets." Moses set his social policy in concrete, and he did it in so many fields that you hardly know where to begin. He built the greatest swimming pools that had ever been built in New York. Immense, imaginatively constructed public swimming pools. But he built them in locations that would separate the races. White children were given sliding boards and swings in the playgrounds; black children still had to play in the streets. Moses built beautiful wading pools for white children; black children had to splash through water from the fire hydrants. He believed in the most terrible generalizations. He believed that black people didn't like cold water—that if he kept the temperature in the pools low, black people would not use them—so the heating systems were designed in that way. He believed that in places like Jones Beach you could discourage black people from coming if you didn't have any black employees, any black lifeguards.

How did he break free of the constraints of elected democracy?

Power in a totalitarian government comes from the barrel of a gun. Power in a monarchy comes from a king's edict. Power in a democracy is supposed to come from the ballot box. It's the will of the people. But Moses was never going to get that power from the ballot box. His arrogance and sense of intellectual superiority gave him a contempt for people, and the contempt was obvious—he couldn't be bothered to conceal it—so people wouldn't vote for him. Robert Moses realized that he would never be elected to anything. He wanted to be mayor of New York but he was never nominated. When he ran as the Republican candidate for governor in 1934, he lost by what is to this day the largest majority any candidate ever lost by in a statewide election in New York. Moses realized he was never going to get power through that normal democratic process, so he had to figure out a different way to get it. And he realized that building public works is power. A bridge is power, because a bridge is money: the bridges that Moses built cost in the hundreds of millions of dollars. A bridge is the contracts that go to politically well connected contractors. A bridge is legal fees for the lawyers who arrange it. It's insurance premiums. A bridge is bonds. Hundreds of millions had to be raised in bonds. Why do banks and investment houses want to invest in them? Because they're the safest bonds—they're insured by the toll revenues, they're going to pay off. Moreover, whoever Moses selected to be the underwriters for these bonds would make guaranteed money in one day, buying the issue when it came out and selling it. And a bridge is jobs—hundreds of jobs—for labor unions. Moses gave the contracts, the legal fees, the insurance premiums, the underwriting fees, and the jobs to the individuals, corporations, and unions who had the most political

influence. So they all had a vested interest in seeing that his project was built. Therefore, if the people of a neighborhood, or their assemblyman or congressman, or a mayor or governor, tried to stop one of his projects, they would find themselves confronted by immense pressure from the very system they were a part of. A huge public work—a bridge or a tunnel or a great highway—is a source of raw power, if it is used right, and no one ever used power with such ingenuity, and such ruthlessness, as Robert Moses.

What was the role of the public authority in Moses's concentration of power?

Moses built and operated his bridges and tunnels through public authorities. For decades, every time you paid a quarter or a dollar or a dime at a toll booth, you were paying it to one of his authorities. There were three members of the Triborough Bridge and Tunnel Authority, but the other two were people who did what Moses told them. On some of the later authorities, he didn't even want to be bothered with other members. The legislation creating the Henry Hudson Parkway Authority states that the authority would have a "sole member." Robert Moses was the "sole member." So whether he had to get two other compliant votes or whether he had to get no other votes, the money that came in through the tolls was spent at his sole discretion. He didn't have to—as mayors do—go to a Board of Estimate or city council or submit his will to the voters. He could spend the authorities' revenues just as he wanted. And these revenues were immense. For decades, he had more money to spend on public works in the city than the city itself had to spend on public works.

Was he addicted to power?

Yes. Power *is* addictive, you know. In a way, it's a drug. The more you have of it the more you want. As a young man, an idealist, a dreamer, Robert Moses couldn't get anything built because he didn't have power. He learned he had to have power, he learned how to get it, and he put the power to work on behalf of his dreams. But then power became the end in itself.

Did Moses benefit financially from his projects?

No. Moses didn't care about money himself; he was personally, totally money honest. He wanted power. A friend of his once said to me, "You know a lot of men want caviar. Robert Moses was satisfied with a ham sandwich if he could have power on the side." Moses also wanted to be immortal. Immortality was terribly important to him. Engineers told him that the life of a suspension bridge is measureless, that it will last indefinitely. Moses loved suspension bridges.

And he believed that his public works, the mark he left on New York, the mark of Moses, would make him immortal. He predicted that in centuries to come, you wouldn't be able to look at New York without seeing his mark. Well, it's fifty years after he wrote that, half a century, and as of today, that prediction is completely true.

What was Moses's impact on the city's postwar housing efforts?

One thing that's forgotten about Robert Moses is that although he was not a member of the New York City Housing Authority, for a period of thirteen years between 1945 and 1958 he completely dominated it. No site was selected for public housing and no brick of a public housing project was laid without his approval. During this period, the Housing Authority—or you might as well say Robert Moses because they're one and the same—built 1,082 separate apartment houses that contained 148,000 apartments and housed, at the time he left power, 550,000 people: more people than live in most cities. As in transportation and parks, in housing his impact was immense. In setting the locations for these housing projects to an astonishing extent he followed a policy of segregating people by race and income. It's going to be very hard to change that.

What was the significance of the expressways that he built in New York in the postwar years?

After the war everyone was beginning to realize that you had to build great arterial routes through the cities. Every city had plans for expressways but nobody was able to build them. There were two reasons for this. One, the staggering cost of these expressways compared to everything that had gone before in public works. Second, they needed to be built through a crowded urban setting. But this is a democracy, and you had to evict from their homes tens of thousands of people for an ordinary expressway. These people were voters, and politicians shied away from the very thought of evictions on such a scale. Moses shied away from nothing. As soon as the war ended, he began to ram six great expressways across the heart of New York. One of these, the Cross-Bronx Expressway, ran right across the Bronx— if you look at it, it's like a gigantic trench that has just been gouged through six and a half miles of crowded apartment houses. He showed politicians that it could be done. Whether it should have been done or not, of course, is a much more complicated question.

How did the expressways differ from the earlier parkways?

The parkways were built through open country. There was very little displacement of people. When you start to build roads, *vast roads*, six lanes, eight lanes, through the heart of the city, you are dealing with a new problem entirely, a problem with people. And the mark of Robert Moses— which is really the mark that Moses has left on all the cities of America—is nowhere more vivid than in what he did to the people who were in the path of these expressways. In all, he built 627 miles of roads. One hundred thirty of those miles ran right through New York City. While I was writing *The Power Broker,* I decided to try to find out what the human cost of a highway was by taking one mile of the 130 miles and examining in great detail what had happened to the people and neighborhoods in the expressway's path. The mile I chose was a mile of the Cross-Bronx Expressway that ran through the East Tremont section of the Bronx. Now, when you look at the Cross-Bronx from a high vantage point from which you can see it all, you are staggered. You realize you are looking at one of the most incredible feats of engineering you have ever seen. This vast trench runs straight through the heart of a congested borough. But when you look at the one mile of East Tremont, you notice something else. Right near the route of this highway is another open area sort of paralleling it and the fact is that this one mile provided another available route to Moses, one that would have required very little displacement of people. He had Crotona Park, which ran east-west, as the Cross-Bronx Expressway runs, and on the north side of Crotona Park was an already broad avenue, Crotona Park North. If he took Crotona Park North and just a little bit of the park, he had the necessary right-of-way to build the expressway. He would have had to tear down only six small tenement buildings. But if he took that route he would also have to tear down the storage barns and facilities of something called the Third Avenue Transit Company, which was a company out of which the Bronx political machine—one of the more corrupt political machines in the United States—reaped a lot of profits. The machine didn't want it torn down. So Moses took another route across East Tremont. He decided to run the Cross-Bronx Expressway through a solid mile of apartment houses, six- and seven-story apartment houses. Fifty-four of them. To build all six of these great highways, Robert Moses threw out of their homes the incredible total of 250,000 persons. East Tremont was just one of twenty separate neighborhoods—communities that had been lively, friendly places to live—that had their centers torn out to make way for his roads. In my opinion, it is neighborhoods like this that make a city a home to its people. And the eviction notices he employed to get people out of their homes were notable for their ruthlessness. The cost of those highways in terms of human suffering was staggering. He used to say, "When you build in a crowded metropolis, you have to hack your way with a meat ax." And he not only used the meat ax, he *loved* using it. He gloried in using it.

How did Moses's projects of the mid-1950s shape the future of the New York region?

The crucial moment came in 1954. In *The Power Broker*, I call it "the point of no return" for New York. He's not just building the Cross-Bronx Expressway but the Long Island Expressway, the Brooklyn-Queens Expressway, the Gowanus Expressway, the Bruckner Expressway, the Staten Island Expressway. He was about to start building all of them. It was the moment when both the city and the public authorities were flush with money because during the war material was not available and they hadn't been building. It was also the moment when the suburbs' great open spaces were about to be filled up with suburbanization. Levittown had started, and all the other developments. So this was a crucial moment in the history of the entire New York region. There were numerous proposals to use this money to improve mass transit: to build new subway lines and to renovate and improve the older subways and the commuter railroads. Moses wouldn't listen to any of these proposals. Instead, he poured all the available resources into highways and not only starved rapid transit but in many ways made it impossible for rapid transit to be improved. He systematically starved the railroads and the commuter lines—during his entire career the city built not one new mile of railroad or subway. And really that set the pattern of the suburbs in a low-density, automobile-oriented framework that may be impossible ever to change.

Was Moses, for all of his faults, a necessary figure?

People are always asking me, "Don't we need another Robert Moses?" If we look at the twenty years before Robert Moses came to power in New York, the city did not manage to build one mile of arterial highway, although it badly needed new highways because of the explosion of the automobile age. Then Moses came in, and from 1924 to 1968 he built 627 miles of arterial highways. Do you know how many miles of arterial highways the city and state have built in and around New York City in the thirty years since Robert Moses left power? Exactly thirteen. So, on the one hand, he had the uniqueness of his vision, the ability to look at a great city whole and to see a network of roads and bridges and parks, and to see it all in an instant. And he had an intensity of purpose—a savage will. He often said, "If the end doesn't justify the means, what does?" The tragedy is that in the later stages of his career, he used his ability for purposes that destroyed the fabric of the city, that destroyed the neighborhoods of the city, that contributed to its ghettoization. When you build something, you're having an impact that lasts for a long time. You can change laws, you can change legislation, you can change social policies; it's much harder to change the physical reality. Moses set the

future of the city in concrete. He skewed the social policy of the city away from the expenditure of money on its people and toward physical construction. And that's a big part of what I mean by setting the future of the city in concrete. Things didn't have to be the way they are. Of course there are great historical forces that make things the way they are, and to an extent every individual is subject to them. But there are some individuals who ride the crest of the social forces and bend and turn them in their direction. Moses was that kind of a person because of his personality, his savage will, the scope of his vision, his energy.

What was Moses's impact beyond the New York region?

When the Long Island park and parkway system was built in the 1920s, no one had ever seen anything like it. And who came to see it? The young urban builders. The people who wanted to build roads, who wanted to build parkways, who wanted to build state parks. They came to Robert Moses to learn how to do it. His office then was in the Belmont mansion out on Long Island. In it he had a huge table that had been August Belmont's great dining table, and he would sit there with his maps and his plans around him talking as he always talked, smacking his hands, palms flat, on the table to emphasize his point. And to that mansion came the people who would later be the state highway engineers and the officials of the Federal Bureau of Public Roads. I remember standing in 1970 with Bertram Tallamy, who was the first director of the Interstate Highway System, and he was telling me, "Every mile of the Interstate Highway System is laid out on principles that I first learned from Robert Moses out at that Belmont mansion in the 1920s." So Robert Moses was not only America's greatest road builder but he was the man who taught other road builders.

Why were you drawn to Moses's story?

I grew up in New York, and when I was young, Robert Moses was the great hero of New York. It was the era when he was opening playgrounds all the time and at each one the children would chant "Two, four, six, eight, Who do we appreciate? Robert Moses!" Later, when I was a student at Horace Mann, I had to write a term paper, and the topic was "Is Robert Moses the perfect example of the white knight in literature?" And I believed that he was. After college I became a reporter; I started doing investigative reporting and I covered politics. I was trying to discover and to explain how power works in a democracy. And I realized I wasn't doing that at all. I had been thinking I was doing it, and I wasn't doing it—and the reason was that I didn't understand where the real power was in New York. No matter what road or path I was following, they all seemed to lead to Robert Moses, but I didn't know—even with all of the articles that had been written about him—I didn't really know the sources of his power, or how he used it. I realized that if I wanted to explain power, I had to explain Robert Moses.

What is your strongest personal memory of Moses?

I can't think back on Robert Moses without thinking of him when he was out of power. They removed him from power when he was eighty years old. But he was totally unimpaired—he'd still swim through the big breakers at Jones Beach. And his mind was so fast. When he delivered these lectures to me, he never forgot anything; he remembered every detail of what had happened years before. And he still had all these plans. Everything that Robert Moses built was as nothing compared to what Robert Moses wanted to build. He had a cottage at Oak Beach, beyond Jones Beach, he had the last cottage, and in it were two picture windows. Framed in one was the tower of Robert Moses State Park. Framed in the other was the Robert Moses Causeway. He would sit in this big leather chair in the middle, Robert Moses framed by his monuments. But he wasn't interested in what he had built. He was interested in what he *wanted* to build. He would grab me by the arm—he had this immensely powerful grip even at eighty— and he'd pull me out onto the porch and point to the road he hadn't built, the Fire Island Parkway. That would be the climax of his Ocean Parkway. "Don't they understand that the Ocean Parkway isn't complete without the Fire Island Parkway?" he would say. "It would be such a beautiful road. You would have the ocean on one side and the bay on the other and so you'd be driving for forty miles between the ocean and the bay." And he would say to me, grabbing my arm and almost snarling in the intensity of his passion, "*Can't you* see *there ought to be a road there?*" As the years passed between the time at the age of eighty when Robert Moses was removed from power and the time he died at the age of ninety-two—he was out of power for twelve years—the realization grew on him that he was never going to get to build again. At first he couldn't believe it: his mind was as filled with ideas as it had been when he was a young man. Thinking back on those years when Moses, the old lion, was out of power, I feel a terrible sadness.

How would you sum up Robert Moses's impact on New York City?

The quote from Sophocles that I use in *The Power Broker* sums it up. Sophocles says, "One must wait until the evening to see how splendid the day has been." Robert Moses's day was splendid. He was cheered by the press for decade after decade—but what is the city that he has left us? Its high-

ways are the most awesome highways ever built, but nothing about the highways is as awesome as the congestion on them. It's a city filled with the public housing he built, public housing that is hated by the people who live in it. It's a city ghettoized because of his policies. But on the other hand, both before and after Robert Moses, the city proved utterly unable to meet the needs of its people in areas requiring large-scale physical construction. The problem of building public works, the gigantic public works needed for a crowded global city—the problem of building in a dense, crowded urban setting—is one that democracy has not solved. It's not right to say that Moses was all wrong or that Jane Jacobs was all right. And it's not really right to contrast the two. What you have to say is that the solution has not been found. I do not say that New York would have been a *better* city had Robert Moses never lived. What I say and believe is that New York would have been a *different* city had Robert Moses never lived.

In 1966, when this photo from the Staten Island Ferry was taken, the downtown skyline— perhaps the best-known city view in the world— had changed remarkably little since the early 1930s, when the last of its soaring, masonry-clad spires had gone up. Within just a few years, however, this familiar sight would become almost unrecognizable, as a belt of massive new office buildings at the water's edge obscured the older skyscrapers at the center. In both lower and midtown Manhattan, the late 1960s would witness a burst of office construction like nothing in the city's history—7 million square feet completed in 1967, 8 million in 1968, 10 million in 1969, 14 million in 1970—the equivalent of adding the entire downtown of a city the size of Kansas City or Pittsburgh every year. (Photo © Fred W. McDarrah)

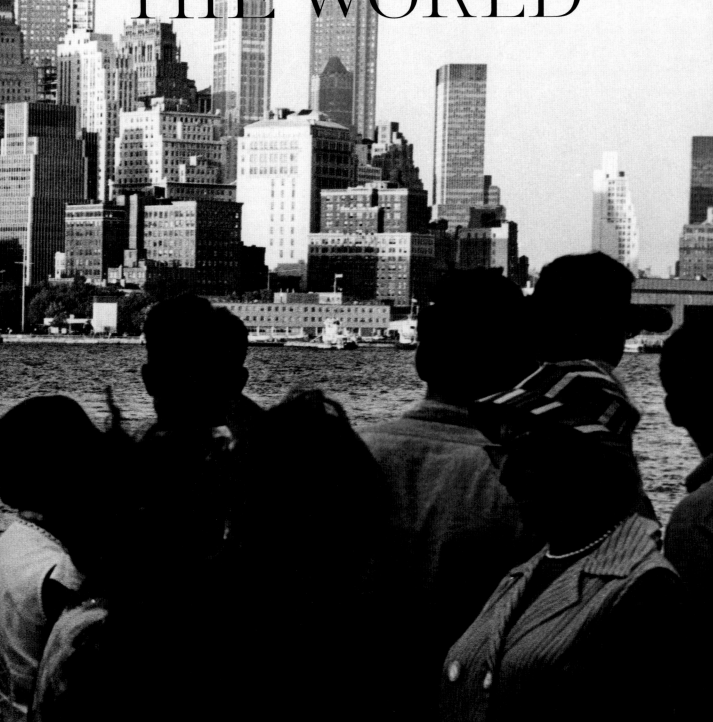

THE CITY AND

1939-1969

THE WORLD

Out for a walk, after a week in bed,
I find them tearing up part of my block. . . .

As usual, in New York, everything is torn down
Before you have had time to care for it. . . .

You would think the simple fact of having lasted
Threatened our cities like mysterious fires.

James Merrill
"An Urban Convalescence," 1962

The main waiting room of Pennsylvania Station being demolished, 1964. Over a period of nearly three years, from 1963 to 1966, McKim, Mead and White's monumental 1910 building was destroyed by its owner, the Pennsylvania Railroad, to make way for a 29-story speculative office building and a new 20,500-seat arena for Madison Square Garden. The railroad station itself—which remained in operation throughout the demolition process—was relocated to a below-ground concourse. In 1999, plans were announced to build a new Pennsylvania Station within the James A. Farley Post Office Building, an imposing classical structure located just across Eighth Avenue—built by McKim, Mead and White in 1913 as a companion to the original station.

THE END OF AN ERA

In the early hours of March 6, 1940, the largest ocean liner ever built slipped silently into its berth along the Hudson River off Manhattan's west side—without fanfare, without a single passenger on board, and after the strangest maiden voyage in history.

For almost half a century, the arrival of a new liner had been a noisy, festive ritual in New York, and a defining civic event. Though virtually all of the great transatlantic ships—the *Mauretania*, the *Lusitania*, the *Rotterdam*, the *Nieuw Amsterdam*, the *Bremen,* and the *Europa*—had been built in Europe, New York was by common consensus their true home: their principal port of call and the only world capital on either side of the Atlantic where they could land directly. Only a few years before, the new arrival's two most distinguished predecessors—the French-built *Normandie* and the British *Queen Mary*—had been cheered into port on their maiden voyages by great crowds of New Yorkers and raucous flotillas of tugboats, ferries, fireboats, and yachts. As nothing else, the arrival of a new ship was a moving reminder of the sheer scale of the modern metropolis—a celebration of the vast harbor from which the city had arisen—and an affirmation of New York's historic role as America's link to Europe and the larger world.

By the spring of 1940, that link had been broken—Europe was in flames—and America's role in the larger world about to change forever. As the somber, unadorned *Queen Elizabeth* pulled into port without a word of welcome, she passed the *Normandie* and the *Queen Mary*, which for more than six months had languished at their slips, unable to risk crossing the war-torn sea lanes of the North Atlantic. The *Queen Elizabeth* herself, which had set sail in total secrecy to avoid being bombed in her British shipyard, had just made it across thanks to her speed and to the cunning of her captain, who with a skeleton crew had raced his immense vessel across the Atlantic one step ahead of German war planes and U-boats. Dressed in drab battle gray, the great ship entered the harbor "like an Empress incognito," one reporter wrote, "veiled for her desperate exploit."

For two weeks, the three greatest passenger ships in the world lay side by side in port, for

the first and only time in their lives. Before the month was out, the *Queen Mary* had shipped out to be refitted as a troop transport, capable of carrying fifteen thousand soldiers at a time; the *Queen Elizabeth* would join her seven months later. By then, France had fallen, and the heartbreakingly beautiful *Normandie*—with no home to return to—would remain in port, her elegant black hull a haunting reminder of a rapidly vanishing world.

For eighteen more months, the United States stayed out of the fighting, but the storm clouds were drawing near. In New York, Robert Moses and Fiorello La Guardia raced to complete as many public works projects as they could before federal resources were diverted to the war effort. By the fall of 1941, Moses had completed the Henry Hudson Bridge, the Bronx-Whitestone Bridge, and the Queens-Midtown Tunnel, and work had begun on another massive tunnel, four miles long, that would connect Brooklyn with lower Manhattan. The New York City Housing Authority, meanwhile, had put up more than sixteen thousand apartments and drawn up plans for tens of thousands more.

Then, in the dwindling days of 1941, Pearl Harbor was attacked and the city and the country mobilized for war. With civilian needs across the country now indefinitely deferred, the Housing Authority's blueprints were rolled up and stored away. The unfinished steel-and-concrete tubes of the Brooklyn-Battery Tunnel would sit empty beneath the harbor, sealed and almost forgotten, for the duration of the war.

In the strange, eventful, and eerily suspended years to come, time itself often seemed to stand still in New York, while beneath it all the forces of change ran faster than ever before.

ON THE TOWN

With the outbreak of war, terror of a kind not felt since the British invasion of 1776 gripped New York, widely presumed to be the number-one target for transatlantic German bomb runs. Day after day, for months, platoons of civilian aircraft spotters anxiously scanned the horizon for enemy planes. Hoping to hide the immense city from enemy attack, the Army Air Corps mounted an experimental camouflage program, flying squadrons of smoke-emitting planes back and forth over Manhattan in an attempt to

For much of the twentieth century, Manhattan's west side offered one of the most stunning urban vistas on earth: a half dozen of the world's greatest passenger ships, docked side by side along their Hudson River piers. This view shows the single busiest day in the history of the port, September 2, 1957, when a dozen liners arrived in the harbor, including (left to right) Cunard's *Britannic, Queen Mary,* and *Mauretania;* the French Line's *Flandre;* Greece's *Olympia;* and the *United States* and *Independence.* That same year brought the first commercial jet service across the Atlantic, a development that would swiftly bring the era of the great transatlantic liners to an end. Within three decades, only a single ship—Cunard's *Queen Elizabeth 2*—would be making regular crossings.

shroud the island from enemy view. Every day, squadrons of fighter planes roared off the runway at Mitchel Field on Long Island, roaming far out over the Atlantic to intercept German war planes and submarines before they reached the harbor.

In the end, the anticipated attack never came, as the Germans never developed a bomber large enough to fly across the Atlantic and back again. And as the fear of enemy attack receded, the immense benefits of a wartime economy began to make themselves felt. Within months, the city's moribund economy began to spring back to life, as the Port of New York—with its 651 miles of active shoreline, 1,800 piers, 40 shipyards, and 36 dry docks—became the principal point of embarkation for the entire European theater of war. By night, endless lines of trucks rumbled through the streets of Brooklyn, carrying troops and matériel to the Brooklyn Army Terminal, where they were loaded onto convoys assembling in the predawn darkness. Before it was over, 3 million soldiers and 63 million tons of supplies would be shipped through New York, which had become the greatest war port in history.

Driven by the demands of war, every sector of the city's economy exploded. On Wallabout Bay in Brooklyn, the New York Navy Yard—birthplace of the *Monitor*, the *Maine*, and the *Arizona*—was swiftly expanded from forty to three hundred acres to become the largest shipyard in the world.

Around the city, factories roared to life, as makers of electronic equipment and precision instruments—from bomb sights to radar to aviation parts—went into overtime, generating work and paychecks for tens of thousands of people. On Madison Avenue, advertising companies drafted war heroes to sell Lucky Strike cigarettes, cranked out ad campaigns for cemeteries, urging families to reserve gravesites before the bad news came, and eventually sold the war itself, fashioning propaganda campaigns for the U.S. Office of War Information. The publishing industry leaped to life, mass producing, for the first time, cheap new paperback editions for the boys overseas, and creating an entirely new genre—the comic book—which featured superheroes like Captain America, often found battling the evil menace of the Axis powers, and Batman and Superman, both of whom worked out of New York—called, respectively, Gotham and Metropolis—itself. With an entire nation anxiously awaiting the latest news from abroad, radio—already knit intimately into the lives of millions of Americans—became an even more powerful force as news broadcasts were expanded to provide listeners with up-to-the-minute coverage of the war. The voice of one CBS correspondent, Edward R. Murrow, broadcast live from a London rooftop during the Blitz, made the newsman a household name across America and set the pattern for news reporting for generations to come.

At night, meanwhile, with the world on fire, New York seemed to turn at an even faster pace, the mood of hectic gaiety made all the more urgent by the war. Even with the bright lights of Broadway dimmed, sometimes to darkness, to reduce the risk of bombardment, the entertainment industry boomed. With consumer goods like cars and appliances at a premium or simply unavailable for the duration, civilians flocked to spend money in nightclubs, restaurants, bars, and shows in record numbers, while

each night servicemen by the thousands swarmed through Times Square, looking for escape or a good time. At theaters like the Paramount on Broadway, huge crowds danced to the intoxicating swing music of Benny Goodman or thrilled to the crooning of Frank Sinatra. At nightclubs up in Harlem, meanwhile, a new generation of jazz musicians, including Charlie Parker, Dizzy Gillespie, and Thelonious Monk, were pioneering a new form called bebop that would transform the genre forever. Broadway itself exploded in a frenzy of hit musicals; some, like *Oklahoma!* and *Carousel*, by old veterans like Rodgers and Hammerstein, others by newcomers like the brilliant young composer Leonard Bernstein, whose huge hit *On the Town* followed the adventures of three sailors on leave for a day in New York.

And yet, for all the willful oblivion and frenzied fun, nothing could dispel for long the chilling arithmetic of the war. By 1944, nearly a million New Yorkers had joined the armed forces, and

Left, the New York Navy Yard on Wallabout Bay in Brooklyn. During the war years, the facility, known popularly as the Brooklyn Navy Yard, became the largest shipyard in the world. In the giant complex, 75,000 employees (including thousands of women riveters, welders, and shipfitters) worked around the clock, in three shifts, seven days a week, to build the mammoth battleships *Missouri* and *Iowa,* five aircraft carriers, and several heavy cruisers, and refit or repair 15,000 smaller vessels. During the war years, the Navy Yard turned out more ships than the entire nation of Japan.

Right, an Italian neighborhood in Brooklyn sending boys off to the army during World War II. During the war, the borough sent 327,000 men into the armed forces, giving rise to the film myth that every bomber crew, every PT boat, and every platoon included at least one young man whose nickname was Brooklyn. By war's end, 7,000 Brooklyn servicemen would be dead.

tens of thousands of families had placed blue stars in their front windows, signifying that a son or brother or husband or father was in service overseas. Before it was over, the families of sixteen thousand New Yorkers would get the news they had been dreading to hear. The grim tidings were marked in front windows by a gold star.

For black New Yorkers, the excitement and ferment and renewed prosperity of the war only served to throw into even sharper relief the appalling inequalities they had faced for generations. To fight the racist dictatorship in Germany, the United States assembled a Jim Crow army, rigidly segregated along racial lines. On

the home front, meanwhile, few of the new job opportunities created by the war went to African Americans, who faced relentless discrimination in public and private sector jobs alike. A survey of seventy-two defense plants in Brooklyn conducted by the Urban League in 1941 revealed that only 234 blacks were employed out of a total workforce of 13,840, and that half of the plants refused to hire blacks at all. When the black labor leader A. Philip Randolph threatened to organize a march on Washington to protest racial discrimination in the army and in defense plants, President Roosevelt urged Mayor La Guardia to step in to stop it. La Guardia balked, and in the summer of 1941, Roosevelt signed into law a bill banning discrimination in any company with a defense contract from the federal government. The first federal civil-rights act of the modern era, it did little to ease discrimination, and in August 1943, for the second time in ten years, riots broke out on the streets of Harlem.

And yet for all the grim headlines and mounting casualty lists at home and abroad, most New Yorkers would look back on the war as a strikingly calm and peaceful time, comfortingly cradled for all the uncertainties of war by oddly abiding realities. By 1944, Franklin Roosevelt and Fiorello La Guardia had been in office for more than a decade, and just as the country seemed never to have had any other president, so the city seemed never to have had any other mayor.

Every summer, the city's attention turned as it always did to baseball. Up in the Bronx—where the Murderer's Row of Gehrig and Ruth had given way to the Bronx Bombers of DiMaggio and Dickey—the implacable Yankee dynasty went on. Each spring, hopes were revived at Ebbets Field in Brooklyn and at the Polo Grounds in upper Manhattan that the Dodgers—or the Giants—would annihilate their National League rivals and seize the World Championship from the Yankees. Each fall, with painful reliability, the hopes of both teams were deferred for another year.

All through the long summer days, radio brought the games into nearly every New York household—along with the clipped intonations of Walter Winchell, the comic routines of Fred Allen and Edgar Bergen, and, on Saturday after-

noons, live performances from the Metropolitan Opera. On Sundays, Fiorello La Guardia dispensed unsolicited advice to nearly 2 million listeners on subjects ranging from the price of chicken to the progress of the war, signing off each wartime broadcast with the bracing exhortation, "Patience and fortitude." During a citywide strike of newspaper deliverymen in 1945, he read the funny pages aloud to his younger constituents, who would otherwise have missed out on their favorite part of the Sunday paper.

Safer and more secure than it had ever been before or than it would ever be again—police statistics for 1945 recorded a mere 292 homicides out of a population of more than 7.5 million—New York had become by the end of the war a city of remarkably stable neighborhoods, most of whose residents enjoyed the same sense of community they would have in any village or small town. Indeed, despite the massive public works that had been thrown up in the 1930s, the city's traditional neighborhoods remained almost entirely intact. Even Robert Moses's sweeping parkways had for the most part either skirted the city entirely or passed through relatively open landscape on its periphery. As they had for generations, the basic units of daily life in New York remained for the vast majority of its citizens the stoop and the sidewalk, the street and the block.

Beneath the surface, however, a fateful shift was under way, as the powerful decentralizing forces unleashed a decade earlier were intensified by the war. Slowly but surely, the relationship between New York and Washington—and between New York and the rest of America—continued to change, as the balance of forces in the nation shifted. To be sure, the city's preeminence had been confirmed once again during the war, just as it had been in the '30s, as a platoon of New Yorkers trooped down to Washington to shape the nation's wartime policy—not social workers and relief experts this time but Wall Street lawyers and investment bankers, including the secretary of defense, Henry Stimson, and senior advisors such as John McCloy, Robert Lovett, and Averell Harriman. Mobilizing the entire country for war, New Yorkers had helped oversee the largest expansion of federal power in the nation's history, and now

This view by Andreas Feininger, looking south on Fifth Avenue in the early 1950s, was one of several images in which the French-born photographer used a telephoto lens to artificially compress the city's congestion. The results, though visually striking, tended to reinforce the era's emerging prejudice against the density and concentration of big cities—the image of New York as a rat race or skyscraper jungle, whose inhabitants were literally piled on top of one another.

looked ahead to a new postwar political and economic order—one which, to a striking degree, would be shaped around the needs of America's multinational economy, headquartered in New York.

And yet, as it had during the New Deal and the Depression, the assertion of the city's influence would come at enormous cost, as the vast wartime expansion of federal power eroded New York's economic supremacy. For all the defense-related dollars flooding into the five boroughs, a far greater percentage of the federal largesse was being directed to regions in the South and West. As the war went on, even the manufacture of uniforms—traditionally the preserve of New York's garment district—was increasingly turned over to manufacturers in the Carolinas, where they were turned out not in high-rise loft buildings but in sprawling modern factories manned for the most part by nonunion workers. Hundreds of millions of dollars in federal funds were being poured into aircraft factories and shipyards along the West Coast and into vast new plants and laboratories in Tennessee, Washington State, and New Mexico—some of them top secret. By the end of the war, the economic infrastructure of the emerging Sun Belt—called into existence by massive public works projects during the Depression—had been given new life as an entire network of government-funded defense industries sprang up from Florida to California.

Indeed, as the Second World War drew to a close much of the fate of the postwar city had been written, though few New Yorkers understood it at the time. With startling speed, the war had lifted the city out of the Depression and ushered in an era of unparalleled prosperity and prestige, a preeminence that would shortly be ratified by its selection as headquarters of the new United Nations. And yet that very prosperity masked the fact that enormously contradictory forces were at work just beneath the surface. In less than five years, the seismic shift in resources and power begun during the depths of the Depression had been dramatically accelerated. In the complex, increasingly dangerous postwar world to come, New York—without surrendering its status as the most important city in the world—would soon be struggling for its very survival.

CRASH

I saw this plane, and it looked like it was coming right at me, and the ceiling was zero. I couldn't believe my eyes.

Army Lieutenant Allen Aiman

On the morning of July 28, 1945—a misty, cloud-covered Saturday just three weeks before the end of World War II—the pilot of a tenton B-25 bomber looking for Newark Airport lost his bearings in the fog, apparently mistook the East River for the Hudson, and banked his huge aircraft into the forest of towers spiking up from midtown Manhattan. Pedestrians below looked up in horror as the big plane—intermittently visible through the broken clouds—narrowly missed the New York Central Building at Park Avenue and Forty-sixth Street, then banked again just in time to avoid a fifty-story tower at 500 Fifth Avenue, rattling windows as it passed.

As the pilot pulled out of the split-second maneuver an immense black form loomed into view straight ahead. At 9:49 a.m. precisely, the great engines roaring as the pilot desperately tried to climb and bank away, the huge plane crashed head-on into the seventy-ninth floor of the Empire State Building.

Horror-stricken occupants of the building, alarmed by the roar of engines, ran to the windows just in time to see the plane loom out of the gray mists that swathed the upper floors of the world's tallest building. . . . It crashed with terrifying impact along the north wall of the building. Its wings were sheared off by the impact, but the motors and fuselage ripped a hole eighteen feet wide and twenty feet high in the outer wall of the structure. Brilliant orange flames shot as high as the observatory as the gasoline tanks exploded. For a moment watchers in the street below saw the tower clearly illumined by the glare. Then it disappeared again in gray murk and smoke of the burning plane.

New York Times, *July 29, 1945*

The crew of the bomber were killed instantly in the crash. So were ten young women working as volunteers in the National Catholic War Relief offices on the seventy-ninth floor, who had offered to come in on a Saturday morning to help with the enormous overflow of paper-

On the morning of July 28, 1945, an army B-25 bomber, which had lost its way in the thick cloud cover above Manhattan, crashed into the 79th floor of the Empire State Building, killing 11 workers and injuring dozens of others. An engine and part of the fuselage tore right through the building and flew out the far side, coming to a rest on top of a penthouse on 32nd Street, while other debris ricocheted off the building to land several blocks away. Miraculously, no one on the street was killed and the building's structure remained intact. "There must be many tenants of the Empire State Building," wrote Frances G. Guilford, who was working in her 34th-floor office at the time of the crash, "who . . . wish to pay tribute to the engineering perfection which enabled this magnificent building to withstand the assault of the bomber. . . . The grand building stood staunch and firm . . . [and returning] to my office . . . [there was] no hint of the chaos not so many floors above." Within 48 hours of the crash, the building was deemed fit for occupancy and was back in business. Within a year—and at a cost of a million dollars—the gaping hole and all the interior damage were repaired, and no visible sign of the tragedy remained.

BOMBER HITS EMPIRE STATE BUILDING, SETTING IT AFIRE AT THE 79TH FLOOR; 13 DEAD, 26 HURT; WIDE AREA ROCKED

WHERE BOMBER CRASHED INTO EMPIRE STATE BUILDING

B-25 CRASHES IN FOG

Hole 18 by 20 Feet Torn Through North Wall by Terrific Impact

BLAZING 'GAS' SCATTERED

Flames Put Out in 40-Minute Fight—2 Women Survive Fall in Elevator

By FRANK ADAMS

A twin-engined B-25 Army bomber, lost in a blinding fog, crashed into the Empire State Building at a point 915 feet above the street level at 9:49 A. M. yesterday. Thirteen persons, including the three occupants of the plane and ten persons at work within the building, were killed in the catastrophe, and twenty-six were injured.

Although the crash and the fire that followed wrecked most of the seventy-eighth and seventy-ninth

work. The body of a male coworker, flung out the window by the impact of the explosion, was found on a setback on the seventy-second floor. In all, fourteen people were killed and several dozen seriously injured by the crash.

But the building itself held firm. Except for one steel beam, bent eighteen inches upward by the sheer force of the crash, there had been no serious structural damage. Many tenants in other parts of the building were unaware that anything had happened. On the eighty-sixth-floor observation deck, the recorded waltz music continued without interruption.

For New Yorkers, the nightmarish accident was a haunting reminder of just how lucky their city had been. Overseas, virtually every other major world capital had been humbled or destroyed by the great conflagration. Berlin and Tokyo had been all but leveled, Moscow starved, Rome and Paris occupied by foreign armies, London battered, first by the Blitz and then by the insidious V-2 rocket. New York, by contrast, had emerged from the world's greatest conflict virtually unscathed, richer than ever, its great walls of stone and steel untouched by the horrors of war.

And now that war was finally coming to an end. Twice a month the *Queen Mary* and the *Queen Elizabeth*, which in four years had ferried more than 2 million men to war, could be seen steaming into port bringing their human cargo back home. As the great sister ships entered the Upper Bay, their decks crammed with American soldiers, a gigantic cheer went up at the sight of New York's breathtaking skyline, which had never seemed more precious or more filled with promise for the future.

Only in the final phases of the war did Americans begin to understand just how profoundly and irrevocably the world had changed. First came the stunning confirmation that Nazi Germany had carried out the most systematic policy of genocide in world history, exterminating three-quarters of the Jewish population of Europe. Then, in August 1945, two blinding flashes of light brought the war in Japan to a sudden end and marked the opening of the nuclear age. In the decades to come, the specter of death by fire raining down from the skies would haunt New Yorkers and city dwellers everywhere.

At 7:01 p.m. on August 14, 1945, after five days of false and conflicting reports, news was received that the Japanese high command had finally surrendered, bringing the most costly war in history to an end. That night, more than 2 million people gathered in Times Square (right)—whose theater marquees and signs blazed with light for the first time in four years—shouting, kissing, crying, and laughing amid a spontaneous celebration that lasted until the early morning hours. "The metropolis exploded its emotions with atomic force," Alexander Feinberg wrote in the *New York Times* the next day. "Restraint was thrown to the winds. Those in the crowds in the streets tossed hats, boxes, and flags into the air. From those leaning perilously out of the windows of office buildings and hotels came a shower of paper, confetti, streamers. Men and women embraced—there were no strangers in New York yesterday."

The subtlest change in New York is something people don't speak much about but that is in everybody's mind. The city, for the first time in its long history, is destructible. A single flight of planes no bigger than a wedge of geese can quickly end this island fantasy, burn the towers, crumble the bridges, turn the underground passages into lethal chambers, cremate the millions. The intimation of mortality is part of New York now: in the sound of jets overhead, in the black headlines of the latest edition.

E. B. White

THE LITTLE FLOWER

Late one night in the waning days of December 1945, Louis E. Yavner, the city's commissioner of investigation, walked up the steps of city hall. After three terms, the long administration of Fiorello La Guardia would be coming to an end on New Year's Eve, and Yavner, who had served the mayor from the start, had some last-minute business to attend to.

As he walked into the darkened building, he was surprised by the sound of a typewriter echoing down the marble corridors. In an office at the end of the hall, he found La Guardia himself, pounding away at his secretary's typewriter.

"Oh, hello, Lou," the mayor said. "I've got these letters to get out and there was no one else around. Say, can you type?"

As he sat down at a nearby desk, Yavner was struck by the poignancy of the moment. Worn to the bone by the end of his third term in office, La Guardia had chosen not to run for a fourth term. After twelve years, the greatest mayoralty in the history of New York was winding down, with a gaunt and haggard man sitting alone in a tiny office late at night, still performing the public service as he saw fit.

By the time he left office, La Guardia was already desperately ill with pancreatic cancer. Two years later, on September 20, 1947, he died at the age of sixty-four—leaving his widow Marie just eight thousand dollars in war bonds and a heavily mortgaged house in the Bronx. Across the city, New Yorkers mourned the death of the Little Flower. Flags were lowered to half-staff, and every fire station in the city marked the great mayor's passing with the tolling of the bells—five chimes, repeated four times—

Fiorello La Guardia (left) on his last day in office, January 1, 1946. The mayor had been worn out by his last term, when wartime constraints made it impossible for him to continue his ambitious reconstruction program. "Why did I take the third term?" he asked friends. "I wanted it the first and second time, and you asked me the third time."

that for generations had honored the death of a fireman.

Whether New Yorkers knew it or not, La Guardia's death spelled the end of an era. For twelve years, he had managed through the breadth of his vision and the sheer force of his personality to balance powerfully conflicting trends and forces that had been building in the city for decades. He had encouraged Robert Moses to build his revolutionary parkways, hastening the dispersal of people and resources to the periphery of the city; yet he had also unified New York's vast subway system and preserved its nickel fare, maintaining the concentration of human energy at the city's center. He had called for a massive effort to level the slums but insisted that the housing that rose in their stead be of the highest possible quality. He had championed his vision of the city of the future, embodied in modern airports, modern parkways, and the World's Fair. But he had also cherished an abiding affection for the streets and blocks of New York's oldest neighborhoods, and for the millions of ordinary New Yorkers who lived there.

During his three terms in office, he had, in short, loved New York and in so doing helped keep its essential identity intact, even as the forces of the modern world threatened to dismantle it.

On September 20, 1947, 45,000 New Yorkers lined up outside the Cathedral of St. John the Divine to pay their last respects to the former mayor, who had died of cancer the night before. "A city of which he was a part as much as any public building awoke to find the little firebrand dead," the *New York Times* reported that morning. "Its people had laughed with him and at him, they had been entertained by his antics and they had been sobered by his warnings, and they found it difficult to believe that the voice he had raised on their behalf in the legislative halls of city and nation, on street corners and on the radio, was stilled forever."

When the light at last went out in the corner office in city hall, something that had held New York together through Depression and war went out with it. Without him, in the years to come, the city would begin to seem to many people, for all its glamour and excitement, an increasingly strange and alien kind of place.

CITY OF NATIONS

Along the East River, from the razed slaughterhouses of Turtle Bay, as though in a race with the spectral flight of planes, men are carving out the permanent headquarters of the United Nations—the greatest housing project of them all. In its stride, New York takes on one more interior city, to shelter, this time, all governments, and to clear the slum called war. New York is not a capital city—it is not a national capital or a state capital. But it is by way of becoming the capital of the world.

E. B. White, 1949

In late 1945, as the world continued to calculate the appalling cost of the war just ended—50 million dead and tens of millions maimed or homeless—a new institution was founded to keep it from ever happening again.

In October, President Roosevelt's dream of a permanent alliance for peace became a reality, and by early 1946, the newly formed United Nations had begun to look for a permanent home.

One place above all seemed supremely fitting—New York, which had emerged from the war as the undisputed financial, cultural, and communications capital of the world. In the aftermath of the bloodiest conflict in history, the great multicultural melting pot seemed to many to be a kind of model or microcosm for the new world order—a crowded island city in which more than sixty ethnic groups coexisted, by and large peacefully, if not always harmoniously.

And yet the great headquarters almost never got built at all.

From the very start, the secretary-general of the United Nations, Trygve Lie, had favored New York City as a permanent home for the organization—but only if the building could be on Manhattan. A headquarters on the densely

built island meant higher housing costs for diplomats and their families, added security concerns, limited space. Yet only in the heart of the city, he felt, could the fledgling group make a real impact. "None of us [are] here on vacation," he said.

But the city government didn't own a suitable site in Manhattan and, with the renewed press of civilian demands on its limited postwar resources, didn't have money to buy one. By late 1946, to the shock of its leading citizens, New York was all but out of the running. On Friday, December 6, the secretary-general told city officials they had exactly five days to come up with a firm offer, or the United Nations would set up shop in Philadelphia, which had already started to condemn land for the buildings.

For Nelson A. Rockefeller—the drivingly ambitious thirty-eight-year-old son of John D. Rockefeller, Jr.—the idea was blasphemous. The old League of Nations had failed, he believed, precisely because its headquarters in Geneva

Born in 1908 to one of the richest families in the world, Nelson A. Rockefeller (above) was fascinated from an early age by large-scale building projects and was closely involved in the development of Rockefeller Center, becoming the corporation's president in 1938, at the age of 30. In December 1946 he played a critical role in bringing the United Nations to New York by arranging for his father, John D. Rockefeller, Jr., to purchase the 17-acre site along the East River that became the institution's home. Elected in 1958 to the first of four terms as governor of New York State, Rockefeller would dramatically reshape the city's landscape through a series of public projects that included the World Trade Center and Battery Park City in lower Manhattan, dozens of new housing projects across the city, and the redevelopment of Roosevelt Island (formerly Blackwell's Island) into a car-free "new town" linked to Manhattan by an aerial tramway. Rockefeller's ambitious construction efforts would increasingly place him in conflict with the city's other great public builder, Robert Moses, leading to a final showdown between the two men in 1968.

had been too far from the center of things. "I wanted the U.N. to fare better," he later declared. "It had to be in the world's financial, cultural, and communications capital. Only by its being near all the media would it be kept in the public's eye and gain its constant support."

Rockefeller was still casting about for a solution when, with only a day to go before the deadline ran out, one of his senior aides, an architect named Wallace Harrison, hit upon a promising idea. For decades, an insalubrious four-block tract of land along the East River filled with slaughterhouses had blighted a stretch of midtown Manhattan. Known as Blood Alley, the seventeen-acre parcel of land had recently been purchased by a freewheeling developer named William Zeckendorf, who dreamed of building a futuristic complex on the site, which he had called X-City. But Zeckendorf was having trouble finding financing for the extravagant project, and Harrison thought he might be willing to sell the property for $8.5 million.

The United Nations didn't have the money. Neither did the city. But Nelson and his thirty-one-year-old brother, David, a banker, knew who did. Reaching their father that same night, the brothers convinced him then and there to donate $8.5 million to the United Nations to be used to purchase the land for its new home.

But they still had to convince Zeckendorf to accept the offer. Late Tuesday night, with

only twelve hours to go, Harrison was dispatched to find the developer, who was celebrating his wedding anniversary in a Madison Avenue nightclub called the Monte Carlo. The architect cornered Zeckendorf at his table and, pulling a map of the site from his side pocket, bluntly asked him if he would sell the property. The cheerfully inebriated developer scrawled his agreement on the map.

The site was theirs, but with hundreds of details still to work out—conveyances of city land, traffic relocations, deed and title transfers—Nelson turned to the only man in New York who could possibly complete the deal in time. In a matter of hours, as the younger man looked on in wonder, Robert Moses displayed his total mastery of the public development process, solving every issue as it arose. The permission of the state legislature would be needed to close down the site's interior streets. Moses made a few phone calls to Albany and it was done. The city would have to surrender its waterfront rights, a complex issue involving municipal, state, and federal regulations. Moses called in a secretary and dictated a lengthy memorandum, which a team of lawyers later determined to be correct to the last comma.

At ten-thirty the next morning, William Zeckendorf was still nursing a hangover when a breathless call came through from Nelson Rockefeller. "It's going to work," Rockefeller said. "The old man is going to give that eight and half million to the U.N. and they're going to take your property. See you soon. . . . Good-bye." Minutes later, the Headquarters Committee officially announced that the site in New York had been chosen, a decision formally accepted three days later.

The breathtaking buildings that now began to rise along the East River were unlike any ever built in New York—or anywhere else for that matter. Shaped largely by the ideas of Le Corbusier, the modern architect who had once called New York "a catastrophe," the new United Nation's headquarters would completely repudiate every aspect of the city's existing character—its density and congestion, its soaring verticality and rigorous orientation to the street—projecting instead a gleaming, abstract composition of modern shapes, which, detached entirely from the city grid about it, seemed to float in a field of open space. The first full-scale embodiment of Le Corbusier's vision of the radiant city of the future, the complex rejected New York's distinctive urban traditions in favor of a clean new "international style," at home everywhere and nowhere.

Le Corbusier himself, with his characteristic blend of impudence and foresight, had no illusions that the new organization or the home he had dreamed up for it could be anything more than interim measures.

Here you can work out the solutions for our modern world without a single day of delay . . . avoiding what might have been too dangerous and too long an interval, were you to have attempted prematurely to build an ideal World Center. . . . It is too soon for a World Center. Therefore, accept in the meanwhile this Battle-Post which is offered to you.

Le Corbusier

By 1950, the first of the U.N.'s buildings was finished, and delegates from around the world were soon convening regularly in their glassy new headquarters along the East River, trying to forge order and a fledgling consensus amid a fractious, deeply divided postwar world. By then, most people had come to realize what Le Corbusier had seen from the start. New York had become the capital of a world-state that did not yet exist—a political union whose power and identity remained largely theoretical.

At that very moment, a genuinely global community *was* beginning to emerge—a commercial community, not a political one—already dominated by gigantic multinational corporations that increasingly ignored traditional political boundaries to move goods and resources around the world at will. That community would make its headquarters in New York, too, not along the East River but in a stunning range of new office buildings already rising a few blocks to the west. In the years to come, they would import Le Corbusier's strange new vision into the very heart of Manhattan itself.

HEADQUARTERS CITY

New York is headquarters town, it's the cerebellum and cerebrum. It is a communications center, processing and exchanging a steadily larger volume of the world's money, information and ideas; and it is a center that determines a large and growing part of the country's production, investment and labor policies—to say nothing of its taste and culture. The . . . wage rates in a factory 2,000 miles away, the fiscal policy of . . . Saudi Arabia, the cut and color of the dress your wife will buy next summer, the sounds that jitterbugs will be vibrating to next fall, the oil production of Libya, the sale of soap in Denver, the future increases in U.S. steel capacity—all . . . are determined or . . . affected by decisions made in New York City.

Gilbert Bruck

By the early 1950s, New York seemed to have entered an economic golden age.

The city was the world's largest manufacturing center, with forty thousand factories and over a million factory workers. It was the nation's largest wholesaling center, accounting for a fifth of all wholesale transactions in America. It had the world's biggest port, handling 40 percent of the nation's waterborne freight—150 million tons a year. And it was the world's greatest financial capital, trading hundreds of millions of dollars each day in its busy markets.

Above all, it had become home to the immense corporations that, having dominated American life for most of the century, were now extending their reach around the globe. One hundred thirty-five of America's five hundred largest industrial companies—including Standard Oil, General Electric, U.S. Steel, Union

New York had always had its share of eccentrics, going back to the colonial era, when New York's governor, Edward Hyde—Lord Cornbury—was reputed to have promenaded along the ramparts of Fort George dressed like his cousin, Queen Anne. Cornbury was widely despised throughout the colony (and the stories about him may have been invented or exaggerated), but the city's later eccentrics were often looked upon with sympathy and even affection. In the 1940s, Joe Gould, a small, thin, unkempt man carrying a greasy pasteboard folder, became a fixture around Greenwich Village. Supported by friends and strangers, Gould had been working for more than 20 years on a manuscript he described as an "oral history" of the city. By 1942, he claimed his work had topped 9 million words, though he died without letting anyone see a word he had written, leading many to wonder whether the work had ever existed at all.

For sheer strangeness, however, no eccentric in the city's history could match the Collyer brothers, whose bizarre story unfolded over several weeks in the spring of 1947.

It began on March 21, when a man identifying himself as Charles Smith phoned the police to report a dead person at 2078 Fifth Avenue, a four-story Victorian brownstone mansion located at the corner of 128th Street in Harlem. The imposing residence was the home of the two bachelor brothers, Homer and Langley Collyer, who had purchased it in 1909, when the neighborhood had been a fashionable outpost of the city's elite. In the decades since, the area had turned into an impoverished slum district. But the Collyers never left.

In the intervening years, the brothers had become a local legend—notorious misers and eccentrics whose ancestors, it was said, had arrived in America a week after the *Mayflower*. Sixty-six-year-old Homer was a talented pianist, a former admiralty lawyer who had become as blind as the poet for whom he was named and hadn't emerged from his house for 15 years. Langley, a thin, courtly, aristocratic man four years his junior, was devoted to caring for his older brother, slipping out of the house late at night in search of food—sometimes walking as far as Brooklyn to buy a single loaf of bread—and attempting to cure

Homer's blindness by feeding him 100 oranges a week. Though the two men were rumored to be millionaires, they lived like squatters in the boarded-up house, surviving without gas, water, electricity, or sewer connections. The city sued regularly to collect unpaid property taxes, and just a few years earlier, a bank had tried to foreclose a mortgage of $6,700. Only when sheriffs, lawyers, and policemen converged upon the house did Langley hand over a check. When asked why they had shut themselves off from the world, Langley said simply, "We don't want to be bothered."

But the Collyer brothers were most notorious for their all-consuming fear of burglars. They had not allowed any outsiders into the house for decades; no one was quite sure how Langley got in and out, since all the doors and windows were boarded up and barricaded. The entire house was said to have been set with dozens of booby traps, designed and built by Langley himself. Only rats and the occasional cat came and went with ease.

Even so, policemen responding to the call that day were unprepared for what they found when they tried to enter the mansion. All the doors were blocked by massive piles of refuse. Several windows wouldn't budge. Finally, Patrolman William Barker forced his way through a second-story window. He emerged a few minutes later and reported that he had found a corpse, emaciated and wearing nothing but a tattered gray bathrobe. It was Homer Collyer, who had been sitting in a small clearing, surrounded by neatly wrapped bundles of newspapers, tied together with string. The police re-entered the house, but could only clear away a narrow space before they were forced to quit for the day. There was no sign of Langley.

By the next morning, a crowd of 500 spectators had gathered on the sidewalk, eager to see the interior of the mansion and to confirm the rumor that the brothers kept hun-

dreds of thousands of dollars in shoe boxes buried in the house. Inside, the police found a honeycomb of narrow passages between ceiling-high piles of junk. Langley had used these passages as he traveled around the house, filling them behind him as he moved forward, to frustrate would-be intruders. Days passed, then weeks, with no sign of Langley. Many of his neighbors believed that he was still in the house, hiding in a room on the third floor. Reported sightings of him came in from every corner of the city.

Working nonstop, police began removing 120 tons of junk from the house, including ten grand pianos, several dressmakers' dummies, bicycles, gas chandeliers, an electric generator, 35-year-old pinups and opera programs, 3,000 books, hundreds of mechanical components, and a Ford Model T. Stacked in piles around the house were every issue of every New York paper since 1918, which Langley had patiently collected, as he had once told a bank official, "so when Homer regains his sight he can catch up on the news." There were also booby traps everywhere. The legends surrounding the Collyer brothers had proved no match for the truth. New York had never seen anything like it.

Finally, on April 8, police uncovered the body of Langley Collyer, just ten feet from the spot where Homer had been found. He had been crushed to death by one of his own booby traps as he carried food to his brother. For several weeks, rats had eaten at the body, sandwiched between a chest of drawers and a bedspring, and flattened underneath a weighted suitcase, three metal bread boxes, and bundles of newspapers. Inspectors determined that Langley had activated the trap himself, accidentally knocking against an overhanging box during a fainting spell.

In the same room, his brother Homer, blind and paralyzed, denied his only source of sustenance, had slowly starved to death.

A New York City policeman emptying the Collyer brothers' house, March 1947.

critics with a phenomenal postwar building boom." On Park Avenue, the epicenter of the explosion, block after block of handsome old apartment houses and venerable hotels were leveled to make way for the shiny new monoliths of steel and glass.

Much of the city seems to be the victim of a roaring, obsessed giantess of a housewife, maniacally energetic, who keeps screaming, "Tear it up! Knock it down! Throw it away! Let's get it cleaned up! Let's make it neat!"

Kate Simon

By 1955, relentless transformation, the dizzying rise and fall of architecture, had long since become an old story in Manhattan, an almost expected feature of life in the city. "Overturn, overturn, overturn, is the maxim of New York," Philip Hone had decreed 110 years before. But there was something different about the newest wave of demolition and reconstruction.

For half a century or more, New York had been the principal headquarters of America's largest corporations. Before the Second World War, however, those companies and the sometimes great architectural structures that housed them, had seemed firmly rooted in the culture of the city. Different as they were, the city's most famous prewar towers—the Singer Building, the Woolworth Building, the Chrysler Building, the Empire State Building, and the RCA Building—had leaped into the sky with an often ostentatious civic pride and daring—urbane and stylish monuments to the bustle and excitement of the city around them.

The postwar buildings, by contrast, were simple, anonymous boxlike shapes that, stripped of the whimsical pinnacles and spires of earlier towers, made no attempt to scrape the sky and were often so similar to one another that an inspection of the corporation's logo was required to determine which was which. Austere shapes indifferent to the city around them, the new corporate headquarters lining Park Avenue, and the even bigger ones to follow along Sixth Avenue, pledged in their form no allegiance to the metropolis, as if such a gesture were unbecomingly parochial and too local for corporate entities with global ambitions. Even when architecturally elegant—as a handful of the best were—their cool, abstract surfaces presented an opaque and, to most New

Carbide, IBM, and RCA—were located in what was now being called headquarters city. And still more were arriving every year.

In 1952, Lever Brothers, a giant multinational corporation that manufactured soap, moved from Cambridge, Massachusetts, to a new headquarters on Park Avenue. Called Lever House, the gleaming structure was the first in the world to bring the glass-and-steel idiom of the United Nations to the service of a sleekly modern corporate image. In the years to come, the International Style would spread around the globe, from Paris to Caracas to Hong Kong, becoming the most familiar symbol of the modern city, and of modernity itself. But nowhere would the new look be more pervasive than in Manhattan, where by the early 1950s a building boom of staggering proportions was under way. Within ten years of the end of the war, 856 new office buildings had been completed, and still the city was adding 2 million square feet of office space each year.

"Manhattan," the editors of *Time* observed in 1953, "written off long ago by city planners . . . because of its jammed-in skyscrapers and canyonlike streets, has defied and amazed its

Yorkers, alien-seeming appearance. Like the U. N. complex itself, these buildings seemed to emerge not from the city's own traditions but from a movement of global proportions, linked no more closely to New York than to anywhere else.

Year by year, as Manhattan's commercial avenues were transformed into formidable chasms of glass and steel, and as the visible connection between the city's commercial culture and public life grew increasingly tenuous, it was becoming less and less clear how firmly linked the corporations themselves were to their home city, or to any geographic location.

Over the next two decades, as advances in transportation and communication continued to bring the world together, and as markets grew increasingly global, New York, which had once had the power to command much of its own destiny, would find itself increasingly at the mercy of larger forces. Within a few years, the city's extraordinary capacity to concentrate within itself the wealth and resources of an entire continent would begin to slow, and then reverse, as the city's industrial base began to fragment with accelerating speed.

Just as that began to happen, huge new populations of impoverished newcomers would be pulled into its orbit—Spanish-speaking immigrants from the Caribbean and blacks from the American South—many of them displaced by the same economic and technological changes beginning to break the old city apart. In a convergence of events that would prove increasingly fateful in the decades to come, New York would soon be repopulated with newcomers in the greatest need of the economic resources the city had traditionally provided—at the very moment those resources were beginning to diminish.

THE GREAT MIGRATION

Going to New York was good-bye to the cotton fields, good-bye to "Massa Charlie," good-bye to the chain-gang, and most of all, good-bye to those sunup-to-sundown working hours. . . . So they came, from all parts of the South. The Georgians came as soon as they were able to pick train fare off the peach trees. They came from South Carolina where the cotton stalks were bare. The North Carolinians came with

tobacco tar beneath their fingernails. They felt as the Pilgrims must have felt when they were coming to America. But [they were] twice as happy, because they had been catching twice the hell. Even while planning the trip, they sang spirituals such as "Jesus Take My Hand" . . . and chanted, "Hallelujah, I'm on my way to the promised land!"

Claude Brown,
Manchild in the Promised Land

On October 2, 1944, on a plantation off Highway 49 near the small town of Clarksdale, Mississippi, a crowd of curious onlookers gathered to watch a remarkable demonstration—eight machines harvesting an entire field of cotton. In the decades to come, the new device—a mechanical cotton picker—would set in motion a chain of events that would transform the nation, from the Mississippi Delta to the streets of New York.

Performing the labor of fifty people at one-eighth the cost, the machine would almost overnight wipe out the jobs of hundreds of thousands of black sharecroppers and field hands, who for generations had scratched out a subsistence living in the cotton fields of the American South. Over the next two decades, in one of the greatest internal migrations in the nation's history, 5 million African Americans would migrate to the industrial cities of the North—to Chicago, Detroit, Cleveland, Philadelphia, Pittsburgh—and to New York.

At the outset of the war, fewer than half a million African Americans made their home in New York. Within five years of the end of the war, three-quarters of a million people were crowded into the traditional black neighborhoods in Brooklyn and Manhattan—and still the numbers grew. Within a dozen years of the end of the war, New York had become the first city in the world with a million black inhabitants.

As they had before, many of the newcomers chose to settle in Harlem, whose very name still conjured visions of the promised land for many American blacks. By 1950, however, the romance and optimism of the Jazz Age had faded to a memory in the capital of black America, which had long since become the most impoverished and overcrowded community in the city.

Adam Clayton Powell, Jr., on June 26, 1944, making a speech at Madison Square Garden during his first campaign for Congress. The son of the pastor of the Abyssinian Baptist Church in Harlem, Powell inherited the influential pulpit from his father in 1937, became the first black New York City councilman in 1941, and was elected Harlem's first black congressman in 1944. Notorious in both New York and Washington for his flamboyant lifestyle, Powell was an outsized personality who delighted in his risqué reputation—a fixture at Broadway openings and Harlem nightclubs, who was married first to a Cotton Club star and then to a beautiful jazz pianist. Yet by the 1950s Powell had become the most influential black politician in the country—an early advocate for civil-rights legislation who was reelected to Congress 12 times by his faithful Harlem constituency.

By midcentury, half of the families in Harlem had slipped below the poverty line, and many were barely able to survive from year to year. As the great migration swelled to a flood, hundreds of thousands of people found themselves crammed into what had become the worst and most dilapidated housing in the city. For those without skills, jobs were hard to come by, and despite modest gains, black unemployment was still twice that of whites. Malnutrition and tuberculosis were rampant.

Harlem, physically at least, has changed very little in my parents' lifetime or in mine. . . . All over Harlem now there is felt the same bitter expectancy with which, in my childhood, we awaited winter; it is coming and it will be hard; there is nothing anyone can do about it.
James Baldwin

While the Apollo Theater on 125th Street still offered live entertainment, the facade had grown shabby from neglect, and most of Harlem's nightclubs had long since closed or moved downtown, unable to rely on white audiences who, since the riots of 1935 and 1943, had grown increasingly wary of Harlem, especially by night. Even the Cotton Club had moved to Times Square. One resident reported that the only white faces one saw on the streets now were those of teachers or social workers.

Despite some small gains in the area of civil rights New York remained as segregated as ever. In 1943, the Metropolitan Life Insurance Com-pany had announced plans to build a housing project called Stuyvesant Town in lower Manhattan. The largest single housing development in the world—built on land cleared with federal funds—it would not, the chairman of the company adamantly declared, even consider admitting blacks as tenants. "Negroes and whites don't mix," he said simply. The storm of protest that ensued would lead to a revolutionary city ordinance, banning racial discrimination in government-assisted housing—the first law of its kind in American history. Over the next few years, New York City would continue to pioneer civil-rights legislation, forbidding racial discrimination in private housing, employment, and education.

But as African Americans soon found, passing a law was one thing, enforcing it another. In spite of the landmark legislation, little had changed by 1950, and true equality seemed as elusive as ever.

The children of these disillusioned colored pioneers inherited the total lot of their parents— the disappointments, the anger. To add to their misery, they had little hope of deliverance. For where does one run to when he's already in the promised land?
Claude Brown

Faced with obstacles at every turn, black New Yorkers had begun to turn to the same avenue of advancement the Irish had pursued a century earlier: politics. Their sheer numbers now represented genuine electoral power, and by the late 1940s a new generation of black politicians had begun to make their way into local, state, and federal government, including Hulan Jack, who became the first black borough president of Manhattan, and Adam Clayton Powell, Jr., the charismatic minister of the Abyssinian Baptist Church who had been representing Harlem in Congress since 1944—one of only a handful of African American members of the House of Representatives. Year after year, he proposed bills to end segregation in federally funded programs; the measures invariably failed to pass, but Powell skillfully managed to keep the issue alive.

Is this the land of the free and the home of the brave? Is this a land of liberty and justice for all? Is this one nation indivisible, under God? Either let us practice the democracy we preach, or shut up!

Adam Clayton Powell, Jr.

By the late 1940s, another great migration had gotten under way, as hundreds of thousands of Spanish-speaking Americans steamed north from the Caribbean island of Puerto Rico.

Though its name meant "rich port" the island was anything but prosperous. Puerto Ricans in small numbers had in fact been coming to New York since the 1898, the year the island was ceded to the United States in the aftermath of the Spanish-American War. In 1917, islanders were finally accorded full American citizenship, and the numbers of newcomers began to rise.

But the real migration began in the 1930s, when Puerto Rico's principal cash crop, sugar, collapsed in the Depression and never recovered. Mired in often hopeless poverty in one of the most densely crowded islands on earth, Puerto Ricans like so many groups before them began to head north in search of a better life.

> *This immigration is different. The Puerto Ricans [have] come not by ship, huddled in the steerage, but by plane. Being U.S. citizens, they beat at no immigration bars, never had their picture taken in colorful native costume behind the wire enclosures of Ellis Island. They simply seeped in, landing by the 20s and 30s from battered planes at La Guardia field and Newark, suddenly appearing beside their cardboard suitcases on the city's sidewalks outside a hole in the wall travel agency. . . . To them, the U.S. means New York City and 300,000 of them now live in its five boroughs.*
>
> *Time*, 1949

Before the outbreak of the Second World War, fewer than sixty thousand Puerto Ricans had made their home in New York. In September 1948, a modern DC-7 left San Juan for the first time, bound for La Guardia Airport, inaugurating the era of direct, low-cost flights. With tickets as cheap as forty dollars, almost anyone could afford the journey, and thousands upon thousands of islanders were soon streaming north every month. Within three decades, the Puerto Rican population in New York had swelled to more than 800,000.

A quarter million of them alone ended up in a single district in upper Manhattan. Once a working-class Italian community—Fiorello La Guardia's old congressional district—East Harlem had always been crowded and poor, but the new Spanish Harlem, or El Barrio, quickly surpassed black Harlem as the most impoverished and overcrowded district in the city.

Spanish now began to rival Yiddish and Italian as New York's second language, as the street life of the city took on a different tone. "Summer is really the kick," the author Piri Thomas wrote, echoing descriptions of the city's crowded tenement streets from decades before. "All the blocks are alive . . . people all over the place. Stoops are occupied like bleacher sections in a game. . . . The block musicians pound out gone beats on tin cans and conga drums and bongos. And kids are all over the place—on fire escapes, under cars, over cars, in alleys, backyards, hallways."

Like most immigrants before them, the new arrivals had come in search of economic opportunity. Nine out of ten newcomers were in fact able to find jobs—most often the menial, low-paying tasks that had been the lot of the city's

Though New York had been home to a substantial Puerto Rican community since the 1920s, the population skyrocketed after inexpensive airline flights from San Juan were introduced in 1947—rising from 61,000 in 1940 to 612,000 20 years later. Though many of the newcomers settled in East Harlem—soon known as El Barrio—large Puerto Rican communities sprouted up on the Upper West Side of Manhattan, in Williamsburg and Red Hook in Brooklyn, and across the South Bronx. Above, a family arrives in New York in 1947. Right, children on the steps of an elementary school in East Harlem, 1947.

newest arrivals since the days of the Irish. "They dig ditches and work ships," one reporter wrote. "They are the city's man behind the scenes. They wash the dishes, make the beds, clean the offices, launder the clothes, change the tablecloths."

Yesterday it was the "brutal and uncouth" Irish; then it was the "knife-wielding" Italians; later it was the "clannish" Jews with their "strange" ways; yesterday it was the Negro; today, it is the Puerto Ricans—and the Negroes—who are relegated to the last step of New York's social ladder.

Jesus Colon

For decades, New York children turned the landscape of city streets, sidewalks, stoops, and alleyways into elaborate playgrounds, handing down traditions one generation to the next. New York street games included a form of jump rope called double dutch as well as marbles, mumblety-peg, hopscotch, touch football, handball, kick the bucket, French tag, squat tag, red rover, and king of the hill. No street game was more popular than stickball, an urban variation of baseball that transformed the city block into a makeshift ballpark. Players used a wooden stick to hit a rubber ball (known as a spaldeen) against a building wall, sending it rebounding across the street to the far sidewalk, where members of the opposite team tried to catch it. Catch basins and manhole covers, both called sewers, served as bases or foul-line markers, while stoops on both sides of the street became bleachers. City boys and girls also spent endless hours drawing in chalk on sidewalks and walls. "In every child's pocket there is a piece of chalk," the urban folklorists Ethel and Oliver Hale observed in 1938. "And with this chalk he liberates his ideas and energies, sketching upon the pavements. . . . Wherever one turns, on every city street, the unfailing patterns may be seen, which at night, after the children have retired from their play, resemble abandoned houses once full of the gusto of life."

Top left, boy in newspaper hat, Harlem, 1947 (© Arthur Leipzig). Bottom left, children playing red rover on the sidewalk, Clauson Avenue, Brooklyn, 1943 (© Arthur Leipzig). Top right, chalk games, Prospect Place, Brooklyn, 1950 (© Arthur Leipzig). Bottom right, boys playing touch football on a Bronx street, 1940s.

I should worry, I should care,
I should marry a millionaire.
He should die, I should cry,
I should marry another guy.

I won't go to Macy's anymore, more, more.
There's a big fat policeman at the door, door, door.
He'll grab you by the collar and make you pay a dollar.
I won't go to Macy's anymore, more, more.

New York street rhymes

By 1950, the underpinnings of a new, and far more troubled, kind of city were in place. In little more than five years following the end of World War II, vast new groups of impoverished newcomers had begun arriving in enormous numbers, straining the city's resources to the breaking point and swelling its already over-crowded slum districts—at the very moment that the city's traditional industrial base was beginning to falter.

For decades, the standard of living had steadily climbed in New York, especially for groups like the Irish, Germans, Italians, and Jews, who had worked their way up the economic ladder, generation by generation, from the wretched conditions of earlier decades. Over the years, they had settled in the middle-class neighborhoods of Manhattan and the outer boroughs or moved on to the suburbs. New Yorkers could take pride in their city's historic capacity to absorb millions of newcomers and bring genuine improvement to their lives.

But by the 1950s, conditions had begun to change. The city's great industrial base—the factories, workshops, and warehouses that had always provided the first step on the ladder for newcomers—was no longer growing. Far from adding thousands of new jobs each year, as they regularly had in earlier decades, the city's manufacturers were struggling to keep the jobs they had, especially in the face of stiff new competition from companies in fast-growing regions in the South and West. Unlike the immigrants before them, the newest arrivals from the American South and Puerto Rico came not to a city of rapid industrial expansion but to a mature economy, with markedly fewer opportunities for blue-collar work.

And there was another, far more intractable problem. The massive influx from the southern United States and Puerto Rico had created a city a quarter of whose citizens—as judged by the majority—were considered nonwhite, and therefore subject to the harshly invidious racial distinctions that had been an elemental feature of American society for hundreds of years.

It was in these troubled circumstances that New York would begin to undergo one of the most massive physical transformations in its history. Driven by the demands of the automobile and by the immense new power of the federal government to intervene in the life of the city, those transformations would shake the very foundations of the metropolis.

To a stunning degree, they would proceed under the aegis of one man, who by 1950 had gathered to himself more power than anyone in the city's history. In the next fifteen years, Robert Moses would wield that power with ferocious intensity, reshaping New York as no one before or since and—for better or for worse, as his biographer Robert A. Caro later wrote—setting much of its future in concrete. Little of that future, as it transpired, would prove to be hospitable for New York's poorest citizens, especially people of color.

One day in 1946, not long before La Guardia's death, a city commissioner named Walter Binger ran into the ex-mayor dining gloomily by himself at the Engineers' Club on Fortieth Street. Binger asked La Guardia what was troubling him. "Moses has got too much power up here now," he replied. When Binger gently reminded La Guardia that it had been he who had granted Moses much of that power, the former mayor looked still more upset, and replied, "Yes, but I could control him. Now no one will be able to control him."

ANTICITIES

Under present redevelopment laws, Macy's could condemn Gimbels—if Robert Moses gave the word.

Charles Abrams

In the years before the war, working first for Al Smith and then Fiorello La Guardia, Robert Moses had developed public projects of extraordinary vision and imagination.

Even then, to be sure, some had questioned his tactics and motives. "He loves the public," his old friend Frances Perkins observed, "but not as people. The public is . . . a great amorphous mass to him; it needs to be bathed, it needs to be aired, it needs better recreation, but not for personal reasons—just to make it a better public."

Now Moses seemed less interested in building for the public than in simply building. With few exceptions, his new projects would incorporate little of the imagination and quality that had marked his efforts before the war. Now they were an end in themselves—or a way to amass still more control over the city and the region.

For all the power that Moses had acquired before the war, it would be nothing compared to the authority he now assumed over the city's future. He had begun to find ways of extending its scope in 1946, when La Guardia's successor—a former police officer and district attorney named William O'Dwyer—found himself overwhelmed by the myriad demands of the postwar metropolis and turned in desperation to Moses. The master builder was perfectly willing to help, if in exchange O'Dwyer would create a new and unheard-of office, that of city construction coordinator, which would give Moses complete command over every public construction project in the five boroughs: not just parks and parkways and tunnels and bridges, as before, but housing projects, schools, community centers—indeed every bit of brick and mortar the city laid down. Moses also insisted that O'Dwyer allow him to be the city's sole liaison with the federal government, a position that within three years would increase his power by an almost unimaginable degree.

In 1949, a federal statute with a deceptively bland name transformed city life in America forever. That year, after decades of promises, Congress turned in earnest to the problem of the nation's slums and to the dilemma that had long thwarted their rebuilding: the indisputable fact that however miserable slum buildings might be for their occupants, they were enormously profitable for their owners. The cost of purchasing thousands of properties in order to clear and rebuild a slum was simply beyond the financial resources of most cities.

The answer was a new housing measure whose modest name, Title I, belied its radical expansion of federal power, especially the power to condemn private property. Over the next fifteen years, Title I would make billions of dollars in federal funds available to local governments to buy or condemn land in the city, not only for government-sponsored projects but for private ones as well.

There was a crucial condition. Experts were convinced that the partial reconstruction of older districts was doomed to failure. Title I funds, it was therefore determined, would only be made available if virtually every structure in a designated area was slated to be destroyed through a process known euphemistically as urban renewal.

In New York, Robert Moses, thanks to O'Dwyer, would soon have control of every one of the federal dollars given out to the city under Title I. In the years to come, the almost demonic maelstrom of destruction and rebuilding that went forth under his signature would beggar anything that had come before in the city's history.

During the war, New Yorkers had trembled at the prospect of an enemy attack that never came. Now, as Robert Moses set to work, one district after another took on an appearance eerily reminiscent of the devastation in Europe and Japan. Month by month, year after year, hundreds of acres of teeming city blocks would be reduced to giant swaths of rubble. What no foreign power had been able to do, New York had begun doing to itself.

"In New York, who needs an atomic bomb?" the novelist Bernard Malamud sardonically wrote. "If you walked away from a place they tore it down."

> Everybody, it would seem, is for the rebuilding of our cities . . . with a unity of approach that is remarkable. . . . But this is not the same thing as liking cities. . . . Most of the rebuilding underway . . . is being designed by people who don't like cities. They do not merely dislike the noise and the dirt and the congestion. They dislike the city's variety and concentration, its tension, its hustle and bustle. . . . The results are not cities within cities, but anti-cities. . . .
>
> William H. Whyte

Much of what rose to take its place would have little to do with the city New Yorkers knew. Rising from the rubble, the new projects put up by the Housing Authority Robert Moses now effectively controlled had nothing in common with anything around them, or for that matter with anything that had been built in the city before—except, perhaps, for the United Nations headquarters. Indeed, without exception, the new developments were shaped to the vision of the anticity that Le Corbusier and other modernist planners had been promoting for years.

That vision was called the tower in the park, and within it, not even the city grid itself would be allowed to remain. Within it, the very streets

The uptown slums are being demolished . . . [b]ut the rectangular tenements that replace them have not a trace of invention. Their bleakness is absolute. No man has ever dreamed of a city of such monotonous severity, and there must be some bond between our houses and our dreams.

John Cheever

One of the first public housing projects to be built in the city after World War II, the James Weldon Johnson Houses in East Harlem (left) revealed the dramatic change in scale from projects built before the war. Named for the Harlem Renaissance writer, the 1947 project housed 1,300 families on a 10.5-acre superblock stretching from 112th Street to 115th Street between Third and Park avenues, in featureless 14-story towers that the critic Lewis Mumford attacked for their "grimness . . . inhuman scale . . . [and] barracks-like air." In the years to come, public housing projects in Harlem, the South Bronx, and other impoverished areas of the city would grow even larger and taller—covering dozens of acres, and reaching 25 stories and more.

and sidewalks themselves would be wiped away, as whole blocks were merged into enormous new tracts called superblocks, reoriented around winding pedestrian paths and suburban-style landscaping. Scattered around each site—often placed at angles to further isolate themselves from their surroundings—were tall, slablike apartment buildings of fifteen stories or more.

Most of [the projects] take in and consolidate adjacent city blocks, forming a superblock. The Housing Authority finds the superblock projects make planning and construction more eco- *nomical and efficient. In addition, the buildings can be widely spaced, exposing them to sunshine and air on all sides; and much of the open spaces can be landscaped and part of it used for playgrounds.*

New York Times

For Robert Moses, no less than for the insurance companies, big labor unions, developers, and government agencies that sponsored urban renewal projects, success was judged by the numbers: the number of housing units built, the number of slum acres cleared. And judged by the numbers, Moses's results were nothing less than astonishing. Every year, for twenty years, he built an average of nearly nine thousand apartments across the city, providing homes for more than 600,000 New Yorkers in all—a population equal to a city the size of Boston or San Francisco. In Harlem alone, he cleared hundreds of acres and built forty thousand new units.

For many New Yorkers, the new apartment units represented a genuine step up, the first decent housing many had ever known. But for those in desperate need of housing—and for the city as a whole—there would be a steep price to pay. By its nature, slum clearance meant tearing down thousands of existing apartments at once, and putting their occupants out of their homes. The families, generally among the city's poorest and least powerful citizens, were supposed to be relocated into nearby housing. As often as not, however, they were left to fend for themselves—hapless victims of the very programs intended to help them.

And there were other drawbacks, in some ways even worse, and certainly longer lasting. Unlike the idealistic officials who had directed La Guardia's programs, Moses mistrusted the very idea of public housing. Like all the public works under his command, the new developments would be built soundly and solidly, and on an enormous scale. But they would be buildings without a soul. Interior amenities would be minimal, and they would be devoid of "luxuries" such as closet doors and toilet seat covers. Outside, their repetitive brick towers would be designed and built without variation, ornament, or detail—anonymous, abstract, and profoundly alienating.

The projects in Harlem are hated. They are hated almost as much as policemen, and this is saying a great deal. And they are hated for the same reason: both reveal, unbearably, the real attitude of the white world, no matter how many liberal speeches are made, no matter how many lofty editorials are written, no matter how many civil-rights commissions are set up.

James Baldwin

"Housing developments instead of replacing slums," the social critic Ernest van der Haag wrote a few years later, "have more often dis-

placed them, i.e. shifted their location. More important, they are no less sterile esthetically than the slums were. In some ways the sterility is more awesome because it seems so orderly, seamless, and therefore ineluctable. Both the physical and social structure of housing developments is designed to prevent spontaneity and variety; they succeed altogether in blocking the communal feeling and the liveliness that was the one redeeming feature of at least some slums."

Moses's concentration of power reached its absolute zenith with the arrival of a new man in city hall—a political nonentity named Vincent Impellitteri, who succeeded O'Dwyer after a corruption scandal forced the mayor out of office in the summer of 1950. That fall, Moses helped the amiable but woefully inexperienced Impellitteri win election in his own right, and in return, the new mayor effectively turned over the city government to his benefactor. For the next forty months, Robert Moses held more official power than anyone in New York's history.

He occupied twelve executive posts simultaneously. He ran the City Park Department, sat on the City Planning Commission and was city construction coordinator. He ran the Long Island State Park Commission, the State Council of Parks, the Jones Beach and Bethpage state park commissions, and the State Power Authority. And he was chairman of the Triborough Bridge and Tunnel Authority, giving him absolute control over the $25 million that flowed through its tollbooths each year.

"With his power," Robert A. Caro wrote, "Robert Moses built himself an empire"—one that stretched the length and breadth of the New York region. He had not one headquarters but three: in a state office building in lower Manhattan, at the Belmont mansion on Long Island, and in an anonymous structure discreetly tucked beneath the Triborough Bridge itself. Each had its own staff of chefs and waiters for private meals. On special occasions, he used Jones Beach as his own resort, treating important guests and dignitaries to lavish feasts and command performances at its outdoor theater. Few could resist his hospitality—or the request for the vote, appropriation, or favor that came with a big smile at the end of the party.

Three professional chauffeurs stood at the ready, around the clock, to transport him any-

where he might need to go—because Robert Moses, the man who built more miles of highways than anyone else in America, had never learned to drive.

But even these imperial trappings tended to understate the impact that Moses, now starting his fourth decade in power, was having on New York and its region. Without quite intending to, he had helped to pioneer a new way of life, one that was rapidly being emulated across the country.

Before the war, Moses had built roads to provide "passports to recreation," in the words of the historian Kenneth T. Jackson—a way for city dwellers to enjoy a weekend drive in the country, or to visit one of his state parks. By the late 1940s, Moses's roads were opening up an entire new world—the suburbs—as more and more families were using the parkways to move out of New York entirely, relocating to the dozens of new residential communities rising beyond the city's borders.

There had long been suburban communities around New York, of course, but the new postwar suburbs were different. They were built not around existing towns but on vast empty tracts of rural land. They were not built one house at a time but instead sprang up wholesale, almost instantly. They were not built for the city's upper classes but for its fast-growing middle class, anxious for more living space and a plot of land they could call their own. Above all, they were laid out not around trains but around cars and Moses's pioneering parkway system, which not only allowed suburbanites to commute to jobs in the city but to move easily around the suburbs themselves.

If the Long Island parkways provided the model for suburban circulation, another Long Island project became the template for the new suburb itself. The brainchild of a Brooklyn-born builder named William J. Levitt, it would turn the construction of houses from a craft into an industry—and change the face of the nation forever. During the war, Levitt had developed an ingenious set of construction techniques that dramatically streamlined the process of house building. In 1947, determined to implement those techniques on a grand scale, he began building the largest private housing project in American history on a four-thousand-acre

potato field on Long Island. Located twenty-five miles east of New York, Levitt's simple and revolutionary housing project—called Levittown—brought assembly-line techniques to the building of houses that were, as Henry Ford's cars had been, all more or less identical. At his peak, Levitt was completing thirty-six new houses each day.

The first tract suburb in America, Levitt's instant town—home to 82,000 people—was only the beginning. Before the '50s were out, the Long Island counties of Nassau and Suffolk would be home to more than 2 million people. Westchester County, to the north of the city, would soon be home to another million, and suburban New Jersey, west of the city, a million and a half. More than half as many people now lived in the city's suburbs as in the city itself, and the numbers were growing.

By the middle of the 1950s, nearly half a million people were commuting to work in New York City each weekday, and the existing parkways—designed, literally, for Sunday drivers—were jammed beyond capacity. To transportation planners, like Robert Moses, it was becoming obvious that the only way to improve the flow of traffic around the region—to link one suburb, in effect, to another—was through an entirely new set of roadways, unlike any ever built before.

From the military highways of the ancient Romans through the early, landscaped parkways of Moses himself, the great highways of history had always run on the outskirts of cities, passing through thinly populated rural areas or farmland. The highways that Robert Moses now proposed would not skirt the city but drive right through the heart of it. They would not be parkways but *expressways,* eight lanes and 225 feet wide, without landscaping or unnecessary curves, thick conduits of concrete through which a torrent of automobile and truck traffic could pass without becoming entangled in local streets and avenues.

Just one of Moses's proposed roads—the seven-mile-long Cross-Bronx Expressway—would have to run across 113 streets and avenues, hundreds of sewer, water, and utility mains, one subway, three railroads, and five elevated transit lines, all of which would have to remain in operation while the road was built. Colonel

In 1956, the Southern State Parkway was widened to accommodate the growing commuter traffic from the new suburbs of Long Island. In a publicity shot taken on July 6, Robert Moses takes the controls of a giant tractor to personally move a house that lay in the path of the road's expanded right-of-way. Covering the story, a *Daily News* reporter noted admiringly that although Moses had several offices around the region, he "would rather be in the field, checking up on jobs and making plans for future ones. Once he makes up his mind about a project, he moves ahead as ruthlessly as the wheels of the big tractor." The anxious-looking man on the left is Henry Hull, the owner of the house being moved.

Thomas Farrell, an army engineer who had built the Burma Road during the war and was now brought in to survey the job, came away staggered by the challenge.

> *You can draw any kind of pictures you like on a clean slate and indulge your every whim in the wilderness. . . . But when you operate in an overbuilt metropolis, you have to hack your way with a meat ax. . . . I'm just going to keep right on building. You do the best you can to stop it.*

> Robert Moses

Something else lay in the path of the Cross-Bronx Expressway: the homes of more than forty thousand people. As Robert A. Caro—examining for the first time ever the sheer human cost of Moses's roads—would later document in detail, a single mile of the Bronx highway, passing through a closely knit working-class community called East Tremont, would require the destruction of fifty-four apartment houses, home to more than fifteen hundred families.

A few of them tried to fight it, hoping not to block the highway's construction but merely to change its course slightly. Organized by an energetic housewife named Lillian Edelstein and assisted by a local engineer who had once worked for Moses himself, East Tremont's citizens mapped out an alternative route that would swing the highway two blocks south,

saving more than fifteen hundred apartments in the process, without increasing the cost of construction.

Victory seemed within reach when the people's committee won the support of the Bronx borough president, James Lyons, but the opposition never had a chance. On April 23, 1953, at a hearing of the Board of Estimate at city hall, Lyons underwent a mysterious change of heart and cast his vote against Lillian Edelstein and her committee. A few months later, the new mayor, Robert F. Wagner, Jr.—who as a candidate had sworn in writing to support the Bronx residents—abruptly switched his position, effectively clearing the way for the road to be built.

The explanation, as it turned out, was not far to seek. By 1953, no politician in the city, not even the mayor, could afford to oppose Robert Moses for long. His power was simply too great. With a phone call, he could call in a favor, threaten to hold back the money for an entire road or park system, or bring pressure to bear from unions, banks, politicians, even clergymen. And if all else failed, as Caro later revealed, he could turn to a set of secret files he kept at his headquarters on Randall's Island, which contained information on the private lives of hundreds of public figures.

The Cross-Bronx Expressway went through as planned. Lillian Edelstein looked on helplessly as her home was bulldozed, along with thousands more all across East Tremont.

"For ten years, through the late 1950s and early 1960s," the writer Marshall Berman later recalled, "the center of the Bronx was pounded and blasted and smashed. My friends and I would stand on the parapet of the Grand Concourse, where 174th Street had been, and survey the work's progress—the immense steam shovels and bulldozers and timber and steel beams, the hundreds of workers in their variously colored hard hats, the giant cranes reaching far above the Bronx's tallest roofs, the dynamite blasts and tremors, the wild, jagged crags of rock newly torn, the vistas of devastation stretching for miles to the east and west as far as the eye could see—and marvel to see our ordinary nice neighborhood transformed into sublime, spectacular ruins."

The story would be repeated throughout the city. Before the rampage of destruction was over, the homes of more than a quarter of a million New Yorkers had been destroyed as Robert Moses rammed one expressway after another across the city—eleven massive roads in all, 130 miles of concrete highways rammed through some of the densest urban communities in the

Left, Fordham Road in the Bronx, on the evening of March 29, 1946.
Right, the interchange of the Cross-Bronx Expressway (right) and Bruckner Boulevard, under construction, mid-1950s. Proposed by Robert Moses in 1946 and begun seven years later, the Cross-Bronx Expressway was one of the most complex and challenging construc-

tion projects ever attempted. Slicing seven miles through some of the most densely built areas of the city, the expressway displaced tens of thousands of people, took 13 years to complete, and cost more than a quarter of a billion dollars, making it the most expensive—and controversial— road ever built.

world. When asked about the difference between his new expressways and his earlier rural parkways, the master builder replied airily, "There are more houses in the way. . . more people in the way—that's all."

Meanwhile, as the new expressways and tract-house suburbs tied the city and its citizens to the automobile, the city itself was being weaned from mass transportation. The entire time Robert Moses's roadways were being built, not a single mile of new subway line was constructed—in large part because Moses, who

worried that rail-based transportation systems would compete with his highways, undermined every effort to build them.

With each passing year, as the entire metropolitan region was increasingly reshaped around the automobile, the culture of the car was becoming an implacable, self-fulfilling prophecy. Unlike the dense and compact multiple dwellings built in older parts of the city, outlying areas of Brooklyn, Queens, and the Bronx consisted—like the new suburbs themselves— almost entirely of sprawling communities of single-family homes, accessible only by auto-mobile. Thanks to Moses's new highways, the new communities could be reached by car—but only by car.

And so from the day each new highway or crossing was complete, it was filled with cars—and soon, jammed with cars. The Brooklyn-Battery Tunnel, built to carry two thousand vehicles an hour, was soon swollen with five or six thousand. The Van Wyck Expressway, designed to handle twenty-six hundred cars an hour, was soon struggling to accommodate seven thousand. The Long Island Expressway, built by Moses to ease congestion on the Southern State and Northern State parkways, itself became so crammed with traffic that it was soon known as the world's longest parking lot, while the older parkways remained as congested as ever.

Each new highway, it seemed, was only encouraging more people to get in their cars and choke the roads, a phenomenon called "traffic generation" by younger planners, who had begun calling for a more balanced approach to the city's transportation needs, one in which new mass-transit lines would complement the arterial highway system. For Robert Moses, however, traffic jams simply proclaimed the need for another road or crossing. The Triborough Bridge, which had carried 13 million cars in 1946, had within four years more than doubled its volume. Moses built a second bridge, the Bronx-Whitestone, to relieve pressure on the Triborough; then, when it grew thick with traffic, he laid out a third bridge, the Throg's Neck, to solve the problem yet again.

And still the flood of cars continued to grow, as ever greater numbers of New Yorkers began relocating to the suburbs from the city, which, in the minds of many, was increasingly being seen as a place from which to escape.

FLIGHT

In the city itself, the influx of people from the American South and Puerto Rico continued, even as another immigration began, this time of newcomers from the West Indies, who for the most part headed not for Harlem but another area of the city.

African Americans had lived in Brooklyn since the 1830s. But the completion in the years before the Second World War of a new subway line, the Independent, offered an avenue of expansion for the city's black population, connecting, in the process, the tenements of upper Manhattan to the spacious brownstones and apartment houses of central Brooklyn in the two adjacent districts of Bedford and Stuyvesant. Duke Ellington and Billy Strayhorn's jazz anthem "Take the A Train" was not only an invitation to come uptown to Harlem but a celebration of the line that linked New York's two great black communities.

By the late 1950s, as the number of blacks in Brooklyn, mostly West Indian, rose to nearly 400,000, Bedford-Stuyvesant surpassed Harlem as the largest black community in New York. The people of "Bed-Stuy," as the district was now called, began spilling into predominantly white areas nearby—Crown Heights, Bushwick, East Flatbush, Brownsville.

For generations, these tough, sometimes shabby neighborhoods had been filled with immigrants from an earlier era—working-class Jewish, Italian, and Irish families for the most part. Now their population began rapidly shifting from white to black. In part, the sudden change was the product of racial prejudice and fear on the part of white New Yorkers. But it was accelerated dramatically when unscrupulous speculators began exploiting those fears for profit, through an insidious real-estate strategy called blockbusting.

"Playing on the fear of white homeowners that blacks would be the first of many," the editor Jason Epstein later wrote, "and that their property would lose its value as [the neighborhood] became a black ghetto, real estate speculators, hoping to turn fear into panic, moved the most 'boisterous, undesirable' people they could find into houses vacated by departing whites. Then they distributed circulars saying, 'Houses wanted. Cash waiting. Don't wait until it's too late.' Buying cheap from panicked whites and selling dear to incoming blacks, these blockbusters soon turned the neighborhood predominantly black."

Block by block, neighborhood by neighborhood, whites fled northern and central Brooklyn—sometimes for other parts of the city, but more often for the new tract suburbs, outside the city limits, where it was easier to control who would be allowed to live in one's community—and who would not.

Fulton and Nostrand, Brooklyn, by Jacob Lawrence, 1958 (right). An African American painter best known for his epic 1941 series, *Migration of the Negro,* Lawrence lived for years in the Bedford-Stuyvesant area of Brooklyn, which by the late 1950s had surpassed Harlem to become the largest black community in the city and—second only to Chicago's South Side—in the United States.

The world's first tract suburb, Levittown (bottom right), was constructed in record time using the revolutionary techniques developed by builder William Levitt and his brother Alfred during the war, which brought the economies of mass production to housebuilding. After the entire site had been cleared flat, trucks dropped off building materials, precisely 60 feet apart, followed by 27 teams moving from house to house, each doing a single job. All complex parts had been preassembled, and new electric-powered hand tools cut construction time still more. At first, Levittown's 17,400 houses were available only to veterans, who could purchase a new house for just $8,000—a price made still more affordable through low-interest loans backed by the GI Bill. On a single day in March 1949, 1,400 houses were sold.

As a Jew I have no room in my mind or heart for racial prejudice. But . . . I have come to know that if we sell one house to a Negro family, then 90 or 95 percent of our white customers will not buy into the community. That is their attitude, not ours. . . . Our position is simply this: We can solve a housing problem, or we can try and solve a racial problem. But we cannot combine the two.

William Levitt

Like most other builders of tract suburbs, the Levitts had simply refused to sell houses to African Americans. In 1960, not one of Levittown's 82,000 residents was black. Instead of prohibiting such discrimination, meanwhile, the federal government actively encouraged it, specifically warning lenders in its housing guidelines about "inharmonious racial or nationality groups." In district maps used to determine credit worthiness, the presence of a single non-white family was sufficient to render the entire block "black."

So strong was the distaste of federal housing agencies for racially mixed city neighborhoods that New Yorkers found it almost impossible to get mortgage assistance to buy or improve a house in an older part of the city. At the same time, federal home loan assistance—established under a second clause in the 1949 Housing Act, called Title II—made financing a house in the suburbs available to millions who had never been able to purchase property before. Thanks to the United States government, it became cheaper to buy in the suburbs than to rent in the city.

> When the American people, through their Congress, voted a little while ago for a twenty-six-billion-dollar highway program, the most charitable thing to assume is that they hadn't the faintest notion of what they were doing. Within the next fifteen years they will doubtless find out, but by that time it will be too late to correct all the damage to our cities and countryside . . . that this ill-conceived and preposterously unbalanced program will have wrought.
>
> Lewis Mumford

No federal action had a greater impact on New York—and every American city—than the passage in June 1956 of the Interstate Highway System: a 41,000-mile network of roads that would impose an immense grid of concrete and asphalt upon the entire continental United States, transforming the nation forever.

The system itself would be openly modeled on New York's pioneering arterial network—not surprisingly, for it had been designed by federal highway engineers who had learned their craft at the foot of Robert Moses, at the Belmont mansion on Long Island, in the '20s. To a striking degree, it would fulfill the car-dominated vision that General Motors had put forth at the 1939 World's Fair—again not surprisingly, for GM itself had led the powerful consortium of business interests—automakers; the rubber, oil, asphalt, and road-building industries; car dealers and renters; truck and bus companies—who had lobbied successfully for the program. The group's foremost spokesman turned out to be Moses himself—"the world's most

vocal, effective, and prestigious apologist for the automobile," in Robert A. Caro's words—whose eloquent speeches and well-reasoned articles were crucial in convincing reluctant government officials to finance the costliest construction effort in the country's history.

Above all, the interstate system would be the greatest and most fateful consequence of the shift in power from New York to Washington that had begun during the New Deal, picked up speed during World War II, and would now come to a peak. Fully 90 percent of the system's gigantic cost was to be borne by the federal government, a provision critical to underdeveloped regions of the South and West, which could never have otherwise afforded the roads.

The most important single public works project in America since the Erie Canal, the Interstate Highway System would work to undo everything that the earlier venture—and the great web of continental railroads that followed it—had brought into being. Where the canal and railroad had concentrated people and goods on a few urban centers—powerfully reinforcing New York's commercial centrality—the highway grid would diffuse resources across the American landscape, diluting the power of New York and almost every other American city.

With astonishing speed, the interstate system accelerated the nationwide shift from public transit and railroads to private cars and trucks. In older communities the highway quickly became the major means of transportation, in newer communities the *only* means. Car ownership soared beyond the most optimistic expectations of the carmakers themselves. In 1939, General Motors's Futurama had daringly predicted that 38 million American autos would be on the road by 1960; the actual total was 61 million.

Although they could be used almost anywhere, automobiles were best suited for low-density environments, spread out across the landscape. Over a period of two decades, beginning in 1950, the suburbs doubled in size, rising from 36 to 74 million inhabitants, while eighteen of the country's twenty-five largest cities lost population.

> *Clearly, the norm of American aspiration is now in suburbia. The happy family of TV com-*

mercials, of magazine covers and ads, lives in suburbia; wherever there is an identifiable background it is the land of blue jeans and shopping centers, of bright new schools, of barbecue-pit participation, garden clubs, P.T.A., do-it-yourself, and green lawns. Here is the place to enjoy the new leisure, and as more people make more money and spend less time making it, the middle-class identification with suburbia will be made more compelling yet. . . . It is not merely that hundreds of thousands have been moving to suburbia, here they are breeding a whole generation that will never have known the city at all.

William H. Whyte, 1957

Once New York had been the leader of an urbanizing nation, the city that other American cities had emulated. Now it was not New York but another city, at the opposite end of the continent, that seemed to provide the prototype for the nation's future—a shift confirmed with almost cruel precision in the summer of 1957, when Walter O'Malley, the owner of the Brooklyn Dodgers, announced that his team would be relocating from Ebbets Field to a new stadium in Los Angeles. That same year, the injury was compounded when the New York Giants announced they, too, would be departing, abandoning the Polo Grounds in upper Manhattan for a new stadium in San Francisco.

New Yorkers felt the loss of the two teams on a deeply personal level, but their departure was just one in a series of staggering blows that now seemed to rain down upon the city without mercy.

The city's industrial core was beginning to erode, as manufacturers in increasing numbers departed New York's cramped multistory loft buildings for efficient, single-floor plants beyond the city limits, where land was cheap, space for truck docks abundant, and highway access easy.

And another revolution was brewing on the waterfront, where the method of handling freight had not fundamentally changed since the days of the clippers: individual crates, hoisted in and out of the holds of ships. The system made theft and pilferage all too easy, and for years, the Port of New York had suffered a reputation for mob-controlled extortion.

Now a new technology promised to diminish the losses: standardized, forty-foot-long locked steel containers that allowed freight to be loaded or unloaded without having to be opened. The Port Authority took an early lead in building container ports but moved most of its operations to the New Jersey side of the bay, to sprawling new facilities in Elizabeth and Newark (thus fulfilling the prediction made by the Regional Plan decades before). Manhattan's Hudson River piers, which had serviced cargo ships for a century, provided no room for the huge storage and trucking areas that container ports required. One by one, shipping companies left the city for New Jersey, taking with them tens of thousands of dock-related jobs. Within a decade, not a single freight pier was still in active service on Manhattan's west side, leaving block after block of rotting piers and pilings along the river's edge.

In the end, industry was leaving the city for the most basic of reasons. New York had never been the cheapest place to do business. Wages and benefits stood well above the national average. The city's tradition of activist government had given New Yorkers the best city hospitals, schools, universities, museums, and libraries in America, but it had also kept taxes relatively high.

In earlier years, the enormous logistical advantages of New York for industry and trade had outweighed the costs. But in the new highway-oriented culture now emerging, those advantages were rapidly disappearing. By the late 1950s, an exodus of manufacturing companies had begun that would not cease for more than two decades, until New York had lost more than three-quarters of its 1 million industrial jobs.

The 1960 census revealed a startling fact. For the first time since 1775—when a colonial population frightened by the prospect of war had deserted the city—New York's population had declined. With 7,781,000 people, it was still by far the largest city in America, still bigger than forty-four of the fifty states. But it was smaller by almost a hundred thousand people than it had been a decade before.

Once F. Scott Fitzgerald had gazed from the top of the Empire State Building onto the distant band of blue and green at the horizon,

In the deepest jungles, on the loneliest islands, in the tiniest settlements scattered around the world, people have heard about Brooklyn. According to the movies, every Brooklyn cab driver was in the Marines, fretting in a foxhole, his brow furrowed, shaking his head as he said, "I wonder how dem Bums are doin'!"

John Richmond

Invented in Manhattan in the late 1840s, baseball had been popularly known in the mid-nineteenth century as the New York game. But it was during the middle years of the following century that the city's hold on the sport seemed all but complete—when baseball, as the writer Roger Angell later remarked, "was almost a private possession of New York City." In the late 1940s and mid-1950s, the trio of teams that made their home in New York—the Yankees in the Bronx, the Giants in Manhattan, the Dodgers in Brooklyn—overpowered their out-of-town opponents with such astounding consistency that seven times in nine years the World's Series turned out to be a battle between two New York boroughs.

Up in the Bronx, the legendary team in pinstripes was not only extending but expanding its historic dominance of the game. If the prewar Yankees had been the most successful club of its time, the postwar Yankees were nothing less than a machine for winning. In the first 18 years after the end of World War II, they captured the American League pennant 15 times and won the World Series ten times. From 1951 to 1953, they won the series three years in a row. "In the 1950s," one man later said, "rooting for the Yankees was like rooting for U.S. Steel."

Yet in the end it was not the Yankees but their National League rivals, the Brooklyn Dodgers, who would become a baseball phenomenon like no other: a team whose

whirlwind of triumph and tragedy in the late 1940s and 1950s offered a powerful, if ultimately heartbreaking, reflection of the changes overtaking the city as a whole.

The Dodgers were everything the Yankees were not. They played not in their league's biggest stadium but in its smallest, Ebbets Field, an aging structure with just 32,000 seats, located on Bedford Avenue, not far from downtown Brooklyn. Notoriously unsuccessful in the decades before the war, the "Brooks" failed to win the pennant for 21 years; then, having won one in 1941, promptly lost the World's Series to the Yankees, a defeat which gave rise to the team's despondent motto: "Wait until next year!" If the Yankees were known as the Bronx Bombers, the Dodgers were "dem Bums."

But no team, anywhere, had a closer bond with its hometown. "In every other American city," one man said, "baseball is a sport. In Brooklyn, it is a religion." During a night game, it was said, one could walk down a Brooklyn street, hear the familiar drawl of the Dodgers's announcer, Red Barber, emanating from one house after another, and never miss a single play. On tens of thousands of Brooklyn streets, boys played stickball—itself an urban version of baseball, adapted to the topography of city sidewalks and gutters—and dreamed of the grass of Ebbets Field. Unlike the Yankees, most members of the Dodgers' lineup lived in Brooklyn itself, in areas like Bay Ridge or Flatbush, making them familiar presences off the field as well as on—neighbors as well as gods.

Everyone agreed there was nothing quite like a Dodgers game, where at least half the fun was in the stands. Intensely critical yet fiercely loyal, Brooklyn fans were known across the country for their wild antics. "They don't pack the bleachers merely to watch a baseball game," one man said. "They

Fans thronging outside Ebbets Field in the early 1950s.

are also there to manage the team." There was Hilda Chester, "the Scarlett O'Hara of Ebbets Field," who sat in the left-field bleachers holding a four-pound cowbell—rung in praise of a good play—and a sign that said HILDA IS HERE. There was the Dodgers Sym-phony: five Italian men from Williamsburg who couldn't read a note of music but invariably played "Three Blind Mice" on their battered instruments whenever the trio of National League umpires came on the field.

Beneath the levity and high spirits, however, was a unique urban relationship. "The thing to remember," John Richmond wrote in 1946, "is that Brooklyn actually has a greater population than thirty states. It is an impressive and complex community of twenty-one principal sections, a kind of patchwork of numerous onetime villages and settlements that date back 300 years. . . . [A] Brooklynite speaks with gruff authority about his own neighborhood but frets like a motherless boy when asked directions about another baliwick in the borough. A resident of Flatbush, for example, possibly knows nothing about the hazards and intracacies of Williamsburg streets. And Red Hook is mighty strange territory to a man from Canarsie." Though they might know little of districts beyond their own, everyone in Brooklyn knew the Dodgers, who provided a rare unifying element

for the sprawling, complex borough. "If you were from Brooklyn," the pitcher Preacher Roe observed, "you were a Dodger fan."

On April 15, 1947, a team mostly known for failure and frivolity was transformed into an extraordinary force for social change, when for the first time in living memory, an African American man stepped onto the field wearing the uniform of a major-league baseball player. In the seasons to come, Jackie Robinson's superb athletic skills and unflappable manners in the face of vitriolic abuse won over the most skeptical fans and teammates—and opened the way for making the team even more representative of its diverse hometown. "The team's roster," the writer Allen Abel later observed, "once as pink and Protestant as the world beyond Gowanus Creek, came to mirror the borough's sense of self: Robinson and Campanella, the blacks; Furillo and Maglie, the Italians; Koufax, the Jew; Snider and Hodges, the valiant all-Americans."

As thousands of Brooklyn fans thrilled to the sight of black and white players meshing seamlessly on the field, the Dodgers became a unique emblem of racial progress. They also became the best team in the league. "When [Jackie] got to Brooklyn," Duke Snider later observed, "we won the pennant. Period." Over the following eight seasons, Brooklyn captured the

National League championship five times. But each year, the victory brought with it an October trip to Yankee Stadium—known in Brooklyn as the Temple of Doom—and a crushing defeat at the hands of the Bronx juggernaut. Then, in the 1955 World Series, to almost everyone's disbelief, the Dodgers finally beat their awesome American League rival. "DODGERS DOOD IT," the *Daily Mirror* announced, "BUMS AIN'T BUMS—ANYMORE!" That afternoon, phone circuits in Brooklyn collapsed from the overload; that evening, parades and fireworks broke out across the borough. "THIS IS NEXT YEAR," the *Daily News* proclaimed.

Yet not even the new world champions could halt the powerful forces now at work across the borough. Despite the proud display of harmony within its ballpark, Brooklyn itself was being wrenched by social change, much of it brought on by growing racial fears and antagonisms. In ever larger numbers, white families were fleeing the row houses and apartments of Brooklyn for new suburban communities in Queens, Staten Island, and Long Island, while African American families from the West Indies or the South

took their place in the borough's older districts.

Superbly oriented to the subway system of an earlier era, Ebbets Field was distant from the city's new arterial highway system and offered parking space for only 700 cars. Night games—which the Dodgers had introduced to baseball in 1938—had helped to raise attendance, but white fans were growing increasingly apprehensive about venturing into the rough neighborhood after dark. African American crowds were on the rise—and the team was still the second largest draw in the league—but in 1956, the Dodgers' owner, Walter O'Malley, informed officials that unless the city built a spectacular new stadium—a domed, 50,000-seat sports center that would sit atop the Long Island Rail Road terminal on Flatbush Avenue in Brooklyn—he would take the Dodgers elsewhere.

Mayor Robert Wagner balked at the $30 million price tag for the new facility. Park Commissioner Robert Moses was prepared to build a new stadium for the team but refused to consider the Flatbush Avenue site—or any location in Brooklyn—proposing instead a spot near Flushing Meadows in

Queens, at the heart of his burgeoning empire of parks and parkways.

As word of the negotiations got out, Brooklynites rose up in fury, staging marches and letter-writing campaigns. BROOKLYN IS THE DODGERS, one sign read, THE DODGERS ARE BROOKLYN. KEEP IT THAT WAY. The president of the Hebrew National frankfurter company seriously offered the site of his plant for a new stadium.

One could not live . . . in Brooklyn and not catch its spirit of devotion to its baseball club, such as no other city in America equalled. Call it loyalty and so it was. It would be a crime against a community of three million people to move the Dodgers. . . . A baseball club in any city in America is a quasi-public institution, and in Brooklyn, the Dodgers were public without the quasi.

Branch Rickey

It was no use. If the Dodgers were no longer to be in Brooklyn, O'Malley felt, they could be almost anywhere, and for more than a year, he had been secretly negotiating with Mayor Norris Poulson of Los Angeles, who—anxious for the

prestige of a major league baseball team—offered to build a new stadium in Southern California. In August 1957, O'Malley announced that the Dodgers would be leaving Brooklyn at the end of the season.

On September 24, 1957, the Dodgers played their last game at Ebbets Field before a minuscule crowd of 6,702 fans—and won. In 1960, using a wrecking ball painted to resemble a baseball, Ebbets Field was demolished and was soon replaced by a 20-story housing project. In the decades to come, Brooklyn, which in quick succession was losing its other great landmarks—the *Daily Eagle* in 1955, Coney Island's Steeplechase Park in 1964, the Navy Yard in 1966—would struggle to regain a sense of borough-wide identity.

In 1962, Dodger Stadium opened in Chavez Ravine, a mile north of downtown Los Angeles. Located near the intersection of two freeways, the structure was surrounded by hundreds of acres of parking lots, with enough space for 24,000 cars. Newspaper editors in Los Angeles decided that the phrase "dem Bums" was never to be used for the new team.

The Dodgers Sym-phony rallies for a game against the Philadelphia Phillies, 1950s.

finding there the crushing proof that the city had limits. Now those patches of green had to a great degree turned gray and brown—no longer signifying the edge of the city but something that for New York was more ominous still: the new realm, neither city nor country, that was *superseding* the city, the seemingly endless agglomeration of highways, parking lots, and tract-housing developments, punctuated by the deteriorating cores of older towns and cities, that stretched almost continuously from Washington to Boston.

New York stood at the center of this "megalopolis," as it had been termed in 1961 by the French demographer Jean Gottman, an area that had become home to 40 million inhabitants, or nearly one in four Americans. But by now, many wondered if the very notion of a center still had any real meaning.

DEATH AND LIFE

There is no place where newness is so continuously pursued. The past is a shame. It must be wrong. New York lives in the present because it is real estate. It has been more for sale than any other city I can think of.

V. S. Pritchett

For nearly two centuries New York had made the continuous process of rebuilding an instrinic part of its character. The demolition of an older building, usually to make way for a larger one, had been always looked upon as a sign of progress,

of vitality, of the transformative energy that made New York unique—a "great place," as the writer O. Henry put it, "if they ever finish it."

In 1961, one of the greatest architectural monuments ever erected in America was slated for destruction, when the Pennsylvania Railroad announced plans to demolish the fifty-one-year-old Penn Station and replace it with an underground station, above which would rise the new Madison Square Garden and a speculative office building.

Use of the station had been declining since its peak in 1945, when an astonishing 109 million passengers passed through the building. But in the years since, the automobile had deeply cut into train travel. The Pennsylvania Railroad—once one of the richest companies in America but now running a $72 million annual deficit—was anxious to shore up revenues by exploiting the station's eight acres of midtown real estate.

At first, few seemed to care about the loss of the old station. News coverage hardly mentioned the existing structure, focusing instead on the shiny new buildings that were to rise in its place.

Then, on August 2, 1962, more than fifty young architects, historians, and critics—including Philip Johnson, codesigner of one of the city's great modernist icons, the Seagram Building—staged a demonstration to denounce the station's destruction. The action drew mostly bemused responses from the press and public, and the demonstrators themselves soon discovered there was nowhere to turn. No government agency in New York—or indeed in any American city—existed to protect older buildings, no matter how magnificent or historically significant. The Planning Commission ruled only over buildings going up, not those coming down. "We thought we were talking to other people," Johnson said, "but we were really only talking to each other." The railroad proceeded with its plans.

At nine o'clock on the rainy Monday morning of October 28, 1963, the demolition of Penn Station began. It would take nearly three full years to pull down the great marble and granite structure that the architect Charles McKim had built to last forever. Much of the stone wreckage—including the enormous Doric

On August 2, 1962, more than 50 protesters gathered on Seventh Avenue to denounce the demolition of Pennsylvania Station (left). "One of the city's strangest and most heartening of picket lines," the editors of the *New York Times* wrote, the demonstration had been organized by six young architects calling themselves the Action Group for Better Architecture in New York. Their cause soon drew the support of dozens of New Yorkers, including the writers Norman Mailer, Lewis Mumford, and Jane Jacobs, and the architects Philip Johnson and I. M. Pei. But the response from the general public was tepid, when not actively antagonistic. "If I were young," one older architect said, "I would be picketing to have it torn down." Irving Felt, the builder of the Madison Square Garden Center that was replacing the station, brusquely dismissed the demonstration, declaring that "fifty years from now, when it's time for our Center to be torn down, there will be a new group of architects who will protest."

By July 1966, demolition was under way on the only section of Pennsylvania Station still standing—the great wall of Doric columns along Seventh Avenue (right). Morris Lipsett, the demolition contractor, was untroubled by his role in destroying the monumental building. "If anybody seriously considered it art," he said, "they would have put up some money to save it." The base and capital of one of the columns was moved to the sculpture garden of the Brooklyn Museum, and two of the oversized eagles were relocated in front of 2 Penn Plaza, the speculative office building that later rose on the site of the station. But the majority of the stone wreckage was dumped in a swamp across the Hudson. "Tossed into the Secaucus graveyard," the *New York Times* architecture critic Ada Louise Huxtable wrote, "are about 25 centuries of classical culture and the standards of style, elegance and grandeur that it gave to the dreams and constructions of Western man. That turns the Jersey wasteland into a pretty classy dump."

What sphinx of cement and aluminum
    bashed open their skulls and ate up
    their brains and imagination? . . .
Moloch the incomprehensible prisons!
    Moloch the crossbone soulless
    jailhouse and Congress of sorrows!
    Moloch whose buildings are
    judgment! . . .
Moloch whose eyes are a thousand blind
    windows! Moloch whose skyscrapers
    stand in the long streets like endless
    Jehovahs!
Moloch whose factories dream and croak
    in the fog! Moloch whose smokestacks
    and antennae crown the cities!
Moloch! Moloch! Robot apartments!
    invisible suburbs! skeleton treasuries!
    blind capitals! demonic industries!
    spectral nations! invincible madhouses!
    granite cocks! monstrous bombs!
They broke their backs lifting Moloch to
    Heaven! Pavements, trees, radios, tons!
    Lifting the city to Heaven which exists
    and is everywhere about us! . . .
Moloch who entered my soul early!
    Moloch in whom I am a consciousness
    without a body! Moloch who
    frightened me out of my natural
    ecstasy! Moloch whom I abandon!
    Wake up in Moloch! Light streaming
    out of the sky!
        Allen Ginsberg, "Howl," 1956

The main concourse of Pennsylvania Station under demolition, 1964 (see page 264). (Photo © Norman McGrath.)

columns and capitals, and the sculpted female angels that had once ornamented its facade—was hastily discarded into a New Jersey swamp called the Secaucus Meadows.

"Until the first blows fell," the editors of the *New York Times* wrote after demolition began, "no one was really convinced that Penn Station would really be demolished or that New York would permit this monumental act of vandalism against one of the largest and finest landmarks of its age.... Any city gets what it admires, and will pay for, and, ultimately, deserves. ... We want and deserve tin-can architecture for a tin-horn culture. And we will probably be judged not by the monuments we build but by those we have destroyed."

Through Penn Station, the architecture historian Vincent Scully wrote, "one entered the city like a god. Perhaps it really was too much. One scuttles in now like a rat."

Looking back, the destruction of Pennsylvania Station marked a low point for the city, which had lost not just an irreplaceable masterpiece but the greatest symbol of the imperial metropolis it had once been. No building had more movingly celebrated the extraordinary concentration of resources and energy that had brought modern New York into being. Its destruction seemed the ultimate confirmation that the culture of highways and cars embraced by Robert Moses would define the future of the city.

Moses himself now looked forward to completing his great arterial system with a pair of elevated highways that would cut straight through Manhattan itself. But as the magnitude of the loss of Penn Station began to sink in, New Yorkers in increasing numbers were calling for an entirely new approach—a new way of thinking about cities and city life. In New York, that approach had already begun to emerge, rising unexpectedly from the blocks of downtown Manhattan to confront directly the prevailing urban mentality of the time—one that had deemed it necessary to destroy the city in order to save it.

Nobody seems to care about New York—except for those of us who live and work here. And we, who do care, believe the time has come to put a stop to the wanton destruction of our greatest buildings, to put a stop to wholesale van-

dalism. It may be too late to save Penn Station.... But it is not too late to save New York.

Action Group for Better
Architecture in New York

The same year that the plan to demolish Penn Station was made public, the city announced that a fourteen-block stretch on the western edge of Greenwich Village had been designated an urban renewal site. Officials declared the area "blighted" and called it a "slum"—the standard language that would make federal funds available to clear the land and put up new high-rise housing. It was the same technique that had been used for a decade to redevelop hundreds of sites around the city and thousands more around the nation.

This time things would turn out differently.

Even by the standards of Manhattan, the West Village was an unusual community. Its cheek-by-jowl mix of shops, bars, restaurants, houses, tenements, factories, and workshops had long drawn an equally complex blend of inhabitants, who enjoyed the area's relatively low rents—and placed a high value on the very variety of people and buildings that so concerned city officials.

A decade before, communities facing urban renewal or highway projects, like East Tremont in the Bronx, had been helpless in the face of official power. But the Villagers were determined to turn the tide. They banded together, forming a Committee to Save the West Village and selecting for its chairman a local resident—a forty-five-year-old working mother who lived at 555 Hudson Street. She was "a particularly skillful and energetic woman," one man said, and "a seasoned veteran of clashes with city officials." She was also, he added, "the author of a book about the mistakes of city planning."

Her name was Jane Jacobs. And her book, *The Death and Life of Great American Cities*, would do more than any other single piece of writing in a century to change the way people looked at New York—and at all cities.

Jacobs had come to New York in the 1940s from Scranton, Pennsylvania, and a few years later moved to Hudson Street with her husband, an architect. Here she kept house, raised her two children, and, day in and day out, watched the workings of her block—the ordinary life of an ordinary city street.

Jane Jacobs with her son Ned in Greenwich Village, 1961. The same year this view was taken, Jacobs published her extraordinarily influential book, *The Death and Life of Great American Cities*—at once an attack on modern urban planning and an appreciation of communities like Greenwich Village, where Jacobs herself had lived and raised a family since 1947. The connection between life and work was crucial to Jacobs, who wrote "out of an intensely lived domesticity," the urbanist Marshall Berman later observed. "She knows her neighborhood in such precise twenty-four hour detail because she has been around it all day.... She knows the shopkeepers, the vast informal networks they maintain.... She portrays the ecology ... of the sidewalks with uncanny fidelity and sensitivity, because she has spent years piloting children ... through these troubled waters, while balancing heavy shopping bags, talking to neighbors, and trying to keep a hold on life.... She makes her readers feel that women know what it is like to live in cities, street by street, day by day, far better than the men who plan and build them."

A little after eight when I put out the garbage can . . . I watch the . . . rituals of the morning: Mr. Halpert unlocking the laundry's handcart . . . Joe Cornacchia's son-in-law stacking out the empty crates from the delicatessen, the barber bringing out his sidewalk folding chair, Mr. Goldstein arranging the coils of wire which proclaim the hardware store is open. . . . Now the primary children, heading for St. Luke's dribble through to the south . . . and the children for P.S. 41 heading toward the east. Two new entrances are being made from the wings: well dressed and even elegant women and men with brief cases emerge from doorways and sidestreets . . . heading for the bus and subways. . . . It is time for me to hurry to work

too, and I exchange my ritual farewell with Mr. Lofaro . . . the fruit man who stands outside his doorway . . . arms folded, his feet planted, looking solid as earth itself. We nod; we each glance quickly up and down the street, then look back to each other and smile. We have done this many a morning for more than ten years, and we both know what it means: All is well.

Jane Jacobs

Working as a writer and editor at *Architectural Forum* magazine, she was surprised to learn that everything she enjoyed about the city had been denounced by planners, architects, and critics. "All was failure," she later wrote. "The great city was Megalopolis, Tyrannopolis, Nekropolis, a monstrosity, a tyranny, a living death. It must go." In 1958, she requested a leave of absence to write a book. Instead of harping on how great cities failed, it would, she hoped, reveal the ways in which they worked.

Published two years later, *The Death and Life of Great American Cities* began by attacking everything the modern planners had done. "Look what [they] have built," she wrote. "Low-income projects that become worse centers of delinquency, vandalism and general social hopelessness than the slums they were supposed to replace . . . Cultural centers that are unable to support a good bookstore. Civic centers that are avoided by everyone but bums. . . . Promenades that go from no place to nowhere and have no promenaders. Expressways that eviscerate great cities. This is not the rebuilding of cities. This is the sacking of cities."

The answer, she said, was right under everyone's nose: the street. The lively city street that had been the prime target of every planner and urban critic for decades. Perhaps more than anyone since Walt Whitman, Jane Jacobs minutely observed—and joyously celebrated—the life of New York's streets.

Under the seeming disorder of the old city, wherever the old city is working successfully, is a marvelous order for maintaining the safety of the streets and the freedom of the city. It is a complex order. Its essence is the intricacy of sidewalk use, bringing with it a constant succession of eyes. This order is all composed of movement and change . . . and we may . . .

liken it to the dance—not to a simple-minded precision dance with everyone kicking up at the same time, twirling in unison . . . but to an intricate ballet in which the individual dancers and ensembles all have distinctive parts which miraculously reinforce each other and compose an orderly whole. The ballet of the good city sidewalk never repeats itself from place to place, and in any one place is always replete with new improvisations.

Jane Jacobs

The book turned conventional wisdom on its head. The very thing that modern planners hated most about the street—its messy mixture of activities—was, she declared, its greatest source of strength. A mixture of different uses, of old buildings as well as newer ones, drew different kinds of people to the street, at different times. Mixture made streets safe and interesting. And safe and interesting streets made a safe and interesting city.

More than an attack on modern city planning, Jacobs's book was a celebration of the everyday successes of cities and of urban life itself. For Jacobs, the city was not a place to escape from but a place to remain, nurture, and preserve. A place to live, and work, and raise a family.

In Jacobs's book, ordinary citizens were for the first time handed a powerful, coherent philosophy to counter the pronouncements of those in power—and in public hearings and in print, Jacobs and the other West Village residents exposed and attacked the underlying assumptions behind the proposed redevelopment project.

"The city has made the mistake of confusing low-rent areas with slums," a writer and community activist named Stephen Zoll observed, "a mistake only possible because the planners have so tenacious a grip on the idea of what a city should look like. Low rent equals slum particularly when a second equation makes urban clutter synonymous with blight. But diversity *is* clutter and no two ways about it."

The residents also prepared an alternative plan for low-rise buildings that would not disrupt the scale of the neighborhood. Gradually, they won allies, including a young city councilman—and future mayor—named Edward I. Koch, and an assemblyman named Louis DeSalvio, who called the original proposal "a return to the dark ages of Robert Moses and his arbitrary and inhuman procedures." In the end, the city killed the high-rise scheme and approved a plan resembling the residents' alternative.

But there was no time to exult. For the Village, another battle was looming, this time with the legendary titan himself.

The current fiction is that . . . any busy housewife who gets her expertise from television, radio and telephone is endowed to plan in detail a huge metropolitan arterial complex good for a century. In the absence of decisions by experts, no work, no arts, parks, no nothing will move. Honest public officials will be denounced as wheelers and dealers, oppressors of the poor, dic-

On February 20, 1961, just as Jane Jacobs was completing work on her book, the West Village community in which she lived was declared by Mayor Robert F. Wagner to be a blighted district, making it eligible for slum clearance under the urban renewal act. Within five days, Jacobs had helped to organize 300 community residents to defeat the city's plans. Over the next several months, local families wrote and signed petitions, shepherded city officials through the area, and on one occasion, chartered a tour bus to stage a demonstration in front of city hall. As the protest gathered strength, Mayor Wagner—campaigning for reelection—reversed his earlier position, and on January 31, 1962, the Planning Commission declared that the West Village was not a slum district after all. Left, Jacobs at a penny sale at St. Luke's Church, held to raise funds for the protest effort.

Robert Moses and Walt Disney review a model of the 1964 New York World's Fair, right. Like Moses a purveyor of vast, wholesome environments for the public, Walt Disney enjoyed a major presence at the 1964 Fair—in the Illinois, Pepsi-Cola, General Electric, and Ford pavilions—and was so thrilled by the public's response that he spoke seriously with Moses about transforming the Flushing Meadows site into an East Coast version of Disneyland. Disney's advisors suggested that although the New York site was feasible, a warm-weather, year-round location would be far more profitable, and within a year, planning and acquisition for Walt Disney World in Florida had begun.

tators, fixers and power brokers. . . . I raise my stein to the builder who can remove ghettos without moving people as I hail the chef who can make omelets without breaking eggs.

Robert Moses

Ever since the late 1920s, traffic planners had dreamed of running an elevated highway across the width of lower Manhattan to link the Manhattan and Williamsburg bridges on the east with the Holland Tunnel on the west. In 1940, Robert Moses had made the Lower Manhattan Expressway a cornerstone of his arterial plan for the region and now, by the mid-1960s, with most of the plan—627 miles of highway—complete or in construction, the time had come to add the finishing touches to the system.

Ten years before, in the Bronx, Moses had been able to silence community opposition. But the array of New Yorkers now marshaling themselves against the new plan could not be stopped so easily. Businessmen attacked the destruction of their plants. Architectural historians pointed to the irreplaceable cast-iron buildings that would be demolished. Jewish radicals from the Lower East Side, Sicilian patriarchs from Little Italy, Chinatown merchants, and avant-garde artists living in loft buildings—everyone, in fact, whose community lay in the path of the proposed roadway—put aside their differences to oppose the plan.

At the head of the unlikely coalition was Jane Jacobs herself. Frustrated at one public hearing, the crowd tore up the stenographer's report—

leading Jacobs to declare that since there was no official record of the hearing, there had been no hearing. She was arrested and charged with riot, inciting to riot, criminal mischief, and obstructing public administration. "Of course Jane Jacobs is disorderly," one critic noted. "That's her job."

As in the West Village, the project's opponents began to find allies—city officials and politicians who were willing as never before to cross Robert Moses in public. Assemblyman Louis DeSalvio, testifying before the city's Board of Estimate, attacked the aging builder with undisguised scorn.

"Except for one old man," he said, "I have been unable to find anyone of technical competence who is for this so-called expressway, and this old man is a cantankerous, stubborn old man who has done many things, which may have, in their time, been good for New York City. . . . I . . . think that the time has come for the stubborn old man to realize that too many of his . . . dreams turn out to be a nightmare for the city. . . . This stubborn old man, by this time, should know that what was bad planning twenty-odd years ago is today so much more bad, that it is rotten, that it stinks. And this board must realize that if it does not . . . kill this stupid example of bad city planning, that the stench of it will haunt them and this great city . . . for many years to come."

However unconventional, Jacobs's tactics worked. In the end, as its opponents grew in

Twenty-five years later, I returned to the New York World's Fair, again riding on the track of the same old Flushing IRT; but by 1964, everything else, from me to the twentieth century, had changed. The World of Tomorrow we had counted on in 1939 had evaporated together with Hiroshima, and only fools and hopeless provincials could look with wide-eyed hope at the future of modernity and the blessings of the Machine Age. . . . I loved the 1964 Fair, too, but for the totally new reason that it provided an extravagant surplus of outrageous kitsch, where the collision of postwar realities and prewar fantasies gave one the choice of weeping or smiling.
Robert Rosenblum

In 1958, a Manhattan lawyer named Robert Kopple—filled with fond

memories of the 1939 World's Fair—proposed that the city host a new international exposition on the same site in 1964, to commemorate the tricentennial of the naming of New York in 1664 by the English.

The idea was swiftly taken up by Robert Moses, who—after quickly easing Kopple himself out of the way—became president of the World's Fair Corporation, a post for which he was forced to relinquish all his city jobs, though he still held on to his five state posts, as well as his chairmanship of the Triborough Authority.

It was clear from the start that Moses had little interest in the fair itself, seeing the project mostly as a means of generating the revenue to achieve one of his oldest ambitions: building the greatest park in New York—a 1,200-acre green space that would eventually rise on the site of the fairgrounds, paid for with the profits of the fair itself.

Located near the geographic heart of the five-borough city, it would be a "central park" not just for Manhattan but for the entire metropolis—the first park worthy of being named Robert Moses Park.

The fair is a funny business—if indeed it can be called a business at all. It involves a strange combination of engineering and showmanship. It is part theater, part traveling carnival, part insubstantial pageant, and part—to me the most important of all—permanent park.
Robert Moses, 1963

Moses's mixed agenda caused problems from the beginning. To provide enough income to build his grand park, the World's Fair would have to run two seasons—putting the event afoul of the Paris-based Bureau of International Expositions, which generally approved

runs of no more than six months. Bending the rules was possible— the 1939 fair had been tacitly approved—but after Moses dismissed the organization as "three people living obscurely in a dumpy apartment in Paris," the group not only refused to approve the fair but explicitly requested its members not to take part. Of the larger European nations, only one, Spain— still under the leadership of Generalissimo Francisco Franco— agreed to participate in the event. It would be a World's Fair, critics noted, without most of the world.

Despite its problems, over the next few years the fair somehow took shape, driven by its master builder's sheer force of will. Covering its square-mile site with 156 pavilions, the fair was an extraordinary mix of high art and low, in which Michelangelo's *Pietà*, installed in the Vatican Pavilion, competed for attention with Walt

Disney's robotic animals. "No one interested in Pop Art should hiss at the hot dog stands," the art historian Katherine Kuh observed, "each topped by what resembles huge scoops of glistening whipped cream. . . or the eighty foot tire . . . turned into a Ferris wheel."

The exposition was "disorganized and hodgepodge," Moses's biographer Robert A. Caro later wrote, "but . . . also somehow vital and vivid, not trend-setting certainly but gay and alive, a scene certainly not boring, a scene that may not have titillated the sophisticated taste of the New York intelligentsia but that would have thrilled the general public."

A product of the space-age optimism of the early 1960s, the fair was devoted in large part to the nation's technological progress—featuring full-size mock-ups of NASA's *Mercury* and *Apollo* spacecraft, and symbolized at its center not by the old Trylon and Perisphere but by an ultramodern Unisphere: a 140-foot stainless-steel globe, ringed by the orbits of NASA's new satellites. The AT&T Pavilion offered a preview of the company's new picturephones, while the IBM exhibit sought to make computers seem more understandable and less intimidating. One computer amazed visitors by translating phrases from Russian to English.

From the first, however, there were signs of friction between the gleaming vision of progress presented by the fair and the increasingly troubled world outside. On opening day, April 22, 1964, civil-rights activists staged a demonstration led by James Farmer, the director of the Congress for Racial Equality, to draw attention to what he called "the melancholy contrast between the idealized, fantasy world of the fair and the real world of brutality, prejudice and violence in which the American Negro is forced to live."

Controversy flared again, less seriously this time, when Philip Johnson, the architect of the New York State Pavilion, commissioned

Among the most popular structures at the fair was the IBM Pavilion, designed by the noted architect Eero Saarinen. After filing into a steeply raked People Wall (above), 500 visitors at a time were lifted to an upper-level auditorium, where a lively multiscreen presentation by the designers Charles and Ray Eames sought to explain the workings of electronic computers in terms of everyday decision making. Bottom left, 50 visiting African dignitaries pose in front of the Unisphere, 1964.

ten avant-garde works for the building's exterior, including pieces by James Rosenquist, Robert Rauschenberg, Roy Lichtenstein, and Andy Warhol. Warhol's silk screen, entitled *Thirteen Most Wanted Men*, consisted of blowups from the police department's mug shots. When officials insisted the offensive images be removed, the artist countered by proposing 25 identical portraits of a smiling Robert Moses. In the end, Warhol's piece was absent from the exhibit.

Whether his image appeared in public or not, Moses's presence could be felt everywhere at the fair. Inside the New York City Pavilion, visitors were offered an extraordinary glimpse of the builder's empire: a 9,000-square-foot scale model showing all of New York's 835,000 buildings, as well as the ribbons of parks, parkways, expressways, tunnels, and bridges that he had created across four decades to knit the region together. Viewing the immense model, visitors could finally grasp something of the sweep and totality of the singular vision that had transformed the twentieth-century city.

[W]hen all is said and done, [Mr. Moses's] Fair is exactly the kind of world we are building all over the U.S. right now . . . the Fair is nothing but the concentrated essence of motel, gas station, shopping center and suburb. Why go to New York to find it, then, when we have it all at home?

Vincent Scully

As in 1939, the most popular exhibit was General Motors's Futurama, whose earlier projection of a highway-oriented America had, to a remarkable degree, come to pass. Now the exhibit proposed extending highways to the most remote regions of the globe—the Sahara desert, the Antarctic, the Amazon jungle. Unlike the original Futurama, which had offered Americans a bold and meaningful vision of their future, the 1964 exhibit presented highway building as an end in itself, extending it almost mindlessly to places that few people would ever care to live. The show embodied "no ideas newer than those . . . in the original Futurama," the architecture critic Vincent Scully noted scornfully. "The 'vision of the future' shown here is stale where not actively revolting, and provides a strong argument against letting auto manufacturers have a say in city planning. All those roads!—the American archetype of movement commercially woven to strangle us all."

In the end, the World's Fair was a financial failure, attracting fewer than than two-thirds of its projected number of visitors. "Rather than showing us the future," the writer George W. S. Trow later said, "it showed us the end of something." Ironically, the very technologies introduced back at the 1939 World's Fair—especially television—were subverting the importance of fairs themselves. "Television shows," the critic Morris Dickstein observed, "are now the corny expositions that aim to bring people together, that satisfy their curiosity about the world beyond their lives. People no longer have to go places; the world comes to them."

Instead of the $29 million in profits he had anticipated, Moses only managed to hold on to $8.6 million—scarcely enough to tear down the temporary pavilions and minimally landscape the large but ordinary park that in the end was not named for Moses but for Flushing Meadow itself.

number and power and support for the project faded, the Lower Manhattan Expressway was defeated. Through her successful challenge, and through the book that stood behind it, Jane Jacobs had powerfully reasserted the value of the city block—and by extension, of the city itself—against the seductive imperative of movement and flow that had mesmerized planners since the dawn of the automobile age.

In the postwar era dominated by Robert Moses, two things above all had symbolized the imposition of the modern, abstract, authoritative vision on the vital, chaotic streets of New York: the expressway and the urban renewal project. Now a determined group in the very core of the city had defeated one of each. They had preserved their neighborhoods and challenged the most basic assumption upon which the city had always proceeded—that the new was always better than the old.

Soon that challenge would be codified in an extraordinary new law. On April 19, 1965, Mayor Robert Wagner authorized the creation of the Landmarks Preservation Commission, the first of its kind in the United States. The agency came two years too late to save Penn Station, but over the coming years the commission would designate hundreds of individual buildings for preservation, as well as entire districts like Greenwich Village and Brooklyn Heights. New York, which had done the most of any American city to destroy its heritage, now moved more vigorously than any other city to protect it.

But even as some parts of the city were being saved, others parts were sinking further into despair, especially the vast black and Puerto Rican ghettos whose residents remained deeply mired in poverty. By the mid-1960s, their anger and frustration at the lack of social and economic progress had grown more intense, building up rapidly into fury, and then, even more swiftly, spilling over into violence.

RIOT AND STRIFE

Rising from the . . . ghettos in the North is a mounting tide of Negro resentment. These blacks feel that they have been bypassed by this year of momentous change in the South; and they are bitter about the double standards of Northern white liberals who give willingly to freedom fighters south of the Mason-Dixon

line but look upon the Negro in the urban slum almost as a permanent fixture.
                    The Nation, August 10, 1964

The black man is mad, mad with the continued police brutality of white policemen. He's been mad as far back as I can remember.
                    Adam Clayton Powell, Jr.

In the summer of 1964, the simmering racial tensions that had plagued New York for nearly two decades exploded onto the streets. On July 15, a fifteen-year-old boy named James Powell was accidentally killed in Harlem by an off-duty policeman. Over the next two days, local residents staged angry but orderly protests. Then, on the hot night of July 18, the crowd turned violent. Shouting "Killer cops!" and "Murderers!" an angry mob gathered outside the 123rd Street police station.

"Almost in a matter of minutes Central Harlem was aflame," *Newsweek* reported. "Rioters raged madly through the streets, scattering as police counterattacked, regrouping to charge again. Rocks, bricks, and garbage-can lids rained down on the cops. Bottles looped down from tenement rooftops, popping on the pavement. . . . Trash cans were set afire. . . . All along 125th Street . . . looters—some in organized gangs—smashed store windows, climbed inside, and crawled out with armloads of trophies: food, clothing, shoes, jewelry, radios—and rifles. Facing a swarm of rioters one night, a sweating, red-faced police captain pleaded through his bullhorn: 'Go home! Go home!' And a voice came back, shrill, taunting, 'We are home, baby!' "

The riot continued for five days in both Harlem and Bedford-Stuyvesant. When it was over, one person had been killed and 520 people arrested. An FBI report asserted that the disturbance was not racial, since the rioters had not targeted whites or white-owned property. Instead, the bureau said, it was "a senseless attack on all constituted authority without purpose or reason."

The riots took a special toll on Mayor Wagner, who had made improved race relations one of the prime goals of his mayoralty. And by 1964, his hopes for New York as a place of civic harmony were being threatened by a different kind of trend.

The son of Robert F. Wagner—the legendary New York senator and New Deal mainstay—Robert F. Wagner, Jr., had moved among the city's highest political circles since childhood and later found himself drawn to city government. Criticized by some as bland and colorless, he was considered by others to be a consummate politician, whose low-key, conciliatory style allowed him to enjoy three terms as mayor—the longest tenure since La Guardia's. "Wagner doesn't have anything," one colleague said, "except the votes on election day." More sensitive to racial concerns than any mayor before him, in 1957 Wagner appointed the city's first Puerto Rican magistrate, and in the following year passed the first law in the nation banning racial discrimination in private housing. Left, Wagner (sitting at left) at a Democratic party fund-raiser in 1956 with former president Harry Truman (right), and Carmine DeSapio, the last boss of Tammany Hall—which ceased being an active force in city politics after Wagner himself challenged its leadership in 1961.

Crime had always been a fact of life in New York, as in all cities. But for two generations or more, New York had by any standards been a remarkably secure place, averaging just over three hundred murders a year—most of them stemming from crimes of passion, gangland attacks, barroom brawls. Most people had felt safe: safe enough to take subways well into the night, to keep their shops open late, to walk the streets at any time.

But during Wagner's third term, crime had begun to rise dramatically—the annual number of murders doubling to more than six hundred a year, with an especially sharp rise in the number of random attacks. By the spring of 1964, the homicide rate had increased to the point where the killing of a young woman on a Queens sidewalk barely rated a small newspaper article. But in the months to come, the event would become an extraordinary symbol of the ominous changes overtaking the city.

At 3:20 a.m. on the morning of March 13, twenty-eight-year-old Catherine "Kitty" Genovese was walking home in her Queens community of Kew Gardens, when she was grabbed and brutally stabbed in three separate assaults by the same man. Thirty-eight neighbors in all saw or heard the murder in progress. One man shouted, "Let that girl alone." Another called the police, thirty minutes after the attack began. The others did nothing at all.

"The incident goes to the heart of whether this is a community or a jungle," one man wrote

the *New York Times*, as the newspaper's extensive coverage of the event unleashed a storm of controversy that not even the quick apprehension of the murderer—a business-machine operator named Winston Moseley—could quiet. Many New Yorkers feared that the city's sense of community, which had long thrived in neighborhoods like Kew Gardens, was unraveling. Reminded that the murder had not occurred in a slum district but in a stable, middle-class neighborhood, many wondered if any part of New York was truly safe.

In 1965, Mayor Wagner—visibly aged by his third term in office—announced that he would not run for a fourth. In November, he was succeeded by John V. Lindsay, a tall, handsome, forty-four-year-old congressman and former corporate lawyer from the patrician "silk-stocking" district on Manhattan's Upper East Side, whose joint Republican and Liberal party candidacy recalled the fusion ticket of Fiorello La Guardia. During the campaign, Lindsay had promised voters a fresh approach to government—including an explicit shift away from the car and highway-oriented policies of Robert Moses—and in a tightly contested three-way race, managed to win election as the 103rd mayor of New York.

"I plan to give New York the most hardworking, the most dedicated, and, I hope, the most exciting administration this city has ever seen," the young mayor-elect declared shortly before his swearing-in.

FUN CITY
The block is burning down on one side of the street, and the kids are trying to build something on the other.

Grace Paley

John Lindsay's two terms in office would be among the strangest and most memorable in the city's history.

In New York, as across the country, the last half decade of the 1960s would often feel like the best of times and the worst of times—a dizzying period of anarchy, confusion, anger, and hope. During Lindsay's administration, wave after wave of social and economic crisis would break over the city—in many cases the consequences of forces unleashed decades before, felt now in all their intensity. And yet before the

decade was done, a new vision of the city would begin to emerge.

For Lindsay, the troubles started instantly. At 5:00 a.m. on January 1, 1966—the very morning he took office—the city's 34,000 transit workers went out on strike, demanding a four-day workweek and a 30 percent pay hike, and completely shutting down the city's subways and buses.

For decades, New York's own municipal employees had been among the lowest-paid workers in the city, forbidden by law from bargaining collectively or going out on strike. An executive order signed in 1958 by Mayor Wagner had changed that, but Wagner himself had always preferred to negotiate quietly with union leaders, to avoid any serious disruption in city services.

Determined to stand fast, Lindsay publicly denounced the union and jailed its leader, a fiery, outspoken Irishman named Michael Quill, who continued to taunt the mayor from behind bars, calling him a "pipsqueak" and "a boy in short pants." As the strike continued day after day, wreaking havoc with the city's economy, Lindsay tried to rally an increasingly exasperated public—voicing the phrase that would haunt him for the rest of his tenure. "It's fun being mayor of New York City," he told reporters. "New York is a fun city."

After twelve days, Lindsay capitulated, agreeing to terms more generous than those the union had demanded at the outset. Emboldened by the outcome, other municipal unions—doctors, nurses, sanitation men, social workers—would soon be staging job actions of their own.

In the fall of 1968, the teachers' union went on strike, not over money but to protest the actions of a black Brooklyn school district called Ocean Hill–Brownsville, which, encouraged by a decentralization program sponsored by the Ford Foundation, had fired fourteen white teachers. Determined to protect their jobs, the union, whose membership was primarily Jewish, refused to return to work until the citywide Board of Education stripped the local district of its power. The mayor refused to take sides, and the three-month strike, one of the most painful and divisive episodes in the city's history, exposed a deep chasm between New York's black and Jewish populations, who had been longtime partners in the struggle for civil rights.

Meanwhile, the city's social problems seemed to worsen with each passing year, as the crime rate rose dramatically, illegal drug use increased, and signs of disorder, from graffiti to vandalism, multiplied everywhere. The city's welfare population, just 4 percent of the city's population at the start of the decade, would be 14 percent by the end.

If there are eight million people in New York, one million live on welfare, no, the figure is higher now, it will be one million two hundred thousand by the end of the year. Fatherless families and motherless families live at the end of an umbilical financial cord which perpetuates them in an embryonic economic state. Poverty lies upon the city like a layer of smog.
Norman Mailer, 1969

Fueled in part by tremendous increases in federal and state funding for social programs, and in part by Lindsay's own eagerness to use government to address the city's ills, New York City's budget spiraled upward, climbing at an average annual rate of 16 percent. By 1969, the city had the second largest governmental budget in the country—bigger than the state of California, bigger than the state of New York, exceeded only by the federal government itself.

To pay for it all, the city and state had instituted twenty-two separate taxes—personal income taxes and commuter taxes, sales taxes, vault taxes and auto use taxes, stock transfer taxes and cigarette taxes. But the base for those tax revenues was now faltering, as the community of multinational corporations that had swelled in size during the postwar years now shifted its allegiance with stunning swiftness. In 1971, six Fortune 500 companies—including American Can, Pepsico, Shell Oil, and U.S. Tobacco—abandoned New York, and fourteen more declared their intention to leave. Within five years, sixteen more major companies had gone.

As the city's revenues failed to keep up with its expenses, Lindsay chose to hide the growing shortfall by expanding the scope of the questionable financial practices that had begun in Mayor Wagner's last term—what observers referred to sarcastically as "inventive account-

On the rainy, cold morning of Monday, January 3, 1966, New Yorkers were forced to get to work without the city's subways or buses, which had been shut down over the weekend by a strike of the city's 34,000 transit workers. In all, more than 1.5 million workers stayed home, crippling businesses in the city. Priding themselves on their ingenuity, other New Yorkers formed car pools, rode bicycles, took cabs, hitchhiked, or simply walked—like this group of hardy commuters, right, setting off on foot across the Brooklyn Bridge.

ing." With the acquiescence of the city comptroller, Abraham Beame, Lindsay placed hundred of millions of dollars of day-to-day operating expenses into the city's capital budget, supposedly reserved for long-term improvements, and drained another $100 million in rainy-day funds set aside for emergencies.

Over the next few years, the city's shaky financial condition would grow far worse when Manhattan's real-estate boom suddenly collapsed, just as federal social spending was scaled back dramatically under President Richard Nixon. Soon the city would be borrowing enormous sums from the bond market and rolling over the mounting debt from one year to another simply to remain solvent. In 1975, it would be Lindsay's successor—the former comptroller, Abraham Beame—who would face

the day of reckoning, when the city was overwhelmed by a fiscal crisis more catastrophic and humiliating than anything in its history.

But the grimmest phenomenon of the era by far was the accelerating decay of the city's poorest districts. New York's slums had always been harsh and unforgiving places. But nothing could compare with the disintegration that began to overtake a number of working-class and poor neighborhoods in the southern half of the Bronx. For years, the city's banks had been categorically refusing to refinance properties in the area, while housing regulations had made it all but impossible for owners to raise rents or evict tenants. Losing money fast, unable to sell, unable to walk away, some landlords now took the extraordinary step of burning down their own buildings to collect insurance money. Within a few years, four blocks a week would be going up in flames. Before the devastation ended, five years later, more than two thousand blocks had been leveled or reduced to empty shells and more than 43,000 apartments lost. The very name of the district, the South Bronx, became a worldwide symbol of urban decline.

> *This muck heaves and palpitates. It is multi-directional and has a mayor.*
> Donald Barthelme

And yet, for all the city's immense and manifold problems, Lindsay would succeed in instilling during his two terms in city hall an exhilarating sense of the city's potential. "Lindsay's presence," the social scientist Andrew Hacker observed a few years later, "awakened the consciousness of people who might otherwise have stayed with the mood and mentality of earlier eras. Whole classes of individuals became more assertive than they had ever been in the past. . . . Sentiments he would arouse lay near the surface. The demography of the city was beginning to fashion the contours of a new civic personality."

Making Jane Jacobs's vision an unofficial cornerstone of city policy, Lindsay, and the urban innovations he pursued, spurred renewed appreciation for the city street and city block, and for the city itself as a liberating force in the lives of its people. In many cases the results of the changes would not be felt for years, their impact muffled as one crisis after another broke over the city. But during Lindsay's two terms, a new respect for the essential strengths of the city's neighborhoods—their complexity and diversity, their vital street life, and their remarkable ability to heal and renew themselves—would be firmly reestablished.

In the long hot summer of 1967, as racial tensions simmered, the mayor began a series of highly publicized walking tours through the most economically depressed parts of the city. "By the end of the summer," the reporter Richard Reeves wrote, "the walks were drawing almost as much attention as the American League pennant race. Chasing along behind Lindsay that night in Harlem were gangs of laughing Negro children, a dozen reporters and photographers, a congressman from Michigan,

John Lindsay walking through the streets of Harlem, on February 9, 1968. Piles of refuse and garbage had mounted on the sidewalk because of a strike by city sanitation workers, one of several municipal strikes that hounded the Lindsay administration.

columnist Art Buchwald and the editor in chief of *Look Magazine*."

Watching televised images of Lindsay touring the ghetto streets in shirtsleeves—tall, aristocratic, his suit jacket casually slung over his shoulder—critics accused the mayor of grandstanding. But his efforts paid off in 1968, when, following the assassination of the Reverend Martin Luther King, Jr., black ghettos across the country exploded into riot. Lindsay's effort to reach out to minority leaders, symbolized by

his highly visible walks, were widely credited with keeping New York calm and helping it to avoid the widespread destruction that permanently scarred the landscape of many American cities.

Though viewed with mistrust by many working-class white voters, Lindsay brought an excitement to municipal politics of a kind not seen since the time of La Guardia. Like John and Robert Kennedy, to whom he was often compared, he succeeded in attracting an entire

generation of young men and women to public service—parks officials, city planners, transportation experts, and urban designers—many of whom shared his passion for new ideas.

Many, too, had cut their teeth on the writings of Jane Jacobs and were eager now to reverse what they saw as the heavy-handed approach of Robert Moses. Nowhere would that effort be more apparent than in the administration of Moses's old fiefdom, the Parks Department. Within days of taking office, Lindsay had replaced a onetime Moses aide with a thirty-four-year-old curator from the Metropolitan Museum of Art named Thomas Hoving. Convinced the parks had been ruled too autocratically under his predecessors, Hoving quickly closed Central Park to automobile traffic on Sundays, opening the lanes to bicyclists and pedestrians. Taxi drivers grumbled, but on the first warm days of spring, New Yorkers by the thousands pulled out their bikes and reveled in the quiet and freshness of a landscape that, for the first time in living memory, was blissfully free of traffic.

Wherever they could, Lindsay's officials sought to counter Moses's antiurban vision—stopping the construction of an expressway he had proposed, which was to cut across Thirtieth Street in Manhattan, establishing a system of community planning boards across the city, and championing new subway lines instead of more highways. In an industrial area of lower Manhattan once known as the Valley, but now called SoHo, where for years artists had been living illegally in the old factory buildings, the City Planning Commission created an innovative zoning category that would allow artists to remain in the loft spaces they had homesteaded. In 1966, Lindsay himself created the Mayor's Office of Film, Theater, and Broadcasting—the first of its kind in the country—to encourage film production in the city, and soon more features were being shot on location in New York than in any other city in the world.

In Brooklyn, meanwhile, thousands of young families who only a few years before might have fled New York for the suburbs began to move instead into nineteenth-century row houses that had long since been divided into boardinghouses and then into small, cheap apartments

for the working class and the poor. To the older populations, often displaced by the newcomers, the trend was less than welcome. Overhearing the new arrivals call themselves pioneers, one man said, "What does that make the rest of us, Indians?"

But to its supporters, brownstoning was seen as a striking testament of faith in the future of the city. White flight might not be the last word, after all.

THE LAST HURRAH

It has yet to be shown that [an] essentially honest, youthful municipal administration based on impulse rather than experience—with tours of the slums, extravagant promises, invitations to disorder in the name of satisfying youth, contrived, uncontrollable events and happenings—can maintain New York's supremacy and livability. We must soon decide whether we want a fun town [or] one guaranteeing outward order and decency.

Robert Moses

Jane Jacobs's ideas and John Lindsay's policies had in large measure repudiated the principles that had shaped Robert Moses's life and work. The old man—nearly eighty now—still held on, but by the late 1960s, he finally faced a real threat to his power, not from John Lindsay, whom Moses dismissed as a "matinee-idol mayor," but from a man and a family capable of challenging Moses's empire as it had never been challenged before.

In the American imagination, the Rockefellers were the very symbol of private wealth. But even more significant than the sheer size of the fortune—estimated in the late 1950s at more than $5 billion—was the family's determination and ability to shape the city in which they lived and worked. In the 1930s, they had built the world's greatest office complex—Rockefeller Center—and sponsored the Museum of Modern Art, which had later helped to make New York the capital of the art world. In the 1950s, the family had been the driving force behind the creation of Lincoln Center for the Performing Arts, which sought to reinforce the city's cultural preeminence by gathering the New York Philharmonic, the Metropolitan Opera, the Juilliard School, and several other

You just don't know how badly I want to reach my hands on a can of spray and touch my big train [that's] set in my yard and feel the voltage running through them trains while I paint my ghetto name on that iron screen for my people of the state of NYC to see and wonder on the art of the ghettos and the backstreets of our times.

Shy 7

In the early 1970s, graffiti on the city's subways exploded in scale from small scrawlings with black markers to the spray painting of entire subway cars with names and patterns in vivid, electric colors. The development sparked a controversy between those who hailed the painted images as an exciting new art form and those who saw in them the ominous loss of civic authority in the city's public spaces. By the early 1980s, when an aggressive campaign by the Transit Authority finally eliminated the painted graffiti from the trains, the distinctive technique and style had emerged as a trend within the city's downtown art community, where several exhibitions and galleries were devoted to the work. (All photographs on pages 528–9 © Martha Cooper.)

You are now in SoHo, one of the most fashionable and expensive neighborhoods in the world, where refurbished floors of century-old lofts go for a million dollars and much more. The streets themselves are a fashion show, day and night. . . . Had Jane Jacobs' example not inspired the neighbors to defend themselves, there would be nothing here today but an eight-lane traffic jam. . . . There would be no mozzarella in the morning . . . no De Sica films on warm summer evenings and no SoHo with its lovely cast-iron buildings, its cobbled streets, its restaurants, its galleries and shops and its millions, indeed, billions of dollars of taxable property.

Jason Epstein

Few transformations in New York's history would be as dramatic, or utterly unexpected, as that which turned an aging manufacturing district in lower Manhattan into one of the best-known and most influential communities in the world. In less than two decades, the 30-block area south of Houston Street would take on a completely new identity, bring a permanent shift to the city's cultural landscape, and become a model of revitalization for cities around the world.

Nothing could have seemed more unlikely in the early 1960s, when the district was slated for demolition to clear a path for Robert Moses's Lower Manhattan Expressway. Not only was the road itself crucial to the health of the city, the great builder argued, but the destruction of the old district would actually be a net gain for New York.

We simply repeat that cities are created by and for traffic. A city without traffic is a ghost town. The area between Canal Street and Third Street, a strip three-quarters of a mile wide, is the most depressed area in lower Manhattan and one of

the worst, if not the worst, slums in the entire city, a ghetto, with the rate of turnover of 14% a year.

Robert Moses

Ironically, it was the threat of the expressway that saved the area from destruction. Since the late 1940s, the proposed highway construction had hung like a death sentence over the entire district, discouraging landlords from improving, or tearing down, their buildings. Built as one of the first industrial districts in the United States, the once bustling area now entered a period of slow but steady decline, as one company after another vacated the upper floors of the old, inefficient loft buildings.

Saddled with the empty space, landlords were delighted when in the late 1950s a new group of tenants—artists—began moving into the unimproved lofts. Traditionally, Greenwich Village had been the artistic center of the city, but the postwar generation of abstract expressionists was producing work too large and bulky for the Village's small walk-up apartments.

The sooty old manufacturing district just south of Houston Street, by contrast, provided ideal studio space for artists. The area's cast-iron buildings, built before the advent of electricity, featured banks of huge windows that flooded the interiors with natural light, while their high ceilings and widely spaced columns easily accommodated the largest canvas and heaviest sculpture. Most important, the upper-floor space, which would have otherwise gone begging, could be rented for almost nothing. "The artists' life," the editors of *Newsweek* reported in 1961, "once carried on in romantic garrets, has moved to the commercial loft."

By then, in complete violation of the building code, some artists had begun living as well as working in the lofts, using ingenuity or bribes to ward away city officials. "One artist . . . would greet a build-

Cast-iron buildings on Broadway and Broome Street in SoHo.

ing inspector on the stairs saying, 'Wait a minute, I have a nude model posing,' the reporter Michael T. Kaufman wrote. "Then he would go inside and using pulleys hoist beds above a false ceiling and camouflage the refrigerator, range and bathtub." Landlords were willing to look the other way because the situation seemed temporary—a makeshift arrangement that would soon come to an end when the artists would be evicted for the expressway.

But opposition to the proposed highway was beginning to grow, and by the 1960s artists had joined

the fight to kill the project, in the process creating a sense of community spirit where there had been none before. Joining forces with Jane Jacobs and the road's other opponents, they formed action committees, lobbied city officials, spoke out at public hearings, and pulled strings within the art world. Fighting for the district's survival, they found themselves growing committed to it, and more and more residents began to envision a permanent future there.

One obstacle to that future was the district's lack of a name. Resi-

Estate, by Robert Rauschenberg, 1963. Among the first artists to live in a downtown loft, Rauschenberg would draw deeply on the city in his work, combining commercial images produced by New York's media industries (in magazines, newspapers, posters, and advertisements) with images of the city itself, such as the lower Manhattan street signs, lamppost, and building facades in *Estate*. (Oil and silkscreened ink on canvas 7 feet 11¾ inches × 5 feet 9¾ inches, Philadelphia Museum of Art. © Untitled Press, Inc. / Licensed by VAGA, New York.)

dents vaguely referred to living "downtown." Firefighters called the area Hell's Hundred Acres because of its frequent factory blazes. Others referred to the district as the Valley—the low-rise stretch between the towers of midtown and downtown. In 1968, a painter and engineer named Aaron Roseman, observing that a City Planning Commission report referred to the area as the South Houston Industrial District, condensed the unwieldy phrase into a short, memorable name—SoHo—that recalled the raffish district in central London.

The turning point for SoHo came in 1971. Having tried to destroy the area and evict the artists, the city government, under John Lindsay, now took the extra-ordinary step of authorizing their presence, modifying the zoning laws to allow "certified artists" to live as well as work in the manu-facturing district. "SoHo," Stephen Koch wrote, "may be the first neighborhood in the history of the Western World to require (it is an article of municipal law) that prospective residents make some plausible claim to the title 'artist.'" Two years later, the Landmarks Preservation Commission declared SoHo's treasury of cast-iron build-ings a historic district, providing a layer of legal protection against their destruction.

With official sanction in place, the neighborhood began to boom. In 1973 there were 40 galleries in the area, and three years later, 70—making SoHo a rival to the tra-ditional gallery district along 57th Street. By the time the decade was out, SoHo had been acknowledged as the emerging center of the art world.

The significance of SoHo's renewal reached well beyond the boundaries of the district itself. As nothing else, its transformation confirmed Jane Jacobs's thesis that city neighborhoods—which she likened to complex living organisms—could rebuild and reinvent themselves without mas-sive outside intervention. "Artists accomplished, without having intended to, what decades of urban renewal had failed to do," the edi-tor Jason Epstein observed. "They restored a neighborhood and became its taxpayers. SoHo's revival shows that the spontaneous generation that once characterized New York's growth remains a pos-sibility."

But the very success of SoHo brought a dilemma of its own, one that soon became an inevitable corollary of urban revitalization. The artistic cachet that had drawn galleries, restaurants, and shops—turning the once forbidding area into a chic and stylish commu-nity—was also driving up rents, pricing out the artists themselves. Though still home to Claes Olden-berg, Robert Rauschenberg, Frank Stella, Christo, Louise Nevelson, and hundreds of other artists, SoHo was increasingly becoming popu-lar among stockbrokers, lawyers, and advertising executives, as loft living emerged as a desirable alternative way of life among the city's upper middle class.

Unable to afford the area that they themselves had helped to make desirable, many artists began searching out cheaper space to the east in Chinatown and the Bowery, to the southwest in an area called TriBeCa—itself shorthand for Tri-angle Below Canal—or across the East River, in Williamsburg and other Brooklyn neighborhoods. The rapidly rising rents, meanwhile, were also driving out the last of the industrial companies that had once filled the area—the machine-part suppliers, textile manufacturers, rope and twine makers—along with the hundreds of blue-collar jobs they had sustained. One by one, the old workshop and ware-house floors gave way to galleries, restaurants, and, increasingly, expensive boutiques and furniture shops.

By the late 1980s, SoHo had become one of the best-known neighborhoods in New York. With 300 galleries and several museums it was almost synonymous with the art world—much as Madison Avenue stood for advertising and Wall Street for finance. Its influ-ence widened, embracing several adjacent districts—NoHo, TriBeCa, the East Village—into what now constituted the city's new "down-town": a series of communities whose complex mix of culture and commerce encompassed not only art but architecture, design, pho-tography, and fashion. When a technologically innovative indus-try—interactive media—sprang up in New York in the mid-1990s, it almost inevitably gravitated to the new downtown districts, whose historic buildings were now rewired with sophisticated telecommunications equipment to adapt them to needs of the hun-dreds of multimedia design and production companies that were arising in the area.

In the 1950s, the modern city had been defined by massive urban renewal projects and arterial high-ways—such as the expressway Robert Moses had hoped to run across lower Manhattan, leveling in the process what he called "one of the worst slums . . . in the entire city." Thirty years later, in a turn of events that Moses himself would have probably found unimaginable, the old industrial district south of Houston Street had become one of the most prosperous and produc-tive parts of New York. Even more astonishingly, it had come to be considered one of the most modern places on earth—a community whose revitalized fabric of nineteenth-century streets and buildings, filled with studios and workspaces and interlaced with high-speed communication net-works, offered a very different defi-nition of modernity and a new model for the future of the city itself.

groups into an imposing set of marble-clad buildings on the Upper West Side.

By the 1960s, the family had grown more powerful than ever. David Rockefeller had become president of the family-held Chase Manhattan Bank, one of the richest financial institutions in the world. Nelson had become the governor of New York State. The brothers' ability to wed public and private resources gave them enormous power, as they proceeded to demonstrate unforgettably in lower Manhattan. David's vigorous effort to reinvigorate the aging business district, symbolized by the construction of a new sixty-story headquarters for Chase, was dramatically reinforced by Nelson's

decision to have the Port Authority build the 110-story, twin-towered World Trade Center, the tallest buildings in the world, just two blocks away.

As a young man, Nelson Rockefeller had watched in wonder as Moses cleared a path, literally overnight, for the United Nations. Later, Moses and the Rockefeller brothers had worked in close collaboration on the building of Lincoln Center and half a dozen other projects. But now the student sought to supplant his master. The governor—himself a "frustrated architect," in the words of a former aide, who was now planning an array of dazzling construction projects for the city and state—increas-

A 1970s demonstration in front of city hall to protest mass layoffs of city workers.

ingly felt the aging power broker standing in his way. In 1962, when Governor Rockefeller publicly suggested that it might be time for Moses to step down from one of his state park posts, Moses threatened to resign all five of his state park commissions, including Jones Beach. It was a tactic that had worked in countless confrontations with previous politicians—but this time it backfired, as Rockefeller coolly accepted all five resignations.

By 1967, Moses's once awesome power had dwindled considerably. Seven years before, he had been forced to surrender his city commissions to become president of the World's Fair. Then, Nelson Rockefeller had bluffed him out of his state commissions. Now all that remained was the chairmanship of the Triborough Bridge and Tunnel Authority, with its eleven huge river crossings.

But even that was too much, in Rockefeller's view. Watching deficits mount with the Long Island Rail Road and the city's subway system, the governor was eager to wrest control of the millions of dollars pouring into the Triborough tollbooths by absorbing it into a new Metropolitan Transportation Authority.

Moses would have no part of it. Triborough was a public authority, he reminded the press and public, beholden only to its bondholders. No one, not even one of the most powerful governors in the state's history, could force him out. Only the bondholders, or their trustee, had that power.

This particular governor, however, had a special advantage. The trustee of the Triborough bondholders happened to be a bank—the Chase Manhattan Bank—the bank his brother ran and his family controlled.

On March 9, 1967, Robert Moses and Governor Rockefeller held a private meeting at the Rockefeller town house on West Fifty-fifth Street. Afterward, Moses announced his support of the proposed merger of the Triborough Authority and the MTA. On February 9, 1968, at another meeting in the Rockefeller town house, Nelson and David Rockefeller signed an agreement by which the Chase Manhattan Bank accepted the merger of Triborough and the removal of Robert Moses, effective at the end of the month. The governor assured Moses he would continue to play a key role in the

merged agency—directing the construction of yet another great crossing over the Long Island Sound—but nothing would ever come of the project.

In the end, it had taken the unique conjunction of public and private power that only Nelson and David Rockefeller possessed, but it had been done. Robert Moses, who had first gained power on April 23, 1924, lost it forever on March 1, 1968. The Moses era had lasted forty-four years. He had left behind twelve major bridges, 658 playgrounds, 627 miles of highways, and more than 2.5 million acres of parks—along with Jones Beach, Shea Stadium, Lincoln Center, the New York Coliseum, and the headquarters of the United Nations. He had also made New York, for better and for worse, the model metropolis of the twentieth-century city, doing as much as anyone to transform it into a sprawling metropolitan region, interwoven by a network of arterial highways and river crossings. He had helped create the transportation template from which, in an astonishingly short period of time, America itself had turned from a nation of cities and countryside to a nation of highways and suburbs.

"In the twentieth century," the urban historian Lewis Mumford said simply, "the influence of Robert Moses on the cities of America was greater than that of any other person."

By the 1970s, the two people who more than any other had framed the debate over the future of New York—Robert Moses and Jane Jacobs—were no longer on the scene. To his immense frustration, Moses never again regained power, and was forced to watch the city's progress from the sidelines. Retiring to a rented cottage on Oak Beach, Long Island, within sight of two of his greatest works, Robert Moses State Park and the Robert Moses Causeway, he remained mentally and physically fit—and as restless and ambitious as ever—until the time of his death in 1981, at the age of ninety-two. By then, Jane Jacobs was gone, too, having left with her family in 1970, at the height of the Vietnam War, for a new life in Canada. She never came back to the great metropolis that had taught her so much about the way cities live.

In the years to come, it would in many ways

be Jacobs's vision that would prevail. In a stunning reversal of policy, New York all but halted new highway construction in the 1970s and '80s, spent billions of dollars to rebuild its subways, and overhauled the structure of its government to make sure no single official would ever amass the power that Robert Moses had once held. Jacobs's hard-won fight to allow ordinary citizens a voice in urban affairs would be institutionalized through a public approval process that for the first time gave communities the power to formally advise on projects in their districts. Her once daring arguments in favor of density, concentration, mixture, and the crucial importance of the street became nothing less than conventional wisdom among planners, architects, and city officials.

Over the years, Jacobs's theory that city neighborhoods were capable of healing and improving themselves was corroborated in ways that would have been unthinkable to Robert Moses. Old loft districts in lower Manhattan, once dismissed as slums, became the most fashionable new parts of town. The South Bronx was brought back to life, not through huge urban renewal projects but by a wave of small-scale, community-driven developments that mixed renovation and new construction. Working-class communities in older parts of Queens and Brooklyn were reborn as local entrepreneurial energy brought new life to once abandoned storefronts and sidewalks.

As time went on, however, the career and contribution of Robert Moses began to be seen in a somewhat different light. Though his methods had often been brutal, Moses had in the end created for New York an arterial highway system that, like it or not, every modern city needed in order to survive. He had, indeed, endowed New York with a system of highways more extensive than any other city in the country, including Los Angeles. And if some of his projects had been horribly destructive, many of the worst had been successfully blocked, so that New Yorkers could point to the fact that Manhattan itself, where Robert Moses lived and worked, had remained virtually unscathed by his depredations, while city centers across the country had been mauled by expressways. And, despite Moses's hostility to mass transportation, the subway system continued to thrive, so that by the end of the century New York could plausibly boast of having the most balanced urban transportation system in the country—the best mass transit system *and* the most arterial highways, the best commuter rail links *and* the largest number of truck and bus routes—the advantages of the highway, in short, and the advantages of the pedestrian street. The testimony of Robert Moses's career, in the end, was not that he had destroyed New York but that New Yorkers had stopped him before he could do so, asserting a corrective balance before he pushed the city too far in one direction. In that regard, the outcome of the contest between Moses and Jacobs represented only the latest episode in an ongoing series of accommodations New Yorkers had historically achieved, balancing the city's need for congestion and traffic with its need for movement and flow. For all his ruthlessness, Robert Moses had found a way to build great public works in the middle of a sprawling urban democracy—works that, however essential they might be to the city's future, were often enormously disruptive and thus deeply unpopular, in the short run, among voters. "Moses is fantastic," an admiring politician once remarked of the builder. "He thinks about places for people in the future, and maybe they'll be thankful in twenty years, but they vote now." The very lack of accountability that made Moses so dangerous was, perhaps, precisely what made him so effective.

In the decades following his fall from power, New York would prove utterly unable to meet the city's needs for large-scale public projects—for improved port facilities, rail systems, affordable housing, regional transit links. To a large degree, it would manage to get by because of the extraordinary inventory of public works built by previous generations, but with each passing year, the need to expand and improve its superb but aging infrastructure would grow more urgent.

Moses's loss of power was seen by many New Yorkers as a victory—and perhaps it was. But it did not resolve an age-old problem that, by the end of the century, would be casting an increasingly long shadow over the city's future: how can a metropolis effectively balance its need for large-scale public works projects with the needs of its local communities and those who live in them?

Taken on December 21, 1971, this aerial view of Brooklyn (foreground) and Manhattan reveals the transformation of the island city into the heart of the most complex urban agglomeration on earth. At the foot of Manhattan Island, where the Dutch first settled 350 years before, now rose the tallest buildings in the world—including the World Trade Center, whose twin 110-story towers, completed in 1973, were the first to eclipse the Empire State Building in height (and would themselves be surpassed a few months later by the Sears Tower in Chicago). An even larger outcropping of skyscrapers rose in midtown, just below the dark green rectangle of Central Park. In Brooklyn, the massive elevated structure of the Gowanus Expressway (lower left)—one of dozens of arterial roadways built by Robert Moses—cuts diagonally across the old city fabric. Linking the city's boroughs to each other is the greatest collection of bridges and tunnels in the world, including the Brooklyn, Manhattan, Williamsburg, Queensborough, and Triborough bridges and Queens-Midtown Tunnel across the East River, the George Washington Bridge (visible near the horizon) and Lincoln and Holland tunnels across the Hudson River, and the Brooklyn-Battery Tunnel running beneath the bay. Not visible in this view is the most recent addition to the city's extraordinary inventory of crossings, the Verrazano-Narrows Bridge, which when completed in 1964 was the longest suspension span in the world.

THE LONELY CROWD:
NEW YORK AFTER THE WAR

MARSHALL BERMAN

The city is a landscape well worth enjoying—damn necessary if you live in the city. Dirt has depth and beauty. I love soot and scorching. From all this can come a positive as well as a negative meaning . . . the beauty and meaning of discarded objects, chance effects . . . the city filth, the evils of advertising, the disease of success, popular culture. . . . Look for beauty where it's not supposed to be found.
Claes Oldenburg, "The Street," 1960

At many moments in its history, the everyday life of New York has generated an environment that imploded on people, natives, and visitors alike, and struck them as just *too much*: too crowded, too dirty, too smelly, too unhealthy, too violent and antagonistic. There seems to be so much surplus trouble that it starts to choke off and smother the city's creative powers. People get demoralized: they feel something must be done, but they don't know what to do, let alone how to do it. At such critical points, the city has usually come through in very different and complementary ways: it has generated simultaneously new construction and new vision, new environments and new ideas. It has constructed magnificent public spaces and amenities that people of all classes and ethnic groups could share, while nourishing innovations in culture and sensibility that uncover new depth and beauty in the old environments that are still there. In the middle of the nineteenth century, for instance, it gave us both Central Park and *Leaves of Grass*. Its Olmsted and Vaux parks created beauty out of wastelands; they gave people new ways of connecting to nature, to their bodies, and to each other; and they managed to be both anticities and supercities. At the same time, above all through Walt Whitman, it imaginatively transformed a walk on crowded, smelly old Broadway or a rush-hour commute to (or from) Brooklyn into an erotic orgy. At the turn of the twentieth century, the city's new environments included Coney Island, Pennsylvania Station and Grand Central Terminal, and Times Square; its new visions were opened up by *Sister Carrie* and *The Age of Innocence*, by the words and pictures of *How the Other Half Lives*, by the 1913 Armory Show and the modernist world of Alfred Stieglitz's 291 Gallery, by the mass culture of Tin Pan Alley and "Alexander's Ragtime Band." For most of New York's history, it has been blessed with a synchronicity of grandeur in construction and in culture.

That synchronicity came to an abrupt end after World War II. There was still much building in and around New York, and there were a few majestic structures, but the great thrust of the new construction struck the city like a curse—a curse that worked in the city's skyscrapers and highways, and then in the emerging suburbs just down those highways, but that finally failed to work in the streets.

Skyscrapers were invented in New York and Chicago at the end of the nineteenth century. They became instant worldwide symbols of modern urban energy, striving, and grandeur. The Woolworth and Singer buildings in the 1910s, the Chrysler and Empire State in the late 1920s, were brilliant theater pieces as well as marvels of engineering. They were designed to thrill people, to promise heights of joy and glory that only New York could give. For generations of men and women who identified themselves with the city, they served as pillars of personal identity.

But the postwar skyscrapers were different, anonymous glass boxes that were home to the dozens of big corporations that, from the '40s through the '60s, established or expanded their headquarters in New York. These companies fueled the greatest long-term capitalist boom in history. Many had close connections to the federal government, especially to defense industries. They did business on a cost-plus basis, with no market incentives to save money; their business culture was bloated and complacent, different from the brutal competitiveness that was typical of New York. They had come here to be close to the Wall Street capital markets and to the city's expanding mass media and its apparatus of publicity; both could help them develop the worldwide horizons they craved and soon achieved. They created many new jobs and shifted the city's employment spectrum toward white-collar and educated labor. Several scathing and brilliant books were written about this corporate culture: David Riesman's *The Lonely Crowd*, C. Wright Mills's *White Collar*, William H. Whyte's *The Organization Man*. There was at least one great film comedy about it, Billy Wilder's *The Apartment*. But there were misunderstandings from the start. Many of the new corporate executives were never comfortable in New York: they found it hard to adapt to its teeming streets, multicultural demography, feverish politics. They longed for environments they could control. IBM, in the early 1960s, was one of the first to create them: it called them campuses. By the late 1960s, real-estate developers began building office parks (usually within an hour of the city by car, in suburban Westchester County, New Jersey, or Connecticut), where corporations would be able to exert far more *control* than they ever could in a metropolis like New York. In the late 1960s, dozens of big companies began to move out. (One corporation president, after his move to the Norwalk area, told *New York* magazine: "Now I can control where they eat lunch.") By that time, the city's economy had grown seriously dependent on them, and it was badly hurt. This set the stage for the fiscal crisis of the 1970s, and also for the recoveries of the 1980s and '90s. Big companies have now learned how to use the *threat* of departure to reap hundreds of millions of dollars in city tax incentives, giving new meaning to the phrase "socialism for the rich."

But even before they left, or even if they stayed, they clashed with one basic feature of the city's environment: *the street*. For much of the twentieth century, people who hated streets have been preoccupied with *disorder*: too many people are running around in too many directions, without any central plan, or else hanging around and not running at all. The most eminent demonizer of the street was the Swiss-born architect Le Corbusier, one of the century's great mad visionaries. He said he loved New York's skyscrapers, but he loathed the way they were tied up in the life of its streets. Streets were his special obsession: they made him foam at the mouth. Again and again his writings declared, in effect, *"We must kill the street!"* Against modern urban street life, he would celebrate "a titanic renaissance of a new phenomenon, TRAFFIC! Cars, cars, fast, fast!" He would clear all the streets and reorganize space into endless rows of great concrete-and-glass slabs, each one a separate world with its own underground garage; the slabs would be linked to each other by broad highways, each slab "a factory for producing traffic," landscaped with plenty of trees and grass. He called his new model "the tower in the park." By the 1940s, Le Corbusier's mythic battle of giants, in which streets are killed by cars, was just a poetic expression of a prosaic consensus among the makers of American urban policy about what was to be done.

The postwar wave of skyscrapers in New York started grandly, with Lever House and the Seagram Building and the United Nations ensemble. But as building after building shot up, it didn't take long to see that something had gone wrong. These great glass slabs were being built with no connection to the streets or to the larger city. They seemed designed to be at home everywhere—though more often they looked out of place and alien everywhere. Lewis Mumford's "Sky Line" pieces in *The New Yorker* exposed the blight with grim brilliance.

What did we do to deserve this? people were always asking. They came up with very different answers. Some people, usually socialists or communists, blamed commercial capitalism. But the argument always came back at them: pre-Depression capitalists were even narrower in their pursuit of profit; yet hadn't they built nobly? Other people—precursors of Tom Wolfe—blamed "foreigners" and European architects. But anyone who knew how to use a library could look and see that, in their heyday before Hitler, those German architects had made brilliant designs that helped cre-

ate the magic of Berlin. President Eisenhower and the mass media kept telling us that, just as the stock market was inexorably rising, so our lives were automatically getting better and better. And sure, plenty of New Yorkers were making money. But money didn't keep people's hearts from sinking every time a construction shed went up. All through the postwar years, whatever they were building, you could be sure it was going to be worse than what they were tearing down.

If we thought construction in the 1950s was bad, in the 1960s it would get even worse—the Pan Am Building, the World Trade Center, the giant tombstones that took possession of Sixth Avenue. Pennsylvania Station was destroyed, and the lovely Singer Building downtown: they died so more slabs could live. The lower Manhattan skyline had for decades been a marvelous ensemble of towers in contrasting sizes and styles, the world's greatest living cubist collage; by the middle of the 1960s, most of the towers were blocked out by slabs that looked like giant containers assembled to ship the old waterfront away. Our city was being stolen from us, and we couldn't even tell by what or whom.

In the case of highways, at least we had somebody to blame. Robert Moses was glad to focus the publicity spotlight on himself. He worked with total ruthlessness and what seemed like amazing efficiency. For the first time anyone could remember, he brought public works projects in not only on time but sometimes even under budget. (The true costs of his projects appeared only after he was gone.) In the postwar years, he was at the height of his powers. He had worked his way into a dozen different directorships. He controlled a variety of city and state agencies and public authorities, and synthesized them into a bureaucratic empire. One thing his favorite projects had in common is that they all followed the vision of Le Corbusier's dictum, "We must kill the street."

Moses's postwar highways broke down the isolation of New York's immigrant neighborhoods and integrated them into an emerging national transportation network. This was the Interstate Highway System, created by President Eisenhower. Kenneth T. Jackson has described the Interstate System as "the largest peacetime construction project in history." By the end of the 1960s, he notes, it completely "remade the nation's metropolitan areas." It drew residents, commerce, industry, and capital out of downtowns and placed the most dynamic activity in new suburbs and suburban neighborhoods of cities. Every American city lost beloved downtown institutions, most strikingly department stores; typically, the flagship store would close, but its new branches would thrive on cheap land in a new building type, the suburban shopping mall, located just off the highway interchange. In 1953, Robert Moses won a $25,000 essay contest, established by General Motors, on "Planning for Better

Highways." He could do so much for New York, and to New York, because he foresaw, over generations, how the traffic was going to be flowing, and he worked tirelessly to get the city into the flow. But he didn't create the flow himself.

Robert Moses accomplished great works in New York's outer boroughs and its suburbs. But in Manhattan, ironically, for all his bombast, he was mostly a failure. For forty years, he dreamed of colossal expressways running all the way across the island: one near Canal Street, another at Thirty-third Street. But there were always too many people making noise in Manhattan; and by the 1960s, his Manhattan opponents, unlike those in Brooklyn and the Bronx, knew how to work the mass media as well as he did. As a result, New York is the one great American city with no expressways running through its downtown, and probably the one American community of any size in which it is possible to live a complete life without a car. Moses's failures helped to give the Manhattan cityscape a paradoxical quality it still has today, ultramodern if you look up, archaic if you look down, full of nineteenth-century streets made for people to move and live on foot or by public transit. It can often be a nightmare to drive through, but its overflowing life on hundreds of blocks makes it a walker's paradise.

The great postwar expressways mark a high point of state assault on city life. In New York, they inflicted enormous suffering on masses of people, but they failed in their profoundest aim: they failed to kill the street. They succeeded, however, nearly everywhere else. In most parts of the country, once the Interstate Highway System was in place, the most ordinary everyday activities—walking to the corner for a quart of milk, taking the bus downtown to see a movie, having a soda under Main Street's bright lights—were suddenly impossible. New York, despite all its postwar billion-dollar blight, kept its classic streetscape and city form remarkably intact. In preserving itself, it became radically different from all the others whose street systems were swept away. Think of Alfred Eisenstadt's famous V-J Day photo in *Life* magazine, where a girl throws her arms around a sailor in Times Square. In 1945, the landscape of Times Square, and of New York City, could easily, naively symbolize America. Never again! The Interstate Highway System failed to transform New York's body but transformed its role: it made us America's Other.

OTHER FACES, OTHER VOICES

They failed to kill the street. New York's streets after World War II were going through great changes: changes in who was on them and changes in our ways of seeing them. Representations of New York street life before the war, in both cinema and photography, had portrayed the street as crowded but clean and orderly. Even when the people appear poor, they are wearing suits (threadbare though these may be); they are standing straight, with good posture; the picture has a Renaissance perspective, with radial symmetry; and the world appears in perfect order, even if the people in the picture are protesting that it's not. In the 1950s, photographers and cinematographers found ways to make the city look as gritty and fluid and kinetic and unbalanced as it really was. Here is a photo of masses of people in Times Square in midwinter. In fact, it's New Year's Eve, 1954. It's by William Klein, from his photographic study, *Life Is Good & Good for You in New York* (a book, ironically, that was first published in Paris and did not appear in the United States until the 1990s). The people in this picture appear mostly Latin, mostly kids, and mostly poor. They are hurtling toward us, or else spilling out of the frame. They are sucking candies shaped like cigarettes, trying to look grown-up. Their faces are split between dark shadows and the lurid tone of the billboards. The photograph places us in the midst of this crowd, about to be enveloped. There's nothing hostile about these kids (they mainly look up-too-late and tired), but we may not want them in our face. However, the image takes us out of the realm of spectators and makes us part of the crowd. In New York demography these are "new people," and they are relating to public space in a new way. Klein gives us no choice about whether we want them to be part of our New York; he answers the question by making us part of *their* New York. This is the achievement of the New York school of photography—Klein, Robert Frank, Bruce Davidson, Gary Winograd, and of the authors of New York film noir, Jules Dassin, Robert Rossen, Abraham Polonsky, Samuel Fuller, Stanley Kubrick, John Cassavetes, and others. The sidewalks of New York were getting more dense and humanly difficult in the 1950s. But a great generation of photographers and filmmakers were at work who could penetrate them and show their underlying structure and their depth and beauty.

Many of these artists and others like them, especially those who worked in film—Dassin and Polonsky—became victims of McCarthyism. Some, like Robert Rossen, became perpetrators as well as victims. Was there anything special about McCarthyism in New York? For one thing, it was so often tied up with the act of betrayal: people were done in by their nearest and dearest—brothers and sisters, parents and children, old lovers and spouses. Thus it tended to be not so much melodramatic, something "they" do to "us," as tragic, something we do to ourselves. There were all sorts of ironic wheels within wheels. Some people felt that, after appearing as a "friendly" witness before the House Un-American Activities Committee, the director Elia Kazan had made *On the Waterfront* as a way of defending his actions. Others believed this great New York movie echoed some

Times Square, 1954–55, photographed by William Klein.

of the plot and "look" of another great New York movie, *Force of Evil*, whose director, Abraham Polonsky, and star, John Garfield, were themselves victims of the HUAC-inspired blacklist. Polonsky was kept from working in America for twenty years; Garfield died of a heart attack within a year. (Although he lived on in the city schoolyards, where everyone knew by heart his last words from *Body and Soul*. Bad Guy: "You'll never get away with this." Garfield: "What are you gonna do? Kill me? Everybody dies.")

Julius and Ethel Rosenberg (betrayed by her brother, cursed by her mother at her grave) were probably the two most prominent faces on display in New York in the early 1950s. What mattered most to me was their homely plainness: they looked like everybody's parents. The point of the plainness, I guessed, was that any ordinary nice folks, even your nearest and dearest, could turn out to be agents of alien powers. I thought they had probably done something, but also that they were being lynched for something they hadn't done. The blacklist reached way down into the working class: nurses, bus drivers, telephone operators, postmen, the man who made change in the subway, everyone was vulnerable. Neither fame nor obscurity could protect you: it was a real system of terror. Once I was talking to a high

school teacher, and I noticed a picture of Paul Robeson on the inside of his locker. "So you're a Paul Robeson fan," I said. He slammed it shut: "Who told you to ask me that?" I never asked him anything again. That was McCarthyism in New York: *People who loved to talk got scared to talk.* They came to see ordinary questions as weapons pointed at them. And sometimes they were right.

Two kinds of creative music were happening in postwar New York: jazz, and rock and roll. The incarnation of jazz that thrived then is called bebop now. Then it was called modern jazz, distinct from 1920s Dixieland and 1930s swing. The alto saxophonist Charlie Parker had invented it, people said. He had died at the age of thirty-four of a heroin overdose, but people venerated his memory, and there was a harvest of great musicians—Dizzy Gillespie, Max Roach, Thelonious Monk, Miles Davis, Charles Mingus, and plenty of others—to carry the flame. It was live, at the Village Vanguard, which is still there, and at a lot of other sweet places that aren't. Bop was played by small groups in small rooms. The ambience was dead serious, more like Beethoven or Schoenberg than like Louis Armstrong. This was no party; these musicians were not entertainers. Although bop was played in nightclubs, you didn't dance or drink to this music: you listened for dear life. The group would play a stanza from some recognizable popular song; then a sax or trumpet player began to develop a variation on the theme, backed by the piano and drums; then, suddenly, the soloist was letting loose floods of notes, amazingly fast, loud, complex, taking people places we'd never dreamed of going, till we felt we would burst, then reaching a climax, then coming down slow, and playing the theme again, while we cheered, before he stopped to rest. Then the other players would take solos, and on great nights they would all have it and they would all help. It was a thrill for the audience to know we were in on the ground floor, even *under* the ground floor, while something uncanny was being made.

Rock and roll was an opposite pole: a music of sociability. In the 1950s it didn't take people deep inside themselves—that didn't happen till Bob Dylan, in the 1960s—but it gave strangers not just a sound but an instant joy they could share, an instant way to feel close. Kids would be singing as they walked down the street, or leaned against lampposts, or rode up in elevators or sat in buses or on subway platforms—until the early 1980s, the trains themselves were too noisy to sing on—and other people, people who didn't know them, would join in. In the 1960s, a bunch of gifted New Yorkers—Dylan, Paul Simon, Lou Reed, Leonard Cohen, Laura Nyro, among others—would use rock as a medium to say the most complex things about life, to a beat. In the 1950s, New York's main contribution was beautiful vocal harmonies, permeated with bittersweet sentimentality, with an input that was heavily black and an audience that was instantly interracial. (Something of the early spirit is preserved in a style called doo-wop, which is still being sung in parks and subways, and which still, if you listen, tears your soul.) Rock broke through in New York not only with Elvis but with Frankie Lymon's "Why Do Fools Fall in Love?" about the same time. Lymon died young—another heroin overdose—but a generation of kids kept his soaring and yearning alive in the streets. Here, like everywhere else in America, public authorities reacted with hysteria to this wild interracial mass of kids. Did they forget their own behavior in the swing era twenty years before? In New York, there were more people who could remember and remind them.

To see art by living artists was a great deal harder in postwar New York than it is today. The Metropolitan Museum of Art and the galleries along Fifty-seventh Street were mostly interested in Europeans and in artists in their sixties or older. Not that there was anything wrong with the school of Paris! But if you were interested in what artists in New York might be doing now, the Museum of Modern Art was pretty much the place to go. MoMA was generous, even extravagant, in displaying the work of the abstract expressionists: Jackson Pollock, Willem de Kooning, Clyfford Still, Franz Kline, David Smith, Mark Rothko, Adolph Gottlieb, Helen Frankenthaler, Joan Mitchell, and others. These artists seemed to tap immense energy sources; they swept across the canvas, or into space, with amazing bursts of energy. Their painting shared with bebop an insistence on the most demanding virtuosity and a common aura of spiritual intensity. Although they were said to have developed a life together, there was a dreadful solitude in their work. I felt they were like boppers, trying to take their solos deeper and deeper into some sort of inner space, hoping somehow to come out the other end where they could laugh and share again. You couldn't look at this art just anytime; your mind had to be prepared. I thought these paintings were like skyscrapers: to see them where they are deepest and most original, you have to look into the sun.

Around 1960, a younger group of artists began showing work that was less intense but more fun. They reached out into the city streets. Their pieces incorporated—or consisted of—found objects, junk, debris. Many of them lived in old factories and warehouses near the Brooklyn Bridge. Their neighborhood was one of many that was supposed to be torn down for Robert Moses's impending Lower Manhattan Expressway. Anticipating total destruction, many factories and warehouses had recently moved away. But apart from the highway, this neighborhood was one of the first in New York to become deindustrialized, and it happens that the deindustrialization process generates an especially rich harvest of junk. These artists prowled around Dumpsters or wrecked buildings; sometimes they lived and worked inside these buildings. They included Robert Rauschenberg, Allan Kaprow, George Segal, James Rosenquist, Claes Oldenburg, Red Grooms. What I loved most in their work was their engagement with the street.

One of Oldenburg's earliest works, shown in 1960 and 1961 on the Lower East Side, is an expressionistic environment that he called *The Street: A Metamorphic Mural. The Street* included a Whitmanesque manifesto:

> *I am for an art that is political-erotical-mystical, that*
> *does something*
> *other than sit on its ass in a museum.*
> *I am for an art that grows up not knowing it is*
> *art at all. . . .*
> *I am for an art that embroils itself with the everyday crap*
> *and still comes out on top. . . .*
> *I am for an art that unfolds like a map, that you can*
> *squeeze like your sweety's arm, or kiss like a pet dog.*
> *Which expands and squeaks like an accordion. . . .*
> *I am for an art you can hammer with, sew with, stitch*
> *with, file with.*

I am for an art that tells you the time of day, or where
such and such a street is.
I am for an art that helps old ladies across the street. . . .

Claes Oldenburg

In the next two decades, a great deal of art responded to this call.

The artist whose sensibility turned out to be most attuned to a street environment was Red Grooms. In the 1960s and '70s Grooms painted dozens of exuberant, intense street scenes. But his visually richest and most imaginative production is *Ruckus Manhattan*, a giant environment he created in the mid-1970s that includes an inhabitable ferry, a surreally twisted Brooklyn Bridge, and a life-size subway car. *Ruckus Manhattan* is like a three-dimensional, interactive Popular Front mural. Spectators are urged to "please touch" Grooms's grungy, flamboyant life-size figures, who come in all colors, sizes, and income groups: businessmen, cab drivers, students, tourists, delivery people with their wares, retirees, ladies of the night, ladies who lunch, housewives, hippies, street musicians, Hasidim, and more. His figures, extravagantly distorted, ooze life. In Grooms's paintings, they reach out and touch each other. In his three-dimensional environments, they even seem to be reaching for *us*. Grooms, Oldenburg, and their friends produced an art that was modern in its intense subjectivity and its cosmopolitan inclusiveness, yet attuned to a place and an urban experience and a distinctive way of being there. These art works were parables of how to live.

Just as this environmental art was coming together, a great book was taking form across town, in the West Village, a book that would bring us a vocabulary to root not only our experience of the city but our whole lives in the life of the street. I'm referring, of course, to Jane Jacobs's *The Death and Life of Great American Cities*, which first appeared in 1961. Jacobs lived on a decrepit block of Hudson Street. Robert Moses, in his incarnation as city construction coordinator, had slated this block for urban renewal. His plans put residents under drastic pressure. Under pressure, Jacobs conceived and unveiled a day in the life of her block, from before dawn to the middle of the night. "No ideas but in things," said the great modern poet William Carlos Williams. Somehow Jacobs's catalog of everyday people, of their names, addresses, and activities, metamorphosed into a luminous vision that made thousands of people feel they were seeing a city for the very first time.

Under the seeming disorder of the old city is a marvelous order for maintaining the safety of the streets and the freedom of the city. It is a complex order. Its essence is intricacy of sidewalk use, bringing with it a constant succession of eyes. This order is composed of movement and change, and though

it is life, not art, we may call it the art form of the city, and liken it to the dance. . . .

Jane Jacobs

Jacobs showed old streets as sources of charm in modern cities. Her book had an instant impact on the planning process, and even on the real-estate market—old blocks gained in value very fast. But she did even more: she showed how the street could be a primary source of human meaning in what seemed like an absurd, meaningless world.

If there is one problem in Jacobs's vision, it is that there may be big troubles between many of the people on that street, and that, while she doesn't deny the existence of these problems, she doesn't exactly proclaim them, either. But there is one moment in our postwar culture that is both a lyrical homage to New York's streets and an indictment of their real troubles, and that is the musical tragedy *West Side Story*, which opened on Broadway in 1957 and ran till 1959. *West Side Story* takes the Broadway musical out of the pastoral world that it has generally thrived in and plunges it into a city that is being raked by ethnic warfare unto death. Ethnic conflict has always marked life in New York, as everywhere else in America, but in New York's "culture of congestion," the conflicting groups are on top of one another with nowhere to run. In those days, people who listened to the city-owned radio station, WNYC, could hear, every hour on the hour, "This is New York, where eight million people live together in peace and harmony and enjoy the benefits of democracy." *West Side Story* casts a cold eye on our official affirmations.

Jerome Robbins's dance routines are breathtaking: he fills and overfills the stage in just the ways that competing ethnic groups are overflowing the streets, streets just around the corner from the comfortable theater where the show goes on. The young men flash and flaunt themselves with moves that are thrilling, and yet, we know, lethal only a few hundred yards away. The play shows not just a love story but a bildungsroman, a drama of growing up, trying to happen on a street that holds out the promise of happiness but throws the people pursuing happiness into a dead end. Leonard Bernstein's gorgeous romantic melodies pull people into identifying the doomed lovers' story with their own. As we in the audience look and listen, we realize that we, too, are part of the overflow, part of the lethal competition, part of the ruckus. In *West Side Story*, postwar New York finally gets a culture that is attuned to its streets, its greatest environmental strength. It is a preview of the 1960s, when so many people's private suffering will play itself out in public space. It discredits postwar New York's official affirmations, yet it is one of the permanent hymns to New York, whose signature style is dancing in the street, skirting ever closer to, twisting the self to overcome, a dance of death.

TRAUMA, APOCALYPSE, BOOM, AFTERMATH:
NEW YORK CITY IN THE LAST THIRTY YEARS

PHILLIP LOPATE

DEFAULT AVERTED

In 1975, the city of New York faced bankruptcy. Business blamed labor for having extracted exorbitant contracts and pensions; the unions and leftists blamed banks for instigating the crisis to reap profits; geographers blamed the population shift to the Sun Belt; economists blamed world inflation; racists blamed minorities for "taking over"; local politicians blamed the federal government for extracting more in taxes than it gave back; all blamed the U.S. Census for not counting illegal aliens.

Had the crisis been physical, a hurricane, one might have gone down to the breakwater and helped repair the levee with sandbags. Had it been military, one might have enlisted. But it was so technical, so abstract, that the average citizen quickly saw it was out of his hands.

Part of its abstract quality was that it lacked temporal borders. No one asks of the fiscal crisis of the 1970s, as with the assassinations of the '60s, where you were when you heard, because the news broke raggedly over months, and meanwhile you went on with your life. But it was an anxious time that shook confidence in the civic order—more so, in a sense, than Watergate, since one had never doubted that candidates used chicanery to get elected, whereas it really seemed surprising that the world's greatest city might be permitted to go under.

It began as a media buzz. We were suddenly told, by television announcers who didn't themselves know whether to treat the matter gravely or comically—what else could possibly happen to this metropolis ravaged by blackouts and garbage strikes?—that New York faced the possibility of fiscal default. Slowly the story made its way from the middle of the broadcast to the top. Even so, few took seriously that the city could run out of money: surely, in those gleaming towers, bank vaults, government offices, there was sufficient cash lying around. Over the years, New Yorkers had become inured to a harlequinade: the transit union, for example, would threaten to go on strike on New Year's Eve, the mayor would insist there was no more money in the till, the clock would tick, the screws would tighten, he would turn around and—voilà, the money had been found.

But now the fear seeped in. Maybe, just this once, the banks *were* right: the city had gone too far, had overstepped its budget in some uniquely heinous way. With liberalism on the decline, New Yorkers were vulnerable to guilt for their generous impulses. Had these social expenditures under attack, which symbolized New York's proud progressive history, actually brought us to the edge of bankruptcy, or was their offensiveness more ideological in nature? The municipal hospital system and the City University of New York's free tuition were special targets, criticized by the banking community as "giveaways" of a liberal local government trying to create "socialism in one city." Would that it were so. The poor were hardly wallowing in benefits, nor, with its high cost of living, could New York be said to resemble a worker's paradise. What did seem valid were the bankers' criticisms of city hall for shoddy, debt-concealing accounting practices.

In retrospect, there was no socialist binge. A study by Paul Peterson and Margaret Weir has shown that the growth of the New York City budget in the late 1960s "was a consequence of two factors for which local officials could hardly be blamed: inflation, and increased assistance from state and federal governments." When Washington cut its funding support to New York in the 1970s, the city was faced with a sudden shortfall, which local officials tried to circumvent with "creative" accounting to roll over mounting debts.

How ironic that the mayor during the crisis, Abraham Beame, should have been the very man who once authorized these legerdemains as city comptroller. The little accountant, a clubhouse politician whom the people had elected almost because of his drabness—tired as they were of their tall, matinee-idol mayor, John V. Lindsay, who had raised expectations too high—was suddenly spouting populist rhetoric and defending the city's autonomy from corporate takeover. Governor Hugh Carey, a portly, enigmatic man, radiating power held in reserve, stood in the background, as though not wanting to intrude on the mayor's jurisdiction.

Meanwhile, we began to see men in business suits—financiers who preferred to stay out of the spotlight, such as Walter Wriston, Richard Shinn, David Rockefeller—stepping out of limousines and going into chambers, while television reporters murmured, "This is the eleventh hour." Tabloids handled the story better. The famous *Daily News* headline, FORD TO CITY: DROP DEAD, told all one needed about Washington's reluctance to bail out the nation's greatest metropolis.

Once serious negotiations got under way and it became clear that Beame could not sustain his single-handed confrontation with the banks, the spectacle shifted to accommodation, as symbolized by the blossoming friendship between the municipal union leader Victor Gotbaum and the investment banker Felix Rohatyn. Behind much of the fiscal crisis's maneuverings lay the restructuring of people's expectations. What had formerly been perceived as a right was now redefined as a privilege—one, moreover, about to be taken away. The fiscal crisis hammered away at the public realm (free zoos, libraries open daily), things that New Yorkers had come to expect, until they responded with the requisite resignation.

The loyal New Yorker was reduced to passive spectator, watching the moves of inside players. Some, like Herman Badillo, argued daringly that New York would be better off going into bankruptcy and shaking loose its fiscal obligations that way. But of course the risk could not be taken. It was like watching one of those blockbuster disaster movies: the city was about to be destroyed by a fireball. At the last moment the comet swerved aside, but the anticipated impact had lodged so deeply in the communal consciousness that one internalized the disaster as if it had actually occurred.

THE POSTINDUSTRIAL CITY

When the dust had settled, the city government was in receivership to a watchdog agency, the Municipal Assistance Corporation, or MAC, which restructured the city's debts more leniently through its own bond sale, and saw to it that social services would be cut and new probusiness policies enacted. For a time, New York became more like Atlanta or Houston, a city run quite openly by a corporate elite.

With the enthusiastic approval of newly elected mayor Edward I. Koch, who took office two years later, city hall did all in its power to please the business community, from zoning policies that encouraged real-estate development, to tax incentives and abatements, to lowering the overall tax burden on businesses. Koch proved an ideal spokesman for the new corporate order: his roots as a reform Democrat left him indifferent to liberal guilt; his colorful, ethnically spiced language made him instantly familiar to the populace. He was your uncle Eddie, who, argumentative and preening, finds a bone to pick with you at your cousin's wedding. His colloquial query, "How'm I doing?" uncannily mirrored the Me Generation's narcissistic insecurities, even as it suggested a clownish self-mockery.

More and more, it was said that the mayor had no real power to set the city's course, which depended on a complex set of events originating in Hong Kong, Haiti, Moscow, Berlin. Koch proved at least an entertaining cheerleader for the surprising economic boom (fueled by foreign investments) that lasted from 1977 to 1987.

Little by little, the pattern of a postindustrial city emerged. The city had lost most of its manufacturing base (over 600,000 factory jobs departing from 1960 to 1975). Foreign

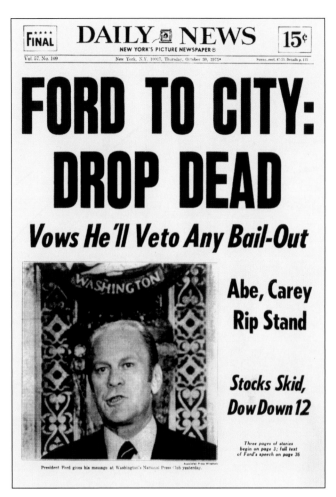

Front page of the *Daily News*, October 30, 1975.

competition had devastated its once regnant garment industry. In industry's place emerged an expanded service economy, built on paper, or pixels: it had a weightless, abstract quality, since you could no longer point to some object produced. New York manufactured "information." Always a place where tips, gossip, the cutting edge mattered, the city now became maniacally obsessed with keeping up. On Wall Street, this inside-tip mentality led to leveraged buyouts, takeovers, and white-collar crimes; in the artistic sphere, its expression was appropriation art, and the high-low mergers of artists such as Julian Schnabel, David Salle, Jean-Michel Basquiat, and Keith Haring.

A giddy, playful, shallow atmosphere prevailed in the art world, far removed from the transcendent austerities of Mark Rothko or David Smith. The superego seemed dead. Gallery owners cast envious eyes on the world of haute couture; art began to seem a subset of fashion. This same epicurean appetite promoted a fascination with cuisine, fancy restaurants, discotheques. The city's new celebrities were master chefs and supermodels. All this froth, it must be admitted, was fun—especially for a city that had been on the ropes a few years earlier. New money for gentrifi-

Brokers and traders on Wall Street nervously awaiting the opening of the market on October 20, 1987, three days after the catastrophic crash known as Black Monday. During that time, the market had lost a third of its overall value—more than a trillion dollars.

cation brought benefits to the housing stock of borderline neighborhoods, such as Columbus Avenue, even as it led to increased rents and co-op conversions, driving poor families into the streets and homeless shelters.

During the Koch years, the poverty rate and income inequality increased noticeably. New York began, as so often in its past, to pull apart into two cities, one of splendor, the other misery. At the time one blamed the short-sightedness of President Reagan, Mayor Koch, and their free market policies. In hindsight, these changes seem part of a juggernaut, a worldwide economic pattern. As Saskia Sassen argued in *The Global City*, manufacturing was increasingly being decentralized—to Taiwan, Korea, and elsewhere. But control was being centralized in cities like New York, London, and Tokyo, thanks to developments in telecommunications and information technology. Multinational firms attracted highly paid service professionals—accountants, lawyers, computer experts, advertising executives—who were high

spenders, creating a demand for luxury goods often produced in sweatshops by part-time labor. Thus, the increasing income disparity in cities like New York or London may not have been so much the product of Ronald Reagan's or Margaret Thatcher's policies as of global trends that promoted the growth of conspicuous consumers and low-paid labor required to service them.

History often appears to us as a local, venal, preventable crime; only later do we come to realize that these changes may have been out of our power. Increasingly New York seemed less like a city in control of its important decisions and more like a tail being waved by a mighty dog, elsewhere.

APOCALYPSE NOW?

The initial effect of the fiscal crisis on New York City was psychological: having grown accustomed to the notion that it was the capital of the twentieth century, as Paris had been

capital of the nineteenth, it encountered a massive insult to its pride, which moved it from teleology (progress) to eschatology (apocalypse). Suddenly its finish was being routinely expected.

"New York makes one think about the collapse of civilization, about Sodom and Gomorrah, the end of the world. The end wouldn't come as a surprise here. Many people already bank on it," Saul Bellow wrote. Undoubtedly, this apocalyptic reading of New York was part of a larger mood. An age that had witnessed the Holocaust and Hiroshima had already seen the worst and could not stop imagining ecological suicide or postnuclear wastelands.

In their more lurid cinematic manifestations, the pessimistic scenarios about Gotham that occurred regularly after 1975 encompassed violent shootouts (*Taxi Driver*) or comic book fantasies of a junkyard civilization (*Escape from New York* or the first, doomy *Batman*). A less flamboyant but no less mournful note was struck by the tabloid columnists who groped to pinpoint some lost "spirit" of innocence the city used to have (the Biltmore clock, the egg cream). In

fact, their New York—a city whose largest social stratum in the mid-1950s had been blue-collar white ethnics—*was* largely gone.

The entire population of New York had been transformed by a wave of immigration from Asia, the Caribbean, and Central America, which rivaled the great infusions of the Irish and German in the 1840s and '50s, the Italians and Jews from 1880 to 1920, and southern blacks and Puerto Ricans in the 1940 to 1970 period. Inevitably, the white ethnic culture of "dese and dose," which had established the archetypal New Yorker in people's minds, could not pass away without some grief. But it was gone—and the new archetypal New Yorker (with a Bengali or Korean accent, perhaps) had not yet coalesced. Hence the sense that the city's heart had "died."

Then there were sober analyses of the "demise" of the city's economy, such as that of Jason Epstein, who—following a line already laid out by Roger Alcaly, David Mermelstein, William K. Tabb, and others—asserted in an article entitled "The Tragical History of New York" that "New York City is adrift on an uncharted sea, and its engine has begun to die." Epstein derived his gloomy prophecy primarily from the incontrovertible fact that the city had gone from being an industrial titan to a service economy, which, he claimed, could never offer a leg up to the undereducated minorities and new immigrants, as factories had done in the past. However, the 1980s apocalyptic projections were also based, like all predictions, on existing elements that were assumed not just to stay put but to intensify. Thus, the city would continue to be polarized between rich and poor, the middle class would be driven out, the costly treatment of AIDS patients and crack cocaine babies would bleed the system dry, younger and younger criminals who had no employable skills would run amok with machine guns, and the murder rate would soar. . . . In fact the crime rate has plummeted dramatically in the past few years. If no complete cure yet exists for AIDS, there are better combinations of drug treatments that promise longer lives. And crack seems far less of a factor than it once was.

For all the distortions attendant on apocalyptic thinking, one advantage is that it circumvents the daily anxiety of wondering whether or how we will come through, by arguing: we won't. The muddledness of daily life may be less dramatically satisfying than the "closure" of apocalypse, but truer. The past twenty-five years have seen a fiscal crisis, cutbacks, a boom, a stock market plunge in 1987, the early 1990s recession, more cutbacks, followed by a substantial boom in the late '90s and a restoration of services. The economic cycles seem to be getting shorter, the extremes closer together. What no one predicted was that the city's economic conditions would keep oscillating between better and worse; that the middle class (at least the middle-class young) would hang on because the promise of city life remained appealing; that the region's structural problems would not disappear but neither would some of its immediate scourges take quite the toll that had been expected; that the new immigrants from overseas would bring a stubborn resiliency and self-reliance back to the city. On a warm day you can go into the street and still see the world.

A CONSERVING MOMENT

The past thirty years have witnessed a flowering of historic self-consciousness about New York: hundreds of books, exhibits, films dedicated to the appreciation of the specific urban aesthetic this city has come to offer. To some degree, the fiscal crisis contributed to the phenomenon by bringing home the fragility of New York's dynamism. What had before seemed haughty and coarsely vital—the city that could crush its inhabitants, but never the other way around—began to take on the fin-de-siècle coloration of a fabulous invalid. After being denigrated for centuries as ugly in comparison to other world cities (especially European capitals), suddenly everyone seemed to "get" New York: the gestalt of the street grid, the charm of the variegated street wall, the advantages, as Jane Jacobs pointed out, of organic growth over sterile city planning.

An important part of this new appreciation was the preservation movement, which gained momentum after the tragic demolition of Pennsylvania Station in 1966. Shortly after, the Landmarks Preservation Law was passed, promising that never again would the city lose so magnificent a treasure.

The downside of this passionate feeling for "Lost New York" was that only the past seemed aesthetically redemptive. A city famous for its commercial creativity suddenly appeared artistically exhausted—unable to come up with a new urban design vocabulary for the end of the twentieth century. Builders scrambled to recapture the protective aura of the city's "most favored" eras: the Olmstedian flagstone of Central Park was employed in Battery Park City's esplanade; the early-twentieth-century municipal lampposts were mimicked along Park Avenue; and the look of art deco lobbies was recaptured in chic bistros all over town. The critique of modernist architecture's glass box had left the profession tentative, afraid to innovate or do much else besides recycle past styles in (more or less) ironically quoted fashion.

Coincidentally or not, the conscious valuing of Old New York peaked at just that moment when the city suffered its worst housing shortage in decades. Where the flaneur might revel in historical fantasy, the real-estate agent's eye was quick to detect ornament as profit. Anything with a venerable facade, touches of prewar "charm," led to steeply rising rents. Grimy warehouses suddenly took on a period cachet, transformable into condominiums and co-ops. By the time their facades had been spiffed up, their brass polished, bricks repointed and ironwork painted, they were so excessively rouged as to create a historically distorting impression. The conversion of much of the South Street Seaport into a shopping mall was one such "revival" that undercut any true connection with the past, though this very dissonance ensured the necessary, alienated crack in consciousness that signified Style.

A more benign aspect of the conserving tendency was that, for the first time in decades, the city government turned substantial resources over to repairing the infrastructure. No doubt they were forced into this move by certain embarrassments—chunks of the Williamsburg Bridge or the FDR Drive falling below—but in any case, a consensus emerged that it was imperative to tend the existing built environment enough so that it could limp on into the next century. Thus began the Caretaker Years, which oversaw relatively unglamorous chores such as painting bridges, reinforcing girders, and repaving avenues.

Another happy result of the conserving impulse was the Koch administration's decision to rehabilitate thousands of city-owned apartment buildings for use as public housing. Ironically, Koch, deservedly attacked for his part in the housing shortage and homeless crisis, probably ended up doing more for public housing in New York than any mayor since Robert Wagner. Aside from the fact that there was no more public housing construction money forthcoming from the federal government, it simply made more sense to repair the prevailing stock—even when that stock contained only a facade over a burnt-out shell—rather than put up high-rise projects. The six-story walk-up was rightly perceived as a vernacular New York building type, whose presence reassured citizens and maintained the urban web much better than did self-enclosed high-rise projects on superblocks. So the city subcontracted to community agencies either to rehabilitate existing structures or erect modular affordable housing. In the Bronx, particularly, the equivalent of a whole city rose, almost invisibly, behind the facades of once abandoned houses: thousands of clean, freshly painted apartments with stripped wooden floors and new kitchen appliances were made available, along with social services such as day care, addiction counseling, employment referral, to a precisely calculated formula of homeless families and the working poor. The South Bronx was brought back to life, returned to that most cherished New York entity, the functioning working-class ghetto. Or almost back to life: virtually no provision had been made for those bars, dance halls, gambling dens, movie theaters, billiard parlors, in which the poor had traditionally found some leisure. Perhaps these would follow.

From time to time, community organizers invoke the examples of Central Park, the Brooklyn Bridge, the New York Public Library, and ask rhetorically whether such noble works are now entirely beyond the city's ken. Perhaps not; but what we do see is a municipal reluctance to take on any public amenity, from a toilet to Governor's Island, unless it is tied to profit-making operations. This notion that the public realm must pay for itself is new and rather worrisome.

Yet what is remarkable about New York in this period is the substantial improvements that *have* been made, without appreciable notice—maybe because the improvements have been more in the way of conservation rather than aesthetic novelties or technological marvels. Typical is the redesign of Bryant Park, done so tastefully and intelligently that a tourist might assume it was ever so—without realizing that this public space close to the city's heart had been virtually given over to drug dealers in the 1970s. Times Square itself, after a long seedy decline and threatened makeover into a character-obliterating office complex, is being restored as an entertainment magnet.

The largest public works project during this era has been New York City Water Tunnel No. 3, a massive waterworks buttressing the older tunnels: necessary, costly, a prodigious engineering feat, invisible to the citizenry. Other, more visible refinements illustrating New York's quiet renewal include the resurgence of Sixth Avenue's Ladies' Mile, the restoration of Union Square, the improvements to Brooklyn's downtown area, the necklace of new parks along the Hudson River, the extensive public school construction, and the renovation of Grand Central Terminal. If none of these causes the heart to flutter—well, there are worse things for a mighty city than to catch its breath and take responsibility for its patrimony.

ONWARD

In New York, politically speaking, the carousel keeps turning. The centrist, frumpy-looking Mayor Koch was followed by the more liberal, dapper David Dinkins, the city's first African American mayor, who unluckily served office during a recession; unable to expand social services, he consoled himself by going to parties. After one term he was replaced by Rudy Giuliani, a dour, hard-nosed moderate who won office with a tough-on-crime platform, and worked hard in his first term to eliminate firecrackers, street vendors, and squeegee men.

Mayor Giuliani's argument was that bearing down on "quality of life" nuisances would improve the general civic tone; in fact, the city did experience an upturn in optimistic feelings, according to all the polls, but whether this was because he had pressured the squeegee operators off the street or because he had the great good fortune to reign during a national economic boom and drop in violent crime remains open to debate. In Giuliani's second term of office, the citizenry went from worrying about disorder to worrying about too much order, too repressive a means of "keeping the peace."

Still, most New Yorkers had to admit that the streets felt safer. The economic picture looked basically good: all the jobs that were lost during the last recession had been gained back. In part due to the development of Silicon Alley, a nexus of entrepreneurial computer-related firms, New York—more than any other city in the world—seemed to have made a full transition to a postindustrial economy. Not that doubts about a prosperity divorced from production ever entirely faded, any more than concerns about whether this brave technological future would find vocational uses for our poorly educated inner-city youth. Sure enough, the boom ended, and the new mayor, Michael J. Bloomberg, inherited a much bleaker fiscal situation, which resulted in serious job loss and service cutbacks. The emotional and economic fallout from 9/11 left New Yorkers scared and traumatized. Yet the city still feels more livable than it did thirty years ago; it has managed to outlive its own death.

Visitors at Ellis Island
view historic photographs
of immigrants, 1995.

CITY OF THE
MILLENNIUM

In the fall of 1975, New York City—city of cities, capital of capitalism, gateway to America—was brought to its knees, humiliated, and left for dead. Languishing in the depths of an economic recession and facing the worst financial crisis of its history, city leaders turned in desperation to the federal government for a $2.3 billion package of loan guarantees that represented New York's only chance to avoid going bankrupt.

President Gerald Ford's stunning response came in a speech on October 29, given to the National Press Club in Washington. Municipal default, the president declared, would be a good thing for New York, forcing it to curtail its traditionally spendthrift ways. No federal guarantees would be forthcoming. The next day, the towering black headline loomed ominously from the front page of the *Daily News*: FORD TO CITY: DROP DEAD.

In its typically blunt and homely way, the *News*'s headline captured the basic assumption behind the president's remarks—an assumption that had been growing more and more commonplace among Americans for years, as the city's social and economic problems multiplied. New York, like most American cities, was plummeting into the abyss. New York—America's extraordinary, unwieldy experiment in capitalism and democracy, hope and greed—had failed. The city was going to die.

But the city did not die. Instead, to the surprise of almost everyone, it got back up off the floor and began to revive. Within a month of his declaration, the president—implored to reconsider by a consortium of bankers, European politicians, and American mayors fearful that a "domino effect" of default would rip across American cities—reversed himself and grudgingly approved the requested loan guarantees. With time now to put its finances in order, the city moved with startling dispatch. By 1981, a year before expected, the city had balanced its budget, had begun to restore services cut during the crisis, and was paying off the last of the federal loans—on time and with interest. In the end, the United States Treasury made millions on the arrangement.

Then, in an even more startling turn of events, New York not only didn't die but flourished again—enjoying a prolonged economic boom in the 1980s, riding out a downturn in the early 1990s, and experiencing an even more striking resurgence later in the 1990s. By the end of the decade and the century, New York had regained an optimism about its future literally unthinkable a quarter of a century before. By nearly every barometer, the city's fortunes had risen. Real-estate values and commercial investment had skyrocketed. Ridership on the subways had increased. The population was growing again. The streets had become dramatically safer, and employment had reached its highest levels in decades. Though crushing problems remained—problems of race and poverty, crumbling infrastructure, and a moribund educational system—a new attitude about the city had emerged not only among New Yorkers but, more strikingly, among Americans generally, who no longer saw New York as a place careening out of control but as the metropolis of America.

The reasons for New York's miraculous revival were many, and they remain the subject of heated, often highly contentious debate. And yet in the end the city's capacity to reinvent itself in the last quarter of the twentieth century derived to a startling degree from the strengths the Dutch themselves had endowed it with four hundred years before: its relentless entrepreneurial drive and energy, its heterogeneity and openness to newcomers, its density and concentration of people and resources, and its openness to experimentation and change.

New York's entrepreneurial spirit asserted itself even before the crisis was fully over. By the 1980s, the city's position within the commercial world had begun to shift as it now took on an expanded role as the clearinghouse of the emerging international economy. With the advent of electronic fund transfers, unimaginably huge sums of money began circulating around the globe—twenty-four hours a day. By the mid-1980s, 40 percent or more of those electronic transactions were passing through New York on any given day. The lights of the great towers of lower Manhattan burned into the small hours of the night as brokers, bankers, and traders communicated with their counterparts in London, Paris, Frankfurt, Tokyo, and Hong Kong—the archipelago of "global cities" where the financial destiny of almost every country was now largely controlled. The new economic city-states were tied far less firmly to their own home countries than to a new worldwide network of trade—whose shape was being increasingly defined by an almost immaterial infrastructure of fiber-optic cables, microwave links, and synchronous satellites.

Down at street level, the impact of the new economic concentration was quickly felt as the city entered a boom era whose frantic pace and spirit of carefree extravagance brought to mind the giddiest years of the 1920s. The rate of new construction outdid previous booms, adding another 45 million square feet of office space to Manhattan alone. In ten years the city's workforce added nearly 400,000 jobs as the financial industries and related "service" professions—law, accounting, computing, management—swelled in size. Built on the accumulation of wealth through the acquisition and merger of companies and the trading of financial instruments, the boom spread extraordinary sums of money through the city's upper classes. A new group of young urban professionals, eager to enjoy and display their sudden wealth, reanimated New York's luxury economy—its restaurants and limousines, condominium apartments and specialty clothing stores. Many parts of the city glittered with an ostentatious wealth that had not been seen since the late 1920s—but as in that era, it was a wealth that often seemed paper-thin and for the most part benefited a narrow spectrum of the elite.

The parallel to the earlier decade seemed all the more apt when the great boom of the '80s came to a sudden end with a market crash of its own. On October 16, 1987, in what was quickly known as Black Monday, the Dow Jones Average dropped 508 points, sparking an economic downturn that severely tested New York's recuperative powers. Over the next five years, the city's economy shed more than 300,000 jobs, erasing almost all the gains of the previous ten years. But by 1993 the stock market, which had stabilized soon after the crash, began rising again, and New York entered yet another period of growth.

This time, the resurgence was driven as much from below—from the city's sidewalk throngs—as from the lofty financial offices above. By the early 1990s, the greatest of all the transformations of the era was evident everywhere in the city, as not only the world's money but the world's people poured into New York. Following the passage of the Hart-Celler Act in 1965—the most radical change to the federal immigration laws since the closing of the golden door in 1924—an extraordinary wave of newcomers began to enter New York, galvanizing every aspect of its economy and making it once again the world capital of heterogeneity, the city of nations.

The numbers were staggering. In the 1970s, 800,000 immigrants arrived in New York; then, in the decade to come, a million more. In 1992, in just one year, while the city was still struggling to pull itself out of recession, 120,000 newcomers took up residence. By the late 1990s, more than a third of all New Yorkers had been born abroad. But even more striking than the sheer quantity of new immigrants was the incredible number of places they came from. During the great immigrations at the turn of the century, the

vast majority had come from Europe. Now they were arriving from every continent—indeed, almost every country: from Ireland, Greece, and Italy; from Eastern Europe; from the West Indies; from Latin America; from Turkey, Israel, and Egypt; from the Indian subcontinent; from Africa; from China, Korea, and the nations of Southeast Asia.

In 1644, a Dutch minister had remarked in astonishment that more than 18 languages were spoken on the streets of New York; 350 years later, the number had risen to nearly 180.

The new immigration laws favored those with skills; furthermore, once admitted, a newcomer could bring his or her entire family. Most of the immigrants were fiercely family-oriented and exhibited "a work ethic," one man said, "beside which the vaunted Protestant Ethic shrinks to limp indolence." Driven, ambitious, and entrepreneurial, the newcomers took over the local shops and services left behind by older groups, from newsstands and grocery stores to taxicabs and dry cleaners. They also entered New York's traditional blue-collar industries, such as the garment business, making up more than half the needle-trade workers by 1990 and sustaining those manufacturing industries that remained in the city.

Unlike many other old American cities—whose populations for the most part were still dominated by large groups of native-born blacks and whites—New York was rapidly assembling the most complex and pluralistic population in the world, one in which no single group was in the majority. By the late 1990s, more than a third of all black New Yorkers traced their immediate roots to the Caribbean, not to the American South. And if the city was home to more than a million Puerto Ricans, it also contained almost as many Latinos from the Dominican Republic, Cuba, and Central and South America. The vast influx also included more than a quarter of a million Europeans—mostly Soviet Jews, settling mainly in Brooklyn communities like Brighton Beach. Asian Americans, meanwhile, were emerging as a major presence in the city and like other groups before them moving up the city's economic ladder with amazing speed.

Yet if the energy and vitality of the newcomers recalled the early years of the century, so did the challenges they confronted. The new immigrant labor fueled a rebirth of the garment industry in lower Manhattan—and with it, a return to the sweatshop, where Asian and Dominican women often worked twelve-hour shifts in conditions not unlike those that reformers and union organizers had struggled to eliminate seventy-five years before. As it had at the turn of the century, New York's burdened public school system struggled to meet the needs of a student population that was growing by twenty thousand a year—including thousands of newcomers who spoke any one of three dozen languages. Housing inspectors found the basements of two-family homes on quiet, leafy streets in Queens crowded with dozens of illegal immigrants—packed in as tightly as tenement dwellers in the late nineteenth century.

As a newly heterogeneous population surged into the city, transforming the human face of New York, the structure of its commercial culture began to change as well—and here, too, the city found itself returning to its entrepreneurial roots. For most of the century, economic life in New York had been dominated by a fleet of large corporations, with more than 135 of the nation's 500 largest companies headquartered in Manhattan in the 1950s. By 1990, that number had dwindled to fewer than 40—but by then the city's economy had already begun to be transformed by an explosive rise in the size and number of companies that sold not products but information and services. All through the 1980s and '90s, hundreds, then thousands, of smaller investment firms, financial service companies, accounting firms, law firms, and brokerage houses sprang up to service an increasingly international commercial culture oriented around the fluid, constantly shifting ebb and flow of trade on Wall Street, where domestic and international markets in commodities, futures, stocks, bonds, and currencies had exploded in size.

With the end of the cold war and advances in computer technology, the world grew steadily more global and more market-driven, and increasingly it was New York, always the most global and market-driven of cities, that again seemed the natural financial capital of the world.

The city's economic comeback was striking. Like other old American cities, it had lost most of its industrial companies and the hundreds of thousands of jobs they sustained. But unlike those cities, it had replaced almost all of those jobs with new positions—office employment, for the most part—that generally offered better wages and working conditions. Though inevitably powered by Wall Street's extraordinary boom, the economic recovery of the 1990s, unlike that of the '80s, was spread widely across the economy, as the growth of the city's traditional industries (publishing, law, advertising, fashion, entertainment, accounting, real estate) was bolstered by the rise of a new industry (multimedia) that quickly became one of the city's largest sources of employment and reasserted New York's place at the cutting edge of the culture.

By the end of the 1990s, the fiscal crisis had dwindled to a memory, and New York City seemed to have reinvented itself once again. Nowhere would the city's self-transformation seem more startlingly complete than in the metamorphosis of its greatest public space—Times

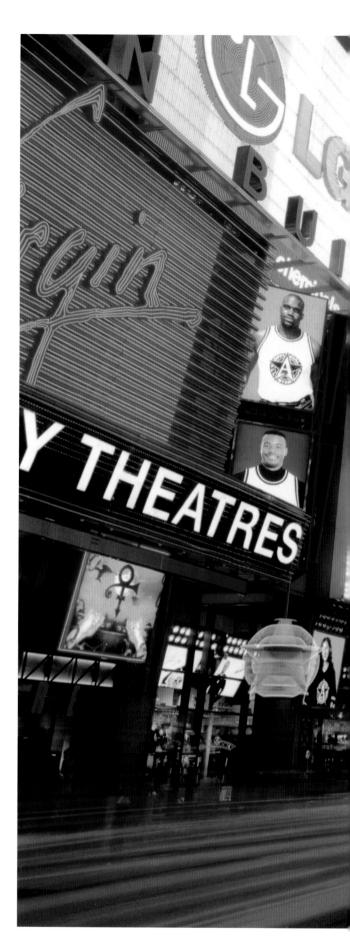

Times Square, looking south from 46th Street, 1999.

Square. In 1975, the legendary entertainment and media district—whose name and glittering image still drew tens of millions of visitors each year—had degenerated in many places into a squalid, crime-ridden twilight zone of sex shops, strip clubs, and seedy bars. New Yorkers themselves often took a kind of ironic civic pride in the fact that the crossroads of the world now looked more like Skid Row than the Great White Way, as prostitutes, drug addicts, alcoholics, and swarms of men in search of sex patrolled 42nd Street and the storied side streets off Broadway and Times Square.

Then in the early 1990s, as the economic resurgence accelerated, decades of debate about whether and how to "clean up" Times Square suddenly gave way to startlingly swift action as a consortium of public and private interests—including the California-based Walt Disney Company and several major New York developers—moved ahead with an aggressive and ambitious program of renewal. Almost overnight, Sodom was transformed. Strict new city zoning ordinances closed down and scattered the warren of X-rated video stores, movie theaters, and peep shows; aggressive policing cleared the sidewalks, side streets, and parking lots of most of the less seemly goings-on. The change was so swift, and so complete, that visitors and residents alike were often bewildered to find that the 42nd Street of Martin Scorsese's Travis Bickel—who yearned, in the 1976 film *Taxi Driver,* for the real rain that would one day come and wash all the scum away—had taken on the air of a historical documentary.

But, without question, the rain had come. One by one, the historic theaters lining 42nd Street were renovated and refurbished, and new theaters were constructed. Office buildings and new commercial buildings shot up, replacing crumbling older structures, while larger and more numerous lighted signs and billboards rapidly filled every available square foot of advertising space in and around the elongated, hourglass-shaped intersection of Times Square. By the late 1990s, a new Times Square had emerged—cleaner, better lit, and more wholesome than it had been in half a century, and busier and more profitable than it had been in decades. Each night as the sun went down, the district was transformed into a glowing, shimmering diaphanous dish of light.

And yet, for some, there was a price attached to the successful transformation of Times Square, which seemed to many people to have traded in its corrupt old soul for a glittering corporate veneer with nothing underneath. As the old offices of press agents and talent scouts and the seedy local shops gave way to spectacular new structures filled with theme restaurants, chain stores, and major media retail outlets, some wondered whether Times Square's identity as

the city's premier public space had been permanently betrayed. As entertainment conglomerates increasingly grasped the marketability of the idea of New York itself, some New Yorkers feared that Times Square and other talismanic way stations in the city were in danger of becoming eerily detached, corporately administered simulacra of their former selves—historic spaces neutered of all idiosyncrasy, cunningly remodeled to fit the idea of what they once had been, then packaged and sold as "the New York experience" to flocks of tourists in a tightly controlled commercial environment.

By the end of the century, a perverse nostalgia for the good old days of sordidness, vice, and crime had become one of the affectations of many long-time city dwellers. And yet, on a balmy night—as throngs of tourists and theatergoers from around the world could now be seen drifting along the sidewalks of Times Square, whose bright signs blazed against the night sky more intensely than they had in living memory—the urban energy of the city seemed to most New Yorkers to have reasserted itself gloriously. The sheer density, the enormous concentration of people and buildings and signage and things, was proclaiming once again the city's fundamental reason for being: the infinite potential for interaction within a densely filled, tightly defined finite space—qualities that have been the city's glory since the Dutch settlers first raised their compact outpost at the tip of the island, three and a half centuries ago.

The experiment is how close can rich and poor live before the fabric completely falls apart? How close can you put ethnic groups that don't like one another much? How much can you promise people about a rich and privileged future, and then not be able to deliver, before they rise up and say enough? And the answer here, over and over and over again, has been that the fabric becomes tattered, that sometimes the fabric even becomes torn, but the fabric survives.
Anna Quindlen, from *New York: A Documentary Film*

To a degree the Dutch and English could never have imagined, the voyages of discovery which gave rise to places like New York were in the end the first fateful steps in a process we now call *globalization.*

Founded as a remote and lonely outpost in a worldwide network of colonies—one node in an incipiently global civilization—New York, whether it knew it or not, was enrolled from the very start in a revolutionary project: the creation of a new kind of human community that would take its identity not from one place, one nationality, one ethnicity, one religion, one way of life, but from the convergence of all places, all nationalities, all ethnicities, all religions, all ways of life. Without intending it, the Dutch set in motion a process with the profoundest implications for life on the planet at the end of the twentieth century. The whole world has now become what New York has been for at least 150 years—helplessly mixed, bewilderingly interconnected, irreducibly commingled, miscegenated in its bloodlines, plural both in its history and in its destiny. With mingling now no longer an option but an inevitability, the experiment founded by the Dutch remains at the dawn of the third millennium more crucial than ever before. Will it be possible for all the peoples of the world to live together in a single place?

For better and for worse, no culture in human history has had more experience grappling with that question. The unique geography of Manhattan itself—both natural and manmade—has only served to intensify over time the baffling, exhilarating, and sometimes frightening experience of congestion and commingling that New York's economic engine and openness to newcomers began conjuring into existence almost two centuries ago. What makes New York unique among public spaces in America is that the narrowness of its geography forces its citizens to confront face-to-face, every day, the diversity of their world. Here, every conceivable age, class, race, profession, political and philosophic viewpoint, sexual persuasion, temperament, and social style is on display. In the city's crowded public spaces—its streets and sidewalks, subways and train stations, museums and bridges, restaurants and theaters—New Yorkers find themselves presented with nothing less than the entire glorious, maddening, imperfect spectacle of the modern world itself.

Not everyone may wish to confront that spectacle on a daily basis, as New Yorkers do. But sooner or later, if Americans are to understand who they are, where they have come from, and where they are going as a people, they must, imaginatively or in fact, come to New York—the capital not only of America and of the American century, but of their own and their culture's becoming. What they will find here—warts and all—is what countless generations of immigrants and newcomers from around the country and the world have found. What the writer Joan Didion, for example, discovered, as she felt herself pulled across the continent from California to Manhattan. Recalling the powerful lure of the city from afar, she wrote: "New York was no mere city. It was instead an infinitely romantic notion, the mysterious nexus of all love and money and power, the shining and perishable dream itself."

And what is that dream—the dream of New York? It is nothing less than the American dream—the restless dream of capitalism and democracy, of opportunity and possibility, of transformation and rising—a dream that to a remarkable degree was born on the banks of the Hudson four hundred years ago, long before America itself began.

No one has described that dream, or the central role New York has played in creatively redefining it generation after generation after generation, better than the historian Kenneth T. Jackson. It is to him therefore, with gratitude and affection, that we leave the last word.

Americans need New York because New York is one of the few places in the country that allows difference to be celebrated, that allows people to reach their full potential. And that's in a sense what drives civilization, what drives freedom, what moves us forward, and what is really the hope of the future. New York is really the hope of the future because it's there for all of us. Whether we never go there, whether we never see New York, whatever small town or small city we're from, it's important that we know that New York is there to welcome us in case we want to be different, in the same way that the idea of the West has always been so important to American history. People didn't have to go to the West to feel that somehow the openness of the country was beckoning them, that somehow it was important in defining what it was to be an American. New York is the same kind of an idea for us all, that somewhere in the country there is a place where we can go, no matter what we believe, no matter who we are, no matter what we want to do, and we can find in that place other people like ourselves, and a possibility of reaching our full potential.

Lower Manhattan and
the World Trade Center,
seen from the Brooklyn
Bridge, 1995.

> America is part of everyone's imaginative life, through movies, music, television, and the Web, whether you grow up in Bilbao, Beijing, or Bombay. Everyone has a New York in their heads, even if they have never been there—which is why the destruction of the twin towers had such an impact.
>
> Timothy Garton Ash

EPILOGUE: THE CENTER OF THE WORLD

PILLARS OF FIRE

On a perfect, almost achingly beautiful late-summer morning in early September 2001, New York City and much of the rest of the contemporary world were changed utterly, in the space of less than two hours. Images of the apocalyptic horror that transpired during that brief time would be burned indelibly into the hearts and minds of all who saw it—the dark, spectral planes bearing down upon the towers, the billowing shrouds of flame and smoke, the horror of the falling bodies, and the immense towers themselves, dissolving into pillars of rubble and dust.

For millions of Americans, and hundreds of millions more around the world, looking on in shock and disbelief as the nightmarish events unfolded in real time on television, time itself seemed to have been rent asunder that day, divided into a before and after permanently defined by the curt and fateful shorthand "9/11."

What the events of September 11 made suddenly and painfully clear was that a new era in New York City's history had already opened by the fall of 2001; indeed, that the city had long since lurched forward into a new and vastly more complex chapter in its long and fateful relationship with the rest of the world.

For almost all of its four-hundred-year history, of course, New York had been a global city. Founded by the Dutch as a crucial link in a worldwide archipelago of European colonies, it had risen to greatness in the nineteenth and twentieth centuries as America itself rose to world stature—emerging at the dawn of the twenty-first century as the undisputed capital of a new and increasingly global economic order. And yet, for most of that time, the city's cosmopolitanism had remained remarkably one-sided—as if globalization in New York mainly meant gathering the world's people and resources and benefiting from them. All that changed on September 11. Along with the towers, the events of that day shattered the illusion that globalization could come without involvement in the world's deepest conflicts and divisions—conflicts and divisions in some measure brought on by the process of globalization itself.

From being the world's melting pot and microcosm, New York suddenly found itself on the front lines of a new global battlefield.

The terrorist attack of September 11 was one of the least random acts of violence ever perpetrated. New York was targeted for reasons that in the end had everything to do with the forces and values the city has harbored for hundreds of years. The twin towers themselves, of course, were the real and symbolic epicenter of an economic, social, and cultural system that in the past two hundred years has come to dominate much of the face of the planet. In the end, every theme and issue in the city's four-century-long history—commerce and diversity, capitalism and democracy, globalization and the creation of a new kind of multicultural society—was put into play in new and harrowing ways by the events of September 11.

To understand those themes and issues, and what happened on that terrible September morning, one must reach back more than half a century before the events of September 11 to the fall of 1946, when the idea of a "world trade center" was first conceived. From start to finish, every aspect of the immense complex would be intricately bound up with a massive projection of American power in the postwar period—a projection that was at once physical, economic, cultural, political, and symbolic; that was centered in New York; and that would ultimately leave the twin towers standing as perhaps its most visible and widely recognized emblems and embodiments.

Indeed, in the end, everything about the story of the World Trade Center—from its origins just after the Second World War, through its construction in the 1960s and '70s, on through its use, impact, meaning, resonance, and demise, can be most powerfully understood within the context of three overlapping narratives: the astonishing extension of American economic power during the second half of the twentieth century; the dramatic changes in the city itself in the fifty years following the war; and the increasingly complex, often deeply conflicted interrelationships between New York, the United States, and the rest of the world.

A WORLD TRADE CENTER

The idea was born in the giddy aftermath of the Second World War, when, in the fall of 1946, as delegates to the brand-new United Nations settled on a site in midtown for their new home, city leaders in New York first proposed building a new complex in lower Manhattan: a "world trade center" that would rise at the very heart of the old port and financial district, booming once again as a decade and a half of depression and world war finally came to a close.

The New York State legislature quickly appointed Winthrop Aldrich, the chairman of the Chase Bank and a member of the Rockefeller family, to look into the project's feasibility. The proposed five-million-square-foot facility—conceived initially as an exposition hall for displaying trade goods from around the globe—would, it was hoped,

exploit the anticipated upsurge in postwar foreign trade and affirm New York's newfound preeminence within a vast and growing global empire.

Thus from the very outset the World Trade Center was intended to be far more than an ordinary office building or urban development. It was instead to be a means of concentrating and accelerating all the forces that had propelled the city from its origins as a tiny outpost on the far edge of the globe to its place at the very center of a world empire. Indeed, in its rationale, in its scale and size—even in its name—the project embodied the visions and ambitions of a postwar America that, emerging triumphant from World War II, stood poised to project its power and influence across a domain more extensive than any in history, including those of ancient Rome and the British Empire.

In contrast to those predecessors, however, postwar American power would be projected primarily not through occupying legions or fleets of battleships but through the extension of its burgeoning commercial interests into markets all around the world, large and small, old and new—markets whose stability would be assured by a new economic and political order.

To a remarkable degree, that global order would be constructed by a group of ambitious and farsighted New Yorkers—cosmopolitan Wall Street lawyers and bankers, for the most part, who had been brought into the government by another patrician New Yorker, President Franklin D. Roosevelt. Tough-minded businessmen who possessed a sweeping vision of America's role in the postwar world, this influential cadre of advisors—including the corporate lawyers Dean Acheson and John J. McCloy and the investment bankers Robert Lovett, Averell Harriman, Henry Morgenthau Jr., and James Forrestal—had come of age during the economic troubles and subsequent political chaos of the 1930s. That turmoil, they believed, had arisen in no small part because the United States had refused to accept the role, first thrust upon it in the years following the First World War, as successor to Great Britain, whose once supreme power as the chief guarantor of international stability was now rapidly waning.

This time, these men resolved, things would be different. The United States, using its unprecedented power and influence in the aftermath of the war, would construct a stable political and economic world order through an ambitious, interlocking series of plans, programs, and institutions, all devised in the last months of the war and in the first few years after it. There was the Bretton Woods Agreement of 1944, named for the tiny New Hampshire town where the terms were hammered out, which fixed the American dollar as the world's central currency, established a general agreement on trades and tariffs, and brought into existence the World Bank and the International Monetary

Fund to provide financial assistance overseas. There was the Marshall Plan, conceived in 1945 and enacted two years later, which would help rebuild the shattered economies of Western Europe, as well as a new military alliance called the North Atlantic Treaty Organization (NATO), founded in 1949, which would protect the continent from the threat of Soviet expansion as it carried out its long-term reconstruction. There was the reshaping of America's own wartime agencies into a permanent national security apparatus, including the Department of Defense and the Central Intelligence Agency, which would prevent the country from ever again turning away from its international responsibilities. And finally there was Franklin Roosevelt's own dream of the United Nations, with its permanent Security Council: a worldwide diplomatic forum that—unlike the prewar League of Nations—America would not only join but host in its largest and most cosmopolitan city.

America's new global order would have a very different cast and character from the waning British Empire it intended to replace. Its strategy would be not the physical dominion of far-flung colonies but the creation and maintenance of stable and prosperous trading partners around the world, an approach that would, in turn, slow the spread of Soviet Communism, encourage international trade, and help American industry—its production capacity swollen by war and in desperate need of new markets—to extend its operations to every corner of the earth.

Constructed in large part by the city's own bankers and lawyers, and shaped by the city's age-old values of trade and commerce, this new global order would, almost inevitably, be headquartered not only in the nation's political capital, Washington, D.C., but as much—or more—in its corporate and financial center, New York, a city that was also America's preeminent gateway and busiest port, handling more than a third of the imports and exports of the nation, which was itself now producing nearly half of the manufactured goods in the world.

SAVING LOWER MANHATTAN

It would take more than a decade for the idea of the World Trade Center to begin to get off the ground—and four decades more to fulfill the lofty promise of its name—but when it did take shape in the mid-1950s, it would begin to move with an all but unstoppable force, propelled above all by two men, sons and brothers of one of the most powerful family dynasties on earth. In the years to come, David and Nelson Rockefeller would seize upon the project not only as a glorious symbol of world trade but as the centerpiece of one of the most fateful and daring real-estate gambles in the history of New York—the effort to save lower Manhattan, the oldest and most historic district in the city, which by 1955 had been almost totally eclipsed by the aston-

ishing postwar building boom in midtown. In the years since the war, even as scores of modern towers had risen on midtown's avenues, not a single new office building had been put up in lower Manhattan, more than a dozen major companies had decamped uptown, and many feared the district was in imminent jeopardy of losing its status as America's major financial center.

In November 1955, intent on ensuring that lower Manhattan remained what he called "the heart pump of the capital blood that sustains the free world," David Rockefeller—now vice-president of his family's bank, Chase Manhattan, and one of the most powerful figures in American business—boldly announced that the bank would construct a new headquarters just one block north of Wall Street: a sixty-story glass-and-steel tower rising from its own raised plaza that would represent the first major commercial construction in the district since the Depression.

Concerned that even that dramatic gesture might not be enough to stem the exodus of business to midtown, David next assembled a powerful coalition of business and real-estate leaders, called the Downtown–Lower Manhattan Association, to come up with a more sweeping proposal. In the fall of 1958, the group released its handiwork: an eighty-page report that was nothing less than a master plan for the salvation of lower Manhattan. Presenting a breathtaking new vision of the oldest part of the city, it called for the complete transformation of the entire downtown area—and the eradication of the old port functions that had defined New York for centuries.

> [The] downtown Manhattan area is one of the most valuable and uniquely situated pieces of real estate in the entire world. The central core area of towering skyscrapers is surrounded by acres of marginal buildings, the majority of which are more than a century old and only partly occupied. . . .
>
> David Rockefeller, 1959

The culmination of nearly half a century of modernism in urban planning (and a reworking, in many respects, of the ideas of the landmark Regional Plan of 1929), the DLMA scheme represented one of the most comprehensive and ambitious urban renewal initiatives ever undertaken.

Under it, virtually no aspect of the old port district would remain unchanged. The fringe of finger piers that had lined the edge of the island for a century—and long cut the city off from the water—would be demolished to make way for new residential and recreational development. Many of the area's ancient winding streets, first laid down in the colonial era, would be widened to accommodate the flow of modern traffic.

Hundreds of blocks along the East and Hudson rivers—home to many of the city's oldest wholesale markets and industrial suppliers—would be wiped clean and consoli-

The twin towers under construction, March 1970. Rising 1,360 feet in the air, the two giant structures dwarfed everything surrounding them—including older skyscrapers that had once been considered the most daring and impressive buildings in the world. Beyond the towers lies the landfill for Battery Park City, created by the 1 million cubic yards of dirt excavated from the Trade Center site, then carried across West Street and dumped in the Hudson River.

Nelson Rockefeller in October 1950, looking out from the top of the RCA Building at Rockefeller Center, with the recently completed United Nations Secretariat building in the distance.

As much as anyone else of their era, David and Nelson Rockefeller embodied the potent mix of pragmatic capitalist drive and visionary internationalist outlook that underlay America's postwar global order. More than anyone else, they took it upon themselves to ensure New York's place at the very center of that burgeoning commercial imperium.

Scions of the immense fortune established by their grandfather, the titan John D. Rockefeller—who in the early twentieth century had built his enormous company, Standard Oil, into one of the first and greatest international conglomerates in the world—the two brothers had in the years since the war come to hold sway over an almost unimaginable concentration of wealth and power. By the 1950s, the Rockefeller family's influence had spread far beyond the oil business to encompass urban redevelopment, international diplomacy, investment banking, and local and national politics.

Nelson, the second and most ambitious of John D. Rockefeller Jr.'s five sons, had begun his career in the Great Depression, helping his father transform midtown Manhattan through the construction and renting of a spectacular office complex, Rockefeller Center, which quickly became the supreme emblem of New York's new role as "headquarters city" for America's big national corporations. In late 1946, when New York had seemed to be out of the running as the permanent headquarters for the United Nations, it had been Nelson who, with the help of his youngest brother, David, had stepped in at the eleventh hour to ensure that the new world organization made its home in the city—by arranging for the purchase of the East River site with $8.5 million of their father's money.

David, the youngest and most determined of the brothers, had worked as an assistant to Mayor Fiorello La Guardia before joining the international loan division of one of his family's banks, Chase, perhaps the most powerful financial institution in the world. By the mid-1950s, he was already becoming known as a "banker-statesman," who understood how to leverage financial resources to achieve larger political and diplomatic ends—and how to leverage those ends, in turn, to amass more riches still.

From their offices on the 56th floor of 30 Rockefeller Plaza, the two brothers—now taking over the reins of the family fortune from their aging father—extended their reach from the very center of the East Coast power establishment. Nelson, preparing a bid for the governorship of New York State, exercised his passion for modern art and architecture by taking over leadership of the Museum of Modern Art, whose spectacular rise in the 1950s reflected the historic postwar shift of the art world from Paris to New York. David, meanwhile, rapidly ascending through Chase's upper ranks, had embarked on an even larger initiative—engineering a merger with the Bank of the Manhattan Company to form Chase Manhattan Bank, a New York–based financial colossus that would soon lead the way for American companies to transcend national boundaries and operate on a truly global basis.

Even as that expansion was getting under way overseas, David turned his sights on a more pressing problem, much closer to home: the ailing fortunes of the old financial district around Wall Street, which was now threatening to unravel completely in the face of the postwar boom remaking its rival four miles to the north, midtown Manhattan. In the end, it would be David who pointed the way toward a dramatic answer to the problem: the creation of an immense new office complex called the World Trade Center—a project so large and ambitious it would require the resources of the state to bring it to fruition. As it happened, by 1959 those resources were under the control of a new governor, David's brother Nelson Aldrich Rockefeller, who would soon take the lead in making his youngest sibling's vision a reality.

David Rockefeller (left) in November 1955, presenting plans and models of the proposed new headquarters for Chase Manhattan Bank, to be built in the heart of the old financial district in lower Manhattan.

dated to make way for huge new office buildings for the vastly expanded white-collar services the new global economy required.

At the center of it all—the anchor and emblem of the entire 550-block redevelopment program—would rise an updated version of the idea first promoted by David Rockefeller's uncle, Winthrop Aldrich, fifteen years earlier, an idea that in the months and years to come would become David's most burning ambition: a world trade center.

If the Empire State Building, rising at the center of the island, had symbolized New York's role in the opening up of the American continent, the World Trade Center—standing at the island's southern tip, and looking out upon the great harbor and the ocean beyond—would symbolize the city's new role as command center and clearinghouse for a truly global economy. "David wanted to build an economic development entity," one aide later recalled, "that would also be a symbol of international business." "We don't want to compete with existing office space," the banker himself declared, defending the idea of the specialized, trade-related office complex. "We want to provide some new use. A World Trade Center seems logical and it seems logical to have it near the banks that service the bulk of U.S. foreign trade."

Originally located at the foot of Wall Street, the immense undertaking called for the demolition of thirteen acres of aging low-rise structures along the East River and their replacement by a massive multibuilding complex that would include not only a hotel and exposition space but several office towers, up to seventy stories high—home to banks, insurance firms, shipping lines, cargo companies, telecommunications operations, and dozens of other firms involved in world trade.

Like Rockefeller Center and the United Nations before it, the complex would be an example of what David Rockefeller called "catalytic bigness"—a project whose sheer size and impact would be large enough to provide the stimulus for further redevelopment.

That very scale, of course, also placed it far beyond the reach of even the most ambitious private developers, a circumstance well understood by David Rockefeller himself, who now turned to the one agency in the region with the power and resources to carry out so vast an undertaking: a relatively low-profile but enormously powerful bistate agency called the Port Authority of New York and New Jersey.

Founded in the years after World War I to coordinate the development of the great harbor the two states shared, the Port Authority had been helping to shape the metropolitan region for nearly half a century, building or expanding one gigantic transportation project after another—including the Lincoln Tunnel and the George Washington Bridge, all

three of the region's major airports, the Port Authority Bus Terminal, and, most recently, two revolutionary container ports at Port Newark and Port Elizabeth in New Jersey. Like all public authorities, the agency was a unique hybrid of public and private power, combining the power of the state to issue bonds and condemn private property with the power of a private corporation to pursue only those projects it believed would turn a profit. Indeed, by the late 1950s, under the direction of its ambitious, canny, publicity-shy executive director, Austin J. Tobin, the flood of annual revenues from its bridges and tunnels had made it one of the wealthiest agencies in the world, with almost unlimited lines of credit with which to build still more ambitious efforts.

But a serious stumbling block stood in the way of the Port Authority's involvement with the proposed complex: the agency's charter, which strictly limited its activities to transportation projects or to facilities directly related to shipping and trade. The Port Authority's own lawyers—along with key members of its board—remained deeply skeptical about the agency taking on what early studies were convinced was "primarily a real-estate operation."

It was precisely at this juncture that the full sweep of the Rockefellers' power was revealed. On January 1, 1959—three months after the publication of the DLMA plan—David's brother Nelson was sworn in as governor of New York State. Henceforth, the public resources of the wealthiest state in the nation would be placed at the disposal of the privately sponsored initiative.

Almost immediately, the new governor began filling the Port Authority's board with his own appointees—senior Wall Street executives, for the most part, who could be counted on to share the Rockefeller vision of lower Manhattan's white-collar future. Within a year, concerns within the agency about the project's compatibility with the Port Authority's mission had melted away—and Austin Tobin's staff had set to work on their own proposal for a five-million-square-foot office complex along the East River, just south of the Brooklyn Bridge.

A few voices of protest were raised at the time. In her landmark book, *The Death and Life of Great American Cities*, published in 1961, Jane Jacobs argued that the real problem with lower Manhattan was not its lack of office space but its failure to provide the variety of uses and amenities—housing, restaurants, shops, entertainment, and cultural activities—found in midtown. "Lower Manhattan is in really serious trouble," she wrote, "and the routine reasoning and remedies of orthodox planning merely compound the trouble." "[The DLMA] plans themselves," she added, "are an exercise in cures irrelevant to the disease."

But it was the early 1960s. Urban renewal was on the rise. Around the globe, as the postwar order took hold from

Established in 1921 by an act of Congress, the Port Authority of New York and New Jersey—the first "public authority" ever created in America—represented a striking innovation in the nation's political life: a regionwide planning and development agency, combining aspects of a government agency and a private corporation, that in the years to come would gain a worldwide reputation for its brilliant engineering and fiercely guarded political independence.

Founded to speed the movement of rail freight around the harbor, by the 1930s the agency shifted its focus to the creation of a series of awesome vehicular river crossings: the Lincoln Tunnel and the George Washington Bridge—spectacular engineering achievements that were also an enormous source of profits, whose steadily rising toll revenues (together with those of the Holland Tunnel, whose operation it took over in 1930) dramatically swelled the Authority's coffers. By the postwar years, as its planners and engineers prepared to build the world's largest bus terminal on Manhattan's West Side, a second deck on the George Washington Bridge, and the longest suspension bridge in the world across the Narrows, the Port Authority—now one of the richest agencies of its kind in the nation—had worked with Robert Moses in the immense effort to reshape the entire region around the needs of the automobile.

> *The structure of our surging metropolitan areas today is being shaped almost exclusively by the motor vehicle.... The suburbanite has been freed from his absolute dependence upon fixed rails with their inflexible routes.*
> Austin J. Tobin
> Chairman, Port of New York
> Authority, 1955

In those same years, the Port Authority had begun pursuing an even more ambitious agenda, thanks to the extraordinary vision and drive of its director, Austin J. Tobin. A brilliant political infighter and tireless coalition builder, Tobin had risen to the top of the Port Authority hierarchy in 1942—a post he would hold for the next 30 years—and possessed a passion for large-scale planning and development that rivaled even the Rockefellers'. Little known to the public—certainly in comparison with his great rival, Robert Moses—he was nonetheless a quiet legend in the city's highest corridors of power, and thought by many observers to be even better at getting his way than Moses himself, in part because he chose his battles more carefully.

Among the first to grasp the significance and implications of the new world order, Tobin was determined to make the Port Authority the leading force in the region—if not the nation—in realizing the postwar dream of a truly global economy. Pioneering new ways to transport and transfer goods, he took it upon himself to wrench New York's aging port into the future: taking over and modernizing the region's three major airports, building the nation's first modern air-cargo facilities at Idlewild (later Kennedy) International Airport, and, in the mid-1950s, bringing forth a global revolution in shipping by constructing the world's first container facilities, at Port Newark and, later, Port Elizabeth, on the New Jersey side of the harbor.

"The world stands today on the brink of a new era in international trade," he declared in 1960. By then, his efforts were well under way to disperse the working port to the distant reaches of the metropolitan region, away from the Manhattan and Brooklyn waterfronts, whose narrow piers and crowded market districts could not possibly accommodate the big new freighters and sprawling storage areas needed for containerized shipping, much less the jet cargo planes that were increasingly bringing goods into the region. No less than the Rockefellers, Tobin believed that the future of lower Manhattan lay not in the handling of physical goods but in the transfer of ideas and information: not in the port itself, but in paperwork.

When, that same year, the Downtown–Lower Manhattan Association plan revived the decade-old idea of a world trade center and proposed that the Port Authority "study" its development, Austin Tobin was not only prepared but eager to take on a project he believed would be the ultimate emblem of the city's place at the forefront of the global economy—as well as the crown jewel of the Port Authority's own empire.

Port Newark, New Jersey, the world's first container port, with the twin towers and lower Manhattan in the distance. Visible from the farthest reaches of the metropolitan area, the World Trade Center was intended by the Port Authority to be the symbol and focal point of the modern port of New York, encompassing not only the city itself but the entire bi-state region.

the Far East to Western Europe, the prospects for world trade had never seemed brighter.

In the heady, can-do optimism of the time, the proposed Trade Center was—at least at the outset—almost universally embraced as a dramatic and glamorous step forward for the city, and as a powerful emblem of a cosmopolitan nation on the move.

THE NEW JERSEY PROBLEM

The first great challenge to the World Trade Center came in the spring of 1961, when planners for the Port Authority released their preliminary study for the East River complex—and ran headlong into a political minefield that almost destroyed it.

By statute, any initiative taken by the Port Authority had to be approved by the two states that controlled it, New York and New Jersey; powerful as he was, Nelson Rockefeller on his own could not simply decree that the agency build the World Trade Center. But when the governor of New Jersey, Richard Meyner, surveyed the Port Authority's model, he reportedly turned to Rockefeller and demanded, "What's in it for me?"

Indeed, at first glance, there was little. Located on the far side of Manhattan, facing Brooklyn, the proposed East River complex would not only be invisible from New Jersey but almost inaccessible to the state's commuters. As Meyner saw it, he was being asked to help build a project whose benefits would accrue almost entirely to his mighty rival across the Hudson.

Soon enough, however, Meyner realized there was something in the project for him: a valuable bargaining tool. The governor told the Port Authority that he would grant his approval for the World Trade Center only if the agency agreed to solve one of his own state's biggest headaches: a deteriorating commuter railroad called the Hudson and Manhattan line, connecting lower Manhattan and New Jersey, that had been losing customers for years and was now on the verge of bankruptcy. Averse to subsidizing mass transit projects of any kind, in large part because of the immense debts associated with them, Tobin demurred. But anxious to get the Trade Center project under way, he reluctantly agreed to have the Port Authority take over the old H&M line if Meyner gave his consent for the East River complex.

When word of the proposed swap reached Albany, however, another obstacle arose, as members of the New York State legislature—adopting perhaps a somewhat parochial attitude—questioned the need for New York to finance a money-losing rail operation that brought New Jersey commuters into the city.

Now it was New Jersey's turn to dig in its heels, and by the fall of 1961, the prospects for the World Trade Center

Austin J. Tobin, the quietly ambitious director of the Port Authority, was responsible for expanding the World Trade Center into the largest single urban development project in history.

ever getting off the ground seemed remote at best. At that very moment, however, a Port Authority staff member— to this day no one seems exactly sure who—came up with an ingenious new concept that seemed to offer an end to the impasse.

Among the property owned by the old H&M line was a pair of enormous but decrepit office buildings along Church Street, located directly above the railroad's Manhattan terminus. Port Authority planners realized they had little use for the aging structures and would probably have to demolish the buildings—only to replace them with something else. But what? Suddenly, what had seemed like two unrelated problems appeared as a single solution, and in the last days before Christmas 1961, a group of Port Authority planners locked themselves into a suite at the Gramercy Park Hotel in Manhattan to give shape to the new idea—which, almost miraculously, seemed to satisfy everyone.

In the Port Authority's revised proposal, the Trade Center would rise not along the East River but on a sixteen-acre parcel along the Hudson River, a site that not only faced New Jersey but sat directly atop the H&M railroad, which would be owned and operated by the Port Authority and renamed PATH (Port Authority Trans-Hudson line). As part of the railroad's upgrade, a new PATH station would be built in the lower levels of the Trade Center itself, allowing residents from across northern New Jersey to commute directly into the complex. As a bonus, the new location was adjacent to five subway lines, making it far more convenient for New Yorkers themselves than the East River site would ever have been. At a single stroke, every objection seemed to be answered, and within three months the legislatures of both states had approved the deal.

THE TALLEST BUILDINGS IN THE WORLD

At 6:30 on the evening of February 13, 1962, the newly elected governor of New Jersey, Richard Hughes, signed into law the historic Hudson Tubes–World Trade Center bill.

Three weeks later, Governor Nelson Rockefeller followed suit, but by then Austin Tobin had already set to work, creating an entire new division within the Port Authority empire called the World Trade Department, and appointing a tireless, unswervingly loyal thirty-two-year-old engineer named Guy Tozzoli to oversee every aspect of the massive operation. "You can pick the best of the Port Authority," Tobin told his eager young director, "because this is our greatest project."

The risks involved with the proposed complex were enormous from the start—as were the challenges, many of which grew from the competing imperatives of the project itself. The same charter that required the Trade Center to turn a profit sharply restricted the range of its potential tenants—three-quarters of whom by law would have to be directly involved in the business or servicing of world trade: shipping lines, customs officials, import-export firms, freight forwarders, admiralty lawyers, naval architects, oil traders, commodity brokers.

When studies showed that demand for such specialized office space would be modest at best, Tobin instructed Tozzoli to increase the size anyway, dramatically, to an almost unheard of total of ten million square feet—nearly five times the floor space of the Empire State Building, or more office space than could be found in the entire cities of Detroit, Houston, or Los Angeles. As Austin Tobin and Guy Tozzoli saw it, only by erecting what one journalist later called "the largest building project since the Egyptian pyramids" could they hope to achieve the catalytic effect that David and Nelson Rockefeller sought to accomplish in lower Manhattan.

In the fall of 1962, as word of the expanding scale of the project raced through the Port Authority, the agency's public relations director, Lee R. Jaffe, circulated an internal memo with a fateful offhanded postscript. "Incidentally," she wrote, "if you're going to build a great project, you should build the world's tallest building." The audacious suggestion instantly caught Tozzoli's imagination—and would stay with him in the months to come.

Meanwhile, his immediate task was to find an architect capable of giving shape to the immense project. In the end, passing over the stable of elite architects in New York, Tozzoli settled on a relative outsider—a forty-nine-year-old Detroit-based designer named Minoru Yamasaki, known for his iron-willed diligence and professionalism, and for putting his client's needs ahead of his own ego.

Yamasaki, who had never designed an office building taller than twenty-eight stories—and had built nothing at

Initial plans for the World Trade Center, presented by the Downtown–Lower Manhattan Association in 1960 and revised a year later by the Port Authority, called for the complex to be located along the East River. By 1962, the project site had been shifted to the Hudson River (upper rectangle), in order to meet the objections of New Jersey officials.

all in New York City—was in many ways a curious choice for the project. A thoughtful, soft-spoken man of Japanese descent, he had attempted in his earlier work to soften the harshness of contemporary architecture through the use of delicate decorative elements and finely textured surfaces, an approach that found little favor among prominent critics—including Yale professor Vincent Scully, who had dismissed one of Yamasaki's projects as a "twittering aviary." Yamasaki's appeal to the Port Authority lay as much in what he was not—"a modernist prima donna," one man later said—as for what he was: a collegial, pragmatic, enormously competent practitioner who was also relatively young—not a trivial consideration for a project that many assumed would take up to twenty years to complete.

For nearly a year, Yamasaki struggled to find the right form for the gargantuan project, working on a scale no architect had ever before confronted. "It was a terrifying program from the standpoint of size," he later remembered. "You just run scared before you get adjusted."

In my opinion, this should not be an overall form which melts into the multi-towered landscape of lower Manhattan but should be unique, have excitement of its own, and yet be respectful to the general area. The great scope of your project demands a way to scale it to the human being so that, rather than be an overpowering group of buildings, it will be inviting, friendly and humane.

Minoru Yamasaki, 1963

Experimenting with one model after another, the architect toyed with the idea of using four smaller structures,

To integrate the vast multiblock project with its complex urban surroundings, the architect Minoru Yamasaki (center) ordered the construction of an enormous site model, showing all of the adjacent buildings as well as the preexisting subway and rail lines that ran beneath the streets.

then one gigantic one, but kept coming back to the image of two slender towers, one offset from the other—a design he hoped would combine the practical requirements of the Port Authority's immense program with the sculptural elegance he admired in the work of his greatest influence, the German-born architect Mies van der Rohe (who had himself pioneered the use of twin towers in several projects along the Chicago lakefront).

In the fall of 1963, after exploring 105 different possibilities for the site, Yamasaki—who stood little more than five feet tall, and who was said to suffer from a pronounced fear of heights—presented Tozzoli with his favored design: two towers, each eighty stories tall, rising starkly from a vast plaza surrounded by four smaller structures.

At that height, the towers themselves were still two hundred feet shorter than the Empire State Building—and two million square feet short of the total Tozzoli had asked for—but as Yamasaki explained to his client, eighty stories had long been agreed upon by architects and builders as the practical upper limit for any tall building.

Tozzoli's response was succinct, emphatic, and emblematic of the era, when no goal seemed out of reach of American enterprise and know-how. "Yama," he said, "President Kennedy is going to put a man on the moon. I want you to build me the tallest buildings in the world."

Huddling with his engineers, Yamasaki satisfied himself that the structural and functional obstacles could be overcome, and agreed to increase the size of the towers.

On January 22, 1964, when the final design was presented to the public at a press conference in the New York Hilton, the officials and reporters assembled for the occasion were stunned. Yamasaki's dramatically revised program called for two identical towers, each 110 stories tall—a full one hundred feet higher than the Empire State Building. With every floor more than an acre in size, each tower alone contained nearly twice the floor space of Al Smith's Depression-era landmark.

Even Nelson Rockefeller was astounded by the plan, gleefully confiding to a senior aide, "My God, these towers will make David's building look like an outhouse."

An editorial in the *New York Times* that ran the next day took a more sober view. "Their impact on New York, for better or for worse, economically and architecturally, is bound to be enormous."

TROUBLE

Well, over one thousand businessmen in this area, thirteen square blocks of lower Manhattan . . . will fight this with all the strength that we have in order to preserve free enterprise in Manhattan. We also feel very reluctant about our city giving up thirteen square blocks to the Port Authority.

Sy Sims, 1964

For two years—while the twin towers spiraled ever higher in Minoru Yamasaki's mind, and while the Port Authority's ambitions vaulted upward—down on the streets below a cataclysmic war had broken out for the body and soul of lower Manhattan.

For all the architect's talk about respecting the integrity of the surrounding neighborhood, the Port Authority's plan for the World Trade Center represented one of the largest and most destructive urban renewal projects ever undertaken. Obedient to the ruling orthodoxies of urban planning, it called for the complete elimination of every street and structure on the sixteen-acre site—nearly two hundred buildings in all, home to more than eight hundred small but thriving businesses, including the world's largest concentration of electronics stores, known as Radio Row—and their replacement by two giant superblocks completely alien to the original ecology of the old port city.

For more than half a decade, the controversy over the project raged on, in and out of court, as the Port Authority battled one opponent after another—including the city itself, which stood to lose millions of dollars in property taxes as a result of the project, and television broadcasters, who feared the massive towers would block reception of their signals. By far the longest and most bitter struggle was waged with hundreds of local businessmen, who—under the leadership of an energetic and impassioned radio store owner named Oscar Nadel—fought the impending displacement of their shopping district with every means at their disposal, from legal challenges to street demonstrations, including a mock funeral for "Mr. Small Business-man," featuring Nadel himself in a casket, being carried through the district.

For the last time I might say with respect to the Port Authority: stay out of private enterprise. You were told to build bridges and tunnels—and airports, build them! Stay in your business and we'll stay in ours!

Oscar Nadel, 1964

Stunned by the amount of press attention and public sympathy the local businessmen were generating, the Port Authority soon found itself facing an even more formidable opponent: New York's major real-estate developers, who attacked the World Trade Center as unfair competition, a

Governor Nelson A. Rockefeller (left) and Mayor John V. Lindsay pose for a publicity photograph with a model of the World Trade Center, 1966. Though seemingly eager in this view to claim credit for the twin towers, the newly elected Mayor Lindsay had scarcely been involved with their development, and he remained skeptical about their impact on the city.

In this aerial view of the World Trade Center construction site, taken in late 1968, the beginnings of the north tower are visible, along with the giant concrete "bathtub" wall that rings the western half of the site. On the site's eastern half, beyond the bathtub, stand the last of the older structures that had once filled the area, including one of the Hudson Terminal buildings. They would all be demolished within a year.

state-subsidized boondoggle that would put millions of square feet of space on the open market, drawing tenants away from their own, unsubsidized buildings. Calling themselves the Committee for a Reasonable World Trade Center, the property owners took out giant newspaper ads criticizing the project and brought lawsuits against the Port Authority, hoping to scale down the size of the complex dramatically—an objective of special concern to the leaders of the opposition, Harry Helmsley and Lawrence Wien, owners of the Empire State Building.

In the end, the superior legal and financial resources of the Port Authority—channeled through Tobin's supreme political skills—managed to prevail on every front, striking a compromise with the city to gain approval to close the needed streets and defeating both the major developers and the small businessmen in one court action after another. In December 1965, the New York State Court of Appeals turned back the last challenge to the legality of the Port Authority's condemnations, and just three months later, on the bright, windswept morning of March 21, 1966—as opponents of the project looked on helplessly—the first redbrick structures on Radio Row, which had stood since the time of the Civil War, began to come down.

After more than twenty years, work on the World Trade Center had finally begun.

INTO THE SKY

One of the most poignant of the many ironies surrounding the story of the World Trade Center was that the saga of its physical rise—by any measure one of the greatest engineering feats of the age—would be largely unnoticed at the time and come to be widely appreciated only after its demise.

And yet from the start, the demands of constructing two towers not only taller but far larger than any other in the world would force Austin Tobin's team of builders and engineers to reinvent almost every aspect of skyscraper technology and design, challenging not only the height but the most basic construction principles of their great rival, the Empire State Building, to produce a uniquely vibrant and responsive structure, every aspect of whose form and function would be ingeniously woven into a single, breathing, dynamic whole.

The first difficulty came with the foundations themselves, which would have to descend through seventy feet of water-saturated landfill, some of it laid down in the colonial era, before reaching bedrock. To ensure a dry basement for the towers (and the sprawling underground parking garages that would surround them), engineers decided to construct a gigantic concrete basin around the entire western portion of the site—two blocks wide and four blocks long, with a perimeter of 3,100 feet in all—that they affectionately dubbed "the bathtub."

On August 5, 1966, using a special "slurry" technique borrowed from the construction of the Milan subway, contractors began sinking the giant bathtub wall, three feet thick and seventy feet deep. Upon its completion fourteen months later, workers excavated the vast sunken pit from which the complex would later rise, unearthing haunting reminders that the stark modern structure was rising from some of the city's oldest and most hallowed land: artifacts dating back to colonial New York, including ship anchors, cannonballs, clay pipes, handblown drinking glasses, and British coins dating back to the reign of King George II. (Archaeologists were disappointed to find no trace of a much greater treasure, the Dutch explorer Adriaen Block's ship, the *Tiger*, which according to legend had burned and sunk at the site in 1613.)

In all, 1.2 million cubic yards of dirt—a hundred thousand truckloads—were removed and hauled away, most of it carried no farther than the other side of West Street, where, following an inspiration that had burst upon Tozzoli while shaving one morning, it was dumped back into the Hudson River to create the first twenty-three acres of landfill for one of Nelson Rockefeller's most cherished ambitions: a ninety-three-acre waterfront development called Battery Park City.

But the greatest challenge for the project by far lay in the engineering of the towers themselves, which would stretch contemporary building technology to its very limit and beyond.

From the start, it was clear that the Port Authority's demand for vast expanses of infinitely flexible office space, and the towering sculptural forms Yamasaki had designed to meet it, would require a complete break with the past. To counteract the greatest natural stress on the tall, sail-like towers—the force not of gravity but of the wind—the structural engineers John Skilling and Leslie Robertson reversed nearly a century of conventional skyscraper practice, which had always relied on an interior framework of steel columns and beams to carry the weight of a building, thus reducing the role of the outer wall to a thin "curtain" keeping out the weather. At the World Trade Center, by contrast, a superstrong lattice of exterior steel columns, placed less than two feet apart and locked tightly together at every floor, would transform each tower into a giant "tube" whose remarkably stiff outer structure could readily resist the force of 150-mile-per-hour winds—far higher than any ever known around New York Harbor.

Pioneering the use of electronic computers in building design, Robertson and his team of young engineers exhaustively analyzed the behavior of their proposed structure, whose dynamic response to the wind and weather was in many ways closer to that of an ocean liner or airplane than a traditional building. Wind tunnels and motion simulators

Taken from an upper floor of the north tower in October 1970, this view shows the prefabricated wall sections (each consisting of three steel columns, connected by three rows of horizontal spandrels) rising along the north face of the building—a spot very close to the point of impact of American Airlines Flight 11 31 years later.

similar to those used in the aerospace and automotive industries were employed for the first time to determine exactly how much the buildings would sway—and, no less critically, how much sway would be acceptable to the buildings' occupants. Another innovation was the placement throughout the buildings of eleven thousand motion dampers—shock absorbers capable of carrying two and a half tons each—intended to dissipate the oscillating movements of the towers in high winds.

Before signing off on the design, Robertson—concerned about the extraordinary height and bulk of the towers—performed one last, unprecedented safety check, to make sure that not even a direct hit by the largest jet aircraft of the time, a Boeing 707, would topple the buildings. The calculations the engineers used, reasonable enough at the time, assumed that the airliner, lost in fog and trying to land, would be traveling relatively slowly, and would have largely emptied its tanks of fuel. However remote, such an event was at least conceivable; no one thought to study the consequences of a fully fueled plane being deliberately rammed into the buildings.

At 10:00 a.m. on August 6, 1968, teams of ironworkers began installing the massive bases for the first steel columns

of the World Trade Center's north tower. Within six months, both immense structures had begun to rise at the foot of lower Manhattan.

As innovative in their construction as they were in their design, the towers were assembled not one column or beam at a time but in huge prefabricated components—exterior wall sections three stories tall and floor decks sixty feet long—which could be lifted into place at once, a daring new technique that dramatically speeded the construction process.

Hidden from view as the buildings rose, meanwhile, was yet another new concept, the one that had made the towers feasible in the first place: an ingenious system of local and express elevators, linked by "sky lobbies" at the forty-fourth and seventy-eighth floors, that allowed the local elevators in the upper floors to be neatly "stacked" above those below, thus saving crucial floor space.

The steelwork on the towers took three years in all, from 1968 to 1971, as the turbulent 1960s came and went, and as the war in Vietnam raged on, wreaking havoc with the American economy, straining the postwar global order, and threatening to tear the nation's social fabric apart.

In April 1970, progress on the towers was briefly slowed when scores of construction workers clashed violently with

In this early-morning view, taken by the structural engineer Leslie Robertson, the back-lighted north tower is almost transparent, revealing not the skeleton of a traditional skyscraper but the innovative structural system devised by Robertson and his colleagues, which relied on a dense core at the center of the building and a thick fence of columns on its exterior, with no intermediate columns in between.

antiwar demonstrators on the streets of lower Manhattan. By then, the enormous structures had begun to dwarf even the highest of the district's old art deco towers, and the early optimism stimulated by their sheer size had begun to wane.

And still the towers rose, as the city below them sank deeper and deeper into social and economic distress. At the peak of construction, more than eight hundred tons of structural steel, converging on the site from Los Angeles, Dallas, Seattle, Pittsburgh, Virginia, Georgia, Canada, and dozens of other locations across the continent, were being raised into the sky by four Australian-built "kangaroo cranes" and bolted into place by Austin Tobin's army of 3,600 men—including Carl Furillo, who had once played right field for the Brooklyn Dodgers, and a New Jersey man named George Nelson, who forty years earlier had helped build the Empire State Building, and who shrugged off his work on the World Trade Center as "just another building." The ironworkers also included a group of Mohawk Indians, whose legendary fearlessness had made them a regular presence on the steel frames of New York skyscrapers since the early twentieth century.

Even as the steel was still rising at the buildings' upper reaches, two and three stories a week, workers on the lower stories began installing the 43,600 windows and adding the anodized aluminum panels that gave the towers their distinctive silvery finish. The astonishing logistics of the World Trade Center's construction, one Port Authority engineer recalled, were "like the D-Day invasion, in terms of intricacy of planning and coordination."

Finally, at 11:30 on the cold, foggy morning of Wednesday, December 23, 1970, the final column of the north tower—a thirty-six-foot-long, four-ton piece of steel draped with a large American flag—was hoisted into place on the 110th floor, and workers held their traditional "topping out" ceremony, raising a thirty-foot-tall Christmas tree on the roof's southeast corner. Seven months later, on July 19, 1971, the ceremony was repeated on the south tower.

In all, eight construction workers, none of them ironworkers, had died in the building of the World Trade Center, a toll considered far better than average for a project of its size. A total of 192,000 tons of structural steel—nearly four times that of the Empire State Building—had been raised 1,360 feet into the sky, twenty-five stories taller than the top floor of Al Smith's beloved uptown landmark, and 110 feet higher than the tip of its mooring mast.

And yet to a remarkable degree, the achievement would go all but ignored, obscured by the growing troubles of the city below, and by the chorus of criticism that now began to engulf the project in the months and years following its completion.

WHITE ELEPHANT

[The towers will throw] the whole of Manhattan . . . into a different scale and ruin what is now one of the most exciting spatial arrangements in the world. If the Chase Manhattan Bank building can be challenged for the destruction of Wall Street's consistency, then the twin towers will add the final touches to this fatal feat.

Eighteen City College architecture students,
in a letter to *Architectural Forum*, 1964

From the outset, it had been clear that the design of the twin towers—a pair of simple, identical shafts, rising in sheer, unbroken lines—shared little of the exuberant, upthrusting quality of the Empire State Building, and from the time of the project's unveiling, critics had questioned the impact of the huge buildings on the intricate, ziggurat-shaped skyline of lower Manhattan, probably the most celebrated urban vista in the world. "Must these structures," the editors of the *Daily News* had wondered in 1964, "be the ugly, boxlike things now planned?" "This fearful instrument of urbicide," the *Washington Post*'s architecture critic lamented two years later, "will be not only the tallest, but unquestionably one of the ugliest buildings in the world. . . . The incredible giants just stand there, artless and dumb, without any relationship to anything, not even to each other."

As they rose over the skyline, the overbearing, almost monstrous structures seemed to symbolize perfectly the distant and remote power establishment that had built them, and even before they were complete, New Yorkers had taken to calling the twin towers Nelson and David. In the *New York Times*, Ada Louise Huxtable, whose early enthusiasm for the project had vanished entirely, referred to them as "tombstones."

The towers are pure technology, the lobbies are pure schmaltz and the impact on New York . . . is pure speculation. . . . The windows [are] so narrow that one of the miraculous benefits of the tall building, the panoramic view out, is destroyed. . . . These are big buildings but they are not great architecture.

Ada Louise Huxtable, 1971

As the project neared completion, the volume and intensity of the criticism only increased. The towers' dense exterior walls, with their thick columns and slotlike windows, came in for special attack: effectively fencing off the commanding views from inside the buildings, they made the towers seem utterly scaleless from the outside. "You know they are office buildings," one critic observed, "yet their design makes it nearly impossible to imagine that they are full of *people*." The towers were "a standing monument to architectural boredom," one man wrote, while another dismissed them as "the largest aluminum siding job in the history of the world."

When the complex at last began to open its doors to the public, in the early 1970s, the critics' ire found a new target: the sprawling, labyrinthine public spaces at ground level. Though the World Trade Center layout—a combination of high-rise and low-rise buildings, arrayed around a central plaza—had plainly been intended to recall the urban glories of Rockefeller Center, many observers found the complex distinctly *anti*urban in spirit. Following modern planning principles in full force when the towers were designed but strongly out of favor by the time they opened, Yamasaki had turned the project away from the surrounding streets, placed almost all of its shops and building entrances in an underground concourse (thus leaving its vast central plaza without any real activity or purpose), and utterly eliminated the city's traditional street grid rather than extending and enhancing the grid, as Rockefeller Center had done. For all its height and density, the project—with its parking garages, its enclosed shopping mall, and its ornate, marble-lined lobbies, finished in a style Ada Louise Huxtable ridiculed as "General Motors Gothic"—struck many New Yorkers as fundamentally suburban in character, an alien intruder in the urban landscape of lower Manhattan.

For the Port Authority itself, meanwhile, a more immediate problem loomed, as the World Trade Center—far from being the moneymaker its sponsors had predicted—threatened to descend into financial insolvency. The towers had scarcely begun rising from the ground when it became evident that the project's basic real-estate premise—the desirability of gathering trade-related businesses under a single roof, which had once seemed so "logical" to David Rockefeller—had little basis in reality.

Despite vigorous efforts to promote it, few private tenants signed up—so few, in fact, that Governor Rockefeller had, early on, ordered forty New York State agencies to occupy more than 20 percent of the available office space in the towers, nearly two million square feet in all—a move that improved the project's balance sheet but sharply increased criticism of it as being (in the words of one of the Port Authority's own commissioners) "a vast white elephant." By the early 1970s, the Trade Center, whose final price tag had soared past a billion dollars, was losing between ten and fifteen million dollars a year, with no end in sight.

And though David Rockefeller had once argued that the project would "not compete with existing office space," it was becoming clear that far from revitalizing lower Manhattan, the World Trade Center—now flooding the market with millions of square feet of unwanted office space—was serving chiefly to depress the district's already sagging real-estate fortunes still further.

Dedication ceremony for the World Trade Center in the lobby of the north tower, April 4, 1973.

All of these problems, however, paled compared to the larger troubles that were now engulfing not only the Trade Center itself but the great world metropolis for which it was to have been the crown jewel. Even as the project opened for business, years of mounting social troubles and financial shortfalls in New York had begun to spiral out of control, bringing forth a tidal wave of problems that would culminate in the fiscal crisis of the mid-1970s. The city, which just a decade before, in the heady days of the Trade Center's planning, seemed to have no limits to growth, was now widely perceived as headed for the abyss.

On the rainy, windswept morning of April 4, 1973, while work in the upper floors of the towers continued, the Port Authority held a dedication ceremony for the World Trade Center, a somber event forced by inclement weather to move from the outdoor plaza to the lobby of the north tower. The guest of honor, U.S. Secretary of Labor Peter J.

It was not for nothing that David and Nelson Rockefeller, the grandsons of the founder of Standard Oil, had played so key a role in the creation of the World Trade Center. In fascinating and ultimately chilling ways, the story of oil, in all of its ramifications, would run like a shining black thread through the epic story of the rise and fall of the twin towers.

No modern industrial economy, of course, could run without oil—something John D. Rockefeller had understood with remarkable foresight in the years following the American Civil War, when he assembled the components of the Standard Oil Company to form one of the most powerful and wealthy corporate conglomerates in the world. Among the earliest and most successful international industries, it was oil, of course—more than any other single commodity—that during the twentieth century fueled the machinery and powered the infrastructure of the new global economy increasingly being directed from New York. The sine qua non of modernization, industrialization, and global expansion, the shining substance called black gold would come to lie at the very heart of the conflicts and divisions globalization would exacerbate in the second half of the twentieth century—deeply entwining the fortunes of the United States and other "first world" countries with the fortunes of third world countries and the developing nations of the Middle East.

Nelson Rockefeller, of course, had learned firsthand the intricacies of the international oil business running the Venezuelan subsidiary of Standard Oil for two years before the outbreak of World War II. The World Trade Center itself—which, with his brother David, he had been so instrumental in bringing about—was in many ways the supreme architectural monument to the postwar vision of an infinitely expanding industrial economy, a vision fatefully dependent upon cheap energy, powered by a presumably infinite supply of cheap oil, and concerned neither for the environment, for the finitude of oil reserves, nor for the complex and often unstable economies and cultures of the nations that provided it. With its lights often burning all through the night, the complex's astonishingly wasteful electrical system—which required all the ceiling lights on half of each floor to be turned on or off at the same time—drained more kilowatts per hour than many medium-sized American cities (the buildings themselves, meanwhile, generated so much waste that they had to be equipped with their own sewage treatment plant).

In 1973, the irony was lost on no one when the opening of the immense, oil-guzzling edifice coincided with the first international oil crisis—a crisis that, in many ways, marked the opening of a new and increasingly tense relationship between the oil-dependent industrial superpowers and the oil-producing nations of the Arab world. In the years to come—eager to keep open the pipelines that fed the insatiable demands of an ever-expanding global commercial empire—most American politicians and captains of industry would turn a blind eye to the mounting social, political, and cultural tensions inside the oil-producing nations they did business with.

In a very real sense, however, as the planes bore down on the World Trade Center in the summer of 2001, the lethal cultural dynamic that helped launch them could be said to have been put in motion decades before, to an important degree by the very commodity that had not only raised the twin towers but also made them an all but inevitable target—oil.

Brennan, never showed up. Nor did New York's mayor, John V. Lindsay. Nor—to the astonishment of many of those present that morning—did the man most responsible for the project, Austin J. Tobin. When a reporter later asked him why he had missed the historic ceremony, Tobin replied, "Because it was raining."

In truth, the endless controversies and conflicts surrounding the development of the Trade Center had sapped even Austin Tobin's superhuman energies and drained his vast reserves of political capital. In early 1972, faced with crises on all fronts and watching his support in the two statehouses beginning to crumble (especially in New Jersey, where a new governor named William Cahill, deeply antagonistic to the Port Authority, had recently taken office), Tobin had chosen to step down—thirty years after he had become director of the agency in 1942, and forty-five years after he had first joined the organization as a bright young law clerk in 1927. Since the Port Authority did not move its headquarters to the World Trade Center until the following year, Tobin himself never got a chance to work in the buildings he had labored so long to create.

For the Trade Center, the months after the official dedication would bring only more troubles, especially after the OPEC oil embargo in late 1973, which set off a worldwide energy crisis, devastated international trade, and forced Americans—for the first time in their history—to confront their dependence on a cheap and seemingly endless supply of fossil fuel. Few buildings seemed to symbolize the carefree attitudes of an earlier time more than the twin towers, whose banks of fluorescently lighted offices, rising high into the night sky, now appeared to many not a romantic gesture (like earlier skyscrapers) but an enormous waste of precious natural resources.

Not only in its extravagant use of energy but in its anti-urban planning, its overweening height, and its sheer bravado and arrogance, the World Trade Center had by dint of its decade-long gestation outlived the era that had given it birth, and by the time of its opening in the early 1970s the complex felt to many observers like something of a dinosaur: the outsized yet somehow forlorn symbol of a more confident, expansive era for New York and, in a larger sense, for America itself.

Nothing captured that sense of poignancy more than an incident that occurred a few years after the towers opened, when Guy Tozzoli arranged for his former boss, Austin Tobin, to visit the completed complex. Of all the extraordinary projects he had been involved with in his long career, Tobin had undoubtedly been proudest of the World Trade Center—and now, stricken with cancer and bound to a wheelchair, he was gently guided by Tozzoli to the center of the vast space that would later be named Austin Tobin Plaza in his honor. Asking to be left by himself, the frail, dying man sat in his wheelchair, looking out upon the immense construction he had all but willed into existence—from the gigantic towers themselves, to the customhouse, hotel, and commodities exchanges surrounding the plaza, to the public artworks that he himself had insisted be an integral part of the project, from Masayuki Nagare's dark granite pyramids to Fritz Koenig's gleaming bronze *Sphere*. For nearly two hours, Tobin sat quietly, saying nothing, looking upon the product of almost two decades of vision, daring, and incredible human effort. Then, at last, he turned away and was helped back into his car.

It was the last time Tozzoli ever saw his friend, employer, and mentor, who died a few weeks later, in his home in Manhattan, at the age of seventy-four.

PROMENADE IN THE CLOUDS

The most sublime and transcendent episode in the forty-year history of the World Trade Center would come in the first dark years after its opening, while the city descended into the worst financial crisis of its history and the towers themselves, still unfinished on the uppermost floors, seemed to stand as a painfully extravagant monument to folly and misguided ambition.

The remarkable event had its beginnings six years before, in 1968, when an eighteen-year-old French street performer and novice wire walker named Philippe Petit—waiting in a dentist's office in Paris to have a toothache treated—came across a newspaper illustration of the twin towers in model form, along with a headline announcing the proposed structures were to be the tallest buildings in the world. In an instant, a daring, almost inconceivable thought came into his head.

"They called me," Petit later explained. "I didn't choose them. I am not attracted by the gigantism, but somehow . . . anything that is giant and manmade strikes me in an awesome way and calls me. I could secretly . . . put my wire, freshly acquired—I was still a naive student of the wire—between the highest towers in the world. It was something that had to be done, and I couldn't explain it. . . . It was a calling of the romantic type."

Under cover of a feigned sneeze, the young man ripped the page out of the paper and, embarrassed, made his way out of the office, protracting his dental agony for days. "But what was it to have a toothache for another week," he later recalled, "when what I had now in my chest was a dream?"

For six years following his epiphany, Philippe Petit nurtured his dream, painstakingly perfecting his skills as a high-wire artist, and devouring everything he could find about the twin towers. In early January 1974, he flew to New York City for the first time in his life to put in motion the next elaborate phase of the illegal escapade he now called simply "the coup."

After seven more months of false starts, last-minute reversals, heartbreaking postponements, and maddening delays, the fateful hour finally arrived.

At six o'clock on the evening of Tuesday, August 6, while one group of colleagues made its way up into the north tower, Petit—delirious with exhaustion and seething with the holy madness of his dream—slipped up to the top of the south tower with two confederates posing as deliverymen, carrying with them three crates filled with equipment, including a disassembled balancing pole, wire for rigging, 250 feet of one-inch braided steel cable, and a bow and arrow.

It took all night to complete the complex job of rigging—to anchor and secure as best he could the cable across the 133-foot gap separating the two towers. One thousand three hundred and sixty feet below, Wall Street was just beginning to come to life when, at a little past seven on the morning of August 7, 1974, Philippe Petit stepped onto the slender, thrumming wire that stretched out across the vast shimmering void. "Whenever other worlds invite us," he would later recall, "whenever we are balancing on the boundaries of our limited human condition, that's where life starts. That's where you start feeling yourself living."

Down on the street below, people stopped in their tracks on the way in to work—first by the tens, then by the hundreds and thousands—staring up in wonder and disbelief at the tiny figure, scarcely more than a dot in the sky, walking on air between the two towers. "Somehow I found myself spending forty-five minutes and doing eight crossings," he later said. "And at some point in one of the crossings, I lay down on the wire and looked at the sky, and I saw a bird above me. And . . . I could see that bird pretty high up, and I saw the eyes were red. And I thought of the myth of Prometheus there. The bird was circling and looking at me as if I was invading his territory, as if I was trespassing, which I was."

Within minutes, police officers were dispatched to the roof of the south tower. Sergeant Charles Daniels of the Port Authority Police Department never forgot what he saw that day:

> *After arriving on the rooftop Officer Meyers and I observed the tightrope "dancer"—because you couldn't call him a "walker"—approximately halfway between the two towers. And upon seeing us he started to smile and laugh and he started going into a dancing routine on the high wire. At this time he then went down to one knee and figuring that maybe the presence of Officer Meyers and myself had broke his concentration we stepped to the background and I said for everyone to be quiet. And at this time he laid down on the high wire and, you know, just lackadaisically rolled around*

The French wire walker Philippe Petit crossing the 133-foot gap between the twin towers, 1,360 feet above the street, on the morning of August 7, 1974.

on the wire . . . and dangled his legs over the wire while he was sitting on a wire, which was incredible. . . . And then when he got up he started walking and laughing and dancing. . . . And when he got to the building we asked him to get off the high wire but instead he turned around and ran back out into the middle. . . . He was bouncing up and down. His feet were actually leaving the wire and then he would resettle back on the wire again. . . . Unbelievable really. To the point that we just . . . everybody was spellbound in the watching of it.

Sgt. Charles Daniels, Port Authority Police, 1974

Coming in off the wire, Petit was immediately taken into custody and manhandled down into an underground police station beneath the south tower, where he was formally charged with fourteen misdemeanors—including criminal trespass, disregarding police orders, reckless endan-

germent, and performing without a permit—then besieged by an army of admiring reporters.

The astonishing feat of high-wire poetry was in many ways the highest point in Philippe Petit's life—and in the life of the towers themselves.

To Guy Tozzoli's delight, the exploit made front-page news around the world, and Petit himself became an instant folk hero, nowhere more so than in New York itself. Thanks to the extraordinary outpouring of public adulation for his performance—and Tozzoli's personal intercession—all charges were dropped, and the twenty-four-year-old was "sentenced" to perform his high-wire act for a group of children in Central Park.

Petit himself never lost his deep love for the towers. Immediately after his walk, the Port Authority presented him with a free lifetime pass to the observation deck atop the south tower, where he was asked to sign his name on a steel beam overlooking the great canyon where he had danced among the clouds.

In the years to come, he would return to the breathtaking perch whenever he could, trying without success to relive the amazing walk in his mind—and to catch a glimpse one more time of the seagull he had once seen sailing above him a quarter of a mile in the sky.

It never came.

REBIRTH

Though no one knew it at the time, Philippe Petit's walk through the clouds in August 1974 would mark a turning point not only for the towers but in many ways for the city itself. In the years to come—slowly at first, and then with growing momentum—the fortunes of New York and the World Trade Center would begin to revive and rebound, in a fashion few could have imagined in the grimmest years of the mid-1970s.

The first changes picked up where Philippe Petit had left off—while the city still toiled in the depths of the fiscal crisis.

In 1975, the observation deck atop the south tower was opened to the public for the first time—and almost overnight became one of the most popular tourist attractions in the city. Three hundred and fifty feet higher than the Empire State Building's outdoor deck, the expansive platform afforded a view that seemed to spread across not only space but time itself: from the great natural harbor that had given birth to the city 350 years before, to the five-borough urban colossus that had risen up two centuries later, to the vast metropolitan region—covering six thousand square miles, in thirty-one counties—that was still in the making.

One year later, on July 4, 1976, the nation's bicentennial celebration came to a stunning climax in New York Harbor, where thousands of small boats and dozens of square-

During Operation Sail, the bicentennial celebration held in New York Harbor on the Fourth of July, 1976, 212 sailing ships from 34 countries—including 169 of the largest square-rigged vessels in the world—paraded past the World Trade Center on their way down the Hudson River and into the Upper Bay.

rigged tall ships could be seen parading majestically against the breathtaking backdrop of the gleaming twin towers.

The same summer as Operation Sail, Windows on the World—which the food critic Gael Greene called "the most spectacular restaurant in the world"—opened for business on the 106th and 107th floors of the Trade Center's north tower. For a city that had just escaped insolvency and was still mired in social and economic trouble, the glamorous new rooftop perch, looking out onto the glittering skyline of Manhattan, came as a welcome omen of better times to come. "Suddenly I knew," Greene wrote, "absolutely *knew*, that New York would survive. . . . If money and power and ego could create this extraordinary pleasure . . . this instant landmark . . . money and power and ego could rescue the city from its ashes."

And yet, for all that, even as late as 1979, more than 10 percent of the offices of the World Trade Center still remained vacant, and the Port Authority was forced to acknowledge that its vision of an immense complex dedicated to trade-related businesses had failed to take hold. By then, however, the effects of another momentous shift began to be felt, as a new kind of global economy—built on the foundations of the postwar world order, but exceeding even the most expansive visions of the bankers and lawyers who had designed it—began to pick up speed.

By the early 1980s, new electronic means of conducting transactions were revolutionizing the nature of international business, and New York—whose central business district contained twice the telecommunications capacity of an average foreign nation—soon became one of a handful of "global cities" (along with London, Tokyo, and Hong Kong) that were concentrating unimaginable amounts of capital and resources. The World Trade Center found its true calling at last, as the most prominent and highly visible headquarters for the new worldwide network of financial industries. Year after year, the old state agencies and original trade-related tenants departed the towers, as the Trade Center's unmatched inventory of acre-sized office floors drew one business giant after another—investment banks, stock brokerages, law firms, insurance companies—including Morgan Stanley, Fuji Bank, Aon, Cantor Fitzgerald, and Marsh & McLennan. Many leased an entire floor, and some as many as six floors, at a time.

And it was not only the world's financial system that was becoming more cosmopolitan. By the 1980s, the working population of the World Trade Center was being dramatically transformed, as newcomers from around the globe streamed into New York City in sheer numbers that rivaled—and with a diversity that far exceeded—the great immigration of a century before. Ironically, the very instability of so much of the world during the decade proved a boon for New York City, which now became a destination point

for wealthy businessmen from South America, for Russian Jews fleeing oppression in the Soviet Union, and for refugees from across Southeast Asia escaping the turmoil that had come to a bloody climax after the American departure from Vietnam. Millions of others—from the Caribbean, the Indian subcontinent, and central Africa, from China, Mexico, Greece, Turkey, and literally dozens of other countries—streamed into New York, drawn by the city's new prosperity and by its age-old promise of economic opportunity, now burning brighter than it had in decades. Nowhere was this electric sense of opportunity more obvious than in the World Trade Center itself, whose floors now resembled a miniature United Nations, filled with Sikh computer programmers and Israeli accountants and financial experts in "emerging markets" who themselves hailed from Malaysia and Syria and Uruguay. By the turn of the millennium, the seventy-nine employees at the Windows on the World restaurant would include immigrants from thirty different countries, including Barbados, Ghana, and Bangladesh, while the buildings' army of window washers would include Poles, Yugoslavs, Albanians, Turks, and Irish.

By the end of the 1980s, it had become evident that the global commercial energies set in motion by the United States after World War II had proved more successful than anyone could have imagined. Indeed, in the fall of 1989, what seemed the last major obstacle to the advancing forces of globalization fell by the wayside, as the Berlin Wall came down and with it the threat of the Soviet Union and its Eastern European bloc. Within a few years, these countries—which had seemed so ominous a presence to the architects of the new world order only a few decades before—would themselves become partners in the international commercial marketplace.

We were aiming at one world with free trade. That was our premise twenty years ago.
> Guy Tozzoli
> Director of the World Trade Center,
> on the anniversary of the
> World Trade Center opening, 1993

The first hint for New Yorkers—and for most Americans—that there might be a hidden cost to the world's rapid globalization came on a sunny Friday afternoon in the winter of 1993. A little after 12:00 p.m. on February 26, a group of fanatical Muslim fundamentalists, attacking what they saw as the heart of the society threatening their absolutist belief system, detonated a van filled with explosives in the underground garage of the World Trade Center. The resulting blast blew a five-story crater through the garage, incinerating three hundred cars and sending smoke billowing up through the structure. Six people were killed and hundreds of others injured, as tenants evacuated the towers by the tens of thousands, down fire stairs filled in some cases with thick smoke. But the structure of the towers themselves remained untouched, thwarting the goal of the terrorists, who had, the Port Authority's chief engineer observed, simply built "the wrong kind of bomb."

The significance of the target was obvious. "A car bomb in a street in New York," the terrorism specialist Bruce Hoffman observed soon after the event, "would doubtless have killed more people. But the World Trade Center is a symbol of Wall Street and the Manhattan skyline and the United States itself, and I think that is very important."

The brief, terrible episode was soon all but forgotten as a new boom took hold in the mid-1990s—this one not only bringing a new round of immigrants and prosperity to the city but reasserting its urban values as never before. Even the World Trade Center, so long seen as an alien presence amid the towers of lower Manhattan, was now being integrated into the city's fabric, as fashionable new residential neighborhoods arose to the north and west, and as the construction of the adjacent World Financial Center (designed by the architect Cesar Pelli and built on the Battery Park City landfill created by the excavation of the Trade Center's "bathtub") provided, in the architect's words, "a set of foothills beside the mountain," locking the twin towers into a new urban composition that extended all the way to the vibrant, revitalized edge of the Hudson.

Indeed, by then a new sense of civic order could be felt all across New York. With the election of a former U.S. district attorney and federal prosecutor, Rudolph Giuliani, to the mayor's office in late 1993, a new emphasis on law and order swept through the city, heralding a drop in crime and vandalism so dramatic and rapid that it stunned New Yorkers and visitors from around the world, many of whom had assumed for nearly three decades that high crime rates and antisocial behavior were an inevitable fact of urban life. As New York acquired the unlikely distinction of being by far the nation's safest big city, its relationship to the country—and to the world—began changing yet again. For Americans, New York regained its former status as the national metropolis, a symbol of American aspiration and ambition as it had not been in nearly half a century. For the larger world, the city seemed to present itself as an astonishing example of the social and economic possibilities of a complex, multicultural society. Whatever its tensions and conflicts, New York—the world's most diverse gathering of nationalities, religions, races, and ethnic groups, home to people speaking 180 languages—had become a remarkably safe, secure, and prosperous place, where most people, most of the time, managed to get along on a daily basis without violence or bloodshed. In 2000, the U.S. Census Bureau reported that New York's population—after shrinking for decades—had shot up by more than seven

The location shoot for the 1976 movie *King Kong,* filmed on June 21, 1976, featured the giant creature lying dead in the center of the World Trade Center's plaza after his fall from the top of the towers.

hundred thousand people in less than a decade, topping the eight million mark for the first time in its history. By then, the half-century-old vision of the city as the unofficial capital of the world, with a "world trade center" at its core, had at last seemed to come true—a city that was not only the crossroads of the world, as the postwar architects had intended, but that seemed now to contain the entire world within it.

As the new century began, even New Yorkers once critical of the World Trade Center had, for the most part, made their peace with it, recognizing that while they themselves might prefer the prewar art deco whimsy of the Chrysler and Empire State buildings, for tourists and visitors from around the world the twin towers had become the symbol of modern New York—in no small part because of a new globalizing force whose sheer power and pervasiveness not even the expansive Rockefeller brothers could have predicted: American popular culture. Since the start of the twentieth century, of course, New York had been the nation's media capital, but now the reach of that mass-media machine—American movies, television, popular music, magazines, and, finally, the Internet and World Wide Web—stretched more widely and deeply than ever before. It penetrated every corner of every nation in the world, and brought with it a vision of American life that entered people's imaginations—and often transformed the way they dressed, spoke, thought, and lived—as no occupying armies could ever do. Many found this vision of American culture

The World Trade Center, rising above the clouds. So tall were the towers that occupants on the uppermost floors often experienced different atmospheric conditions from those below and, when preparing to leave their offices, would sometimes call downstairs to find out what the weather was like.

The date . . . now has a certain permanence, graven on our collective memory, like a very few others . . . dates which seem to separate yesterday from today, and then from now. They become the rarest of moments; ordinary people will forever be able to tell you where they were and what they were doing when they first heard the news, as if the terrible deed had happened to them, which in some ways it did.

David Halberstam, 2001

From the very break of dawn, it was obvious that Tuesday, September 11, 2001, would be one of the most beautiful days of the year in New York: a day of "seemingly infinite visibility," one man later said, whose blue sky stretched from horizon to horizon, without a cloud in sight—the unusual, exquisite conditions that pilots call "severe clear."

In the city itself, it was the day of the primary elections, when Democrats and Republicans went to the polls to choose their parties' candidates for the general election, two months in the future. Because of the city's strict term limits rule, Mayor Giuliani's two-term, eight-year tenure was coming to an end, and four Democratic and two Republican candidates were now vying for a chance to replace him. Polls opened across the city at 6:00 a.m., and many New Yorkers planned to stop and vote in their neighborhoods before coming to work that morning.

It was also the first day of classes at many private and parochial schools in the city, and parents across town spent the early-morning hours reassuring their young children—at once excited and nervous at the prospect of starting a new grade—before dropping them off at school entrances.

In every other way, September 11, 2001, seemed a perfectly ordinary Tuesday in New York, a city that had risen from its decades of troubles into an astonishing renaissance that had left it safer, larger, and more prosperous than it had been in almost half a century. "The city was as beautiful as it has ever been," the writer Adam Gopnik observed. "The protective bubble that for the past decade or so had settled over the city, with a bubble's transparency and bright highlights, still seemed to be in place above us."

Downtown, at the World Trade Center, as 7:00 a.m. arrived and rush hour approached, computers automatically directed all fifty-five express elevators in the two towers to descend to the building lobbies, to prepare for the typical morning flood of passengers heading for the upper levels of the buildings. Over the next hour, thousands of New Yorkers boarded the enormous express cars—each capable of carrying more than fifty people at a time—to reach their workplaces: corporate lawyers and civil engineers, stock analysts and commodities brokers, waiters and dishwashers, window cleaners and broadcasting technicians. Soon the buildings had begun to hum with life, though

seductive, thrilling, even liberating. Others envied it, and resented its seemingly unstoppable power. Still others feared it and despised it, and regarded it as the greatest threat to everything they held dear. They vowed to thwart it, any way they could.

At the very heart of that vision, in the end, was New York itself, the supreme urban embodiment of the global culture that the United States had now projected across the earth. And the heart of that image, in turn, was the twin towers, the most familiar buildings in the most familiar skyline in the world, whose size, visibility, and proximity to Wall Street made them the ultimate emblem of the forces of globalization, still making its restless way across the globe.

only a fraction of their typical daytime population of fifty thousand workers and eighty thousand visitors had yet arrived (among other things, the observation deck on the south tower was not scheduled to open for another forty-five minutes). In the spacious 107th-floor dining room of the Windows on the World restaurant, near the top of the north tower, breakfast patrons included Neil Levin, the newly appointed executive director of the Port Authority of New York and New Jersey. A floor below, in the restaurant's bright, well-appointed banquet rooms, an early-morning conference on information technology, sponsored by a British firm called the Risk Waters Group and attended by eighty-seven high-ranking executives from UBS Warburg, Merrill Lynch, and other financial giants, began on schedule, at 8:00 a.m.

At precisely that moment, American Airlines Flight 11— a Boeing 767 filled with eighty-one passengers and eleven crew members—departed Logan Airport in Boston, en route to Los Angeles. Sitting in first class were a thirty-one-year-old Egyptian-born man named Mohammed Atta and four other men who, unknown to the crew or other passengers, were the vanguard of a carefully choreographed terrorist plot involving four different airplanes—departing Logan, Newark, and Dulles airports in the same hour and all bound for the West Coast—that had been in the planning for over a year. The terrorists, part of the fanatical Islamic organization called Al Qaeda, had chosen transcontinental flights to ensure that the planes were loaded with as much jet fuel as possible. They had chosen a midweek day to minimize the number of passengers who might interfere with their plans. And they had chosen a clear day to help them locate their targets, and to ensure maximum visibility for what they were about to do.

About twenty minutes into the flight, the five men, armed with razor-edged box cutters, got up from their seats, attacked passengers and flight attendants, broke into the cockpit, overpowered the flight crew, and took the pilots' seats themselves. Following the student flight training they had received months before, they changed the aircraft's westerly course and headed south for New York.

Around 8:46 a.m., people all across the West Side of Manhattan heard the loud whine of a jet plane coming down the Hudson. Everything about it was wrong. Moving south along a flight path that always heads north, it was traveling far too low—just nine hundred feet—and much too fast, nearly five hundred miles per hour (or more than twice the speed ever permitted for civilian aircraft under ten thousand feet). On West Broadway at Thomas Street, eight blocks north of the Trade Center, a fire truck from the First Battalion had been called out to inspect a gas leak in the street, accompanied by a filmmaker named Jules Naudet, who with his brother Gideon was making a documentary about

life in a city firehouse. Naudet thus happened to be shooting when a fireman first heard the screaming sound and, startled by its intensity, looked up; the filmmaker then instinctively trained his video camera to the south, catching sight of the plane as it emerged from behind a nearby building and headed straight for the top of the north tower.

At 8:46:26 a.m., the big Boeing 767, 156 feet wide and loaded with more than nine thousand gallons of highly inflammable Jet-A aviation fuel, tore into the north wall of the north tower, 1 World Trade Center. At the last minute, the pilot banked the plane slightly—perhaps to ensure it would hit the building, or perhaps to hit several floors at once, maximizing the damage. Smashing into floors ninety-four to ninety-eight—the offices of the financial services company Marsh & McLennan—the aircraft was transformed into a 137-ton missile of aluminum and steel, destroying everything and everyone in its path. The landing gear ripped through the building with such force that it flew out the opposite wall and ended up on Rector Street, five blocks to the south. The plane's heavier parts, including its engines, flew straight into the heart of the building, destroying or seriously damaging half the columns in the core of the structure. Most of the rest of the aircraft was shredded into fragments of aluminum no larger than a person's fist. All ninety-two passengers and crew members on Flight 11, and dozens, perhaps hundreds, of people working on the ninety-fourth to ninety-eighth floors— no one will ever know for sure—were killed instantly upon impact. Witnesses on the upper floors of the south tower were stunned to see balls of fire bursting through windows, followed by desks, files, furniture—and bodies.

For a split second after the collision (as a detailed reconstruction of the morning's events by reporters from the *New York Times* would later reveal), nothing in the building moved. On the ninety-first floor, just three stories beneath the impact, a naval architect named Steve McIntyre, sitting in his office at the American Bureau of Shipping, heard the terrific explosion above him and was startled to see everything on his desk, from family pictures to a heavy stone paperweight in the shape of a ship, remain perfectly in place. A moment later, however, the tower's three hundred thousand tons of steel and concrete began to lurch to the south as a shock wave ripped through the building from top to bottom. The huge structure swayed in one direction for four long seconds—then swayed back for another four—then repeated the terrifying motion another five times, like a ship heaving in rough seas.

Astonishingly, the tower stood. Though a giant gash now ran across much of the north wall of the building—severing no fewer than thirty-five of that wall's fifty-nine columns—the building's steel frame redistributed the load to undamaged columns on either side of the enormous

As office workers watch helplessly from the upper floors of a building in lower Manhattan, United Airlines Flight 175 approaches the south tower at nearly 600 miles per hour.

opening and managed to maintain its integrity, as engineers had foreseen it would decades earlier. That simple structural miracle would mean that nearly everyone below the ninety-second floor—six or seven thousand people, or more—would escape with their lives.

But no one had ever planned for the willful attack by a jet plane loaded with fuel, which now meant that everyone above the point of impact was doomed—as was the tower itself. At the moment of impact, three thousand gallons of jet fuel ripped out of the plane's wing tanks, atomized in the air, and—ignited by friction, sparks, and short circuits in the building's wiring—burst into a giant fireball that exploded through the northern, western, and eastern walls of the building. Though it stunned everyone who saw its explosive force, the spectacular ball of flame—which burned off about a third of the plane's fuel load, and vaporized anyone unlucky enough to be caught in its path—nonetheless did relatively little structural damage to the building. It was

the six thousand gallons still remaining that proved fatal, as they began making their lethal way through the building, pouring down stairways and elevator shafts into hallways and offices on floor after floor, igniting everything in their path: carpet, curtains, desks, chairs, paper, phones, computers. Like all modern high-rises in New York, the World Trade Center boasted an extensive fire-suppression system—a network of sprinklers, standpipes, and water hoses capable of putting out the worst possible fire that could ever be fed by the interior furnishings alone. But those systems had never been designed for a fire fed by a full planeload of jet fuel, a fire that reached temperatures as high as 2,000 degrees Fahrenheit. And in any case, that fire-suppression system had itself been destroyed or rendered useless. Ripping through the building, the aircraft had cut nearly all of the structure's lifelines, severing the water pipes that supplied the sprinklers and hoses, as well as disabling all of the elevators and blocking all three staircases.

The building's structure had performed magnificently. But nothing could stop the inferno now building up inside from sealing the tower's fate.

On the floors nearest the plane's impact, tenants who were still alive made a desperate scramble for the emergency stairs. On the ninety-first floor, Steven McIntyre made his way to the least damaged of the tower's three stairwells, in the northwest corner of the building's core, and was stunned to see that the gypsum wallboard that normally protected the staircase had been completely ripped from its metal framing, leaving the staircase exposed and filled with scattered debris. Looking up, he saw the stairway to the floor above was completely blocked. Though he had no way of knowing it at the time, McIntyre was looking at the dividing line between life and death. Beneath him lay ninety floors of offices, whose thousands of tenants were already beginning to make their way down to the street, frightened and shaken but otherwise unhurt. Above the obstruction were 1,344 people on nineteen floors, most of them still alive and many of them uninjured—none of whom would live. McIntyre himself stood at the very edge of survival; he and most of his colleagues at the Bureau of Shipping were able to make their way through the debris-filled staircase and escape. But just one floor above, on ninety-two, employees of Carr Futures, attempting the same maneuver, were unable to get out. Conditions were even worse higher up. As the fires raged, thick black smoke began to fill the topmost floors of the building, making it almost impossible to breathe, and reducing visibility to less than ten feet. People began gravitating to the hundreds of broken windows, bending their bodies into space a thousand feet up, desperate for air. Police in helicopters could see an even more terrifying sight behind the windows that had not broken—"about 50 people," one officer later reported, "with their faces pressed against the window, trying to breathe."

From almost the moment that Flight 11 hit the north tower, the city's phone lines had been flooded with calls from New Yorkers reporting the incident to the 911 emergency response center in downtown Brooklyn, and now officials gave the order to activate the city's new emergency operations center—located, ironically, in 7 World Trade Center, just across the street from the twin towers. The center had been a special project of Mayor Giuliani, who during his time in office had been deeply concerned—in the eyes of his critics, obsessed—with the city's capacity to respond to major security risks. Thanks to his preoccupations, no city in the country and perhaps the world was better prepared for a terrorist incident than New York, and in the wake of the attack, the speed and scope of the city's response was stunning. Within one minute of the plane's impact, firefighters were on their way to the site. Within three and a half minutes, officials ordered all bridges and tunnels leading into Manhattan to be secured for the use of emergency vehicles, and initiated police procedures for crowd control in the area. Within ten minutes, the fire department's central dispatcher declared a "level-five" alarm, the highest possible; all local hospitals were informed of the disaster and told to prepare for large numbers of incoming patients; and every available ambulance was dispatched to the vicinity of the Trade Center. Within half an hour, the Statue of Liberty, United Nations, and Empire State Building would be evacuated, the region's three airports shut down, and the airspace over New York declared off-limits to all private traffic.

As the initial firefighters reached the scene (including the Rescue 2 company from Brooklyn, who managed to receive the alarm, suit up, race through the Brooklyn-Battery Tunnel, and arrive at the towers in less than fifteen minutes), they quickly established a command post in the lobby of the north tower and prepared to do what firemen in New York have always done: head straight into the inferno to put out the flames or, failing that, to save as many lives as possible. But the crews quickly determined that the impact of the plane had disabled every one of the building's ninety-nine elevators, which left no alternative but the daunting prospect of climbing up ninety flights of stairs, each man carrying more than sixty pounds' worth of gear—hatchets, shovels, oxygen tanks, pickaxes—and negotiating the same steps that thousands of occupants were now using to make their way out of the building. As the first men began making their way up the stairs, the thousands coming down made room for them, thanked them, wished them good luck—and continued their escape.

Nearby, the big underground shopping concourse at the foot of the towers was rapidly emptying out, as nearly everyone who had been there at the time of the attack quickly made for the exits. Marco Haber, a writer for Marsh & McLennan—who on a typical day would have been at his desk by 8:50 a.m.—had run into an acquaintance in the subway and had joined him for breakfast in a coffee shop in the concourse. Following a mob of people out onto the street, he was puzzled to see small bits of paper raining down. "The first paper that I saw close up," Haber recalled, said "Marsh—right there, the letterhead." It had fallen from his own company's office, a hundred stories up. Others watched in terror as pieces of concrete began falling from the building, some the size of an alarm clock, one man recalled, others the size of a desk.

Meanwhile, the thousands who remained in the undamaged south tower of the complex, 2 World Trade Center, could only look on in horror at the awful scene outside their windows. They could feel the heat on their faces from the fires roaring through the other building, 130 feet away—"like an oven door," recalled a secretary named Marissa

Panigrosso, who worked in the offices of the Aon company on the ninety-eighth floor. "There has been an explosion in World Trade One," an office worker named Sean Rooney said in a phone message to his wife, "that's the other building. It looks like a plane struck it. And it's, it's—horrible."

From the very moment Flight 11 flew into the north tower, people all over New York began calling each other, sending e-mails, and frantically posting online, trying to communicate what was happening in their city. All over the region, people looked out windows, or climbed onto their roofs, or went into the street for a better view—the World Trade Center being the most visible building not only in the city but in the entire metropolitan area, home to more than twenty-five million people. Many witnesses assumed at first that it was simply a horrible accident, one that recalled the July 1945 crash of an Army B-25 bomber into the upper stories of the Empire State Building. Others wondered immediately how it was possible for an airline pilot to accidentally fly into a building on a sparkling clear morning. It was not long before the three major television networks—all headquartered in New York—and global cable channels such as CNN established live video feeds, broadcasting the riveting sight not only to viewers across the city but also across the whole country and, just as quickly, the whole world. In little more than ten minutes, the remarkable worldwide communications system that had arisen in the past three decades was fully up and running—a fact that was about to take on a new and horrendous significance. For it would soon become apparent that the attack of Flight 11, despite the inconceivable devastation and carnage it had wrought, was in some sense merely the prologue or stage setter, as the terrorists had surely intended, drawing the attention of the entire world—in real time—to what was about to happen. In tracing the rise of modern urban civilization, scholars have pointed to three new technological and cultural forces that came to the fore in New York in the 1920s, each exemplifying what the cultural historian Ann Douglas has called air-mindedness, New York's infinite capacity for ambition and upward mobility: skyscrapers, airplanes, and the broadcast media. In a kind of awful inversion, the terrorists had already set one of those forces against another in order to fulfill their goal of wreaking maximum havoc—and were about to enlist the third to spread the psychological impact of that havoc as broadly as possible.

At 9:02 a.m., a public address message was broadcast throughout the south tower urging tenants to stay in their offices, a decision made on the assumption that it would be less dangerous to remain in the still-intact tower than evacuate outside into a rain of falling debris. An employee named Stanley Prainmath, who had evacuated the building, had already returned to his office at Fuji Bank on the eighty-first floor when his eye caught something outside the window, to the south—a jet, flying far too low, racing across New York Harbor, passing the Statue of Liberty, then growing larger and larger, until Prainmath could clearly see its gray fuselage with a big "U" and "A" logo on its side. It was United Airlines Flight 175, which had departed Logan Airport fourteen minutes after Flight 11: another Boeing 767, also bound for Los Angeles and also holding five terrorists. It was now racing at a blistering 586 miles per hour across the Upper Bay, piloted by a twenty-three-year-old man named Marwan al-Shehhi from the United Arab Emirates, who, with his partners, had hijacked the plane above New Jersey and looped around to approach from the south.

For those thousands looking up from the streets below, or the millions more watching the scene live on television, the plane appeared to come out of nowhere—a sudden blur that seemed to move as fast as a rifle bullet, and seemed equally impossible to deflect or stop. At 9:02:54 a.m., before anyone could react, the huge plane sliced into the south face of the south tower, not in the center of the building this time, but toward the eastern edge—a difference that would have immense consequences for the structural fate of the building. At the last minute, the pilot had banked the plane to the left, more sharply than at the north tower, spreading the impact zone from the seventy-eighth to the eighty-fourth floors, seven stories in all.

As before, the plane's ten thousand gallons of aviation fuel exploded instantly into a vast fireball that turned the remnants of the plane into white-hot fragments of metal. The higher speed of the second plane meant that the kinetic energy it released was half again greater than that of the first attack, deflecting the enormous steel structure for several seconds to the north and west, straining every beam, column, and connection before it bent back again.

The plane's fuselage and wings, cutting a path this time not into the dense core of the building but into relatively open expanses of office space, acted like giant plows, pushing everything toward the northeast corner of the floor and sending fragments of the plane flying out the north side of the building as far as Murray Street, six blocks uptown. The fireball, even bigger than the first, exploded out of three sides of the building—a searing, brilliant cloud of orange and gray and black that once again consumed about a third of the plane's fuel, sending the rest flowing into the plumbing risers and elevator shafts, burning as intensely and unstoppably as in the north tower. In all, the heat energy released by the attack was estimated to be upward of five billion watts, more than three times the energy output of a standard nuclear power plant. Yet here too, despite the severing of thirty of the fifty-nine columns along its south face, the tower managed to stand. The thick fence of exterior columns,

New Yorkers race up Church Street, six blocks north of the World Trade Center, to escape the giant billowing cloud of dust and debris brought on by the collapse of the south tower.

firmly linked by heavy steel spandrels on every floor—a design built to resist the worst hurricane winds imaginable—allowed the exterior to efficiently redistribute its load to undamaged columns on either side of the seventy-foot-wide gash, effectively forming an arch over the hideous opening.

Though the impact of the plane instantly killed everyone on board as well as scores of others in the building, a few people near the center of the impact zone somehow managed to survive the huge explosion—including Stanley Prainmath, who, through the door frame of his office, could glimpse the surreal sight of one of the plane's wingtips burning just thirty feet away. He ran across the wrecked floor to the fire stairs, but found the entrances to all three completely blocked with debris. Then he caught sight of a flashlight shining through a break in the damaged wall of a stairwell and, pounding on the gypsum-board surface, caught the attention of a fellow worker named Brian Clark, who was inside the staircase. Together, the two men slammed their bare hands through the gypsum board until they could carve an opening large enough for Prainmath to squeeze through to safety.

The scene was grimmer still on the seventy-eighth floor, one of the building's "sky lobbies," which had been filled moments before the impact with hundreds of people waiting, more or less calmly, for the express elevators that would take them to the ground floor. In an instant—and seemingly out of nowhere—the left wingtip of the second plane sliced through the space, killing more than a hundred people in a matter of seconds. One woman, named Mary Jos, amazed to find herself severely injured but still alive, managed to crawl over the bodies of her co-workers, determined to find a way out. Higher up in the building, employees who could see that there was no escape now used their last minutes to make final plans. Edmund McNally, an employee at Fiduciary Trust on the ninety-seventh floor, spoke on the phone with his wife, Liz, reviewing his life insurance and employee bonus plans, even as the floors above him were beginning to buckle. "He said that I meant the world to him and he loved me," she recalled. Then McNally hung up—only to call back a minute later to mention that he had made reservations for a holiday in Rome for her upcoming birthday: "Liz, you have to cancel that," he said.

In the upper floors of the south tower, time as well as space created a sharp dividing line between life and death. Almost all of those who decided to leave immediately after the first tower was hit survived; most of those who stayed died. Many who were only mildly injured sought to help others before they descended themselves, only to be lost alongside them. Edgar Emery patiently led five colleagues down a stairwell, encouraging a co-worker named Anne

Foodim, who had recently undergone a series of chemotherapy treatments and was worn out by the climb down. "If you can finish chemo," he said, "then you can get down those steps." After making sure everyone was safe, Emery made his way back upstairs to find other colleagues who might be in trouble. He was never seen again.

In both towers now, thousands of people on the lower floors were making their way downstairs, walking calmly, in single file, in order to leave room for the firemen heading upstairs. (In the wake of the 1993 bombing, the Port Authority had substantially enhanced the safety features of the complex, and insisted on regular evacuation drills.) "Dozens and dozens of firefighters were running past us," an office worker named Julie Davis said, "telling us to stay calm and keep moving. I remember looking into their eyes, thinking how brave they were." The evacuees included a blind man named Mike Hingson who, with his seeing-eye golden retriever, Roselle, was working his way down the crowded stairwell from the seventy-eighth floor of the north tower, where everyone moved to the side to make way for the pair. The crowd also made way for burn victims, some walking "like zombies," one man later said, with clothes and skin peeling from their arms and faces. As people exited the north tower, they saw—or tried to avert their eyes from—the awful sight of the plaza strewn with dozens of bodies, including a number still wearing wide black seat belts, passengers on Flight 11. "There were corpses everywhere," a lawyer named Quinlan Kato recalled. Everything in sight—bodies, trees, the plaza surface itself—was covered in a thick layer of gray dust. So real was the danger of being hit (one firefighter was killed when a falling body slammed on top of him) that most evacuees were told to escape by way of the underground concourse.

Less than an hour after the initial impact, it had become obvious that this was a day like no other in the history of New York City, or America, or for that matter, the world. In the city, ordinary life had all but ceased, as millions of people stood transfixed by a sight they could scarcely comprehend—both towers of the World Trade Center burning like some kind of fantastic chimney, sending a thick shroud of black smoke wafting across lower Manhattan and Brooklyn. Within the hour, in almost every town and village around the country and the world, daily life would slow or stop, as people huddled in front of televisions, horrified yet mesmerized by the situation unfolding in New York as they watched.

And suddenly there was more horrific news to absorb. At 9:38 a.m., the Pentagon in Washington, D.C., was hit by a third plane—American Airlines Flight 77, which had taken off from Dulles Airport bound for Los Angeles but had reversed course over Ohio, headed back to Washington, violated the "no-fly" zones protecting the nation's capital and rammed into the western face of the giant military complex, killing everyone on board and 126 people working in the building. And reports soon arrived of yet another crash, this one in rural Pennsylvania. Hijackers had commandeered United Airlines Flight 93 from Newark to San Francisco and were headed straight for Washington—presumably to destroy the Capitol or the White House—when a group of passengers, hearing about the Trade Center attack on their cell phones, had decided to foil the terrorists' plot any way they could. The plane had gone down in an empty field near a town called Shanksville; everyone in it had been killed instantly. For the first time in the nation's history, at 9:40 a.m., officials of the Federal Aviation Administration ordered every airliner over the United States to land immediately—more than four thousand planes in all—and shut down the country's entire airspace.

Americans could not believe what was happening—and with good reason. Not since the British invaded Washington, D.C., during the War of 1812, 187 years earlier, had the mainland of the United States been attacked by a foreign power. The terrorists had targeted the prime centers and symbols of American economic and political might—Wall Street and Washington—but fate and the heroism of the passengers on Flight 93 had managed to limit the damage in the nation's capital, leaving the country's biggest city to bear the brunt of the attack.

In New York, all eyes now turned to Mayor Rudolph Giuliani, who had raced downtown from a midtown meeting after the first tower was hit. In a measure of how unimaginably devastating the attack had been, the staff of the city's new high-tech emergency command center in 7 World Trade Center had itself been forced to evacuate; the mayor and his deputies attempted to set up a temporary office at 75 Barclay Street, just north of the twin towers, but the building was so badly damaged by the second attack that for a terrifying fifteen minutes the mayor and his aides were trapped by debris. Yet when he finally emerged, covered with dust and ash, the mayor remained remarkably calm and firmly in command—setting the tone for what by common consent would be his finest hour, and one of the most extraordinary demonstrations of leadership in memory. In statements that were invariably authoritative and carefully factual, the mayor neither heightened the public's fears nor minimized them, offering a much-needed sense of reassurance even as he made plain that he, too, was emotionally devastated and stunned by what had happened. Seeming to intuitively sense the deepest feelings coursing through the city, his comments remained perfectly on-key throughout the disaster, at times achieving a striking eloquence. Asked to estimate how many casualties were expected, he refused to hazard a guess and instead simply answered, "more than any of us can bear."

"Who knew Giuliani was Churchill?" one New York newspaper headline wondered a week or so later, revealing the complex feelings of surprise and awe shared by almost everyone in the city. "Seen up close," *The New Yorker* magazine observed, "it is possible to sense the real source of [Giuliani's] authority: he lacks imagination, genuinely does not care about appearances, is not self-conscious about the effect he is making, and has the crucial ability to know just how grave things are and, at some decent level, not to be overwhelmed. . . . Giuliani rises to the occasion because he is not ruled by a sense of occasion. He is not a good actor. He is just a public man, a mayor."

As the mayor was the first to point out, however, his courage was only a reflection of that being shown by the city's uniformed personnel—the firefighters and police officers and emergency workers—as the disaster continued to grow worse. With more than a hundred fire engines now surrounding the World Trade Center, firefighters continued to rush into the buildings, hoping to help in any way possible. When fireman Peter Biefield, suiting up outside his truck, was asked "How's it going?," by an old friend, he answered, "We're going into the burning towers, what else?" He then put on his helmet and walked into the complex, headed for the south tower. He would never emerge.

After nearly an hour of continuous burning, the fires in the south tower had grown so intense that on the northeast corner of the building, a stream of molten metal could be seen pouring down from the broken windows of the eightieth floor. It was the aluminum of the plane's fuselage and wings, heated beyond the metal's 1,220-degree-Fahrenheit melting point and literally turned into liquid. Those fires were now having a lethal effect on the building's structure—especially, many experts would later conclude, on its most vulnerable elements: the long steel trusses linking the columns of the outside wall to those at the center of the building. Located underneath each floor, the trusses served not only to carry the weight of the office floors but to provide crucial bracing for the building's outer columns, keeping them from buckling under the enormous load of the structure above. They were fireproofed with a sprayed-on coating of mineral fiber, but much of that covering had been jarred loose by the initial impact, leaving

Pedestrians in Times Square, watching large-screen projections of the burning towers. Almost from the moment the first plane hit the north tower, images of the disaster in lower Manhattan were being beamed, in real time, to every part of the world—and every corner of the city itself.

the open, weblike trusses exposed to the intense heat, which was steadily robbing the steel of its strength. As the trusses sagged, engineers would later speculate, they began pulling away from their connections, fatally uncoupling the building's structural system. Whatever the precise sequence of events within, at a few moments after 9:58 a.m., along the east wall of the eighteenth floor, the building's exterior columns began buckling, initiating a catastrophic process that, once begun, could not possibly be stopped. Moments later, as witnesses below looked on in staggered disbelief, the top thirty stories of the south tower suddenly twisted to the east and south, and the entire building began to collapse, each floor slamming down on the floor below it and causing that floor, in turn, to fall onto the one below—a phenomenon known as pancaking. Fifty-six minutes and ten seconds after being hit, the south tower—1,362 feet in height—came down at a speed of 125 miles per hour, equivalent almost to the rate of free fall. From start to finish, the building's collapse took less than fifteen seconds.

Hit after the north tower, the south tower had fallen first because of the greater force of the second attack and because of the location of the impact: to one side rather than at the center of the building, and more than ten stories lower, thus causing a far greater load—110,000 tons versus 45,000 tons—to bear on the damaged portion of the structure.

As the quarter-mile-tall structure dissolved into a massive shroud of smoke and dust, thousands of people who had been massed around the base of the towers and on nearby streets—looking on with horrified fascination—now ran for their lives, trying to keep ahead of the billowing cloud that had begun to race down the surrounding streets and avenues after them.

A firefighter named Rick Picciotto, hearing on the radio that the south tower had collapsed, yelled into the microphone, uncomprehending, "What tower, what tower? The TV antenna on the north tower, a water tower, what tower?" The response over the channel was unbelievable: "The entire south tower."

Within minutes the smoke began to clear slightly—revealing the bizarre sight of the north tower, standing all by itself, still burning. The last people coming down the north tower's stairs had heard a strange groaning noise that lasted more than a minute—a sound they did not realize was the collapse of the other building. "I'm sure the firefighters knew from their radio what had happened," a Port Authority engineer named Stewart Sloan said, "but they didn't tell us, and they stayed at their posts to guide us out."

By a few minutes after 10:00 a.m., the only people left in the north tower below the ninety-sixth floor were firefighters, who, realizing with infinite frustration that their task was hopeless and that the north tower was in danger of imminent collapse, began themselves to evacuate the building. But on the seven highest occupied floors of the north tower—101 to 107—more than a thousand people still remained. Some had tried to make for the roof, recalling that in 1993, police helicopters had rescued people from the top of the north tower, and unaware that the Port Authority and fire department, fearful that the intense heat and smoke rising from the building would endanger pilots, had decided not to attempt a rooftop evacuation. Those who sought to escape upward had met with a terrible discovery. "I've gone to the roof and the rooftop doors are locked," an office worker named Frank Doyle reported to his wife. "You need to call nine-one-one and tell them we're trapped."

And then there were those who, unable to withstand the flames and heat, made perhaps the most horrific decision of all. It had begun soon after the building was hit. On the 104th floor, stockbroker Andrew Rosenblum was on the phone with his wife when he suddenly said, "Oh, my God." He had seen the first bodies start to fly by outside the window. An hour later, dozens were falling to their deaths—including some who may have deliberately jumped to avoid being burned or asphyxiated, and others who may have been pushed out, unintentionally, by people piling up behind them at the broken windows, desperate for air. "I saw three people jump holding hands," a construction worker named Tony Bristow recalled. "Then the wind took them in different directions. It was boom, boom, boom, as they hit different buildings coming down." A writer who lived thirteen blocks north of the towers described the incredible sight to a reporter:

> When I went up to the roof, a bunch of workers and residents from our building said, "People are jumping," and I didn't believe them. I looked with my binoculars, and what they were saying were people were clearly debris—sheets of metal, chairs, unidentifiable stuff, and then a . . . oh God, a man in khakis and an open suit jacket, feet up in the air, falling down the side of the building facing the river, three, four, five seconds, vanished between a low silver-skinned building and World Trade No. 7 in the foreground. Then more people began to jump out the river side of the tower, and then out the front, where they fell against the backdrop of windows, almost in sequence, like paratroopers bustling out of an aircraft.

At 10:28 a.m., the television antenna atop the north tower began to give way, followed a fraction of a second later by the upper floors of the building itself. "I turned around and watched the top of my building coming down," recalled Stewart Sloan, who had made it to safety. "I stood and watched one floor after another, after another, after another." Eight feet taller than its twin, the north tower fell in about the same amount of time, throwing up a similar mountain of debris, smoke, and dust. But unlike the south tower, whose exterior columns had given way, the north tower had collapsed from within, as its core of structural columns, weakened by the intense heat and the devastating damage caused by the impact, finally buckled and fell. It had taken 102 minutes.

Looking at the mountain of smoldering, burning wreckage that stood where the towers had just been, a tenant named John Maloney said, "I don't know what the gates of hell look like, but it's got to be like this. I'm a combat veteran, Vietnam, and I never saw anything like this."

With the collapse of the second tower, a strange calm descended over much of the city, especially on the blocks north of Fourteenth Street, where the streets, normally filled with cars and trucks, were almost empty. Things were quieter still below Houston Street, which had been declared off-limits to everyone except local residents. But below Canal Street, the upper boundary of lower Manhattan, the city was a disaster zone, the streets filled with thousands of emergency personnel—firemen, policemen, medics, and volunteers—and hundreds of vehicles, including dozens of ambulances, standing at the ready. And below Chambers Street, and west of Broadway, the blocks surrounding the Trade Center were transformed into an eerie moonscape, streets and buildings covered in two to three inches of dust and filled with chunks of debris. At the corner of Church and Murray streets, near an abandoned bagel cart, stood a giant twisted cylinder of metal that, passersby realized with a shock, was an engine from the jet that hit the south tower.

At the city's downtown hospitals—Beekman, Bellevue, St. Vincent's, New York University—thousands of doctors and nurses had been alerted and trauma rooms mobilized to receive a flood of injuries. On the sidewalks outside stood dozens of orderlies with stretchers, waiting for the first wave of ambulances. But the wave never arrived, and relatively few patients came in. "Those who got out, got out," one nurse explained. "Those who didn't, they died."

By eleven o'clock, thousands of people, dazed and terrified and covered in dust, were making their way on foot from the Trade Center, many heading for the Brooklyn Bridge, others straggling up the West Side Highway. "There are no words to describe this," the CBS anchorman Dan Rather observed, as he watched the hordes of gray figures clutching water bottles and staggering down the sidewalks. Tens of thousands were evacuating the rest of lower Manhattan, crossing the East River bridges to Brooklyn and Queens, walking dozens of blocks to midtown and the Upper East and West Sides, catching ferries to New Jersey.

By the early afternoon, New Yorkers—cringing at the fresh sound of jet engines above—looked up to see something they had never seen in their lives: American F-16

fighter planes, soaring above Manhattan, attempting to protect the city from further attacks. Meanwhile, the USS *John F. Kennedy* and the USS *George Washington*—giant aircraft carriers, escorted by eight additional warships—were steaming at top speed from Newport News, Virginia, ready to enter New York Harbor and protect the homeland for the first time in modern history.

All afternoon, people kept looking downtown, amazed not by what they saw but by what they didn't—the twin towers, which had been a fixture in the Manhattan skyline for more than three decades. All that remained now was a giant column of smoke, as the ruins of the buildings continued to burn with incredible intensity. A southwesterly wind carried the smoke across lower Manhattan and Brooklyn, along with thousands of papers from the offices of the Trade Center. For the rest of the day, and into the next, people in Brooklyn found their backyards and sidewalks littered with memoranda, business correspondence, and fragments of financial and engineering reports from the companies that had occupied the upper floors of the towers.

By the middle of the afternoon, all of the buildings in the Trade Center and the immediate vicinity had been completely evacuated, including several that had been seriously damaged by the avalanche of steel and concrete that came down when the towers collapsed. The Marriott Hotel, adjacent to the towers, had been all but destroyed, as were a number of the lower buildings in the Trade Center complex. Fires had been raging within 7 World Trade Center for hours, and officials now cleared everyone from the area, warning that its collapse was imminent. It took several more hours, but at 5:20 p.m., the forty-seven-story building finally came down, creating yet another eight-story mound of smoldering rubble. In time, it would be the failure of Number 7—which unlike the towers had not been hit by a plane—that would puzzle engineers and investigators the most. Never in history had a steel-frame building collapsed from a fire alone. Though inconclusive, later investigations would point to a giant tank of diesel fuel placed on a lower floor of the building, to provide a backup source of power for the mayor's emergency command center.

All seven buildings in the World Trade Center—comprising twelve million square feet—had been destroyed. Another nine million square feet of space, located in surrounding buildings, had been rendered unusable without substantial reconstruction. In less than two hours, twenty-one million square feet of office space had been lost, a total greater than that found in the downtowns of most major cities in the United States.

But as unimaginable as the physical damage had been, it was the toll in human life that was on everyone's mind as the sun began to set that day. Estimates ran as high as six thousand dead, and based on that number, officials in New

Because of fears that the sound of heavy machinery would drown out the cries of victims trapped in the rubble, the early phases of rescue work were done almost entirely by hand, by long chains of volunteers reminiscent of traditional bucket brigades.

New York City firefighters searching the ruins of the World Trade Center.

York placed an initial order for six thousand body bags, praying they would not need more.

As time went on, as accurate counts were obtained and duplications were eliminated, the number would decrease, to five thousand, then four, then three. In the end, the confirmed toll for the World Trade Center attacks would be 2,792 men and women, including 156 passengers aboard the two airplanes. It would remain the second single deadliest day in American history—surpassing the casualties of Pearl Harbor, D-Day, and, except for one terrible day of fighting at Antietam, the worst battles of the Civil War. And here, unlike the carnage of those earlier events, the victims were primarily civilians.

Included in the overall total was one particularly staggering figure. Three hundred and forty-three members of the Fire Department of New York had lost their lives that day, including most of the department's top leadership: the chief, Peter Ganci; the first deputy commissioner, Bill Feehan; and the department's chaplain, a Franciscan friar named Father Mychal Judge, who was administering last rites in the north tower when he suddenly died of a heart attack. Three specially trained units, Rescue 1, 2 (the Brooklyn company that had managed to reach the towers so quickly), and 3, were wiped out completely. No fire department in

the country had ever suffered anything remotely like it. Indeed, in its entire 136-year history, from 1865 to September 10, 2001, the New York fire department had lost a total of 778 men. The impact on the close-knit fraternity of firefighters was inconceivable. One of them, sitting afterward with reddened eyes on the ground at the site, said simply, "My boss and all my buddies died and I don't think there is anything else to say."

For the firefighters, and for the police and other emergency workers who had placed themselves in harm's way, there was only the knowledge that the day also represented the greatest single rescue operation in American history, a day when no fewer than twenty thousand people were safely evacuated from the devastated complex and its surroundings.

As dusk fell and an end finally came to the most wrenching day in the city's history, New Yorkers could only try and take comfort from that fact, and from the brave words of the city's mayor, Rudolph Giuliani, who, asked about the future of New York, did not hesitate. "We're going to rebuild," he replied. "We are going to come out of this emotionally stronger, politically stronger, much closer together as a city, and we're going to come out of this economically stronger, too. . . . The people in New York City will be whole again."

AFTERMATH

When Tower Two came down, we just started digging. We keep on going because that's what we do.

A New York City firefighter

By all accounts, few people in New York—or, for that matter, across the country—slept well on the night of September 11, and on the following Wednesday morning, many reported feeling as if they were awakening from a nightmare, only to remember with a terrible sinking sensation in the heart that what had happened the previous day was no dream.

In lower Manhattan, on the site of what twenty-four hours before had been the gleaming towers of the World Trade Center, an apocalyptic wasteland of tangled steel and concrete smoldered with subterranean fires.

All through the night, machinery and supplies and an army of men and women—rescue workers, firefighters, engineers, heavy-equipment operators, and countless volunteers—had converged on the site of the disaster, hoping above all to save any survivors who might somehow still be alive.

As day broke on Wednesday, September 12, however, the full horror of the spectacle became apparent. Sixteen acres of lower Manhattan's urban landscape, an area so large that it was all but impossible to capture in a single ground-level view, stood in ruins. At the center were the remains of the towers themselves, fragments of walls and columns jutting into the sky—shards of steel rising eight and nine stories tall—surrounded by the remnants of the complex's lower buildings, which looked as if some kind of monstrous hand had come down from above and smashed them to pieces.

Hundreds of rescue workers crawled gingerly across the mountains of debris, pulling bodies—or, more often, fragments of bodies—from the torn and twisted wreckage, placing the remains in black plastic body bags, and carrying them over to the lobby of the American Express headquarters in the World Financial Center, across West Street, which had been transformed into a provisional morgue. When one of the workers found human remains, an alert was sounded and all work halted for a moment as the nearby workers took off their hard hats and placed them over their hearts.

Other workers, meanwhile, carefully combed the ruins, listening for the cries of anyone who might be buried within. In order that those faint sounds might not be drowned out by the roar of construction machinery, most of the early rescue and recovery work was done by hand. "What you've got is daisy chains of guys—hundreds of guys," said a carpenter named Robert Doremus who, like scores of other construction workers across the city, had abandoned his building site to join the effort downtown. "Pulling stuff out, handing it off the old-fashioned way, the way they used to bring water in to a fire." Despite high hopes, however, only a handful of survivors were found on the first day, and with each passing hour, experts knew, the chances of finding other victims alive diminished dramatically.

A few days after the attack, in order to begin to tame the inconceivable chaos the press had begun to call Ground Zero, officials divided the vast area of devastation into four zones, each with its own private contractor in charge, and work began in earnest on the unimaginably monumental task of clearing away over a million tons of rubble and debris. For over a century, since the days of the first suspension bridges and skyscrapers, New York had been known around the world for the skill and daring of its builders. Now, responding to a challenge as daunting as—and far more heartbreaking than—any they had ever faced, the city's construction crews leapt into the effort with a kind of controlled fury that stunned everyone who witnessed it. Working nonstop, seven days a week, in grueling twelve-hour shifts that went on all day and then all night under the ghastly glare of portable floodlights, teams of workers armed with picks, hand shovels, acetylene torches, cranes, backhoes, and mammoth excavators—"every piece of equipment known to man," one worker said—began making their way through the rubble, wearing respirators to fight off the thick fog of dust and smoke that filled the air, watching for flames that could suddenly flare up when debris was removed and oxygen reignited the smoldering ruins below, and listening constantly for the claxon horn that warned of the imminent structural collapse of some half-destroyed structure. Physically backbreaking, the work was even more challenging psychologically; many of the men toiling in what they called "the pile" reported feeling zombielike and obsessed, utterly disconnected from the rest of the world and all but unable to eat and sleep when they got off the site. Soon, large tents would be set up near the site, where the men could take their meals and shower and sleep. A temporary chapel would also be established, manned by religious officials from various congregations around the city. Many of the rescue and recovery volunteers, hardly able to stand working at the site, were even less able to stay away, and found themselves driven to return to "the pile" before their rest shift was done.

By Wednesday, tens of thousands of people throughout the metropolitan area—people whose family members worked in the towers and had failed to show up Tuesday night—had gravitated to the New York State Armory at Twenty-sixth Street and Lexington Avenue, which had been pressed into service as a central information post. Distraught relatives brought photographs, documents, and locks of hair (or other items containing DNA samples) to help locate their loved ones—or, failing that, to help identify their remains. Lines outside the building soon stretched around the block. Photocopied posters, meanwhile, began to appear by the tens of thousands on lampposts and walls around Manhattan, each showing a picture of a missing person, details of their appearance, their last known location, a contact number, and, in many cases, a heartrending plea for help:

"We're looking for Kevin M. Williams, 104th Fl. WTC."

"Have you seen him? Robert 'Bob' Dewitt."

"Ayuda!! Manuel Emilio Mesia. 740-0496 'Por Favor.'"

"Please help us find Jennifer Y. Wong, Location: 96th floor of 1 WTC. Thank you. God bless you."

"Roger Mark Rasweiler. Missing. One WTC 100th floor."

"We Need Your Help: Giovanna 'Gennie' Gambale."

By then, bouquets of flowers and display boards covered with heartfelt thank-you notes were being placed in front of the city's firehouses, which had become instant shrines and community gathering places. Nearly all of the fire companies in lower Manhattan had suffered casualties; many were missing half their complement or more. Dazed and numbed by their loss, surviving firefighters stood in the open doors of their firehouses, in front of the empty spaces where their big red ladder trucks and engines had stood a few days before.

By unspoken agreement, the center for mourning in the city was Union Square on Fourteenth Street, where, since the opening days of the Civil War in 1861, New Yorkers had gathered in times of crisis. Now, once again, the park became a citywide gathering place, as thousands converged for candlelight vigils and prayer services, and the pathways filled with makeshift memorials and shrines.

While New Yorkers wept and mourned, they also rushed to help, any way they could—donating food and supplies until warehouses bulged, and giving blood until hospitals and clinics asked them to stop, pointing out that there was simply not enough need and that unused blood would only have to be discarded. The chefs and staffs of lower Manhattan's restaurants—including some of the nation's greatest culinary landmarks—now worked overtime to provide nourishing meals for the hundreds of rescue workers at the site, meals that hundreds of other New Yorkers volunteered day and night to serve. Other citizens showed up at the emergency centers that had quickly been set up in the piers along the Hudson River, and offered to help grieving families. "I'm here to do whatever," declared thirty-two-year-old Grace Spence, who had herself once worked in the towers. "I can hold hands, listen to stories, sweep the streets, whatever." Meanwhile, out on the West Side High-

way—the primary vehicular route to and from the site—crowds lined the roadway night and day, waving American flags and cheering on rescue and emergency workers as they headed down to Ground Zero. Some would still be coming out to stand there and cheer, flags in hand, four and five months later.

"New York seems to know how to survive an unspeakable trauma," the *New York Times* columnist Joyce Purnick observed, "how, when visited with a tragedy, to turn itself, temporarily, into a small town. Anyone who walked around the city yesterday could have no doubt that New York would overcome the horror that was worse than any it had ever experienced." For all of the city's proud tradition of coming together in time of crisis, never before in its history had the everyday tensions and divisions among its people—of widely differing classes, races, and ethnicities—seemed to melt away so thoroughly. The mayor had promised that New York would "come out of this emotionally stronger . . . much closer together as a city," but few could have guessed how powerful a sense of unity would arise in the days after the attacks, when a protective cloak of tolerance seemed to be extended over every group in the city—including, to the surprise of some observers, New York's substantial Arab-American population. "It was almost as if the city had turned tender," the reporters Jim Dwyer and Susan Sachs observed, "as if people wanted to tip-toe around each other so as not to cause any upset." Even the ordinary sense of urban detachment maintained by New Yorkers fell away, as perfect strangers casually struck up conversations in the street and other public places, everyone linked by a common experience and common emotions.

Nowhere was the new mood more evident or more striking than among the city's political leaders, among whom, in the light of the tragedy, ancient differences and enmities seemed to vanish. New Yorkers looked on in amazement as the state's liberal Democratic senator Charles Schumer deferred thoughtfully to its conservative Republican governor, George Pataki, who in turn deferred to him; still more remarkably, they watched Senator Hillary Clinton and Mayor Rudy Giuliani—long-standing political opponents who just a year earlier had fought an unusually bitter campaign against each other—now sharing hugs and conferring warmly as they walked side by side down West Street. As he had from the first hours of the catastrophe, the mayor himself continued to set a remarkable standard of leadership. "Acting at once as chief operating officer of the city," the reporter Jennifer Steinhauer wrote, "personally monitoring how many pounds of debris have been removed . . . [and as] city psychologist, trying to assure a grief-stricken and terrified population he knows they are safe and he knows they are hurting, the mayor has almost unilaterally managed to create a sense that the city and by

In the hours and days after the disaster, families and friends posted handmade flyers all around the city in a desperate attempt to locate their loved ones.

Within hours of the attacks, spontaneous shrines to the victims began appearing in dozens of locations around the city, as well as in cities and towns across the country and around the world.

its proxy, the nation, are scratching their way to normalcy." Indeed, for millions of Americans outside the city, Giuliani's careful pronouncements and steady course of action in the first days after the attacks provided a firm sense of authority that many found lacking in the relatively inconsistent initial statements of President George W. Bush.

The sudden swell of affection and respect for New York's mayor was the harbinger of an even greater shift in national attitudes toward the city. Almost overnight, the complex and sometimes difficult relationship between America and its largest metropolis took a new and dramatic turn. While New York's striking renaissance in the 1980s and 1990s had muted much of the open antagonism that had prevailed between the city and nation in the 1960s and 1970s, a certain skepticism had remained, especially among rural Americans, about the cosmopolitan city and its values. But the attacks on the World Trade Center brought forth an astonishing outpouring of sympathy by Americans for New York

City, as well an outright pride, in every corner of the country, in the heroism and valor of its emergency workers and ordinary citizens. New Yorkers, meanwhile, expressed their patriotism more openly and directly than at any time since World War II—especially through the display of American flags, which sprouted from countless rooftops and fire escapes, appeared in doors and shop windows, and in some cases covered the faces of entire buildings. Ironically, it had taken an attack on what was perceived to be a prime emblem of America to transform New York, unequivocally, into that very emblem. "It will be a . . . supreme irony," the columnist Michael Wolff wrote, "if now, after generations of disenfranchisement, New York City becomes the great symbol of Americanism." Shrines for the victims—and expressions of encouragement and even love for the city and its people—could be found in cities, towns, and villages across America. Volunteers poured into New York from around the country—nurses from Kentucky, firefighters from San

Francisco, medical workers from Atlanta. Fund-raising drives were begun in half a dozen cities to purchase new trucks for the New York fire department. And foundations and corporations in every part of the country as well as millions of individuals donated money for the families of the New York City and Port Authority personnel lost in the attacks.

When New York senators Schumer and Clinton sat down with President Bush in Washington to discuss emergency aid for the city two days after the attacks, they were unsure what to expect—especially given that Bush had been heavily defeated in the city and state in the election the year before. But the president asked simply, "What do you need?" and when Schumer answered that the immediate recovery costs would total at least twenty billion dollars, Bush responded instantly, "You've got it." "There was a lump in my throat," Schumer later admitted.

That sense of sympathy and pride in the city, of course, resonated not only across the country but throughout the world. In England, officials at Lloyds of London, the insurance giant, ordered the ringing of the Lutine Bell, a ritual that for over a century and a half had marked news of a missing ship; at Buckingham Palace, a special Changing of the Guard was held in honor of those who had died in the attacks, the military band playing "The Star-Spangled Banner" as tourists and Britons holding American flags looked on and wept. That same day, the Parisian newspaper *Le Monde*, known for its often harsh criticism of the United States and its policies, ran a headline that said simply, *"Nous sommes tous Américains"*—"We are all Americans now—" while from Havana came an expression of sympathy for the victims of the attack from Cuban president Fidel Castro. The author Thomas Keneally, who had watched the events in Australia, where it was almost midnight, wrote of the profound and strikingly personal impact the attacks on lower Manhattan had on people around the globe. "I don't think New Yorkers realize the extent to which the world sees their city as everyone's city," he said. "Had a New Yorker been present, I like to believe he or she would have been comforted by the intimacy of our outrage."

RECOVERY

On the morning of the attacks, the New York Stock Exchange—the heart of the city and the country's financial system, located just a few blocks from the collapsing towers—had ordered a halt to trading and sent its members home. It would remain closed for the next five and a half days—the longest shutdown since World War I. But on Friday afternoon, officials announced that the market would reopen for business on the morning of Monday, September 17, as a symbol of the financial world's determination to rebuild and persevere. Over the weekend, thousands of

workers labored frantically to make it possible for the financial district to come back to life on Monday morning. Street cleaners swept through the district, hosing down sidewalks and building facades of the dust and debris that had accumulated for days. Hundreds of crews from telephone and power companies worked eighteen-hour days to restore telephone and data links and electric power. "The magnitude of this is so huge," electrical engineer Mark Bauer said, "all the work that has to be done at one time. The manpower, the tooling, the coordination is tremendous." The district's streets were still closed to traffic, but officials ensured that the subway system was functioning to carry more than three hundred thousand workers into the area on Monday morning and take them home again that evening. "There's a certain amount of apprehension," a financial services executive named Andrew Goldman declared, "but there's also a strong feeling of wanting to come back to work."

At 9:30 a.m., the president of the New York Stock Exchange, Richard Grasso, rang the bell that traditionally marks the start of the day's trading. As was widely expected, the market dropped dramatically: the Dow Jones Industrial Average lost 684 points that day, in absolute terms the largest single-day point drop in history. But to everyone's relief, the market did not plunge out of control, setting off a financial crisis. Indeed, within days the market stabilized and, as talk turned to the country's military response to the attacks, began to rise again.

The return of activity to the financial district that Monday marked a turning point, but it would be many months before even a semblance of normalcy returned to much of lower Manhattan. Thousands of homes and offices in the vicinity of Ground Zero would remain without electric power for weeks, and without phone service for months. For months, too, the terrible odor of the ruins would remain strong in many areas downtown, as fires continued to smolder beneath the rubble, flaring up regularly as portions of the debris were removed. In the end, it would take one hundred days, exactly, for the last of the fires to finally burn out.

And even as some parts of the city began to return to normal on the second week after the attacks, other parts of the city and the region were only starting to confront the full impact of what had happened. That week, the funerals began—firefighters and police officers and ordinary citizens, two and three each weekday, and ten or more on weekends, some taking place in the city itself, but many in suburban towns in New Jersey and Long Island where the majority of the city's emergency workers, and many who worked in the buildings, made their homes. The *New York Times*, trying to bring human scale to the incalculable enormity of the disaster, began running brief obituaries of the victims, "Portraits in Grief," each describing the distinctive quirks and qualities of an individual who had been killed in the attacks. Day after day the articles appeared, fifteen and twenty at a time, week after week, month after month, as New Yorkers awakened each morning to read about another group of people they would never get a chance to know. A quick glimpse at the very first few names—McLaughlin, Fazio, DeChavez, Sam-Dinoo, Dowling—served as a reminder of the extraordinary diversity of contemporary New York. There could be no greater or more moving testament to the city's extraordinary everyday internationalism, however, than the simple fact that the victims of the attacks included citizens from no fewer than ninety-two foreign countries.

In the city, many people remained fearful, frightened to go into parts of town—the subways, or large, crowded public spaces, such as Penn Station or Times Square—that they had always taken for granted. But others sought to remain hopeful about the city and its future. "I think New York will rebuild," a money manager named Paul R. Beirne declared. "I think the economy will be able to absorb this, both here locally as well as nationally. And you know, it certainly makes me nervous, and a little scared, but there's resilience. I'm optimistic." Many shops and homes displayed a poster by the graphic designer Milton Glaser that updated his famous "I love New York" image, with the red heart that stood for the word "love" now revealing a slight singe, and with the words "more than ever" added at the bottom. "The city . . . naked now in a new way," the writer Adam Gopnik observed a week after the attacks, "not startling but vulnerable—seemed somehow to increase in our affection and allegiance."

The sense of loss would not only linger, of course, but would reemerge again and again, triggered by something as simple and unavoidable as glancing downtown. Even those who had disliked the design of the World Trade Center had always relied on the twin towers—so unusually prominent and distinctive—as a way to find their bearings around the city, making the structures' absence not only psychologically but literally disorienting. "It's eerie," a transit worker named Monet Harris said. "You always look for those two buildings. You always know where you are when you see those two buildings. And now they're gone."

REBUILDING

When you destroy an ant's nest, immediately the ants start rebuilding it. And though the destruction is very fast, and the reconstruction is very slow, the ants always win. A sense of purpose and determination always wins in the end.
Cesar Pelli, architect of the World Financial Center

Even as the city was coming to terms with the human cost of the attacks, officials and planners were confronting the staggering damage to the physical infrastructure of the city.

The attack had destroyed or seriously damaged several major switching hubs for land-based telephone and cellular lines. The destruction of the giant television antenna that had stood atop the north tower left much of the city unable to receive broadcast signals. The collapse of 7 World Trade Center had wrecked a major electrical substation that had been located beneath it, as well as eliminating the multimillion-dollar Emergency Command Center that Mayor Giuliani had placed on the building's twenty-third floor. And two mass transit lines—a spur of the IRT subway and the PATH commuter train that ran beneath the World Trade Center—had been destroyed when the towers came down. (One of the stranger sights during the excavation of the debris at Ground Zero had been the discovery and removal of several relatively undamaged PATH train cars that had been sitting on their tracks, far beneath the complex, since the time of the attacks.)

Within months, work began on the replacement or restoration of many of these essential systems. Having seen so much loss, office workers in lower Manhattan were especially cheered to see something new appearing, when a box-like tube of girders began appearing in the giant hole left by the collapse of the towers—the start of a thousand-foot stretch of subway line that would return to service a few months later. Planning had begun, too, on the reconstruction of the PATH line whose main Manhattan terminal had once been located under the World Trade Center, and many New Yorkers were heartened to hear that the project would not only restore what had once been, but offer a genuine improvement for the riding public by providing a new connection to the city's subway system. It was the start of what planners intended to be a new downtown "Grand Central" that would link not only several existing subway lines and the PATH train but new high-speed lines to Kennedy Airport and the Long Island Rail Road, fulfilling a goal that had been talked about for decades but never acted upon, to furnish lower Manhattan with the kind of regional transportation hub that midtown had enjoyed since the start of the twentieth century.

It was in that same spirit that planners began discussing the future of Ground Zero itself, hoping to find new possibilities for the future in the terrible tragedy. Everyone recognized that the meaning of the sixteen-acre site had been indelibly changed by the attacks, and that a significant part of it—including the area where the towers themselves had stood—would need to be set aside as a memorial to the thousands who had been lost there. (Indeed, as plans for an international design competition took shape, planners anticipated that the completed memorial would become one of the most heavily visited places in the world.)

But much of the site would need to be rebuilt as urban fabric, not only to replace the revenues generated by the

Trade Center but as a way of making lower Manhattan whole again. By the start of 2002, with the arrival of a new mayor, the wealthy businessman Michael J. Bloomberg, at City Hall, city and state officials had begun to put in place a mechanism and a process for reenvisioning the future of the site. As many observers pointed out, the sudden loss of the World Trade Center posed not only a challenge but an extraordinary, if unasked-for, opportunity to reconceive a major portion of New York's urban landscape.

Even as the early proposals began to take shape, it was obvious that the Trade Center's 1960s superblock planning, which effectively turned its back on the rest of the city, would be superseded by an approach that harkened back to a time when even the tallest skyscrapers in the city rose from the streets and blocks of the urban grid. At the very least, Greenwich Street and Fulton Street—which had been wiped off the grid in 1968—would be restored to allow pedestrians the major north-south and east-west paths that had been blocked for decades by the World Trade Center.

In the months to come, a lengthy, convoluted planning process—by turns inspiring and frustrating—would get under way as state and city officials, civic groups, and private developers attempted to determine not only what should be built but how to go about making the decision. The release of six massing studies for the site (developed by local planning consultants) would provoke so vocal an outcry—especially from five thousand New Yorkers at an unusual daylong public forum at the Javits Center—that the project sponsors, rapidly changing gears, would choose to cast their net more widely, inviting noted architects from around the world to submit proposals. The new approach would eventually yield nine initial designs, then two developed schemes, then a single striking proposal by the Polish-born architect Daniel Libeskind that, officials hoped, would provide a basis for moving forward.

But it would be years before new structures began rising from the site, and even as the planning process proceeded, New Yorkers looking downtown in the spring of 2002 were inspired and comforted by a remarkable sight: twin towers of light, rising side by side from a spot in lower Manhattan not far from the former World Trade Center. A concept developed by a group of young artists, it relied on ninety-six powerful floodlights, arrayed in two enormous squares reminiscent of the towers' footprints, and pointed straight into the skies. It was switched off after exactly a month in operation, according to the original terms of its installation, but many hoped that the hauntingly beautiful concept would make a reappearance in the permanent reconstruction of the site.

Experts had originally predicted that the removal of the debris at Ground Zero would require more than a year to complete, but the dedication and intensity of the recovery workers—who had never stopped working seven days a week, twenty-four hours a day—accelerated that timetable dramatically. By April 2002, as workers began clearing the last of the 1.8 million tons of debris they had swept away from the site, the vast mountains of rubble had been reduced to small hills, and the day was fast approaching when the final pieces of debris would be removed, a fact that brought both relief and sadness to the men who had toiled so tirelessly there. Of the 2,792 people killed in the attacks, remains had been identified for little more than 1,000.

On Thursday, May 30, 2002, just eight and a half months after the attack, a ceremony was held at Ground Zero to commemorate the removal of the last piece of the towers and the formal end of the recovery effort. The unforgettable landscape of devastation had been replaced by something that looked far more like a conventional construction site—indeed, like the original construction site of the Trade Center itself: after nearly forty years, the giant sunken "bathtub," which after the construction of the towers no one had ever expected to see again, was now plainly visible.

That morning, at 10:29—the time of the collapse of the second tower—as bells tolled and thousands stood in silence, an empty stretcher was ceremonially carried up the ramp from the six-story-deep pit and along West Street, past friends and relatives of the victims and hundreds of firefighters and policemen standing at attention. Behind the stretcher came a truck, a yellow cab pulling a flatbed, on which rested Column Number 1001 from 2 World Trade Center, a fifty-eight-ton steel column that was the final piece of the buildings to be removed. The column, draped in black muslin and an American flag, slowly made its way up the ramps and along West Street past the weeping thousands.

It was impossible not to think of a day nearly thirty-two years before when, on a cold morning in December 1970, another steel column, it too draped in an American flag and it too the last of its kind, had ceremonially made its way up the side of the rising towers to be lifted into place at the very top, well over a thousand feet above the street.

Now those towers were gone, leaving a great void that could be filled, at least for the time being, only with dreams of the city that might again rise someday—perhaps higher than before—into the limitless sky.

"Tribute of Light" memorial,
March 2002.

ACKNOWLEDGMENTS

We were so immeasurably aided in our work on this book, as on the series it accompanies, by so many extraordinarily gifted people—scholars, writers, researchers, archivists, producers, editors, designers, and fact-checkers—that the task of merely enumerating them, let alone trying to express how deeply grateful we are to them for their assistance, is humbling.

A number of people in particular had an especially profound impact on the project, and it is with enormous pleasure and gratitude that we take this opportunity to express our indebtedness to them—beginning with the immensely gifted writers and historians who contributed essays to this volume. The series would not have been possible without the help on-camera and off of Kenneth T. Jackson, the editor in chief of *The Encyclopedia of New York City* and one of the greatest urban historians working today. His enormous erudition, his love for the city and for the way cities work, along with his worldliness, tact, and generosity, influenced the series and book in more ways than we can describe. We also owe a very special debt of thanks to Mike Wallace, coauthor of *Gotham: A History of New York City to 1898.* His exhaustive knowledge of every period of the city's history—and his profound insights into the underlying forces at work in its unfolding—proved invaluable in helping us shape a coherent narrative out of New York's sprawling four-century-long history. The project would also have been inconceivable without the extraordinary contributions—on-camera and off—of our other contributors: Robert A. Caro, whose landmark biography of Robert Moses, *The Power Broker,* remains one of the greatest works of urban history ever written; Phillip Lopate, whose intimate familiarity with the city's history and literature were matched by his love for film and the filmmaking process and his unique feel for the life and texture of the city's streets; Robert A. M. Stern, whose immense passion, razor-sharp wit, and verbal flair on-camera were matched by an encyclopedic knowledge of New York's history, architecture, and public spaces; Carol Berkin, whose passion for the character and drama of New York in the eighteenth and early nineteenth centuries brought that period alive as no one else; Daniel Czitrom, whose vast knowledge of the interrelationships uniting the city's social, political, and cultural history helped deepen our understanding in more ways than we can possibly enumerate; David Levering Lewis, whose extremely nuanced sense of the way the politics of race,

culture, class, and creativity have interacted in the life of the city gave us new insight into New York in the 1920s; and Marshall Berman, whose brilliant and imaginative reflections on the culture and politics and experience of modernity in New York remain an inspiration.

We are also immensely and forever indebted to the scholarship, passion, wit, and sensitivity of our extremely gifted consultants and historical advisors who—in addition to the above—included Thomas Bender, Lois Bianchi, Patricia Bonomi, Hope Cooke, Graham Hodges, Margo Jefferson, John Kuo Wei Tchen, Virginia Sanchez Korrol, John Hull Mollenkopf, Kathy Peiss, Richard Snow, Sam Bass Warner, and Steven Zeitlin—all of whom reviewed drafts of the scripts and shared with us their immense knowledge of the city and its history. Many, many thanks to them all.

Along the way, a number of gifted writers contributed material that one way or the other found its way into the text of our film script and book. We're particularly grateful in this respect to the immensely talented Ronald Blumer—a wonderful documentary film writer with a unique nose for story and detail—and to Mike Bryan, who at the eleventh hour helped us blast a road through the last fifty years of the city's history. Their work significantly influenced the final three chapters of the book. Amid all her other enormous contributions, our inimitable executive editor and mentor, Judy Crichton, frequently took pen in hand to help untangle obstinately graceless or obtuse passages of our own. At key points along the way, Phillip Lopate and Richard Rubin also provided additional material that made the film and book better than they would otherwise have been, and we thank them all.

We also owe a very special debt of gratitude to our tremendously gifted and infinitely resourceful associate producer, Steve Rivo. From the very beginning of the series itself through the completion of this book, he was an invaluable colleague in a thousand ways—coordinating the massive database of historical quotes and facts, creating treatments for specific scenes, drafting many of the captions, offering insightful comments and critiques on the scripts and manuscripts-in-progress, amid other duties too numerous to mention but always carried out with imagination and flair.

The textual research for the project was an immense and often daunting undertaking that in the course of six years involved a small army of peo-

ple. We are humbly indebted to our extremely gifted senior research associates, Jeanne Houck and Robert W. Snyder, who constructed much of the essential base of information and interpretation from which the treatments and scripts were written. The visual archive was a vast labyrinth of its own, and we are very grateful to Anya Sirota, Helen Kaplan, Katherine Bourbeau, and, above all, to Robin Espinola, for the immense skill and diligence with which they tracked down and acquired literally tens of thousands of archival images of the city, many of them never before published. Meghan Horvath, with Justine Bertucelli and Lily Thorne—who also helped research and acquire many of the images—organized and cataloged them with discipline and dispatch for use in the film and book. The project would simply have been impossible without their efforts.

We are very grateful as well to Mike Berk, who, with the help early on of Virginia Heffernan, painstakingly fact-checked the book and scripts with an eagle eye and strikingly critical intelligence. Many thanks, too, to Bonnie Lynn Lafave, who read the text with a penetrating editorial eye and a keen ear for language, and thus saved us from numerous infelicities.

The project would not have been possible without the extraordinary resources of a number of distinguished historical and cultural institutions in New York and across the country. Many thanks in particular are due our wonderful partners at the New-York Historical Society, especially Betsy Gotbaum, and her colleagues Dale Neighbors, Mary Beth Betts, and Nicole Wells. We are also grateful to the Museum of the City of New York, especially Robert MacDonald and his colleagues Peter Simmons, Eileen Kennedy, and Marguerite Lavin; the Library of Congress, especially Mary Ison and Maia Keech; and the New York Public Library, especially Alice Hudson. A very special thank-you is due to Arthur O. Sulzberger for guiding us through and then generously making available the unique—and uniquely beautiful—collection of antique lithographs that graces the corridors of the *New York Times.* We are also immensely indebted to Barbara Cohen and Judith Stonehill from New York Bound, Paul Cohen (author of *Manhattan in Maps*), Eric Fettmann, and Jeffrey Kraus, whose breathtaking private collections enormously enriched the book and series. We are especially grateful to Roger Whitehouse, who so generously opened to us his entire archive of extraordinary historic photographs.

The length, design, and copious imagery of the book, along with the foibles of its authors, have not made it

an easy one for our publisher, Alfred A. Knopf, to bring to press. With this in mind, we're all the more grateful to our wonderful editor, Ashbel Green, and inspiring managing editor, Katherine Hourigan, who—along with an incredible team that included the director of manufacturing Andy Hughes, art director Carol Devine Carson, production editor Kathleen Fridella, Asya Muchnick, and Geoff Martin—oversaw the book's production with great intelligence, sensitivity, and patience. To the incomparable Wendy Byrne, who designed the book with the superb taste and elegant eye she brings to every project, our deepest thanks for making the book look as good as it does. Many thanks as well to Knopf's associate publisher, Pat Johnson, and the promotion and publicity team—including Paul Bogaards, Anne-Lise Spitzer, William Loverd, Nicholas Latimer, and Sheila O'Shea—who did such a marvelous job of getting this book out to the public. We are very grateful, as well, to Andrew Wylie, Liza Walworth, and the Wylie Agency for shepherding the book so expertly from the outset, and to our attorney, Robert Gold, whose advice and wisdom have been crucial throughout.

In the most fundamental way, this book could not exist without the series upon which it was based, and with that in mind, we would like to extend our heartfelt thanks to a number of people whose contributions to the film were inestimable. We are extremely grateful to two extraordinary cinematographers, Buddy Squires and Allen Moore, who made the city come alive on screen with their exquisite photography. Many thanks as well to our senior creative consultant, Geoffrey C. Ward—the best film writer and storyteller working in documentaries today—who, as always, brought his unique sensibility and exquisite taste to countless screenings and script sessions.

Our narrator, David Ogden Stiers, brought an elegance, authority, and sensitivity to the series it would otherwise not have had; we are eternally grateful to him for bringing the narration to life so wonderfully.

From the start, we could not have gone forward without the invaluable and bolstering encouragement, advice—and stunning on-camera contribution—of David McCullough, master historian, peerless storyteller, and friend.

It would be hard to express how deeply indebted we are to our extraordinary editing staff—our beloved supervising editor Li-Shin Yu, and our senior editors Edward Barteski, David Hanser and Nina Schulman; our heroic associate editors Michael Balabuch (who did double duty as post-production supervisor as well), Janet Cristenfeld, and Syndi Pilar; our assistant editors, Roxanne Yamashiro, Anna Josenhans, June Shiiki, Samara Smith, Josh Sternfeld, and Sarah Kaylor; our apprentice editors, Judd Erlich and Kramer O'Neill; our sound editors, Ira Spiegel and Marlena Grzaslewicz; and our post-production assistant, Julia Wilk.

In the course of a very long project, we were blessed with a truly extraordinary production staff, whose work and spirit in countless ways have been permanently knit into the film and book. Our most heartful thanks to our valiant and dedicated associate producer, Ray Segal, who provided invaluable critical commentary and ideas, who oversaw with enormous flair and an infinitely painstaking attention to detail the most elaborate of shoots, and who took the lead in producing—with the mapmakers Justin and Tracey Morrill—the superb original maps that grace the film and this book; to our coordinating producer, Kerry Herman; to our supervising producer, Kate Roth Knull; to our production coordinator, Justine Bertucelli; to our assistant producer, Lily Thorne; to our archival film researchers, Daniel Vatsky, Corrinne Collette, and Hilary Klotz; to our production assistants, Jenks Whittenburg, Marijke Smit, and Zachary Kaiman; to our associate producer, Helen Kaplan, and assistant producer, Danna Liebert, and to Phyllis Schwartz and Michael Shepley, whose strategic advice and wise counsel helped us immeasurably.

The film series would not have been possible without the generous support of the Chase Manhattan Corporation, especially Fred Hill, Aubrey Hawes, and David Nowlen; the National Endowment for the Humanities, especially Jim Dougherty, Karen Miles, and Nancy Rogers; PBS, especially Erwin Duggan, Kathy Quattrone, John Wilson, and Sandy Heberer; the Corporation for Public Broadcasting; the Ford Foundation; the Arthur Vining Davis Foundations; the Rosalind P. Walter Foundation; and the J. M. Kaplan Fund.

Many, many thanks to Sheryl Shade and Shade Global, whose indefatigable efforts on our behalf, with her colleague, David Bober, brought us corporate underwriting.

In the course of this project, we have had not one but two great public television stations as our allies—WNET in New York and WGBH in Boston. Many, many thanks to our friends at Thirteen/WNET, especially Bill Baker, Ward Chamberlin, Tammy Robinson, and Audrey Koota, for all they've done for us. Without their extraordinary commitment and steadfast support this project would not have been possible.

To our longstanding partners in Boston at WGBH—they know better than anyone how deep and unpayable our debt runs on this one. To Margaret Drain and Mark Samels and Susie Mottau at *The American Experience,* please accept our deepest gratitude for steady support, invaluable editorial insight, and friendship of every kind.

To Judy Crichton and to Peter McGhee—there really aren't the words to express what we feel. From start to finish, their extraordinary and unflagging friendship and support—creative, editorial, strategic, and moral—held the project, and its producers, together. In return, we offer our deepest and most heartfelt thanks, along with this—the work they sustained and made possible over seven long years—in the hope that it represents some compensation.

Ric Burns
James Sanders
Lisa Ades
July 1999

Like the film upon which it was based, the new epilogue of this book—chronicling the rise and fall of the World Trade Center—was created over the course of a year, from June 2002 to June 2003. Space does not permit us to acknowledge the contributions of everyone who helped us with this final chapter of the film and book. But it would be remiss not to acknowledge a few published works that were especially helpful in preparing this narrative, including Philippe Petit's account of his 1974 high-wire adventure and William Langewiesche's historic reporting on September 11 and its aftermath.

In this respect, we also wish to acknowledge the extraordinary journalistic achievement of James Glanz, Eric Lipton, and their colleagues at the *New York Times,* whose painstaking reconstruction of the complex sequence of devastating human and physical events that transpired within the towers that morning provided an incomparable window into an all but incomprehensible moment in the city's history.

Ric Burns
James Sanders
June 2003

SELECTED BIBLIOGRAPHY

WORKS CITED

Abbott, Berenice. *New York in the Thirties.* New York: Dover, 1973.

Adams, Henry. *The Education of Henry Adams.* Boston: Houghton Mifflin, 1918.

Auchincloss, Louis. *The Hone and Strong Diaries of Old Manhattan.* New York: Abbeville Press, 1989.

Barnum, P. T. *Struggles and Triumphs.* New York: Viking Penguin, 1987.

Bourget, Paul. *Outre-Mer: Impressions of America.* New York: Charles Scribner's Sons, 1895.

Brace, Charles Loring. *The Dangerous Classes of New York and Twenty Years' Work among Them.* New York: Wynkoop & Hallenbeck, Publishers, 1995.

Brown, Claude. *Manchild in the Promised Land: A Modern Classic of the Black Experience.* New York: Penguin Group, 1965.

Bruccoli, Matthew J., Scottie Fitzgerald Smith, and Joan P. Kerr, eds. *The Romantic Egoists: A Pictorial Autobiography from the Scrapbooks and Albums of Scott and Zelda Fitzgerald.* Columbia, South Carolina: Bruccoli Clark, 1974.

Campbell, Helen, Thomas Byrnes, and Thomas W. Knox. *Darkness and Daylight.* Hartford, Conn.: The Hartford Publishing Co., 1899.

Clinton, De Witt. *Remarks on the Canal, from Lake Gore to the Hudson River.* New York: Samuel Wood & Sons, 1816.

Cowley, Malcolm. *Exile's Return.* New York: Norton, 1934.

Donnan, Elizabeth. *Documents Relative to the History of the Slave Trade in America.* Washington, D.C.: Carnegie Institute, 1932.

Dos Passos, John. *Manhattan Transfer.* New York: Houghton Mifflin, 1953.

———. *U.S.A.* New York: Penguin Books, 1938.

Dreiser, Theodore. *The Color of a Great City.* Syracuse, N.Y.: Syracuse University Press, 1996.

Ellington, Duke. *Music Is My Mistress.* New York: Da Capo, 1973.

Federal Writers' Project. *New York Panorama* (companion to *The WPA Guide to New York City*). New York: Pantheon Books, 1984.

———. *The WPA Guide to New York City,* introduction by William Whyte. New York: The New Press, 1992.

Feininger, Andreas. *New York in the Forties.* New York: Dover, 1978.

Fitzgerald, F. Scott. *The Crack Up.* New York: New Directions Publishing Corp., 1964.

———. *The Great Gatsby.* New York: Charles Scribner's Sons, 1953.

———. *The Stories of F. Scott Fitzgerald.* New York: Collier Books, 1986.

Foster, George G. *New York by Gas-Light and Other Urban Sketches.* Berkeley: University of California Press, 1990.

Ganz, Marie, and Nat J. Ferber. *Rebels: Into Anarchy and Out Again.* New York: Dodd, Mead & Company, 1920.

Gold, Michael. *Jews without Money.* New York: Carroll & Graf Publishers, Inc., 1993.

Hapgood, Hutchins. *The Spirit of the Ghetto.* New York: Funk and Wagnalls Co., 1965.

Harper's Magazine. New York. New York: Gallery Books, 1991.

Hine, Lewis W. *Men at Work.* New York: Dover, 1977.

Horsmanden, Daniel, and Thomas J. Davis, eds. *The New York Conspiracy.* Reprint: Boston: Beacon Press, 1971.

Howells, William Dean, and Mildred Howells, eds. *Life in Letters of William Dean Howells.* Garden City, N.Y.: Doubleday, 1928.

Hughes, Langston. *The Big Sea.* New York: Hill & Wang, 1940.

———. *Shakespeare in Harlem.* New York: Alfred A. Knopf, 1942.

Irving, Washington. *Diedrich Knickerbocker's History of New York.* New York: Heritage Press, 1940.

Jacobs, Jane. *The Death and Life of Great American Cities.* New York: Vintage, 1961.

James, Bartlett Burleigh, and Jameson J. Franklin, eds. *Journal of Jasper Danckaerts, 1679–1680.* New York: Charles Scribner's Sons, 1913.

James, Henry. *New York Revisited.* New York: Franklin Square Press, 1994.

Jameson, J. Franklin, ed. *Narratives of New Netherland: 1609–1664.* New York: Charles Scribner's Sons, 1909.

Johnson, James Weldon. *Autobiography of an Ex-Colored Man.* New York: Alfred A. Knopf, 1927.

Kazin, Alfred. *New York Jew.* New York: Vintage Books, 1978.

———. *Starting Out in the Thirties.* Boston: Little, Brown, 1965.

———. *A Walker in the City.* New York: Harcourt, Brace, 1951.

Koolhaas, Rem. *Delirious New York: A Retroactive Manifesto for Manhattan.* New York: Oxford University Press, 1978.

Le Corbusier. *When the Cathedrals Were White.* New York: Reynal and Hitchcock, 1947.

Locke, Alain, ed. *The New Negro.* New York: Simon & Schuster, 1997.

Lopate, Phillip, ed. *Writing New York: A Literary Anthology.* New York: Library of America, 1998.

Mackay, Alexander. *The Western World.* New York: Negro Universities Press, 1968.

Malkiel, Theresa A. *The Diary of a Shirtwaist Striker.* Ithaca, N.Y.: ILR Press, Cornell University, 1910.

McCabe, James D., Jr. *Lights and Shadows of New York Life.* Reprint: New York: Farrar, Straus & Giroux, 1970.

McCullough, Esther Morgan, ed. *As I Pass, O Manhattan: An Anthology of Life in New York.* North Bennington, Vt.: Coley Taylor Publishers, 1956.

Miller, Edwin Haviland. *Selected Letters of Walt Whitman.* Iowa City: University of Iowa Press, 1990.

Miller, John. *Historical Chronicles of New Amsterdam: Colonial New York and Early Long Island.* New York: Ira J. Friedman, 1968.

Moses, Robert. *Public Works: A Dangerous Trade.* New York: McGraw-Hill, 1970.

Moss, Howard, ed. *New York: Poems.* New York: Avon, 1980.

Nevins, Allan, ed. *The Diary of Philip Hone: 1828–1851.* Vols. 1 and 2. New York: Dodd, Mead & Co., 1927.

———, and Milton Halsey Thomas, eds. *The Diary of George Templeton Strong: 1835–1875.* New York: The Macmillan Co., 1952.

O'Callaghan, E. B. *Documents Relative to the Colonial History of the State of New York,* 15 vols. Albany, N.Y.: 1853–1887.

Oppel, Frank. *Gaslight New York Revisited.* New York: Castle, 1989.

———. *Tales of Gaslight New York.* New York: Castle, 1985.

Pintard, John. *Letters from John Pintard to His Daughter.* Vols. 1–4. New York: New-York Historical Society, 1940.

Redfield, J. S. *Redfield's Traveler's Guide to the City of New York.* New York: J. S. Redfield, 1871.

Richmond, John, and Abril Lamarque. *Brooklyn U.S.A.* New York: Creative Age Press, 1946.

Riis, Jacob A. *Children of the Tenements.* New York: 1903.

———. *How the Other Half Lives.* New York: Charles Scribner's Sons, 1890.

———. *The Making of an American,* edited by Roy Lubove. New York: Harper Torchbooks, 1966.

Ringel, Fred J., ed. *America: As Americans See It.* New York: The Literary Guild, 1932.

Riordon, William L. *Plunkitt of Tammany Hall: A Series of Very Plain Talks on Very Practical Politics.* New York: McClure, Phillips & Co., 1905.

Ross, Joel H., M.D. *What I Saw in New York; or, A Bird's Eye View of City Life.* Auburn, N.Y.: Derby & Miller, 1851.

Schaukirk, Ewald Gustav. *Occupation of New York City by the British.* New York: Arno Press, 1969.

Sloan, John. *New York Etchings, 1905–1949.* New York: Dover, 1978.

Smith, Alfred E. *Up to Now.* New York: Viking, 1929.

Steffens, Lincoln. *Autobiography.* New York: 1931.

Sterling, Dorothy. *We Are Your Sisters: Black Women in the Nineteenth Century.* New York: W. W. Norton & Co., 1984.

Suriano, Gregory R., ed. *Gershwin in His Time: A Biographical Scrapbook, 1919–1937.* New York: Gramercy Books, 1998.

Sweetser, M. F. *How to Know New York City.* New York: Press of J. J. Little & Co., 1895.

Tocqueville, Alexis de. *Democracy in America.* Vols. 1 and 2. New York: Alfred A. Knopf, 1945.

Trotsky, Leon. *My Life.* New York: Grosset & Dunlap, 1930.

Trow, George W. S. *Within the Context of No Context.* Boston: Little, Brown, 1978.

Valentine, D. T. *Manual of the Common Council of the City of New York.* New York: Edmund Jones & Co., 1864.

Wald, Lillian. *The House on Henry Street.* New York: Henry Holt & Co., 1915.

Weegee. *Naked City.* New York: Da Capo Press, 1945.

Whalen, Grover. *Mr. New York: The Autobiography of Grover Whalen.* New York: G. P. Putnam's Sons, 1955.

Wharton, Edith. *The Age of Innocence.* New York: Charles Scribner's Sons, 1968.

White, E. B. *Here Is New York.* New York: Harper & Brothers, 1949.

Whitehouse, Roger. *Sunshine and Shadow: A Photographic Record of the City and Its People from 1850 to 1915.* New York: Harper & Row, 1974.

Whitman, Walt. *The Complete Poems.* New York: Penguin Books, 1977.

———. *Complete Poetry and Collected Prose.* Cambridge: University of Cambridge, 1982.

Whyte, William H., ed. *The Exploding Metropolis.* Garden City, N.Y.: Doubleday & Co., 1958.

Yezierska, Anzia. *Bread Givers.* New York: Persea Books, 1952.

———. *How I Found America.* New York: Persea Books, 1991.

ADDITIONAL SOURCES

Abbot, Wilber C. *New York in the American Revolution.* New York: Charles Scribner's Sons, 1929.

Albion, Robert Greenhalgh. *The Rise of New York Port, 1815–1860.* New York: Charles Scribner's Sons, 1939.

Allen, Irving Lewis. *The City in Slang: New York Life in Popular Speech.* New York: Oxford University Press, 1993.

Allen, Leslie. *Liberty: The Statue and the American Dream.* New York: The Statue of Liberty. Ellis Island Foundation, 1985.

Allen, Max, ed. *Ideas That Matter: The Worlds of Jane Jacobs.* Ontario, Canada: The Gonger Press, 1997.

Allen, Oliver E. *New York, New York.* New York: Atheneum, 1990.

Alpern, Andrew. *New York's Fabulous Luxury Apartments.* New York: Dover, 1975.

American Heritage Magazine. "New York in the 1920s: Supreme City." Vol. 39, no. 7, November 1988.

American Social History Project. *Who Built America?* New York: Pantheon Books, 1992.

Anderson, Jervis. *This Was Harlem: A Cultural Portrait, 1900–1950.* New York: Farrar, Straus & Giroux, 1981.

Asbury, Herbert. *The Gangs of New York: An Informal History of the Underworld.* New York: Alfred A. Knopf, 1927.

Astor, Gerald. *The New York Cops: An Informal History.* New York: Charles Scribner's Sons, 1971.

Augustyn, Robert, and Paul Cohen, eds. *Manhattan in Maps, 1527–1995.* New York: Rizzoli International Publications, 1997.

Aylesworth, Thomas G., and Virginia L. Aylesworth. *New York: The Glamour Years, 1919–1945.* New York: Bison Books, 1987.

Baldwin, Neil. *Edison: Inventing the Century.* New York: Hyperion, 1995.

Barlow, Elizabeth. *Frederick Law Olmsted's New York.* New York: Praeger Publishers, 1972.

Bayor, Ronald H., and Timothy J. Meagher, eds. *The New York Irish.* Baltimore: The Johns Hopkins University Press, 1996.

Beard, Rick, and Leslie Cohen Berlowitz. *Greenwich Village: Culture and Counterculture.* New Brunswick, N.J.: Rutgers University Press, 1993.

Bender, Thomas. *New York Intellect.* New York: Alfred A. Knopf, 1987.

———, and Carl E. Schorske. *Budapest and New York: Studies in Metropolitan Transformation: 1870–1930.* New York: Russell Sage Foundation, 1994.

Bergmann, Hans. *God in the Street: New York Writing from the Penny Press to Melville.* Philadelphia: Temple University Press, 1995.

Berman, Marshall. *All That Is Solid Melts into Air: The Experience of Modernity.* New York: Simon & Schuster, 1982.

Bernstein, Iver. *The New York City Draft Riots.* New York: Oxford University Press, 1990.

Berrol, Selma. *New York and Its People, 1624–1996.* Westport, Conn.: Praeger, 1997.

Binder, Frederick M., and David M. Reimers. *All the Nations under Heaven: An Ethnic and Racial History of New York City.* New York: Columbia University Press, 1995.

Birmingham, Stephen. *"Our Crowd": The Great Jewish Families of New York.* New York: Harper & Row, 1967.

Black, Mary. *Old New York in Early Photographs.* New York: Dover, 1976.

Blackmar, Elizabeth. *Manhattan for Rent, 1785–1850.* Ithaca, N.Y.: Cornell University Press, 1989.

Bleecker, Samuel E. *The Politics of Architecture: A Perspective on Nelson A. Rockefeller.* New York: The Rutledge Press, 1981.

Bliven, Bruce, Jr. *Under the Guns; New York: 1775–1776.* New York: Harper & Row, 1972.

Bobbe, Dorothie. *De Witt Clinton.* New York: Minton, Balch & Co., 1933.

Bonomi, Patricia. *A Factious People: Politics and Society in Colonial New York.* New York: Columbia University Press, 1971.

———. *The Lord Cornbury Scandal: The Politics of Reputation in British America.* Chapel Hill, N.C.: University of North Carolina Press, 1998.

Bookbinder, Bernie. *City of the World: New York and Its People.* New York: Harry N. Abrams, 1989.

Bowling, Kenneth R. *The Creation of Washington, D.C.: The Idea and Location of the American Capital.* Fairfax, Va.: George Mason University Press, 1991.

Boyer, M. Christine. *Manhattan Manners: Architecture and Style, 1850–1900.* New York: Rizzoli, 1985.

Brooklyn Museum, The. *The Great East River Bridge, 1883–1983.* New York: Harry N. Abrams, Inc., 1983.

Brown, Henry Collins. *The Story of Old New York.* New York: E. P. Dutton & Co., c. 1934.

Brownstone, David M., Irene M. Franck, and Douglas Brownstone. *Island of Hope, Island of Tears.* New York: Rawson, Wade Publishers, 1979.

Buck, James E., ed. *The New York Stock Exchange: The First 200 Years.* Essex, Conn.: Greenwich Publishing Group, 1992.

Buckley, Peter George. "To the Opera House: Culture and Society in New York City, 1820–1860." Ph.D. dissertation, SUNY at Stonybrook, 1984.

Burrows, Edwin G., and Mike Wallace. *Gotham: A History of New York City to 1898.* New York: Oxford University Press, 1999.

Callow, Alexander B., Jr. *The Tweed Ring.* New York: Oxford University Press, 1966.

Caro, Robert A. *The Power Broker: Robert Moses and the Fall of New York.* New York: Alfred A. Knopf, 1974.

Chambers, Veronica. *The Harlem Renaissance.* Philadelphia: Chelsea House, 1998.

Charters, Samuel B., and Leonard Kunstadt. *Jazz: A History of the New York Scene*. New York: Da Capo Press, 1981.

Chase, W. Parker. *New York: The Wonder City, 1932*. New York: New York Bound, 1983.

Chermayeff, Ivan, Fred Wasserman, and Mary J. Shapiro. *Ellis Island: An Illustrated History of the Immigrant Experience*. New York: Macmillan Publishing Co., 1991.

Chernow, Ron. *The Death of the Banker: The Decline and Fall of the Great Financial Dynasties and the Triumph of the Small Investor*. New York: Vintage Books, 1997.

———. *The House of Morgan: An American Banking Dynasty and the Rise of Modern Finance*. New York: Simon & Schuster, 1990.

———. *Titan: The Life of John D. Rockefeller, Sr*. New York: Random House, 1998.

Crichton, Judy. *America 1900: The Turning Point*. New York: Henry Holt & Co., 1998.

Condit, Carl W. *The Port of New York*. Chicago: University of Chicago Press, 1980.

Connable, Alfred, and Edward Silberfarb. *Tigers of Tammany: Nine Men Who Ran New York*. New York: Holt, Rinehart & Winston, 1967.

Cooke, Hope. *Seeing New York: History Walks for Armchair and Footloose Travelers*. Philadelphia: Temple University Press, 1995.

Covello, Leonard, with Guido D'Agostino. *The Heart Is the Teacher*. New York: McGraw-Hill, 1958.

Czitrom, Daniel J. *Media and the American Mind: From Morse to McLuhan*. Chapel Hill, N.C.: University of North Carolina Press, 1982.

Daniels, Doris Groshen. *Always a Sister: The Feminism of Lilian Wald*. New York: The Feminist Press, 1989.

Dargan, Amanda, and Steven Zeitlin. *City Play*. New Brunswick, N.J.: Rutgers University Press, 1990.

Davis, Thomas J. *A Rumor of Revolt: The "Great Negro Plot" in Colonial New York*. New York: The Free Press, 1985.

———. "Slavery in Colonial New York City." Ph.D dissertation, Columbia University, 1974.

Diehl, Lorraine B. *The Late, Great Pennsylvania Station*. New York: American Heritage Press, 1985.

Douglas, Ann. *Terrible Honesty: Mongrel Manhattan in the 1920s*. New York: Farrar, Straus & Giroux, 1995.

Duffus, R. L. *Lillian Wald: Neighbor and Crusader*. New York: The Macmillan Co., 1938.

Edmiston, Susan, and Linda D. Cirino. *Literary New York: A History and Guide*. New York: Houghton Mifflin Co., 1976.

Elkins, Stanley, and Eric McKittrick. *The Age of Federalism*. New York: Oxford University Press, 1993.

Elliot, Lawrence. *Little Flower: The Life and Times of Fiorello La Guardia*. New York: William Morrow & Co., 1983.

Ellis, Edward Robb. *The Epic of New York City: A Narrative History*. New York: Coward-McCann, 1966.

Elzea, Rowland, and Elizabeth Hawkes. *John Sloan: Spectator of Life*. Wilmington: Delaware Art Museum, 1988.

Erenberg, Lewis A. *Steppin' Out: New York Nightlife and the Transformation of American Culture, 1890–1930*. Chicago: University of Chicago Press, 1981.

Erie, Steven P. *Rainbow's End: Irish-Americans and the Dilemmas of Urban Machine Politics, 1840–1985*. Berkeley: University of California Press, 1988.

Ernst, Robert. *Immigrant Life in New York City: 1825–1863*. New York: King's Crown Press, 1949.

Ewen, Elizabeth. *Immigrant Women in the Land of Dollars: Life and Culture on the Lower East Side, 1890–1925*. New York: Monthly Review Press, 1985.

Federal Writers' Project. *The WPA Guide to New York City: The Federal Writers' Project Guide to 1930s New York*. New York: Pantheon Books, 1982.

Fitch, Robert. *The Assassination of New York*. New York: Verso, 1993.

Flexner, James Thomas. *The Young Hamilton: A Biography*. Boston: Little, Brown & Company, 1978.

Foner, Nancy, ed. *New Immigrants in New York*. New York: Columbia University Press, 1987.

Ford, James. *Slums and Housing: With Special Reference to New York City. History, Conditions, Policy*, 2 vols. Cambridge, Mass.: Howard University Press, 1936.

Fowler, Gene. *Beau James: The Life and Times of Jimmy Walker*. New York: Viking Press, 1949.

Gabler, Neal. *Winchell: Gossip, Power, and the Culture of Celebrity*. New York: Alfred A. Knopf, 1995.

Garmey, Stephen. *Gramercy Park: An Illustrated History of a New York Neighborhood*. New York: Balsam Press, 1984.

Garrett, Charles. *The La Guardia Years: Machine and Reform Politics in New York City*. New Brunswick, N.J.: Rutgers University Press, 1961.

Geist, Charles R. *Wall Street: A History*. New York: Oxford University Press, 1997.

Gelernter, David. *1939: The Lost World of the Fair*. New York: The Free Press, 1995.

Gilfoyle, Timothy. *City of Eros: New York City, Prostitution, and the Commercialization of Sex, 1790–1920*.

New York: W. W. Norton & Co., 1992.

Gilmartin, Gregory F. *Shaping the City: New York and the Municipal Art Society*. New York: Potter, 1995.

Glueck, Grace. *New York: The Painted City*. Salt Lake City, Utah: Peregrine Smith, 1992.

Goldman, Jonathan. *The Empire State Building Book*. New York: St. Martin's, 1980.

Goodfriend, Joyce D. *Before the Melting Pot: Society and Culture in Colonial New York*. Princeton, N.J.: Princeton University Press, 1992.

Gordon, John Steele. *Hamilton's Blessing*. New York: Penguin Books, 1998.

Grafton, John. *New York in the Nineteenth Century*. New York: Dover, 1980.

Green, Martin. *New York 1913: The Armory Show and the Paterson Strike Pageant*. New York: Charles Scribner's Sons, 1988.

Greenberg, Cheryl Lynn. *Or Does it Explode?: Black Harlem in the Great Depression*. New York: Oxford University Press, 1991.

Greenberg, Rodney. *George Gershwin*. London: Phaidon Press, 1998.

Gronowicz, Anthony. *Race and Class Politics in New York City before the Civil War*. Boston: Northeastern University Press, 1998.

Haegler, John Denis. *John Jacob Astor: Business and Finance in the Early Republic*. Detroit: Wayne State University Press, 1991.

Hammack, David C. *Power and Society: Greater New York at the Turn of the Century*. New York: Columbia University Press, 1987.

Hawes, Elizabeth. *New York, New York*. New York: Henry Holt & Co., 1993.

Heinze, Andrew R. *Adapting to Abundance: Jewish Immigrants, Mass Consumption, and the Search for American Identity*. New York: Columbia University Press, 1990.

Henderson, Thomas M. *Tammany Hall and the New Immigrants: The Progressive Years*. New York: Arno Press, 1976.

Henderson, Mary C. *The City and the Theater: New York Playhouses from the Bowling Green to Times Square*. Clifton, N.J.: James T. White & Co., 1973.

Hershkowitz, Leo. *Tweed's New York: Another Look*. Garden City, N.Y.: Anchor Press, 1977.

Hill, Marilyn Wood. *Their Sisters' Keepers: Prostitution in New York City, 1830–1870*. Berkeley: University of California Press, 1993.

Hindus, Milton, ed. *The Old East Side, An Anthology*. Philadelphia: Jewish Publications Society of America, 1969.

Hodges, Graham Russel. *New York City Cartmen, 1667–1850*. New York: New York University Press, 1986.

Homberger, Eric. *The Historical Atlas of New York City: A Visual Celebration of Nearly 400 Years of New York City's History*. New York : Henry Holt & Co., 1994.

———. *Scenes from the Life of a City: Corruption and Conscience in Old New York*. New Haven: Yale University Press, 1994.

Hood, Clifton. *722 Miles: The Building of the Subways and How They Transformed New York*. New York: Simon & Schuster, 1993.

Horlick, Allan Stanley. *Country Boys and Merchant Princes: The Social Control of Young Men in New York*. Lewisberg, Penn.: Bucknell University Press, 1975.

Howe, Irving. *World of Our Fathers*. New York: Schocken Books, 1979.

———, and Kenneth Libo. *How We Lived: A Documentary History of Immigrant Jews in America*. New York: Richard Marek Publishers, 1979.

Huthmacher, Joseph J. *Senator Robert F. Wagner and the Rise of Urban Liberalism*. New York: Atheneum, 1968.

Huxtable, Ada Louise. *Will They Ever Finish Bruckner Boulevard?* New York: Collier Books, 1972.

Jablonski, Edward. *Irving Berlin: American Troubadour*. New York: Henry Holt & Co., 1999.

———, and Lawrence D. Stewart. *The Gershwin Years: George and Ira*. New York: Da Capo Press, 1996.

Jackson, Kenneth T. *Crabgrass Frontier: The Suburbanization of the U.S.* New York: Oxford University Press, 1985.

———, ed. *The Encyclopedia of New York City*. New Haven: Yale University Press, 1995.

———, ed. *The Neighborhoods of Brooklyn*. New Haven: Yale University Press, 1998.

———, ed. *Sodom on the Hudson: Poverty and Society in New York City*. New York: American Heritage Custom Publishing Group, 1993.

Jonas, Susan, ed. *Ellis Island*. New York: Aperture Books, 1989.

Josephson, Matthew, and Hannah Josephson. *Al Smith: Hero of the Cities*. Boston: Houghton Mifflin Co., 1969.

Kammen, Michael. *Colonial New York: A History*. New York: Charles Scribner's Sons, 1975.

Kaplan, Justin. *Walt Whitman: A Life*. New York: Simon & Schuster, 1986.

Karatzas, Daniel. *Jackson Heights: A Garden in the City*. Jackson Heights, New York: Daniel Karatzas, 1988.

Kasson, John F. *Amusing the Million: Coney Island at the Turn of the Century*. New York: Hill & Wang, 1978.

Katz, William. *Black Legacy: A History of New York's African Americans*. New York: Ethrac Publications, 1997.

Kazin, Alfred. *A Writer's America: Landscape in Literature.* New York: Alfred A. Knopf, 1988.

Kelly, Bruce, Gail Travis Guillet, and Mary Ellen W. Hern. *Art of the Olmsted Landscape.* New York: New York City Landmarks Preservation Commission, 1981.

Kessner, Thomas. *Fiorello H. La Guardia and the Making of Modern New York.* New York: Penguin Group, 1989.

——. *The Golden Door: Italian and Jewish Immigrant Mobility in New York City, 1880–1915.* New York: Oxford University Press, 1977.

Kinkead, Eugene. *Central Park.* New York: W. W. Norton & Co., 1990.

Kisseloff, Jeff. *You Must Remember This.* New York: Harcourt Brace Jovanovich, 1989.

Klein, Alexander. *The Empire City: A Treasury of New York.* New York: Rinehart and Co., 1955.

Klein, Carole. *Gramercy Park: An American Bloomsbury.* New York: Houghton Mifflin Co., 1987.

Kobler, John. *Ardent Spirits: The Rise and Fall of Prohibition.* New York: G. P. Putnam's Sons, 1973.

Kouwenhoven, John A. *The Columbia Historical Portrait of New York: An Essay in Graphic History.* New York: Doubleday & Co., Inc., 1953.

Kraut, Alan M. *Silent Travelers: Germs, Genes, and the "Immigrant Menace."* New York: Basic Books, 1994.

Krieg, Joann P., ed. *Robert Moses: Single-Minded Genius.* Interlaken, N.Y.: Heart of the Lakes Publishing, 1989.

Krinsky, Carol Herselle. *Rockefeller Center.* New York: Oxford University Press, 1978.

Kunhardt, Philip B., Jr., Philip B. Kunhardt III, and Peter W. Kunhardt. *Lincoln: An Illustrated Biography.* New York: Alfred A. Knopf, 1993.

——. *P. T. Barnum: America's Greatest Showman.* New York: Alfred A. Knopf, 1995.

La Guardia, Fiorello H. *The Making of an Insurgent: An Autobiography, 1882–1919.* New York: J. B. Lippincott, 1948.

La Sorte, Michael. *La Merica: Images of Italian Greenhorn Experience.* Philadelphia: Temple University Press, 1985.

Lancaster, Clay. *Old Brooklyn Heights: New York's First Suburb.* New York: Dover, 1979.

Landau, Sarah Bradford, and Carl W. Condit. *Rise of the New York Skyscraper: 1865–1913.* New Haven: Yale University Press, 1996.

Lankevich, George J. *American Metropolis: A History of New York City.* New York: New York University Press, 1998.

Leach, William. *Land of Desire: Merchants, Power, and the Rise of a New American Culture.* New York: Pantheon Books, 1993.

Levinson, Leonard Louis. *Wall Street: A Pictorial History.* New York: Ziff-Davis Publishing, 1961.

Lewis, David Levering. *When Harlem Was in Vogue.* New York: Alfred A. Knopf, 1979.

Lewis, Tom. *Empire of the Air: The Men Who Made Radio.* New York: HarperCollins, 1991.

Lightfoot, Frederick. *Nineteenth-Century New York in Rare Photographic Views.* New York: Dover, 1981.

Livington, E. A. (Bud). *President Lincoln's Third Largest City: Brooklyn and the Civil War.* Glendale, New York: Budd Press, 1994.

Lockwood, Charles. *Bricks and Brownstone: The New York Row House, 1783–1929.* New York: McGraw-Hill, 1972.

——. *Manhattan Moves Uptown: An Illustrated History.* New York: Barnes & Noble, 1976.

Lowe, David Garrard. *Stanford White's New York.* New York: Doubleday, 1992.

Lubove, Roy. *The Progressives and the Slums: Tenement House Reform in New York City.* Pittsburgh: University of Pittsburgh Press, 1962.

Maeder, Jay, ed. *Big Town, Big Time.* New York: Daily News Books, 1999.

Maffi, Mario. *Gateway to the Promised Land: Ethnic Cultures in New York's Lower East Side.* New York: New York University Press, 1995.

Manglone, Jerre, and Ben Morreance. *La Storia: Five Centuries of the Italian American Experience.* New York: Harper Collins, 1992.

Mann, Arthur. *La Guardia: A Fighter Against His Times, 1882–1933.* New York: J. B. Lippincott Co., 1959.

Manners, William. *Patience and Fortitude: Fiorello La Guardia.* New York: Harcourt Brace Jovanovich, 1976.

Marqusee, Michael. *New York: An Illustrated Anthology.* Salem, Mass.: Salem House, 1988.

——, and Bill Harris. *New York: An Anthology.* New York: Little, Brown & Co., 1985.

Martin, George. *Madam Secretary: Frances Perkins.* Boston: Houghton Mifflin Co., 1976.

Mast, Gerard. *Can't Help Singing: The American Musical on Stage and Screen.* Woodstock, N.Y.: Overlook, 1987.

Maxtone-Graham, John. *The Only Way to Cross.* New York: Macmillan, 1972.

Mayer, Grace M. *Once Upon a City.* New York: The Macmillan Co., 1985.

McCullough, David. *The Great Bridge: The Epic Story of the Building of the Brooklyn Bridge.* New York: Avon Books, 1972.

McKay, Ernest A. *The Civil War and New York City.* Syracuse, N.Y.: Syracuse University Press, 1990.

McKay, Richard C. *South Street: A Maritime History of New York.* New York: G. P. Putnam's Sons, 1934.

McNickle, Chris. *To Be Mayor of New York: Ethnic Politics in the City.* New York: Columbia University Press, 1993.

Ment, David. *The Shaping of a City: A Brief History of Brooklyn.* Brooklyn: Brooklyn Educational and Cultural Alliance, 1979.

Metzker, Isaac, ed. *A Bintel Brief: Sixty Years of Letters from the Lower East Side to the* Jewish Daily Forward. New York: Ballantine Books, 1971.

Metropolitan Museum of Art. *American Impressionism and Realism: The Painting of Modern Life, 1885–1915.* New York: Harry N. Abrams, 1994.

Middleton, William D. *Manhattan Gateway: New York's Pennsylvania Station.* Waukesha, Wisc.: Kalmbach Books, 1996.

Milford, Nancy. *Zelda: A Biography.* New York: Harper Perennial, 1992.

Miller, Byron S. *Sail, Steam, and Splendor.* New York: Times Books, 1977.

Miller, Terry. *Greenwich Village and How It Got That Way.* New York: Crown Publishers, 1990.

Mizener, Arthur. *Scott Fitzgerald and His World.* New York: G. P. Putnam's Sons, 1972.

Mollenkopf, John Hill, ed. *Power, Culture and Place: Essays on New York City.* New York: Russell Sage Foundation, 1988.

Moore, Deborah Dash. *At Home in America: Second Generation New York Jews.* New York: Columbia University Press, 1981.

Morris, Jan. *Manhattan '45.* New York: Oxford University Press, 1986.

Morrison, John H. *History of New York Ship Yards.* New York: W. M. F. Sametz & Co., 1909.

Morton, Margaret. *The Tunnel.* New Haven: Yale University Press, 1995.

Moscow, Henry. *The Street Book.* New York: Fordham University Press, 1978.

Moscow, Warren. *What Have You Done for Me Lately? The Ins and Outs of New York City Politics.* Englewood Cliffs, N.J.: Prentice-Hall, 1967.

Mumford, Lewis. *The Brown Decades: A Study of the Arts in America 1865–1895.* New York: Dover, 1955.

Murphy, May Ellen, Mark Murphy, and Ralph Foster Weld. *A Treasury of Brooklyn.* New York: William Sloane Assoc., Inc., 1949.

Naison, Mark. *Communists in Harlem during the Depression.* New York: Grove, 1985.

Nasaw, David. *Children of the City: At Work and at Play.* New York: Oxford University Press, 1985.

——. *Going Out: The Rise and Fall of Public Amusements.* New York: Basic Books, 1993.

O'Neill, Hank. *Berenice Abbott: American Photographer.* New York: McGraw-Hill, 1982.

O'Neill, William, ed. *Echoes of Revolt: The Masses, 1911–1917.* Chicago: Quadrangle Books, 1966.

Ogren, Kathy J. *The Jazz Revolution: Twenties America and the Meaning of Jazz.* New York: Oxford University Press, 1989.

Osofsky, Gilbert. *Harlem: The Making of a Ghetto.* 2nd ed. New York: Harper & Row, 1971.

Patterson, Jerry E. *The City of New York: A History Illustrated from the Collections of the Museum of the City of New York.* New York: Harry N. Abrams, 1978.

Peiss, Kathy. *Cheap Amusements: Working Women and Leisure in Turn of the Century New York.* Philadelphia: Temple University Press, 1986.

Pomerantz, Sidney I. *New York: An American City 1783–1803.* Port Washington, N.Y.: Ira J. Friedman, Inc., 1965.

Porter, Kenneth Wiggins. *John Jacob Astor: Business Man,* Vol. 2. Cambridge, Mass.: Harvard University Press, 1931.

Queens Museum. *Dawn of a New Day: The World's Fair, 1939–40.* New York: NYU Press, 1980.

——. *Remembering the Future: The New York World's Fair from 1939 to 1964.* New York: Rizzoli, 1989.

Ramirez, Jan Seidler. *Within Bohemia's Borders: Greenwich Village 1830–1930.* New York: Museum of the City of New York, 1990.

Reed, Henry Hope, and Sophia Duckworth. *Central Park: A History and a Guide.* New York: Clarkson N. Potter, 1972.

Reeves, Pamela. *Ellis Island: Gateway to the American Dream.* New York: Crescent Books, 1991.

Reynolds, David S. *Walt Whitman's America: A Cultural Biography.* New York: Vintage Books, 1996.

Rink, Oliver A. *Holland on the Hudson: An Economic and Social History of Dutch New York.* Ithaca, N.Y.: Cornell University Press, 1986.

Riordon, William C. *Plunkitt of Tammany Hall.* New York: E. P. Dutton, 1963.

Rischin, Moses. *The Promised City: New York's Jews, 1870–1914.* Cambridge, Mass.: Harvard University Press, 1977.

Rosebrock, Ellen Fletcher. *South Street: A Photographic Guide.* New York: Dover, 1977.

Rosenberg, Carroll Smith. *Religion and the Rise of the American City: The New York City Mission Movement, 1812–1870.* Ithaca, N.Y.: Cornell University Press, 1971.

Rosenberg, Charles E. *The Cholera Years: The United States in 1832, 1849, and 1866.* Chicago: University of Chicago Press, 1987.

Rosenfeld, Lulla Adler. *The Yiddish Theatre and Jacob P. Adler.* New York: Shapolsky Publishers, 1977.

Rosenwaike, Ira. *Population History of New York City.* Syracuse, N.Y.: Syracuse University Press, 1972.

Rosenzweig, Roy and Elizabeth Blackmar. *The Park and the People: A History of Central Park.* Ithaca, N.Y.: Cornell University Press, 1992.

Roth, Leland M. *McKim, Mead and White, Architects.* New York: Harper & Row, 1983.

Rutterbaum, Steven. *Mansions in the Clouds: The Skyscraper Palazzi of Emery Roth.* New York: Balsam Press, 1986.

Salins, Peter D., ed. *New York Un-bound: The City and Politics of the Future.* New York: Basil Blackwell, 1988.

Salwen, Peter. *Upper West Side Story.* New York: Abbeville Press, 1989.

Sanchez Korrol, Virginia. *From Colonia to Community: The History of Puerto Ricans in New York City.* Berkeley: University of California Press, 1994.

Sanders, Ronald. *The Downtown Jews: Portraits of an Immigrant Generation.* New York: Harper & Row, 1969.

Sante, Luc. *Low Life: The Lures and Snares of Old New York.* New York: Farrar, Straus & Giroux, 1991.

Schoener, Allon. *New York: An Illustrated Hisotry of the People.* New York: Norton, 1998.

———, ed. *Portal to America: The Lower East Side, 1870–1925.* New York: Holt, Rinehart & Winston, 1967.

Scully, Vincent. *American Architecture and Urbanism.* 1969. New York: Henry Holt & Co., 1969.

Shanor, Rebecca Read. *The City That Never Was.* New York: Viking, 1988.

Shapiro, Mary J. *Gateway to Liberty: The Study of the Statue of Liberty and Ellis Island.* New York: Vintage, 1986.

Shaw, Ronald E. *Erie Water West: A History of the Erie Canal, 1792–1854.* Lexington, Ky.: University of Kentucky Press, 1966.

Shefter, Martin. *Capital of the American Century: The National and International Influence of New York City.* New York: Russell Sage Foundation, 1993.

Sherrow, Victoria. *The Triangle Factory Fire.* Brookfield, Conn.: Millbrook Press, 1995.

Siegel, Beatrice. *Lillian Wald of Henry Street.* New York: Macmillan Publishing Co., 1983.

Silver, Nathan. *Lost New York.* New York: American Legacy Press, 1967.

Simon, Kate. *Fifth Avenue: A Very Social History.* New York: Harcourt Brace Jovanovich, 1978.

Slide, Anthony. *The Vaudevillians: A Dictonary of Vaudeville Performers.* Westport, Conn.: Arlington House, 1981.

Snow, Richard. *Coney Island: A Postcard Journey to the City of Fire.* New York: Brightwaters Press, 1984

Snyder-Grenier, Ellen M. *Brooklyn! An Illustrated History.* Philadelphia: Temple University Press, 1996.

Snyder, Robert W. *The Voice of the City: Vaudeville and Popular Culture in New York.* New York: Oxford University Press, 1989.

Stansell, Christine. *City of Women: Sex and Class in New York, 1789–1860.* New York: Alfred A. Knopf, 1986.

Stasz, Clarice. *The Vanderbilt Women: Dynasty of Wealth, Glamour and Tragedy.* New York: St. Martin's Press, 1991.

Stein, Charles W. *American Vaudeville as Seen by Its Contemporaries.* New York: Alfred A. Knopf, 1984.

Stein, Leon, ed. *Out of the Sweatshop: The Struggle for Industrial Democracy.* New York: Quadrangle/The New York Times Book Co., 1977.

Stern, Robert A. M., with Thomas P. Catalano. *Raymond Hood.* New York: Rizzoli International Publications, 1982.

———, Gregory Gilmartin, and John Montague Massengale. *New York 1900: Metropolitan Architecture and Urbanism, 1890–1915.* New York: Rizzoli, 1992.

———, Gregory Gilmartin and Thomas Mellins. *New York 1930: Architecture and Urbanism between the Two World Wars.* New York: Rizzoli, 1987.

———, Thomas Mellins, and David Fishman. *New York 1960: Architecture and Urbanism between the Second World War and the Bicentennial.* New York: Monacelli Press, Inc., 1995.

Still, Bayrd. *Mirror for Gotham.* New York: New York University Press, 1956.

Stokes, I. N. Phelps. *The Iconography of Manhattan Island, 1498–1909,* Vols. 1 and 2. New York: Arno Press, 1967.

Strickland, Roy, and James Sanders. *At Home in the City: Housing in New York, 1810–1983.* New York: Graduate Center of City University of New York, 1983.

Strouse, Jean. *Morgan: American Financier.* New York: Random House, 1999.

Tauranac, John. *The Empire State Building.* New York: St. Martin's Griffin, 1995.

Tax, Meredith. *The Rising of the Women: Feminist Solidarity as Class Conflict, 1880–1917.* New York: Monthly Review Press, 1980.

Taylor, George Rogers. *The Transportation Revolution, 1815–1860.* White Plains, N.Y.: M. E. Sharpe, 1951.

Taylor, William R. *In Pursuit of Gotham: Culture and Commerce in New York.* New York: Oxford University Press, 1992.

———, ed. *Inventing Times Square: Commerce and Culture at the Crossroads of the World.* New York: Russell Sage Foundation, 1991.

Tchen, John Kuo Wei. "New York before Chinatown: Orientalism, Identity, Formation, and Political Culture in the American Metropolis, 1784–1822." Ph.D. dissertation, New York University, 1992.

Toll, Robert C. *On with the Show: The First Century of Show Business in America.* New York: Oxford University Press, 1976.

Tomkins, Calvin. *Merchants and Masterpieces: The Story of the Metropolitan Museum of Art.* New York: E. P. Dutton and Co., 1970.

Trachtenberg, Marvin. *The Statue of Liberty.* New York: Penguin Books, 1977.

Turnbull, Andrew. *Scott Fitzgerald.* New York: Charles Scribner's Sons, 1962.

Tyler, Gus. *Look for the Union Label: A History of the International Ladies' Garment Workers' Union.* Armonk, N.Y.: M. E. Sharpe, 1995.

Ultan, Lloyd. *The Beautiful Bronx, 1920–1950.* New York: Arlington House, 1979.

———, and Gary Hermalyn. *The Bronx in the Innocent Years, 1890–1925.* New York: Harper & Row, 1985.

Van Der Zee, Henri, and Barbara Van Der Zee. *A Sweet and Alien Land: The Story of Dutch New York.* New York: Viking, 1978.

Van Leeuwen, Thomas A. P. *The Skyward Trend of Thought: The Metaphysics of the American Skyscraper.* Cambridge, Mass.: Massachusetts Institute of Technology Press, 1988.

Walsh, George. *Gentleman Jimmy Walker: Mayor of the Jazz Age.* New York: Praeger, 1974.

Ward, David, and Olivier Zunz. *The Landscape of Modernity: Essays on New York City, 1900–1940.* New York: Russell Sage Foundation, 1992.

Watson, Steven. *The Harlem Renaissance: Hub of African-American Culture, 1920–1930.* New York: Pantheon Books, 1995.

Weatherford, Doris. *Foreign and Female: Immigrant Women in America, 1840–1930.* New York: Facts on File, 1995.

Wilentz, Sean. *Chants Democratic: New York City and the Rise of the American Working Class, 1788–1850.* New York: Oxford University Press, 1984.

Willensky, Elliot, and Norval White. *AIA Guide to New York City.* New York: Harcourt Brace Jovanovich, 1988.

Williams, Beryl. *Lillian Wald: Angel of Henry Street.* New York: Julian Messner, 1948.

Willis, Carol. *Form Follows Finance: Skyscrapers and Skylines in New York and Chicago.* New York: Princeton Architectural Press, 1995.

———, ed. *Building the Empire State.* New York: W. W. Norton & Co. 1998.

Wilson, Richard Guy. *McKim, Mead, & White.* New York: Rizzoli, 1983.

———. *American Renaissance.* New York: Brooklyn Museum, 1979.

Wurts, Richard. *New York World's Fair.* New York: Dover, 1977.

ADDITIONAL SOURCES FOR REVISED EDITION

Aust, Stefan, Cordt Schnibben, et al. *Inside 9-11: What Really Happened.* New York: St. Martin's Press, 2001.

Darton, Eric. *Divided We Stand: A Biography of New York's World Trade Center.* New York: Basic Books, 1999.

Gillespie, Angus Kress. *Twin Towers: The Life of New York City's World Trade Center.* New Brunswick, N.J.: Rutgers University Press, 1999.

Glanz, James, Jim Dwyer, Eric Lipton, et al. "102 Minutes," *New York Times,* May 26, 2002, A1.

Glanz, James, and Eric Lipton. "Height of Ambition," *New York Times Magazine,* September 8, 2002, 32.

———. "In Data Trove, a Graphic Look at Towers' Fall," *New York Times,* October 29, 2002, A1.

Langewiesche, William. *American Ground.* New York: Simon & Schuster, 2002.

Petit, Philippe. *To Reach the Clouds: My High Wire Walk Between the Twin Towers.* New York: North Point Press, 2002.

Numbers in *italics* refer to illustrations.

ILLUSTRATION CREDITS

Unless otherwise noted, when there is more than one credit for a page, left to right is separated by a semicolon, top to bottom by two dashes.

ABBREVIATIONS

BPL	Brooklyn Public Library
BB	Brown Brothers, Sterling, PA
CB	Corbis-Bettmann
CP	Culver Pictures
LC	Library of Congress
LA	Lisa Ades
MCNY	Museum of the City of New York
NA	National Archives, Still Pictures
NPG	National Portrait Gallery, Smithsonian Institution
NYHS	Collection of the New-York Historical Society
NYPL	The New York Public Library, Astor, Lenox and Tilden Foundations
SC	Steeplechase Films

FRONT MATTER

i: SC. ii–iii: New York City Municipal Archives. iv–v: BB. vi–vii: LA. viii: LC. ix: (detail) MCNY, 40.140.198. x–xii: CP.

INTRODUCTION: CITY OF DESIRE

xiv: CB.

THE COUNTRY AND THE CITY

2–3: David David Gallery, Philadelphia/Superstock. 4: SC. 6: LC. 7: Courtesy of Richard B. Arkway, Inc. 8: MCNY. 10: Collection of Eric Homberger. 10–11: LC. 12–13: Courtesy of Paul Cohen, *Manhattan in Maps.* 13: (inset) NYHS, 1909.2. 14–15: (lower) MCNY, 29.100.2424. 15: (upper) NYHS, 1950.335. 16–17: MCNY, 29.100.709. 18: NYHS, 3233—MCNY, J. Clarence Davies Scrapbook. 19: By Courtesy of the National Portrait Gallery, London. 20: NYHS, 44137; Copyright © The British Museum. 21: NYHS, 1952.80. 22–23: NYHS, 1904.1. 23: (upper) SC. 24: NYHS, 32102. 26: Stokes Collection, NYPL. 27: LC— Collection of Eric Homberger. 28: The Pierpont Morgan Library/ Art Resource, NY. 29: (both) The New York Public Library Picture Collection. 31: Courtesy of Paul Cohen, *Manhattan in Maps.* 32: Stokes Collection, NYPL.

33: MCNY, 29.100.2025. 35: MCNY, 29.100.2024—Stokes Collection, NYPL. 36: NYHS, 53357. 38–39: NYHS, 54615. 40: NPG. 41: White House Collection, Courtesy White House Historical Association. 42: Stokes Collection, NYPL. 43: MCNY, 29.100.2335. 44–45: NYHS, 1907.32. 47: (inset) NYHS, 1859.7—(lower) Stokes Collection, NYPL. 48–49: MCNY, 33.83.3. 50: NYHS, 1948.576. 51: NPG/Art Resource, NY—Historic Hudson Valley, Tarrytown, NY. 52–53: Courtesy of Paul Cohen, *Manhattan in Maps*/LC. 53: (upper) NYHS, 1854.1. 54: Print Collection, NYPL. 55: SC. 56: NYHS, 1967.6. 57: (all four) SC. 58–59: NYHS, 34684. 60: NYHS, 1875.3—Arthur Ochs Sulzberger/ The New York Times. 64–65: NYHS, 1864.14. 66: NYHS, 1864.16.

ORDER AND DISORDER

68–69: Print Collection, NYPL. 70: NYHS. 73: NYHS, 66756. 74–75: New York State Historical Association, Cooperstown, NY. 76: MCNY, 85.205.1. 77: NYHS, 44668. 78: NYHS, 1926.78. 79: NYHS, 28609. 80: The Eric Fettmann Collection—LC. 81: General Research Division, NYPL—NYHS—LC. 82: (upper right) Ed Folsom Collection— (lower left) MCNY, 42.121. 83: Stephen O. Saxe. 84: MCNY, 57.300.519. 85: (upper) NYHS, 72452—(lower left) NPG; (inset) NYHS, 63929. 86–87: MCNY, 33.169. 88: MCNY. 89: MCNY. 90: SC. 91: NYHS, Box 51. 92: NYHS, 72359. 93: NYHS, 71367. 94: (upper right) NYHS, 48541— (middle) SC—(lower left) Gilman Paper Company Collection. 95: MCNY, 38.93.1—Collection Matthew Isenburg. 96–97: MCNY, 29.100.2373. 98: LA. 98–99: MCNY, 29.100.2374. 100: SC—Jeffrey Kraus Collection. 101: Avery Architectural and Fine Arts Library, Columbia University in the City of New York. 102: NYHS, 36561. 103: (upper left) Oscar Lion Collection, Rare Books Division, NYPL—(lower left and lower right) Berg Collection, NYPL. 104: LA; LA; SC. 105: MCNY, 31.24. 106: Collection of the Museum of American Financial History. 107: MCNY, 40.54. 108: (both) SC. 109: Rare Books Division, NYPL. 110: (left inset)

Courtesy of the National Park Service, Frederick Law Olmsted National Historic Site; (right inset) Courtesy of the Society for Preservation of New England Antiquities. 110–11: NYHS, 7245. 112: NYHS, 2829. 113: (left) MCNY; (right upper and lower) LA. 114: MCNY. 115: Jeffrey Kraus Collection—SC—LA. 116: NYHS, Meserve Collection. 118: NYHS, 58247. 120: NYHS, 1773—Print Collection, NYPL. 122: The Eric Fettmann Collection. 123: Print Collection, NYPL—NYHS, 59133. 124: NYHS, 40416. 125: MCNY, 53.53.8. 126: NYHS, 46085. 128–29: NYHS, 60714. 130: NYHS, 21184. 133: Lightfoot Collection/Archive Photos. 134–35: NYHS, 16930. 136: NYHS, Bagoe Collection.

SUNSHINE AND SHADOW

138–39: Arthur Ochs Sulzberger/The New York Times. 140: MCNY. 142–43: CP. 144: MCNY. 145: Jeffrey Kraus Collection. 146: SC—LA. 147: Courtesy AT&T Archives. 148: NYHS, 1971.104. 149: (middle left) NYHS, 50457; (upper right) NYHS. 150: NYHS—SC. 151: SC; LA—NYHS, 8046. 152: (upper left) Jeffrey Kraus Collection; (lower right) MCNY. 154: The Brooklyn Historical Society. 155: The Brooklyn Historical Society. 156: (upper left) The New York Public Library Picture Collection; (upper right) NYHS; (lower) Rutgers University Libraries. 158: LA. 159: MCNY. 160: NYHS, 220; NYHS. 161: (all three) The Eric Fettmann Collection. 162: (upper left) NYHS, 31106; (lower right) MCNY, G.W. Pach. 163: NYHS, 64914. 164: MCNY, 45.117.262; MCNY, 45.117.269. 166–67: NYHS, 475. 168: SC. 169: MCNY, 57.15; MCNY. 170–71: MCNY—MCNY, 42.410. 172–73: MCNY, 57.15.15. 174: (both) LC. 175: © 1999 Macy's East, Inc., All rights reserved. 176: MCNY, The Byron Collection. 178–79: MCNY, L779. 180: LC. 182: MCNY, 55.53.28. 183: (upper) CP—(middle) LC—(lower) NYHS, 29500. 184: NYHS, 6670. 185: LC. 186: NPG; LC. 187: LC. 188: BPL, Brooklyn Collection. 189: NYHS, 70221—Local History and Genealogy, NYPL. 190: CP—BPL, Brooklyn Collection. 191: (left) NPG; (right) MCNY, The Jacob A. Riis Collection. 193: MCNY, The Jacob A. Riis Collection. 194: MCNY, The Jacob A. Riis Collection; LC.

195: MCNY, The Jacob A. Riis Collection. 196: MCNY, The Jacob A. Riis Collection. 197: (all three) BPL, Brooklyn Collection. 198: Collection Roger Whitehouse. 199: (upper left) MCNY; (upper right) Courtesy George Eastman House, Rochester, NY—(inset) CP—(lower) MCNY, The Jacob A. Riis Collection. 200: MCNY. 201: MCNY. 202: NYHS, 72688. 203: NYHS, 69050. 204–5: MCNY, 93.91.138. 206: The Eric Fettmann Collection—BPL, Brooklyn Collection. 207: Alice Austen Collection, Staten Island Historical Society. 208–9: MCNY. 210–11: MCNY, 32.275.2. 212: General Research Division, NYPL. 215: CP.

THE POWER AND THE PEOPLE

216–17: LC. 218: LA. 220–21: BB. 221: (lower) LC. 222: CB—Edwin Levick Collection/Archive Photos. 223: LC. 224–25: CP. 226: LA. 227: CP. 228: CP. 229: National Park Service, Statue of Liberty National Monument—LC. 230–31: NYHS, 72726. 232: BPL, Brooklyn Collection. 233: (both) LA. 234: (upper right) LC; (far left) LC; (lower right) U.S. Department of the Interior, National Park Service, Edison National Historic Site. 235: CP. 236: MCNY—NYHS, 48180. 237: MCNY. 238: LC. 239: SC. 240–41: SC. 242: LA. 243: LC. 244: (both) LC. 245: MCNY, The Byron Collection. 246: MCNY, The Jacob A. Riis Collection. 247: NYHS, 72723—NYHS, 72724. 249: LC. 250–51: BB. 252: BB. 253: LC. 254: MCNY, Theater Collection. 255: NYHS, 61876. 256: Local History and Genealogy, NYPL—NA. 257: LA. 258–59: LC. 259: LA—LC. 260: SC—LC. 260–61: Local History and Genealogy, NYPL. 262: Courtesy of The Bronx County Historical Society Collection, The Bronx, New York. 263: Avery Architectural and Fine Arts Library, Columbia University in the City of New York. 264: MCNY—NYHS, 59044. 265: MCNY. 266: CP. 267: CB. 268–69: CB. 270: BB. 271: MCNY. 272: Photographic Services of the Consolidated Edison Company of New York, Inc. 273: Courtesy Visiting Nurse Service of New York. 274: LC. 275: LC—BB. 277: Courtesy of Cornell University. 278: Courtesy of Cornell University. 278–79: Courtesy of the Kheel Center, Cornell University. 280: CP. 281: Courtesy of the Kheel Center,

Cornell University. 282–83: BB. 284: Courtesy of the Kheel Center, Cornell University. 285: CP. 286: LC. 287: CB; The Eric Fettmann Collection—BB. 288: CB. 289: CB. 290: CB; BB. 291: CP. 292: Courtesy AT&T Archives. 294: MCNY. 295: CB—LA. 296: MCNY, 93.91.276. 297: SC. 298–99: MCNY, William Hassler. 299: (lower) Local History and Genealogy, NYPL. 302–3: LC.

COSMOPOLIS

308–9: CP. 310: CB. 312–13: CB. 314: CB. 316: (upper) CB. 316–17: (lower) New York State Archives. 318: CB—Courtesy "21." 319: The Newark Museum/Art Resource, NY. 320–21: MCNY, 38.299.12. 322: CP. 323: LC. 324: BB. 325: Photographs and Prints, Schomburg Center, NYPL. 326: Photographs and Prints, Schomburg Center, NYPL. 327: (detail) Photographs and Prints, Schomburg Center, NYPL. 328: Photographs and Prints, Schomburg Center, NYPL; BB—Photographs and Prints, Schomburg Center, NYPL. 329: CB. 330: Photographs and Prints, Schomburg Center, NYPL—CB. 331: From the collection of Dr. Meredith and Gail Wright Sirmans, with the permission of Ms. Ruth Robinson-Deen, Executor, Miriam Hayden Estate, M. Hanks Gallery. 332–33: CB. 333: © William Bolin/Vanity Fair, Condé Nast Publications, Inc. 335: Gift of Helen Farr Sloan, Photograph © 1998 Board of Trustees, National Gallery of Art, Washington. 336: NYHS, 61201. 337: MCNY, 91.53.5. 338: NYHS, 58073. 339: © Lepape/Vogue, Condé Nast Publications, Inc. 341: (upper left and right) The Eric Fettmann Collection; (lower left) The Eric Fettmann Collection; (lower right) Courtesy Professor Harold A. Layer, San Francisco State University. 342: New York City Municipal Archives; CB. 343: BB. 344: The J. Paul Getty Museum, Los Angeles, reprinted with the permission of the Georgia O'Keeffe Foundation. 345: New Jersey State Museum Collection, Purchased by the Friends of the New Jersey State Museum with a gift from Mary Lea Johnson, FA 1972.229/©1999 The Georgia O'Keeffe Foundation/Artists Rights. 346: Frank Driggs/Archive Photos. 348–49: MCNY, Robert R. Preato Collection, 91.76.15. 350–51: CP. 352: SC—MCNY. 353: Courtesy of Sandy Marrone. 355: CB. 357: The Eric Fettmann Collection. 358–59: CB.

360: Collection of the late Mario Cavagnaro. 361: NPG. 362: MCNY. 363: Smithsonian Institution. 365: CB. 368: CB. 369: Local History and Genealogy, NYPL. 370–71: LC. 371: NYPL. 372: Estate of Margaret Bourke-White/The Margaret Bourke-White Papers, Syracuse University. 375: *The Regional Plan of New York and Its Environs, 1929*, Regional Plan Association. 376: CB. 377: CB. 380: Avery Architectural and Fine Arts Library, Columbia University in the City of New York. 381: MCNY, L638.3. 382: CB. 383: CB. 385: CP. 386–87: Rem Koolhaas, *Delirious New York*/Courtesy Office for Metropolitan Architecture. 389: CB. 393: LC.

THE CITY OF TOMORROW

394–95: CB. 396: Rockefeller Center Archive. 399: Edward E. Rutter/New York City Parks Photo Archive. 400: Local History and Genealogy, NYPL. 403: CB. 405: AP/Wide World Photos. 406–7: Long Island State Park Region, New York State Office of Parks, Recreation and Historic Preservation. 408: (all three) Margaret Basara McGowan. 409: CP. 410–11: MCNY, Monroe-Pritchard Collection. 412: (both) Long Island State Park Region, New York State Office of Parks, Recreation and Historical Preservation. 414: Courtesy Seymour Durst, Old York Library. 415: CB. 416: MCNY, Gift of Peter Hopkins, 68.82. 417: CB. 418: CB. 419: © 1932 by The New York Times Co. Reprinted by permission. 421: LC. 423: AP/Wide World Photos. 424: (both) Courtesy Whitney Museum of American Art. 425: (both) Courtesy Whitney Museum of American Art. 426: CB. 427: New York City Parks Photo Archive—The La Guardia and Wagner Archives, La Guardia Community College/The City University of New York. 428: (both) New York City Parks Photo Archive. 430–31: CB. 432: Local History and Genealogy, NYPL. 433: LC. 434: Archive Photos. 435: AP/Wide World Photos. 436: National Museum of American Art, Washington, DC/Art Resource, NY. 438: Archives, City College of New York, CUNY. 439: MTA Bridges and Tunnels Special Archive. 440–41: Local History and Genealogy, NYPL. 442–43: CB. 445: The La Guardia and Wagner Archives, La Guardia Community College/The City University of New York. 448–49: © 1999:

Whitney Museum of American Art. 450: MCNY, 94.64.28. 451: CB. 452: SC. 453: CB—Rockefeller Center Archive. 454: (both) LA. 455: MCNY, Gift of Mr. John J. Soble, 72.5.1. 456: MCNY, 68.107.97. 457: Photographic Services of the Consolidated Edison Company of New York, Inc. 460–61: © Arnold Newman.

THE CITY AND THE WORLD

466–67: © Fred W. McDarrah. 468: John Barrington Bayley, Archive New York City Landmarks Preservation Commission. 470–71: CB. 472: NYHS, 73028. 473: LC. 474: NYHS. 477: © 1945 by The New York Times Co. Reprinted by permission. 478–79: BB. 480: CB. 481: AP/Wide World Photos. 482: CB. 483: Popperfoto/Archive Photos; LA. 485: New York Daily News. 486: Ezra Stoller © Esto. 487: AKG London. 489: CB. 490: CP. 491: CB. 492: (both) © Arthur Leipzig. 493: © Arthur Leipzig—CB. 496: New York City Housing Authority. 498–99: NYHS, 69963. 501: AP/Wide World Photos. 502: CB. 502–3: CB. 505: (tempera on hardboard, 24 x 30 inches) Collection of Joyce and George Wein, Courtesy DC Moore Gallery, NYC—AP/Wide World Photos. 508: BPL, Brooklyn Collection. 509: National Baseball Hall of Fame Library, Cooperstown, NY. 510: AP/Wide World Photos. 511: CB. 512–13: © Norman McGrath. 515: Reprinted with the permission of Jane Jacobs/Courtesy of Boston College, John J. Burns Library. 516: Reprinted with the permission of Jane Jacobs/Courtesy of Boston College, John J. Burns Library. 517: MTA Bridges and Tunnels Special Archive. 518: 1964 World's Fair Records, Manuscripts and Archives Division, NYPL. 519: IBM Corporation. 521: AP/Wide World Photos. 523: New York Times Pictures. 524–25: AP/Wide World Photos. 526–27: © Lehnartz Fotografie. 528–29: (all three) © Martha Cooper. 530: Corbis/G. E. Kidder Smith. 531: Philadelphia Museum of Art: Gift of the Friends of the Philadelphia Museum of Art/© Untitled Press, Inc./Licensed by VAGA, New York, NY. 532–33: CB. 535: MCNY. 539: © William Klein, Courtesy Howard Greenberg Gallery, NYC. 543: New York Daily News/AP Wide World Photos. 544–45: © Gilles Peress/Magnum Photos, Inc. 548–49: © Erich Hartmann/Magnum Photos, Inc.

CITY OF THE MILLENNIUM

552–53: Bill Ross/Corbis Images. 556–57: © Norman McGrath.

EPILOGUE

561: MCNY, Collection of The New York Port Authority. 562: (upper left) Courtesy of the Rockefeller Archive Center; (lower right) Courtesy JP Morgan Chase Archives. 564: Port Authority of New York and New Jersey. 565: AP/Wide World Photos. 566: AP/Wide World Photos. 567: Balthazar Korab Photography, Ltd. 568: New York Daily News/Phil Stanziola. 569: MCNY, Collection of The New York Port Authority. 571: New York Daily News/John Duprey. 572-73: Leslie E. Robertson Associates, R.L.L.P. Consulting Structural Engineers. 575: New York Daily News/Frank Hurley. 578: Jean-Louis Blondeau/Polaris. 579: Burt Glinn/Magnum. 581: New York Daily News/Robert Rosamilio. 582–83; Katherine D. Weisberger. 585: William Nunez. 588–89: Susan Meiselas/Magnum. 591: Shannon Stapleton/Reuters. 594–95: Maria Tama/Getty Images. 596: Carolina Salguero/Sipa Press. 599: Gregory DiBisceglie. 600: Michel Lorenzini. 604–5: Sean Hemmerle/CONTACT.

ENDPAPERS

MCNY, 56.323.47.

TEXT CREDITS

Grateful acknowledgment is made to the following for permission to reprint previously published material:

Irving Berlin Music: excerpt from "Jimmy" by Irving Berlin. Copyright © 1927 by Irving Berlin. Copyright renewed. International copyright secured. All rights reserved. Used by permission.

Carlin America, Inc.: excerpt from "Manhattan" by Lorenz Hart and Richard Rodgers. Copyright 1925 by Piedmont Music Company. Copyright renewed. Used by permission. All rights reserved.

Harcourt, Inc.: excerpts from *When the Cathedrals Were White* by Edouard Le Corbusier. Copyright © 1947 by Harcourt, Inc., copyright renewed 1975 by Francis E. Hyslop Jr. Reprinted by permission of Harcourt, Inc.

HarperCollins Publishers, Inc.: excerpt from "Howl" by Allen Ginsberg from *Collected Poems, 1947–1980* by Allen Ginsberg. Copyright © 1955 by Allen Ginsberg. Reprinted by permission of HarperCollins Publishers, Inc.

Alfred A. Knopf, a division of Random House, Inc.: excerpt from *The Autobiography of an Ex-Colored Man* by James Weldon Johnson. Copyright © 1927 by Alfred A. Knopf, a division of Random House, Inc.; excerpt from "An Urban Convalescence" from *Selected Poems, 1946–1985* by James Merrill. Copyright © 1992 by James Merrill; excerpt from *Collected Poems* by Langston Hughes. Copyright © 1994 by the Estate of Langston Hughes. Reprinted by permission of Alfred A. Knopf, a division of Random House, Inc.

Claes Oldenburg: excerpt from "The Street" by Claes Oldenburg. Copyright © 1960, 1961 by Claes Oldenburg. Reprinted by permission of the author.

New Directions Publishing Corporation: excerpts from *The Crack Up* by F. Scott Fitzgerald. Copyright © 1945 by New Directions Publishing Corporation. Reprinted by permission of New Directions Publishing Corporation.

Random House, Inc.: excerpt from *The Death and Life of Great American Cities* by Jane Jacobs. Copyright © 1961 and renewed 1989 by Jane Jacobs. Reprinted by permission of Random House, Inc.

A NOTE ABOUT THE AUTHORS

Ric Burns is best known for his work on the acclaimed PBS series *The Civil War*, which he produced with Ken Burns and wrote with Geoffrey C. Ward and Ken Burns, and for which he received two Emmy Awards and the Producer of the Year award of the Producers Guild of America. For public television, he has also directed the award-winning documentaries *Coney Island, The Donner Party, The Way West*, and *Ansel Adams*.

James Sanders, an architect, is the author of *Celluloid Skyline: New York and the Movies* and has written for the *New York Times,* the *Los Angeles Times, Vanity Fair,* and *Architectural Record*. He has completed design and development projects for the Port Authority of New York and New Jersey, the Parks Council, the Landmarks Preservation Commission, and other civic groups and commercial clients in New York and Los Angeles.

Lisa Ades has produced several award-winning films with Ric Burns for public television, including *The Way West,* a six-hour documentary broadcast nationally on PBS, and *The Donner Party,* which received Peabody and D. W. Griffith awards. Before coproducing *Coney Island* in 1990, she was a producer at New York's public television station WNET.

A NOTE ABOUT THE CONTRIBUTORS

Carol Berkin is a professor of history at Baruch College and the Graduate Center of the City University of New York and is the author of several books, including *Jonathan Sewall: Odyssey of an American Loyalist*.

Marshall Berman is a professor of political theory at the graduate center of the City University of New York and is the author of *All That Is Solid Melts into Air: The Experience of Modernity*.

Robert A. Caro has written *The Power Broker: Robert Moses and the Fall of New York* and *The Path to Power, Means of Ascent,* and *Master of the Senate,* the first three volumes of *The Years of Lyndon Johnson*. Among other awards, he has won two Pulitzer Prizes, the National Book Award, the National Book Critics Circle Award (twice), and the Francis Parkman Prize, awarded by the Society of American Historians.

Daniel Czitrom is a professor of history and chair of the American Studies Program at Mount Holyoke

College and is the author of *Media and the American Mind: From Morse to McLuhan.*

Kenneth T. Jackson is Jacques Barzun Professor of History, Columbia University, Editor in Chief of the *Encyclopedia of New York City,* and the author of several books, including *Crabgrass Frontier: The Suburbanization of the United States.*

David Levering Lewis is Martin Luther King, Jr. Professor of History, Rutgers University, and is the author of *When Harlem Was in Vogue* and the two-volume *W. E. B. DuBois: Biography of a Race,* for which he was awarded the Pulitzer Prize.

Phillip Lopate is a professor of English at Hofstra University, editor of *Writing New York* and *The Art of the Essay,* and the author of several books, including *Totally, Tenderly, Tragically: Essays and Criticism from a Lifelong Love Affair with the Movies.*

Robert A. M. Stern is an architect, the dean of the Yale University School of Architecture, and the coauthor of *New York 1900, New York 1930,* and *New York 1960.*

Mike Wallace is a professor of history at John Jay College of Criminal Justice and the Graduate Center of City University of New York and is the coauthor of *Gotham: A History of New York City to 1898,* for which he was awarded the Pulitzer Prize.

NEW YORK: A DOCUMENTARY FILM

Directed by
Ric Burns

Produced by
Lisa Ades and Ric Burns

Written by
Ric Burns and James Sanders

Edited by
Li-Shin Yu, Edward Barteski, David Hanser, Nina Schulman

Narrated by
David Ogden Stiers

Co-Directed by
Lisa Ades

Cinematography
Buddy Squires and Allen Moore

Original Music Composed and Arranged by
Brian Keane

**Associate Producers (Episodes 1–4)
Coproducers (Episode 5)**
Steve Rivo and Ray Segal

Voices
Joan Allen, Philip Bosco, Andre

Codrescu, Keith David, Janeane Garofalo, Paul Giamatti, Spalding Gray, Gene Jones, James Hazeldine, Frederic Kimball, Robert Sean Leonard, David Margulies, Frank McCourt, Patrick McGrath, Joe Morton, George Plimpton, Isaiah Sheiffer, Ron Silver, Frances Sternhagen, Callie Thorne, Eli Wallach, Harris Yulin

Additional Writing
Ronald Blumer

Associate Editor/Post-Production Supervisor
Michael Balabuch

Additional Editing
Richard Hankin

Associate Editors
Janet Cristenfeld, Syndi Pilar

Sound Editors
Ira Spiegel and Marlene Grzaslewicz

Supervising Producer
Kate Roth Knull

Coordinating Producer
Kerry Herman

Production Coordinator
Justine Bertucelli

Associate Producer
Helen Kaplan

Series Archivist
Robin Espinola

Footage Archivists
Daniel Vatsky and Hilary Klotz

Assistant Producers
Lily Thorne and Danna Liebert

Researchers
Meghan Horvath and Anya Sirota

Research Assistants
Marijke Smit; Zachary Kaiman; Jenks Whittenburg

Assistant Editors
Roxanne Yamashiro, Anna Josenhans, June Shiiki, Josh Sternfeld, Samara Smith, Sarah Kaylor Mick Gormaley

Apprentice Editors
Judd Erlich, Kramer O'Neill

Assistant Sound Editor
Mariusz Gladinski

Additional Cinematography
Roger Sherman, David Ford, Stephen McCarthy, Don Lenzer

Sound Recording
John Zecca, Andrew Yarme, Mark Mandler

Re-recording Mixer
Dominick Tavella

Sound Engineer
Lou Verricho

Base Map Design
Justin and Tracey Morrill, Mapquest.com, inc.

Senior Creative Consultant
Geoffrey C. Ward

Senior Historical Consultants
Kenneth T. Jackson and Mike Wallace

Senior Research Consultants
Jeanne Houck and Robert W. Snyder

Historical Consultants
Thomas Bender, Marshall Berman, Lois Bianchi, Patricia Bonomi, Hope Cooke, Daniel Czitrom, Graham Hodges, David Levering Lewis, Phillip Lopate, Kathy Peiss, Richard Snow, Robert A. M. Stern, Sam Bass Warner, Steve Zeitlin

On-Screen Commentators
Ruth J. Abram, Thomas Bender, Carol Berkin, Marshall Berman, Rev. Calvin O. Butts III, Robert A. Caro, Caleb Carr, Daniel Czitrom, Ann Douglas, E. L. Doctorow, Joshua Freeman, Brendan Gill, Allen Ginsberg, John Steele Gordon, Mayor Rudy Giuliani, Nancy Groce, Pete Hamill, Kenneth T. Jackson, Margo Jefferson, Alfred Kazin, Tony Kushner, Fran Lebowitz, David Levering Lewis, Phillip Lopate, David McCullough, Senator Daniel Patrick Moynihan, Albert Murray, Kathy Peiss, Peter Quinn, Luc Sante, Gretchen Sullivan Sorin, Robert A. M. Stern, Martin Scorsese, Joel Silverman, Christine Stansell, Jean Strouse, John Kuo Wei Tchen, George W. S. Trow, Donald Trump, Mike Wallace, Craig Steven Wilder, Carol Willis

Executive Editor
Judy Crichton

Executive Producer
Ric Burns

NEW YORK is a production of Steeplechase Films in association with WGBH Boston, Thirteen/WNET, and the New-York Historical Society. It is a special presentation of *The American Experience.*

This project would not have been possible without the extraordinary collections and assistance of the New-York Historical Society, the Museum of the City of New York, the Library of Congress, and the New York Public Library.

Major funding provided by The Chase Manhattan Corporation, the National Endowment for the Humanities, PBS/CPB, the Ford Foundation, and the Arthur Vining Davis Foundations.

We would also like to express our enormous appreciation to Morgan Stanley for their crucial support of the final episode of the series.